LOEB CLASSICAL LIBRARY

FOUNDED BY JAMES LOEB 1911

EDITED BY

JEFFREY HENDERSON

THUCYDIDES

II

LCL 109

THUCYDIDES

HISTORY OF THE
PELOPONNESIAN WAR
BOOKS III–IV

WITH AN ENGLISH TRANSLATION BY

CHARLES FORSTER SMITH

HARVARD UNIVERSITY PRESS
CAMBRIDGE, MASSACHUSETTS
LONDON, ENGLAND

First published 1920
Reprinted and revised 1930

LOEB CLASSICAL LIBRARY® is a registered trademark
of the President and Fellows of Harvard College

ISBN 978-0-674-99121-7

Printed on acid-free paper and bound by
The Maple-Vail Book Manufacturing Group

CONTENTS

THUCYDIDES

BOOK III

ΘΟΥΚΥΔΙΔΟΥ ΙΣΤΟΡΙΑΙ

Γ

I. Τοῦ δ' ἐπιγιγνομένου θέρους Πελοποννήσιοι καὶ οἱ ξύμμαχοι ἅμα τῷ σίτῳ ἀκμάζοντι ἐστράτευσαν ἐς τὴν Ἀττικήν (ἡγεῖτο δὲ αὐτῶν Ἀρχίδαμος ὁ Ζευξιδάμου, Λακεδαιμονίων βασιλεύς), καὶ ἐγκαθεζόμενοι ἐδῄουν τὴν γῆν· καὶ προσβολαί, ὥσπερ εἰώθεσαν, ἐγίγνοντο τῶν Ἀθηναίων ἱππέων ὅπῃ παρείκοι, καὶ τὸν πλεῖστον ὅμιλον τῶν ψιλῶν εἶργον τὸ μὴ προεξιόντας τῶν ὅπλων τὰ ἐγγὺς 2 τῆς πόλεως κακουργεῖν. ἐμμείναντες δὲ χρόνον οὐ εἶχον τὰ σιτία ἀνεχώρησαν καὶ διελύθησαν κατὰ πόλεις.

II. Μετὰ δὲ τὴν ἐσβολὴν τῶν Πελοποννησίων εὐθὺς Λέσβος πλὴν Μηθύμνης ἀπέστη ἀπὸ Ἀθηναίων, βουληθέντες μὲν καὶ πρὸ τοῦ πολέμου (ἀλλ' οἱ Λακεδαιμόνιοι οὐ προσεδέξαντο), ἀναγκασθέντες δὲ καὶ ταύτην τὴν ἀπόστασιν πρότερον 2 ἢ διενοοῦντο ποιήσασθαι. τῶν τε γὰρ λιμένων τὴν χῶσιν καὶ τειχῶν οἰκοδόμησιν καὶ νεῶν

---

[1] Mytilene was an oligarchical state, with dependent towns, Antissa, Pyrrha, and Eresus, only Methymna on the northern coast retaining its democratic constitution and its connection with Athens. For the revolt, *cf.* Diod. Sic. xii.

THUCYDIDES

BOOK III

I. DURING the following summer, when the grain was ripening, the Peloponnesians and their allies made an expedition into Attica under the leadership of Archidamus son of Zeuxidamus, king of the Lacedaemonians, and settling in camp proceeded to ravage the land. And sallies were made as usual by the Athenian cavalry wherever opportunity offered, thus preventing the great mass of the enemy's light-armed troops from going beyond their watch-posts and laying waste the districts near the city. The invaders remained as long as their provisions lasted, then withdrew and dispersed to their several cities.

II. Directly after the invasion of the Peloponnesians, all Lesbos,[1] except Methymna, revolted from Athens. The Lesbians had wished to do this even before the war, but the Lacedaemonians had not taken them into their alliance, and even in this instance they were forced to revolt sooner than they had intended. For they were waiting until the work should be finished of blocking their harbours,

45. The complaint of the Mytilenaeans was founded on the Athenian attempt to prevent their centralisation. See W. Herbst, *Der Abfall Mytilenes*, 1861; Leithäuser, *Der Abfall Mytilenes*, 1874.

ποίησιν ἐπέμενον τελεσθῆναι, καὶ ὅσα ἐκ τοῦ
Πόντου ἔδει ἀφικέσθαι, τοξότας τε καὶ σῖτον,
3 καὶ ἃ μεταπεμπόμενοι ἦσαν. Τενέδιοι γὰρ ὄντες
αὐτοῖς διάφοροι καὶ Μηθυμναῖοι καὶ αὐτῶν Μυτιληναίων ἰδίᾳ ἄνδρες κατὰ στάσιν, πρόξενοι
Ἀθηναίων, μηνυταὶ γίγνονται τοῖς Ἀθηναίοις
ὅτι ξυνοικίζουσί τε τὴν Λέσβον ἐς τὴν Μυτιλήνην
βίᾳ καὶ τὴν παρασκευὴν ἅπασαν μετὰ Λακεδαιμονίων καὶ Βοιωτῶν ξυγγενῶν ὄντων ἐπὶ ἀποστάσει ἐπείγονται· καὶ εἰ μή τις προκαταλή-
ψεται ἤδη, στερήσεσθαι αὐτοὺς Λέσβου.

III. Οἱ δ᾽ Ἀθηναῖοι (ἦσαν γὰρ τεταλαιπωρη-
μένοι ὑπό τε τῆς νόσου καὶ τοῦ πολέμου ἄρτι
καθισταμένου καὶ ἀκμάζοντος) μέγα μὲν ἔργον
ἡγοῦντο εἶναι Λέσβον προσπολεμώσασθαι ναυτικὸν ἔχουσαν καὶ δύναμιν ἀκέραιον, καὶ οὐκ
ἀπεδέχοντο τὸ πρῶτον τὰς κατηγορίας μεῖζον
μέρος νέμοντες τῷ μὴ βούλεσθαι ἀληθῆ εἶναι·
ἐπειδὴ μέντοι καὶ πέμψαντες πρέσβεις οὐκ
ἔπειθον τοὺς Μυτιληναίους τήν τε ξυνοίκισιν
καὶ τὴν παρασκευὴν διαλύειν, δείσαντες προκατα-
2 λαβεῖν ἐβούλοντο. καὶ πέμπουσιν ἐξαπιναίως
τεσσαράκοντα ναῦς, αἳ ἔτυχον περὶ Πελοπόννησον παρεσκευασμέναι πλεῖν. Κλεϊππίδης δὲ
3 ὁ Δεινίου τρίτος αὐτὸς ἐστρατήγει. ἐσηγγέλθη
γὰρ αὐτοῖς ὡς εἴη Ἀπόλλωνος Μαλόεντος ἔξω

---

[1] The word means literally "public guest," or "friend."
Under the condition of entertaining and assisting ambassa-
dors and citizens of the state they represented they enjoyed

building walls, and constructing ships, and until
the arrival of what they needed from the Pontus—
archers and grain, and whatever else they were
sending for. But the people of Tenedos, who
were at variance with them, and of Methymna,
and some of the Mytilenaeans themselves, men in
private station who were *proxeni*[1] of the Athenians,
were moved by partisanship to turn informers and
notify the Athenians that the Mytilenaeans were
attempting to bring all Lesbos into a political union
centred in Mytilene; that all their preparations were
being hurried forward, in concert with the Lacedaemonians and with their kinsmen the Boeotians, with
the purpose of revolting; and that unless someone
should forestall them forthwith, Lesbos would be lost
to Athens.

III. But the Athenians, distressed by the plague
as well as by the war, which had recently broken out
and was now at its height, thought it a serious
matter to make a new enemy of Lesbos, which had
a fleet and power unimpaired; and so at first they
would not listen to the charges, giving greater weight
to the wish that they might not be true. When,
however, the envoys whom they sent could not persuade the Mytilenaeans to stop their measures for
political union and their preparations, they became
alarmed and wished to forestall them. So they suddenly despatched forty ships, which happened to be
ready for a cruise around the Peloponnesus, under
the command of Cleïppides son of Deinias and two
others; for word had come to them that there was a

certain privileges from that state, and answered pretty nearly
to our *Consuls* and *Residents*, though the *proxenus* was always
a member of the state where he served.

τῆς πόλεως ἑορτή, ἐν ᾗ πανδημεὶ Μυτιληναῖοι
ἑορτάζουσι, καὶ ἐλπίδα εἶναι ἐπειχθέντας ἐπι-
πεσεῖν ἄφνω· καὶ ἢν μὲν ξυμβῇ ἡ πεῖρα· εἰ δὲ
μή, Μυτιληναίοις εἰπεῖν ναῦς τε παραδοῦναι
καὶ τείχη καθελεῖν, μὴ πειθομένων δὲ πολεμεῖν.
4 καὶ αἱ μὲν νῆες ᾤχοντο· τὰς δὲ τῶν Μυτιληναίων δέκα τριήρεις, αἳ ἔτυχον βοηθοὶ παρὰ
σφᾶς κατὰ τὸ ξυμμαχικὸν παροῦσαι, κατέσχον
οἱ Ἀθηναῖοι καὶ τοὺς ἄνδρας ἐξ αὐτῶν ἐς
5 φυλακὴν ἐποιήσαντο. τοῖς δὲ Μυτιληναίοις
ἀνὴρ ἐκ τῶν Ἀθηνῶν διαβὰς ἐς Εὔβοιαν καὶ
πεζῇ ἐπὶ Γεραιστὸν ἐλθών, ὁλκάδος ἀναγομένης
ἐπιτυχών, πλῷ χρησάμενος καὶ τριταῖος ἐκ τῶν
Ἀθηνῶν ἐς Μυτιλήνην ἀφικόμενος ἀγγέλλει τὸν
6 ἐπίπλουν. οἱ δὲ οὔτε ἐς τὸν Μαλόεντα[1] ἐξῆλθον
τά τε ἄλλα τῶν τειχῶν καὶ λιμένων περὶ τὰ
ἡμιτέλεστα φαρξάμενοι ἐφύλασσον.

IV. Καὶ οἱ Ἀθηναῖοι οὐ πολὺ ὕστερον κατα-
πλεύσαντες ὡς ἑώρων, ἀπήγγειλαν μὲν οἱ στρατηγοὶ τὰ ἐπεσταλμένα, οὐκ ἐσακουόντων δὲ τῶν
2 Μυτιληναίων ἐς πόλεμον καθίσταντο. ἀπαρά-
σκευοι δὲ οἱ Μυτιληναῖοι καὶ ἐξαίφνης ἀναγκασθέντες πολεμεῖν ἔκπλουν μέν τινα ἐποιήσαντο
τῶν νεῶν ὡς ἐπὶ ναυμαχίαν ὀλίγον πρὸ τοῦ
λιμένος, ἔπειτα καταδιωχθέντες ὑπὸ τῶν
Ἀττικῶν νεῶν λόγους ἤδη προσέφερον τοῖς
στρατηγοῖς, βουλόμενοι τὰς ναῦς τὸ παραυτίκα,
εἰ δύναιντο, ὁμολογίᾳ τινὶ ἐπιεικεῖ ἀποπέμψα-
3 σθαι. καὶ οἱ στρατηγοὶ τῶν Ἀθηναίων ἀπεδέ-

---

[1] *i.e.* Apollo, god of Malea, the place north of the city
(*cf.* ch. iv. 5), where Apollo had a temple.

festival of Apollo Maloeis[1] outside Mytilene at which the whole populace kept holiday, and that they might hope to take them by surprise if they should make haste. And if the attempt succeeded, well and good ; but if not, the generals were to order the Mytilenaeans to deliver up their ships and pull down their walls, and if they disobeyed, to go to war. So the ships set off; and as there happened to be at Athens at the time ten Mytilenaean triremes serving as auxiliaries in accordance with the terms of their alliance, the Athenians detained them, placing their crews in custody. But the Mytilenaeans got word of the expedition through a man who crossed over from Athens to Euboea, went thence by land to Geraestus, and, chancing there upon a merchantman that was putting to sea, took ship and on the third day after leaving Athens reached Mytilene. The Mytilenaeans, accordingly, not only did not go out to the temple of Apollo Maloeis, but barricaded the half-finished portions of the walls and harbours and kept guard.[2]

IV. When not long afterwards the Athenians arrived and saw the state of affairs, their generals delivered their orders, and then, as the Mytilenaeans did not hearken to them, began hostilities. But the Mytilenaeans, being unprepared for war and forced to enter upon it without warning, merely sailed out a short distance beyond their harbour, as though offering battle ; then, when they had been chased to shore by the Athenian ships, they made overtures to the generals, wishing, if possible, to secure some sort of reasonable terms and thus to get rid of the fleet for the present. The Athenian commanders accepted

---

[2] Or, with Krüger, " but also guarded the other points after throwing barricades around the half-finished portions of the walls and harbours."

ξαντο, καὶ αὐτοὶ φοβούμενοι μὴ οὐχ ἱκανοὶ ὦσι
4 Λέσβῳ πάσῃ πολεμεῖν. καὶ ἀνοκωχὴν ποιησάμενοι πέμπουσιν ἐς τὰς Ἀθήνας οἱ Μυτιληναῖοι
τῶν τε διαβαλλόντων ἕνα, ᾧ μετέμελεν ἤδη, καὶ
ἄλλους, εἴ πως πείσειαν τὰς ναῦς ἀπελθεῖν ὡς
5 σφῶν οὐδὲν νεωτεριούντων. ἐν τούτῳ δὲ ἀποστέλλουσι καὶ ἐς τὴν Λακεδαίμονα πρέσβεις
τριήρει λαθόντες τὸ τῶν Ἀθηναίων ναυτικόν, οἳ
ὥρμουν ἐν τῇ Μαλέᾳ πρὸς βορέαν τῆς πόλεως·
οὐ γὰρ ἐπίστευον τοῖς ἀπὸ τῶν Ἀθηναίων προ-
6 χωρήσειν. καὶ οἱ μὲν ἐς τὴν Λακεδαίμονα
ταλαιπώρως διὰ τοῦ πελάγους κομισθέντες αὐτοῖς
ἔπρασσον ὅπως τις βοήθεια ἥξει.

V. Οἱ δ᾽ ἐκ τῶν Ἀθηνῶν πρέσβεις ὡς οὐδὲν
ἦλθον πράξαντες, ἐς πόλεμον καθίσταντο οἱ
Μυτιληναῖοι καὶ ἡ ἄλλη Λέσβος πλὴν Μη-
θύμνης· οὗτοι δὲ τοῖς Ἀθηναίοις ἐβεβοηθήκεσαν
καὶ Ἴμβριοι καὶ Λήμνιοι καὶ τῶν ἄλλων ὀλίγοι
2 τινὲς ξυμμάχων. καὶ ἔξοδον μέν τινα πανδημεὶ
ἐποιήσαντο οἱ Μυτιληναῖοι ἐπὶ τὸ τῶν Ἀθηναίων
στρατόπεδον, καὶ μάχη ἐγένετο, ἐν ᾗ οὐκ ἔλασσον
ἔχοντες οἱ Μυτιληναῖοι οὔτε ἐπηυλίσαντο οὔτε
ἐπίστευσαν σφίσιν αὐτοῖς, ἀλλ᾽ ἀνεχώρησαν·
3 ἔπειτα οἱ μὲν ἡσύχαζον, ἐκ Πελοποννήσου καὶ
μετ᾽ ἄλλης παρασκευῆς βουλόμενοι εἰ προσ-
4 γένοιτό τι κινδυνεύειν· καὶ γὰρ αὐτοῖς Μελέας
Λάκων ἀφικνεῖται καὶ Ἑρμαιώνδας Θηβαῖος,
οἳ προαπεστάλησαν μὲν τῆς ἀποστάσεως, φθάσαι
δὲ οὐ δυνάμενοι τὸν τῶν Ἀθηναίων ἐπίπλουν
κρύφα μετὰ τὴν μάχην ὕστερον ἐσπλέουσι
τριήρει, καὶ παρῄνουν πέμπειν τριήρη ἄλλην καὶ

their proposals, being themselves afraid that they were
not strong enough to make war against all Lesbos
So the Mytilenaeans, having concluded an armistice,
sent envoys to Athens, among whom was one of the
informers who was by now repentant, in the hope
that they might persuade them to recall their fleet,
on the understanding that they themselves would
not start a revolution. Meanwhile they also sent
envoys to Lacedaemon in a trireme, which eluded
the Athenian fleet lying at anchor at Malea north of
the town ; for they had no confidence in the success
of their negotiations with the Athenians. These
envoys, arriving at Lacedaemon after a hard voyage
through the open sea, began negotiating for some aid
for their countrymen.

V. But when the envoys to Athens returned without having accomplished anything, the people of
Mytilene and the rest of Lesbos, except Methymna,
began war ; the Methymnaeans, however, supported
the Athenians, as did also the Imbrians, Lemnians,
and a few of the other allies. The Mytilenaeans made
a sortie in full force against the camp of the Athenians, and a battle occurred in which the Mytilenaeans had the advantage ; nevertheless they did not
have enough confidence in themselves to bivouack on
the field, but withdrew. From this time on they kept
quiet, being unwilling to risk an engagement without reinforcements from Peloponnesus and elsewhere.
Such reinforcements they expected, for there had
come to them Meleas a Laconian and Hermaeondas
a Theban, who had been sent out before the revolt,
but being unable to arrive before the Athenian
expedition, had sailed in secretly after the battle in
a trireme, and now advised them to send a second

πρέσβεις μεθ' ἑαυτῶν· καὶ ἐκπέμπουσιν. VI. οἱ
δὲ Ἀθηναῖοι πολὺ ἐπιρρωσθέντες διὰ τὴν τῶν
Μυτιληναίων ἡσυχίαν ξυμμάχους τε προσε-
κάλουν, οἳ πολὺ θᾶσσον παρῆσαν ὁρῶντες οὐδὲν
ἰσχυρὸν ἀπὸ τῶν Λεσβίων, καὶ περιορμισάμενοι
καὶ¹ τὸ πρὸς νότον τῆς πόλεως ἐτείχισαν στρατόπεδα δύο ἑκατέρωθεν τῆς πόλεως καὶ τοὺς
ἐφόρμους ἐπ' ἀμφοτέροις τοῖς λιμέσιν ἐποιοῦντο.
2 καὶ τῆς μὲν θαλάσσης εἶργον μὴ χρῆσθαι τοὺς
Μυτιληναίους, τῆς δὲ γῆς τῆς μὲν ἄλλης ἐκράτουν οἱ Μυτιληναῖοι καὶ οἱ ἄλλοι Λέσβιοι
προσβεβοηθηκότες ἤδη, τὸ δὲ περὶ τὰ στρατόπεδα οὐ πολὺ κατεῖχον οἱ Ἀθηναῖοι, ναύσταθ-
μον δὲ μᾶλλον ἦν αὐτοῖς πλοίων καὶ ἀγορᾶς ἡ
Μαλέα. καὶ τὰ μὲν περὶ Μυτιλήνην οὕτως
ἐπολεμεῖτο.

VII. Κατὰ δὲ τὸν αὐτὸν χρόνον τοῦ θέρους
τούτου Ἀθηναῖοι καὶ περὶ Πελοπόννησον ναῦς
ἀπέστειλαν τριάκοντα καὶ Ἀσώπιον τὸν Φορμίωνος στρατηγόν, κελευσάντων Ἀκαρνάνων τῶν
Φορμίωνός τινα σφίσι πέμψαι ἢ υἱὸν ἢ ξυγγενῆ
2 ἄρχοντα. καὶ παραπλέουσαι αἱ νῆες τῆς Λακω-
3 νικῆς τὰ ἐπιθαλάσσια χωρία ἐπόρθησαν. ἔπειτα
τὰς μὲν πλείους ἀποπέμπει τῶν νεῶν πάλιν ἐπ'
οἴκου ὁ Ἀσώπιος, αὐτὸς δ' ἔχων δώδεκα ἀφικ-
4 νεῖται ἐς Ναύπακτον, καὶ ὕστερον Ἀκαρνᾶνας
ἀναστήσας πανδημεὶ στρατεύει ἐπ' Οἰνιάδας καὶ
ταῖς τε ναυσὶ κατὰ τὸν Ἀχελῷον ἔπλευσε καὶ
5 ὁ κατὰ γῆν στρατὸς ἐδῄου τὴν χώραν. ὡς δ' οὐ
προσεχώρουν, τὸν μὲν πεζὸν ἀφίησιν, αὐτὸς δὲ

---

¹ <καὶ>, so Hude with Steup, as a part of the fleet must
have continued at anchor north of the city.

trireme and some envoys to accompany them. And
this the Mytilenaeans did. VI. Meanwhile the Athenians, much encouraged by the inactivity of the Mytilenaeans, summoned their allies, who put in an
appearance the more quickly as they saw that no energetic measures were being taken by the Lesbians.
They also placed their ships at anchor round the
southern part of the town, and established a blockade against both harbours. Thus they excluded the
Mytilenaeans from the use of the sea; but as for the
land, the Mytilenaeans and the other Lesbians, who
had now come to their aid, dominated all the island,
except the small strip held by the Athenians in the
neighbourhood of their camps, and it was Malea
rather than their camps that they used as a station
for boats and supplies. Such was the course of the
war at Mytilene.

VII. About the same time during this summer
the Athenians sent also on a cruise round the Peloponnesus thirty ships with Asopius son of Phormio
as commander; for the Acarnanians had requested
them to send them as commander either a son or
some other kinsman of Phormio's. And the ships as
they sailed past ravaged the coast of Laconia. Afterwards Asopius sent most of the ships back home,
but had twelve with him when he reached Naupactus.
Then later, having called out all the forces of the
Acarnanians, he made an expedition against Oeniadae, sailing with the ships up the Achelous, while his
army on land ravaged the country. As, however, the
inhabitants would not come over to him, he dismissed

πλεύσας ἐς Λευκάδα καὶ ἀπόβασιν ἐς Νήρικον
ποιησάμενος ἀναχωρῶν διαφθείρεται αὐτός τε
καὶ τῆς στρατιᾶς τι μέρος ὑπὸ τῶν αὐτόθεν τε
ξυμβοηθησάντων καὶ φρουρῶν τινων ὀλίγων.
6 καὶ ὕστερον ὑποσπόνδους τοὺς νεκροὺς ἀποπλεύσαντες οἱ Ἀθηναῖοι παρὰ τῶν Λευκαδίων ἐκομί-
σαντο.

VIII. Οἱ δὲ ἐπὶ τῆς πρώτης νεὼς ἐκπεμφθέντες
Μυτιληναίων πρέσβεις, ὡς αὐτοῖς οἱ Λακεδαιμόνιοι εἶπον Ὀλυμπίαζε παρεῖναι, ὅπως καὶ οἱ
ἄλλοι ξύμμαχοι ἀκούσαντες βουλεύσωνται, ἀφικνοῦνται ἐς τὴν Ὀλυμπίαν· ἦν δὲ Ὀλυμπιὰς ᾗ
Δωριεὺς Ῥόδιος τὸ δεύτερον ἐνίκα. καὶ ἐπειδὴ
μετὰ τὴν ἑορτὴν κατέστησαν ἐς λόγους, εἶποι
τοιάδε.

IX. "Τὸ μὲν καθεστὸς τοῖς Ἕλλησι νόμιμον,
ὦ Λακεδαιμόνιοι καὶ ξύμμαχοι, ἴσμεν· τοὺς γὰρ
ἀφισταμένους ἐν τοῖς πολέμοις καὶ ξυμμαχίαν
τὴν πρὶν ἀπολείποντας οἱ δεξάμενοι, καθ᾽ ὅσον
μὲν ὠφελοῦνται, ἐν ἡδονῇ ἔχουσι, νομίζοντες δὲ
εἶναι προδότας τῶν πρὸ τοῦ φίλων χείρους
2 ἡγοῦνται. καὶ οὐκ ἄδικος αὕτη ἡ ἀξίωσίς ἐστιν,
εἰ τύχοιεν πρὸς ἀλλήλους οἵ τε ἀφιστάμενοι καὶ
ἀφ᾽ ὧν διακρίνοιντο ἴσοι μὲν τῇ γνώμῃ ὄντες καὶ
εὐνοίᾳ, ἀντίπαλοι δὲ τῇ παρασκευῇ καὶ δυνάμει,

---

[1] Foreigners (φρουρῶν as opposed to τῶν αὐτόθεν ξυμβοηθησάντων), possibly Corinthians.

[2] Dorieus son of Diagoras was victor three times in succession at Olympia (Paus. VI. vii. 1), as well as in numerous

his army, but himself sailed to Leucas and made a descent upon Nericus. On his way back from Nericus he and part of his army were slain by the people of that place, who rallied to its defence, and by a few guards.[1] The Athenians first stood out to sea and then later recovered their dead from the Leucadians under a truce.

VIII. Meanwhile the Mytilenaean envoys who had been sent on the first ship, having been told by the Lacedaemonians to present themselves at Olympia, in order that the other members of the alliance also might hear them and take counsel, came to Olympia. It was the Olympiad in which Dorieus[2] the Rhodian won his second victory. After the festival the Peloponnesians met in council, and the envoys spoke as follows :

IX. " We are not unaware, men of Lacedaemon and members of the alliance, of the traditional feeling of the Hellenes towards men who revolt in time of war and abandon their former alliance : those who accept them as allies are indeed pleased with them in so far as they derive advantage, but they regard them as traitors to their former friends and therefore think the worse of them. And this estimate is not unjust, provided that those who revolt and those from whom they secede held the same political views and were actuated by the same feeling of good will toward one another, and were evenly matched in preparation for war and in power, and provided also

other contests (Paus. vi. vii. 4). He fought in the Decelean war on the Spartan side (viii. xxxv. 1 ; Xen. *Hell.* i. i. 2), and was captured by the Athenians, but on account of his fame as an athlete was released without ransom (Xen. *Hell.* i. v. 19 ; Paus. vi. vii. 4, 5).

πρόφασίς τε ἐπιεικὴς μηδεμία ὑπάρχοι τῆς ἀπο-
στάσεως· ὃ καὶ ἡμῖν καὶ Ἀθηναίοις οὐκ ἦν, μηδέ
τῳ χείρους δόξωμεν εἶναι, εἰ ἐν τῇ εἰρήνῃ τιμώμενοι ὑπ' αὐτῶν ἐν τοῖς δεινοῖς ἀφιστάμεθα.

X. "Περὶ γὰρ τοῦ δικαίου καὶ ἀρετῆς πρῶτον,
ἄλλως τε καὶ ξυμμαχίας δεόμενοι, τοὺς λόγους
ποιησόμεθα, εἰδότες οὔτε φιλίαν ἰδιώταις βέβαιον
γιγνομένην οὔτε κοινωνίαν πόλεσιν ἐς οὐδέν, εἰ
μὴ μετ' ἀρετῆς δοκούσης ἐς ἀλλήλους γίγνοιντο
καὶ τἆλλα ὁμοιότροποι εἶεν· ἐν γὰρ τῷ διαλλάσ-
σοντι τῆς γνώμης καὶ αἱ διαφοραὶ τῶν ἔργων
καθίστανται.

2   "'Ἡμῖν δὲ καὶ Ἀθηναίοις ξυμμαχία ἐγένετο
πρῶτον ἀπολιπόντων μὲν ὑμῶν ἐκ τοῦ Μηδικοῦ
πολέμου, παραμεινάντων δὲ ἐκείνων πρὸς τὰ
3   ὑπόλοιπα τῶν ἔργων. ξύμμαχοι μέντοι ἐγενόμεθα οὐκ ἐπὶ καταδουλώσει τῶν Ἑλλήνων
Ἀθηναίοις, ἀλλ' ἐπ' ἐλευθερώσει ἀπὸ τοῦ Μήδου
4   τοῖς Ἕλλησιν. καὶ μέχρι μὲν ἀπὸ τοῦ ἴσου
ἡγοῦντο, προθύμως εἱπόμεθα· ἐπειδὴ δὲ ἑωρῶμεν
αὐτοὺς τὴν μὲν τοῦ Μήδου ἔχθραν ἀνιέντας, τὴν
δὲ τῶν ξυμμάχων δούλωσιν ἐπειγομένους,[1] οὐκ
5   ἀδεεῖς ἔτι ἦμεν. ἀδύνατοι δὲ ὄντες καθ' ἓν γενόμενοι διὰ πολυψηφίαν ἀμύνασθαι οἱ ξύμμαχοι
6   ἐδουλώθησαν πλὴν ἡμῶν καὶ Χίων· ἡμεῖς δὲ
αὐτόνομοι δὴ ὄντες καὶ ἐλεύθεροι τῷ ὀνόματι
ξυνεστρατεύσαμεν. καὶ πιστοὺς οὐκέτι εἴχομεν
ἡγεμόνας Ἀθηναίους, παραδείγμασι τοῖς προγενο-

[1] ἐπειγομένους, Ross' conjecture for ἐπαγομένους of the MSS.

that there were no reasonable excuse for their revolt. But these conditions did not obtain between us and the Athenians; therefore, let no one think the worse of us on the ground that we were honoured by them in time of peace and now revolt from them in time of danger.

X. "We will first discuss the question of justice and rectitude, especially as we are seeking an alliance, for we know that neither does friendship between men prove lasting, nor does a league between states come to aught, unless they comport themselves with transparent honesty of purpose towards one another and in general are of like character and way of thinking; for differences in men's actions arise from the diversity of their convictions.

"Now between us and the Athenians an alliance was first made when you withdrew from the Persian war but they remained to finish the work. We became allies, however, not to the Athenians for the enslavement of the Hellenes, but to the Hellenes for their emancipation from the Persians. And as long as they maintained their hegemony on terms of equality we heartily followed their lead; but when we saw them relaxing their hostility to the Persians and eager for the enslavement of the allies, we were no longer without alarm. And the allies, being unable, on account of the number of those who had votes, to unite for self-defence, were all enslaved except ourselves and the Chians; while we shared their campaigns as presumably "independent" and enjoying at least the name of freedom. And we could no longer regard the Athenians as trustworthy leaders, taking as warning examples the

μένοις χρώμενοι· οὐ γὰρ εἰκὸς ἦν αὐτοὺς οὓς μὲν
μεθ' ἡμῶν ἐνσπόνδους ἐποιήσαντο καταστρέψασθαι, τοὺς δὲ ὑπολοίπους, εἴ ποτε ἄρα δυνηθεῖεν,[1] μὴ δρᾶσαι τοῦτο.

XI. " Καὶ εἰ μὲν αὐτόνομοι ἔτι ἦμεν ἅπαντες,
βεβαιότεροι ἂν ἡμῖν ἦσαν μηδὲν νεωτεριεῖν· ὑπο-
χειρίους δὲ ἔχοντες τοὺς πλείους, ἡμῖν δὲ ἀπὸ τοῦ
ἴσου ὁμιλοῦντες, χαλεπώτερον εἰκότως ἔμελλον
οἴσειν καὶ πρὸς τὸ πλέον ἤδη εἶκον τοῦ ἡμετέρου
ἔτι μόνου ἀντισουμένου, ἄλλως τε καὶ ὅσῳ
δυνατώτεροι αὐτοὶ αὑτῶν ἐγίγνοντο καὶ ἡμεῖς
ἐρημότεροι. τὸ δὲ ἀντίπαλον δέος μόνον πιστὸν
ἐς ξυμμαχίαν· ὁ γὰρ παραβαίνειν τι βουλόμενος
2 τῷ μὴ προύχων ἂν ἐπελθεῖν ἀποτρέπεται. αὐτόνομοί τε ἐλείφθημεν οὐ δι' ἄλλο τι ἢ ὅσον αὐτοῖς
ἐς τὴν ἀρχὴν εὐπρεπείᾳ τε λόγου καὶ γνώμης
μᾶλλον ἐφόδῳ ἢ ἰσχύος τὰ πράγματα ἐφαίνετο
3 καταληπτά. ἅμα μὲν γὰρ μαρτυρίῳ ἐχρῶντο
μὴ ἂν τούς γε ἰσοψήφους ἄκοντας, εἰ μή τι
ἠδίκουν οἷς ἐπῇσαν, ξυστρατεύειν· ἐν τῷ αὐτῷ
δὲ καὶ τὰ κράτιστα ἐπί τε τοὺς ὑποδεεστέρους
πρώτους ξυνεπῆγον καὶ τελευταῖα[2] λιπόντες τοῦ
ἄλλου περιῃρημένου ἀσθενέστερα ἔμελλον ἕξειν.
εἰ δὲ ἀφ' ἡμῶν ἤρξαντο, ἐχόντων ἔτι τῶν πάντων

---

[1] δυνηθεῖεν, Dobree's conjecture for ἐδυνήθησαν of the MSS.
[2] [τὰ] τελευταῖα : τὰ deleted with Krüger.

events of the past; for it was not likely that they, after subjugating those with whom they had entered into treaty relations together with us, would not do the same to those who were left, if ever they should possibly have the power.

XI. "Again if we had all remained independent we should have had better assurance that they would make no violent change in our status; having, however, the majority under their hands, while still associating with us on an equal footing, they would naturally find it more irksome that our state alone still maintained its equality as compared with the majority that had already yielded, especially since they were becoming more powerful in proportion as we became more isolated. Indeed it is only the fear that arises from equality of power that constitutes a firm basis for an alliance; for he that would transgress is deterred by the feeling that he has no superiority wherewith to make an attack. And we were left independent for no other reason than because they clearly saw that with a view to empire they must get control of affairs by fair-seeming words and by attacks of policy rather than of force. For, on the one hand, they had as evidence in their favour that surely those who have an equal voice with themselves would never have taken part in their campaigns had not those whom they attacked been guilty of some wrong; and on the other hand, they also brought the united strength of the strongest states against the less powerful first, and leaving the former to the last they counted upon finding them weaker when all the rest had been removed from around them. But if they had begun with us, while the whole body of allies were not only still strong in

αὐτῶν τε ἰσχὺν καὶ πρὸς ὅ τι χρὴ στῆναι, οὐκ
4 ἂν ὁμοίως ἐχειρώσαντο. τό τε ναυτικὸν ἡμῶν
παρεῖχέ τινα φόβον μή ποτε καθ' ἓν γενόμενον
ἢ ὑμῖν ἢ ἄλλῳ τῳ προσθέμενον κίνδυνον σφίσι
5 παράσχῃ. τὰ δὲ καὶ ἀπὸ θεραπείας τοῦ τε
κοινοῦ αὐτῶν καὶ τῶν αἰεὶ προεστώτων περιεγι-
6 γνόμεθα. οὐ μέντοι ἐπὶ πολύ γ' ἂν ἐδοκοῦμεν
δυνηθῆναι, εἰ μὴ ὁ πόλεμος ὅδε κατέστη, παραδείγμασι χρώμενοι τοῖς ἐς τοὺς ἄλλους.

XII. "Τίς οὖν αὕτη ἡ φιλία ἐγίγνετο ἢ ἐλευ-
θερία πιστή, ἐν ᾗ παρὰ γνώμην ἀλλήλους ὑπε-
δεχόμεθα καὶ οἱ μὲν ἡμᾶς ἐν τῷ πολέμῳ δεδιότες
ἐθεράπευον, ἡμεῖς δὲ ἐκείνους ἐν τῇ ἡσυχίᾳ τὸ
αὐτὸ ἐποιοῦμεν· ὅ τε τοῖς ἄλλοις μάλιστα εὔνοια
πίστιν βεβαιοῖ, ἡμῖν τοῦτο ὁ φόβος ἐχυρὸν
παρεῖχε, δέει τε τὸ πλέον ἢ φιλίᾳ κατεχόμενοι
ξύμμαχοι ἦμεν· καὶ ὁποτέροις θᾶσσον παράσχοι
ἀσφάλεια θάρσος, οὗτοι πρότεροί τι καὶ παρα-
2 βήσεσθαι ἔμελλον. ὥστε εἴ τῳ δοκοῦμεν ἀδικεῖν
προαποστάντες διὰ τὴν ἐκείνων μέλλησιν τῶν ἐς
ἡμᾶς δεινῶν, αὐτοὶ οὐκ ἀνταναμείναντες σαφῶς
3 εἰδέναι εἴ τι αὐτῶν ἔσται, οὐκ ὀρθῶς σκοπεῖ. εἰ
γὰρ δυνατοὶ ἦμεν ἐκ τοῦ ἴσου καὶ ἀντεπιβου-
λεῦσαι, καὶ ἀντιμελλῆσαί τι ἔδει ἡμᾶς ἐκ τοῦ
ὁμοίου ἐπ' ἐκείνους ἰέναι· ἐπ' ἐκείνοις δὲ ὄντος
αἰεὶ τοῦ ἐπιχειρεῖν καὶ ἐφ' ἡμῖν εἶναι δεῖ τὸ
προαμύνασθαι.

their own strength, but also had a leader to rally to, they would not have got the mastery so easily. Besides, our navy caused them some fear, lest it should some day be augmented by being united either with yours or another's and thus become a menace to themselves. To some extent also we owe our salvation to the court we paid to the Athenian people and to the political leaders of the day. But we could not have expected to be able to survive for long, if we may judge by their conduct toward the other allies, unless this war had broken out.

XII. "Was this then a friendship or a freedom to put faith in, where we violated our real feelings whenever we treated each other as friends? They courted us in time of war only because they were afraid of us, while we acted in the same manner toward them in time of peace; and good faith, which in most cases is made steadfast by good will, was in our case made secure by fear, and it was fear rather than friendship that held us both to the alliance; and whichever of us should soonest gain boldness through a feeling of security was bound to be the first to commit some act of transgression also. If, therefore, anyone thinks that, just because they postponed the measures we dread, we do wrong in revolting first, without having waited on our side until we were quite sure that any of our suspicions would come true, he is in error. For if we were in a position to meet their plotting by counter-measures on equal terms with them, it was indeed incumbent upon us on our part to postpone likewise our offensive against them; but since the power of attack is always in their hands, the right of acting betimes in our own defence must necessarily be in ours.

XIII. "Τοιαύτας ἔχοντες προφάσεις καὶ αἰ-
τίας, ὦ Λακεδαιμόνιοι καὶ ξύμμαχοι, ἀπέστημεν,
σαφεῖς μὲν τοῖς ἀκούουσι γνῶναι ὡς εἰκότως
ἐδράσαμεν, ἱκανὰς δὲ ἡμᾶς ἐκφοβῆσαι καὶ πρὸς
ἀσφάλειάν τινα τρέψαι, βουλομένους μὲν καὶ
πάλαι, ὅτε ἔτι ἐν τῇ εἰρήνῃ ἐπέμψαμεν ὡς ὑμᾶς
περὶ ἀποστάσεως, ὑμῶν δὲ οὐ προσδεξαμένων
κωλυθέντας· νῦν δὲ ἐπειδὴ Βοιωτοὶ προυκαλέ-
σαντο, εὐθὺς ὑπηκούσαμεν, καὶ ἐνομίζομεν ἀπο-
στήσεσθαι διπλῆν ἀπόστασιν, ἀπό τε τῶν Ἑλλήνων μὴ ξὺν κακῶς ποιεῖν αὐτοὺς μετ' Ἀθηναίων,
ἀλλὰ ξυνελευθεροῦν, ἀπό τε Ἀθηναίων μὴ αὐτοὶ
διαφθαρῆναι ὑπ' ἐκείνων ἐν ὑστέρῳ, ἀλλὰ προ-
2 ποιῆσαι. ἡ μέντοι ἀπόστασις ἡμῶν θᾶσσον
γεγένηται καὶ ἀπαράσκευος· ᾗ καὶ μᾶλλον
χρὴ ξυμμάχους δεξαμένους ἡμᾶς διὰ ταχέων
βοήθειαν ἀποστέλλειν, ἵνα φαίνησθε ἀμύνοντές
τε οἷς δεῖ καὶ ἐν τῷ αὐτῷ τοὺς πολεμίους βλάπ-
3 τοντες. καιρὸς δὲ ὡς οὔπω πρότερον. νόσῳ τε
γὰρ ἐφθάραται Ἀθηναῖοι καὶ χρημάτων δαπάνῃ,
νῆές τε αὐτοῖς αἱ μὲν περὶ τὴν ὑμετέραν εἰσίν
4 αἱ δ' ἐφ' ἡμῖν τετάχαται· ὥστε οὐκ εἰκὸς αὐτοὺς
περιουσίαν νεῶν ἔχειν, ἢν ὑμεῖς ἐν τῷ θέρει τῷδε
ναυσί τε καὶ πεζῷ ἅμα ἐπεσβάλητε τὸ δεύτερον,
ἀλλ' ἢ ὑμᾶς οὐκ ἀμυνοῦνται ἐπιπλέοντας ἢ ἀπ'
5 ἀμφοτέρων ἀποχωρήσονται. νομίσῃ τε μηδεὶς

---

[1] This has not been definitely stated above, but it is
implied in ch. ii. 3, v. 4.

XIII. " Such were the motives and reasons, Lacedaemonians and allies, which led us to revolt, and
they are clear enough to convince all who hear them
that we had good grounds for our action, and cogent
enough to alarm us and impel us to seek some means
of safety. This we long ago wished to do while you
were still at peace, when we sent envoys to you
suggesting that we should revolt, but were prevented from doing so because you would not receive us. But now, when the Boeotians invited[1]
us we responded promptly. It was our intention
to make at once a double withdrawal—from the
Hellenes[2] and thus aid in liberating them instead
of joining the Athenians to do them wrong ; and
from the Athenians, and thus destroy them first instead of being ourselves destroyed by them afterwards. Our revolt, however, has been made pre-
maturely and without preparation ; wherefore it is
the more incumbent upon you to receive us as allies
and quickly send us aid, in order that all men may
see that you protect those whom you ought to
protect and at the same time harm your enemies.
And it is an opportunity such as never has been
before. For the Athenians have been ruined by
pestilence as well as by heavy expenses. Part of
their fleet is cruising about your coasts,[3] part is
arrayed against us ; so that it is not likely that they
have any ships to spare if you attack them this
coming summer a second time, by sea as well as by
land ; but they will either not resist you when you
sail against them, or else they will have to withdraw
their fleets both from our waters and from yours.
And let no one think that he will be incurring a risk

[2] *i.e.* from the Delian Confederacy.
[3] *cf.* ch. vii. 2.

ἀλλοτρίας γῆς πέρι[1] οἰκεῖον κίνδυνον ἕξειν. ᾧ
γὰρ δοκεῖ μακρὰν ἀπεῖναι ἡ Λέσβος, τὴν ὠφελίαν
αὐτῷ ἐγγύθεν παρέξει. οὐ γὰρ ἐν τῇ Ἀττικῇ
ἔσται ὁ πόλεμος, ὥς τις οἴεται, ἀλλὰ δι᾽ ἣν ἡ
6 Ἀττικὴ ὠφελεῖται. ἔστι δὲ τῶν χρημάτων ἀπὸ
τῶν ξυμμάχων ἡ πρόσοδος, καὶ ἔτι μείζων ἔσται,
εἰ ἡμᾶς καταστρέψονται· οὔτε γὰρ ἀποστήσεται
ἄλλος τά τε ἡμέτερα προσγενήσεται, πάθοιμέν
7 τ᾽ ἂν δεινότερα ἢ οἱ πρὶν δουλεύοντες. βοηθη-
σάντων δὲ ὑμῶν προθύμως πόλιν τε προσλήψεσθε
ναυτικὸν ἔχουσαν μέγα, οὗπερ ὑμῖν μάλιστα
προσδεῖ, καὶ Ἀθηναίους ῥᾷον καθαιρήσετε ὑφαι-
ροῦντες αὐτῶν τοὺς ξυμμάχους (θρασύτερον γὰρ
πᾶς τις προσχωρήσεται), τήν τε αἰτίαν ἀπο-
φεύξεσθε ἣν εἴχετε μὴ βοηθεῖν τοῖς ἀφισταμένοις,
ἢν δὲ ἐλευθεροῦντες φαίνησθε, τὸ κράτος τοῦ
πολέμου βεβαιότερον ἕξετε.

XIV. "Αἰσχυνθέντες οὖν τάς τε τῶν Ἑλλήνων
ἐς ἡμᾶς ἐλπίδας καὶ Δία τὸν Ὀλύμπιον, ἐν οὗ τῷ
ἱερῷ ἴσα καὶ ἱκέται ἐσμέν, ἐπαμύνατε Μυτιληναίοις ξύμμαχοι γενόμενοι, καὶ μὴ πρόησθε ἡμᾶς,
ἴδιον μὲν τὸν κίνδυνον τῶν σωμάτων παραβαλλο-
μένους, κοινὴν δὲ τὴν ἐκ τοῦ κατορθῶσαι ὠφελίαν
ἅπασι δώσοντας, ἔτι δὲ κοινοτέραν τὴν βλάβην,
2 εἰ μὴ πεισθέντων ὑμῶν σφαλησόμεθα. γίγνεσθε
δὲ ἄνδρες οἷοσπερ ὑμᾶς οἵ τε Ἕλληνες ἀξιοῦσι
καὶ τὸ ἡμέτερον δέος βούλεται."

[1] οὐκ is inserted by Hude.

of his own for the country of another. For though Lesbos seems to him to be a long way off, the help she will bring him will be close at hand. For the war will not be in Attica,[1] as some think, but in those countries from which Athens derives its support. The revenues of Athens come from her allies, and they will be still greater if they shall subdue us; for not only will no one else revolt, but our resources will be added to hers, and we should be treated with greater rigour[2] than those who have long been slaves. But if you give us your hearty support, you will add to your league a state that has a large navy, a thing of which you still stand most in need, and you will find it easier to overthrow the Athenians by gradually drawing their allies away from them—for every one will be emboldened to come over to your side—and you will free yourselves of the reproach under which you have heretofore laboured, of refusing[3] to aid those who revolt from the Athenians. But if you openly play the part of liberators,[4] the more certain will be your victory in the war.

XIV. "Reverencing, then, not only the hopes which the Hellenes place in you, but also that Olympian Zeus in whose temple we are even as suppliants, succour the Mytilenaeans by entering on this alliance; and do not abandon us when we are hazarding our lives in a risk all our own, but shall bring to all a general benefit if we succeed—and a still more general injury if through your refusal we shall fail. Prove yourselves, therefore, men such as the Hellenes account you and our fears would have you be."

---

[1] *i.e.* the war will not be decided in Attica.
[2] Especially as regards the tribute which would be exacted.
[3] *cf.* I. lxix. 1, 5.   [4] *cf.* II. viii. 4.

XV. Τοιαῦτα μὲν οἱ Μυτιληναῖοι εἶπον. οἱ δὲ Λακεδαιμόνιοι καὶ οἱ ξύμμαχοι ἐπειδὴ ἤκουσαν, προσδεξάμενοι τοὺς λόγους ξυμμάχους τε τοὺς Λεσβίους ἐποιήσαντο καὶ τὴν ἐς τὴν Ἀττικὴν ἐσβολὴν τοῖς τε ξυμμάχοις παροῦσι κατὰ τάχος ἔφραζον ἰέναι ἐς τὸν ἰσθμὸν τοῖς δύο μέρεσιν ὡς ποιησόμενοι, καὶ αὐτοὶ πρῶτοι ἀφίκοντο, καὶ ὁλκοὺς παρεσκεύαζον τῶν νεῶν ἐν τῷ ἰσθμῷ ὡς ὑπεροίσοντες ἐκ τῆς Κορίνθου ἐς τὴν πρὸς Ἀθήνας θάλασσαν καὶ ναυσὶ καὶ πεζῷ ἅμα 2 ἐπιόντες. καὶ οἱ μὲν προθύμως ταῦτα ἔπρασσον· οἱ δὲ ἄλλοι ξύμμαχοι βραδέως τε ξυνελέγοντο καὶ ἐν καρποῦ ξυγκομιδῇ ἦσαν καὶ ἀρρωστίᾳ τοῦ στρατεύειν.

XVI. Αἰσθόμενοι δὲ αὐτοὺς οἱ Ἀθηναῖοι διὰ κατάγνωσιν ἀσθενείας σφῶν παρασκευαζομένους, δηλῶσαι βουλόμενοι ὅτι οὐκ ὀρθῶς ἐγνώκασιν, ἀλλ' οἷοί τέ εἰσι μὴ κινοῦντες τὸ ἐπὶ Λέσβῳ ναυτικὸν καὶ τὸ ἀπὸ Πελοποννήσου ἐπιὸν ῥᾳδίως ἀμύνεσθαι, ἐπλήρωσαν ναῦς ἑκατὸν ἐσβάντες αὐτοί τε πλὴν ἱππέων καὶ πεντακοσιομεδίμνων καὶ οἱ μέτοικοι, καὶ παρὰ τὸν ἰσθμὸν ἀναγαγόντες ἐπίδειξίν τε ἐποιοῦντο καὶ ἀπο-2 βάσεις τῆς Πελοποννήσου ᾗ δοκοίη αὐτοῖς. οἱ δὲ Λακεδαιμόνιοι ὁρῶντες πολὺν τὸν παράλογον τά τε ὑπὸ τῶν Λεσβίων ῥηθέντα ἡγοῦντο οὐκ

---

[1] cf. II. x. 2.

[2] Of citizens usually only the θῆτες, who were light-armed troops on land, served in the fleet (VI. xliii) ; but in critical

XV. Thus spoke the Mytilenaeans. The Lacedaemonians and their allies, after they had heard them,
accepted their proposals, and received the Lesbians as
allies. Those allies who were there present were
directed to assemble with all speed at the Isthmus
with two-thirds [1] of their forces for the purpose of
making the proposed invasion of Attica; and the
Lacedaemonians themselves arrived first and proceeded to construct on the Isthmus hauling-machines
with which to transfer the ships from Corinth to the
sea on the Athenian side, in order to attack Athens
both by sea and by land. They set to work zealously
at these things, but the rest of the allies collected
slowly, since they were busy gathering in their
harvest and were in no mood for campaigning.

XVI. Meanwhile the Athenians, perceiving that
the enemy, in making their preparations, were acting
upon a conviction of their own weakness, and wishing
to show that they were mistaken in their judgment,
and that without moving the fleet at Lesbos they could
easily ward off the new force coming from the Peloponnesus, manned one hundred ships, the citizens,[2]
—except the knights and the highest class—em-
barking as well as the resident aliens. Then putting
out to sea they displayed their strength along the
coast of the Isthmus and made descents upon the
Peloponnesus wherever they pleased. As for the
Lacedaemonians, when they saw how greatly they
had miscalculated, they concluded that the reports
of the Lesbians [3] were untrue, and regarding the

---

times members of the three upper classes, whose regular
duty was hoplite service, might be pressed into service in the
fleet (VIII. xxiv 2).

[3] cf. ch. xiii. 3, 4.

ἀληθῆ καὶ ἄπορα νομίζοντες, ὡς αὐτοῖς καὶ οἱ
ξύμμαχοι ἅμα οὐ παρῆσαν καὶ ἠγγέλλοντο καὶ
αἱ περὶ τὴν Πελοπόννησον τριάκοντα νῆες τῶν
Ἀθηναίων τὴν περιοικίδα αὐτῶν πορθοῦσαι, ἀνε-
3 χώρησαν ἐπ᾽ οἴκου. ὕστερον δὲ ναυτικὸν παρεσκεύαζον ὅ τι πέμψουσιν ἐς τὴν Λέσβον καὶ
κατὰ πόλεις ἐπήγγελον τεσσαράκοντα νεῶν
πλῆθος καὶ ναύαρχον προσέταξαν Ἀλκίδαν, ὃς
4 ἔμελλεν ἐπιπλεύσεσθαι. ἀνεχώρησαν δὲ καὶ οἱ
Ἀθηναῖοι ταῖς ἑκατὸν ναυσίν, ἐπειδὴ καὶ ἐκείνους
εἶδον.

XVII. Καὶ[1] κατὰ τὸν χρόνον τοῦτον ὃν αἱ
νῆες ἔπλεον ἐν τοῖς πλεῖσται δὴ νῆες ἅμ᾽
αὐτοῖς ἐνεργοὶ κάλλει[2] ἐγένοντο, παραπλήσιαι
2 δὲ καὶ ἔτι πλείους ἀρχομένου τοῦ πολέμου. τήν
τε γὰρ Ἀττικὴν καὶ Εὔβοιαν καὶ Σαλαμῖνα
ἑκατὸν ἐφύλασσον καὶ περὶ Πελοπόννησον ἕτεραι
ἑκατὸν ἦσαν, χωρὶς δὲ αἱ περὶ Ποτίδαιαν καὶ
ἐν τοῖς ἄλλοις χωρίοις, ὥστε αἱ πᾶσαι ἅμα
ἐγίγνοντο ἐν ἑνὶ θέρει διακόσιαι καὶ πεντήκοντα.
3 καὶ τὰ χρήματα τοῦτο μάλιστα ὑπανάλωσε μετὰ
Ποτιδαίας. τήν τε γὰρ Ποτίδαιαν δίδραχμοι
ὁπλῖται ἐφρούρουν (αὐτῷ γὰρ καὶ ὑπηρέτῃ
δραχμὴν ἐλάμβανε τῆς ἡμέρας), τρισχίλιοι μὲν
οἱ πρῶτοι, ὧν οὐκ ἐλάσσους διεπολιόρκησαν,
ἑξακόσιοι δὲ καὶ χίλιοι μετὰ Φορμίωνος, οἳ
προαπῆλθον· νῆές τε αἱ πᾶσαι τὸν αὐτὸν μισθὸν

---

[1] This whole chapter is condemned as spurious by Steup,
followed by Hude.
[2] Untranslatable in this context: Stahl writes καὶ ἄλλη,
van Herwerden ἄλλαι ἄλλῃ, Cullinan κάλλαι, L. Herbst σ᾽
καὶ λ᾽.

expedition as impracticable, since their allies had not yet arrived, and, besides, word had come to them that the thirty[1] ships which were cruising around the Peloponnese were ravaging their own country districts, they went back home. Later,[2] however, they prepared a fleet which was to be dispatched to Lesbos and sent orders to the allied states for forty ships, appointing Alcidas who was to sail as admiral of this fleet. And when the Athenians saw that the enemy had withdrawn, they also returned home with their hundred ships.

XVII. At the time when these ships were at sea about the largest number the Athenians ever had at once were on active service, though there were as many or even more at the beginning of the war. For one hundred ships were guarding Attica, Euboea and Salamis, and another hundred were cruising off the Peloponnesus, besides those at Potidaea and in other places, so that the number in service at the same time in a single summer was all told two hundred and fifty. It was this effort, together with Potidaea, that chiefly exhausted their resources of money. For in the siege of Potidaea the hoplite received a wage of two drachmas a day, one for himself and one for his attendant; and there were at first three thousand of these, and the number was not less than this throughout the siege, besides sixteen hundred who came with Phormio, but went away before the siege was over; and the sailors on the ships all drew the same pay as the soldiers.

[1] cf. ch. vii. 1.   [2] cf. ch. xxv. 1; xxvi. 1.

4 ἔφερον. τὰ μὲν οὖν χρήματα οὕτως ὑπαναλώθη
τὸ πρῶτον, καὶ νῆες τοσαῦται δὴ πλεῖσται
ἐπληρώθησαν.

XVIII. Μυτιληναῖοι δὲ κατὰ τὸν αὐτὸν χρόνον ὃν οἱ Λακεδαιμόνιοι περὶ τὸν ἰσθμὸν ἦσαν
ἐπὶ Μήθυμναν ὡς προδιδομένην ἐστράτευσαν
κατὰ γῆν αὐτοί τε καὶ οἱ ἐπίκουροι· καὶ προσβαλόντες τῇ πόλει, ἐπειδὴ οὐ προυχώρει ᾗ
προσεδέχοντο, ἀπῆλθον ἐπ' Ἀντίσσης καὶ Πύρρας
καὶ Ἐρέσου, καὶ καταστησάμενοι τὰ ἐν ταῖς
πόλεσι ταύταις βεβαιότερα καὶ τείχη κρατύ-
2 ναντες διὰ τάχους ἀπῆλθον ἐπ' οἴκου. ἐστράτευσαν δὲ καὶ οἱ Μηθυμναῖοι ἀναχωρησάντων
αὐτῶν ἐπ' Ἄντισσαν· καὶ ἐκβοηθείας τινὸς γενομένης πληγέντες ὑπό τε τῶν Ἀντισσαίων καὶ
τῶν ἐπικούρων ἀπέθανόν τε πολλοὶ καὶ ἀνεχώ-
3 ρησαν οἱ λοιποὶ κατὰ τάχος. οἱ δὲ Ἀθηναῖοι
πυνθανόμενοι ταῦτα, τούς τε Μυτιληναίους τῆς
γῆς κρατοῦντας καὶ τοὺς σφετέρους στρατιώτας
οὐχ ἱκανοὺς ὄντας εἴργειν, πέμπουσι περὶ τὸ
φθινόπωρον ἤδη ἀρχόμενον Πάχητα τὸν Ἐπι-
κούρου στρατηγὸν καὶ χιλίους ὁπλίτας ἑαυτῶν.
4 οἱ δὲ αὐτερέται πλεύσαντες τῶν νεῶν ἀφικνοῦνται
καὶ περιτειχίζουσι Μυτιλήνην ἐν κύκλῳ ἁπλῷ
τείχει· φρούρια δ' ἔστιν ᾗ ἐπὶ τῶν καρτερῶν
5 ἐγκατοικοδομεῖται. καὶ ἡ μὲν Μυτιλήνη κατὰ
κράτος ἤδη ἀμφοτέρωθεν καὶ ἐκ γῆς καὶ ἐκ
θαλάσσης εἴργετο, καὶ ὁ χειμὼν ἤρχετο γίγνεσθαι.

XIX. Προσδεόμενοι δὲ οἱ Ἀθηναῖοι χρημάτων
ἐς τὴν πολιορκίαν, καὶ αὐτοὶ ἐσενεγκόντες τότε

It was in this way, then, that their money was exhausted at first, and this was the largest number of ships manned by them.

XVIII. While the Lacedaemonians were at the Isthmus, the Mytilenaeans and their auxiliaries [1] marched with their army against Methymna, which they supposed was being betrayed into their hands; and they assaulted the city, but when their attempt did not succeed as they had expected, they went off to Antissa, Pyrrha and Eresus, and after establishing their interests in these cities on a firmer basis and strengthening the walls, went home in haste. As soon, however, as they had withdrawn, the Methymnaeans in their turn made an expedition against Antissa; but a sortie was made by the inhabitants of Antissa and the auxiliary troops in which the Methymnaeans were defeated and many of them slain, whereupon the rest withdrew in haste. Now when the Athenians learned that the Mytilenaeans were masters of the country and that their own soldiers were not numerous enough to keep them within their walls, about the beginning of autumn they sent Paches son of Epicurus in command of a thousand Athenian hoplites, who also served as rowers.[2] When they arrived at Mytilene, they encircled it with a single wall, in which forts were built at a number of strong positions. Mytilene was thus at last completely cut off both by sea and land just as the winter set in.

XIX. Now the Athenians, finding themselves in need of additional funds for the siege, having then

[1] Foreign mercenaries; cf. ch. ii. 2.
[2] The fact of hoplites serving at the oars—evidently for economical reasons (cf. ch. xix. 1)—is especially emphasised. cf. i. x. 4 ; vi. xci. 4.

πρῶτον ἐσφορὰν διακόσια τάλαντα, ἐξέπεμψαν
καὶ ἐπὶ τοὺς ξυμμάχους ἀργυρολόγους ναῦς
δώδεκα καὶ Λυσικλέα πέμπτον αὐτὸν στρατηγόν.
2 ὁ δὲ ἄλλα τε ἠργυρολόγει καὶ περιέπλει, καὶ
τῆς Καρίας ἐκ Μυοῦντος ἀναβὰς διὰ τοῦ
Μαιάνδρου πεδίου μέχρι τοῦ Σανδίου λόφου,
ἐπιθεμένων τῶν Καρῶν καὶ Ἀναιιτῶν, αὐτός τε
διαφθείρεται καὶ τῆς ἄλλης στρατιᾶς πολλοί.

XX. Τοῦ δ᾽ αὐτοῦ χειμῶνος οἱ Πλαταιῆς (ἔτι
γὰρ ἐπολιορκοῦντο ὑπὸ τῶν Πελοποννησίων καὶ
Βοιωτῶν) ἐπειδὴ τῷ τε σίτῳ ἐπιλείποντι ἐπιέζοντο
καὶ ἀπὸ τῶν Ἀθηνῶν οὐδεμία ἐλπὶς ἦν τιμωρίας
οὐδὲ ἄλλη σωτηρία ἐφαίνετο, ἐπιβουλεύουσιν
αὐτοί τε καὶ Ἀθηναίων οἱ ξυμπολιορκούμενοι
πρῶτον μὲν πάντες ἐξελθεῖν καὶ ὑπερβῆναι τὰ
τείχη τῶν πολεμίων, ἢν δύνωνται βιάσασθαι,
ἐσηγησαμένων τὴν πεῖραν αὐτοῖς Θεαινέτου τε
τοῦ Τολμίδου, ἀνδρὸς μάντεως, καὶ Εὐπομπίδου
2 τοῦ Δαϊμάχου, ὃς καὶ ἐστρατήγει· ἔπειτα οἱ μὲν
ἡμίσεις ἀπώκνησάν πως τὸν κίνδυνον μέγαν
ἡγησάμενοι, ἐς δὲ ἄνδρας διακοσίους καὶ εἴκοσι
μάλιστα ἐνέμειναν τῇ ἐξόδῳ ἐθελονταὶ τρόπῳ
3 τοιῷδε. κλίμακας ἐποιήσαντο ἴσας τῷ τείχει
τῶν πολεμίων· ξυνεμετρήσαντο δὲ ταῖς ἐπιβολαῖς
τῶν πλίνθων, ᾗ ἔτυχε πρὸς σφᾶς οὐκ ἐξαλη-
λιμμένον τὸ τεῖχος αὐτῶν. ἠριθμοῦντο δὲ πολλοὶ
ἅμα τὰς ἐπιβολὰς καὶ ἔμελλον οἱ μέν τινες

for the first time resorted to a property tax[1] upon themselves to the amount of two hundred talents, also sent to the allies twelve ships under the command of Lysicles and four others, to collect money from them. He cruised about and collected money at various places; but on his way inland from Myus in Caria through the plain of the Meander, after he had reached the hill of Sandius, he was attacked by the Carians and the Anaeitans and slain, together with many of his army.

XX. During the same winter the Plataeans, who were still[2] being besieged by the Peloponnesians and the Boeotians, began to be distressed by failure of their supply of food, and since there was no hope of aid from Athens nor any other means of safety in sight, they and the Athenians who were besieged with them planned to leave the city and climb over the enemy's walls, in the hope that they might be able to force a passage. The attempt was suggested to them by Theaenetus son of Tolmides, a soothsayer, and Eupompidas son of Daïmachus, who was one of the generals. At first all were to take part, but afterwards half of them somehow lost heart, thinking the risk too great, and only about two hundred and twenty voluntarily persisted in making the sortie, which was carried out in the following way. They made ladders equal in height to the enemy's wall, getting the measure by counting the layers of bricks at a point where the enemy's wall on the side facing Plataea happened not to have been plastered over. Many counted the layers at the same time, and while

---

[1] The ἐσφορά was an extraordinary tax levied only in war time. See Boeckh, *Public Economy*, p. 612.

[2] For previous discussion of this siege, see II. lxxi.-lxxviii.

ἁμαρτήσεσθαι, οἱ δὲ πλείους τεύξεσθαι τοῦ
ἀληθοῦς λογισμοῦ, ἄλλως τε καὶ πολλάκις
ἀριθμοῦντες καὶ ἅμα οὐ πολὺ ἀπέχοντες, ἀλλὰ
ῥᾳδίως καθορωμένου ἐς ὃ ἐβούλοντο τοῦ τείχους.
4 τὴν μὲν οὖν ξυμμέτρησιν τῶν κλιμάκων οὕτως
ἔλαβον ἐκ τοῦ πάχους τῆς πλίνθου εἰκάσαντες
τὸ μέτρον.

XXI. Τὸ δὲ τεῖχος ἦν τῶν Πελοποννησίων
τοιόνδε τῇ οἰκοδομήσει. εἶχε μὲν δύο τοὺς περι-
βόλους, πρός τε Πλαταιῶν καὶ εἴ τις ἔξωθεν ἀπ'
Ἀθηνῶν ἐπίοι, διεῖχον δὲ οἱ περίβολοι ἑκκαίδεκα
2 πόδας μάλιστα ἀπ' ἀλλήλων. τὸ οὖν μεταξὺ
τοῦτο οἱ ἑκκαίδεκα πόδες [1] τοῖς φύλαξιν οἰκήματα
διανενεμημένα ᾠκοδόμητο, καὶ ἦν ξυνεχῆ [2] ὥστε
ἓν φαίνεσθαι τεῖχος παχὺ ἐπάλξεις ἔχον ἀμφο-
3 τέρωθεν. διὰ δέκα δὲ ἐπάλξεων πύργοι ἦσαν
μεγάλοι καὶ ἰσοπλατεῖς τῷ τείχει, διήκοντες ἔς
τε τὸ ἔσω μέτωπον αὐτοῦ οἱ αὐτοὶ καὶ τὸ ἔξω,
ὥστε πάροδον μὴ εἶναι παρὰ πύργον,[3] ἀλλὰ δι'
4 αὐτῶν μέσων διῇσαν. τὰς οὖν νύκτας, ὁπότε
χειμὼν εἴη νοτερός, τὰς μὲν ἐπάλξεις ἀπέλειπον,
ἐκ δὲ τῶν πύργων ὄντων δι' ὀλίγου καὶ ἄνωθεν
στεγανῶν τὴν φυλακὴν ἐποιοῦντο. τὸ μὲν οὖν
τεῖχος ᾧ περιεφρουροῦντο οἱ Πλαταιῆς τοιοῦτον ἦν.

XXII. Οἱ δ', ἐπειδὴ παρεσκεύαστο αὐτοῖς,
τηρήσαντες νύκτα χειμέριον ὕδατι καὶ ἀνέμῳ καὶ
ἅμ' ἀσέληνον ἐξῇσαν· ἡγοῦντο δὲ οἵπερ καὶ τῆς

[1] οἱ ἑκκαίδεκα πόδες deleted by van Herwerden, followed
by Hude.
[2] ξυνεχῆ with all MSS. except C, which Hude follows.
[3] παρὰ πύργον deleted by Naber, followed by Hude.

some were sure to make a mistake, the majority were likely to hit the true count, especially since they counted time and again, and, besides, were at no great distance, and the part of the wall they wished to see was easily visible. The measurement of the ladders, then, they got at in this way, reckoning the measure from the thickness of the bricks.

XXI. The wall of the Peloponnesians was built in the following fashion. It had two encircling lines, the inner looking towards Plataea, the outer to guard against attack from the direction of Athens, and the two circuits were distant about sixteen feet from one another. This interval of sixteen feet had in building been divided up into rooms assigned to the guards; and the whole structure was continuous,[1] so as to appear to be a single thick wall furnished with battlements on both sides. And at every tenth battlement there were high towers of the same width as the wall, extending both to the inner and outer faces of it, so that there was no passage left at the sides of the towers, but the guards had to go through the middle of them. Now at night when the weather was rainy the guards left the battlements and kept watch from the towers, which were not far apart and were roofed overhead. Such, then, was the wall by which the Plataeans were beleaguered.

XXII. After the Plataeans had finished their preparations, they waited for a night that was stormy with rain and wind and at the same time moonless, and then went forth. They were led by the men

---

[1] *i.e.* the two περίβολοι were joined together by a roof.

πείρας αἴτιοι ἦσαν. καὶ πρῶτον μὲν τὴν τάφρον
διέβησαν ἣ περιεῖχεν αὐτούς, ἔπειτα προσέμειξαν
τῷ τείχει τῶν πολεμίων λαθόντες τοὺς φύλακας,
ἀνὰ τὸ σκοτεινὸν μὲν οὐ προϊδόντων αὐτῶν, ψόφῳ
δὲ τῷ ἐκ τοῦ προσιέναι αὐτοὺς ἀντιπαταγοῦντος
2 τοῦ ἀνέμου οὐ κατακουσάντων· ἅμα δὲ καὶ διέ-
χοντες πολὺ ἦσαν, ὅπως τὰ ὅπλα μὴ κρουόμενα
πρὸς ἄλληλα αἴσθησιν παρέχοι. ἦσαν δὲ εὐστα-
λεῖς τε τῇ ὁπλίσει καὶ τὸν ἀριστερὸν μόνον πόδα
ὑποδεδεμένοι ἀσφαλείας ἕνεκα τῆς πρὸς τὸν
3 πηλόν. κατὰ οὖν μεταπύργιον προσέμισγον πρὸς
τὰς ἐπάλξεις εἰδότες ὅτι ἐρῆμοί εἰσι, πρῶτον μὲν
οἱ τὰς κλίμακας φέροντες, καὶ προσέθεσαν· ἔπειτα
ψιλοὶ δώδεκα ξὺν ξιφιδίῳ καὶ θώρακι ἀνέβαινον,
ὧν ἡγεῖτο Ἀμμέας ὁ Κοροίβου καὶ πρῶτος ἀνέβη,
μετὰ δὲ αὐτὸν οἱ ἑπόμενοι ἐξ ἐφ' ἑκάτερον τῶν
πύργων ἀνέβαινον· ἔπειτα ψιλοὶ ἄλλοι μετὰ
τούτους ξὺν δορατίοις ἐχώρουν, οἷς ἕτεροι κατόπιν
τὰς ἀσπίδας ἔφερον, ὅπως ἐκεῖνοι ῥᾷον προσβαί-
νοιεν, καὶ ἔμελλον δώσειν ὁπότε πρὸς τοῖς πολε-
4 μίοις εἶεν. ὡς δὲ ἄνω πλείους ἐγένοντο, ᾔσθοντο
οἱ ἐκ τῶν πύργων φύλακες· κατέβαλε γάρ τις τῶν
Πλαταιῶν ἀντιλαμβανόμενος ἀπὸ τῶν ἐπάλξεων
5 κεραμίδα, ἣ πεσοῦσα δοῦπον ἐποίησεν. καὶ
αὐτίκα βοὴ ἦν, τὸ δὲ στρατόπεδον ἐπὶ τὸ τεῖχος
ὥρμησεν· οὐ γὰρ ᾔδει ὅ τι ἦν τὸ δεινὸν σκοτεινῆς
νυκτὸς καὶ χειμῶνος ὄντος, καὶ ἅμα οἱ ἐν τῇ πόλει
τῶν Πλαταιῶν ὑπολελειμμένοι ἐξελθόντες προσέβαλλον τῷ τείχει τῶν Πελοποννησίων ἐκ τοὔμ-

who were the authors of the enterprise. First they crossed the ditch which surrounded the town, then reached the foot of the enemy's wall unobserved by the guards, who in the all-pervading darkness could not see ahead and could not hear because the clatter of the wind drowned the noise of their approach; and, besides, they kept a good distance apart as they advanced, in order that their arms might not rattle against each other and cause detection. And they were not only lightly armed but also had only the left foot sandalled, for security against slipping in the mud. So they came up to the battlements at a space between two towers, knowing that the battlements were deserted. First came the men with the ladders, who set them against the wall; next came twelve light-armed men, with dagger and corslet only, who mounted the ladders. These were led by Ammeas son of Coroebus, who was the first to ascend, and after him his followers ascended, six men going against each of the adjoining towers. Next after these came other light troops armed with short spears, their shields being borne by another group which followed, that the former might advance more easily; and their shields were to be handed them when they were close to the enemy. Now when several had got up, the sentinels on the towers became aware of their presence; for one of the Plataeans in laying hold of the battlements threw down a tile, which fell with a thud. And immediately there was an outcry, and the garrison rushed to the wall; for they did not know what the danger was, as the night was dark and stormy, and at the same time the Plataeans who had been left behind in the town went out and attacked the wall of the Peloponnesians on the side

πάλιν ἢ οἱ ἄνδρες αὐτῶν ὑπερέβαινον, ὅπως
6 ἥκιστα πρὸς αὐτοὺς τὸν νοῦν ἔχοιεν. ἐθορυβοῦντο
μὲν οὖν κατὰ χώραν μένοντες, βοηθεῖν δὲ οὐδεὶς
ἐτόλμα ἐκ τῆς ἑαυτῶν φυλακῆς, ἀλλ᾽ ἐν ἀπόρῳ
7 ἦσαν εἰκάσαι τὸ γιγνόμενον. καὶ οἱ τριακόσιοι
αὐτῶν, οἷς ἐτέτακτο παραβοηθεῖν εἴ τι δέοι,
ἐχώρουν ἔξωθεν τοῦ τείχους πρὸς τὴν βοήν,
8 φρυκτοί τε ἤροντο ἐς τὰς Θήβας πολέμιοι· παραν-
ῖσχον δὲ καὶ οἱ ἐκ τῆς πόλεως Πλαταιῆς ἀπὸ
τοῦ τείχους φρυκτοὺς πολλοὺς πρότερον παρε-
σκευασμένους ἐς αὐτὸ τοῦτο, ὅπως ἀσαφῆ τὰ
σημεῖα τῆς φρυκτωρίας τοῖς πολεμίοις ᾖ καὶ μὴ
βοηθοῖεν, ἄλλο τι νομίσαντες τὸ γιγνόμενον εἶναι
ἢ τὸ ὄν, πρὶν σφῶν οἱ ἄνδρες οἱ ἐξιόντες διαφύγοιεν καὶ τοῦ ἀσφαλοῦς ἀντιλάβοιντο.

XXIII. Οἱ δ᾽ ὑπερβαίνοντες τῶν Πλαταιῶν ἐν
τούτῳ, ὡς οἱ πρῶτοι αὐτῶν ἀνεβεβήκεσαν καὶ
τοῦ πύργου ἑκατέρου τοὺς φύλακας διαφθείραντες
ἐκεκρατήκεσαν, τάς τε διόδους τῶν πύργων
ἐνστάντες αὐτοὶ ἐφύλασσον μηδένα δι᾽ αὐτῶν
ἐπιβοηθεῖν, καὶ κλίμακας προσθέντες ἀπὸ τοῦ
τείχους τοῖς πύργοις καὶ ἐπαναβιβάσαντες ἄνδρας
πλείους, οἱ μὲν ἀπὸ τῶν πύργων τοὺς ἐπιβοηθοῦν-
τας καὶ κάτωθεν καὶ ἄνωθεν εἶργον βάλλοντες,
οἱ δ᾽ ἐν τούτῳ οἱ πλείους πολλὰς προσθέντες
κλίμακας ἅμα καὶ τὰς ἐπάλξεις ἀπώσαντες διὰ
2 τοῦ μεταπυργίου ὑπερέβαινον. ὁ δὲ διακομιζό-
μενος αἰεὶ ἵστατο ἐπὶ τοῦ χείλους τῆς τάφρου

opposite that over which their men were climbing,
to distract attention from them as far as possible. Now
the sentinels remained at their posts, though in a
state of excitement, no one daring to leave his station
and lend aid, but all being at a loss to conjecture
what was going on. Furthermore, the three hundred,
who had been appointed to bring aid wherever it was
needed, proceeded outside of the wall in the direction
of the outcry, and beacon fires indicating danger
from the enemy were flashed towards Thebes. But the
Plataeans in the town at the same time raised from
their wall many beacons, which had been prepared
beforehand for this very purpose, that the enemy's
beacon signals might be rendered unintelligible and
that the Thebans, thinking that the situation was
different from what it really was, might defer bringing aid until the Plataeans who were leaving should
have made good their escape and reached safety.

XXIII. Meanwhile, when the foremost of the
Plataeans who were scaling the walls had mounted,
slain the guards, and got possession of the two towers,
they themselves took position inside the towers and
guarded the passageways, that no one might come
through these against them. Then from the top of
the wall they placed ladders against the towers,
got up a number of men, and kept all assailants
away from the towers, shooting at them from below
and above.[1] Meanwhile the others, the main body,
had put up a large number of ladders and thrown
down the battlements, and were climbing over
through the space between the towers. And as each
one got over he halted on the edge of the ditch; and

[1] *i.e.* from the tops of the towers and from the wall at
their base.

καὶ ἐντεῦθεν ἐτόξευόν τε καὶ ἠκόντιζον, εἴ τις
παραβοηθῶν παρὰ τὸ τεῖχος κωλυτὴς γίγνοιτο
3 τῆς διαβάσεως. ἐπεὶ δὲ πάντες διεπεπεραίωντο,
οἱ ἀπὸ τῶν πύργων χαλεπῶς οἱ τελευταῖοι κατα-
βαίνοντες ἐχώρουν ἐπὶ τὴν τάφρον, καὶ ἐν τούτῳ οἱ τριακόσιοι αὐτοῖς ἐπεφέροντο λαμπάδας
4 ἔχοντες. οἱ μὲν οὖν Πλαταιῆς ἐκείνους ἑώρων
μᾶλλον ἐκ τοῦ σκότους ἑστῶτες ἐπὶ τοῦ χείλους
τῆς τάφρου, καὶ ἐτόξευόν τε καὶ ἐσηκόντιζον ἐς
τὰ γυμνά, αὐτοὶ δὲ ἐν τῷ ἀφανεῖ ὄντες ἧσσον διὰ
τὰς λαμπάδας καθεωρῶντο, ὥστε φθάνουσι τῶν
Πλαταιῶν καὶ οἱ ὕστατοι διαβάντες τὴν τάφρον,
5 χαλεπῶς δὲ καὶ βιαίως· κρύσταλλός τε γὰρ
ἐπεπήγει οὐ βέβαιος ἐν αὐτῇ ὥστ' ἐπελθεῖν, ἀλλ'
οἷος ἀπηλιώτου ἢ βορέου [1] ὑδατώδης μᾶλλον, καὶ
ἡ νὺξ τοιούτῳ ἀνέμῳ ὑπονειφομένη πολὺ τὸ ὕδωρ
ἐν αὐτῇ ἐπεποιήκει, ὃ μόλις ὑπερέχοντες ἐπεραιώθησαν. ἐγένετο δὲ καὶ ἡ διάφευξις αὐτοῖς μᾶλλον
διὰ τοῦ χειμῶνος τὸ μέγεθος.

XXIV. Ὁρμήσαντες δὲ ἀπὸ τῆς τάφρου οἱ
Πλαταιῆς ἐχώρουν ἀθρόοι τὴν ἐς Θήβας φέρουσαν ὁδὸν ἐν δεξιᾷ ἔχοντες τὸ τοῦ Ἀνδροκράτους
ἡρῷον, νομίζοντες ἥκιστ' ἂν σφᾶς ταύτην αὐτοὺς
ὑποτοπῆσαι τραπέσθαι τὴν ἐς τοὺς πολεμίους·
καὶ ἅμα ἑώρων τοὺς Πελοποννησίους τὴν πρὸς
Κιθαιρῶνα καὶ Δρυὸς κεφαλὰς τὴν ἐπ' Ἀθηνῶν
2 φέρουσαν μετὰ λαμπάδων διώκοντας. καὶ ἐπὶ
μὲν ἓξ ἢ ἑπτὰ σταδίους οἱ Πλαταιῆς τὴν ἐπὶ τῶν
Θηβῶν ἐχώρησαν, ἔπειθ' ὑποστρέψαντες ᾖσαν
τὴν πρὸς τὸ ὄρος φέρουσαν ὁδὸν ἐς Ἐρύθρας καὶ

[1] ἢ βορέου, deleted by Dobree, followed by Hude. Poppo
would transpose ὑδατώδης μᾶλλον, or bracket ὑδατώδης.

from there they shot arrows and hurled javelins at any enemy who tried to approach along the wall and interfere with their crossing. And when all these had reached the other side, the men who had held the towers, the last of whom descended with difficulty, advanced toward the ditch ; and at the same time the three hundred bore down upon them, carrying torches. Now the Plataeans, as they stood on the edge of the ditch, saw them better out of the darkness, and kept launching arrows and javelins at their uncovered sides, while they themselves, being in the shadow, were rendered less visible by the enemy's torches. Consequently even the last of the Plataeans got safely across the ditch, though only with difficulty and after a hard struggle; for in the ditch ice had formed that was not firm enough to walk on but mushy, such as is formed when the wind is east instead of north ; and since the night, the wind being from that quarter, was somewhat snowy, the water in the ditch had become so deep that they could scarcely keep their heads above it as they crossed. It was, however, chiefly the violence of the storm that enabled them to escape at all.

XXIV. Starting from the ditch, the Plataeans advanced in a body along the road toward Thebes, having on their right the shrine of the hero Androcrates; for they thought that no one would ever suspect them of having taken this road, which led towards their enemies; besides, they saw the Peloponnesians, torches in hand, taking in pursuit the road toward Cithaeron and Dryoscephalae, which is the road to Athens. And for six or seven stadia the Plataeans proceeded on the road toward Thebes, then turned and followed that leading towards Erythrae and

39

Ὑσιάς, καὶ λαβόμενοι τῶν ὁρῶν διαφεύγουσιν ἐς
τὰς Ἀθήνας, ἄνδρες δώδεκα καὶ διακόσιοι ἀπὸ
πλειόνων· εἰσὶ γάρ τινες αὐτῶν οἳ ἀπετράποντο
ἐς τὴν πόλιν πρὶν ὑπερβαίνειν, εἷς δ' ἐπὶ τῇ ἔξω
3 τάφρῳ τοξότης ἐλήφθη. οἱ μὲν οὖν Πελοποννήσιοι κατὰ χώραν ἐγένοντο τῆς βοηθείας
παυσάμενοι· οἱ δ' ἐκ τῆς πόλεως Πλαταιῆς τῶν
μὲν γεγενημένων εἰδότες οὐδέν, τῶν δὲ ἀποτραπο-
μένων σφίσιν ἀπαγγειλάντων ὡς οὐδεὶς περίεστι,
κήρυκα ἐκπέμψαντες, ἐπεὶ ἡμέρα ἐγένετο, ἐσπένδοντο ἀναίρεσιν τοῖς νεκροῖς, μαθόντες δὲ τὸ
ἀληθὲς ἐπαύσαντο. οἱ μὲν δὴ τῶν Πλαταιῶν
ἄνδρες οὕτω ὑπερβάντες ἐσώθησαν.

XXV. Ἐκ δὲ τῆς Λακεδαίμονος τοῦ αὐτοῦ χειμῶνος τελευτῶντος ἐκπέμπεται Σάλαιθος ὁ Λακεδαιμόνιος ἐς Μυτιλήνην τριήρει. καὶ πλεύσας ἐς
Πύρραν καὶ ἐξ αὐτῆς πεζῇ κατὰ χαράδραν τινά,
ᾗ ὑπερβατὸν[1] ἦν τὸ περιτείχισμα, διαλαθὼν
ἐσέρχεται ἐς τὴν Μυτιλήνην, καὶ ἔλεγε τοῖς
προέδροις ὅτι ἐσβολή τε ἅμα ἐς τὴν Ἀττικὴν
ἔσται καὶ αἱ τεσσαράκοντα νῆες παρέσονται
ἃς ἔδει βοηθῆσαι αὐτοῖς, προαποπεμφθῆναί τε
αὐτὸς τούτων ἕνεκα καὶ ἅμα τῶν ἄλλων ἐπιμελη-
2 σόμενος. καὶ οἱ μὲν Μυτιληναῖοι ἐθάρσουν τε
καὶ πρὸς τοὺς Ἀθηναίους ἧσσον εἶχον τὴν
γνώμην ὥστε ξυμβαίνειν. ὅ τε χειμὼν ἐτελεύτα
οὗτος, καὶ τέταρτον ἔτος τῷ πολέμῳ ἐτελεύτα
τῷδε ὃν Θουκυδίδης ξυνέγραψεν.

XXVI. Τοῦ δ' ἐπιγιγνομένου θέρους οἱ Πελοποννήσιοι ἐπειδὴ τὰς ἐς τὴν Μυτιλήνην[2] τεσ-

---

[1] Van Herwerden suggests ὑποβατόν, followed by Hude.
[2] δύο καὶ of the MSS. before τεσσαράκοντα suspected by
Krüger and deleted by van Herwerden.

Hysiae, and reaching the mountains escaped to Athens. They were only two hundred and twelve men out of a larger number; for some had turned back to the town without trying to climb the wall, and one man, an archer, had been taken at the outer ditch. The Peloponnesians, then, desisted from the pursuit and returned to their post. But the Plataeans in the town, knowing nothing of what had really happened, but informed by those who had turned back that no one survived, sent a herald at daybreak and asked for a truce that they might take up their dead ; on learning the truth however, they desisted. So these Plataeans got over the wall in the manner described and reached safety.[1]

XXV. Toward the close of the same winter, Salae-thus the Lacedaemonian was sent in a trireme from Lacedaemon to Mytilene. Landing at Pyrrha and proceeding thence on foot, he followed the bed of a ravine, where the circuit-wall could be crossed, and came undetected into Mytilene. He told the magistrates that there would be an invasion of Attica and that simultaneously the forty ships[2] which were to come to their aid would arrive, adding that he himself had been sent ahead to make these announcements and also to take charge of matters in general. Accordingly the Mytilenaeans were encouraged and were less inclined than ever to make terms with the Athenians. So this winter ended, and with it the fourth year of this war of which Thucydides wrote the history.

XXVI. During the following summer the Peloponnesians first despatched the forty ships which they

423 B.C.

427 B.C.

---

[1] For the fate of the city and of the Plataeans who remained in it, see chs. lii.–lxviii.

[2] cf. ch. xvi. 3.

σαράκοντα ναῦς ἀπέστειλαν ἄρχοντα Ἀλκίδαν,
ὃς ἦν αὐτοῖς ναύαρχος, προστάξαντες, αὐτοὶ ἐς
τὴν Ἀττικὴν καὶ οἱ ξύμμαχοι ἐσέβαλον, ὅπως
οἱ Ἀθηναῖοι ἀμφοτέρωθεν θορυβούμενοι ἧσσον
ταῖς ναυσὶν ἐς τὴν Μυτιλήνην καταπλεούσαις
2 ἐπιβοηθήσωσιν. ἡγεῖτο δὲ τῆς ἐσβολῆς ταύτης
Κλεομένης ὑπὲρ Παυσανίου τοῦ Πλειστοάνακτος
υἱέος βασιλέως ὄντος καὶ νεωτέρου ἔτι, πατρὸς
3 δὴ ἀδελφὸς ὤν. ἐδῄωσαν δὲ τῆς Ἀττικῆς τά
τε πρότερον τετμημένα,[1] εἴ τι ἐβεβλαστήκει,
καὶ ὅσα ἐν ταῖς πρὶν ἐσβολαῖς παρελέλειπτο·
καὶ ἡ ἐσβολὴ αὕτη χαλεπωτάτη ἐγένετο τοῖς
4 Ἀθηναίοις μετὰ τὴν δευτέραν. ἐπιμένοντες γὰρ
αἰεὶ ἀπὸ τῆς Λέσβου τι πεύσεσθαι τῶν νεῶν
ἔργον ὡς ἤδη πεπεραιωμένων ἐπεξῆλθον τὰ πολλὰ
τέμνοντες. ὡς δ' οὐδὲν ἀπέβαινεν αὐτοῖς ὧν
προσεδέχοντο καὶ ἐπελελοίπει ὁ σῖτος, ἀνεχώρησαν καὶ διελύθησαν κατὰ πόλεις.

XXVII. Οἱ δὲ Μυτιληναῖοι ἐν τούτῳ, ὡς αἵ τε
νῆες αὐτοῖς οὐχ ἧκον ἀπὸ τῆς Πελοποννήτου, ἀλλὰ
ἐνεχρόνιζον, καὶ ὁ σῖτος ἐπελελοίπει, ἀναγκά-
2 ζονται ξυμβαίνειν πρὸς τοὺς Ἀθηναίους διὰ τάδε.
ὁ Σάλαιθος καὶ αὐτὸς οὐ προσδεχόμενος ἔτι τὰς
ναῦς ὁπλίζει τὸν δῆμον πρότερον ψιλὸν ὄντα ὡς

---

[1] καὶ of the MSS. before εἴ τι deleted by Dindorf.

---

[1] cf. II. lvii 2.
[2] It is implied that the Lacedaemonians planned this
summer, as on previous invasions, to ravage certain districts

had promised to Mytilene, appointing in command of
them Alcidas, who was the Lacedaemonian admiral,
and then invaded Attica, themselves and their allies,
in order that the Athenians, threatened on both sea
and land, might be deterred from sending a force to
attack the fleet that was on its way to Mytilene.
The leader of this invasion was Cleomenes, regent for
his nephew Pausanias son of Pleistoanax, who was
king but still a minor. And they ravaged the parts
of Attica that had been laid waste before, wherever
any new growth had sprung up, as well as those that
had been left untouched in the former invasions.
And this invasion proved more grievous to the
Athenians than any except the second;[1] for the
enemy, who were momentarily expecting to hear
from Lesbos of some achievement of their fleet,
which they supposed had already got across, went
on and on, ravaging most of the country. But when
they found that nothing turned out as they expected and their food was exhausted, they withdrew
and dispersed to their several cities.[2]

XXVII. Meanwhile the Mytilenaeans, seeing that
the fleet had not arrived from the Peloponnesus but
was loitering on the way, and that their food was
exhausted, were compelled to make terms with the
Athenians by the following circumstances. Salaethus,
who himself no longer expected the fleet to come,
equipped the commons with heavy armour,[3] instead
of their former light arms, intending to attack the

and then, after hearing of the success of the fleet at Lesbos,
to withdraw. But they were kept in Attica longer than they
had intended by the delay on the part of the fleet.

[3] With shield and spears and breast-plate. The light-
armed troops wore no defensive armour and carried spear
or bow.

43

3 ἐπεξιὼν τοῖς Ἀθηναίοις· οἱ δὲ ἐπειδὴ ἔλαβον
ὅπλα, οὔτε ἠκροῶντο ἔτι τῶν ἀρχόντων, κατὰ
ξυλλόγους τε γιγνόμενοι ἢ τὸν σῖτον ἐκέλευον
τοὺς δυνατοὺς φέρειν ἐς τὸ φανερὸν καὶ διανέμειν
ἅπασιν, ἢ αὐτοὶ ξυγχωρήσαντες πρὸς Ἀθηναίους
ἔφασαν παραδώσειν τὴν πόλιν. XXVIII. γνόντες
δὲ οἱ ἐν τοῖς πράγμασιν οὔτ᾽ ἀποκωλύειν δυνατοὶ
ὄντες, εἴ τ᾽ ἀπομονωθήσονται τῆς ξυμβάσεως, κιν-
δυνεύσοντες, ποιοῦνται κοινῇ ὁμολογίαν πρός τε
Πάχητα καὶ τὸ στρατόπεδον, ὥστε Ἀθηναίοις
μὲν ἐξεῖναι βουλεῦσαι περὶ Μυτιληναίων ὁποῖον
ἄν τι βούλωνται καὶ τὴν στρατιὰν ἐς τὴν πόλιν
δέχεσθαι αὐτούς, πρεσβείαν δὲ ἀποστέλλειν ἐς
τὰς Ἀθήνας Μυτιληναίους περὶ ἑαυτῶν· ἐν ὅσῳ
δ᾽ ἂν πάλιν ἔλθωσι, Πάχητα μήτε δῆσαι
Μυτιληναίων μηδένα μηδὲ ἀνδραποδίσαι μήτε
2 ἀποκτεῖναι. ἡ μὲν ξύμβασις αὕτη ἐγένετο. οἱ
δὲ πράξαντες πρὸς τοὺς Λακεδαιμονίους μάλιστα
τῶν Μυτιληναίων περιδεεῖς ὄντες, ὡς ἡ στρατιὰ
ἐσῆλθεν, οὐκ ἠνέσχοντο, ἀλλ᾽ ἐπὶ τοὺς βωμοὺς
ὅμως καθίζουσιν· Πάχης δ᾽ ἀναστήσας αὐτοὺς
ὥστε μὴ ἀδικῆσαι, κατατίθεται ἐς Τένεδον μέχρι
3 οὗ τοῖς Ἀθηναίοις τι δόξῃ. πέμψας δὲ καὶ ἐς
τὴν Ἄντισσαν τριήρεις προσεκτήσατο καὶ τἆλλα
τὰ περὶ τὸ στρατόπεδον καθίστατο ᾗ αὐτῷ ἐδόκει.

XXIX. Οἱ δ᾽ ἐν ταῖς τεσσαράκοντα ναυσὶ
Πελοποννήσιοι, οὓς ἔδει ἐν τάχει παραγενέσθαι,
πλέοντες περί τε αὐτὴν τὴν Πελοπόννησον ἐνδιέ-

Athenians; but the commons, as soon as they had got arms, would no longer obey their commanders, but gathered in groups and ordered the aristocrats to bring out whatever food there was and distribute it to all; otherwise, they said, they would come to terms with the Athenians independently and deliver up the city. XXVIII. Thereupon the men in authority, realizing that they could not prevent this and that they would be in peril if excluded from the capitulation, joined the commons in making an agreement with Paches and his army. The conditions were that the Athenian state should have the power to decide as they pleased about the fate of the Mytileneans and that the besieging army should be admitted into the city; but it was conceded that the Mytilenaeans might send an embassy to Athens to treat for terms, Paches, meanwhile, until the return of the embassy, agreeing not to imprison or enslave or put to death any Mytilenaean. Such was the agreement. But those of the Mytilenaeans who had been most involved in the intrigue with the Lacedaemonians were in great terror when the army entered the town, and could not keep quiet, but notwithstanding the agreement took refuge at the altars. Paches, however, induced them to leave the altars, promising to do them no injury, and placed them for safe keeping in Tenedos until the Athenians should reach a decision. He also sent triremes to Antissa and took possession of it, and made such other dispositions with reference to the army as seemed best to him.

XXIX. Meanwhile the Peloponnesians in the forty ships, who ought to have arrived speedily at Mytilene, wasted time on their voyage round the

τριψαν καὶ κατὰ τὸν ἄλλον πλοῦν σχολαῖοι κομισθέντες τοὺς μὲν ἐκ τῆς πόλεως ᾿Αθηναίους
λανθάνουσι, πρὶν δὴ τῇ Δήλῳ ἔσχον, προσμεί-
ξαντες δὲ ἀπ' αὐτῆς τῇ ᾿Ικάρῳ καὶ Μυκόνῳ πυν-
2 θάνονται πρῶτον ὅτι ἡ Μυτιλήνη ἑάλωκεν. βουλόμενοι δὲ τὸ σαφὲς εἰδέναι κατέπλευσαν ἐς
῎Εμβατον τῆς ᾿Ερυθραίας· ἡμέραι δὲ μάλιστα
ἦσαν τῇ Μυτιλήνῃ ἑαλωκυίᾳ ἑπτὰ ὅτε ἐς τὸ
῎Εμβατον κατέπλευσαν. πυθόμενοι δὲ τὸ σαφὲς
ἐβουλεύοντο ἐκ τῶν παρόντων· καὶ ἔλεξεν αὐτοῖς
Τευτίαπλος ἀνὴρ ᾿Ηλεῖος τάδε.

XXX. "᾿Αλκίδα καὶ Πελοποννησίων ὅσοι πάρ-
εσμεν ἄρχοντες τῆς στρατιᾶς, ἐμοὶ δοκεῖ πλεῖν
ἡμᾶς ἐπὶ Μυτιλήνην πρὶν ἐκπύστους γενέσθαι,
2 ὥσπερ ἔχομεν. κατὰ γὰρ τὸ εἰκὸς ἀνδρῶν νεωστὶ
πόλιν ἐχόντων πολὺ τὸ ἀφύλακτον εὑρήσομεν,
κατὰ μὲν θάλασσαν καὶ πάνυ, ᾗ ἐκεῖνοί τε ἀνέλ-
πιστοι ἐπιγενέσθαι ἄν τινα σφίσι πολέμιον καὶ
ἡμῶν ἡ ἀλκὴ τυγχάνει μάλιστα οὖσα· εἰκὸς δὲ καὶ
τὸ πεζὸν αὐτῶν κατ' οἰκίας ἀμελέστερον ὡς κεκρα-
3 τηκότων διεσπάρθαι. εἰ οὖν προσπέσοιμεν ἄφνω
τε καὶ νυκτός, ἐλπίζω μετὰ τῶν ἔνδον, εἴ τις ἄρα
ἡμῖν ἐστιν ὑπόλοιπος εὔνους, καταληφθῆναι ἂν
4 τὰ πράγματα. καὶ μὴ ἀποκνήσωμεν τὸν κίνδυνον,
νομίσαντες οὐκ ἄλλο τι εἶναι τὸ καινὸν τοῦ
πολέμου ἢ τὸ τοιοῦτον· ὃ εἴ τις στρατηγὸς ἔν τε

Peloponnesus and on the rest of the way proceeded leisurely. They were unobserved by the Athenian home fleet until they reached Delos; but when after leaving Delos they touched at Icaros and Myconos they received the first tidings that Mytilene had been taken. Wishing however to know the exact situation they sailed to Embatum in Erythraea; and it was about seven days after the capture of Mytilene that they came to Embatum. Now that they had learned the truth, they took counsel in view of the present emergency, and Teutiaplus, an Elean, spoke to them as follows:

XXX. "Alcidas, and you who, like myself, are present here as commanders of the Peloponnesian forces, it seems to me that we should sail to Mytilene before our approach becomes known, without a moment's delay. For in all probability we shall find that men who have but lately come into possession of a city are very much off their guard. At sea, indeed, they will be altogether so, where they have no expectation of any possible hostile attack and our rôle is chiefly to act on the defensive;[1] and on land also their forces are probably scattered among the houses all the more carelessly because they believe that they are victors. If, then, we should fall upon them suddenly and at night, I believe that, in concert with our supporters inside, if any are left, we should find ourselves masters of the situation. And let us not shrink from the danger, remembering that the element of surprise in warfare is precisely of this nature.[2] And if a general guards against such surprises in his own case, and, whenever he

---

[1] Or, "while on our side it is just here that our strength lies." [2] i.e. dangerous.

αὐτῷ φυλάσσοιτο καὶ τοῖς πολεμίοις ἐνορῶν
ἐπιχειροίη, πλεῖστ' ἂν ὀρθοῖτο."

XXXI. Ὁ μὲν τοσαῦτα εἰπὼν οὐκ ἔπειθε τὸν
Ἀλκίδαν. ἄλλοι δέ τινες τῶν ἀπ' Ἰωνίας φυγάδων
καὶ οἱ Λέσβιοι οἱ [1] ξυμπλέοντες παρῄνουν, ἐπειδὴ
τοῦτον τὸν κίνδυνον φοβεῖται, τῶν ἐν Ἰωνίᾳ πόλεων καταλαβεῖν τινα ἢ Κύμην τὴν Αἰολίδα, ὅπως
ἐκ πόλεως ὁρμώμενοι τὴν Ἰωνίαν ἀποστήσωσιν
(ἐλπίδα δ' εἶναι· οὐδενὶ γὰρ ἀκουσίως ἀφῖχθαι),
καὶ τὴν πρόσοδον ταύτην μεγίστην οὖσαν
Ἀθηναίων ἵν' ὑφέλωσι καὶ ἅμα, ἢν ἐφορμῶσι
σφίσιν, αὐτοῖς δαπάνη γίγνηται· [2] πείσειν τε
2 οἴεσθαι καὶ Πισσούθνην ὥστε ξυμπολεμεῖν. ὁ
δὲ οὐδὲ ταῦτα ἐνεδέχετο, ἀλλὰ τὸ πλεῖστον τῆς
γνώμης εἶχεν, ἐπειδὴ τῆς Μυτιλήνης ὑστερήκει,
ὅτι τάχιστα τῇ Πελοποννήσῳ πάλιν προσμεῖξαι.

XXXII. Ἄρας δὲ ἐκ τοῦ Ἐμβάτου παρέπλει,
καὶ προσσχὼν Μυοννήσῳ τῇ Τηίων τοὺς αἰχμα-
λώτους οὓς κατὰ πλοῦν εἰλήφει ἀπέσφαξε τοὺς

---

[1] οἱ before ξυμπλέοντες added by Madvig, followed by
Hude.
[2] καὶ τὴν πρόσοδον . . . γίγνηται. The first part of this
vexed passage is in accord with the essentially unanimous
tradition of the MSS., except that Dobree's conjecture, ἵν'
ὑφέλωσι, is substituted for ἢν ὑφέλωσι. The second part
(καὶ ἅμα . . . γίγνηται) is in agreement with van Herwerden
and Müller-Strübing, Thuk. Forsch., p. 97, after Codex M
and a Schol. (τὸ σφίσιν αὐτοῖς οὐχ ἅμα ἀναγνωστέον, ἀλλὰ
διαιρετέον, καὶ κατὰ τὸ σφίσιν ὑποστικτέον). Most MSS. have
ἐφορμῶσι αὐτοῖς (or αὐτοὺς) δαπάνη σφίσι γίγνηται (Β γίγνεται);
G ἐφορμῶσιν αὐτοῖς σφιςι δαπάνη γίγνηται. Dobree's conjecture (ἵνα) not only gives a good construction for ὑφέλωσι—

sees an opportunity to employ them in the case of the enemy, makes the attempt, he will win the greatest success."

XXXI. Thus he spoke, but could not win Alcidas to his plan. Then some others, exiles from Ionia, and the Lesbians[1] who were with the fleet, advised him, since he feared the risk of this enterprise, to seize one of the cities in Ionia, or Cyme in Aeolia, in order that they might have a city as their base and bring Ionia to revolt (and that there was a prospect of success, seeing that everyone welcomed his coming) and might thus steal from the Athenians this the greatest source of their revenue, and at the same time the Athenians might be put to expense, in case they should attempt to blockade their base. They thought, moreover, that they could persuade Pissuthnes to join them in the war. Alcidas, however, would not accept these proposals, either, but his chief concern, now that he was too late for Mytilene, was to get back to Peloponnesus as quickly as possible.

XXXII. So he set sail from Embatum and skirted the coast; and putting in at Myonnesus in the country of the Teians he butchered most of the captives whom he had taken on the voyage. Then

[1] The πρέσβεις of chs. iv., v.

without altering the essential meaning of the sentence—but obviates the necessity of making γίγνηται dependent on ὅπως, which is too far off and separated from it by too many subordinate clauses. If ἦν ὑφέλωσι be retained, with most editors, the sense would be: "and if they could steal from the Athenians this the greatest source of their revenue, these might also at the same time, in case they should blockade them [the Peloponnesians], be put to expense."

2 πολλούς. καὶ ἐς τὴν Ἔφεσον καθορμισαμένου
αὐτοῦ Σαμίων τῶν ἐξ Ἀναίων ἀφικόμενοι πρέσβεις ἔλεγον οὐ καλῶς τὴν Ἑλλάδα ἐλευθεροῦν
αὐτόν, εἰ ἄνδρας διέφθειρεν οὔτε χεῖρας ἀνταιρο-
μένους οὔτε πολεμίους, Ἀθηναίων δὲ ὑπὸ ἀνάγκης
ξυμμάχους· εἴ τε μὴ παύσεται, ὀλίγους μὲν αὐτὸν
τῶν ἐχθρῶν ἐς φιλίαν προσάξεσθαι, πολὺ δὲ
3 πλείους τῶν φίλων πολεμίους ἕξειν. καὶ ὁ μὲν
ἐπείσθη τε καὶ Χίων ἄνδρας ὅσους εἶχεν ἔτι
ἀφῆκε καὶ τῶν ἄλλων τινάς· ὁρῶντες γὰρ τὰς
ναῦς οἱ ἄνθρωποι οὐκ ἔφευγον, ἀλλὰ προσεχώρουν
μᾶλλον ὡς Ἀττικαῖς καὶ ἐλπίδα οὐδὲ τὴν
ἐλαχίστην εἶχον μή ποτε Ἀθηναίων τῆς
θαλάσσης κρατούντων ναῦς Πελοποννησίων ἐς
Ἰωνίαν παραβαλεῖν.

XXXIII. Ἀπὸ δὲ τῆς Ἐφέσου ὁ Ἀλκίδας ἔπλει
κατὰ τάχος καὶ φυγὴν ἐποιεῖτο· ὤφθη γὰρ ὑπὸ τῆς
Σαλαμινίας καὶ Παράλου ἔτι περὶ Κλάρον ὁρμῶν
(αἱ δ' ἀπ' Ἀθηνῶν ἔτυχον πλέουσαι), καὶ δεδιὼς
τὴν δίωξιν ἔπλει διὰ τοῦ πελάγους ὡς γῇ ἑκούσιος
2 οὐ σχήσων ἄλλῃ ἢ Πελοποννήσῳ. τῷ δὲ Πάχητι
καὶ τοῖς Ἀθηναίοις ἦλθε μὲν καὶ ἀπὸ τῆς
Ἐρυθραίας ἀγγελία, ἀφικνεῖτο δὲ καὶ πανταχόθεν·
ἀτειχίστου γὰρ οὔσης τῆς Ἰωνίας μέγα τὸ δέος

---

[1] These were probably the Samians who settled at Anaea,
on the coast opposite the island, after the overthrow of
Samos in 439 B.C. (cf. I. cxvii. 3). They are referred to in
ch. xix. 2 as " Anaeitans."

he anchored at Ephesus, where he was visited by
envoys of the Samians who were settled at Anaea,[1]
who said that it was an ill way he had of freeing
Hellas, to destroy men who were not lifting their
hands against him and were not enemies, but were
merely allies of the Athenians under compulsion;
and unless he abandoned this course he would win
few enemies over into friendship and would turn
far more friends into enemies. Alcidas was persuaded, and set free all the Chians whom he still
held and some of the others. It should be explained that the people of the coast,[2] when they
saw the Peloponnesian ships, made no attempt to flee,
but came near, supposing that they were Athenian
ships; and they had not the slightest expectation
that while the Athenians dominated the sea the
Peloponnesian fleet would ever venture over to Ionia.

XXXIII. From Ephesus Alcidas sailed in haste
and took to flight; for while still at anchor near
Clarus[3] he had been sighted by the Salaminia and
Paralus,[4] which happened to be on a voyage from
Athens, and in fear of pursuit he sailed through the
open sea, determined that he would not, unless
obliged to do so, put into land anywhere except in
the Peloponnesus. Reports of him had been brought
from Erythraea to Paches and the Athenians, and
now kept coming from all quarters. For since Ionia
was unfortified, a great alarm arose everywhere lest

[2] *i.e.* the Greeks of whom Alcidas had taken so many
prisoners.
[3] *i.e.* while on his way from Embatum to Ephesus.
[4] The two swift Athenian state triremes kept always
manned ready for extraordinary service. Alcidas knew that
these two boats would notify the main Athenian fleet under
Paches of his whereabouts, and that Paches would make
pursuit.

ἐγένετο μὴ παραπλέοντες οἱ Πελοποννήσιοι, εἰ
καὶ ὡς μὴ διενοοῦντο μένειν, πορθῶσιν ἅμα
προσπίπτοντες τὰς πόλεις. αὐτάγγελοι δ᾽ αὐτὸν
ἰδοῦσαι ἐν τῇ Κλάρῳ ἥ τε Πάραλος καὶ ἡ
3 Σαλαμινία ἔφρασαν. ὁ δὲ ὑπὸ σπουδῆς ἐποιεῖτο
τὴν δίωξιν· καὶ μέχρι μὲν Πάτμου τῆς νήσου
ἐπεδίωξεν, ὡς δ᾽ οὐκέτι ἐν καταλήψει ἐφαίνετο,
ἐπανεχώρει. κέρδος δὲ ἐνόμισεν, ἐπειδὴ οὐ
μετεώροις περιέτυχεν, ὅτι οὐδαμοῦ ἐγκαταλη-
φθεῖσαι ἠναγκάσθησαν στρατόπεδόν τε ποιεῖσθαι
καὶ φυλακὴν σφίσι καὶ ἐφόρμησιν παρασχεῖν.

XXXIV. Παραπλέων δὲ πάλιν ἔσχε καὶ ἐς Νότιον τὸ Κολοφωνίων, οὗ κατῴκηντο Κολοφώνιοι
τῆς ἄνω πόλεως ἑαλωκυίας ὑπὸ Ἰταμάνους καὶ τῶν
βαρβάρων κατὰ στάσιν ἰδίᾳ ἐπαχθέντων· ἑάλω
δὲ μάλιστα αὕτη ὅτε ἡ δευτέρα Πελοποννησίων
2 ἐσβολὴ ἐς τὴν Ἀττικὴν ἐγίγνετο. ἐν οὖν τῷ
Νοτίῳ οἱ καταφυγόντες καὶ κατοικήσαντες αὐτόθι
αὖθις στασιάσαντες, οἱ μὲν παρὰ Πισσούθνου
ἐπικούρους Ἀρκάδων τε καὶ τῶν βαρβάρων
ἐπαγαγόμενοι ἐν διατειχίσματι εἶχον (καὶ τῶν
ἐκ τῆς ἄνω πόλεως Κολοφωνίων οἱ μηδίσαντες
ξυνεσελθόντες ἐπολίτευον), οἱ δὲ ὑπεξελθόντες
τούτους καὶ ὄντες φυγάδες τὸν Πάχητα ἐπάγονται.

---

[1] *i.e.* since they were only cruising.
[2] Such a blockade would not only have been costly, but
would also have kept the fleet from carrying on its work at
Lesbos.

the Peloponnesians, while following the coast—even
if, under the circumstances,[1] they had no intention of
remaining—might in passing fall upon their cities
and plunder them.   And finally the Paralus and the
Salaminia brought the news that they had themselves seen him at Clarus.   So Paches eagerly undertook the pursuit; and he followed him as far as the
island of Patmos, but when it was clear that Alcidas
could no longer be overtaken he turned back again.
And since he had not come up with the Peloponnesian fleet in the open sea, he considered it a piece
of good fortune that they had not been overtaken in
some port and compelled to set up a camp there,
thus giving the Athenian fleet the trouble of watching and blockading them.[2]

XXXIV. On the way back as he sailed along the
coast he put in at Notium, the port of the Colophonians, where the Colophonians had settled when the
upper town had been taken by Itamenes and the
barbarians,[3] who had been called in on account of
party discord by one of the factions.   And this place
had been taken about the time when the second
Peloponnesian invasion of Attica was made.[4]   Now
those who had fled for refuge to Notium and
settled there again fell into sedition.   One party
called in mercenaries, both Arcadian and barbarian,
whom they had obtained from Pissuthnes, and kept
them in a space walled off from the rest of the city,
and the Colophonians from the upper town who
were in sympathy with the Persians joined them
there and were admitted to citizenship; the other
party had secretly made their escape, and, being

---

[3] *i.e.* the Persians.   Itamenes is otherwise unknown.
[4] In the spring of 430 B.C.

3 ὁ δὲ προκαλεσάμενος ἐς λόγους Ἱππίαν τῶν ἐν τῷ
διατειχίσματι Ἀρκάδων ἄρχοντα, ὥστε, ἢν μηδὲν
ἀρέσκον λέγῃ, πάλιν αὐτὸν καταστήσειν ἐς τὸ
τεῖχος σῶν καὶ ὑγιᾶ, ὁ μὲν ἐξῆλθε παρ᾽ αὐτόν,
ὁ δ᾽ ἐκεῖνον μὲν ἐν φυλακῇ ἀδέσμῳ εἶχεν, αὐτὸς δὲ
προσβαλὼν τῷ τειχίσματι ἐξαπιναίως καὶ οὐ
προσδεχομένων αἱρεῖ, τούς τε Ἀρκάδας καὶ τῶν
βαρβάρων ὅσοι ἐνῆσαν διαφθείρει· καὶ τὸν
Ἱππίαν ὕστερον ἐσαγαγὼν ὥσπερ ἐσπείσατο·
ἐπειδὴ ἔνδον ἦν, ξυλλαμβάνει καὶ κατατοξεύει.
4 Κολοφωνίοις δὲ Νότιον παραδίδωσι πλὴν τῶν
μηδισάντων. καὶ ὕστερον Ἀθηναῖοι οἰκιστὰς
πέμψαντες κατὰ τοὺς ἑαυτῶν νόμους κατῴκισαν
τὸ Νότιον, ξυναγαγόντες πάντας ἐκ τῶν πόλεων,
εἴ πού τις ἦν Κολοφωνίων.

XXXV. Ὁ δὲ Πάχης ἀφικόμενος ἐς τὴν Μυτιλήνην τήν τε Πύρραν καὶ Ἔρεσον παρεστήσατο,
καὶ Σάλαιθον λαβὼν ἐν τῇ πόλει τὸν Λακεδαι-
μόνιον κεκρυμμένον ἀποπέμπει ἐς τὰς Ἀθήνας
καὶ τοὺς ἐκ τῆς Τενέδου Μυτιληναίων ἄνδρας ἅμα
οὓς κατέθετο καὶ εἴ τις ἄλλος αὐτῷ αἴτιος ἐδόκει
2 εἶναι τῆς ἀποστάσεως· ἀποπέμπει δὲ καὶ τῆς
στρατιᾶς τὸ πλέον. τοῖς δὲ λοιποῖς ὑπομένων
καθίστατο τὰ περὶ τὴν Μυτιλήνην καὶ τὴν ἄλλην
Λέσβον ᾗ αὐτῷ ἐδόκει.

XXXVI. Ἀφικομένων δὲ τῶν ἀνδρῶν καὶ τοῦ
Σαλαίθου οἱ Ἀθηναῖοι τὸν μὲν Σάλαιθον εὐθὺς
ἀπέκτειναν, ἔστιν ἃ παρεχόμενον τά τ᾽ ἄλλα καὶ
ἀπὸ Πλαταιῶν (ἔτι γὰρ ἐπολιορκοῦντο) ἀπάξειν

now in exile, called in Paches. And he summoned Hippias, the commander of the Arcadians in the fortified quarter, to a conference, on condition that if his proposals were unsatisfactory he would restore him safe and sound to the fortress. But when Hippias came out to him, he kept him under guard but unfettered while he himself made a sudden and unexpected attack upon the fortress, captured it, and put to death all the Arcadians and barbarians that were in it. As for Hippias, he afterward took him into the fortress just as he had agreed to do, and as soon as he was inside seized him and shot him down. He then delivered Notium to the Colophonians, excepting, however, the Persian sympathizers. The Athenians afterwards sent a commission and recolonized Notium, giving it their own institutions, after they had first brought together all the Colophonians from cities where any of them were to be found.

XXXV. After returning to Mytilene Paches reduced Pyrrha and Eresus, and having caught Salaethus the Lacedaemonian in hiding in the town sent him off to Athens, as also the Mytilenaean men whom he had placed for safe-keeping in Tenedos, and any others who seemed to him to blame for the revolt. He also sent back most of his army; with the rest he remained, and proceeded to settle the affairs of Mytilene and of Lesbos in general as seemed best to him. 427 B.C.

XXXVI. When Salaethus and the others arrived at Athens, the Athenians at once put Salaethus to death, although he offered among other things to induce the Peloponnesians to abandon Plataea, which

55

2 Πελοποννησίους· περὶ δὲ τῶν ἀνδρῶν γνώμας
ἐποιοῦντο, καὶ ὑπὸ ὀργῆς ἔδοξεν αὐτοῖς οὐ τοὺς
παρόντας μόνον ἀποκτεῖναι, ἀλλὰ καὶ τοὺς
ἅπαντας Μυτιληναίους ὅσοι ἡβῶσι, παῖδας δὲ
καὶ γυναῖκας ἀνδραποδίσαι, ἐπικαλοῦντες τήν τε
ἄλλην ἀπόστασιν ὅτι οὐκ ἀρχόμενοι ὥσπερ οἱ
ἄλλοι ἐποιήσαντο, καὶ προσξυνελάβοντο οὐκ
ἐλάχιστον τῆς ὁρμῆς αἱ Πελοποννησίων νῆες ἐς
Ἰωνίαν ἐκείνοις βοηθοὶ τολμήσασαι παρακιν-
δυνεῦσαι· οὐ γὰρ ἀπὸ βραχείας διανοίας ἐδόκουν
3 τὴν ἀπόστασιν ποιήσασθαι. πέμπουσιν οὖν
τριήρη ὡς Πάχητα ἄγγελον τῶν δεδογμένων, κατὰ
τάχος κελεύοντες διαχρήσασθαι Μυτιληναίους·
4 καὶ τῇ ὑστεραίᾳ μετάνοιά τις εὐθὺς ἦν αὐτοῖς
καὶ ἀναλογισμὸς ὠμὸν τὸ βούλευμα καὶ μέγα
ἐγνῶσθαι, πόλιν ὅλην διαφθεῖραι μᾶλλον ἢ οὐ
5 τοὺς αἰτίους. ὡς δ᾽ ᾔσθοντο τοῦτο τῶν Μυτιληναίων οἱ παρόντες πρέσβεις καὶ οἱ αὐτοῖς τῶν
Ἀθηναίων ξυμπράσσοντες, παρεσκεύασαν τοὺς
ἐν τέλει ὥστε αὖθις γνώμας προθεῖναι· καὶ
ἔπεισαν ῥᾷον, διότι καὶ ἐκείνοις ἔνδηλον ἦν βουλόμενον τὸ πλέον τῶν πολιτῶν αὖθίς τινας σφίσιν
6 ἀποδοῦναι βουλεύσασθαι. καταστάσης δ᾽ εὐθὺς
ἐκκλησίας ἄλλαι τε γνῶμαι ἀφ᾽ ἑκάστων ἐλέγοντο καὶ Κλέων ὁ Κλεαινέτου, ὅσπερ καὶ τὴν
προτέραν ἐνενικήκει ὥστε ἀποκτεῖναι, ὢν καὶ ἐς
τὰ ἄλλα βιαιότατος τῶν πολιτῶν τῷ τε δήμῳ

was still under siege; as to the others they held a debate, and under the impulse of anger finally determined to put to death, not only the Mytilenaeans who were there in Athens, but also all who were of adult age, and to enslave their women and children. The general charge which they brought against them was that they had made this revolt in spite of the fact that they were not held in subjection like the other allies; and what contributed not least to their fury was that the Peloponnesian fleet had dared to venture over to Ionia to their support; for from this they thought the revolt had been made after long deliberation. Accordingly they sent a trireme to Paches to announce what had been determined upon, and bidding him to despatch the Mytilenaeans with all haste; but on the very next day a feeling of repentance came over them and they began to reflect that the design which they had formed was cruel and monstrous, to destroy a whole city instead of merely those who were guilty. And when this became known to the Mytilenaean [1] envoys who were present and their Athenian supporters, they induced those in authority to bring the question before the people again; and they found less difficulty in persuading them because it was evident to them also that the greater part of the citizens wished that another opportunity should be given them to consider the matter. A meeting of the assembly was held immediately, at which various opinions were expressed by the several speakers. One of these was Cleon son of Cleaenetus, who had been successful in carrying the earlier motion to put the Mytilenaeans to death. He was not only the most violent of the citizens, but at that

[1] cf. ch. xxviii. 1.

παρὰ πολὺ ἐν τῷ τότε πιθανώτατος, παρελθὼν
αὖθις ἔλεγε τοιάδε.

XXXVII. "Πολλάκις μὲν ἤδη ἔγωγε καὶ ἄλλοτε ἔγνων δημοκρατίαν ὅτι ἀδύνατόν ἐστιν
ἑτέρων ἄρχειν, μάλιστα δ' ἐν τῇ νῦν ὑμετέρᾳ
2 περὶ Μυτιληναίων μεταμελείᾳ. διὰ γὰρ τὸ καθ'
ἡμέραν ἀδεὲς καὶ ἀνεπιβούλευτον πρὸς ἀλλήλους
καὶ ἐς τοὺς ξυμμάχους τὸ αὐτὸ ἔχετε, καὶ ὅ τι
ἂν ἢ λόγῳ πεισθέντες ὑπ' αὐτῶν ἁμάρτητε ἢ
οἴκτῳ ἐνδῶτε, οὐκ ἐπικινδύνως ἡγεῖσθε ἐς ὑμᾶς
καὶ οὐκ ἐς τὴν τῶν ξυμμάχων χάριν μαλακίζεσθαι,
οὐ σκοποῦντες ὅτι τυραννίδα ἔχετε τὴν ἀρχὴν
καὶ πρὸς ἐπιβουλεύοντας αὐτοὺς καὶ ἄκοντας
ἀρχομένους, οἳ[1] οὐκ ἐξ ὧν ἂν χαρίζησθε βλαπτόμενοι αὐτοὶ ἀκροῶνται ὑμῶν, ἀλλ' ἐξ ὧν ἂν
ἰσχύι μᾶλλον ἢ τῇ ἐκείνων εὐνοίᾳ περιγένησθε.
3 πάντων δὲ δεινότατον εἰ βέβαιον ἡμῖν μηδὲν
καθεστήξει ὧν ἂν δόξῃ πέρι, μηδὲ γνωσόμεθα ὅτι
χείροσι νόμοις ἀκινήτοις χρωμένη πόλις κρείσσων
ἐστὶν ἢ καλῶς ἔχουσιν ἀκύροις, ἀμαθία τε μετὰ
σωφροσύνης ὠφελιμώτερον ἢ δεξιότης μετὰ ἀκο-
λασίας, οἵ τε φαυλότεροι τῶν ἀνθρώπων πρὸς
τοὺς ξυνετωτέρους ὡς ἐπὶ τὸ πλέον ἄμεινον
4 οἰκοῦσι τὰς πόλεις. οἱ μὲν γὰρ τῶν τε νόμων
σοφώτεροι βούλονται φαίνεσθαι τῶν τε αἰεὶ
λεγομένων ἐς τὸ κοινὸν περιγίγνεσθαι, ὡς ἐν
ἄλλοις μείζοσιν οὐκ ἂν δηλώσαντες τὴν γνώμην,

---

[1] οἳ wanting in all better MSS., but adopted by Bekker,
Krüger, and Hude.

time had by far the greatest influence with the people. He now came forward a second time and spoke as follows:

XXXVII. "On many other occasions in the past I have realized that a democracy is incompetent to govern others, but more than ever to-day, when I observe your change of heart concerning the Mytilenaeans. The fact is that, because your daily life is unaffected by fear and intrigue in your relations to each other,[1] you have the same attitude towards your allies also, and you forget that whenever you are led into error by their representations or yield out of pity, your weakness involves you in danger and does not win the gratitude of your allies. For you do not reflect that the empire you hold is a despotism[2] imposed upon subjects who, for their part, do intrigue against you and submit to your rule against their will, who render obedience, not because of any kindnesses you may do them to your own hurt, but because of such superiority as you may have established by reason of your strength rather than of their goodwill. But quite the most alarming thing is, if nothing we have resolved upon shall be settled once for all, and if we shall refuse to recognize that a state which has inferior laws that are inviolable is stronger than one whose laws are good but without authority; that ignorance combined with self-restraint is more serviceable than cleverness combined with recklessness; and that simpler people for the most part make better citizens than the more shrewd. The latter always want to show that they are wiser than the laws, and to dominate all public discussions, as if there could never be weightier

[1] cf. II. xxxvii. 2.   [2] cf. II. lxiii. 2.

THUCYDIDES

καὶ ἐκ τοῦ τοιούτου τὰ πολλὰ σφάλλουσι τὰς
πόλεις· οἱ δ' ἀπιστοῦντες τῇ ἐξ ἑαυτῶν ξυνέσει
ἀμαθέστεροι μὲν τῶν νόμων ἀξιοῦσιν εἶναι, ἀδυ-
νατώτεροι δὲ τὸν[1] τοῦ καλῶς εἰπόντος μέμψασθαι
λόγον, κριταὶ δὲ ὄντες ἀπὸ τοῦ ἴσου μᾶλλον ἢ
5 ἀγωνισταὶ ὀρθοῦνται τὰ πλείω. ὡς οὖν χρὴ καὶ
ἡμᾶς ποιοῦντας μὴ δεινότητι καὶ ξυνέσεως ἀγῶνι
ἐπαιρομένους παρὰ δόξαν τῷ ὑμετέρῳ πλήθει
παραινεῖν.

XXXVIII. ''Ἐγὼ μὲν οὖν ὁ αὐτός εἰμι τῇ
γνώμῃ καὶ θαυμάζω μὲν τῶν προθέντων αὖθις
περὶ Μυτιληναίων λέγειν καὶ χρόνου διατριβὴν
ἐμποιησάντων, ὅ ἐστι πρὸς τῶν ἠδικηκότων
μᾶλλον (ὁ γὰρ παθὼν τῷ δράσαντι ἀμβλυτέρα
τῇ ὀργῇ ἐπεξέρχεται, ἀμύνεσθαι δὲ τῷ παθεῖν
ὅτι ἐγγυτάτω κείμενον ἀντίπαλον ὂν[2] μάλιστα
τὴν τιμωρίαν λαμβάνει[3]), θαυμάζω δὲ καὶ ὅστις
ἔσται ὁ ἀντερῶν καὶ ἀξιώσων ἀποφαίνειν τὰς μὲν
Μυτιληναίων ἀδικίας ἡμῖν ὠφελίμους οὔσας, τὰς
δ' ἡμετέρας ξυμφορὰς τοῖς ξυμμάχοις βλάβας
2 καθισταμένας. καὶ δῆλον ὅτι ἢ τῷ λέγειν
πιστεύσας τὸ πάνυ δοκοῦν ἀνταποφῆναι ὡς οὐκ
ἔγνωσται ἀγωνίσαιτ' ἄν, ἢ κέρδει ἐπαιρόμενος τὸ
εὐπρεπὲς τοῦ λόγου ἐκπονήσας παράγειν πειρά-
3 σεται. ἡ δὲ πόλις ἐκ τῶν τοιῶνδε ἀγώνων τὰ
μὲν ἆθλα ἑτέροις δίδωσιν, αὐτὴ δὲ τοὺς κινδύνους
4 ἀναφέρει. αἴτιοι δ' ὑμεῖς κακῶς ἀγωνοθετοῦντες,

---

[1] τὸν, added from Stobaeus by Naber, followed by Hude.
[2] ὂν is deleted by Haase, followed by Hude, and generally.
[3] λαμβάνει, for ἀναλαμβάνει of the MSS., Reiske, followed by Hude.

questions on which to declare their opinions, and as a consequence of such conduct they generally bring their states to ruin; the former, on the contrary, mistrusting their own insight, are content to be less enlightened than the laws and less competent than others to criticise the words of an able speaker, but being impartial judges rather than interested contestants they generally prosper. Thus, then, we ought to act and not be so excited by eloquence and combat of wits as to advise the Athenian people contrary to our own judgment.

XXXVIII. "As for me, I have not changed my opinion, and I wonder at those who propose to debate again the question of the Mytilenaeans and thus interpose delay, which is in the interest of those who have done the wrong; for thus the edge of the victim's wrath is duller when he proceeds against the offender, whereas the vengeance that follows upon the very heels of the outrage exacts a punishment that most nearly matches the offence. And I wonder, too, who will answer me and undertake to prove that the wrong-doings of the Mytilenaeans are beneficial to us but that our misfortunes prove injurious to our allies. Manifestly he must either have such confidence in his powers of speech as to undertake to show that what is universally accepted as true has not been established,[1] or else, incited by gain, will by an elaborate display of specious oratory attempt to mislead you. But in contests of that kind the city bestows the prizes upon others, while she herself undergoes all the risks. And you are yourselves to blame, for your management of

---

[1] Or, "your absolute resolve has really not been adopted."

οἵτινες εἰώθατε θεαταὶ μὲν τῶν λόγων γίγνεσθαι,
ἀκροαταὶ δὲ τῶν ἔργων, τὰ μὲν μέλλοντα ἔργα
ἀπὸ τῶν εὖ εἰπόντων σκοποῦντες ὡς δυνατὰ
γίγνεσθαι, τὰ δὲ πεπραγμένα ἤδη, οὐ τὸ δρασθὲν
πιστότερον ὄψει λαβόντες ἢ τὸ ἀκουσθέν, ἀπὸ
5 τῶν λόγῳ καλῶς ἐπιτιμησάντων· καὶ μετὰ καινό-
τητος μὲν λόγου ἀπατᾶσθαι ἄριστοι, μετὰ δεδοκι-
μασμένου δὲ μὴ ξυνέπεσθαι ἐθέλειν, δοῦλοι ὄντες
τῶν αἰεὶ ἀτόπων, ὑπερόπται δὲ τῶν εἰωθότων,
6 καὶ μάλιστα μὲν αὐτὸς εἰπεῖν ἕκαστος βουλόμενος
δύνασθαι, εἰ δὲ μή, ἀνταγωνιζόμενοι τοῖς τοιαῦτα
λέγουσι μὴ ὕστεροι ἀκολουθῆσαι δοκεῖν τῇ γνώμῃ,
ὀξέως δέ τι λέγοντος προεπαινέσαι, καὶ προαισθέσθαι τε πρόθυμοι [1] τὰ λεγόμενα καὶ προ-
νοῆσαι βραδεῖς τὰ ἐξ αὐτῶν ἀποβησόμενα,
7 ζητοῦντές τε ἄλλο τι ὡς εἰπεῖν ἢ ἐν οἷς ζῶμεν,
φρονοῦντες δὲ οὐδὲ περὶ τῶν παρόντων ἱκανῶς·
ἁπλῶς τε ἀκοῆς ἡδονῇ ἡσσώμενοι καὶ σοφιστῶν
θεαταῖς ἐοικότες καθημένοις μᾶλλον ἢ περὶ πόλεως
βουλευομένοις.

XXXIX. "Ὧν ἐγὼ πειρώμενος ἀποτρέπειν
ὑμᾶς ἀποφαίνω Μυτιληναίους μάλιστα δὴ μίαν
2 πόλιν ἠδικηκότας ὑμᾶς. ἐγὼ γάρ, οἵτινες μὲν
μὴ δυνατοὶ φέρειν τὴν ὑμετέραν ἀρχὴν ἢ οἵτινες
ὑπὸ τῶν πολεμίων ἀναγκασθέντες ἀπέστησαν,
ξυγγνώμην ἔχω· νῆσον δὲ οἵτινες ἔχοντες μετὰ
τειχῶν καὶ κατὰ θάλασσαν μόνον φοβούμενοι
τοὺς ἡμετέρους πολεμίους, ἐν ᾧ καὶ αὐτοὶ τριήρων
παρασκευῇ οὐκ ἄφαρκτοι ἦσαν πρὸς αὐτούς,

---

[1] εἶναι after πρόθυμοι, deleted by Poppo, followed by
Hude.

these contests is wrong. It is your wont to be spectators of words and hearers of deeds, forming your judgment of future enterprises according as able speakers represent them to be feasible, but as regards accomplished facts, not counting what has been done more credible, because you have seen it, than what you have heard, you are swayed in judgment by those who have made an eloquent invective. You are adepts not only at being deceived by novel proposals but also at refusing to follow approved advice, slaves as you are of each new paradox and scorners of what is familiar. Each of you wishes above all to be an orator himself, or, failing that, to vie with those dealers in paradox by seeming not to lag behind them in wit but to applaud a smart saying before it is out of the speaker's mouth; you are as quick to forestall what is said as you are slow to foresee what will come of it. You seek, one might say, a world quite unlike that in which we live, but give too little heed to that which is at hand. In a word, you are in thrall to the pleasures of the ear and are more like men who sit as spectators at exhibitions of sophists than men who take counsel for the welfare of the state.

XXXIX. "And it is from these ways that I seek to turn you when I attempt to prove that Mytilene has done you more injury than any single state. I can make allowance for men who resorted to revolt because they were unable to bear your rule or because they were compelled by your enemies to do so; but men who inhabited a fortified island and had no fear of our enemies except by sea, and even there were not without the protection of a force of their own triremes, who moreover were independent and

αὐτόνομοί τε οἰκοῦντες καὶ τιμώμενοι ἐς τὰ πρῶτα
ὑπὸ ἡμῶν τοιαῦτα εἰργάσαντο, τί ἄλλο οὗτοι ἢ
ἐπεβούλευσάν τε καὶ ἐπανέστησαν μᾶλλον ἢ
ἀπέστησαν (ἀπόστασις μέν γε τῶν βίαιόν τι
πασχόντων ἐστίν), ἐζήτησάν τε μετὰ τῶν πολε-
μιωτάτων ἡμᾶς στάντες διαφθεῖραι; καίτοι δεινότερόν ἐστιν ἢ εἰ καθ᾽ αὑτοὺς δύναμιν κτώμενοι
3 ἀντεπολέμησαν. παράδειγμα δὲ αὐτοῖς οὔτε αἱ
τῶν πέλας ξυμφοραὶ ἐγένοντο, ὅσοι ἀποστάντες
ἤδη ἡμῶν ἐχειρώθησαν, οὔτε ἡ παροῦσα εὐδαι-
μονία παρέσχεν ὄκνον μὴ ἐλθεῖν ἐς τὰ δεινά·
γενόμενοι δὲ πρὸς τὸ μέλλον θρασεῖς καὶ ἐλπίσαντες μακρότερα μὲν τῆς δυνάμεως, ἐλάσσω δὲ
τῆς βουλήσεως, πόλεμον ἤραντο, ἰσχὺν ἀξιώ-
σαντες τοῦ δικαίου προθεῖναι· ἐν ᾧ γὰρ ᾠήθησαν περιέσεσθαι, ἐπέθεντο ἡμῖν οὐκ ἀδικούμενοι.
4 εἴωθε δὲ τῶν πόλεων αἷς ἂν μάλιστα ἀπροσδόκητος καὶ δι᾽ ἐλαχίστου εὐπραξία ἔλθῃ, ἐς ὕβριν
τρέπειν· τὰ δὲ πολλὰ κατὰ λόγον τοῖς ἀνθρώποις
εὐτυχοῦντα ἀσφαλέστερα ἢ παρὰ δόξαν, καὶ
κακοπραγίαν ὡς εἰπεῖν ῥᾷον ἀπωθοῦνται ἢ εὐδαι-
5 μονίαν διασῴζονται. χρῆν δὲ Μυτιληναίους καὶ
πάλαι μηδὲν διαφερόντως τῶν ἄλλων ὑφ᾽ ἡμῶν
τετιμῆσθαι, καὶ οὐκ ἂν ἐς τόδε ἐξύβρισαν· πέφυκε
γὰρ καὶ ἄλλως ἄνθρωπος τὸ μὲν θεραπεῦον
ὑπερφρονεῖν, τὸ δὲ μὴ ὑπεῖκον θαυμάζειν.
6   "Κολασθέντων δὲ καὶ νῦν ἀξίως τῆς ἀδικίας
καὶ μὴ τοῖς μὲν ὀλίγοις ἡ αἰτία προστεθῇ, τὸν δὲ
64

were treated by us with the highest consideration, when these men have acted thus, what else is it but conspiracy and rebellion rather than revolt—for revolt is the work of those who suffer oppression—and a deliberate attempt by taking their stand on the side of our bitterest enemies to bring about our destruction? And yet this is assuredly a more heinous thing than if they had gone to war against us by themselves for the acquisition of power. The calamities of their neighbours who had already revolted from us and been subdued proved no warning to them; nor did the good fortune which they enjoyed make them hesitate to take the perilous step; on the contrary, becoming over-confident as to the future, and conceiving hopes which, though greater than their powers, were less than their ambition, they took up arms, presuming to put might before right; for the moment they thought they should prove superior they attacked us unprovoked. And indeed it is the rule, that such states as come to unexpected prosperity most fully and most suddenly, do turn to insolence, whereas men generally find success less precarious when it comes in accordance with reasonable calculations than when it surpasses expectation, and more easily, as it seems, they repel adversity than maintain prosperity. But the Mytilenaeans from the first ought never to have been treated by us with any more consideration than our other allies, and then they would not have broken out into such insolence; for it is human nature in any case to be contemptuous of those who pay court but to admire those who will not yield.

"Let them be punished, therefore, even now, in a manner befitting their crime, and do not put the

δῆμον ἀπολύσητε. πάντες γὰρ ὑμῖν γε ὁμοίως
ἐπέθεντο, οἷς γ᾽ ἐξῆν ὡς ἡμᾶς τραπομένοις νῦν
πάλιν ἐν τῇ πόλει εἶναι· ἀλλὰ τὸν μετὰ τῶν
ὀλίγων κίνδυνον ἡγησάμενοι βεβαιότερον ξυναπ-
7 έστησαν. τῶν τε ξυμμάχων σκέψασθε εἰ τοῖς
τε ἀναγκασθεῖσιν ὑπὸ τῶν πολεμίων καὶ τοῖς
ἑκοῦσιν ἀποστᾶσι τὰς αὐτὰς ζημίας προσθήσετε,
τίνα οἴεσθε ὅντινα οὐ βραχείᾳ προφάσει ἀποστή-
σεσθαι, ὅταν ἢ κατορθώσαντι ἐλευθέρωσις ᾖ ἢ
8 σφαλέντι μηδὲν παθεῖν ἀνήκεστον; ἡμῖν δὲ πρὸς
ἑκάστην πόλιν ἀποκεκινδυνεύσεται τά τε χρήματα
καὶ αἱ ψυχαί· καὶ τυχόντες μὲν πόλιν ἐφθαρμένην παραλαβόντες τῆς ἔπειτα [1] προσόδου, δι᾽
ἣν ἰσχύομεν, τὸ λοιπὸν στερήσεσθε, σφαλέντες
δὲ πολεμίους πρὸς τοῖς ὑπάρχουσιν ἕξομεν, καὶ
ὃν χρόνον τοῖς νῦν καθεστηκόσι δεῖ ἐχθροῖς ἀν-
θίστασθαι, τοῖς οἰκείοις ξυμμάχοις πολεμήσομεν.

XL. " Οὔκουν δεῖ προθεῖναι [2] ἐλπίδα οὔτε λόγῳ
πιστὴν οὔτε χρήμασιν ὠνητήν, ὡς ξυγγνώμην
ἁμαρτεῖν ἀνθρωπίνως λήψονται. ἄκοντες μὲν
γὰρ οὐκ ἔβλαψαν, εἰδότες δὲ ἐπεβούλευσαν· ξύγ-
2 γνωμον δ᾽ ἐστὶ τὸ ἀκούσιον. ἐγὼ μὲν οὖν καὶ
τότε πρῶτον καὶ νῦν διαμάχομαι μὴ μεταγνῶναι
ὑμᾶς τὰ προδεδογμένα, μηδὲ τρισὶ τοῖς ἀξυμ-
φορωτάτοις τῇ ἀρχῇ, οἴκτῳ καὶ ἡδονῇ λόγων καὶ

---

[1] ἔπειτα, Hude adopts ἐπετείας, van Herwerden and H.
Weil ἐπετείου.
[2] προθεῖναι, Hude retains προσθεῖναι, with BC.

blame upon the aristocrats and exonerate the common people. For they all alike attacked you, even the commons, who, if they had taken our side, might now have been reinstated in their city; but they thought there was less risk in sharing the dangers of the oligarchs, and so joined them in the revolt. Consider, moreover, your allies: if you inflict upon those who wilfully revolt no greater punishment than upon those who revolt under compulsion from our foes, which of them, think you, will not revolt on a slight pretext, when the alternatives are liberty if he succeeds or a fate not irreparable if he fails? We, on the other hand, shall have to risk our money and our lives against each separate state, and when we succeed we shall recover a ruined state and be deprived for the future of its revenue, the source of our strength, whereas if we fail we shall be adding fresh enemies to those we have already, and when we should be resisting our present foes we shall be fighting our own allies.

XL. "We must not, therefore, hold out to them any hope, either to be secured by eloquence or purchased by money, that they will be excused on the plea that their error was human. For their act was no unintentional injury but a deliberate plot; and it is that which is unintentional which is excusable. Therefore, I still protest, as I have from the first,[1] that you should not reverse your former decision or be led into error by pity, delight in eloquence, or clemency, the three

___

[1] Referring to what happened in the assembly of the day before, in which, however, he had urged the action that was taken; its reconsideration was not urged till the present meeting.

3 ἐπιεικείᾳ, ἁμαρτάνειν. ἔλεός τε γὰρ πρὸς τοὺς
ὁμοίους δίκαιος ἀντιδίδοσθαι καὶ μὴ πρὸς τοὺς
οὔτ' ἀντοικτιοῦντας ἐξ ἀνάγκης τε καθεστῶτας
αἰεὶ πολεμίους· οἵ τε τέρποντες λόγῳ ῥήτορες [1]
ἕξουσι καὶ ἐν ἄλλοις ἐλάσσοσιν ἀγῶνα, καὶ μὴ
ἐν ᾧ ἡ μὲν πόλις βραχέα ἡσθεῖσα μεγάλα ζημιώ-
σεται, αὐτοὶ δὲ ἐκ τοῦ εὖ εἰπεῖν τὸ παθεῖν εὖ
ἀντιλήψονται· καὶ ἡ ἐπιείκεια πρὸς τοὺς μέλλοντας ἐπιτηδείους καὶ τὸ λοιπὸν ἔσεσθαι μᾶλλον
δίδοται ἢ πρὸς τοὺς ὁμοίως τε καὶ οὐδὲν ἧσσον
πολεμίους ὑπολειπομένους.

4   "Ἔν τε ξυνελὼν λέγω· πιθόμενοι μὲν ἐμοὶ
τά τε δίκαια ἐς Μυτιληναίους καὶ τὰ ξύμφορα
ἅμα ποιήσετε, ἄλλως δὲ γνόντες τοῖς μὲν οὐ
χαριεῖσθε, ὑμᾶς δὲ αὐτοὺς μᾶλλον δικαιώσεσθε.
εἰ γὰρ οὗτοι ὀρθῶς ἀπέστησαν, ὑμεῖς ἂν οὐ
χρεὼν ἄρχοιτε. εἰ δὲ δὴ καὶ οὐ προσῆκον ὅμως
ἀξιοῦτε τοῦτο δρᾶν, παρὰ τὸ εἰκός τοι καὶ τούσδε
ξυμφόρως δεῖ κολάζεσθαι, ἢ παύεσθαι τῆς ἀρχῆς
5 καὶ ἐκ τοῦ ἀκινδύνου ἀνδραγαθίζεσθαι. τῇ τε
αὐτῇ ζημίᾳ ἀξιώσατε ἀμύνασθαι καὶ μὴ ἀναλγη-
τότεροι οἱ διαφυγόντες τῶν ἐπιβουλευσάντων
φανῆναι, ἐνθυμηθέντες ἃ εἰκὸς ἦν αὐτοὺς ποιῆσαι
κρατήσαντας ὑμῶν, ἄλλως τε καὶ προϋπάρξαντας

[1] ῥήτορες, deleted by Naber, followed by Hude

influences most prejudicial to a ruling state. For
compassion may rightly be bestowed upon those who
are likewise compassionate and not upon those who
will show no pity in return but of necessity are
always enemies. As to the orators who charm by
their eloquence, they will have other opportunities
of display in matters of less importance, and not
where the city for a brief pleasure will pay a heavy
penalty while they themselves get a fine fee for
their fine speaking. And clemency would better be
reserved for those who will afterwards be faithful
allies than be shown to those who remain just what
they were before and no whit the less our enemies.

"I can sum up what I have to say in a word. If
you take my advice, you will do not only what is just
to the Mytilenaeans but also at the same time what
is expedient for us; but if you decide otherwise, you
will not win their gratitude but will rather bring a
just condemnation upon yourselves; for if these
people had a right to secede, it would follow that
you are wrong in exercising dominion. But if, right
or wrong, you are still resolved to maintain it, then
you must punish these people in defiance of equity as
your interests require; or else you must give up your
empire and in discreet safety practise the fine virtues
you preach.[1] Resolve also to punish them with the
same penalty that has already been voted,[2] and that
those who have escaped the plot shall not appear to
have less feeling than those who framed it, bearing in
mind what they would probably have done to you
had they won the victory, especially since they

[1] For the thought, cf. II. lxiii. 2.
[2] So Steup explains. Most editors explain, "with the
same penalty they would have inflicted," following the schol.
ἢ ἂν ἐτιμωρήσαντο καὶ αὐτοὶ ὑμᾶς, περιγενόμενοι ὑμῶν.

6 ἀδικίας. μάλιστα δὲ οἱ μὴ ξὺν προφάσει τινὰ κακῶς ποιοῦντες ἐπεξέρχονται καὶ διολλύναι,[1] τὸν κίνδυνον ὑφορώμενοι τοῦ ὑπολειπομένου ἐχθροῦ· ὁ γὰρ μὴ ξὺν ἀνάγκῃ τι παθὼν χαλεπώτερος διαφυγὼν τοῦ ἀπὸ τῆς ἴσης ἐχθροῦ.

7 "Μὴ οὖν προδόται γένησθε ὑμῶν αὐτῶν, γενόμενοι δ' ὅτι ἐγγύτατα τῇ γνώμῃ τοῦ πάσχειν καὶ ὡς πρὸ παντὸς ἂν ἐτιμήσασθε αὐτοὺς χειρώσασθαι, νῦν ἀνταπόδοτε μὴ μαλακισθέντες πρὸς τὸ παρὸν αὐτίκα μηδὲ τοῦ ἐπικρεμασθέντος ποτὲ

8 δεινοῦ ἀμνημονοῦντες. κολάσατε δὲ ἀξίως τούτους τε καὶ τοῖς ἄλλοις ξυμμάχοις παράδειγμα σαφὲς καταστήσατε, ὃς ἂν ἀφίστηται, θανάτῳ ζημιωσόμενος. τόδε γὰρ ἢν γνῶσιν, ἧσσον τῶν πολεμίων ἀμελήσαντες τοῖς ὑμετέροις αὐτῶν μαχεῖσθε ξυμμάχοις."

XLI. Τοιαῦτα μὲν ὁ Κλέων εἶπεν. μετὰ δ' αὐτὸν Διόδοτος ὁ Εὐκράτους, ὅσπερ καὶ ἐν τῇ προτέρᾳ ἐκκλησίᾳ ἀντέλεγε μάλιστα μὴ ἀποκτεῖναι Μυτιληναίους, παρελθὼν καὶ τότε ἔλεγε τοιάδε.

XLII. "Οὔτε τοὺς προθέντας τὴν διαγνώμην αὖθις περὶ Μυτιληναίων αἰτιῶμαι οὔτε τοὺς μεμφομένους μὴ πολλάκις περὶ τῶν μεγίστων βουλεύεσθαι ἐπαινῶ, νομίζω δὲ δύο τὰ ἐναντιώτατα εὐβουλίᾳ εἶναι, τάχος τε καὶ ὀργήν, ὧν τὸ μὲν μετὰ ἀνοίας φιλεῖ γίγνεσθαι, τὸ δὲ μετὰ ἀπαι-

2 δευσίας καὶ βραχύτητος γνώμης. τούς τε λόγους ὅστις διαμάχεται μὴ διδασκάλους τῶν πραγμά-

---

[1] διολλύναι, Stahl's conjecture, followed by Hude and others, for διόλλυνται of the MSS.

were the aggressors. Indeed it is generally those who wrong another without cause that follow him up to destroy him utterly, perceiving the danger that threatens from an enemy who is left alive; for one who has been needlessly injured is more dangerous if he escape than an avowed enemy who expects to give and take.

"Do not, then, be traitors to your own cause, but recalling as nearly as possible how you felt when they made you suffer and how you would then have given anything to crush them, now pay them back. Do not become tender-hearted at the sight of their present distress, nor unmindful of the danger that so lately hung over you, but chastise them as they deserve, and give to your other allies plain warning that whoever revolts shall be punished with death. For if they realise this, the less will you have to neglect your enemies and fight against your own allies."

XLI. Such was Cleon's speech. After him Diodotus son of Eucrates, who in the earlier meeting had been the principal speaker against putting the Mytilenaeans to death, came forward now also and spoke as follows:

XLII. "I have no fault to find with those who have proposed a reconsideration of the question of the Mytilenaeans, nor do I commend those who object to repeated deliberation on matters of the greatest moment; on the contrary, I believe the two things most opposed to good counsel are haste and passion, of which the one is wont to keep company with folly, the other with an undisciplined and shallow mind. As for words, whoever contends[1] that they are not to be guides of our actions is either dull

---

[1] Directed at Cleon's remarks, ch. xxxviii. 4 ff.

των γίγνεσθαι, ἢ ἀξύνετός ἐστιν ἢ ἰδίᾳ τι αὑτῷ
διαφέρει· ἀξύνετος μέν, εἰ ἄλλῳ τινὶ ἡγεῖται
περὶ τοῦ μέλλοντος δυνατὸν εἶναι καὶ μὴ ἐμ-
φανοῦς φράσαι, διαφέρει δ᾽ αὑτῷ, εἰ βουλόμενός
τι αἰσχρὸν πεῖσαι εὖ μὲν εἰπεῖν οὐκ ἂν ἡγεῖται
περὶ τοῦ μὴ καλοῦ δύνασθαι, εὖ δὲ διαβαλὼν
ἐκπλῆξαι ἂν τούς τε ἀντεροῦντας καὶ τοὺς ἀκου-
3 σομένους. χαλεπώτατοι δὲ καὶ οἱ ἐπὶ χρήμασι
προκατηγοροῦντες ἐπίδειξίν τινα. εἰ μὲν γὰρ
ἀμαθίαν κατῃτιῶντο, ὁ μὴ πείσας ἀξυνετώτερος
ἂν δόξας εἶναι ἢ ἀδικώτερος ἀπεχώρει· ἀδικίας
δ᾽ ἐπιφερομένης πείσας τε ὕποπτος γίγνεται καὶ
4 μὴ τυχὼν μετὰ ἀξυνεσίας καὶ ἄδικος. ἥ τε
πόλις οὐκ ὠφελεῖται ἐν τῷ τοιῷδε· φόβῳ γὰρ
ἀποστερεῖται τῶν ξυμβούλων. καὶ πλεῖστ᾽ ἂν
ὀρθοῖτο ἀδυνάτους λέγειν ἔχουσα τοὺς τοιούτους
τῶν πολιτῶν· ἐλάχιστα γὰρ ἂν πεισθεῖεν[1]
5 ἁμαρτάνειν. χρὴ δὲ τὸν μὲν ἀγαθὸν πολίτην μὴ
ἐκφοβοῦντα τοὺς ἀντεροῦντας, ἀλλ᾽ ἀπὸ τοῦ ἴσου
φαίνεσθαι ἄμεινον λέγοντα, τὴν δὲ σώφρονα πόλιν
τῷ τε πλεῖστα εὖ βουλεύοντι μὴ προστιθέναι
τιμήν, ἀλλὰ μηδ᾽ ἐλασσοῦν τῆς ὑπαρχούσης, καὶ
τὸν μὴ τυχόντα γνώμης οὐχ ὅπως ζημιοῦν, ἀλλὰ
6 μηδ᾽ ἀτιμάζειν. οὕτω γὰρ ὅ τε κατορθῶν ἥκιστα
ἂν ἐπὶ τῷ ἔτι μειζόνων ἀξιοῦσθαι παρὰ γνώμην

---

[1] πεισθείησαν, Hude adopts Madvig's conjecture πεισθείη
ξυναμαρτάνειν.

of wit or has some private interest at stake—dull,
if he thinks it possible by any other means to throw
light on that which still belongs to the dim and
distant future; self-interested, if, wishing to put
through a discreditable measure, he realizes that
while he cannot speak well in a bad cause, he
can at least slander well and thus intimidate both
his opponents and his hearers. Most dangerous of
all, however, are precisely those who[1] charge a
speaker beforehand with being bribed to make a
display of rhetoric. For if they merely imputed
ignorance, the speaker who failed to carry his
audience might go his way with the repute of being
dull but not dishonest; when, however, the charge
is dishonesty, the speaker who succeeds becomes an
object of suspicion, whereas if he fails he is regarded
as not only dull but dishonest as well. And all
this is a detriment to the state, which is thus robbed
of its counsellors through fear. Indeed it would
prosper most if its citizens of this stamp had no
eloquence at all, for then the people would be least
likely to blunder through their influence. But the
good citizen ought to show himself a better speaker,
not by trying to browbeat those who will oppose
him, but by fair argument; and while the wise city
should not indeed confer fresh honours upon the
man whose advice is most often salutary, it certainly
should not detract from those which he already has,
and as for him whose suggestion does not meet with
approval, so far from punishing him, it should not
even treat him with disrespect. For then it would
be least likely that a successful speaker, with a view
to being counted worthy of still greater honours,

---

[1] Like Cleon, ch. xxxviii. 2; xl. 1, 3.

τι καὶ πρὸς χάριν λέγοι, ὅ τε μὴ ἐπιτυχὼν ὀρέ-
γοιτο τῷ αὐτῷ, χαριζόμενός τι καὶ αὐτός, προσάγεσθαι τὸ πλῆθος.

XLIII. Ὧν ἡμεῖς τἀναντία δρῶμεν, καὶ προσέτι, ἤν τις καὶ ὑποπτεύηται κέρδους μὲν ἕνεκα,
τὰ βέλτιστα δὲ ὅμως λέγειν, φθονήσαντες τῆς
οὐ βεβαίου δοκήσεως τῶν κερδῶν τὴν φανερὰν
2 ὠφελίαν τῆς πόλεως ἀφαιρούμεθα. καθέστηκε
δὲ τἀγαθὰ ἀπὸ τοῦ εὐθέος λεγόμενα μηδὲν ἀνυ-
ποπτότερα εἶναι τῶν κακῶν, ὥστε δεῖν ὁμοίως
τόν τε τὰ δεινότατα βουλόμενον πεῖσαι ἀπάτῃ
προσάγεσθαι τὸ πλῆθος καὶ τὸν τὰ ἀμείνω λέ-
3 γοντα ψευσάμενον πιστὸν γενέσθαι. μόνην τε
πόλιν διὰ τὰς περινοίας εὖ ποιῆσαι ἐκ τοῦ προφανοῦς μὴ ἐξαπατήσαντα ἀδύνατον· ὁ γὰρ διδοὺς
φανερῶς τι ἀγαθὸν ἀνθυποπτεύεται ἀφανῶς πῃ
4 πλέον ἕξειν. χρὴ δὲ πρὸς τὰ μέγιστα καὶ ἐν τῷ
τοιῷδε ἀξιοῦν τι[1] ἡμᾶς περαιτέρω προνοοῦντας
λέγειν ὑμῶν τῶν δι᾽ ὀλίγου σκοπούντων, ἄλλως
τε καὶ ὑπεύθυνον τὴν παραίνεσιν ἔχοντας πρὸς
5 ἀνεύθυνον τὴν ὑμετέραν ἀκρόασιν. εἰ γὰρ ὅ τε
πείσας καὶ ὁ ἐπισπόμενος ὁμοίως ἐβλάπτοντο,
σωφρονέστερον ἂν ἐκρίνετε· νῦν δὲ πρὸς ὀργὴν

---

[1] Conjecture of Krüger and Haase, confirmed by ABFM,
for the Vulgate ἀξιοῦντι, with CEG.

would speak insincerely and for the purpose of winning favour and that the unsuccessful speaker would employ the same means, by courting favour in his turn in an effort to win the multitude to himself.

XLIII. But we pursue the opposite course, and, moreover, if a man be even suspected of corruption, albeit he give the best counsel, we conceive a grudge against him because of the dubious surmise that he is corrupt and thus deprive the state of an indubitable advantage. And it has come to such a pass that good advice frankly given is regarded with just as much suspicion as the bad, and that, in consequence, a speaker who wants to carry the most dangerous measures must resort to deceit in order to win the people to his views, precisely as the man whose proposals are good must lie in order to be believed. And because of this excessive cleverness Athens is the only state where a man cannot do a good service to his country openly and without deceiving it; for whenever he openly offers you something good you requite him by suspecting that in some way he will secretly profit by it. Yet even so, in view of the very great interests at stake, and in so grave a matter, we who advise must regard it as our duty to look somewhat further ahead than you who give matters only a brief consideration, especially since we are responsible advisers,[1] while you are irresponsible listeners. Indeed, if not only those who gave advice but also those who followed it had to suffer alike, you would show greater prudence in your decisions; but as it is, whenever you meet with

---

[1] It was open to any Athenian citizen to impeach any law or decree, as contrary to some existing law or as unjust or inexpedient, by a proceeding called γραφὴ παρανόμων.

ἥντιν᾿ ἂν τύχητε ἔστιν ὅτε σφαλέντες τὴν τοῦ πείσαντος μίαν γνώμην ζημιοῦτε καὶ οὐ τὰς ὑμετέρας αὐτῶν, αἳ πολλαὶ οὖσαι ξυνεξήμαρτον.

XLIV. "Ἐγὼ δὲ παρῆλθον οὔτε ἀντερῶν περὶ Μυτιληναίων οὔτε κατηγορήσων. οὐ γὰρ περὶ τῆς ἐκείνων ἀδικίας ἡμῖν ὁ ἀγών, εἰ σωφρονοῦμεν, 2 ἀλλὰ περὶ τῆς ἡμετέρας εὐβουλίας. ἤν τε γὰρ ἀποφήνω πάνυ ἀδικοῦντας αὐτούς, οὐ διὰ τοῦτο καὶ ἀποκτεῖναι κελεύσω, εἰ μὴ ξυμφέρον, ἤν τε καὶ ἔχοντάς τι ξυγγνώμης, ἐᾶν,[1] εἰ τῇ πόλει μὴ 3 ἀγαθὸν φαίνοιτο. νομίζω δὲ περὶ τοῦ μέλλοντος ἡμᾶς μᾶλλον βουλεύεσθαι ἢ τοῦ παρόντος. καὶ τοῦτο ὃ μάλιστα Κλέων ἰσχυρίζεται, ἐς τὸ λοιπὸν ξυμφέρον ἔσεσθαι πρὸς τὸ ἧσσον ἀφίστασθαι θάνατον ζημίαν προθεῖσι, καὶ αὐτὸς περὶ τοῦ ἐς τὸ μέλλον καλῶς ἔχοντος ἀντισχυριζόμενος τἀ- 4 ναντία γιγνώσκω. καὶ οὐκ ἀξιῶ ὑμᾶς τῷ εὐ- πρεπεῖ τοῦ ἐκείνου λόγου τὸ χρήσιμον τοῦ ἐμοῦ ἀπώσασθαι. δικαιότερος γὰρ ὢν αὐτοῦ ὁ λόγος πρὸς τὴν νῦν ὑμετέραν ὀργὴν ἐς Μυτιληναίους τάχ᾿ ἂν ἐπισπάσαιτο· ἡμεῖς δὲ οὐ δικαζόμεθα πρὸς αὐτούς, ὥστε τῶν δικαίων δεῖν, ἀλλὰ βουλευό- μεθα περὶ αὐτῶν, ὅπως χρησίμως ἕξουσιν.

XLV. "Ἐν οὖν ταῖς πόλεσι πολλῶν θανάτου ζημίαι πρόκεινται καὶ οὐκ ἴσων τῷδε, ἀλλ᾿ ἐλασσόνων ἁμαρτημάτων· ὅμως δὲ τῇ ἐλπίδι

[1] ἐᾶν, Lindau's conjecture for εἶεν of the MSS.

a reverse you give way to your first impulse and
punish your adviser for his single error of judgment
instead of yourselves, the multitude who shared in
the error.

XLIV. "But I have come forward neither as an
advocate of the Mytilenaeans in opposition to Cleon
nor as their accuser. For the question for us to
consider, if we are sensible, is not what wrong they
have done, but what is the wise course for us. For
no matter how guilty I show them to be, I shall not
on that account bid you to put them to death,
unless it is to our advantage; and if I show that they
have some claim for forgiveness, I shall not on that
account advise you to spare their lives, if this should
prove clearly not to be for the good of the state. In
my opinion we are deliberating about the future
rather than the present. And as for the point
which Cleon especially maintains, that it will be to
our future advantage to inflict the penalty of death,
to the end that revolts may be less frequent, I also
in the interest of our future prosperity emphatically
maintain the contrary. And I beg you not to be led
by the speciousness of his argument to reject the
practical advantages in mine. For embittered as you
are toward the Mytilenaeans, you may perhaps be
attracted by his argument, based as it is on the more
legal aspects of the case ; we are, however, not
engaged in a law-suit with them, so as to be concerned about the question of right and wrong ; but
we are deliberating about them, to determine what
policy will make them useful to us.

XLV. "Now the death-penalty has been prescribed in various states for many offences which are
not so serious as this is, nay, for minor ones ; but

ἐπαιρόμενοι κινδυνεύουσι, καὶ οὐδείς πω κατα-
γνοὺς ἑαυτοῦ μὴ περιέσεσθαι τῷ ἐπιβουλεύματι
2 ἦλθεν ἐς τὸ δεινόν. πόλις τε ἀφισταμένη τίς πω
ἥσσω τῇ δοκήσει ἔχουσα τὴν παρασκευήν, ἢ
οἰκείαν ἢ ἄλλων ξυμμαχίᾳ, τούτῳ ἐπεχείρησε;
3 πεφύκασί τε ἅπαντες καὶ ἰδίᾳ καὶ δημοσίᾳ
ἁμαρτάνειν, καὶ οὐκ ἔστι νόμος ὅστις ἀπείρξει
τούτου, ἐπεὶ διεξεληλύθασί γε διὰ πασῶν τῶν
ζημιῶν οἱ ἄνθρωποι προστιθέντες,[1] εἴ πως ἧσσον
ἀδικοῖντο ὑπὸ τῶν κακούργων. καὶ εἰκὸς τὸ
πάλαι τῶν μεγίστων ἀδικημάτων μαλακωτέρας
κεῖσθαι αὐτάς, παραβαινομένων δὲ τῷ χρόνῳ ἐς
τὸν θάνατον αἱ πολλαὶ ἀνήκουσιν· καὶ ταῦτα[2]
4 ὅμως παραβαίνεται. ἢ τοίνυν δεινότερόν τι
τούτου δέος εὑρετέον ἐστὶν ἢ τόδε γε οὐδὲν
ἐπίσχει, ἀλλ᾽ ἡ μὲν πενία ἀνάγκῃ τὴν τόλμαν
παρέχουσα, ἡ δ᾽ ἐξουσία ὕβρει τὴν πλεονεξίαν
καὶ φρονήματι, αἱ δ᾽ ἄλλαι ξυντυχίαι ὀργῇ[3] τῶν
ἀνθρώπων, ὡς ἑκάστη τις κατέχεται ὑπ᾽ ἀνη-
κέστου τινὸς κρείσσονος, ἐξάγουσιν ἐς τοὺς
5 κινδύνους. ἥ τε ἐλπὶς καὶ ὁ ἔρως ἐπὶ παντί, ὁ
μὲν ἡγούμενος, ἡ δ᾽ ἐφεπομένη, καὶ ὁ μὲν τὴν
ἐπιβουλὴν ἐκφροντίζων, ἡ δὲ τὴν εὐπορίαν τῆς
τύχης ὑποτιθεῖσα πλεῖστα βλάπτουσι, καὶ ὄντα
6 ἀφανῆ κρείσσω ἐστὶ τῶν ὁρωμένων δεινῶν. καὶ
ἡ τύχη ἐπ᾽ αὐτοῖς οὐδὲν ἔλασσον ξυμβάλλεται
ἐς τὸ ἐπαίρειν· ἀδοκήτως γὰρ ἔστιν ὅτε παρι-
σταμένη καὶ ἐκ τῶν ὑποδεεστέρων κινδυνεύειν τινὰ

---

[1] προστιθέντες MSS., Krüger προτιθέντες, followed by Hude.
[2] Hude's correction. Or, reading καὶ τοῦτο with the MSS.,
"and still even this is disregarded."
[3] ὀργῇ MSS., Stahl ὀργήν, followed by Hude.

nevertheless men are so inspired by hope as to take the risk; indeed, no one ever yet has entered upon a perilous enterprise with the conviction that his plot was condemned to failure. And as to states, what one that was meditating revolt ever took the decisive step in the belief that the resources at hand, whether its own or contributed by its allies, were inadequate for success? All men are by nature prone to err, both in private and in public life, and there is no law which will prevent them; in fact, mankind has run the whole gamut of penalties, making them more and more severe, in the hope that the transgressions of evil-doers might be abated. It is probable that in ancient times the penalties prescribed for the greatest offences were relatively mild, but as transgressions still occurred, in course of time the penalty was seldom less than death. But even so there is still transgression. Either, then, some terror more dreadful than death must be discovered, or we must own that death at least is no prevention. Nay, men are lured into hazardous enterprises by the constraint of poverty, which makes them bold, by the insolence and pride of affluence, which makes them greedy, and by the various passions engendered in the other conditions of human life as these are severally mastered by some mighty and irresistible impulse. Then, too, Hope and Desire are everywhere; Desire leads, Hope attends; Desire contrives the plan, Hope suggests the facility of fortune; the two passions are most baneful, and being unseen phantoms prevail over seen dangers. Besides these, fortune contributes in no less degree to urge men on; for she sometimes presents herself unexpectedly and thus tempts men

προάγει καὶ οὐχ ἧσσον τὰς πόλεις, ὅσῳ περὶ τῶν
μεγίστων τε, ἐλευθερίας ἢ ἄλλων ἀρχῆς, καὶ μετὰ
πάντων ἕκαστος ἀλογίστως ἐπὶ πλέον τι αὑτὸν
7 ἐδόξασεν. ἁπλῶς τε ἀδύνατον καὶ πολλῆς εὐη-
θείας, ὅστις οἴεται, τῆς ἀνθρωπείας φύσεως
ὁρμωμένης προθύμως τι πρᾶξαι, ἀποτροπήν τινα
ἔχειν ἢ νόμων ἰσχύι ἢ ἄλλῳ τῳ δεινῷ.

XLVI. "Οὔκουν χρὴ οὔτε τοῦ θανάτου τῇ
ζημίᾳ ὡς ἐχεγγύῳ πιστεύσαντας χεῖρον βουλεύσασθαι, οὔτε ἀνέλπιστον καταστῆσαι τοῖς ἀπο-
στᾶσιν ὡς οὐκ ἔσται μεταγνῶναι καὶ ὅτι ἐν
2 βραχυτάτῳ τὴν ἁμαρτίαν καταλῦσαι. σκέψασθε
γὰρ ὅτι νῦν μέν, ἤν τις καὶ ἀποστᾶσα πόλις γνῷ
μὴ περιεσομένη, ἔλθοι ἂν ἐς ξύμβασιν δυνατὴ
οὖσα ἔτι τὴν δαπάνην ἀποδοῦναι καὶ τὸ λοιπὸν
ὑποτελεῖν· ἐκείνως δὲ τίνα οἴεσθε ἥντινα οὐκ
ἄμεινον μὲν ἢ νῦν παρασκευάσεσθαι, πολιορκίᾳ
δὲ παρατενεῖσθαι ἐς τοὔσχατον, εἰ τὸ αὐτὸ δύνα-
3 ται σχολῇ καὶ ταχὺ ξυμβῆναι; ἡμῖν τε πῶς οὐ
βλάβη δαπανᾶν καθημένοις διὰ τὸ ἀξύμβατον, καὶ
ἢν ἕλωμεν, πόλιν ἐφθαρμένην παραλαβεῖν καὶ τῆς
προσόδου τὸ λοιπὸν ἀπ' αὐτῆς στέρεσθαι; ἰσχύ-
4 ομεν δὲ πρὸς τοὺς πολεμίους τῇδε. ὥστε οὐ δικα-
στὰς ὄντας δεῖ ἡμᾶς μᾶλλον τῶν ἐξαμαρτανόντων
ἀκριβεῖς βλάπτεσθαι ἢ ὁρᾶν ὅπως ἐς τὸν ἔπειτα

to take risks even when their resources are inadequate, and states even more than men, inasmuch as the stake is the greatest of all—their own freedom or empire over others—and the individual, when supported by the whole people, unreasonably overestimates his own strength. In a word, it is impossible, and a mark of extreme simplicity, for anyone to imagine that when human nature is wholeheartedly bent on any undertaking it can be diverted from it by rigorous laws or by any other terror.

XLVI. "We must not, therefore, so pin our faith to the penalty of death as a guarantee against revolt as to make the wrong decision, or lead our rebellious subjects to believe that there will be no chance for them to repent and in the briefest time possible put an end to their error. Consider now: according to your present policy[1] if a city has revolted and then realizes that it will fail, it may come to terms while still able to pay the indemnity and to keep up its tribute in the future; but, in the other case, what city, think you, will not prepare itself more thoroughly than now, and hold out in siege to the last extremity, if it makes no difference whether it capitulates quickly or at its leisure? And as for us, how can we fail to suffer loss, incurring the expense of besieging a city because it will not surrender, and, if we capture it, recovering one that is ruined, and losing thereafter the revenue from it— the source of our strength against our enemies? We must not, therefore, be such rigorous judges of the delinquents as to suffer harm ourselves, but we must rather see how for the time to come, by punishing

---

[1] Athens had not been accustomed to treat secession from the alliance as treason punishable with death for the men and slavery for the women and children.

χρόνον μετρίως κολάζοντες ταῖς πόλεσιν ἕξομεν
ἐς χρημάτων λόγον ἰσχυούσαις χρῆσθαι, καὶ τὴν
φυλακὴν μὴ ἀπὸ τῶν νόμων τῆς δεινότητος ἀξιοῦν
ποιεῖσθαι, ἀλλ' ἀπὸ τῶν ἔργων τῆς ἐπιμελείας.
5 οὗ νῦν τοὐναντίον δρῶντες, ἤν τινα ἐλεύθερον καὶ
βίᾳ ἀρχόμενον εἰκότως πρὸς αὐτονομίαν ἀπο-
στάντα χειρωσώμεθα, χαλεπῶς οἰόμεθα χρῆναι
6 τιμωρεῖσθαι. χρὴ δὲ τοὺς ἐλευθέρους οὐκ ἀφισταμένους σφόδρα κολάζειν, ἀλλὰ πρὶν ἀποστῆναι
σφόδρα φυλάσσειν καὶ προκαταλαμβάνειν ὅπως
μηδ' ἐς ἐπίνοιαν τούτου ἴωσι, κρατήσαντάς τε ὅτι
ἐπ' ἐλάχιστον τὴν αἰτίαν ἐπιφέρειν.

XLVII. "Ὑμεῖς δὲ σκέψασθε ὅσον ἂν καὶ τοῦτο
2 ἁμαρτάνοιτε Κλέωνι πειθόμενοι. νῦν μὲν γὰρ
ὑμῖν ὁ δῆμος ἐν πάσαις ταῖς πόλεσιν εὔνους
ἐστὶ καὶ ἢ οὐ ξυναφίσταται τοῖς ὀλίγοις ἤ, ἐὰν
βιασθῇ, ὑπάρχει τοῖς ἀποστήσασι πολέμιος
εὐθύς, καὶ τῆς ἀντικαθισταμένης πόλεως τὸ
πλῆθος ξύμμαχον ἔχοντες ἐς πόλεμον ἐπέρχεσθε.
3 εἰ δὲ διαφθερεῖτε τὸν δῆμον τὸν Μυτιληναίων,
ὃς οὔτε μετέσχε τῆς ἀποστάσεως, ἐπειδή τε
ὅπλων ἐκράτησεν, ἑκὼν παρέδωκε τὴν πόλιν,
πρῶτον μὲν ἀδικήσετε τοὺς εὐεργέτας κτείνοντες,
ἔπειτα καταστήσετε τοῖς δυνατοῖς τῶν ἀνθρώπων
ὃ βούλονται μάλιστα· ἀφιστάντες γὰρ τὰς πόλεις
τὸν δῆμον εὐθὺς ξύμμαχον ἕξουσι προδειξάντων
ὑμῶν τὴν αὐτὴν ζημίαν τοῖς τε ἀδικοῦσιν ὁμοίως

moderately, we may have at our service dependent cities that are strong in material resources; and we must deem it proper to protect ourselves against revolts, not by the terror of our laws, but rather by the vigilance of our administration. At present we do just the opposite: whenever a free people that is forced into subjection revolts, as it naturally will, in order to recover its independence, we think that, as soon as we have subdued it, we must punish it severely. We ought, on the contrary, instead of rigorously chastising free peoples when they revolt, to watch them rigorously before they revolt, and thus forestall their even thinking of such a thing; and when we have subdued a revolt, we ought to put the blame on as few as possible.[1]

XLVII. "And do you consider, too, how great a mistake you would make in another point also by following Cleon's advice. At the present time the populace of all the cities is well disposed to you, and either does not join with the aristocrats in revolting, or, if forced to do so, is hostile from the beginning to those who stirred up the revolt; and so, when you go to war, you have the populace of the rebellious city as your allies. If, however, you destroy the populace in Mytilene, which took no part in the revolt, and which voluntarily put the city into your hands as soon as it got hold of arms, in the first place you will be guilty of killing your benefactors, and, in the second place, you will bring about what the influential men most wish: the next time they instigate a revolt among our allies they will at once have the populace on their side, because you will have published it abroad that the same punishment

[1] In answer to Cleon's demand, ch. xxxix. 6.

4 κεῖσθαι καὶ τοῖς μή. δεῖ δέ, καὶ εἰ ἠδίκησαν, μὴ
προσποιεῖσθαι, ὅπως ὃ μόνον ἡμῖν ἔτι ξύμμαχόν
5 ἐστι μὴ πολέμιον γένηται. καὶ τοῦτο πολλῷ
ξυμφορώτερον ἡγοῦμαι ἐς τὴν κάθεξιν τῆς ἀρχῆς,
ἑκόντας ἡμᾶς ἀδικηθῆναι ἢ δικαίως οὓς μὴ δεῖ
διαφθεῖραι· καὶ τὸ Κλέωνος τὸ αὐτὸ δίκαιον καὶ
ξύμφορον τῆς τιμωρίας οὐχ εὑρίσκεται ἐν αὐτῷ
δυνατὸν ὂν ἅμα γίγνεσθαι.

XLVIII. "Ὑμεῖς δὲ γνόντες ἀμείνω τάδε εἶναι
καὶ μήτε οἴκτῳ πλέον νείμαντες μήτ' ἐπιεικείᾳ,
οἷς οὐδὲ ἐγὼ ἐῶ προσάγεσθαι, ἀπ' αὐτῶν δὲ τῶν
παραινουμένων πείθεσθέ μοι Μυτιληναίων οὓς
μὲν Πάχης ἀπέπεμψεν ὡς ἀδικοῦντας κρῖναι καθ'
2 ἡσυχίαν, τοὺς δ' ἄλλους ἐᾶν οἰκεῖν. τάδε γὰρ
ἔς τε τὸ μέλλον ἀγαθὰ καὶ τοῖς πολεμίοις ἤδη
φοβερά· ὅστις γὰρ εὖ βουλεύεται πρὸς τοὺς
ἐναντίους κρείσσων ἐστὶν ἢ μετ' ἔργων ἰσχύος
ἄνοια ἐπιών."

XLIX. Τοιαῦτα δὲ ὁ Διόδοτος εἶπεν. ῥη-
θεισῶν δὲ τῶν γνωμῶν τούτων μάλιστα ἀντι-
πάλων πρὸς ἀλλήλας οἱ Ἀθηναῖοι ἦλθον μὲν
ἐς ἀγῶνα ὅμως[1] τῆς δόξης καὶ ἐγένοντο ἐν τῇ
χειροτονίᾳ ἀγχώμαλοι, ἐκράτησε δὲ ἡ τοῦ Διο-
2 δότου. καὶ τριήρη εὐθὺς ἄλλην ἀπέστελλον
κατὰ σπουδήν, ὅπως μὴ φθασάσης τῆς προτέρας[2]
εὕρωσι διεφθαρμένην τὴν πόλιν· προεῖχε δὲ
3 ἡμέρᾳ καὶ νυκτὶ μάλιστα. παρασκευασάντων δὲ
τῶν Μυτιληναίων πρέσβεων τῇ νηὶ οἶνον καὶ

---

[1] ὅμως, with MSS. Bredow emends to ὁμοίως, followed
by Hude.
[2] προτέρας, generally adopted, Valla and a few MSS.,
against δευτέρας or ἑτέρας of other MSS.

is ordained for the innocent and for the guilty. Why, even if they were guilty, you should pretend not to know it, to the end that the only class that is still friendly to us may not become hostile. And it is, I think, far more conducive to the maintenance of our dominion, that we should willingly submit to be wronged, than that we should destroy, however justly, those whom we ought not to destroy. And whereas Cleon claims[1] that this punishment combines justice and expediency, it appears that in such a policy the two cannot be combined.

XLVIII. "Do you, then, recognize that mine is the better course, and without being unduly swayed by either pity or clemency—for neither would I have you influenced by such motives—but simply weighing the considerations I have urged, accede to my proposal: pass sentence at your leisure upon the Mytilenaeans whom Paches sent here as guilty,[2] but let the rest dwell in peace. Such a course will be best for the future, and will cause alarm among our enemies at once; for he who is wise in counsel is stronger against the foe than he who recklessly rushes on with brute force."

XLIX. Such was the speech of Diodotus. And after these opinions had been maintained with nearly equal force, the one against the other, the Athenians, in spite of the reaction, experienced such a conflict of opinion that in the show of hands they were about equally divided; but the view of Diodotus prevailed. They then immediately despatched a second trireme with all haste, hoping that the first trireme, which had the start by about a day and a night, might not arrive first and the city be found destroyed. The Mytilenaean envoys provided wine

---

[1] cf. ch. xl. 4.   [2] cf. ch. xxxv. 1.

ἄλφιτα καὶ μεγάλα ὑποσχομένων, εἰ φθάσειαν, ἐγένετο σπουδὴ τοῦ πλοῦ τοιαύτη ὥστε ἤσθιόν τε ἅμα ἐλαύνοντες οἴνῳ καὶ ἐλαίῳ ἄλφιτα πεφυρμένα, καὶ οἱ μὲν ὕπνον ᾑροῦντο κατὰ μέρος, οἱ 4 δὲ ἤλαυνον. κατὰ τύχην δὲ πνεύματος οὐδενὸς ἐναντιωθέντος καὶ τῆς μὲν προτέρας νεὼς οὐ σπουδῇ πλεούσης ἐπὶ πρᾶγμα ἀλλόκοτον, ταύτης δὲ τοιούτῳ τρόπῳ ἐπειγομένης, ἡ μὲν ἔφθασε τοσοῦτον ὅσον Πάχητα ἀνεγνωκέναι τὸ ψήφισμα καὶ μέλλειν δράσειν τὰ δεδογμένα, ἡ δ᾽ ὑστέρα αὐτῆς ἐπικατάγεται καὶ διεκώλυσε μὴ διαφθεῖραι. παρὰ τοσοῦτον μὲν ἡ Μυτιλήνη ἦλθε κινδύνου.

L. Τοὺς δ᾽ ἄλλους ἄνδρας οὓς ὁ Πάχης ἀπέπεμψεν ὡς αἰτιωτάτους ὄντας τῆς ἀποστάσεως Κλέωνος γνώμῃ διέφθειραν οἱ Ἀθηναῖοι (ἦσαν δὲ ὀλίγῳ πλείους χιλίων), καὶ Μυτιληναίων τείχη 2 καθεῖλον καὶ ναῦς παρέλαβον. ὕστερον δὲ φόρον μὲν οὐκ ἔταξαν Λεσβίοις, κλήρους δὲ ποιήσαντες τῆς γῆς πλὴν τῆς Μηθυμναίων τρισχιλίους, τριακοσίους μὲν τοῖς θεοῖς ἱεροὺς ἐξεῖλον, ἐπὶ δὲ τοὺς ἄλλους σφῶν αὐτῶν κληρούχους τοὺς λαχόντας ἀπέπεμψαν· οἷς ἀργύριον Λέσβιοι ταξάμενοι τοῦ κλήρου ἑκάστου τοῦ ἐνιαυτοῦ δύο μνᾶς φέρειν

---

[1] Usually the barley-meal was mixed with water and oil.

[2] A crew ordinarily stopped for meals and rested at anchor at night.

[3] Paches was accused of shameful deeds of violence toward Lesbian men and women (Agath. *Epigr.* lvii.), and when

and barley for the crew and promised a large reward
if they should arrive in time; and such was their
haste on the voyage that they kept on rowing as
they ate their barley-cakes, kneaded with wine and
oil,[1] and took turns at sleeping and rowing.[2] And
since by good fortune no contrary wind arose, and
the earlier ship was sailing in no hurry on so horrible
a business, while the second pressed on in the
manner described, although the former did in fact
arrive first, so that Paches had just time enough to
read the decree and was about to execute the orders,
the second put in close after it and prevented the
destruction of the city. By just so much did
Mytilene escape its peril.

L. The rest of the men, however, whom Paches[3]
had sent to Athens as chief authors of the revolt,
numbering somewhat more than a thousand,[4] were
put to death by the Athenians on the motion of
Cleon. They also pulled down the walls of Mytilene
and took possession of the Mytilenaean fleet. After-
awards, instead of imposing a tribute upon the
Lesbians, they divided all the land except that of the
Methymnaeans into three thousand allotments, and
reserving three hundred of these as sacred to the
gods they sent out Athenian colonists, chosen by
lot. to occupy the rest. With these the Lesbians
made an arrangement to pay a rental of two minas a
year[5] for each lot, they themselves to cultivate the

brought to trial committed suicide in the presence of his
judges.

  [4] On the ground that so large a number is incompatible
with ch. xxviii. 1, 2; xxxv. 1, Steup conjectures τριάκοντα
(Λ' for ,Λ).

  [5] The whole rental amounting to 90 talents; £18,000;
$87,300.

3 αὐτοὶ εἰργάζοντο τὴν γῆν. παρέλαβον δὲ καὶ τὰ
ἐν τῇ ἠπείρῳ πολίσματα οἱ Ἀθηναῖοι ὅσων
Μυτιληναῖοι ἐκράτουν, καὶ ὑπήκουον ὕστερον
Ἀθηναίων. τὰ μὲν κατὰ Λέσβον οὕτως ἐγένετο.

LI. Ἐν δὲ τῷ αὐτῷ θέρει μετὰ τὴν Λέσβου
ἅλωσιν Ἀθηναῖοι Νικίου τοῦ Νικηράτου στρατηγοῦντος ἐστράτευσαν ἐπὶ Μινῴαν τὴν νῆσον, ἣ
κεῖται πρὸ Μεγάρων· ἐχρῶντο δὲ αὐτῇ πύργον
2 ἐνοικοδομήσαντες οἱ Μεγαρῆς φρουρίῳ. ἐβούλετο δὲ Νικίας τὴν φυλακὴν αὐτόθεν δι' ἐλάσ-
σονος τοῖς Ἀθηναίοις καὶ μὴ ἀπὸ τοῦ Βουδόρου
καὶ τῆς Σαλαμῖνος εἶναι, τούς τε Πελοποννησίους ὅπως μὴ ποιῶνται ἔκπλους αὐτόθεν λαν-
θάνοντες τριήρων τε, οἷον καὶ τὸν πρὶν γενόμενον,
καὶ λῃστῶν ἐκπομπαῖς, τοῖς τε Μεγαρεῦσιν
3 ἅμα μηδὲν ἐσπλεῖν. ἑλὼν οὖν ἀπὸ τῆς Νισαίας πρῶτον δύο πύργω προύχοντε μηχαναῖς
ἐκ θαλάσσης καὶ τὸν ἔσπλουν ἐς τὸ μεταξὺ τῆς
νήσου ἐλευθερώσας ἀπετείχιζε καὶ τὸ ἐκ τῆς ἠπείρου, ᾗ κατὰ γέφυραν διὰ τενάγους ἐπιβοήθεια
4 ἦν τῇ νήσῳ οὐ πολὺ διεχούσῃ τῆς ἠπείρου. ὡς δὲ
τοῦτο ἐξειργάσαντο ἐν ἡμέραις ὀλίγαις, ὕστερον
δὴ καὶ ἐν τῇ νήσῳ τεῖχος[1] ἐγκαταλιπὼν καὶ
φρουρὰν ἀνεχώρησε τῷ στρατῷ.

[1] τεῖχος—the text is probably corrupt, the verb being omitted.

---

[1] cf. IV. lii. 3, where they are called ἀκταῖαι πόλεις.
[2] Referring to Brasidas' attempt, described II. xciii., xciv.

land. The Athenians also took possession of all the towns on the mainland which the Mytilenaeans controlled,[1] and these were thereafter subject to the Athenians. Such was the course of events at Lesbos.

LI. In the same summer, after the capture of Lesbos, the Athenians, under the command of Nicias son of Niceratus, made an expedition against the island of Minoa, which lies in front of Megara and was used as a garrison-station by the Megarians, who had built a tower upon it. But Nicias was desirous that the watch which the Athenians kept should be maintained at that point, which would be at closer range for them, instead of at Budorum in Salamis, the purpose of the watch being to prevent the Peloponnesians from using the harbour of Megara as a base from which to send out unobserved either triremes, as they had done once before,[2] or expeditions of privateers, and at the same time to see to it that nothing was brought in by sea for the Megarians. Accordingly, by an attack from the sea he took by means of engines of war two projecting towers—first that on the island opposite Nisaea—and when he had thus cleared the way into the channel between the island and the mainland he walled off also the point on the side toward the mainland, where by a bridge across a morass aid could be brought to the island, which is not far distant from the mainland.[3] And when, after a few days, this work was completed, Nicias built a fort on the island also, left a garrison in it, and then withdrew his army to Athens.

[3] This seems to be the sense intended. The passage is very much condensed or corrupt. The two towers seem to have stood on the strait between Minoa and the mainland, one on each side, at the end of dams built out to narrow the strait.

LII. Ὑπὸ δὲ τοὺς αὐτοὺς χρόνους τοῦ θέρους τούτου καὶ οἱ Πλαταιῆς οὐκέτι ἔχοντες σῖτον οὐδὲ δυνάμενοι πολιορκεῖσθαι ξυνέβησαν τοῖς 2 Πελοποννησίοις τοιῷδε τρόπῳ. προσέβαλον αὐτῶν τῷ τείχει, οἱ δὲ οὐκ ἐδύναντο ἀμύνεσθαι. γνοὺς δὲ ὁ Λακεδαιμόνιος ἄρχων τὴν ἀσθένειαν αὐτῶν βίᾳ μὲν οὐκ ἐβούλετο ἑλεῖν (εἰρημένον γὰρ ἦν [1] αὐτῷ ἐκ Λακεδαίμονος, ὅπως, εἰ σπονδαὶ γίγνοιντό ποτε πρὸς Ἀθηναίους καὶ ξυγχωροῖεν ὅσα πολέμῳ χωρία ἔχουσιν ἑκάτεροι ἀποδίδοσθαι, μὴ ἀνάδοτος εἴη ἡ Πλάταια ὡς αὐτῶν ἑκόντων προσχωρησάντων), προσπέμπει δὲ αὐτοῖς κήρυκα λέγοντα, εἰ βούλονται παραδοῦναι τὴν πόλιν ἑκόντες τοῖς Λακεδαιμονίοις καὶ δικασταῖς ἐκείνοις χρήσασθαι, τούς τε ἀδίκους κολάσειν, παρὰ δίκην 3 δὲ οὐδένα. τοσαῦτα μὲν ὁ κῆρυξ εἶπεν· οἱ δέ (ἦσαν γὰρ ἤδη ἐν τῷ ἀσθενεστάτῳ) παρέδοσαν τὴν πόλιν. καὶ τοὺς Πλαταιᾶς ἔτρεφον οἱ Πελοποννήσιοι ἡμέρας τινάς, ἐν ὅσῳ οἱ ἐκ τῆς Λακεδαίμονος δικασταί, πέντε ἄνδρες, ἀφίκοντο. 4 ἐλθόντων δὲ αὐτῶν κατηγορία μὲν οὐδεμία προυτέθη, ἠρώτων δὲ αὐτοὺς ἐπικαλεσάμενοι τοσοῦτον μόνον, εἴ τι Λακεδαιμονίους καὶ τοὺς ξυμμάχους ἐν τῷ πολέμῳ τῷ καθεστῶτι ἀγαθόν τι εἰργασ- 5 μένοι εἰσίν. οἱ δ' ἔλεγον αἰτησάμενοι μακρότερα εἰπεῖν καὶ προτάξαντες σφῶν αὐτῶν Ἀστύμαχόν τε τὸν Ἀσωπολάου καὶ Λάκωνα τὸν Αἰειμνήστου,

[1] ἦν, bracketed by Hude, as not read by the Scholiast.

LII. During this summer and about the same time, the Plataeans,[1] who were now without food and could endure the siege no longer, surrendered to the Peloponnesians. It happened in the following manner. An assault was in progress upon their wall and they were unable to repel it. The Lacedaemonian commander recognised their weakness; but he did not wish to take Plataea by storm, for he had received orders to this effect from Sparta, to the end that, if ever a treaty of peace should be made with the Athenians and the Lacedaemonians should consent that all the places each had taken in war should be given back, Plataea might not have to be given up, on the ground that its inhabitants had gone over to Sparta voluntarily. So he sent a herald to them to say that if they would of their own accord deliver their city into the hands of the Lacedaemonians and submit to their decisions they would punish the guilty, but none contrary to justice. The herald made this proposal, and they, since they were now in the last stage of weakness, surrendered the city. And the Peloponnesians fed the Plataeans for some days, until the judges, five in number, arrived from Lacedaemon. When they came no accusation was brought against the Plataeans, but they were summoned by the judges and asked this single question: "Have you rendered any good service to the Lacedaemonians and their allies in the present war?" The Plataeans, however, begged to be allowed to speak at greater length, and appointed as their spokesmen Astymachus son of Asopolaus and Lacon son of Aeimnestus, who was a proxenus of the

---

[1] Resuming the narrative from the end of ch. xxiv.

πρόξενον ὄντα Λακεδαιμονίων· καὶ ἐπελθόντες
ἔλεγον τοιάδε.

LIII. "Τὴν μὲν παράδοσιν τῆς πόλεως, ὦ
Λακεδαιμόνιοι, πιστεύσαντες ὑμῖν ἐποιησάμεθα,
οὐ τοιάνδε δίκην οἰόμενοι ὑφέξειν, νομιμωτέραν
δέ τινα ἔσεσθαι, καὶ ἐν δικασταῖς οὐκ ἂν ἄλλοις
δεξάμενοι, ὥσπερ καὶ ἐσμέν, γενέσθαι ἢ ὑμῖν,[1]
2 ἡγούμενοι τὸ ἴσον μάλιστ' ἂν φέρεσθαι. νῦν δὲ
φοβούμεθα μὴ ἀμφοτέρων ἅμα ἡμαρτήκαμεν·
τόν τε γὰρ ἀγῶνα περὶ τῶν δεινοτάτων εἶναι εἰκότως ὑποπτεύομεν καὶ ὑμᾶς μὴ οὐ κοινοὶ ἀποβῆτε,
τεκμαιρόμενοι προκατηγορίας τε ἡμῶν οὐ προγε-
γενημένης ᾗ χρὴ ἀντειπεῖν (ἀλλ' αὐτοὶ λόγον
ᾐτησάμεθα) τό τε ἐπερώτημα βραχὺ ὄν, ᾧ τὰ
μὲν ἀληθῆ ἀποκρίνασθαι ἐναντία γίγνεται, τὰ δὲ
3 ψευδῆ ἔλεγχον ἔχει. πανταχόθεν δὲ ἄποροι
καθεστῶτες ἀναγκαζόμεθα καὶ ἀσφαλέστερον
δοκεῖ εἶναι εἰπόντας τι κινδυνεύειν· καὶ γὰρ ὁ μὴ
ῥηθεὶς λόγος τοῖς ὧδ' ἔχουσιν αἰτίαν ἂν παρά-
4 σχοι ὡς, εἰ ἐλέχθη, σωτήριος ἂν ἦν. χαλεπῶς
δὲ ἔχει ἡμῖν πρὸς τοῖς ἄλλοις καὶ ἡ πειθώ.
ἀγνῶτες μὲν γὰρ ὄντες ἀλλήλων ἐπεσενεγκάμενοι
μαρτύρια ὧν ἄπειροι ἦτε ὠφελούμεθ' ἄν· νῦν δὲ
πρὸς εἰδότας πάντα λελέξεται,[2] καὶ δέδιμεν οὐχὶ

---

[1] ἢ ὑμῖν, bracketed by Hude, as seemingly not read by the
Scholiast.   [2] λελέξεται, Hude reads λέξεται with C.

---

[1] Public host or consul.   He had commanded the Plataean
contingent at Marathon.

Lacedaemonians.[1] These men came forward and spoke as follows:

LIII. "When we surrendered our city, Lacedaemonians, trusting in your good faith, we had no thought that we should have to undergo a trial like this, but supposed it would be a more regular procedure; and when we consented to be on trial before you and you alone as judges, as we now are, we believed that we should be most likely to obtain fair treatment. But now we fear that we have been disappointed in both expectations; for we have good reason to suspect, not only that the issues involved in the trial are of the gravest nature [2] but also that you will not prove to be impartial judges. These inferences we draw from the fact that no accusation was first brought against us requiring a plea in defence, but we have had to ask leave to speak, and that the question which is put to us is so curt that a truthful answer to it is against our interests, while a false one can be exposed at once. But beset as we are with perplexities on every hand, we are forced, as indeed seems to be the safer course, to say something and take the risk; for to men in our condition not to have spoken would cause us afterwards to reproach ourselves with the thought that, had the word been spoken, it would have saved us. A further difficulty in our position is the task of convincing you. For if we were strangers to each other, we might find it to our advantage to introduce evidence on matters with which you were unacquainted; but as it is, anything that we shall say is already known to you, and what we fear is, not that

[2] *i.e.* that their very lives were at stake, whereas they had expected, after capitulation, that in the formal trial there could be no question of capital punishment.

THUCYDIDES

μὴ προκαταγνόντες ἡμῶν τὰς ἀρετὰς ἥσσους εἶναι
τῶν ὑμετέρων ἔγκλημα αὐτὸ ποιῆτε, ἀλλὰ μὴ
ἄλλοις χάριν φέροντες ἐπὶ διεγνωσμένην κρίσιν
καθιστώμεθα.

LIV. '' Παρεχόμενοι δὲ ὅμως ἃ ἔχομεν δίκαια
πρός τε τὰ Θηβαίων διάφορα καὶ ἐς ὑμᾶς καὶ
τοὺς ἄλλους Ἕλληνας, τῶν εὖ δεδραμένων ὑπόμνησιν ποιησόμεθα καὶ πείθειν πειρασόμεθα.
2 φαμὲν γὰρ πρὸς τὸ ἐρώτημα τὸ βραχύ, εἴ τι
Λακεδαιμονίους καὶ τοὺς ξυμμάχους ἐν τῷ πολέμῳ τῷδε ἀγαθὸν πεποιήκαμεν, εἰ μὲν ὡς πολεμίους ἐρωτᾶτε, οὐκ ἀδικεῖσθαι ὑμᾶς μὴ εὖ παθόν-
τας, φίλους δὲ νομίζοντας αὐτοὺς ἁμαρτάνειν
3 μᾶλλον τοὺς ἡμῖν ἐπιστρατεύσαντας. τὰ δ' ἐν
τῇ εἰρήνῃ καὶ πρὸς τὸν Μῆδον ἀγαθοὶ γεγενήμεθα,
τὴν μὲν οὐ λύσαντες νῦν πρότεροι, τῷ δὲ ξυνεπι-
θέμενοι τότε ἐς ἐλευθερίαν τῆς Ἑλλάδος μόνοι
4 Βοιωτῶν. καὶ γὰρ ἠπειρῶταί τε ὄντες ἐναυμαχή-
σαμεν ἐπ᾽ Ἀρτεμισίῳ, μάχῃ τε τῇ ἐν τῇ ἡμετέρᾳ
γῇ γενομένῃ παρεγενόμεθα ὑμῖν τε καὶ Παυσανίᾳ·
εἴ τέ τι ἄλλο κατ᾽ ἐκεῖνον τὸν χρόνον ἐγένετο
ἐπικίνδυνον τοῖς Ἕλλησι, πάντων παρὰ δύναμιν
5 μετέσχομεν. καὶ ὑμῖν, ὦ Λακεδαιμόνιοι, ἰδίᾳ,
ὅπερ δὴ μέγιστος φόβος περιέστη τὴν Σπάρτην
μετὰ τὸν σεισμὸν τῶν ἐς Ἰθώμην Εἱλώτων ἀπο-

---

[1] Referring to the achievements of the Plataeans in the
Persian wars.
[2] i.e. the Thebans. With bitter irony the Plataeans
ascribe to themselves the evident purpose of the

you have already judged our virtues[1] to be inferior to your own and now make that a charge against us, but that in order to gratify others[2] we are to appear before a court that has already decided against us.

LIV. "Nevertheless, we shall present whatever just claims we have, both as regards our quarrel with the Thebans and as touching you and the rest of the Hellenes, and thus, by reminding you of our public services, shall try to persuade you. In reply to the curt inquiry of yours, whether we have rendered any good service to the Lacedaemonians and their allies in this war, if you ask us as enemies, we say that you are not wronged if you did not receive benefit at our hands; but if in asking it you regard us as friends, we reply that you yourselves rather than we are at fault, in that you made war upon us. But in the war against the Persians and during the peace which followed we have proved ourselves good and true men; we have not now been the first to break the peace, and then we were the only Boeotians[3] who rallied to defend the freedom of Hellas. For though we are an inland people, we took part in the sea-fight at Artemisium; in the battle that was fought here in our own land[4] we stood side by side with you and Pausanias; and whatever perils arose to threaten the Hellenes in those days, we bore our part in them all beyond our strength. And to you in particular, Lacedaemonians, at that critical moment when after the earthquake Sparta was encompassed by a mighty terror owing to the revolt of the Helots

Lacedaemonians—by standing trial before a prejudiced court they will "do a favour to the Thebans."

[3] Rhetorical inaccuracy, for the Thespians did the same (Hdt. VII. cxxxii.; VIII. l.).

[4] The battle of Plataea, 479 B.C. See Hdt. IX. lxii. ff.

στάντων, τὸ τρίτον μέρος ἡμῶν αὐτῶν ἐξεπέμψα-
μεν ἐς ἐπικουρίαν· ὧν οὐκ εἰκὸς ἀμνημονεῖν.

LV. "Καὶ τὰ μὲν παλαιὰ καὶ μέγιστα τοιοῦτοι
ἠξιώσαμεν εἶναι, πολέμιοι δὲ ἐγενόμεθα ὕστερον.
ὑμεῖς δὲ αἴτιοι· δεομένων γὰρ ξυμμαχίας ὅτε
Θηβαῖοι ἡμᾶς ἐβιάσαντο, ὑμεῖς ἀπεώσασθε καὶ
πρὸς Ἀθηναίους ἐκελεύετε τραπέσθαι ὡς ἐγγὺς
2 ὄντας, ὑμῶν δὲ μακρὰν ἀποικούντων. ἐν μέντοι
τῷ πολέμῳ οὐδὲν ἐκπρεπέστερον ὑπὸ ἡμῶν οὔτε
3 ἐπάθετε οὔτε ἐμελλήσατε. εἰ δ' ἀποστῆναι
Ἀθηναίων οὐκ ἠθελήσαμεν ὑμῶν κελευσάντων,
οὐκ ἠδικοῦμεν· καὶ γὰρ ἐκεῖνοι ἐβοήθουν ἡμῖν
ἐναντία Θηβαίοις ὅτε ὑμεῖς ἀπωκνεῖτε, καὶ προδοῦναι αὐτοὺς οὐκέτι ἦν καλόν, ἄλλως τε καὶ οὓς
εὖ παθών τις καὶ αὐτὸς δεόμενος προσηγάγετο
ξυμμάχους καὶ πολιτείας μετέλαβεν, ἰέναι δὲ ἐς
4 τὰ παραγγελλόμενα εἰκὸς ἦν προθύμως. ἃ δὲ
ἑκάτεροι ἐξηγεῖσθε τοῖς ξυμμάχοις, οὐχ οἱ ἑπόμενοι αἴτιοι εἴ τι μὴ καλῶς ἐδρᾶτο, ἀλλ' οἱ ἄγοντες
ἐπὶ τὰ μὴ ὀρθῶς ἔχοντα.

LVI. "Θηβαῖοι δὲ πολλὰ μὲν καὶ ἄλλα ἡμᾶς
ἠδίκησαν, τὸ δὲ τελευταῖον αὐτοὶ ξύνιστε, δι' ὅπερ
2 καὶ τάδε πάσχομεν. πόλιν γὰρ αὐτοὺς τὴν ἡμετέραν καταλαμβάνοντας ἐν σπονδαῖς καὶ προσέτι
ἱερομηνίᾳ ὀρθῶς τε ἐτιμωρησάμεθα κατὰ τὸν πᾶσι
νόμον καθεστῶτα, τὸν ἐπιόντα πολέμιον ὅσιον

and their occupation of Ithome, we sent a third part of our citizens to bring aid. These are things you ought not to forget.

LV. "Such was the part we were proud to play in the great actions of the past. It was not until later that we became your enemies, and for this you yourselves were to blame; for when the Thebans oppressed us and we sought alliance with you, you rebuffed us and bade us apply to the Athenians, because they were near, whereas you lived far away. In the course of this war, however, you have neither suffered, nor were ever in danger of suffering, any extraordinary harm at our hands. And if we refused to revolt from the Athenians at your bidding, we were not in the wrong; for they helped us against the Thebans when you held back. After that it would not have been honourable for us to desert them, above all when we were their debtors and when at our own request we had been admitted to their alliance and had shared the rights of citizenship with them. On the contrary, there was every reason why we should heartily obey their commands. And whatever measures either you or they have initiated for your allies, it is not the followers who are to blame for any wrong that has been done, but those who have led them into evil courses.

LVI. "As for the Thebans, they have done us many wrongs in the past, and you yourselves are well aware of this crowning outrage, which has brought us into our present plight. They attempted to seize our city in time of peace, and furthermore on a day of festival; therefore we were justified in punishing them in accordance with the law which has universal sanction, that it is right to repel him who comes

εἶναι ἀμύνεσθαι, καὶ νῦν οὐκ ἂν εἰκότως δι' αὐτοὺς
3 βλαπτοίμεθα. εἰ γὰρ τῷ αὐτίκα χρησίμῳ ὑμῶν
τε καὶ ἐκείνων πολεμίῳ[1] τὸ δίκαιον λήψεσθε, τοῦ
μὲν ὀρθοῦ φανεῖσθε οὐκ ἀληθεῖς κριταὶ ὄντες, τὸ
4 δὲ ξυμφέρον μᾶλλον θεραπεύοντες. καίτοι εἰ νῦν
ὑμῖν ὠφέλιμοι δοκοῦσιν εἶναι, πολὺ καὶ ἡμεῖς καὶ
οἱ ἄλλοι Ἕλληνες μᾶλλον τότε ὅτε ἐν μείζονι
κινδύνῳ ἦτε. νῦν μὲν γὰρ ἑτέροις ὑμεῖς ἐπέρχεσθε
δεινοί, ἐν ἐκείνῳ δὲ τῷ καιρῷ, ὅτε πᾶσι δουλείαν
5 ἐπέφερεν ὁ βάρβαρος, οἵδε μετ' αὐτοῦ ἦσαν. καὶ
δίκαιον ἡμῶν τῆς νῦν ἁμαρτίας, εἰ ἄρα ἡμάρτηταί
τι, ἀντιθεῖναι τὴν τότε προθυμίαν, καὶ μείζω τε
πρὸς ἐλάσσω εὑρήσετε καὶ ἐν καιροῖς οἷς σπάνιον
ἦν τῶν Ἑλλήνων τινὰ ἀρετὴν τῇ Ξέρξου δυνάμει
ἀντιτάξασθαι, ἐπῃνοῦντό τε μᾶλλον οἱ μὴ τὰ
ξύμφορα πρὸς τὴν ἔφοδον αὐτοῖς[2] ἀσφαλείᾳ
πράσσοντες, ἐθέλοντες δὲ τολμᾶν μετὰ κινδύνων
6 τὰ βέλτιστα. ὧν ἡμεῖς γενόμενοι καὶ τιμηθέντες
ἐς τὰ πρῶτα νῦν ἐπὶ τοῖς αὐτοῖς δέδιμεν μὴ δια-
φθαρῶμεν, Ἀθηναίους ἑλόμενοι δικαίως μᾶλλον ἢ
7 ὑμᾶς κερδαλέως. καίτοι χρὴ ταὐτὰ περὶ τῶν
αὐτῶν ὁμοίως φαίνεσθαι γιγνώσκοντας καὶ τὸ
ξυμφέρον μὴ ἄλλο τι νομίσαι, ἢ τῶν ξυμμάχων
τοῖς ἀγαθοῖς ὅταν αἰεὶ βέβαιον τὴν χάριν τῆς

---

[1] πολεμίῳ, bracketed by Hude, as derived from a gloss
(πολεμίων).
[2] αὐτοῖς, Bekker and most editors with M, Hude αὑτοῖς.

against you as an enemy; and now we cannot reasonably be made to suffer on their account. For if you shall decide the question of justice by such considerations as your immediate advantage and their hostility, you will show yourselves to be, not true judges of what is right, but rather to be mere slaves of expediency. And yet if the Thebans seem serviceable to you now, we and the rest of the Hellenes were of far greater service to you when you were in greater danger. For now you are attacking others and are a menace to them, but in that crisis, when the barbarian was threatening us all with slavery, these men were on his side. And it is only fair that you should set our present error, if error there has been, over against the zeal we showed then; if you do, you will find, not only that the zeal outweighs the offence, but also that it was shown at a time when it was a rare thing for Hellenes to oppose their courage to the power of Xerxes. At that time the greater praise was given to those who, instead of intriguing in security for their own advantage with reference to the invasion,[1] were ready to hazard the noblest course though fraught with danger. With these we took our stand and were honoured among the foremost; but now, for the same conduct, we fear lest we are to be destroyed, in that we have chosen the Athenians from regard to right rather than you for profit. And yet you ought to show yourselves consistent, giving the same judgment concerning the same things, and to consider your true advantage to be only this—to cherish an ever-enduring gratitude

---

[1] As the Thebans did. If αὐτοῖς be read, with nearly all MSS., it must be construed with ἔφοδον, "working to further the invasion of the enemy."

ἀρετῆς ἔχουσι[1] καὶ τὸ παραυτίκα που ὑμῖν[2] ὠφέλιμον καθίσταται.

LVII. "Προσσκέψασθέ[3] τε ὅτι νῦν μὲν παράδειγμα τοῖς πολλοῖς τῶν Ἑλλήνων ἀνδραγαθίας νομίζεσθε· εἰ δὲ περὶ ἡμῶν γνώσεσθε μὴ τὰ εἰκότα (οὐ γὰρ ἀφανῆ κρινεῖτε τὴν δίκην τήνδε, ἐπαινούμενοι δὲ περὶ οὐδ' ἡμῶν μεμπτῶν), ὁρᾶτε ὅπως μὴ οὐκ ἀποδέξωνται ἀνδρῶν ἀγαθῶν πέρι αὐτοὺς ἀμείνους ὄντας ἀπρεπές τι ἐπιγνῶναι, οὐδὲ πρὸς ἱεροῖς τοῖς κοινοῖς σκῦλα ἀπὸ ἡμῶν τῶν εὐεργετῶν 2 τῆς Ἑλλάδος ἀνατεθῆναι. δεινὸν δὲ δόξει εἶναι Πλάταιαν Λακεδαιμονίους πορθῆσαι, καὶ τοὺς μὲν πατέρας ἀναγράψαι ἐς τὸν τρίποδα τὸν ἐν Δελφοῖς δι' ἀρετὴν τὴν πόλιν, ὑμᾶς δὲ καὶ ἐκ παντὸς τοῦ Ἑλληνικοῦ πανοικησίᾳ διὰ Θηβαίους ἐξαλεῖψαι. 3 ἐς τοῦτο γὰρ δὴ ξυμφορᾶς προκεχωρήκαμεν, οἵτινες Μήδων τε κρατησάντων ἀπωλλύμεθα καὶ νῦν ἐν ὑμῖν τοῖς πρὶν φιλτάτοις Θηβαίων ἡσσώμεθα καὶ δύο ἀγῶνας τοὺς μεγίστους ὑπέστημεν, τότε μέν, τὴν πόλιν εἰ μὴ παρέδομεν, λιμῷ δια- 4 φθαρῆναι, νῦν δὲ θανάτου δίκῃ κρίνεσθαι. καὶ περιεώσμεθα ἐκ πάντων Πλαταιῆς, οἱ παρὰ δύναμιν πρόθυμοι ἐς τοὺς Ἕλληνας, ἔρημοι καὶ ἀτιμώρητοι· καὶ οὔτε τῶν τότε ξυμμάχων ὠφελεῖ οὐδείς, ἡμεῖς τε, ὦ Λακεδαιμόνιοι, ἡ μόνη ἐλπίς, δέδιμεν μὴ οὐ βέβαιοι ἦτε.

---

[1] Heilmann's correction for ἔχωσι of the MSS.

[2] Jowett prefers ἡμῖν, with M, in which case the sense would be general : "while (as a matter of course) our own immediate interests are sufficiently secured." With ὑμῖν there is a return to the particular, *i.e.* the case of the Lacedaemonians.

[3] προσσκέψασθε, Meineke's conjecture for προσκέψασθε of the MSS.

toward the best of your allies for their valour, while also securing what may be to your advantage at the present moment.

LVII. "Consider, too, that you are now regarded by most of the Hellenes as an example of uprightness; but if the verdict you give concerning us shall be inequitable, beware (since the case you are deciding here is not obscure, but you the judges are the object of men's praise and we the defendants are of no mean repute), beware, I say, lest men repudiate an unseemly sentence passed upon good men by men still better and resent the dedication in the common temples of spoils taken from us, the benefactors of Hellas. Monstrous will it seem that the Lacedaemonians should sack Plataea, and that you, whose fathers inscribed the name of our city on the tripod at Delphi in commemoration of her valour, should blot her out, house and home, from the map of Hellas—to please the Thebans! For to this depth of misfortune have we come, we who, when the Persians prevailed, were on the verge of ruin,[1] and now when we plead before you, formerly our closest friends, we are beaten by Thebans; and we have had to face two supreme dangers, at that time of perishing by starvation if we had not surrendered our city, and now of standing trial for our lives. And we have been thrust aside by all, we men of Plataea, who were zealous toward the Hellenes beyond our strength, and are now desolate and undefended. No one of our former allies now aids us, and as for you, Lacedaemonians, our only hope, we fear that you are not steadfast.

[1] The reference is to the burning of their city by Xerxes; see Hdt. VIII. l.

THUCYDIDES

LVIII. "Καίτοι ἀξιοῦμέν γε καὶ θεῶν ἕνεκα τῶν ξυμμαχικῶν ποτε γενομένων καὶ τῆς ἀρετῆς τῆς ἐς τοὺς Ἕλληνας καμφθῆναι ὑμᾶς καὶ μεταγνῶναι εἴ τι ὑπὸ Θηβαίων ἐπείσθητε, τήν τε δωρεὰν ἀνταπαιτῆσαι αὐτοὺς μὴ κτείνειν οὓς μὴ ὑμῖν πρέπει, σώφρονά τε ἀντὶ αἰσχρᾶς κομίσασθαι χάριν, καὶ μὴ ἡδονὴν δόντας ἄλλοις κακίαν αὐ-
2 τοὺς ἀντιλαβεῖν. βραχὺ γὰρ τὸ τὰ ἡμέτερα σώματα διαφθεῖραι, ἐπίπονον δὲ τὴν δύσκλειαν αὐτοῦ ἀφανίσαι· οὐκ ἐχθροὺς γὰρ ἡμᾶς[1] εἰκότως τιμωρήσεσθε, ἀλλ᾽ εὔνους, κατ᾽ ἀνάγκην πολεμή-
3 σαντας. ὥστε καὶ τῶν σωμάτων ἄδειαν ποιοῦντες ὅσια ἂν δικάζοιτε καὶ προνοοῦντες ὅτι ἑκόντας τε ἐλάβετε καὶ χεῖρας προϊσχομένους (ὁ δὲ νόμος τοῖς Ἕλλησι μὴ κτείνειν τούτους), ἔτι δὲ καὶ
4 εὐεργέτας γεγενημένους διὰ παντός. ἀποβλέψατε γὰρ ἐς πατέρων τῶν ὑμετέρων θήκας, οὓς ἀποθανόντας ὑπὸ Μήδων καὶ ταφέντας ἐν τῇ ἡμετέρᾳ ἐτιμῶμεν κατὰ ἔτος ἕκαστον δημοσίᾳ ἐσθήμασί τε καὶ τοῖς ἄλλοις νομίμοις, ὅσα τε ἡ γῆ ἡμῶν ἀνεδίδου ὡραῖα, πάντων ἀπαρχὰς ἐπιφέροντες, εὖνοι μὲν ἐκ φιλίας χώρας, ξύμμαχοι δὲ ὁμαίχμοις ποτὲ γενομένοις. ὧν ὑμεῖς τοὐναντίον ἂν
5 δράσαιτε μὴ ὀρθῶς γνόντες. σκέψασθε δέ·[2] Παυ-

[1] ἡμᾶς, bracketed by Hude, because omitted in M.
[2] δέ, Hude reads τε, with C.

---

[1] The Thebans had demanded that the Plataeans be put to death.

LVIII. "And yet we adjure you, for the sake of the gods who of old sanctioned our alliance and for our good service in the cause of the Hellenes, to relent and change your minds, if you have been in any way won over by the Thebans,[1] and in your turn to ask of them the boon not to put to death those whom it ill becomes you to slay, that you may thus receive an honest instead of a shameful gratitude, and may not in giving pleasure to others get in return ignominy for yourselves. It is a simple matter to take our lives, but a grievous task to blot out the infamy of it; for we are not enemies whom you would have a right to punish, but good friends who were forced into war with you. You would, therefore, render a righteous judgment if you guaranteed us security of life and if you bore in mind, before it is too late, that it was in voluntary surrender and with outstretched hands that you received us (and the usage of the Hellenes forbids the slaying of suppliants); and, moreover, that we have always been your benefactors. Turn your eyes upon the sepulchres of your fathers, slain by the Persians and buried in our land, whom we have honoured year by year with a public offering of raiment[2] and other customary gifts; the first fruits, too, of all that the earth each year has produced have been brought them, the tribute of kindly hands from a friendly land and of allies to those who were once their companions in arms. All this you would reverse by an unjust verdict. Reflect: when Pausanias buried

---

[2] For garments as offerings to the dead, cf. Soph. El. 452; Eur. Or. 123, 1436; Tac. A. iii. 2. But some understand ἐσθήμασι to refer to mourning garments. See also Plut. Aristides, xxi.

σανίας μὲν γὰρ ἔθαπτεν αὐτοὺς νομίζων ἐν γῇ τε
φιλίᾳ τιθέναι καὶ παρ' ἀνδράσι τοιούτοις· ὑμεῖς
δὲ εἰ κτενεῖτε ἡμᾶς καὶ χώραν τὴν Πλαταιίδα
Θηβαΐδα ποιήσετε, τί ἄλλο ἢ ἐν πολεμίᾳ τε καὶ
παρὰ τοῖς αὐθένταις πατέρας τοὺς ὑμετέρους καὶ
ξυγγενεῖς ἀτίμους γερῶν ὧν νῦν ἴσχουσι κατα-
λείψετε; πρὸς δὲ καὶ γῆν ἐν ᾗ ἠλευθερώθησαν
οἱ Ἕλληνες δουλώσετε, ἱερά τε θεῶν οἷς εὐξά-
μενοι Μήδων ἐκράτησαν ἐρημοῦτε[1] καὶ θυσίας
τὰς πατρίους τῶν ἐσσαμένων καὶ κτισάντων
ἀφαιρήσεσθε.

LIX. "Οὐ πρὸς τῆς ὑμετέρας δόξης, ὦ Λακεδαιμόνιοι, τάδε, οὔτε ἐς τὰ κοινὰ τῶν Ἑλλήνων
νόμιμα καὶ ἐς τοὺς προγόνους ἁμαρτάνειν οὔτε
ἡμᾶς τοὺς εὐεργέτας ἀλλοτρίας ἕνεκα ἔχθρας μὴ
αὐτοὺς ἀδικηθέντας διαφθεῖραι, φείσασθαι δὲ καὶ
ἐπικλασθῆναι τῇ γνώμῃ οἴκτῳ σώφρονι λαβόντας
μὴ ὧν πεισόμεθα μόνον δεινότητα κατανοοῦντας,
ἀλλ' οἷοί τε ἂν ὄντες πάθοιμεν καὶ ὡς ἀστάθμητον τὸ τῆς ξυμφορᾶς ᾦτινί ποτ' ἂν καὶ ἀναξίῳ
2 ξυμπέσοι. ἡμεῖς τε, ὡς πρέπον ἡμῖν καὶ ὡς ἡ
χρεία προάγει, αἰτούμεθα ὑμᾶς, θεοὺς τοὺς
ὁμοβωμίους καὶ κοινοὺς τῶν Ἑλλήνων ἐπιβοώμενοι, πεῖσαι τάδε, προφερόμενοι[2] θ' ὅρκους οὓς
οἱ πατέρες ὑμῶν ὤμοσαν μὴ ἀμνημονεῖν ἱκέται

---

[1] ἐρημοῦτε, Hude adopts Stahl's conjecture ἐρημοῦντες,
because of the striking present between two futures.
[2] θ' after προφερόμενοι is Stahl's conjecture, adopted by
Hude.

them he thought he was laying them in a friendly land and among friends; but you, if you put us to death and make the territory of Plataea a Theban province, will you not be leaving them in a hostile land and among their murderers [1]—these your fathers and kinsmen—and dispossessed of the honours they now enjoy? Nay more, you will be enslaving the very land in which the Hellenes gained their liberty; you will be bringing desolation upon the temples of the gods to whom they prayed when they conquered the Persians; and you will be robbing of their hereditary sacrifices the people who founded and established them.

LIX. "These things are not consistent with your honour, Lacedaemonians, nor can it be so to offend against the common usage of the Hellenes and against your ancestors, or to put us, your benefactors, to death because of the enmity of others, when you have not been wronged yourselves. Nay, your good name demands that you should spare us and be softened in heart, regarding us with a dispassionate pity and bearing in mind, not only how terrible will be our fate, but who we are that must suffer, and how uncertain is fortune, whose strokes sometimes fall even upon the innocent. And we, as befits our condition and as our sore need demands, entreat you in the name of the common gods of the Hellenic race whom we invoke, gods worshipped by us all at the same altars, to listen to our prayers; and at the same time, appealing to the oaths wherein your fathers swore that they would never forget us, we become suppliants

---

[1] The Thebans are called their murderers because they had sided with the Persians against the Hellenic allies.

THUCYDIDES

γιγνόμεθα ὑμῶν τῶν πατρῴων τάφων καὶ ἐπι-
καλούμεθα τοὺς κεκμηκότας μὴ γενέσθαι ὑπὸ
Θηβαίοις μηδὲ τοῖς ἐχθίστοις φίλτατοι ὄντες
παραδοθῆναι, ἡμέρας τε ἀναμιμνήσκομεν ἐκείνης
ᾗ τὰ λαμπρότατα μετ' αὐτῶν πράξαντες νῦν ἐν
3 τῇδε τὰ δεινότατα κινδυνεύομεν παθεῖν. ὅπερ
δὲ ἀναγκαῖόν τε καὶ χαλεπώτατον τοῖς ὧδε
ἔχουσι, λόγου τελευτᾶν, διότι καὶ τοῦ βίου ὁ
κίνδυνος ἐγγὺς μετ' αὐτοῦ, παυόμενοι λέγομεν ἤδη
ὅτι οὐ Θηβαίοις παρέδομεν τὴν πόλιν (εἱλόμεθα
γὰρ ἂν πρό γε τούτου τῷ αἰσχίστῳ ὀλέθρῳ λιμῷ
τελευτῆσαι), ὑμῖν δὲ πιστεύσαντες προσήλθομεν
(καὶ δίκαιον, εἰ μὴ πείθομεν, ἐς τὰ αὐτὰ καταστή-
σαντας τὸν ξυντυχόντα κίνδυνον ἐᾶσαι ἡμᾶς
4 αὐτοὺς ἑλέσθαι), ἐπισκήπτομέν τε ἅμα μὴ Πλαταιῆς ὄντες, οἱ προθυμότατοι περὶ τοὺς Ἕλληνας
γενόμενοι, Θηβαίοις τοῖς ἡμῖν ἐχθίστοις ἐκ τῶν
ὑμετέρων χειρῶν καὶ τῆς ὑμετέρας πίστεως ἱκέται
ὄντες, ὦ Λακεδαιμόνιοι, παραδοθῆναι, γενέσθαι
δὲ σωτῆρας ἡμῶν καὶ μὴ τοὺς ἄλλους Ἕλληνας
ἐλευθεροῦντας ἡμᾶς διολέσαι."

LX. Τοιαῦτα μὲν οἱ Πλαταιῆς εἶπον. οἱ δὲ
Θηβαῖοι δείσαντες πρὸς τὸν λόγον αὐτῶν μὴ οἱ
Λακεδαιμόνιοί τι ἐνδῶσι, παρελθόντες[1] ἔφασαν
καὶ αὐτοὶ βούλεσθαι εἰπεῖν, ἐπειδὴ καὶ ἐκείνοις
παρὰ γνώμην τὴν αὐτῶν μακρότερος λόγος ἐδόθη
τῆς πρὸς τὸ ἐρώτημα ἀποκρίσεως. ὡς δ' ἐκέ-
λευσαν, ἔλεγον τοιάδε.

LXI. "Τοὺς μὲν λόγους οὐκ ἂν ᾐτησάμεθα

[1] παρελθόντες, Hude adopts Ullrich's conjecture προσελ-
θόντες.

before your ancestral tombs and call upon the departed not to suffer us to come into the power of Thebans or permit us, who were their dearest friends, to be delivered into the hands of their bitterest foes. We also remind you of that day on which we shared with them in the most brilliant deeds, we who now on this day are on the brink of the most awful fate. And now, bringing our plea to an end—and this must be, howbeit for men in our condition it is the hardest thing of all, seeing that with its ending our mortal peril also draws near—we say that we did not surrender our city to the Thebans—in preference to that our choice would have been to die of starvation, the most horrible of deaths—but capitulated to you because we trusted you. And it is but right, if we fail in our plea, that you should restore us to our former position and let us choose for ourselves the danger that shall confront us. And we likewise adjure you, Plataeans that we are, people who were most zealous for the cause of Hellas, and are now your suppliants, O Lacedaemonians, not to deliver us out of your hands and your good faith to the Thebans, our bitterest foes, but to become our saviours, and not, while liberating the rest of the Hellenes, to bring utter destruction upon us."

LX. Thus the Plataeans spoke. And the Thebans, fearing lest the Lacedaemonians might be so moved by their plea as to yield somewhat, came forward and said that they, too, wished to speak, since, against their own judgment, the Plataeans had been granted leave to speak at greater length than the answer to the question required. And when the judges assented, they spoke as follows:

LXI. "We should not have asked permission to

εἰπεῖν, εἰ καὶ αὐτοὶ βραχέως τὸ ἐρωτηθὲν ἀπεκρίναντο καὶ μὴ ἐπὶ ἡμᾶς τραπόμενοι κατηγορίαν
ἐποιήσαντο καὶ περὶ αὑτῶν ἔξω τῶν προκειμένων
καὶ ἅμα οὐδὲ ᾐτιαμένων πολλὴν τὴν ἀπολογίαν
καὶ ἔπαινον ὧν οὐδεὶς ἐμέμψατο. νῦν δὲ πρὸς
μὲν τὰ ἀντειπεῖν δεῖ, τῶν δὲ ἔλεγχον ποιήσασθαι,
ἵνα μήτε ἡ ἡμετέρα αὐτοὺς κακία ὠφελῇ μήτε ἡ
τούτων δόξα, τὸ δ᾽ ἀληθὲς περὶ ἀμφοτέρων
ἀκούσαντες κρίνητε.

2 "Ἡμεῖς δὲ αὐτοῖς διάφοροι ἐγενόμεθα τὸ
πρῶτον ὅτι ἡμῶν κτισάντων Πλάταιαν ὕστερον
τῆς ἄλλης Βοιωτίας καὶ ἄλλα χωρία μετ᾽ αὐτῆς,
ἃ ξυμμείκτους ἀνθρώπους ἐξελάσαντες ἔσχομεν,
οὐκ ἠξίουν οὗτοι, ὥσπερ ἐτάχθη τὸ πρῶτον,
ἡγεμονεύεσθαι ὑφ᾽ ἡμῶν, ἔξω δὲ τῶν ἄλλων
Βοιωτῶν παραβαίνοντες τὰ πάτρια, ἐπειδὴ προσ-
ηναγκάζοντο, προσεχώρησαν πρὸς Ἀθηναίους
καὶ μετ᾽ αὐτῶν πολλὰ ἡμᾶς ἔβλαπτον, ἀνθ᾽ ὧν
καὶ ἀντέπασχον. LXII. ἐπειδὴ δὲ καὶ ὁ βάρβαρος ἦλθεν ἐπὶ τὴν Ἑλλάδα, φασὶ μόνοι
Βοιωτῶν οὐ μηδίσαι, καὶ τούτῳ μάλιστα αὐτοί
2 τε ἀγάλλονται καὶ ἡμᾶς λοιδοροῦσιν. ἡμεῖς δὲ
μηδίσαι μὲν αὐτοὺς οὔ φαμεν διότι οὐδ᾽ Ἀθηναίους, τῇ μέντοι αὐτῇ ἰδέᾳ ὕστερον ἰόντων
Ἀθηναίων ἐπὶ τοὺς Ἕλληνας μόνους αὖ Βοιωτῶν
3 ἀττικίσαι. καίτοι σκέψασθε ἐν οἵῳ εἴδει ἑκάτεροι

---

[1] Strabo mentions Pelasgians, Thracians, Hyantians.

make this speech, if the Plataeans had briefly
answered the question, and had not turned upon us
and accused us, at the same time setting up a long
defence of themselves on matters foreign to the issue
and on which no charge whatever had been made
against them, and praising themselves where nobody
had blamed them.   But as it is, we must answer
their charges and expose their self-praise, in order
that neither our baseness nor their good repute may
help them, but that you may hear the truth about us
both before you decide.

"The quarrel we had with them began in this
way: after we had settled the rest of Boeotia and
had occupied Plataea and other places of which we
got possession by driving out a mixed population,[1]
these Plataeans disdained to submit to our leadership,
as had been agreed upon at first, and separating
themselves from the rest of the Boeotians and
breaking away from the traditions of our fathers
went over to the Athenians as soon as an attempt was
made to force them into obedience, and in conjunction
with the Athenians did us much harm, for which
they also suffered in return.   LXII. Again, they say
that when the barbarians came against Hellas they
were the only Boeotians who did not medize, and for
this especially they plume themselves and abuse us.
We say, however, that the only reason they did not
medize was because the Athenians also did not, and
that, moreover, on the same principle, when the
Athenians afterwards assailed all Hellas, they were
the only Boeotians who atticized.[2]   And yet consider

---

[2] Ever since the Persian war *medize* and *medism* had been
terms of bitter reproach in Hellas; in the mouths of the
Thebans *atticize* and *atticism* have a like invidious meaning.

ἡμῶν τοῦτο ἔπραξαν. ἡμῖν μὲν γὰρ ἡ πόλις τότε
ἐτύγχανεν οὔτε κατ᾽ ὀλιγαρχίαν ἰσόνομον πολι-
τεύουσα οὔτε κατὰ δημοκρατίαν· ὅπερ δέ ἐστι
νόμοις μὲν καὶ τῷ σωφρονεστάτῳ ἐναντιώτατον,
ἐγγυτάτω δὲ τυράννου, δυναστεία ὀλίγων ἀνδρῶν
4 εἶχε τὰ πράγματα. καὶ οὗτοι ἰδίας δυνάμεις
ἐλπίσαντες ἔτι μᾶλλον σχήσειν, εἰ τὰ τοῦ Μήδου
κρατήσειε, κατέχοντες ἰσχύι τὸ πλῆθος ἐπηγά-
γοντο αὐτόν· καὶ ἡ ξύμπασα πόλις οὐκ αὐτοκράτωρ οὖσα ἑαυτῆς τοῦτ᾽ ἔπραξεν, οὐδ᾽ ἄξιον
αὐτῇ ὀνειδίσαι ὧν μὴ μετὰ νόμων ἥμαρτεν.
5 ἐπειδὴ γοῦν ὅ τε Μῆδος ἀπῆλθε καὶ τοὺς νόμους
ἔλαβε, σκέψασθαι χρή, Ἀθηναίων ὕστερον ἐπιόντων τήν τε ἄλλην Ἑλλάδα καὶ τὴν ἡμετέραν
χώραν πειρωμένων ὑφ᾽ αὑτοῖς ποιεῖσθαι καὶ κατὰ
στάσιν ἤδη ἐχόντων αὐτῆς τὰ πολλά, εἰ μαχόμενοι ἐν Κορωνείᾳ καὶ νικήσαντες αὐτοὺς ἠλευ-
θερώσαμεν τὴν Βοιωτίαν καὶ τοὺς ἄλλους νῦν
προθύμως ξυνελευθεροῦμεν, ἵππους τε παρέχοντες
καὶ παρασκευὴν ὅσην οὐκ ἄλλοι τῶν ξυμμάχων.
6 καὶ τὰ μὲν ἐς τὸν μηδισμὸν τοσαῦτα ἀπολο-
γούμεθα.

LXIII. "Ὡς δὲ ὑμεῖς μᾶλλόν τε ἠδικήκατε
τοὺς Ἕλληνας καὶ ἀξιώτεροί ἐστε πάσης ζημίας,
2 πειρασόμεθα ἀποφαίνειν. ἐγένεσθε ἐπὶ τῇ ἡμε-

---

[1] *i.e.* where, as at Sparta, the ὀλίγοι, or ruling class,
possessed equal rights.

the circumstances under which we each acted as we did. For the constitution of our city at that time was, as it happened, neither an oligarchy under equal laws[1] nor yet a democracy; but its affairs were in the hands of a small group of powerful men—the form which is most opposed to law and the best regulated polity, and most allied to a tyranny. These men, hoping to win still greater power for themselves if the fortunes of the Persian should prevail, forcibly kept the people down and brought him in. The city as a whole was not in control of its own actions when Thebes took the course it did, nor is it fair to reproach it for the mistakes it made when not under the rule of law. At any rate, after the Persian departed and Thebes obtained its lawful government, and when subsequently the Athenians became aggressive and were trying to bring not only the rest of Hellas but also our country under their own sway and, owing to factions amongst us, were already in possession of most of it,[2] pray observe whether we fought and defeated them at Coronea[3] and thus liberated Boeotia, and whether we are now zealously helping[4] to liberate the other peoples, furnishing more cavalry and munitions of war than any of the other allies. Such is our defence against the charge of medism.

LXIII. "We will now try to show that you Plataeans have wronged the Hellenes more than we and are more deserving of any punishment, however severe. You became allies and citizens of Athens

---

[2] After the battle at Oenophyta, 458 B.C. *cf.* I. cviii. 2, 3.
[3] 446 B.C. *cf.* I. cxiii. 2.
[4] This is mentioned with a view to influencing Spartan judges.

τέρᾳ τιμωρίᾳ, ὡς φατέ, Ἀθηναίων ξύμμαχοι καὶ
πολῖται. οὐκοῦν χρῆν τὰ πρὸς ἡμᾶς μόνον ὑμᾶς
ἐπάγεσθαι αὐτοὺς καὶ μὴ ξυνεπιέναι μετ' αὐτῶν
ἄλλοις, ὑπάρχον γε ὑμῖν, εἴ τι καὶ ἄκοντες προσ-
ήγεσθε ὑπ' Ἀθηναίων, τῆς τῶν Λακεδαιμονίων
τῶνδε ἤδη ἐπὶ τῷ Μήδῳ ξυμμαχίας γεγενημένης,
ἣν αὐτοὶ μάλιστα προβάλλεσθε· ἱκανή γε [1]
ἦν ἡμᾶς τε ὑμῶν ἀποτρέπειν καί, τὸ μέγιστον,
ἀδεῶς παρέχειν βουλεύεσθαι. ἀλλ' ἑκόντες καὶ
οὐ βιαζόμενοι ἔτι εἴλεσθε μᾶλλον τὰ Ἀθηναίων.
3 καὶ λέγετε ὡς αἰσχρὸν ἦν προδοῦναι τοὺς εὐερ-
γέτας· πολὺ δέ γε αἴσχιον καὶ ἀδικώτερον τοὺς
πάντας Ἕλληνας καταπροδοῦναι, οἷς ξυνωμόσατε,
ἢ Ἀθηναίους μόνους, τοὺς μὲν καταδουλουμένους
4 τὴν Ἑλλάδα, τοὺς δὲ ἐλευθεροῦντας. καὶ οὐκ
ἴσην αὐτοῖς τὴν χάριν ἀνταπέδοτε οὐδὲ αἰσχύνης
ἀπηλλαγμένην· ὑμεῖς μὲν γὰρ ἀδικούμενοι αὐτούς,
ὡς φατέ, ἐπηγάγεσθε, τοῖς δὲ ἀδικοῦσιν ἄλλους
ξυνεργοὶ κατέστητε. καίτοι τὰς ὁμοίας χάριτας
μὴ ἀντιδιδόναι αἰσχρὸν μᾶλλον ἢ τὰς μετὰ
δικαιοσύνης μὲν ὀφειληθείσας, ἐς ἀδικίαν δὲ
ἀποδιδομένας.

---

[1] ἱκανή γε, Hude reads ἱκανὴ γάρ, with Cod. Graev.

---

[1] cf. ch. lv. 1.

[2] The alliance of the Lacedaemonians that is in mind here
would seem to be the general league of the Hellenes in the
Persian War, in which the Lacedaemonians were leaders;
but in ch. lviii. 1 the Plataeans use the words θεῶν τῶν
ξυμμαχικῶν ποτε γενομένων especially with reference to the
compact mentioned in II. lxxi , where it is said that the
allies, at the instance of Pausanias, after the battle of

that you might, as you claim,[1] obtain protection against us. In that case you ought only to have invoked their aid against us, instead of assisting them in their aggressions against others; such a course was certainly open to you, in case you were ever being led on by the Athenians against your will, since the alliance of the Lacedaemonians here had already been organized against the Persians—the alliance of which you are always reminding us.[2] That would have been enough to keep us from interfering with you, and, what is more important, to enable you to take your own counsel without fear. Nay, it was willingly and not now under compulsion that you embraced the Athenian cause. You say, however, that it would have been dishonourable to betray your benefactors; but it was far more dishonourable and wicked to betray to their destruction all the Hellenes, with whom you had sworn alliance, than merely the Athenians, when they were endeavouring to enslave Hellas, the others to liberate her. And the recompense you made them is not equal, nor indeed free from dishonour. For you were being wronged, as you claim, when you invoked their aid, but they were wronging others when you became their helpers. And yet, surely, not to repay favours with like favours is dishonourable; but it is not so when, though the debt was incurred in a just matter, it can only be repaid by wrong-doing.[3]

Plataea, mutually guaranteed the independence of all the Hellenic states, and of the Plataeans in particular.

[3] *cf.* Cicero, *de Off.* 1. 15. 48, *non reddere viro bono non licet, modo id facere possit sine injuria.* The whole sentence serves to substantiate the words οὐδὲ αἰσχύνης ἀπηλλαγμένην, the charge τὰς ὁμοίας χάριτας μὴ ἀντιδιδόναι being, according to the Theban speakers, applicable to the Plataeans.

THUCYDIDES

LXIV. " Δῆλόν τε ἐποιήσατε οὐδὲ τότε τῶν
Ἑλλήνων ἕνεκα μόνοι οὐ μηδίσαντες, ἀλλ' ὅτι
οὐδ' Ἀθηναῖοι ἡμεῖς¹ δέ, τοῖς μὲν ταὐτὰ βουλό-
2 μενοι ποιεῖν, τοῖς δὲ τἀναντία. καὶ νῦν ἀξιοῦτε,
ἀφ' ὧν δι' ἑτέρους ἐγένεσθε ἀγαθοί, ἀπὸ τούτων
ὠφελεῖσθαι. ἀλλ' οὐκ εἰκός· ὥσπερ δὲ Ἀθηναίους εἵλεσθε, τούτοις ξυναγωνίζεσθε, καὶ μὴ προ-
φέρετε τὴν τότε γενομένην ξυνωμοσίαν ὡς χρὴ
3 ἀπ' αὐτῆς νῦν σῴζεσθαι. ἀπελίπετε γὰρ αὐτὴν
καὶ παραβάντες ξυγκατεδουλοῦσθε μᾶλλον Αἰγινήτας καὶ ἄλλους τινὰς τῶν ξυνομοσάντων ἢ
διεκωλύετε, καὶ ταῦτα οὔτε ἄκοντες ἔχοντές τε
τοὺς νόμους οὕσπερ μέχρι τοῦ δεῦρο καὶ οὐδενὸς
ὑμᾶς βιασαμένου, ὥσπερ ἡμᾶς. τὴν τελευταίαν
τε πρὶν περιτειχίζεσθαι πρόκλησιν ἐς ἡσυχίαν
ἡμῶν, ὥστε μηδετέροις ἀμύνειν, οὐκ ἐδέχεσθε.
4 τίνες ἂν οὖν ὑμῶν δικαιότερον πᾶσι τοῖς Ἕλλησι
μισοῖντο, οἵτινες ἐπὶ τῷ ἐκείνων κακῷ ἀνδραγα-
θίαν προύθεσθε; καὶ ἃ μέν ποτε χρηστοὶ ἐγένεσθε, ὡς φατέ, οὐ προσήκοντα νῦν ἐπεδείξατε, ἃ
δὲ ἡ φύσις αἰεὶ ἐβούλετο, ἐξηλέγχθη ἐς τὸ ἀλη-
θές· μετὰ γὰρ Ἀθηναίων ἄδικον ὁδὸν ἰόντων
5 ἐχωρήσατε. τὰ μὲν οὖν ἐς τὸν ἡμέτερόν τε ἀκούσιον μηδισμὸν καὶ τὸν ὑμέτερον ἑκούσιον ἀττικι-
σμὸν τοιαῦτα ἀποφαίνομεν.

LXV. " Ἃ δὲ τελευταῖά φατε ἀδικηθῆναι
(παρανόμως γὰρ ἐλθεῖν ἡμᾶς ἐν σπονδαῖς καὶ

¹ ἡμεῖς, with the majority of the best MSS.; Hude reads
ὑμεῖς with CG.

LXIV. "You have, therefore, made it clear that even then it was not for the sake of the Hellenes that you alone of the Boeotians refused to medize, but merely because the Athenians also refused while we did not, and you preferred to act with the one party and against the other. And now you expect to be rewarded for the virtuous conduct that was due to the inspiration of others! But that is unreasonable; as you chose the Athenians, continue to fight on their side. And do not keep reminding us of the alliance you made then, and claim that it ought to save you now. For you have abandoned it and in violation of its principles have constantly aided, instead of trying to prevent, the enslavement of the Aeginetans[1] and other members of the alliance; and that, too, not against your will, since you then enjoyed the laws under which you have lived till now and were not, like us, under compulsion by another. Moreover, you refused to accept the last proposal we made you before Plataea was invested [2]—to leave you unmolested if you would aid neither side. Who, then, would more justly be hated by all the Hellenes than you, who displayed your virtue in order to compass their injury? Furthermore, those noble qualities which, as you claim, you once displayed you have now made plain were not properly yours, but your natural longings have been put to the proof and shown in their reality; for you have followed the Athenians when they walked in the way of iniquity. Such, then, is our affirmation regarding our unwilling medism and your willing atticism.

LXV. "As to your last charge of wrong-doing on our part—that we unlawfully attacked your city in

[1] cf. I. cv., cviii.; II. xxvii.   [2] cf. II. lxxii. 1.

ἱερομηνίᾳ ἐπὶ τὴν ὑμετέραν πόλιν), οὐ νομίζομεν
2 οὐδ ἐν τούτοις ὑμῶν μᾶλλον ἁμαρτεῖν. εἰ μὲν
γὰρ ἡμεῖς αὐτοὶ πρός τε τὴν πόλιν ἐλθόντες ἐμαχόμεθα καὶ τὴν γῆν ἐδῃοῦμεν ὡς πολέμιοι, ἀδι-
κοῦμεν· εἰ δὲ ἄνδρες ὑμῶν οἱ πρῶτοι καὶ χρήμασι
καὶ γένει, βουλόμενοι τῆς μὲν ἔξω ξυμμαχίας
ὑμᾶς παῦσαι, ἐς δὲ τὰ κοινὰ τῶν πάντων Βοιωτῶν
πάτρια καταστῆσαι, ἐπεκαλέσαντο ἑκόντες, τί
ἀδικοῦμεν; οἱ γὰρ ἄγοντες παρανομοῦσι μᾶλλον
3 τῶν ἑπομένων. ἀλλ' οὔτ' ἐκεῖνοι, ὡς ἡμεῖς κρί-
νομεν, οὔτε ἡμεῖς· πολῖται δὲ ὄντες ὥσπερ ὑμεῖς
καὶ πλείω παραβαλλόμενοι, τὸ ἑαυτῶν τεῖχος
ἀνοίξαντες καὶ ἐς τὴν αὑτῶν πόλιν φιλίους, οὐ
πολεμίους [1] κομίσαντες ἐβούλοντο τούς τε ὑμῶν
χείρους μηκέτι μᾶλλον γενέσθαι, τούς τε ἀμείνους
τὰ ἄξια ἔχειν, σωφρονισταὶ ὄντες τῆς γνώμης καὶ
τῶν σωμάτων τὴν πόλιν οὐκ ἀλλοτριοῦντες, ἀλλ'
ἐς τὴν ξυγγένειαν οἰκειοῦντες, ἐχθροὺς οὐδενὶ
καθιστάντες, ἅπασι δ' ὁμοίως ἐνσπόνδους.

LXVI. "Τεκμήριον δὲ ὡς οὐ πολεμίως ἐπράσ-
σομεν· οὔτε γὰρ ἠδικήσαμεν οὐδένα, προείπομέν
τε τὸν βουλόμενον κατὰ τὰ τῶν πάντων Βοιωτῶν
2 πάτρια πολιτεύειν ἰέναι πρὸς ἡμᾶς. καὶ ὑμεῖς
ἄσμενοι χωρήσαντες καὶ ξύμβασιν ποιησάμενοι
τὸ μὲν πρῶτον ἡσυχάζετε, ὕστερον δὲ κατανοή-

---

[1] φιλίους οὐ πολεμίους, Steup's correction for φιλίως οὐ
πολεμίως of the MSS.

[1] cf. II. ii. 2.   [2] Parody on ch. lv. 4.

time of peace and on a day of festival—we do not think that in this matter, either, we are more at fault than you. If it was of our own motion that we went to your city, fought you, and ravaged your land as enemies, we are in the wrong; but if some of your countrymen, the leading men in both wealth and family,[1] wishing to put an end to your alliance with an outsider and to restore you to the traditions of our fathers which are common to all the Boeotians, of their own free will invoked our aid, of what wrong are we guilty? For it is those who lead that break the laws rather than those who follow.[2] But in my judgment neither they nor we did wrong. They, who are just as much citizens as you and had more at stake, opened their gates and conducted into their own city friends, not enemies, because they wished that the baser sort among you should not become still worse, and that the better sort should have their deserts, being the censors of your political principles[3] and not seeking to deprive the state of your persons, but rather bringing you back into a natural union with your kindred, and that without making you an enemy of anyone but restoring you to peace with all alike.

LXVI. "The proof that we acted in no hostile spirit is that we wronged nobody, and made a proclamation that anyone who wished to be a citizen according to the hereditary ways of all the Boeotians should come over to us. And you came gladly, and entering into an agreement with us you kept quiet at first; but afterwards, when you became aware that

---

[3] σωφρονισταί, regulators or censors, those who bring others to a right mind and are a check on vice and lawlessness. It was a technical term applied to magistrates, ten in number, at Athens, who superintended the morals of the youth.

σαντες ἡμᾶς ὀλίγους ὄντας, εἰ ἄρα καὶ ἐδοκοῦμέν
τι ἀνεπιεικέστερον πρᾶξαι οὐ μετὰ τοῦ πλήθους
ὑμῶν ἐσελθόντες, τὰ μὲν ὅμοια οὐκ ἀνταπέδοτε
ἡμῖν, μήτε νεωτερίσαι ἔργῳ λόγοις τε πείθειν
ὥστε ἐξελθεῖν, ἐπιθέμενοι δὲ παρὰ τὴν ξύμβασιν, οὓς μὲν ἐν χερσὶν ἀπεκτείνατε, οὐχ
ὁμοίως ἀλγοῦμεν (κατὰ νόμον γὰρ δή τινα ἔπα-
σχον), οὓς δὲ χεῖρας προϊσχομένους καὶ ζωγρή-
σαντες ὑποσχόμενοί τε ἡμῖν ὕστερον[1] μὴ κτενεῖν
παρανόμως διεφθείρατε, πῶς οὐ δεινὰ εἴργασθε;
3 καὶ ταῦτα τρεῖς ἀδικίας ἐν ὀλίγῳ πράξαντες, τήν
τε λυθεῖσαν ὁμολογίαν καὶ τῶν ἀνδρῶν τὸν ὕστερον θάνατον καὶ τὴν περὶ αὐτῶν ἡμῖν μὴ κτενεῖν
ψευσθεῖσαν ὑπόσχεσιν, ἢν τὰ ἐν τοῖς ἀγροῖς
ὑμῖν μὴ ἀδικῶμεν, ὅμως φατὲ ἡμᾶς παρανομῆσαι
4 καὶ αὐτοὶ ἀξιοῦτε μὴ ἀντιδοῦναι δίκην. οὔκ, ἤν
γε οὗτοι τὰ ὀρθὰ γιγνώσκωσιν· πάντων δὲ αὐτῶν
ἕνεκα κολασθήσεσθε.

LXVII. "Καὶ ταῦτα, ὦ Λακεδαιμόνιοι, τούτοι
ἕνεκα ἐπεξήλθομεν καὶ ὑπὲρ ὑμῶν καὶ ἡμῶν, ἵνα
ὑμεῖς μὲν εἰδῆτε καὶ δικαίως αὐτῶν καταγνωσό-
2 μενοι, ἡμεῖς δὲ ἔτι ὁσιώτερον τετιμωρημένοι. καὶ
μὴ παλαιὰς ἀρετάς, εἴ τις ἄρα καὶ ἐγένετο, ἀκούοντες ἐπικλασθῆτε, ἃς χρὴ τοῖς μὲν ἀδικουμένοις
ἐπικούρους εἶναι, τοῖς δὲ αἰσχρόν τι δρῶσι δι-
πλασίας ζημίας, ὅτι οὐκ ἐκ προσηκόντων ἁμαρ-
τάνουσι, μηδὲ ὀλοφυρμῷ καὶ οἴκτῳ ὠφελείσθων,

---

[1] ὕστερον μὴ κτενεῖν, Hude transposes μὴ κτενεῖν ὕστερον,
against the MSS.

we were few in number—even supposing we might seem to have acted somewhat inconsiderately in entering your town without the consent of the popular party—you did not repay us in kind, resorting to no act of violence but endeavouring by arguments to induce us to withdraw, but you assailed us in violation of your agreement. Now as to those whom you killed in hand-to-hand conflict we are not so much grieved—for they suffered, we grant you, by a kind of law—but as regards those whom you spared when they stretched out their hands to you, and then, though you afterwards promised us that you would not kill them, lawlessly butchered—was not that an abominable deed? And after committing these three wrongs within a short space of time—the violation of your agreement, the subsequent murder of our men, and the breaking of your promise to us not to kill them if we spared your property in the fields—you nevertheless assert that we were the transgressors, and claim exemption from punishment for yourselves! No, not if these judges decide aright; but for all these crimes you must be chastised.

LXVII. "We have discussed these matters at length, Lacedaemonians, both for your sakes and our own, in order that you, for your part, may know that you will justly condemn them, and we that we have still more righteously exacted vengeance. And let not your hearts be softened when you hear them speak of their ancient virtues, if indeed they ever had any; for virtues might well be a succour to the victims of wrong, but should bring a two-fold penalty upon the authors of a shameful deed, because their offence is out of keeping with their character. And let not their lamentation and pitiful wailing

πατέρων τε τάφους τῶν ὑμετέρων ἐπιβοώμενοι
3 καὶ τὴν σφετέραν ἐρημίαν. καὶ γὰρ ἡμεῖς ἀνταπο-
φαίνομεν πολλῷ δεινότερα παθοῦσαν τὴν ὑπὸ
τούτων ἡλικίαν ἡμῶν διεφθαρμένην, ὧν πατέρες
οἱ μὲν πρὸς ὑμᾶς τὴν Βοιωτίαν ἄγοντες ἀπέθανον
ἐν Κορωνείᾳ, οἱ δὲ πρεσβῦται λελειμμένοι κατ᾽ [1]
οἰκίας ἐρῆμοι πολλῷ δικαιοτέραν ὑμῶν ἱκετείαν
4 ποιοῦνται τούσδε τιμωρήσασθαι. οἴκτου τε
ἀξιώτεροι τυγχάνειν οἱ ἀπρεπές τι πάσχοντες
τῶν ἀνθρώπων, οἱ δὲ δικαίως, ὥσπερ οἵδε, τὰ
5 ἐναντία ἐπίχαρτοι εἶναι. καὶ τὴν νῦν ἐρημίαν
δι᾽ ἑαυτοὺς ἔχουσιν· τοὺς γὰρ ἀμείνους ξυμμάχους ἑκόντες ἀπεώσαντο. παρενόμησάν τε οὐ
προπαθόντες ὑφ᾽ ἡμῶν, μίσει δὲ πλέον ἢ δίκῃ
κρίναντες, καὶ οὐκ [2] ἂν ἀνταποδόντες νῦν τὴν
ἴσην τιμωρίαν· ἔννομα γὰρ πείσονται καὶ οὐχὶ ἐκ
μάχης χεῖρας προϊσχόμενοι, ὥσπερ φασίν, ἀλλ᾽
ἀπὸ ξυμβάσεως ἐς δίκην σφᾶς αὐτοὺς παραδόντες.
6 ἀμύνατε οὖν, ὦ Λακεδαιμόνιοι, καὶ τῷ τῶν Ἑλλήνων νόμῳ ὑπὸ τῶνδε παραβαθέντι καὶ ἡμῖν ἄνομα
παθοῦσιν ἀνταπόδοτε [3] χάριν δικαίαν ὧν πρόθυμοι γεγενήμεθα· καὶ μὴ τοῖς τῶνδε λόγοις
περιωσθῶμεν ἐν ὑμῖν, ποιήσατε δὲ τοῖς Ἕλλησι
παράδειγμα οὐ λόγων τοὺς ἀγῶνας προθήσοντες,
ἀλλ᾽ ἔργων, ὧν ἀγαθῶν μὲν ὄντων βραχεῖα ἡ

---

[1] κατ᾽ οἰκίας, Stahl's emendation for καὶ οἰκίαι of the MSS.
[2] ἂν ἀνταποδόντες, Dobree added ἄν.
[3] ἀνταπόδοτε, Hude ἀνταπόδοτέ τε, after Gertz.

avail them, nor their appeals to the sepulchres of
your fathers and their own desolate state. For
in answer we too would point out that a far more
dreadful fate befell our young men who were
butchered by them, of whose fathers some died at
Coronea[1] trying to win Boeotia to your cause, while
others, left desolate at home in their old age, with
far greater justice make supplication to you to take
vengeance upon these men. Pity is more worthily
bestowed upon those who suffer an unseemly fate,
but those who, like these Plataeans, deserve their
fate afford on the contrary a subject for rejoicing.
As for their present desolation, that also is their
own fault; for of their own free will they rejected
the better alliance. They acted unlawfully without
having received provocation at our hands, but
through hatred rather than according to a just
judgment, and they could not possibly pay now a
penalty equal to their guilt, for they will suffer a
lawful sentence; and they are not, as they claim,[2]
stretching out suppliant hands on the field of battle,
but have delivered themselves up to justice under
formal agreement. Vindicate, therefore, Lacedaemonians, the law of the Hellenes which has been
transgressed by these men, and render to us who
have suffered by their lawlessness a just recompense
for the services we have zealously given, and let us
not because of their words be thrust aside when we
plead before you,[3] but make it plain to the Hellenes
by an example that the trials you institute will be of
deeds, not words, and that, if the deeds are good, a

---

[1] As at ch. lxii. 5, a reminder flattering to the Lacedaemonians.　　[2] *cf.* ch. lviii. 3.

[3] Note the mocking quotation of phrases in the speech of
the Plataeans, ch. lvii. 3, 4.

ἀπαγγελία ἀρκεῖ, ἁμαρτανομένων δὲ λόγοι ἔπεσι
7 κοσμηθέντες προκαλύμματα γίγνονται. ἀλλ' ἢν
οἱ ἡγεμόνες, ὥσπερ νῦν ὑμεῖς, κεφαλαιώσαντες
πρὸς τοὺς ξύμπαντας διαγνώμας ποιήσησθε,
ἧσσόν τις ἐπ' ἀδίκοις ἔργοις λόγους καλοὺς
ζητήσει."

LXVIII. Τοιαῦτα δὲ οἱ Θηβαῖοι εἶπον. οἱ δὲ
Λακεδαιμόνιοι δικασταὶ νομίζοντες τὸ ἐπερώτημα
σφίσιν ὀρθῶς ἕξειν, εἴ τι ἐν τῷ πολέμῳ ὑπ' αὐτῶν
ἀγαθὸν πεπόνθασι, διότι τόν τε ἄλλον χρόνον
ἠξίουν δῆθεν αὐτοὺς κατὰ τὰς παλαιὰς Παυσανίου μετὰ τὸν Μῆδον σπονδὰς ἡσυχάζειν καὶ
ὅτε ὕστερον ἃ πρὸ τοῦ περιτειχίζεσθαι προεί-
χοντο αὐτοῖς, κοινοὺς εἶναι κατ' ἐκείνας,[1] οὐκ ἐδέξαντο, ἡγούμενοι τῇ ἑαυτῶν δικαίᾳ βουλήσει
2 ἔκσπονδοι ἤδη ὑπ' αὐτῶν κακῶς πεπονθέναι,
αὖθις τὸ αὐτὸ ἕνα ἕκαστον παραγαγόντες καὶ
ἐρωτῶντες, εἴ τι Λακεδαιμονίους καὶ τοὺς ξυμμάχους ἀγαθὸν ἐν τῷ πολέμῳ δεδρακότες εἰσίν,
ὁπότε μὴ φαῖεν, ἀπάγοντες ἀπέκτεινον καὶ ἐξαί-
3 ρετον ἐποιήσαντο οὐδένα. διέφθειραν δὲ Πλαταιῶν μὲν αὐτῶν οὐκ ἐλάσσους διακοσίων, Ἀθηναίων δὲ πέντε καὶ εἴκοσι, οἳ ξυνεπολιορκοῦντο·
γυναῖκας δὲ ἠνδραπόδισαν. τὴν δὲ πόλιν ἐνιαυ-

---

[1] κατ' ἐκείνας, Badham's conjecture for κατ' ἐκεῖνα ὡς of
the MSS.

---

[1] Referring to the ἐπερώτημα βραχύ of ch. lii. 4; liii. 2.
Possibly πρὸς τοὺς ξύμπαντας goes with διαγνώμας ποιήσησθε,
"and then as a warning to all pass sentence."

brief recital of them suffices, but if they are wrong, speeches decked out with phrases are but veils to hide the truth. Nay, if all leaders, like you in the present instance, should first state the facts briefly for all concerned,[1] and then pass sentence, there will be less seeking of fair words after foul deeds."

LXVIII. Such was the speech of the Thebans. And the Lacedaemonian judges decided that their question, whether they had received any benefit from the Plataeans in the war, would be a fair one for them to put; for they had at all other times urged them, they claimed, to maintain neutrality in accordance with the old covenant which they had made with Pausanias after the Persian defeat; and when afterwards, before the investment of Plataea was undertaken, their proposal to the Plataeans that they remain neutral in accordance with the earlier agreement had not been accepted,[2] they thought themselves thenceforth released from all obligations of the treaty because their own intentions had been honourable, and considered that they had been wronged by the Plataeans. So they caused them to come forward again, one at a time, and asked them the same question, whether they had rendered any good service to the Lacedaemonians and their allies in the war, and when they said " no " they led them off and slew them, exempting no one. The number of the Plataeans that perished was not less than two hundred, and of the Athenians who had taken part in the siege twenty-five; and the women were sold as slaves. As for the city itself, they gave occupation of

---

[2] The text is certainly corrupt. Badham's slight change, adopted by Hude, seems to be the simplest solution of the difficulty.

τὸν μέν τινα[1] Μεγαρέων ἀνδράσι κατὰ στάσιν
ἐκπεπτωκόσι καὶ ὅσοι τὰ σφέτερα φρονοῦντες
Πλαταιῶν περιῆσαν ἔδοσαν ἐνοικεῖν· ὕστερον δὲ
καθελόντες αὐτὴν ἐς ἔδαφος πᾶσαν ἐκ τῶν θεμελίων ᾠκοδόμησαν πρὸς τῷ Ἡραίῳ καταγώγιον
διακοσίων ποδῶν πανταχῇ κύκλῳ οἰκήματα ἔχον
κάτωθεν καὶ ἄνωθεν, καὶ ὀροφαῖς καὶ θυρώμασι
τοῖς τῶν Πλαταιῶν ἐχρήσαντο, καὶ τοῖς ἄλλοις ἃ
ἦν ἐν τῷ τείχει ἔπιπλα, χαλκὸς καὶ σίδηρος,
κλίνας κατασκευάσαντες ἀνέθεσαν τῇ Ἥρᾳ, καὶ
νεὼν ἑκατόμπεδον λίθινον ᾠκοδόμησαν αὐτῇ. τὴν
δὲ γῆν δημοσιώσαντες ἀπεμίσθωσαν ἐπὶ δέκα
4 ἔτη, καὶ ἐνέμοντο Θηβαῖοι. σχεδὸν δέ τι καὶ τὸ
ξύμπαν περὶ Πλαταιῶν οἱ Λακεδαιμόνιοι οὕτως
ἀποτετραμμένοι ἐγένοντο Θηβαίων ἕνεκα, νομίζοντες ἐς τὸν πόλεμον αὐτοὺς ἄρτι τότε καθιστά-
5 μενον ὠφελίμους εἶναι. καὶ τὰ μὲν κατὰ Πλάταιαν ἔτει τρίτῳ καὶ ἐνενηκοστῷ ἐπειδὴ Ἀθηναίων ξύμμαχοι ἐγένοντο οὕτως ἐτελεύτησεν.

LXIX. Αἱ δὲ τεσσαράκοντα νῆες τῶν Πελοποννησίων αἱ Λεσβίοις βοηθοὶ ἐλθοῦσαι, ὡς τότε
φεύγουσαι διὰ τοῦ πελάγους ἔκ τε τῶν Ἀθηναίων
ἐπιδιωχθεῖσαι καὶ πρὸς τῇ Κρήτῃ χειμασθεῖσαι
καὶ[2] ἀπ' αὐτῆς σποράδες πρὸς τὴν Πελοπόννησον
κατηνέχθησαν, καταλαμβάνουσιν ἐν τῇ Κυλλήνῃ
τρεῖς καὶ δέκα τριήρεις Λευκαδίων καὶ Ἀμπρακιωτῶν καὶ Βρασίδαν τὸν Τέλλιδος ξύμβουλον
2 Ἀλκίδᾳ ἐπεληλυθότα. ἐβούλοντο γὰρ οἱ Λακεδαιμόνιοι, ὡς τῆς Λέσβου ἡμαρτήκεσαν, πλέον τὸ

---

[1] Θηβαῖοι before Μεγαρέων, deleted by Classen.
[2] καὶ, omitted by Classen, followed by Hude.

it for about a year to some men of Megara who had been driven out in consequence of a sedition, and also to such of the surviving Plataeans as favoured the Lacedaemonian cause. Afterwards, however, they razed it entirely[1] to the ground, and built, in the neighbourhood of the sanctuary of Hera, an inn two hundred feet square, with rooms all around, above and below, using for this purpose the roofs and doors of the Plataeans; and with the rest of the material inside the walls, articles of copper and iron, they fashioned couches, which they dedicated to Hera; and they also built for her a stone temple one hundred feet long. But the land they confiscated and leased for ten years, and the Thebans occupied it. Indeed it was almost wholly for the sake of the Thebans that the Lacedaemonians in all their dealings with the Plataeans showed themselves so thoroughly hostile to them, thinking that the Thebans would be serviceable in the war then just beginning. Such was the fate of Plataea, in the ninety-third year after they became allies of Athens. 519 B.C.

LXIX. Meanwhile[2] the forty Peloponnesian ships, which had gone to the relief of the Lesbians and were at that time traversing the open sea in flight, after they had first been pursued by the Athenians and had been caught in a storm off Crete, had come straggling back to the Peloponnesus, where they found, at Cyllene, thirteen Leucadian and Ambraciot triremes and Brasidas son of Tellis, who had come as adviser to Alcidas. For after they had failed to capture Lesbos the Lacedaemonians wished to strengthen

---

[1] Or, taking ἐκ τῶν θεμελίων with ᾠκοδόμησαν, as Steup and others do, "they built on the old foundations."

[2] Resuming the narrative interrupted at ch. xxxiii. 1.

ναυτικὸν ποιήσαντες ἐς τὴν Κέρκυραν πλεῦσαι
στασιάζουσαν, δώδεκα μὲν ναυσὶ μόναις παρόντων
Ἀθηναίων περὶ Ναύπακτον, πρὶν δὲ πλέον τι
ἐπιβοηθῆσαι ἐκ τῶν Ἀθηνῶν ναυτικόν, ὅπως
προφθάσωσι, καὶ παρεσκευάζοντο ὅ τε Βρασίδας
καὶ ὁ Ἀλκίδας πρὸς ταῦτα.

LXX. Οἱ γὰρ Κερκυραῖοι ἐστασίαζον, ἐπειδὴ
οἱ αἰχμάλωτοι ἦλθον αὐτοῖς οἱ ἐκ τῶν περὶ
Ἐπίδαμνον ναυμαχιῶν ὑπὸ Κορινθίων ἀφεθέντες,
τῷ μὲν λόγῳ ὀκτακοσίων ταλάντων τοῖς προξένοις
διηγγυημένοι, ἔργῳ δὲ πεπεισμένοι Κορινθίοις
Κέρκυραν προσποιῆσαι. καὶ ἔπρασσον οὗτοι
ἕκαστον τῶν πολιτῶν μετιόντες, ὅπως ἀποστή-
2 σωσιν Ἀθηναίων τὴν πόλιν. καὶ ἀφικομένης
Ἀττικῆς τε νεὼς καὶ Κορινθίας πρέσβεις ἀγου-
σῶν καὶ ἐς λόγους καταστάντων ἐψηφίσαντο
Κερκυραῖοι Ἀθηναίοις μὲν ξύμμαχοι εἶναι κατὰ
τὰ ξυγκείμενα, Πελοποννησίοις δὲ φίλοι ὥσπερ
3 καὶ πρότερον. καὶ (ἦν γὰρ Πειθίας ἐθελοπρόξενός
τε τῶν Ἀθηναίων καὶ τοῦ δήμου προειστήκει)
ὑπάγουσιν αὐτὸν οὗτοι οἱ ἄνδρες ἐς δίκην, λέγοντες
4 Ἀθηναίοις τὴν Κέρκυραν καταδουλοῦν. ὁ δὲ
ἀποφυγὼν ἀνθυπάγει αὐτῶν τοὺς πλουσιωτάτους
πέντε ἄνδρας, φάσκων τέμνειν χάρακας ἐκ τοῦ τε
Διὸς τοῦ τεμένους καὶ τοῦ Ἀλκίνου· ζημία δὲ
5 καθ' ἑκάστην χάρακα ἐπέκειτο στατήρ. ὀφλόντων

---

[1] cf. I. xlvii.–lv.   [2] £160,000, $776,000.
[3] The agreement was for a defensive alliance (ἐπιμαχία);
cf. I. xliv. 1.

their fleet and to sail to Corcyra, which was in the throes of a revolution. The Athenians had a fleet of only twelve ships at Naupactus, and the Lacedaemonians desired to reach Corcyra before a larger fleet could come from Athens to re-enforce them. It was with this end in view that Brasidas and Alcidas set about making their preparations.

LXX. The Corcyraeans had been in a state of revolution ever since the home-coming of the captives who had been taken in the two sea-fights off Epidamnus[1] and had been released by the Corinthians. They had nominally been set free on bail in the sum of eight hundred talents[2] pledged by their proxeni, but in fact they had been bribed to bring Corcyra over to the Corinthian side. And these men had been going from citizen to citizen and intriguing with them, with a view to inducing the city to revolt from Athens. And on the arrival of an Attic and Corinthian ship bringing envoys, and after the envoys had held conferences with them, the Corcyraeans voted to continue to be allies to the Athenians according to their agreement,[3] but on the other hand to renew their former friendship with the Peloponnesians. Thereupon the returned prisoners brought Peithias, a volunteer proxenus of the Athenians and leader of the popular party, to trial, charging him with trying to bring Corcyra into servitude to Athens. But he, being acquitted, brought suits in turn against the five wealthiest men of their number, alleging that they were cutting vine-poles from the sacred precincts of Zeus and Alcinous, an offence for which a fine of a stater[4] for each stake was fixed by

[4] If of gold, about 16s.; if the silver Athenian stater, about 2s. 8d.; if the silver Corinthian stater, about 1s. 4d.

δὲ αὐτῶν καὶ πρὸς τὰ ἱερὰ ἱκετῶν καθεζομένων
διὰ πλῆθος τῆς ζημίας, ὅπως ταξάμενοι ἀποδῶσιν,
ὁ Πειθίας (ἐτύγχανε γὰρ καὶ βουλῆς ὤν) πείθει
6 ὥστε τῷ νόμῳ χρήσασθαι. οἱ δ' ἐπειδὴ τῷ τε
νόμῳ ἐξείργοντο καὶ ἅμα ἐπυνθάνοντο τὸν Πειθίαν,
ἕως ἔτι βουλῆς ἐστι, μέλλειν τὸ πλῆθος ἀνα-
πείσειν τοὺς αὐτοὺς Ἀθηναίοις φίλους τε καὶ
ἐχθροὺς νομίζειν, ξυνίσταντό τε καὶ λαβόντες
ἐγχειρίδια ἐξαπιναίως ἐς τὴν βουλὴν ἐσελθόντες
τόν τε Πειθίαν κτείνουσι καὶ ἄλλους τῶν τε
βουλευτῶν καὶ ἰδιωτῶν ἐς ἑξήκοντα· οἱ δέ τινες
τῆς αὐτῆς γνώμης τῷ Πειθίᾳ ὀλίγοι ἐς τὴν Ἀττικὴν τριήρη κατέφυγον ἔτι παροῦσαν.

LXXI. Δράσαντες δὲ τοῦτο καὶ ξυγκαλέσαντες
Κερκυραίους εἶπον ὅτι ταῦτα καὶ βέλτιστα εἴη
καὶ ἥκιστ' ἂν δουλωθεῖεν ὑπ' Ἀθηναίων, τό τε
λοιπὸν μηδετέρους δέχεσθαι ἀλλ' ἢ μιᾷ νηὶ ἡσυχά-
ζοντας, τὸ δὲ πλέον πολέμιον ἡγεῖσθαι. ὡς δὲ
εἶπον, καὶ ἐπικυρῶσαι ἠνάγκασαν τὴν γνώμην.
2 πέμπουσι δὲ καὶ ἐς τὰς Ἀθήνας εὐθὺς πρέσβεις
περί τε τῶν πεπραγμένων διδάξοντας ὡς ξυνέφερε
καὶ τοὺς ἐκεῖ καταπεφευγότας πείσοντας μηδὲν
ἀνεπιτήδειον πράσσειν, ὅπως μή τις ἐπιστροφὴ
γένηται. LXXII. ἐλθόντων δὲ οἱ Ἀθηναῖοι τούς

---

[1] Or, perhaps, ἐπιστροφή = animadversio, "that no attention should be paid"—by way of punishment for the change
in Corcyraean policy.

law. When they had been convicted and because of
the excessive amount of the fine took refuge at the
temples as suppliants, that they might arrange for
the payment of the fine by instalments, Peithias persuaded the senate, of which he was also a member, to
let the law take its course. The condemned men,
seeing that they were debarred by the law from carrying out their proposal and at the same time learning
that Peithias, so long as he continued to be a member
of the senate, would persist in his attempt to persuade the populace to conclude an offensive and defensive alliance with the Athenians, banded together
and suddenly rushing into the senate with daggers
in their hands killed Peithias and others, both sena-
tors and private persons, to the number of sixty. A
few, however, who held the same political views as
Peithias, took refuge in the Attic trireme that was
still in the harbour.

LXXI. After they had taken these measures the
conspirators called the Corcyraeans together and
told them that it was all for the best, and that
now they would be least likely to be enslaved by the
Athenians; and in future they should remain neutral
and receive neither party if they came with more
than one ship, regarding any larger number as
hostile. Having thus spoken they compelled the
people to ratify their proposal. They also sent at
once to Athens envoys to explain recent events at
Corcyra, showing how these were for the interests
of Athens, and to persuade those who had taken
refuge there to do nothing prejudicial to them, in
order that there might not be a reaction against
Corcyra.[1] LXXII. But when the envoys arrived,
the Athenians arrested them as revolutionists, and

τε πρέσβεις ὡς νεωτερίζοντας ξυλλαβόντες καὶ
ὅσους ἔπεισαν κατέθεντο ἐς Αἴγιναν.

2 Ἐν δὲ τούτῳ τῶν Κερκυραίων οἱ ἔχοντες τὰ
πράγματα ἐλθούσης τριήρους Κορινθίας καὶ Λακεδαιμονίων πρέσβεων ἐπιτίθεντα τῷ δήμῳ καὶ
3 μαχόμενοι ἐνίκησαν. ἀφικομένης δὲ νυκτὸς ὁ
μὲν δῆμος ἐς τὴν ἀκρόπολιν καὶ τὰ μετέωρα τῆς
πόλεως καταφεύγει καὶ αὐτοῦ ξυλλεγεὶς ἱδρύθη,
καὶ τὸν Ὑλλαϊκὸν λιμένα εἶχον· οἱ δὲ τήν τε
ἀγορὰν κατέλαβον, οὗπερ οἱ πολλοὶ ᾤκουν αὐτῶν,
καὶ τὸν λιμένα τὸν πρὸς αὐτῇ καὶ πρὸς τὴν
ἤπειρον. LXXIII. τῇ δ᾽ ὑστεραίᾳ ἠκροβολίσαντό
τε ὀλίγα καὶ ἐς τοὺς ἀγροὺς περιέπεμπον ἀμφότεροι, τοὺς δούλους παρακαλοῦντές τε καὶ ἐλευθερίαν ὑπισχνούμενοι· καὶ τῷ μὲν δήμῳ τῶν
οἰκετῶν τὸ πλῆθος παρεγένετο ξύμμαχον, τοῖς δ᾽
ἑτέροις ἐκ τῆς ἠπείρου ἐπίκουροι ὀκτακόσιοι.
LXXIV. διαλιπούσης δ᾽ ἡμέρας μάχη αὖθις
γίγνεται, καὶ νικᾷ ὁ δῆμος χωρίων τε ἰσχύι καὶ
πλήθει προύχων· αἵ τε γυναῖκες αὐτοῖς τολμηρῶς
ξυνεπελάβοντο βάλλουσαι ἀπὸ τῶν οἰκιῶν τῷ
κεράμῳ καὶ παρὰ φύσιν ὑπομένουσαι τὸν θόρυ-
2 βον. γενομένης δὲ τῆς τροπῆς περὶ δείλην ὀψίαν
δείσαντες οἱ ὀλίγοι μὴ αὐτοβοεὶ ὁ δῆμος τοῦ τε
νεωρίου κρατήσειεν ἐπελθὼν καὶ σφᾶς διαφθεί-
ρειεν, ἐμπιπρᾶσι τὰς οἰκίας τὰς ἐν κύκλῳ τῆς
ἀγορᾶς καὶ τὰς ξυνοικίας, ὅπως μὴ ᾖ ἔφοδος,
φειδόμενοι οὔτε οἰκείας οὔτε ἀλλοτρίας, ὥστε καὶ

deposited them in Aegina, together with such of the fugitives as they had won over.

Meanwhile the dominant party at Corcyra, on the arrival of a Corinthian trireme with Lacedaemonian envoys, attacked the people and were victorious in the fight. But when night came on the people fled for refuge to the acropolis and the high places of the city, and getting together in a body established themselves there. They held also the Hyllaïc harbour,[1] while the other party seized the quarter of the market-place where most of them lived, and the harbour[2] adjacent to it which faces the mainland. LXXIII. On the next day they skirmished a little, and both parties sent messengers round into the fields, calling upon the slaves and offering them freedom; and a majority of the slaves made common cause with the people, while the other party gained the support of eight hundred mercenaries from the mainland. LXXIV. After a day's interval another battle occurred, and the people won, as they had the advantage in the strength of their position as well as in numbers. The women also boldly took part with them in the fight, hurling tiles from the houses and enduring the uproar with a courage beyond their sex. But about twilight, when their forces had been routed, the oligarchs, fearing lest the people, if they came on, might at the first onset get possession of the arsenal and put them to the sword, set fire to the dwelling-houses around the market-place and to the tenements,[3] in order to prevent an assault, sparing neither their own houses nor those of others. The result was that much merchandise

---

[1] Probably the present bay Chalikiopulon.   [2] Now bay of Kastradu.   [3] Large buildings rented to several poor families (= *insulae* at Rome).

χρήματα πολλὰ ἐμπόρων κατεκαύθη καὶ ἡ πόλις
ἐκινδύνευσε πᾶσα διαφθαρῆναι, εἰ ἄνεμος ἐπε-
3 γένετο τῇ φλογὶ ἐπίφορος ἐς αὐτήν. καὶ οἱ μὲν
παυσάμενοι τῆς μάχης ὡς ἑκάτεροι ἡσυχάσαντες
τὴν νύκτα ἐν φυλακῇ ἦσαν· καὶ ἡ Κορινθία ναῦς
τοῦ δήμου κεκρατηκότος ὑπεξανήγετο, καὶ τῶν
ἐπικούρων οἱ πολλοὶ ἐς τὴν ἤπειρον λαθόντες
διεκομίσθησαν.

LXXV. Τῇ δὲ ἐπιγιγνομένῃ ἡμέρᾳ Νικόστρατος
ὁ Διειτρέφους, Ἀθηναίων στρατηγός, παρα-
γίγνεται βοηθῶν ἐκ Ναυπάκτου δώδεκα ναυσὶ
καὶ Μεσσηνίων πεντακοσίοις ὁπλίταις· ξύμβασίν
τε ἔπρασσε καὶ πείθει ὥστε ξυγχωρῆσαι ἀλλήλοις δέκα μὲν ἄνδρας τοὺς αἰτιωτάτους κρῖναι, οἳ
οὐκέτι ἔμειναν, τοὺς δ᾽ ἄλλους οἰκεῖν σπονδὰς
πρὸς ἀλλήλους ποιησαμένους καὶ πρὸς Ἀθηναίους
ὥστε τοὺς αὐτοὺς ἐχθροὺς καὶ φίλους νομίζειν.
2 καὶ ὁ μὲν ταῦτα πράξας ἔμελλεν ἀποπλεύσεσθαι·
οἱ δὲ τοῦ δήμου προστάται πείθουσιν αὐτὸν πέντε
μὲν ναῦς τῶν αὐτοῦ σφίσι καταλιπεῖν, ὅπως
ἧσσόν τι ἐν κινήσει ὦσιν οἱ ἐναντίοι, ἴσας δὲ
αὐτοὶ πληρώσαντες ἐκ σφῶν αὐτῶν ξυμπέμψειν.
3 καὶ ὁ μὲν ξυνεχώρησεν, οἱ δὲ τοὺς ἐχθροὺς κατέ-
λεγον ἐς τὰς ναῦς. δείσαντες δὲ ἐκεῖνοι μὴ ἐς τὰς
Ἀθήνας ἀποπεμφθῶσι καθίζουσιν ἐς τὸ τῶν
4 Διοσκόρων ἱερόν. Νικόστρατος δὲ αὐτοὺς ἀνίστη
τε καὶ παρεμυθεῖτο. ὡς δ᾽ οὐκ ἔπειθεν, ὁ δῆμος
ὁπλισθεὶς ἐπὶ τῇ προφάσει ταύτῃ, ὡς οὐδὲν

was burned up and that the whole city was in imminent danger of being entirely destroyed if a wind blowing toward the city had sprung up to reinforce the flames. And during the night, after they had desisted from battle, both parties rested but remained on the alert; and now that the people had got the upper hand the Corinthian ship slipped out to sea, and most of the mercenaries were secretly conveyed over to the mainland.

LXXV. On the following day Nicostratus son of Diitrephes, general of the Athenians, came to their assistance from Naupactus with twelve ships and five hundred Messenian hoplites. He tried to negotiate a settlement between the factions, and succeeded in persuading them to come to a mutual agreement: that the twelve men who were chiefly to blame should be brought to trial (whereupon they fled at once) and that the rest should make peace with each other and dwell together, and enter into an offensive and defensive alliance with the Athenians. When he had accomplished this, he was about to sail away; but the leaders of the people persuaded him to leave them five of his ships, that their opponents might be somewhat less inclined to disturbance, agreeing on their part to man and send with him an equal number of their own ships. He agreed, and they began to tell off their personal enemies as crews for the ships. But these, fearing that they might be sent off to Athens, sat down as suppliants in the temple of the Dioscuri. Nicostratus, however, urged them to rise and tried to reassure them. But when he could not induce them to rise, the people took this pretext to arm themselves, interpreting their distrust and refusal to sail

αὐτῶν ὑγιὲς διανοουμένων τῇ τοῦ μὴ ξυμπλεῖν
ἀπιστίᾳ, τά τε ὅπλα αὐτῶν ἐκ τῶν οἰκιῶν ἔλαβε
καὶ αὐτῶν τινας οἷς ἐπέτυχον, εἰ μὴ Νικόστρατος
5 ἐκώλυσε, διέφθειραν ἄν. ὁρῶντες δὲ οἱ ἄλλοι
τὰ γιγνόμενα καθίζουσιν ἐς τὸ Ἥραιον ἱκέται
καὶ γίγνονται οὐκ ἐλάσσους τετρακοσίων. ὁ δὲ
δῆμος δείσας μή τι νεωτερίσωσιν ἀνίστησί τε
αὐτοὺς πείσας καὶ διακομίζει ἐς τὴν πρὸ τοῦ
Ἡραίου νῆσον καὶ τὰ ἐπιτήδεια ἐκεῖσε αὐτοῖς
διεπέμπετο.

LXXVI. Τῆς δὲ στάσεως ἐν τούτῳ οὔσης τε-
τάρτῃ ἢ πέμπτῃ ἡμέρᾳ μετὰ τὴν τῶν ἀνδρῶν ἐς
τὴν νῆσον διακομιδὴν αἱ ἐκ τῆς Κυλλήνης Πελοποννησίων νῆες, μετὰ τὸν ἐκ τῆς Ἰωνίας πλοῦν
ἔφορμοι οὖσαι, παραγίγνονται τρεῖς καὶ πεντή-
κοντα· ἦρχε δὲ αὐτῶν Ἀλκίδας, ὅσπερ καὶ πρότερον, καὶ Βρασίδας αὐτῷ ξύμβουλος ἐπέπλει.
ὁρμισάμενοι δὲ ἐς Σύβοτα λιμένα τῆς ἠπείρου
ἅμα ἔῳ ἐπέπλεον τῇ Κερκύρᾳ. LXXVII. οἱ δὲ
πολλῷ θορύβῳ καὶ πεφοβημένοι τά τ' ἐν τῇ
πόλει καὶ τὸν ἐπίπλουν παρεσκευάζοντό τε ἅμα
ἑξήκοντα ναῦς καὶ τὰς αἰεὶ πληρουμένας ἐξέ-
πεμπον πρὸς τοὺς ἐναντίους, παραινούντων Ἀθηναίων σφᾶς τε ἐᾶσαι πρῶτον ἐκπλεῦσαι καὶ
2 ὕστερον πάσαις ἅμα ἐκείνους ἐπιγενέσθαι. ὡς δὲ
αὐτοῖς πρὸς τοῖς πολεμίοις ἦσαν σποράδες αἱ
νῆες, δύο μὲν εὐθὺς ηὐτομόλησαν, ἐν ἑτέραις δὲ
ἀλλήλοις οἱ ἐμπλέοντες ἐμάχοντο· ἦν δὲ οὐδεὶς

with Nicostratus as proof that their intentions were anything but good. Accordingly they took arms from their houses, and would have slain some of the oligarchs whom they chanced to meet, if Nicostratus had not prevented them. The rest, seeing what was going on, sat down as suppliants in the temple of Hera, and they were not less than four hundred in number. But the people, fearing that they might start a revolution, persuaded them to rise and conveyed them over to the island which lies in front of the temple of Hera; and provisions were regularly sent to them there.

LXXVI. At this stage of the revolution, on the fourth or fifth day after the transfer of the men to the island, the Peloponnesian ships arrived[1] from Cyllene, where they had been lying at anchor since their voyage from Ionia, being fifty-three in number; and Alcidas was in command of them as before, with Brasidas on board as his adviser. They came to anchor first at Sybota, a harbour of the mainland, and then at daybreak sailed for Corcyra. LXXVII. But the Corcyraeans,[2] being in great confusion and thrown into a panic by the state of affairs in the city as well as by the approaching fleet, proceeded to equip sixty ships and at the same time to send them out against the enemy as fast as they were manned, although the Athenians urged that they themselves be permitted to sail out first, and that the Corcyraeans should come out afterwards with all their ships in a body. But when their ships were near the enemy, scattered here and there, two of them deserted immediately, while in others the crews were fighting one another; and there was no order in anything

[1] cf. ch. lxix. 1.
[2] i.e. the democratic party, now in control.

THUCYDIDES

3 κόσμος τῶν ποιουμένων. ἰδόντες δὲ οἱ Πελοποννήσιοι τὴν ταραχὴν εἴκοσι μὲν ναυσὶ πρὸς τοὺς
Κερκυραίους ἐτάξαντο, ταῖς δὲ λοιπαῖς πρὸς τὰς
δώδεκα ναῦς τῶν Ἀθηναίων, ὧν ἦσαν αἱ δύο ἤ [1]
Σαλαμινία καὶ Πάραλος.

LXXVIII. Καὶ οἱ μὲν Κερκυραῖοι κακῶς τε
καὶ κατ' ὀλίγας προσπίπτοντες ἐταλαιπώρουν τὸ
καθ' αὑτούς· οἱ δ' Ἀθηναῖοι φοβούμενοι τὸ
πλῆθος καὶ τὴν περικύκλωσιν ἀθρόαις μὲν οὐ
προσέπιπτον οὐδὲ κατὰ μέσον ταῖς ἐφ' ἑαυτοὺς
τεταγμέναις, προσβαλόντες δὲ κατὰ κέρας κατα-
δύουσι μίαν ναῦν. καὶ μετὰ ταῦτα κύκλον ταξα-
μένων αὐτῶν περιέπλεον καὶ ἐπειρῶντο θορυβεῖν.
2 γνόντες δὲ οἱ πρὸς τοῖς Κερκυραίοις καὶ δείσαντες
μὴ ὅπερ ἐν Ναυπάκτῳ γένοιτο, ἐπιβοηθοῦσι,
καὶ γενόμεναι ἀθρόαι αἱ νῆες ἅμα τὸν ἐπίπλουν
3 τοῖς Ἀθηναίοις ἐποιοῦντο. οἱ δ' ὑπεχώρουν ἤδη
πρύμναν κρουόμενοι καὶ ἅμα τὰς τῶν Κερκυραίων
ἐβούλοντο προκαταφυγεῖν ὅτι μάλιστα, ἑαυτῶν
σχολῇ τε ὑποχωρούντων καὶ πρὸς σφᾶς τεταγ-
4 μένων τῶν ἐναντίων. ἡ μὲν οὖν ναυμαχία
τοιαύτη γενομένη ἐτελεύτα ἐς ἡλίου δύσιν.

LXXIX. Καὶ οἱ Κερκυραῖοι δείσαντες μὴ
σφίσιν ἐπιπλεύσαντες ἐπὶ τὴν πόλιν ὡς κρατοῦντες οἱ πολέμιοι ἢ τοὺς ἐκ τῆς νήσου ἀναλά-
βωσιν ἢ καὶ ἄλλο τι νεωτερίσωσι, τούς τε ἐκ τῆς
νήσου πάλιν ἐς τὸ Ἥραιον διεκόμισαν καὶ τὴν

[1] ἤ added by Krüger.

136

they did. And when the Peloponnesians saw their
confusion they arrayed only twenty ships against
the Corcyraeans, and all the rest against the twelve
Athenian ships, among which were the two sacred
ships, the Salaminia and the Paralos.

LXXVIII. Now the Corcyraeans, since they were
attacking in disorder and with few ships at a time,
were having trouble in their part of the battle; and
the Athenians, fearing the enemy's superior numbers
and seeing the danger of being surrounded, did not
attack the whole body together nor the centre of
the ships that were arrayed against them, but charged
upon one of the wings and sank a single ship. And
then, when the Peloponnesians after this move
formed their ships in a circle, they kept sailing round
the Peloponnesian fleet, trying to throw it into
confusion. But those who were facing the Corcyraeans, perceiving this manœuvre and fearing a
repetition of what happened at Naupactus,[1] came to
the rescue, and the whole fleet, now united, advanced
simultaneously upon the Athenians. Thereupon the
Athenians began to retire, backing water,[2] hoping at
the same time that the Corcyraean ships might as
far as possible escape into harbour,[3] as they themselves retired slowly and the enemy's attacks were
directed only against them. Such then was the
course of the battle, which lasted till sunset.

LXXIX. The Corcyraeans, fearing that the
enemy, confident of victory, might sail against the
city and either take on board the prisoners on the
island or commit some other act of violence, transferred these prisoners once more to the temple of

[1] cf. II. lxxxiv.   [2] i.e. keeping their faces to the enemy.
[3] i.e. with as many ships as possible; as it was they lost
thirteen ships.

2 πόλιν ἐφύλασσον. οἱ δ' ἐπὶ μὲν τὴν πόλιν οὐκ
ἐτόλμησαν πλεῦσαι κρατοῦντες τῇ ναυμαχίᾳ,
τρεῖς δὲ καὶ δέκα ναῦς ἔχοντες τῶν Κερκυραίων
ἀπέπλευσαν ἐς τὴν ἤπειρον ὅθενπερ ἀνηγάγοντο.
3 τῇ δ' ὑστεραίᾳ ἐπὶ μὲν τὴν πόλιν οὐδὲν μᾶλλον
ἐπέπλεον, καίπερ ἐν πολλῇ ταραχῇ καὶ φόβῳ
ὄντας καὶ Βρασίδου παραινοῦντος, ὡς λέγεται,
Ἀλκίδᾳ, ἰσοψήφου δὲ οὐκ ὄντος· ἐπὶ δὲ τὴν
Λευκίμνην τὸ ἀκρωτήριον ἀποβάντες ἐπόρθουν
τοὺς ἀγρούς.

LXXX. Ὁ δὲ δῆμος τῶν Κερκυραίων ἐν τούτῳ
περιδεὴς γενόμενος μὴ ἐπιπλεύσωσιν αἱ νῆες, τοῖς
τε ἱκέταις ἦσαν ἐς λόγους καὶ τοῖς ἄλλοις ὅπως
σωθήσεται ἡ πόλις. καί τινας αὐτῶν ἔπεισαν
ἐς τὰς ναῦς ἐσβῆναι· ἐπλήρωσαν γὰρ ὅμως τριά-
2 κοντα.[1] οἱ δὲ Πελοποννήσιοι μέχρι μέσου ἡμέρας
δῃώσαντες τὴν γῆν ἀπέπλευσαν, καὶ ὑπὸ νύκτα
αὐτοῖς ἐφρυκτωρήθησαν ἑξήκοντα νῆες Ἀθηναίων
προσπλέουσαι ἀπὸ Λευκάδος· ἃς οἱ Ἀθηναῖοι
πυνθανόμενοι τὴν στάσιν καὶ τὰς μετ' Ἀλκίδου
ναῦς ἐπὶ Κέρκυραν μελλούσας πλεῖν ἀπέστειλαν
καὶ Εὐρυμέδοντα τὸν Θουκλέους στρατηγόν.

LXXXI. Οἱ μὲν οὖν Πελοποννήσιοι τῆς
νυκτὸς εὐθὺς κατὰ τάχος ἐκομίζοντο ἐπ' οἴκου
παρὰ τὴν γῆν· καὶ ὑπερενεγκόντες τὸν Λευκαδίων
ἰσθμὸν τὰς ναῦς, ὅπως μὴ περιπλέοντες ὀφθῶσιν,

---

[1] Some MSS. give προσδεχόμενοι τὸν ἐπίπλουν after τριάκοντα, most editors omit.

Hera and then took measures to protect the city. The Peloponnesians, however, although they were the victors in the naval battle, did not venture to attack the city, but with thirteen Corcyraean ships which they had taken sailed back to the harbour on the mainland from which they had set out. On the next day they were no more inclined to attack the city, though the inhabitants were in a state of great confusion and fear, and though Brasidas, it is said, urged Alcidas to do so, but did not have equal authority with him. Instead, they merely landed on the promontory of Leucimne and ravaged the fields.

LXXX. Meanwhile the people of Corcyra, becoming alarmed lest the ships should attack them, conferred with the suppliants and also with the other members of the opposite faction on the best means of saving the city. And some of them they persuaded to go on board the ships; for in spite of all the Corcyraeans had manned thirty ships. But the Peloponnesians, after ravaging the land till midday, sailed away, and toward night a signal was flashed to them that sixty Athenian ships were approaching from Leucas. These ships had been sent by the Athenians, under the command of Eurymedon son of Thucles, when they learned of the revolution at Corcyra and that the fleet under Alcidas was about to sail thither.

LXXXI. The Peloponnesians accordingly set sail that very night for home, going with all speed and keeping close to the shore; and hauling their ships across the Leucadian isthmus,[1] in order to avoid being seen, as they would be if they sailed around, they got

---

[1] This isthmus was the ἀκτὴ ἠπείρου of Homer (ω 378), now Santa Maura, the neck of land, about three stadia in width, joining Leucas with the mainland.

2 ἀποκομίζονται. Κερκυραῖοι δὲ αἰσθόμενοι τάς τε
Ἀττικὰς ναῦς προσπλεούσας τάς τε τῶν πολεμίων οἰχομένας, λαθόντες[1] τούς τε Μεσσηνίους ἐς
τὴν πόλιν ἤγαγον πρότερον ἔξω ὄντας, καὶ τὰς
ναῦς περιπλεῦσαι κελεύσαντες ἃς ἐπλήρωσαν ἐς
τὸν Ὑλλαϊκὸν λιμένα, ἐν ὅσῳ περιεκομίζοντο, τῶν
ἐχθρῶν εἴ τινα λάβοιεν, ἀπέκτεινον· καὶ ἐκ τῶν
νεῶν ὅσους ἔπεισαν ἐσβῆναι ἐκβιβάζοντες ἀπε-
χρῶντο, ἐς τὸ Ἥραιόν τε ἐλθόντες τῶν ἱκετῶν
ὡς πεντήκοντα ἄνδρας δίκην ὑποσχεῖν ἔπεισαν
3 καὶ κατέγνωσαν πάντων θάνατον. οἱ δὲ πολλοὶ
τῶν ἱκετῶν, ὅσοι οὐκ ἐπείσθησαν, ὡς ἑώρων τὰ
γιγνόμενα, διέφθειρον αὐτοῦ ἐν τῷ ἱερῷ ἀλλήλους
καὶ ἐκ τῶν δένδρων τινὲς ἀπήγχοντο, οἱ δ' ὡς
4 ἕκαστοι ἐδύναντο ἀνηλοῦντο. ἡμέρας τε ἑπτά, ἃς
ἀφικόμενος ὁ Εὐρυμέδων ταῖς ἑξήκοντα ναυσὶ
παρέμεινε, Κερκυραῖοι σφῶν αὐτῶν τοὺς ἐχθροὺς
δοκοῦντας εἶναι ἐφόνευον, τὴν μὲν αἰτίαν ἐπιφέροντες τοῖς τὸν δῆμον καταλύουσιν, ἀπέθανον
δέ τινες καὶ ἰδίας ἔχθρας ἕνεκα, καὶ ἄλλοι χρημάτων σφίσιν ὀφειλομένων ὑπὸ τῶν λαβόντων·
5 πᾶσά τε ἰδέα κατέστη θανάτου, καὶ οἷον φιλεῖ ἐν
τῷ τοιούτῳ γίγνεσθαι, οὐδὲν ὅ τι οὐ ξυνέβη καὶ
ἔτι περαιτέρω. καὶ γὰρ πατὴρ παῖδα ἀπέ-

[1] λαθόντες, Hude's conjecture for λαβόντες of the MSS.

[1] The 500 whom Nicostratus had brought, the object
being doubtless merely the intimidation of the oligarchs.

away. Now the Corcyraeans had no sooner perceived that the Athenian fleet was approaching and that the enemy's fleet had gone than they secretly brought the Messenians,[1] who had till then been outside the walls, into the city, and ordered the ships which they had manned to sail round into the Hyllaic harbour[2]; then while these were on their way thither they slew any of their personal enemies whom they could lay hands upon. They also put ashore and despatched all those on board the ships whom they had persuaded to go aboard, then went into the temple of Hera, persuaded about fifty of the suppliants there to submit to trial, and condemned them all to death. But most of the suppliants, not having consented to be tried, when they saw what was happening set about destroying one another in the sacred precinct itself, while a few hanged themselves on trees, and still others made away with themselves as best they could. And during the seven days that Eurymedon, after his arrival, stayed there with his sixty ships, the Corcyraeans continued slaughtering such of their fellow-citizens as they considered to be their personal enemies. The charge they brought was of conspiring to overthrow the democracy, but some were in fact put to death merely to satisfy private enmity, and others, because money was owing to them, were slain by those who had borrowed it. Death in every form ensued, and whatever horrors are wont to be perpetrated at such times all happened then—aye, and even worse. For father slew son, men were dragged

---

[2] The object was that the oligarchs on them might be cut off from their friends in the neighbourhood of the agora and in the temple of Hera.

κτεινε καὶ ἀπὸ τῶν ἱερῶν ἀπεσπῶντο καὶ πρὸς
αὐτοῖς ἐκτείνοντο, οἱ δέ τινες καὶ περιοικοδομη-
θέντες ἐς τοῦ Διονύσου τῷ ἱερῷ ἀπέθανον.

LXXXII. Οὕτως ὠμὴ ἡ στάσις[1] προυχώρησε,
καὶ ἔδοξε μᾶλλον, διότι ἐν τοῖς πρώτη ἐγένετο,
ἐπεὶ ὕστερόν γε καὶ πᾶν ὡς εἰπεῖν τὸ Ἑλληνικὸν
ἐκινήθη διαφορῶν οὐσῶν ἑκασταχοῦ τοῖς τε τῶν
δήμων προστάταις τοὺς Ἀθηναίους ἐπάγεσθαι
καὶ τοῖς ὀλίγοις τοὺς Λακεδαιμονίους. καὶ ἐν μὲν
εἰρήνῃ οὐκ ἂν ἐχόντων πρόφασιν οὐδ' ἑτοίμων
παρακαλεῖν αὐτούς, πολεμουμένων δὲ καὶ ξυμμαχίας ἅμα ἑκατέροις τῇ τῶν ἐναντίων κακώσει
καὶ σφίσιν αὐτοῖς ἐκ τοῦ αὐτοῦ προσποιήσει
ῥᾳδίως αἱ ἐπαγωγαὶ τοῖς νεωτερίζειν τι βουλο-
2 μένοις ἐπορίζοντο. καὶ ἐπέπεσε πολλὰ καὶ
χαλεπὰ κατὰ στάσιν ταῖς πόλεσι, γιγνόμενα μὲν
καὶ αἰεὶ ἐσόμενα, ἕως ἂν ἡ αὐτὴ φύσις ἀνθρώπων
ᾖ, μᾶλλον δὲ καὶ ἡσυχαίτερα καὶ τοῖς εἴδεσι
διηλλαγμένα, ὡς ἂν ἕκασται[2] αἱ μεταβολαὶ τῶν
ξυντυχιῶν ἐφιστῶνται. ἐν μὲν γὰρ εἰρήνῃ καὶ
ἀγαθοῖς πράγμασιν αἵ τε πόλεις καὶ οἱ ἰδιῶται
ἀμείνους τὰς γνώμας ἔχουσι διὰ τὸ μὴ ἐς ἀκου-
σίους ἀνάγκας πίπτειν· ὁ δὲ πόλεμος ὑφελὼν τὴν
εὐπορίαν τοῦ καθ' ἡμέραν βίαιος διδάσκαλος καὶ
πρὸς τὰ παρόντα τὰς ὀργὰς τῶν πολλῶν ὁμοιοῖ.
3 Ἐστασίαζέ τε οὖν τὰ τῶν πόλεων καὶ τὰ
ἐφυστερίζοντά που πύστει τῶν προγενομένων

---

[1] ἡ στάσις, for στάσις of the MSS., Krüger with Schol.
[2] ἕκασται, Hude alters to ἑκάσταις.

from the temples and slain near them, and some were even walled up in the temple of Dionysus and perished there.

LXXXII. To such excesses of savagery did the revolution go; and it seemed the more savage, because it was among the first that occurred; for afterwards practically the whole Hellenic world was convulsed, since in each state the leaders of the democratic factions were at variance with the oligarchs, the former seeking to bring in the Athenians, the latter the Lacedaemonians. And while in time of peace they would have had no pretext for asking their intervention, nor any inclination to do so, yet now that these two states were at war, either faction in the various cities, if it desired a revolution, found it easy to bring in allies also, for the discomfiture at one stroke of its opponents and the strengthening of its own cause. And so there fell upon the cities on account of revolutions many grievous calamities, such as happen and always will happen while human nature is the same, but which are severer or milder, and different in their manifestations, according as the variations in circumstances present themselves in each case. For in peace and prosperity both states and individuals have gentler feelings, because men are not then forced to face conditions of dire necessity; but war, which robs men of the easy supply of their daily wants, is a rough schoolmaster and creates in most people a temper that matches their condition.

And so the cities began to be disturbed by revolutions, and those that fell into this state later, on hearing of what had been done before, carried to

πολὺ ἐπέφερε τὴν ὑπερβολὴν τοῦ και·ιοῦσθαι τὰς
διανοίας τῶν τ' ἐπιχειρήσεων περιτεχνήσει καὶ
4 τῶν τιμωριῶν ἀτοπίᾳ. καὶ τὴν εἰωθυῖαν ἀξίωσιν
τῶν ὀνομάτων ἐς τὰ ἔργα ἀντήλλαξαν τῇ δικαιώσει. τόλμα μὲν γὰρ ἀλόγιστος ἀνδρεία
φιλέταιρος ἐνομίσθη, μέλλησις δὲ προμηθὴς
δειλία εὐπρεπής, τὸ δὲ σῶφρον τοῦ ἀνάνδρου
πρόσχημα, καὶ τὸ πρὸς ἅπαν ξυνετὸν ἐπὶ πᾶν
ἀργόν· τὸ δ' ἐμπλήκτως ὀξὺ ἀνδρὸς μοίρᾳ προσ-
ετέθη, ἀσφαλείᾳ δὲ τὸ ¹ ἐπιβουλεύσασθαι ἀπο-
5 τροπῆς πρόφασις εὔλογος. καὶ ὁ μὲν χαλε-
παίνων πιστὸς αἰεί, ὁ δ' ἀντιλέγων αὐτῷ ὕποπτος.
ἐπιβουλεύσας δέ τις τυχὼν ξυνετὸς καὶ ὑπονοή-
σας ἔτι δεινότερος· προβουλεύσας δὲ ὅπως μηδὲν
αὐτῶν δεήσει, τῆς τε ἑταιρίας διαλυτὴς καὶ τοὺς
ἐναντίους ἐκπεπληγμένος. ἁπλῶς τε ὁ φθάσας
τὸν μέλλοντα κακόν τι δρᾶν ἐπῃνεῖτο καὶ ὁ ἐπι-
6 κελεύσας τὸν μὴ διανοούμενον. καὶ μὴν καὶ τὸ
ξυγγενὲς τοῦ ἑταιρικοῦ ἀλλοτριώτερον ἐγένετο διὰ
τὸ ἑτοιμότερον εἶναι ἀπροφασίστως τολμᾶν· οὐ
γὰρ μετὰ τῶν κειμένων νόμων ὠφελίᾳ ² αἱ τοιαῦ-
ται ξύνοδοι, ἀλλὰ παρὰ τοὺς καθεστῶτας πλεονεξίᾳ. καὶ τὰς ἐς σφᾶς αὐτοὺς πίστεις οὐ τῷ
θείῳ νόμῳ μᾶλλον ἐκρατύνοντο ἢ τῷ κοινῇ τι
7 παρανομῆσαι. τά τε ἀπὸ τῶν ἐναντίων καλῶς
λεγόμενα ἐνεδέχοντο ἔργων φυλακῇ, εἰ προύχοιεν,
καὶ οὐ γενναιότητι. ἀντιτιμωρήσασθαί τέ τινα

---

¹ ἀσφάλεια δὲ τοῦ ἐπιβουλεύσασθαι Hude.
² ὠφελίᾳ, Poppo for ὠφελίας of the MSS.

---

¹ i.e. either of plotting or of detecting plots.
² Or, "Fair words proffered by their opponents they re-

still more extravagant lengths the invention of new devices, both by the extreme ingenuity of their attacks and the monstrousness of their revenges. The ordinary acceptation of words in their relation to things was changed as men thought fit. Reckless audacity came to be regarded as courageous loyalty to party, prudent hesitation as specious cowardice, moderation as a cloak for unmanly weakness, and to be clever in everything was to do naught in anything. Frantic impulsiveness was accounted a true man's part, but caution in deliberation a specious pretext for shirking. The hot-headed man was always trusted, his opponent suspected. He who succeeded in a plot was clever, and he who had detected one was still shrewder; on the other hand, he who made it his aim to have no need of such things [1] was a disrupter of party and scared of his opponents. In a word, both he that got ahead of another who intended to do something evil and he that prompted to evil one who had never thought of of it were alike commended. Furthermore, the tie of blood was weaker than the tie of party, because the partisan was more ready to dare without demur; for such associations are not entered into for the public good in conformity with the prescribed laws, but for selfish aggrandisement contrary to the established laws. Their pledges to one another were confirmed not so much by divine law as by common transgression of the law. Fair words proffered by opponents, if these had the upper hand, were received with caution as to their actions and not in a generous spirit. [2] To get revenge on some one was

ceived, if they had the upper hand, by vigilant action rather than with frank generosity."

περὶ πλείονος ἦν ἢ αὐτὸν μὴ προπαθεῖν. καὶ
ὅρκοι εἴ που ἄρα γένοιντο ξυναλλαγῆς, ἐν τῷ
αὐτίκα πρὸς τὸ ἄπορον ἑκατέρῳ διδόμενοι ἴσχυον,
οὐκ ἐχόντων ἄλλοθεν δύναμιν· ἐν δὲ τῷ παρα-
τυχόντι ὁ φθάσας θαρσῆσαι, εἰ ἴδοι ἄφαρκτον,
ἥδιον διὰ τὴν πίστιν ἐτιμωρεῖτο ἢ ἀπὸ τοῦ προφανοῦς, καὶ τό τε ἀσφαλὲς ἐλογίζετο καὶ ὅτι
ἀπάτῃ περιγενόμενος ξυνέσεως ἀγώνισμα προσε-
λάμβανεν. ῥᾷον δ᾽ οἱ πολλοὶ κακοῦργοι ὄντες
δεξιοὶ κέκληνται ἢ ἀμαθεῖς ἀγαθοί, καὶ τῷ μὲν
αἰσχύνονται, ἐπὶ δὲ τῷ ἀγάλλονται.

8   Πάντων δ᾽ αὐτῶν αἴτιον [1] ἀρχὴ ἡ [2] διὰ πλεονεξίαν καὶ φιλοτιμίαν, ἐκ δ᾽ αὐτῶν καὶ ἐς τὸ
φιλονικεῖν καθισταμένων τὸ πρόθυμον. οἱ γὰρ
ἐν ταῖς πόλεσι προστάντες μετ᾽ ὀνόματος ἑκάτεροι εὐπρεποῦς, πλήθους τε ἰσονομίας πολιτικῆς
καὶ ἀριστοκρατίας σώφρονος προτιμήσει, τὰ μὲν
κοινὰ λόγῳ θεραπεύοντες ἆθλα ἐποιοῦντο, παντὶ
δὲ τρόπῳ ἀγωνιζόμενοι ἀλλήλων περιγίγνεσθαι
ἐτόλμησάν τε τὰ δεινότατα, ἐπεξῆσάν τε τὰς
τιμωρίας ἔτι μείζους, οὐ μέχρι τοῦ δικαίου καὶ
τῇ πόλει ξυμφόρου προστιθέντες,[3] ἐς δὲ τὸ ἑκατέροις που αἰεὶ ἡδονὴν ἔχον ὁρίζοντες, καὶ ἢ μετὰ

[1] αἴτιον, Hude deletes, with Madvig.
[2] ἡ, Hude deletes.
[3] προστιθέντες, Dion. Hal. for προτιθέντες of the MSS.

---

[1] Or, omitting ὄντες, "And in general men are more
willing to be called clever rogues than good simpletons."

more valued than never to have suffered injury oneself. And if in any case oaths of reconcilement were exchanged, for the moment only were they binding, since each side had given them merely to meet the emergency, having at the time no other resource; but he who, when the opportunity offered and he saw his enemy off his guard, was the first to pluck up courage, found his revenge sweeter because of the violated pledge than if he had openly attacked, and took into account not only the greater safety of such a course, but also that, by winning through deceit, he was gaining besides the prize of astuteness. And in general it is easier for rogues to get themselves called clever than for the stupid to be reputed good,[1] and they are ashamed of the one but glory in the other.

The cause of all these evils was the desire to rule which greed and ambition inspire, and also, springing from them, that ardour [2] which belongs to men who once have become engaged in factious rivalry. For those who emerged as party leaders in the several cities, by assuming on either side a fair-sounding name, the one using as its catch-word " political equality for the masses under the law," the other " temperate aristocracy," [3] while they pretended to be devoted to the common weal, in reality made it their prize; striving in every way to get the better of each other they dared the most awful deeds, and sought revenges still more awful, not pursuing these within the bounds of justice and the public weal, but limiting them, both parties alike, only by the moment's

---

[2] Or, τὸ πρόθυμον, " party-spirit."
[3] For the objectionable terms " democracy " (δημοκρατία) and " oligarchy " (ὀλιγαρχία).

ψήφου ἀδίκου καταγνώσεως [1] ἢ χειρὶ κτώμενοι τὸ
κρατεῖν ἑτοῖμοι ἦσαν τὴν αὐτίκα φιλονικίαν
ἐκπιμπλάναι. ὥστε εὐσεβείᾳ μὲν οὐδέτεροι ἐνόμιζον, εὐπρεπείᾳ δὲ λόγου οἷς ξυμβαίη ἐπιφθόνως
τι διαπράξασθαι, ἄμεινον ἤκουον. τὰ δὲ μέσα
τῶν πολιτῶν ὑπ' ἀμφοτέρων ἢ ὅτι οὐ ξυνηγωνί-
ζοντο ἢ φθόνῳ τοῦ περιεῖναι διεφθείροντο.

LXXXIII. Οὕτω πᾶσα ἰδέα κατέστη κακο-
τροπίας διὰ τὰς στάσεις τῷ Ἑλληνικῷ, καὶ τὸ
εὔηθες, οὗ τὸ γενναῖον πλεῖστον μετέχει, κατα-
γελασθὲν ἠφανίσθη, τὸ δὲ ἀντιτετάχθαι ἀλλήλοις
2 τῇ γνώμῃ ἀπίστως ἐπὶ πολὺ διήνεγκεν· οὐ γὰρ
ἦν ὁ διαλύσων οὔτε λόγος ἐχυρὸς οὔτε ὅρκος φο-
βερός, κρείσσους δὲ ὄντες ἅπαντες λογισμῷ ἐς τὸ
ἀνέλπιστον τοῦ βεβαίου μὴ παθεῖν μᾶλλον πρου-
3 σκόπουν ἢ πιστεῦσαι ἐδύναντο. καὶ οἱ φαυλότεροι γνώμην ὡς τὰ πλείω περιεγίγνοντο· τῷ γὰρ
δεδιέναι τό τε αὐτῶν ἐνδεὲς καὶ τὸ τῶν ἐναντίων
ξυνετόν, μὴ λόγοις τε ἥσσους ὦσι καὶ ἐκ τοῦ
πολυτρόπου αὐτῶν τῆς γνώμης φθάσωσι προεπι-
βουλευόμενοι, τολμηρῶς πρὸς τὰ ἔργα ἐχώρουν.
4 οἱ δὲ καταφρονοῦντες κἂν προαισθέσθαι καὶ ἔργῳ
οὐδὲν σφᾶς δεῖν λαμβάνειν ἃ γνώμῃ ἔξεστιν,
ἄφαρκτοι μᾶλλον διεφθείροντο.

---

[1] καταγνώσεως, Hude deletes, with van Herwerden.

---

[1] Or, as Shilleto, "leaning in calculation to considering
that security was hopeless, they rather took precautions . . ."
cf. Schol., ῥέποντες δὲ οἱ ἄνθρωποι τοῖς λογισμοῖς πρὸς τὸ μὴ
ἐλπίζειν τινὰ πίστιν καὶ βεβαιότητα.

caprice; and they were ready, either by passing an unjust sentence of condemnation or by winning the upper hand through acts of violence, to glut the animosity of the moment. The result was that though neither had any regard for true piety, yet those who could carry through an odious deed under the cloak of a specious phrase received the higher praise. And citizens who belonged to neither party were continually destroyed by both, either because they would not make common cause with them, or through mere jealousy that they should survive.

LXXXIII. So it was that every form of depravity showed itself in Hellas in consequence of its revolutions, and that simplicity, which is the chief element of a noble nature, was laughed to scorn and disappeared, while mutual antagonism of feeling, combined with mistrust, prevailed far and wide. For there was no assurance binding enough, no oath terrible enough, to reconcile men; but always, if they were stronger,[1] since they accounted all security hopeless, they were rather disposed to take precautions against being wronged than able to trust others. And it was generally those of meaner intellect who won the day; for being afraid of their own defects and of their opponents' sagacity, in order that they might not be worsted in words, and, by reason of their opponents' intellectual versatility find themselves unawares victims of their plots, they boldly resorted to deeds. Their opponents, on the other hand, contemptuously assuming that they would be aware in time and that there was no need to secure by deeds what they might have by wit, were taken off their guard and perished in greater numbers.

LXXXIV. Ἐν δ' οὖν τῇ Κερκύρᾳ τὰ πολλὰ
αὐτῶν προετολμήθη, καὶ ὁπόσ' ἂν[1] ὕβρει μὲν
ἀρχόμενοι τὸ πλέον ἢ σωφροσύνῃ ὑπὸ τῶν τὴν
τιμωρίαν παρασχόντων οἱ ἀνταμυνόμενοι δράσειαν, πενίας δὲ τῆς εἰωθυίας ἀπαλλαξείοντές
τινες, μάλιστα δ' ἂν διὰ πάθους ἐπιθυμοῦντες
τὰ τῶν πέλας ἔχειν, παρὰ δίκην γιγνώσκοιεν, ἅ
τε μὴ ἐπὶ πλεονεξίᾳ, ἀπὸ ἴσου δὲ μάλιστα ἐπιόντες ἀπαιδευσίᾳ ὀργῆς πλεῖστον ἐκφερόμενοι
2 ὠμῶς καὶ ἀπαραιτήτως ἐπέλθοιεν. ξυνταραχ-
θέντος τε τοῦ βίου ἐς τὸν καιρὸν τοῦτον τῇ πόλει
καὶ τῶν νόμων κρατήσασα ἡ ἀνθρωπεία φύσις,
εἰωθυῖα καὶ παρὰ τοὺς νόμους ἀδικεῖν, ἀσμένη
ἐδήλωσεν ἀκρατὴς μὲν ὀργῆς οὖσα, κρείσσων δὲ
τοῦ δικαίου, πολεμία δὲ τοῦ προύχοντος. οὐ γὰρ
ἂν τοῦ τε ὁσίου τὸ τιμωρεῖσθαι προυτίθεσαν τοῦ
τε μὴ ἀδικεῖν τὸ κερδαίνειν, ἐν ᾧ μὴ βλάπτουσαν
3 ἰσχὺν εἶχε τὸ φθονεῖν. ἀξιοῦσί τε τοὺς κοινοὺς
περὶ τῶν τοιούτων οἱ ἄνθρωποι νόμους, ἀφ' ὧν
ἅπασιν ἐλπὶς ὑπόκειται σφαλεῖσι κἂν αὐτοὺς
διασώζεσθαι, ἐν ἄλλων τιμωρίαις προκαταλύειν
καὶ μὴ ὑπολείπεσθαι, εἴ ποτε ἄρα τις κινδυνεύσας
τινὸς δεήσεται αὐτῶν.

---

[1] ὁπόσ' ἂν, Hude's correction for ὁπόσα of the MSS.

---

[1] This chapter is bracketed as spurious by Hude and
nearly all recent commentators, because it is condemned by

LXXXIV.[1] It was in Corcyra, then, that most of these atrocities were first committed—all the acts of retaliation which men who are governed with high-handed insolence rather than with moderation are likely to commit upon their rulers when these at last afford them opportunity for revenge; or such as men resolve upon contrary to justice when they seek release from their accustomed poverty, and in consequence of their sufferings are likely to be most eager for their neighbours' goods;[2] and assaults of pitiless cruelty, such as men make, not with a view to gain, but when, being on terms of complete equality with their foe, they are utterly carried away by uncontrollable passion. At this crisis, when the life of the city had been thrown into utter confusion, human nature, now triumphant over the laws, and accustomed even in spite of the laws to do wrong, took delight in showing that its passions were ungovernable, that it was stronger than justice and an enemy to all superiority. For surely no man would have put revenge before religion, and gain before innocence of wrong, had not envy swayed him with her blighting power. Indeed, men do not hesitate, when they seek to avenge themselves upon others, to abrogate in advance the common principles observed in such cases—those principles upon which depends every man's own hope of salvation should he himself be overtaken by misfortune—thus failing to leave them in force against the time when perchance a man in peril shall have need of some one of them.

the ancient grammarians, is not mentioned by Dionysius of Halicarnassus, and is obelised in Codex F.

[2] Or, μάλιστα δ' ἂν διὰ πάθους ἐπιθυμοῦντες, "would be above all men passionately eager for . . ."

LXXXV. Οἱ μὲν οὖν κατὰ τὴν πόλιν Κερκυραῖοι τοιαύταις ὀργαῖς ταῖς πρώταις ἐς ἀλλήλους ἐχρήσαντο, καὶ ὁ Εὐρυμέδων καὶ οἱ Ἀθηναῖοι ἀπέπλευσαν ταῖς ναυσίν· ὕστερον δὲ οἱ φεύγοντες
2 τῶν Κερκυραίων (διεσώθησαν γὰρ αὐτῶν ἐς πεντακοσίους) τείχη τε λαβόντες, ἃ ἦν ἐν τῇ ἠπείρῳ, ἐκράτουν τῆς πέραν οἰκείας γῆς καὶ ἐξ αὐτῆς ὁρμώμενοι ἐλῄζοντο τοὺς ἐν τῇ νήσῳ καὶ πολλὰ ἔβλαπτον, καὶ λιμὸς ἰσχυρὸς ἐγένετο ἐν τῇ πόλει.
3 ἐπρεσβεύοντο δὲ καὶ ἐς τὴν Λακεδαίμονα καὶ Κόρινθον περὶ καθόδου· καὶ ὡς οὐδὲν αὐτοῖς ἐπράσσετο, ὕστερον χρόνῳ πλοῖα καὶ ἐπικούρους παρασκευασάμενοι διέβησαν ἐς τὴν νῆσον ἑξακό-
4 σιοι μάλιστα οἱ πάντες, καὶ τὰ πλοῖα ἐμπρήσαντες, ὅπως ἀπόγνοια ᾖ τοῦ ἄλλο τι ἢ κρατεῖν τῆς γῆς, ἀναβάντες ἐς τὸ ὄρος τὴν Ἰστώνην, τεῖχος ἐνοικοδομησάμενοι ἔφθειρον τοὺς ἐν τῇ πόλει καὶ τῆς γῆς ἐκράτουν.

LXXXVI. Τοῦ δ᾽ αὐτοῦ θέρους τελευτῶντος Ἀθηναῖοι εἴκοσι ναῦς ἔστειλαν ἐς Σικελίαν καὶ Λάχητα τὸν Μελανώπου στρατηγὸν αὐτῶν καὶ
2 Χαροιάδην τὸν Εὐφιλήτου. οἱ γὰρ Συρακόσιοι καὶ Λεοντῖνοι ἐς πόλεμον ἀλλήλοις καθέστασαν. ξύμμαχοι δὲ τοῖς μὲν Συρακοσίοις ἦσαν πλὴν Καμαριναίων αἱ ἄλλαι Δωρίδες πόλεις, αἵπερ καὶ πρὸς τὴν τῶν Λακεδαιμονίων τὸ πρῶτον ἀρχομένου τοῦ πολέμου ξυμμαχίαν ἐτάχθησαν, οὐ μέντοι ξυνεπολέμησάν γε· τοῖς δὲ Λεοντίνοις αἱ Χαλκιδικαὶ πόλεις καὶ Καμάρινα· τῆς δὲ Ἰταλίας Λοκροὶ μὲν Συρακοσίων ἦσαν, Ῥηγῖνοι δὲ κατὰ
3 τὸ ξυγγενὲς Λεοντίνων. ἐς οὖν τὰς Ἀθήνας

LXXXV. Such then were the first outbreaks of passion which the Corcyraeans who remained at home indulged in toward each other; and Eurymedon sailed away with the Athenian fleet. Later, however, the Corcyraean fugitives, of whom about five hundred[1] had got safely across to the mainland, seized some forts there, and thus dominating the territory belonging to Corcyra on the opposite coast made it a base from which they plundered the people of the island and did them much harm, so that a severe famine arose in the city. They also sent envoys to Lacedaemon and Corinth to negotiate for their restoration; but since nothing was accomplished by these they afterwards procured boats and mercenaries and crossed over to the island, about six hundred in all. They then burned their boats, in order that they might despair of success unless they dominated the country, and went up to Mt. Istone, and after building a fort there began to destroy the people in the city, exercising dominion over the country.

LXXXVI. Toward the close of the same summer the Athenians sent twenty ships to Sicily under the command of Laches son of Melanopus and Charoeades son of Euphiletus. For the Syracusans and the Leontines were now at war with each other. In alliance with the Syracusans were all the Dorian cities except Camarina—the cities which at the outbreak of the war had joined the Lacedaemonian alliance, although they had taken no active part in the war—while the Chalcidian cities and Camarina were allies of the Leontines. In Italy the Locrians allied themselves with the Syracusans, and the Rhegians with the Leontines, because they were kinsmen.[2] The Leontines and their allies sent an

[1] cf. ch. xx. 2.   [2] cf. vi. xliv. 3.

πέμψαντες οἱ τῶν Λεοντίνων ξύμμαχοι κατά τε
παλαιὰν ξυμμαχίαν καὶ ὅτι Ἴωνες ἦσαν, πεί-
θουσι τοὺς Ἀθηναίους πέμψαι σφίσι ναῦς· ὑπὸ
γὰρ τῶν Συρακοσίων τῆς τε γῆς εἴργοντο καὶ τῆς
4 θαλάσσης. καὶ ἔπεμψαν οἱ Ἀθηναῖοι τῆς μὲν
οἰκειότητος προφάσει, βουλόμενοι δὲ μήτε σῖτον
ἐς τὴν Πελοπόννησον ἄγεσθαι αὐτόθεν πρόπειράν
τε ποιούμενοι εἰ σφίσι δυνατὰ εἴη τὰ ἐν τῇ
5 Σικελίᾳ πράγματα ὑποχείρια γενέσθαι. καταστάντες οὖν ἐς Ῥήγιον τῆς Ἰταλίας τὸν πόλεμον
ἐποιοῦντο μετὰ τῶν ξυμμάχων. καὶ τὸ θέρος
ἐτελεύτα.

LXXXVII. Τοῦ δ᾽ ἐπιγιγνομένου χειμῶνος ἡ
νόσος τὸ δεύτερον ἐπέπεσε τοῖς Ἀθηναίοις, ἐκλι-
ποῦσα μὲν οὐδένα χρόνον τὸ παντάπασιν, ἐγένετο
2 δέ τις ὅμως διοκωχή. παρέμεινε δὲ τὸ μὲν ὕστερον οὐκ ἔλασσον ἐνιαυτοῦ, τὸ δὲ πρότερον καὶ
δύο ἔτη, ὥστε Ἀθηναίους γε μὴ εἶναι ὅ τι μᾶλλον τούτου ἐπίεσε καὶ ἐκάκωσε τὴν δύναμιν.
3 τετρακοσίων γὰρ ὁπλιτῶν καὶ τετρακισχιλίων
οὐκ ἐλάσσους ἀπέθανον ἐκ τῶν τάξεων καὶ τρια-
κοσίων ἱππέων, τοῦ δὲ ἄλλου ὄχλου ἀνεξεύρετος
4 ἀριθμός. ἐγένοντο δὲ καὶ οἱ πολλοὶ σεισμοὶ τότε
τῆς γῆς ἔν τε Ἀθήναις καὶ ἐν Εὐβοίᾳ καὶ ἐν
Βοιωτοῖς καὶ μάλιστα ἐν Ὀρχομενῷ τῷ Βοιωτίῳ.

LXXXVIII. Καὶ οἱ μὲν ἐν Σικελίᾳ Ἀθηναῖοι
καὶ Ῥηγῖνοι τοῦ αὐτοῦ χειμῶνος τριάκοντα ναυσὶ

---

[1] At the head of this embassy was the celebrated rhetori-
cian Gorgias.
[2] cf. *C.I.A.* i. 33 for some fragments of treaties of alliance
renewed under the archon Apseudes (433–432 B.C.).
[3] cf. II. xlvii. ff.

embassy[1] to Athens and urged them, both on the ground of an earlier alliance[2] and because they were Ionians, to send them ships; for they were being excluded from both the land and the sea by the Syracusans. And the Athenians sent the ships, professedly on the ground of their relationship, but really because they wished to prevent the importation of grain from Sicily into the Peloponnesus, and also to make a preliminary test whether the affairs of Sicily could be brought under their own control. So they established themselves at Rhegium in Italy and proceeded to carry on the war in concert with their allies. And the summer ended.

LXXXVII. In the course of the following winter 427 B.C. the plague again[3] fell upon the Athenians; and indeed it had not died out at any time entirely, though there had been a period of respite. And it continued the second time not less than a year, having run for two full years on the previous occasion, so that the Athenians were more distressed by it than by any other misfortune and their power more crippled.[4] For no fewer than four thousand four hundred of those enrolled as hoplites died and also three hundred cavalry, and of the populace a number that could not be ascertained. It was at this time also that the great number of earthquakes occurred at Athens, in Euboea, and in Boeotia, and especially at Orchomenus in Boeotia.

LXXXVIII. The same winter the Athenians in Sicily and the Rhegians made an expedition with thirty

[4] This statement may have been written without a knowledge of the later events of the war, especially the unhappy issue of the Sicilian expedition (see Introd. p. xiii.)—unless δύναμις be taken to mean "fighting strength," or something narrower than "power."

στρατεύουσιν ἐπὶ τὰς Αἰόλου νήσους καλουμένας·
θέρους γὰρ δι' ἀνυδρίαν ἀδύνατα ἦν ἐπιστρατεύειν.
2 νέμονται δὲ Λιπαραῖοι αὐτάς, Κνιδίων ἄποικοι
ὄντες. οἰκοῦσι δ' ἐν μίᾳ τῶν νήσων οὐ μεγάλῃ,
καλεῖται δὲ Λιπάρα· τὰς δὲ ἄλλας ἐκ ταύτης
ὁρμώμενοι γεωργοῦσι, Διδύμην καὶ Στρογγύλην
3 καὶ Ἱεράν. νομίζουσι δὲ οἱ ἐκείνῃ ἄνθρωποι ἐν
τῇ Ἱερᾷ ὡς ὁ Ἥφαιστος χαλκεύει, ὅτι τὴν νύκτα
φαίνεται πῦρ ἀναδιδοῦσα πολὺ καὶ τὴν ἡμέραν
καπνόν. κεῖνται δὲ αἱ νῆσοι αὗται κατὰ τὴν
Σικελῶν καὶ Μεσσηνίων γῆν, ξύμμαχοι δ' ἦσαν
4 Συρακοσίων· τεμόντες δ' οἱ Ἀθηναῖοι τὴν γῆν,
ὡς οὐ προσεχώρουν, ἀπέπλευσαν ἐς τὸ Ῥήγιον.
καὶ ὁ χειμὼν ἐτελεύτα, καὶ πέμπτον ἔτος τῷ
πολέμῳ ἐτελεύτα τῷδε ὃν Θουκυδίδης ξυνέγραψεν.

LXXXIX. Τοῦ δ' ἐπιγιγνομένου θέρους Πελοποννήσιοι καὶ οἱ ξύμμαχοι μέχρι μὲν τοῦ ἰσθμοῦ
ἦλθον ὡς ἐς τὴν Ἀττικὴν ἐσβαλοῦντες, Ἄγιδος
τοῦ Ἀρχιδάμου ἡγουμένου, Λακεδαιμονίων βασιλέως, σεισμῶν δὲ γενομένων πολλῶν ἀπετράποντο
2 πάλιν καὶ οὐκ ἐγένετο ἐσβολή. καὶ περὶ τούτους
τοὺς χρόνους, τῶν σεισμῶν κατεχόντων, τῆς
Εὐβοίας ἐν Ὀροβίαις ἡ θάλασσα ἐπανελθοῦσα
ἀπὸ τῆς τότε οὔσης γῆς καὶ κυματωθεῖσα ἐπῆλθε
τῆς πόλεως μέρος τι, καὶ τὸ μὲν κατέκλυσε, τὸ δ'
ὑπενόστησε, καὶ θάλασσα νῦν ἐστι πρότερον οὖσα

---

[1] Strabo names three more, modern geographers eleven or
twelve. Strongyle, the modern Stromboli, seat of an active

ships against the islands of Aeolus, as they are called; for it was impossible to invade them in the summer time on account of the lack of water there. These islands are occupied by the Liparaeans, who are colonists of the Cnidians. They have their homes on one of the islands, which is not large, called Lipara, and from this go out and cultivate the rest, namely Didyme, Strongyle and Hiera.[1] The people of this region believe that Hephaestus has his forge in Hiera, because this island is seen to send up a great flame of fire at night and smoke by day. The islands lie over against the territory of the Sicels and the Messenians, and were in alliance with the Syracusans; the Athenians, therefore, laid waste their land, but since the inhabitants would not come over to their side they sailed back to Rhegium. And the winter ended, and with it the fifth year of this war of which Thucydides wrote the history.

LXXXIX. In the following summer the Pelopon- 426 B.C.
nesians and their allies, led by Agis son of Archidamus, king of the Lacedaemonians, advanced as far as the Isthmus with the intention of invading Attica; but a great many earthquakes occurred, causing them to turn back again, and no invasion took place. At about the same time, while the earthquakes prevailed, the sea at Orobiae in Euboea receded from what was then the shore-line, and then coming on in a great wave overran a portion of the city. One part of the flood subsided, but another engulfed the shore, so that what was land before is

volcano, has recently become especially notable on account of its nearness to Messina and Reggio, where the great earthquake occurred, Dec. 28, 1908.

γῇ· καὶ ἀνθρώπους διέφθειρεν ὅσοι μὴ ἐδύναντο
3 φθῆναι πρὸς τὰ μετέωρα ἀναδραμόντες. καὶ
περὶ Ἀταλάντην τὴν ἐπὶ Λοκροῖς τοῖς Ὀπουντίοις
νῆσον παραπλησία γίγνεται ἐπίκλυσις, καὶ τοῦ
τε φρουρίου τῶν Ἀθηναίων παρεῖλε καὶ δύο νεῶν
4 ἀνειλκυσμένων τὴν ἑτέραν κατέαξεν. ἐγένετο δὲ
καὶ ἐν Πεπαρήθῳ κύματος ἐπαναχώρησίς τις, οὐ
μέντοι ἐπέκλυσέ γε· καὶ σεισμὸς τοῦ τείχους τι
κατέβαλε καὶ τὸ πρυτανεῖον καὶ ἄλλας οἰκίας
5 ὀλίγας. αἴτιον δ' ἔγωγε νομίζω τοῦ τοιούτου,
ᾗ ἰσχυρότατος ὁ σεισμὸς ἐγένετο, κατὰ τοῦτο
ἀποστέλλειν τε τὴν θάλασσαν καὶ ἐξαπίνης πάλιν
ἐπισπωμένην[1] βιαιότερον τὴν ἐπίκλυσιν ποιεῖν·
ἄνευ δὲ σεισμοῦ οὐκ ἄν μοι δοκεῖ τὸ τοιοῦτο
ξυμβῆναι γενέσθαι.

XC. Τοῦ δ' αὐτοῦ θέρους ἐπολέμουν μὲν καὶ
ἄλλοι, ὡς ἑκάστοις ξυνέβαινεν, ἐν τῇ Σικελίᾳ καὶ
αὐτοὶ οἱ Σικελιῶται ἐπ' ἀλλήλους στρατεύοντες
καὶ οἱ Ἀθηναῖοι ξὺν τοῖς σφετέροις ξυμμάχοις·
ἃ δὲ λόγου μάλιστα ἄξια ἢ μετὰ τῶν Ἀθηναίων
οἱ ξύμμαχοι ἔπραξαν ἢ πρὸς τοὺς Ἀθηναίους
2 οἱ ἀντιπόλεμοι, τούτων μνησθήσομαι. Χαροιάδου
γὰρ ἤδη τοῦ Ἀθηναίων στρατηγοῦ τεθνηκότος
ὑπὸ Συρακοσίων πολέμῳ, Λάχης ἅπασαν ἔχων
τῶν νεῶν τὴν ἀρχὴν ἐστράτευσε μετὰ τῶν ξυμμάχων ἐπὶ Μύλας τὰς Μεσσηνίων. ἔτυχον δὲ

[1] Madvig reads ἐπισπώμενον, after Schol., followed by
Hude.

---

[1] cf. II. xxxii.
[2] "Thucydides is pointing out the connection between the
earthquake and the inundation. Where the earthquake was
most violent, there the inundation was greatest. But the

now sea; and it destroyed of the people as many
as could not run up to the high ground in time.
In the neighbourhood also of the island of Atalante,
which lies off the coast of Opuntian Locris, there
was a similar inundation, which carried away a part
of the Athenian fort there,[1] and wrecked one of
two ships which had been drawn up on the shore.
At Peparethos likewise there was a recession of the
waters, but no inundation; and there was an earthquake, which threw down a part of the wall as well
as the prytaneum and a few other houses.   And the
cause of such a phenomenon, in my own opinion, was
this: at that point where the shock of the earthquake
was greatest the sea was driven back, then, suddenly
returning [2] with increased violence, made the inundation; but without an earthquake, it seems to me, such a
thing would not have happened,

XC. During the same summer war was being waged
in Sicily, not only by other peoples as they each had
occasion to do so, but also by the Siceliots themselves, who were campaigning against one another,
and likewise by the Athenians in concert with their
allies; but I shall mention only the most memorable
things done by the Athenians in concert with their
allies, or against the Athenians by their opponents.
After Charoeades, the Athenian general, had been
slain in battle by the Syracusans, Laches, being now
in sole command of the fleet, made an expedition
with the allies against Mylae, a town belonging to
the Messenians.   It so happened that two divisions

---

effect was indirect, being immediately caused by the recoil
of the sea after the earthquake was over ; hence τὴν θάλασσαν, and not, as we might expect, τὸν σεισμόν, is the subject
of ποιεῖν.   ἀποστέλλειν either active or neuter." (Jowett.)

δύο φυλαὶ ἐν ταῖς Μύλαις τῶν Μεσσηνίων φρου-
ροῦσαι καί τινα καὶ ἐνέδραν πεποιημέναι τοῖς ἀπὸ
3 τῶν νεῶν. οἱ δὲ Ἀθηναῖοι καὶ οἱ ξύμμαχοι τούς
τε ἐκ τῆς ἐνέδρας τρέπουσι καὶ διαφθείρουσι
πολλούς, καὶ τῷ ἐρύματι προσβαλόντες ἠνάγκασαν ὁμολογίᾳ τήν τε ἀκρόπολιν παραδοῦναι καὶ
4 ἐπὶ Μεσσήνην ξυστρατεῦσαι. καὶ μετὰ τοῦτο
ἐπελθόντων οἱ Μεσσήνιοι τῶν τε Ἀθηναίων καὶ
τῶν ξυμμάχων προσεχώρησαν καὶ αὐτοί, ὁμήρους
τε δόντες καὶ τὰ ἄλλα πιστὰ παρασχόμενοι.

XCI. Τοῦ δ' αὐτοῦ θέρους οἱ Ἀθηναῖοι τριάκοντα μὲν ναῦς ἔστειλαν περὶ Πελοπόννησον, ὧν
ἐστρατήγει Δημοσθένης τε ὁ Ἀλκισθένους καὶ
Προκλῆς ὁ Θεοδώρου, ἑξήκοντα δὲ ἐς Μῆλον καὶ
δισχιλίους ὁπλίτας, ἐστρατήγει δὲ αὐτῶν Νικίας
2 ὁ Νικηράτου. τοὺς γὰρ Μηλίους ὄντας νησιώτας
καὶ οὐκ ἐθέλοντας ὑπακούειν οὐδὲ ἐς τὸ αὑτῶν
3 ξυμμαχικὸν ἰέναι ἐβούλοντο προσαγαγέσθαι. ὡς
δὲ αὐτοῖς δῃουμένης τῆς γῆς οὐ προσεχώρουν,
ἄραντες ἐκ τῆς Μήλου αὐτοὶ μὲν ἔπλευσαν ἐς
Ὠρωπὸν τῆς Γραϊκῆς, ὑπὸ νύκτα δὲ σχόντες εὐθὺς
ἐπορεύοντο οἱ ὁπλῖται ἀπὸ τῶν νεῶν πεζῇ ἐς
4 Τάναγραν τῆς Βοιωτίας. οἱ δὲ ἐκ τῆς πόλεως
πανδημεὶ Ἀθηναῖοι, Ἱππονίκου τε τοῦ Καλλίου
στρατηγοῦντος καὶ Εὐρυμέδοντος τοῦ Θουκλέους,
5 ἀπὸ σημείου ἐς τὸ αὐτὸ κατὰ γῆν ἀπῆντων. καὶ
στρατοπεδευσάμενοι ταύτην τὴν ἡμέραν ἐν τῇ
Τανάγρᾳ ἐδῄουν καὶ ἐνηυλίσαντο. καὶ τῇ ὑστε-

of the Messenians were in garrison at Mylae, and
that these had laid an ambush against the men who
had landed from the ships. The Athenians and their
allies, however, put to rout the ambushing troops,
slaying many of them; then, assaulting the fortification, they compelled its defenders to surrender
the acropolis by agreement and march with them
against Messene. After this, on the approach of the
Athenians and their allies, the Messenians also sub-
mitted, giving hostages and offering the other
customary pledges of good faith.

XCI. That same summer the Athenians sent thirty
ships round the Peloponnesus under the command
of Demosthenes son of Alcisthenes and Procles son
of Theodorus, and sixty ships and two thousand
hoplites under the command of Nicias son of Niceratus, to Melos. For the Melians, although they were
islanders,[1] were unwilling to be subject to Athens
or even to join their alliance, and the Athenians
wished to bring them over. But when they would
not submit, even after their land had been ravaged,
the Athenians left Melos and sailed to Oropus in the
territory of Graïa, and the hoplites, landing there at
nightfall, proceeded at once by land to Tanagra in
Boeotia. There they were met by the Athenians
from the city in full force, who, under the command
of Hipponicus son of Callias and Eurymedon son of
Thucles, came overland upon a concerted signal and
joined them. And after they had made camp they
spent that day in ravaging the territory of Tanagra,
and also passed the night there. On the next day

---

[1] The Melians and Theraeans, as Laconian colonists (v.
lxxxiv. 2), alone in the Cyclades held aloof from the Athenian alliance.

ραίᾳ μάχῃ κρατήσαντες τοὺς ἐπεξελθόντας τῶν
Ταναγραίων καὶ Θηβαίων τινὰς προσβεβοηθη-
κότας καὶ ὅπλα λαβόντες καὶ τροπαῖον στήσαντες
ἀνεχώρησαν, οἱ μὲν ἐς τὴν πόλιν, οἱ δὲ ἐπὶ τὰς
6 ναῦς. καὶ παραπλεύσας ὁ Νικίας ταῖς ἑξήκοντα
ναυσὶ τῆς Λοκρίδος τὰ ἐπιθαλάσσια ἔτεμε καὶ
ἀνεχώρησεν ἐπ᾽ οἴκου.

XCII. Ὑπὸ δὲ τὸν χρόνον τοῦτον Λακεδαιμόνιοι
Ἡράκλειαν τὴν ἐν Τραχινίᾳ ἀποικίαν καθίσταντο
2 ἀπὸ τοιᾶσδε γνώμης. Μηλιῆς οἱ ξύμπαντες εἰσὶ
μὲν τρία μέρη, Παράλιοι, Ἱερῆς, Τραχίνιοι· τούτων δὲ οἱ Τραχίνιοι πολέμῳ ἐφθαρμένοι ὑπὸ
Οἰταίων ὁμόρων ὄντων, τὸ πρῶτον μελλήσαντες
Ἀθηναίοις προσθεῖναι σφᾶς αὐτούς, δείσαντες δὲ
μὴ οὐ σφίσι πιστοὶ ὦσι, πέμπουσιν ἐς Λακε-
3 δαίμονα ἑλόμενοι πρεσβευτὴν Τεισαμενόν. ξυνε-
πρεσβεύοντο δὲ αὐτοῖς καὶ Δωριῆς, ἡ μητρόπολις
τῶν Λακεδαιμονίων, τῶν αὐτῶν δεόμενοι· ὑπὸ γὰρ
4 τῶν Οἰταίων καὶ αὐτοὶ ἐφθείροντο. ἀκούσαντες
δὲ οἱ Λακεδαιμόνιοι γνώμην εἶχον τὴν ἀποικίαν
ἐκπέμπειν, τοῖς τε Τραχινίοις βουλόμενοι καὶ τοῖς
Δωριεῦσι τιμωρεῖν. καὶ ἅμα τοῦ πρὸς Ἀθηναίους
πολέμου καλῶς αὐτοῖς ἐδόκει ἡ πόλις καθίστα-
σθαι· ἐπί τε γὰρ τῇ Εὐβοίᾳ ναυτικὸν παρα-
σκευασθῆναι ἄν, ὥστ᾽ ἐκ βραχέος τὴν διάβασιν
γίγνεσθαι, τῆς τε ἐπὶ Θρᾴκης παρόδου χρησίμως
ἕξειν. τό τε ξύμπαν ὥρμηντο τὸ χωρίον κτίζειν.
5 πρῶτον μὲν οὖν ἐν Δελφοῖς τὸν θεὸν ἐπήροντο,
κελεύοντος δὲ ἐξέπεμψαν τοὺς οἰκήτορας αὐτῶν

they defeated in battle the men of Tanagra who came out against them, as well as some Thebans who had come to their aid, then taking possession of the arms of the fallen and setting up a trophy they returned, the one party to the city, the other to the ships. And Nicias sailed along the coast with his sixty ships, ravaged the seaboard of Locris, and then returned home.

XCII. It was about this time that the Lacedaemonians established Heracleia, their colony in Trachinia, with the following object in view. The people of Malia, considered as a whole, consist of three divisions, Paralians, Hiereans, and Trachinians. Of these the Trachinians, after they had been ruined in war by their neighbours the Oetaeans, at first intended to attach themselves to the Athenians, but, fearing that these might not be loyal, sent to Lacedaemon, choosing Teisamenus as their envoy. And envoys from Doris, the mother city of the Lacedaemonians, also took part in the embassy, making the same request, for they too were being ruined by the Oetaeans. After hearing their appeal, the Lacedaemonians were of the opinion that they should send out the colony, wishing to aid both the Trachinians and the Dorians. At the same time, the site of the proposed city seemed to them well adapted for carrying on the war against Athens; for a fleet could be equipped there for an attack upon Euboea and the crossing thus made from a short distance away, and the place would also be useful for expeditions along the coast towards Thrace. In short, they were eager to found the settlement. They therefore first consulted the god at Delphi, and at his bidding sent out the colonists, consisting of both Spartans and

τε καὶ τῶν περιοίκων, καὶ τῶν ἄλλων Ἑλλήνων
τὸν βουλόμενον ἐκέλευον ἕπεσθαι πλὴν Ἰώνων
καὶ Ἀχαιῶν καὶ ἔστιν ὧν ἄλλων ἐθνῶν. οἰκισταὶ
δὲ τρεῖς Λακεδαιμονίων ἡγήσαντο, Λέων καὶ
6 Ἀλκίδας καὶ Δαμάγων. καταστάντες δὲ ἐτείχισαν
τὴν πόλιν ἐκ καινῆς, ἣ νῦν Ἡράκλεια καλεῖται,
ἀπέχουσα Θερμοπυλῶν σταδίους μάλιστα τεσσαράκοντα, τῆς δὲ θαλάσσης εἴκοσι. νεώριά τε
παρεσκευάζοντο καὶ εἶρξαν τὸ κατὰ Θερμοπύλας
κατ᾽ αὐτὸ τὸ στενόν, ὅπως εὐφύλακτα αὐτοῖς
εἴη.

XCIII. Οἱ δὲ Ἀθηναῖοι τῆς πόλεως ταύτης
ξυνοικιζομένης τὸ πρῶτον ἔδεισάν τε καὶ ἐνόμισαν
ἐπὶ τῇ Εὐβοίᾳ μάλιστα καθίστασθαι, ὅτι βραχύς
ἐστιν ὁ διάπλους πρὸς τὸ Κήναιον τῆς Εὐβοίας.
ἔπειτα μέντοι παρὰ δόξαν αὐτοῖς ἀπέβη· οὐ γὰρ
2 ἐγένετο ἀπ᾽ αὐτῆς δεινὸν οὐδέν. αἴτιον δὲ ἦν· οἵ
τε Θεσσαλοὶ ἐν δυνάμει ὄντες τῶν ταύτῃ χωρίων
καὶ ὧν ἐπὶ τῇ γῇ ἐκτίζετο, φοβούμενοι μὴ σφίσι
μεγάλῃ ἰσχύι παροικῶσιν, ἔφθειρον καὶ διὰ
παντὸς ἐπολέμουν ἀνθρώποις νεοκαταστάτοις,
ἕως ἐξετρύχωσαν γενομένους τὸ πρῶτον καὶ πάνυ
πολλούς (πᾶς γάρ τις Λακεδαιμονίων οἰκιζόντων
3 θαρσαλέως ᾔει, βέβαιον νομίζων τὴν πόλιν)· οὐ
μέντοι ἥκιστα οἱ ἄρχοντες αὐτῶν τῶν Λακεδαιμονίων οἱ ἀφικνούμενοι τὰ πράγματά τε ἔφθειρον
καὶ ἐς ὀλιγανθρωπίαν κατέστησαν, ἐκφοβήσαντες

Perioeci,[1] and they invited any other Hellenes who so desired to accompany them, except Ionians and Achaeans and certain other races. The founders of the colony in charge of the expedition were three Lacedaemonians, Leon, Alcidas, and Damagon. When they had established themselves they built a new wall about the city, which is now called Heracleia, and is about forty stadia distant from Thermopylae and twenty from the sea. They then proceeded to build dockyards, and in order that the place might be easy to guard fenced off the approach on the side toward Thermopylae by a wall across the pass itself.

XCIII. As for the Athenians, while the colonists were being gathered for this city, they at first became alarmed, thinking it was being established chiefly as a menace to Euboea, because it is only a short distance across from here to Cenaeum in Euboea. Afterwards, however, the matter turned out contrary to their expectations; for no harm came from the city. And the reasons were as follows: the Thessalians, who were the paramount power in those regions and whose territory was being menaced by the settlement, fearing that their new neighbours might become very powerful, began to harry and make war continually upon the new settlers, until they finally wore them out, although they had at first been very numerous; for, since the Lacedaemonians were founding the colony, everybody came boldly, thinking the city secure. One of the principal causes, however, was that the governors sent out by the Lacedaemonians themselves ruined the undertaking and reduced the population to a handful, frightening most of the settlers away by

[1] The old inhabitants, chiefly of Achaean stock, who had been reduced to a condition of dependence (not slavery) by the Dorians.

τοὺς πολλοὺς χαλεπῶς τε καὶ ἔστιν ἃ οὐ καλῶς
ἐξηγούμενοι, ὥστε ῥᾷον ἤδη αὐτῶν οἱ πρόσοικοι
ἐπεκράτουν.

XCIV. Τοῦ δ' αὐτοῦ θέρους, καὶ περὶ τὸν αὐτὸν
χρόνον ὃν ἐν τῇ Μήλῳ οἱ Ἀθηναῖοι κατείχοντο,
καὶ οἱ ἀπὸ τῶν τριάκοντα νεῶν Ἀθηναῖοι περὶ
Πελοπόννησον ὄντες πρῶτον ἐν Ἑλλομενῷ τῆς
Λευκαδίας φρουρούς τινας λοχήσαντες διέφθειραν, ἔπειτα ὕστερον ἐπὶ Λευκάδα μείζονι στόλῳ
ἦλθον, Ἀκαρνᾶσί τε πᾶσιν, οἳ πανδημεὶ πλὴν
Οἰνιαδῶν ξυνέσποντο, καὶ Ζακυνθίοις καὶ Κεφαλλῆσι καὶ Κερκυραίων πέντε καὶ δέκα ναυσίν.
2 καὶ οἱ μὲν Λευκάδιοι, τῆς τε ἔξω γῆς δῃουμένης
καὶ τῆς ἐντὸς τοῦ ἰσθμοῦ, ἐν ᾗ καὶ ἡ Λευκάς ἐστι
καὶ τὸ ἱερὸν τοῦ Ἀπόλλωνος, πλήθει βιαζόμενοι
ἡσύχαζον· οἱ δὲ Ἀκαρνᾶνες ἠξίουν Δημοσθένη
τὸν στρατηγὸν τῶν Ἀθηναίων ἀποτειχίζειν αὐτούς, νομίζοντες ῥᾳδίως γ' ἂν ἐκπολιορκῆσαι καὶ
3 πόλεως αἰεὶ σφίσι πολεμίας ἀπαλλαγῆναι. Δημοσθένης δ' ἀναπείθεται κατὰ τὸν χρόνον τοῦτον
ὑπὸ Μεσσηνίων ὡς καλὸν αὐτῷ στρατιᾶς τοσαύ-
της ξυνειλεγμένης Αἰτωλοῖς ἐπιθέσθαι, Ναυπάκτῳ τε πολεμίοις οὖσι, καὶ ἢν κρατήσῃ αὐτῶν,
ῥᾳδίως καὶ τὸ ἄλλο ἠπειρωτικὸν τὸ ταύτῃ Ἀθη-
4 ναίοις προσποιήσειν. τὸ γὰρ ἔθνος μέγα μὲν

---

[1] This isthmus, which at this time connected the island
with the mainland, had been previously cut through by the
Corinthians (Strabo, p. 452 c) ; but it had been filled with

their harsh and sometimes unjust administration, so that at length their neighbours more easily prevailed over them.

XCIV. During the same summer, and at about the time when the Athenians were detained at Melos, the troops of the thirty Athenian ships that were cruising round the Peloponnesus first set an ambush at Ellomenus in Leucadia and killed some of the garrison, and then, later on, went against Leucas with a greater armament, which consisted of all the Acarnanians, who joined the expedition with their entire forces (with the exception of the people of Oeniadae), some Zacynthians and Cephallenians, and fifteen ships from Corcyra. The Leucadians, finding themselves outnumbered, were obliged to remain quiet, although their lands were being ravaged both without and within the isthmus,[1] where stands Leucas and the temple of Apollo; but the Acarnanians tried to induce Demosthenes, the Athenian general, to shut them in by a wall, thinking they could easily reduce them by siege and thus rid themselves of a city that was always hostile to them. But just at this time Demosthenes was persuaded by the Messenians that it was a fine opportunity for him, seeing that so large an army was collected, to attack the Aetolians, because they were hostile to Naupactus, and also because, if he defeated them, he would find it easy to bring the rest of the mainland in that region into subjection to the Athenians. The Aetolians, they explained, were, it was true, a great and warlike

---

sand before the Peloponnesian war, as is evident from constant allusions to hauling ships across. It is clear from the context that the territory of the Leucadians included a part of the mainland of Acarnania.

εἶναι τὸ τῶν Αἰτωλῶν καὶ μάχιμον, οἰκοῦν δὲ
κατὰ κώμας ἀτειχίστους, καὶ ταύτας διὰ πολλοῦ,
καὶ σκευῇ ψιλῇ χρώμενον οὐ χαλεπὸν ἀπέφαινον,
5 πρὶν ξυμβοηθῆσαι, καταστραφῆναι. ἐπιχειρεῖν
δ᾽ ἐκέλευον πρῶτον μὲν Ἀποδωτοῖς, ἔπειτα δὲ
Ὀφιονεῦσι, καὶ μετὰ τούτους Εὐρυτᾶσιν, ὅπερ
μέγιστον μέρος ἐστὶ τῶν Αἰτωλῶν, ἀγνωστότατοι
δὲ γλῶσσαν καὶ ὠμοφάγοι εἰσίν, ὡς λέγονται.
τούτων γὰρ ληφθέντων ῥᾳδίως καὶ τἆλλα προσ-
χωρήσειν.

XCV. Ὁ δὲ τῶν Μεσσηνίων χάριτι πεισθεὶς
καὶ μάλιστα νομίσας ἄνευ τῆς τῶν Ἀθηναίων
δυνάμεως τοῖς ἠπειρώταις ξυμμάχοις μετὰ τῶν
Αἰτωλῶν δύνασθαι ἂν κατὰ γῆν ἐλθεῖν ἐπὶ Βοιωτοὺς διὰ Λοκρῶν τῶν Ὀζολῶν ἐς Κυτίνιον τὸ
Δωρικόν, ἐν δεξιᾷ ἔχων τὸν Παρνασσόν, ἕως
καταβαίη ἐς Φωκέας, οἳ προθύμως ἐδόκουν κατὰ
τὴν Ἀθηναίων αἰεί ποτε φιλίαν ξυστρατεύσειν ἢ
κἂν βίᾳ προσαχθῆναι (καὶ Φωκεῦσιν ἤδη ὅμορος
ἡ Βοιωτία ἐστίν), ἄρας οὖν ξύμπαντι τῷ στρατεύματι ἀπὸ τῆς Λευκάδος ἀκόντων τῶν Ἀκαρνάνων
2 παρέπλευσεν ἐς Σόλλιον. κοινώσας δὲ τὴν ἐπίνοιαν τοῖς Ἀκαρνᾶσιν, ὡς οὐ προσεδέξαντο διὰ
τῆς Λευκάδος τὴν οὐ περιτείχισιν, αὐτὸς τῇ λοιπῇ
στρατιᾷ, Κεφαλλῆσι καὶ Μεσσηνίοις καὶ Ζακυνθίοις καὶ Ἀθηναίων τριακοσίοις τοῖς ἐπιβάταις
τῶν σφετέρων νεῶν (αἱ γὰρ πέντε καὶ δέκα τῶν

people, but as they lived in unwalled villages, which, moreover, were widely separated, and as they used only light armour, they could be subdued without difficulty before they could unite for mutual defence. And they advised him to attack the Apodotians first, then the Ophioneans, and after them the Eurytanians. These last constitute the largest division of the Aetolians, their speech is more unintelligible than that of the other Aetolians, and, according to report, they are eaters of raw flesh. If these tribes were subdued, they said, the rest would readily yield.

XCV. Demosthenes was induced to make this decision, not only by his desire to please the Messenians, but chiefly because he thought that, without help from Athens, he would be able with his allies from the mainland, once the Aetolians had joined him, to make an overland expedition against the Boeotians by passing through the country of the Ozolian Locrians to Cytinium in Doris, keeping Parnassus on the right, until he should descend into Phocian territory. The Phocians would presumably be eager to join the expedition in view of their traditional friendship with Athens, or else could be forced to do so; and Phocis is on the very borders of Boeotia. So he set sail from Leucas with his whole armament in spite of the unwillingness of the Acarnanians and went along the coast to Sollium. There he made his plan known to the Acarnanians, but they would not agree to it because of his refusal to invest Leucas; he therefore set out upon his expedition against the Aetolians without them, taking the rest of his army, which consisted of Cephallenians, Messenians, Zacynthians, and three hundred Athenian marines from his own ships—for

Κερκυραίων ἀπῆλθον νῆες), ἐστράτευσεν ἐπ'
3 Αἰτωλούς. ὡρμᾶτο δὲ ἐξ Οἰνεῶνος τῆς Λοκρίδος.
οἱ δὲ Ὀζόλαι οὗτοι Λοκροὶ ξύμμαχοι ἦσαν, καὶ
ἔδει αὐτοὺς πανστρατιᾷ ἀπαντῆσαι τοῖς Ἀθηναίοις ἐς τὴν μεσόγειαν· ὄντες γὰρ ὅμοροι τοῖς
Αἰτωλοῖς καὶ ὁμόσκευοι μεγάλη ὠφελία ἐδόκουν
εἶναι ξυστρατεύοντες μάχης τε ἐμπειρίᾳ τῆς ἐκείνων καὶ χωρίων.

XCVI. Αὐλισάμενος δὲ τῷ στρατῷ ἐν τοῦ
Διὸς τοῦ Νεμείου τῷ ἱερῷ, ἐν ᾧ Ἡσίοδος ὁ ποιη-
τὴς λέγεται ὑπὸ τῶν ταύτῃ ἀποθανεῖν, χρησθὲν
αὐτῷ ἐν Νεμέᾳ τοῦτο παθεῖν, ἅμα τῇ ἔῳ ἄρας
2 ἐπορεύετο ἐς τὴν Αἰτωλίαν. καὶ αἱρεῖ τῇ πρώτῃ
ἡμέρᾳ Ποτιδανίαν καὶ τῇ δευτέρᾳ Κροκύλειον καὶ
τῇ τρίτῃ Τείχιον, ἔμενέ τε αὐτοῦ καὶ τὴν λείαν ἐς
Εὐπάλιον τῆς Λοκρίδος ἀπέπεμψεν· τὴν γὰρ γνώμην εἶχε τὰ ἄλλα καταστρεψάμενος οὕτως ἐπὶ
Ὀφιονέας, εἰ μὴ βούλοιντο ξυγχωρεῖν, ἐς Ναύ-
3 πακτον ἐπαναχωρήσας στρατεῦσαι ὕστερον. τοὺς
δὲ Αἰτωλοὺς οὐκ ἐλάνθανεν αὕτη ἡ παρασκευὴ
οὔτε ὅτε τὸ πρῶτον ἐπεβουλεύετο, ἐπειδή τε ὁ
στρατὸς ἐσεβεβλήκει, πολλῇ χειρὶ ἐπεβοήθουν
πάντες, ὥστε καὶ οἱ ἔσχατοι Ὀφιονέων οἱ πρὸς
τὸν Μηλιακὸν κόλπον καθήκοντες, Βωμιῆς καὶ
Καλλιῆς, ἐβοήθησαν.

XCVII. Τῷ δὲ Δημοσθένει τοιόνδε τι οἱ Μεσσήνιοι παρήνουν, ὅπερ καὶ τὸ πρῶτον· ἀναδιδά-
σκοντες αὐτὸν τῶν Αἰτωλῶν ὡς εἴη ῥᾳδία ἡ

the fifteen Corcyraean ships had gone back home. The base from which he started was Oeneon in Locris. The people of this country, Ozolian Locris, were allies, and they with their whole force were to meet the Athenians in the interior; for since they were neighbours of the Aetolians and used the same sort of arms, it was believed that their help would be of great service on the expedition on account of their knowledge both of the Aetolian manner of fighting and of the country.

XCVI. He bivouacked with his army in the precinct of Nemean Zeus, where the poet Hesiod[1] is said to have been killed by the men of that region, an oracle having foretold to him that he should suffer this fate at Nemea; then he set out at daybreak for Aetolia. On the first day he took Potidania, on the second Crocyleum, on the third Teichium. There he remained, sending his booty back to Eupalium in Locris; for his intention was to subdue the other places first, and then, in case the Ophioneans would not submit, to return to Naupactus and make a second expedition against them. But all these preparations did not escape the notice of the Aetolians, either when the design was first being formed or afterwards; indeed his army had no sooner invaded their country than they all began to rally in great force, so that help came even from the remotest tribes of the Ophioneans, who stretch as far as the Maliac Gulf, and from the Bomians and Callians.

XCVII. The Messenians, however, gave Demosthenes about the same advice as at first: informing him that the conquest of the Aetolians was easy,

---

[1] For the particulars of the tradition, cf. Plut. *Sept. Sap. Conv.* xix.

αἵρεσις, ἰέναι ἐκέλευον ὅτι τάχιστα ἐπὶ τὰς κώμας καὶ μὴ μένειν ἕως ἂν ξύμπαντες ἀθροισθέντες
ἀντιτάξωνται, τὴν δ᾽ ἐν ποσὶν αἰεὶ πειρᾶσθαι
2 αἱρεῖν. ὁ δὲ τούτοις τε πεισθεὶς καὶ τῇ τύχῃ
ἐλπίσας, ὅτι οὐδὲν αὐτῷ ἠναντιοῦτο, τοὺς Λοκροὺς οὐκ ἀναμείνας οὓς αὐτῷ ἔδει προσβοηθῆσαι
(ψιλῶν γὰρ ἀκοντιστῶν ἐνδεὴς ἦν μάλιστα) ἐχώρει ἐπὶ Αἰγιτίου, καὶ κατὰ κράτος αἱρεῖ ἐπιών.
ὑπέφευγον γὰρ οἱ ἄνθρωποι καὶ ἐκάθηντο ἐπὶ τῶν
λόφων τῶν ὑπὲρ τῆς πόλεως· ἦν γὰρ ἐφ᾽ ὑψηλῶν
χωρίων ἀπέχουσα τῆς θαλάσσης ὀγδοήκοντα
3 σταδίους μάλιστα. οἱ δὲ Αἰτωλοί (βεβοηθηκότες
γὰρ ἤδη ἦσαν ἐπὶ τὸ Αἰγίτιον) προσέβαλλον τοῖς
Ἀθηναίοις καὶ τοῖς ξυμμάχοις καταθέοντες ἀπὸ
τῶν λόφων ἄλλοι ἄλλοθεν καὶ ἐσηκόντιζον, καὶ
ὅτε μὲν ἐπίοι τὸ τῶν Ἀθηναίων στρατόπεδον,
ὑπεχώρουν, ἀναχωροῦσι δὲ ἐπέκειντο· καὶ ἦν ἐπὶ
πολὺ τοιαύτη ἡ μάχη, διώξεις τε καὶ ὑπαγωγαί,
ἐν οἷς ἀμφοτέροις ἥσσους ἦσαν οἱ Ἀθηναῖοι.

XCVIII. Μέχρι μὲν οὖν οἱ τοξόται εἶχόν τε τὰ
βέλη αὐτοῖς καὶ οἷοί τε ἦσαν χρῆσθαι, οἱ δὲ
ἀντεῖχον (τοξευόμενοι γὰρ οἱ Αἰτωλοί, ἄνθρωποι
ψιλοί, ἀνεστέλλοντο)· ἐπειδὴ δὲ τοῦ τε τοξάρχου
ἀποθανόντος οὗτοι διεσκεδάσθησαν καὶ αὐτοὶ
ἐκεκμήκεσαν καὶ ἐπὶ πολὺ τῷ αὐτῷ πόνῳ ξυνε-
χόμενοι, οἵ τε Αἰτωλοὶ ἐνέκειντο καὶ ἐσηκόντιζον,
οὕτω δὴ τραπόμενοι ἔφευγον, καὶ ἐσπίπτοντες ἔς
τε χαράδρας ἀνεκβάτους καὶ χωρία ὧν οὐκ ἦσαν

they urged him to proceed as quickly as possible against the villages, not waiting until they should all unite and array themselves against him, but trying to take the first village in his way. Yielding to their advice and being hopeful because of his good fortune, since he was meeting with no opposition, he did not wait for the Locrians, who were to have brought him reinforcements—for he was greatly in need of light-armed men that were javelin-throwers—but advanced against Aegitium and took it by storm at the first onset. For the inhabitants secretly fled and took post on the hills above the city, which stood on high ground about eighty stadia from the sea. But the Aetolians, who by this time had come to the rescue of Aegitium, attacked the Athenians and their allies, running down from the hills on every side and showering javelins upon them, then retreating whenever the Athenian army advanced and advancing whenever they retreated. Indeed, the battle continued for a long time in this fashion, alternate pursuits and retreats, and in both the Athenians had the worst of it.

XCVIII. Now so long as their bowmen had arrows and were able to use them the Athenians held out, for the Aetolian troops were light-armed and so, while they were exposed to the arrows, they were constantly driven back. But when the captain of the archers had been killed and his men scattered, and the hoplites were worn out, since they had been engaged for a long time in the unremitting struggle and the Aetolians were pressing them hard and hurling javelins upon them, they at last turned and fled, and falling into ravines from which there was no way out and into places with which they were unacquainted,

ἔμπειροι διεφθείροντο· καὶ γὰρ ὁ ἡγεμὼν αὐτοῖς
τῶν ὁδῶν Χρόμων ὁ Μεσσήνιος ἐτύγχανε τεθνη-
2 κώς. οἱ δὲ Αἰτωλοὶ ἐσακοντίζοντες πολλοὺς μὲν
αὐτοῦ ἐν τῇ τροπῇ κατὰ πόδας αἱροῦντες, ἄνθρωποι ποδώκεις καὶ ψιλοί, διέφθειρον, τοὺς δὲ
πλείους τῶν ὁδῶν ἁμαρτάνοντας καὶ ἐς τὴν ὕλην
ἐσφερομένους, ὅθεν διέξοδοι οὐκ ἦσαν, πῦρ κομι-
3 σάμενοι περιεπίμπρασαν· πᾶσά τε ἰδέα κατέστη
τῆς φυγῆς καὶ τοῦ ὀλέθρου τῷ στρατοπέδῳ τῶν
Ἀθηναίων, μόλις τε ἐπὶ τὴν θάλασσαν καὶ τὸν
Οἰνεῶνα τῆς Λοκρίδος, ὅθενπερ καὶ ὡρμήθησαν,
4 οἱ περιγενόμενοι κατέφυγον. ἀπέθανον δὲ τῶν τε
ξυμμάχων πολλοὶ καὶ αὐτῶν Ἀθηναίων ὁπλῖται
περὶ εἴκοσι μάλιστα καὶ ἑκατόν. τοσοῦτοι μὲν
τὸ πλῆθος καὶ ἡλικία ἡ αὐτὴ[1] οὗτοι βέλτιστοι δὴ
ἄνδρες ἐν τῷ πολέμῳ τῷδε ἐκ τῆς Ἀθηναίων
πόλεως διεφθάρησαν· ἀπέθανε δὲ καὶ ὁ ἕτερος
5 στρατηγὸς Προκλῆς. τοὺς δὲ νεκροὺς ὑποσπόνδους ἀνελόμενοι παρὰ τῶν Αἰτωλῶν καὶ ἀναχωρήσαντες ἐς Ναύπακτον ὕστερον ἐς τὰς Ἀθήνας
ταῖς ναυσὶν ἐκομίσθησαν. Δημοσθένης δὲ περὶ
Ναύπακτον καὶ τὰ χωρία ταῦτα ὑπελείφθη τοῖς
πεπραγμένοις φοβούμενος τοὺς Ἀθηναίους.

XCIX. Κατὰ δὲ τοὺς αὐτοὺς χρόνους καὶ οἱ
περὶ Σικελίαν Ἀθηναῖοι πλεύσαντες ἐς τὴν Λοκρίδα ἐν ἀποβάσει τέ τινι τοὺς προσβοηθήσαντας
Λοκρῶν ἐκράτησαν καὶ περιπόλιον αἱροῦσιν ὃ ἦν
ἐπὶ τῷ Ἄληκι ποταμῷ.

C. Τοῦ δ᾿ αὐτοῦ θέρους Αἰτωλοὶ προπέμψαντες
πρότερον ἔς τε Κόρινθον καὶ ἐς Λακεδαίμονα
πρέσβεις, Τόλοφόν τε τὸν Ὀφιονέα καὶ Βοριάδην

---

[1] ἡ αὐτή, Hude ἡ ῥύτη.

they perished; for Chromon, the Messenian, who had been their guide on the way, had unfortunately been killed. The Aetolians kept plying their javelins, and being swift of foot and lightly equipped, following at their heels they caught many there in the rout and slew them; but the greater number missed the roads and got into the forest, from which there were no paths out, and the Aetolians brought fire and set the woods ablaze around them. Then every manner of flight was essayed and every manner of destruction befell the army of the Athenians, and it was only with difficulty that the survivors escaped to the sea at Oeneon in Locris, whence they had set out. Many of the allies were slain, and of the Athenians themselves about one hundred and twenty hoplites. So great a number of men, and all of the same age, perished here, the best men in truth whom the city of Athens lost in this war; and Procles, one of the two generals, perished also. When they had received back their dead from the Aetolians under a truce and had retreated to Naupactus, they were afterwards taken back by the fleet to Athens. Demosthenes, however, remained behind in Naupactus and the region round about, for he was afraid of the Athenians because of what had happened.

XCIX. About the same time the Athenian forces over in Sicily sailed to Locris[1] and disembarking there defeated the Locrians who came against them and took a guard-house which was situated on the river Halex.

C. During the same summer the Aetolians, who had previously sent three envoys to Corinth and Lacedaemon, namely Tolophus the Ophionean, Boriades

[1] *i.e.* the territory of the Epizephyrian Locri, north of Rhegium in Italy.

τὸν Εὐρυτᾶνα καὶ Τείσανδρον τὸν ᾿Αποδωτόν,
πείθουσιν ὥστε σφίσι πέμψαι στρατιὰν ἐπὶ Ναύ-
2 πακτον διὰ τὴν τῶν ᾿Αθηναίων ἐπαγωγήν. καὶ
ἐξέπεμψαν Λακεδαιμόνιοι περὶ τὸ φθινόπωρον
τρισχιλίους ὁπλίτας τῶν ξυμμάχων. τούτων
ἦσαν πεντακόσιοι ἐξ ῾Ηρακλείας, τῆς ἐν Τραχῖνι
πόλεως τότε νεοκτίστου οὔσης· Σπαρτιάτης δ᾿
ἦρχεν Εὐρύλοχος τῆς στρατιᾶς, καὶ ξυνηκολού-
θουν αὐτῷ Μακάριος καὶ Μενεδάϊος οἱ Σπαρτιᾶται. CI. ξυλλεγέντος δὲ τοῦ στρατεύματος
ἐς Δελφοὺς ἐπεκηρυκεύετο Εὐρύλοχος Λοκροῖς
τοῖς ᾿Οζόλαις· διὰ τούτων γὰρ ἡ ὁδὸς ἦν ἐς Ναύπακτον, καὶ ἅμα τῶν ᾿Αθηναίων ἐβούλετο ἀπο-
2 στῆσαι αὐτούς. ξυνέπρασσον δὲ μάλιστα αὐτῷ
τῶν Λοκρῶν ᾿Αμφισσῆς διὰ τὸ τῶν Φωκέων
ἔχθος δεδιότες· καὶ αὐτοὶ πρῶτοι δόντες ὁμήρους
καὶ τοὺς ἄλλους ἔπεισαν δοῦναι φοβουμένους τὸν
ἐπιόντα στρατόν, πρῶτον μὲν οὖν τοὺς ὁμόρους
αὐτοῖς Μυονέας (ταύτῃ γὰρ δυσεσβολώτατος ἡ
Λοκρίς), ἔπειτα ᾿Ιπνέας καὶ Μεσσαπίους καὶ
Τριταιέας καὶ Χαλαίους· καὶ Τολοφωνίους καὶ
῾Ησσίους καὶ Οἰανθέας. οὗτοι καὶ ξυνεστράτευον
πάντες. ᾿Ολπαῖοι δὲ ὁμήρους μὲν ἔδοσαν, ἠκολούθουν δὲ οὔ· καὶ ῾Υαῖοι οὐκ ἔδοσαν ὁμήρους πρὶν
αὐτῶν εἶλον κώμην Πόλιν ὄνομα ἔχουσαν.
CII. ᾿Επειδὴ δὲ παρεσκεύαστο πάντα καὶ τοὺς
ὁμήρους κατέθετο ἐς Κυτίνιον τὸ Δωρικόν, ἐχώρει
τῷ στρατῷ ἐπὶ τὴν Ναύπακτον διὰ τῶν Λοκρῶν,
καὶ πορευόμενος Οἰνεῶνα αἱρεῖ αὐτῶν καὶ Εὐ-
2 πάλιον· οὐ γὰρ προσεχώρησαν. γενόμενοι δ᾿ ἐν
τῇ Ναυπακτίᾳ καὶ οἱ Αἰτωλοὶ ἅμα ἤδη προσβε-

the Eurytanian, and Teisander the Apodotian, urged them to send an army against Naupactus because this city had brought the Athenians against them. So towards autumn the Lacedaemonians sent three thousand hoplites of their allies, among whom were six hundred from Heracleia, the city which had recently been founded in Trachis. The commander of the expedition was Eurylochus a Spartan, who was accompanied by the Spartans Macarius and Menedaïus, CI. And when the army was collected at Delphi, Eurylochus sent a herald to the Ozolian Locrians; for the road to Naupactus lay through their territory, and he also wished to induce them to revolt from Athens. Of the Locrians the people of Amphissa co-operated with him chiefly, these being afraid on account of their enmity to the Phocians; and after these had taken the lead in giving him hostages they persuaded the rest, who were afraid of the invading army, to do likewise—first their neighbours the Myoneans, who held the country from which Locris was most difficult of access, then the Ipneans, Messapians, Tritaeeans, Chalaeans, Tolophonians, Hessians and Oeantheans. All these tribes also took part in the expedition. The Olpaeans gave hostages, but did not take the field with the others; and the Hyaeans refused to give hostages until a village of theirs, Polis by name, was taken.

CII. When all preparations had been made, and the hostages had been deposited at Cytinium in Doris, Eurylochus advanced with his army against Naupactus through the Locrian territory, taking on his march two of their towns, Oeneon and Eupalium, which refused to yield. And when they reached the territory of Naupactus, the Aetolians meanwhile

βοηθηκότες, ἐδῄουν τὴν γῆν καὶ τὸ προάστειον
ἀτείχιστον ὂν εἷλον· ἐπί τε Μολύκρειον ἐλθόντες,
τὴν Κορινθίων μὲν ἀποικίαν, Ἀθηναίων δὲ ὑπή-
3 κοον, αἱροῦσιν. Δημοσθένης δὲ ὁ Ἀθηναῖος (ἔτι
γὰρ ἐτύγχανεν ὢν μετὰ τὰ ἐκ τῆς Αἰτωλίας περὶ
Ναύπακτον) προαισθόμενος τοῦ στρατοῦ καὶ
δείσας περὶ αὐτῆς, ἐλθὼν πείθει Ἀκαρνᾶνας,
χαλεπῶς διὰ τὴν ἐκ τῆς Λευκάδος ἀναχώρησιν,
4 βοηθῆσαι Ναυπάκτῳ. καὶ πέμπουσι μετ' αὐτοῦ
ἐπὶ τῶν νεῶν χιλίους ὁπλίτας, οἳ ἐσελθόντες
περιεποίησαν τὸ χωρίον· δεινὸν γὰρ ἦν μή, μεγάλου ὄντος τοῦ τείχους, ὀλίγων δὲ τῶν ἀμυνομένων,
5 οὐκ ἀντίσχωσιν. Εὐρύλοχος δὲ καὶ οἱ μετ' αὐτοῦ
ὡς ᾔσθοντο τὴν στρατιὰν ἐσεληλυθυῖαν καὶ ἀδύνατον ὂν τὴν πόλιν βίᾳ ἑλεῖν, ἀνεχώρησαν οὐκ
ἐπὶ Πελοποννήσου, ἀλλ' ἐς τὴν Αἰολίδα τὴν νῦν
καλουμένην, Καλυδῶνα καὶ Πλευρῶνα καὶ ἐς τὰ
ταύτῃ χωρία, καὶ ἐς Πρόσχιον τῆς Αἰτωλίας.
6 οἱ γὰρ Ἀμπρακιῶται ἐλθόντες πρὸς αὐτοὺς πείθουσιν ὥστε μετὰ σφῶν Ἄργει τε τῷ Ἀμφιλο-
χικῷ καὶ Ἀμφιλοχίᾳ τῇ ἄλλῃ ἐπιχειρῆσαι καὶ
Ἀκαρνανίᾳ ἅμα, λέγοντες ὅτι, ἢν τούτων κρα-
τήσωσι, πᾶν τὸ ἠπειρωτικὸν Λακεδαιμονίοις ξύμ-
7 μαχον καθεστήξει. καὶ ὁ μὲν Εὐρύλοχος πεισθεὶς
καὶ τοὺς Αἰτωλοὺς ἀφεὶς ἡσύχαζε τῷ στρατῷ
περὶ τοὺς χώρους τούτους, ἕως τοῖς Ἀμπρακιώταις ἐκστρατευσαμένοις περὶ τὸ Ἄργος δέοι βοηθεῖν. καὶ τὸ θέρος ἐτελεύτα.

---

[1] i.e. the fleet of the Acarnanians themselves; the thirty
Athenian ships, which Demosthenes had commanded, had

having come to their support, they ravaged the land and took the outer town, which was not fortified; and advancing against Molycreium, a colony founded by the Corinthians but subject to Athens, they took it. But Demosthenes the Athenian, who happened to have remained in the neighbourhood of Naupactus after his retreat from Aetolia, got information of the expedition, and fearing for the town went and persuaded the Acarnanians, though with difficulty on account of his withdrawal from Leucas, to come to the aid of Naupactus. And they sent with him on board the fleet [1] one thousand hoplites, who entered the place and saved it; for there was danger that they might not be able to hold out, since the walls were extensive and the defenders few in number. Eurylochus and his men, perceiving that the army had entered and that it was impossible to take the town by storm, now withdrew, not to the Peloponnesus, but to the district of Aeolis, as it is now called, to Calydon, namely, and Pleuron, and the other towns of that region, and to Proschium in Aetolia. For the Ambraciots came and urged him to join them in an attack upon Amphilochian Argos and the rest of Amphilochia, and at the same time upon Acarnania, saying that if they got control of these places all the mainland would be brought into alliance with the Lacedaemonians. Eurylochus was persuaded, and dismissing the Aetolians remained inactive, keeping his army in these regions until the Ambraciots should take the field and the time should come for him to join them in the neighbourhood of Argos. And the summer ended.

---

[1] returned to Athens (ch. xcviii. 5), while those mentioned ch. cv. 3 did not come till later.

CIII. Οἱ δ' ἐν τῇ Σικελίᾳ Ἀθηναῖοι τοῦ ἐπιγιγνομένου χειμῶνος ἐπελθόντες μετὰ τῶν Ἑλλήνων ξυμμάχων καὶ ὅσοι Σικελῶν κατὰ κράτος ἀρχόμενοι
ὑπὸ Συρακοσίων καὶ ξύμμαχοι ὄντες ἀποστάντες
αὐτοῖς [1] ξυνεπολέμουν, ἐπ' Ἴνησσαν τὸ Σικελικὸν
πόλισμα, οὗ τὴν ἀκρόπολιν Συρακόσιοι εἶχον,
προσέβαλλον, καὶ ὡς οὐκ ἐδύναντο ἑλεῖν, ἀπῆσαν.
2 ἐν δὲ τῇ ἀναχωρήσει ὑστέροις Ἀθηναίων τοῖς
ξυμμάχοις ἀναχωροῦσιν ἐπιτίθενται οἱ ἐκ τοῦ
τειχίσματος Συρακόσιοι, καὶ προσπεσόντες τρέ-
πουσί τε μέρος τι τοῦ στρατοῦ καὶ ἀπέκτειναν
3 οὐκ ὀλίγους. καὶ μετὰ τοῦτο ἀπὸ τῶν νεῶν ὁ
Λάχης καὶ οἱ Ἀθηναῖοι ἐς τὴν Λοκρίδα ἀποβάσεις
τινὰς ποιησάμενοι κατὰ τὸν Καίκινον ποταμὸν
τοὺς προσβοηθοῦντας Λοκρῶν μετὰ Προξένου τοῦ
Καπάτωνος ὡς τριακοσίους μάχῃ ἐκράτησαν καὶ
ὅπλα λαβόντες ἀπεχώρησαν.

CIV. Τοῦ δ' αὐτοῦ χειμῶνος καὶ Δῆλον ἐκά-
θηραν Ἀθηναῖοι κατὰ χρησμὸν δή τινα. ἐκάθηρε
μὲν γὰρ καὶ Πεισίστρατος ὁ τύραννος πρότερον
αὐτήν, οὐχ ἅπασαν, ἀλλ' ὅσον ἀπὸ τοῦ ἱεροῦ
ἐφεωρᾶτο τῆς νήσου· τότε δὲ πᾶσα ἐκαθάρθη
2 τοιῷδε τρόπῳ. θῆκαι ὅσαι ἦσαν τῶν τεθνεώτων
ἐν Δήλῳ, πάσας ἀνεῖλον, καὶ τὸ λοιπὸν προεῖπον
μήτε ἐναποθνῄσκειν ἐν τῇ νήσῳ μήτε ἐντίκτειν,
ἀλλ' ἐς τὴν Ῥήνειαν διακομίζεσθαι. ἀπέχει δὲ
ἡ Ῥήνεια τῆς Δήλου οὕτως ὀλίγον ὥστε Πολυ-
κράτης, ὁ Σαμίων τύραννος, ἰσχύσας τινὰ χρόνον
ναυτικῷ καὶ τῶν τε ἄλλων νήσων ἄρξας καὶ τὴν
Ῥήνειαν ἑλὼν ἀνέθηκε τῷ Ἀπόλλωνι τῷ Δηλίῳ

---

[1] ἀπὸ Συρακοσίων after αὐτοῖς, deleted by van Herwerden.

CIII. The following winter the Athenians in 426 B.C.
Sicily, with their Hellenic allies and such of the
Sicels as had been unwilling subjects and allies of
the Syracusans but had now revolted from them and
were taking sides with the Athenians, attacked the
Sicel town Inessa, the acropolis of which was held
by the Syracusans, but being unable to take it they
departed. On their retreat, however, the allies, who
were in the rear of the Athenians, were attacked by
the Syracusan garrison of the fort, who fell upon them
and put to flight part of the army, killing not a few
of them. After this Laches and the Athenians took
the fleet and made several descents upon Locris; and
at the river Caïcinus they defeated in battle about
three hundred Locrians who came out against them,
under the command of Proxenus son of Capato, took
the arms of the fallen, and returned to Rhegium.

CIV. During the same winter the Athenians purified Delos in compliance with a certain oracle. It
had been purified before by Peisistratus the tyrant,[1]
not indeed the whole of the island but that portion of
it which was visible from the temple ; but at this
time the whole of it was purified, and in the following
manner. All the sepulchres of the dead that were
in Delos they removed, and proclaimed that thereafter no one should either die or give birth to a child
on the island, but should first be carried over to
Rheneia. For Rheneia is so short a distance from
Delos that Polycrates the tyrant of Samos, who for
some time was powerful on the sea and not only
gained control of the other islands[2] but also seized
Rheneia, dedicated this island to the Delian Apollo,

[1] First tyranny 560 B.C.; death 527 B.C.
[2] The Cyclades.

ἀλύσει δήσας πρὸς τὴν Δῆλον. καὶ τὴν πεντε-
τηρίδα τότε πρῶτον μετὰ τὴν κάθαρσιν ἐποίησαν
3 οἱ Ἀθηναῖοι.[1] ἦν δέ ποτε καὶ τὸ πάλαι μεγάλη
ξύνοδος ἐς τὴν Δῆλον τῶν Ἰώνων τε καὶ περικτιό-
νων νησιωτῶν· ξύν τε γὰρ γυναιξὶ καὶ παισὶν
ἐθεώρουν, ὥσπερ νῦν ἐς τὰ Ἐφέσια Ἴωνες, καὶ
ἀγὼν ἐποιεῖτο αὐτόθι καὶ γυμνικὸς καὶ μουσικός,
4 χορούς τε ἀνῆγον αἱ πόλεις. δηλοῖ δὲ μάλιστα
Ὅμηρος ὅτι τοιαῦτα ἦν ἐν τοῖς ἔπεσι τοῖσδε, ἅ
ἐστιν ἐκ προοιμίου Ἀπόλλωνος·

ἄλλοτε[2] Δήλῳ, Φοῖβε, μάλιστά γε θυμὸν ἐτέρ-
   φθης,
ἔνθα τοι ἑλκεχίτωνες Ἰάονες ἠγερέθονται
σὺν σφοῖσιν τεκέεσσι γυναιξί τε σὴν ἐς ἄγυιαν·
ἔνθα σε πυγμαχίῃ καὶ ὀρχηστυῖ καὶ ἀοιδῇ
μνησάμενοι τέρπουσιν, ὅταν καθέσωσιν ἀγῶνα.

5 ὅτι δὲ καὶ μουσικῆς ἀγὼν ἦν καὶ ἀγωνιούμενοι
ἐφοίτων ἐν τοῖσδε αὖ δηλοῖ, ἅ ἐστιν ἐκ τοῦ αὐτοῦ
προοιμίου. τὸν γὰρ Δηλιακὸν χορὸν τῶν γυναι-

---

[1] τὰ Δήλια, after οἱ Ἀθηναῖοι, deleted by van Herwerden,
followed by Hude.
[2] ἄλλοτε, Camerarius' conjecture, now generally adopted,
for the Vulgate ἀλλ' ὅτε, which Hude retains.

---

[1] "As a symbolical expression of indissoluble union"
(Curtius).
[2] i.e. celebrated every fifth year.
[3] Homer is clearly regarded by Thucydides as the author
of the hymn here cited. How definite a personality he was

and bound it with a chain to Delos.[1]   It was at this
time, after the purification, that the Athenians first
celebrated their penteteric[2] festival in Delos.   There
had indeed in ancient times been a great gathering
at Delos of the Ionians and the inhabitants of the
neighbouring islands; and they used to resort to the
festival with their wives and children, as the Ionians
now do to the Ephesian games; and a contest was
formerly held there, both gymnastic and musical, and
choruses were sent thither by the cities.   The best
evidence that the festival was of this character is
given by Homer[3] in the following verses, which are
from the hymn to Apollo :[4]

> " At other times, Phoebus, Delos is dearest to
> thy heart, where the Ionians in trailing robes
> are gathered together with their wives and
> children in thy street; there they delight thee
> with boxing and dancing and song, making
> mention of thy name, whenever they ordain the
> contest."

And that there was a musical contest also to which
men resorted as competitors Homer once more
makes clear in the following verses from the same
hymn.   After commemorating the Delian chorus of

to Thucydides is shown by the words "in which he also
mentions himself."

[4] προοίμιον, *proem* or *introduction.*   In connection with
epic poems the hymns were called προοίμια, because they
were sung before other poems, *i.e.* by the rhapsodists as
preludes to their rhapsodies.   Schol. ἐξ ὕμνου· τοὺς γὰρ ὕμνους
προοίμια ἐκάλουν.   The question has been raised whether the
hymn was a prelude to the rhapsodies or was, as *e.g.* here,
in itself a rhapsody.   The citations here made by Thucydides
are from the *Hymn to the Delian Apollo,* 146 ff. and 165 ff.

THUCYDIDES

κῶν ὑμνήσας ἐτελεύτα τοῦ ἐπαίνου ἐς τάδε τὰ
ἔπη, ἐν οἷς καὶ ἑαυτοῦ ἐπεμνήσθη·

ἀλλ' ἄγεθ', ἱλήκοι μὲν Ἀπόλλων Ἀρτέμιδι ξύν,
χαίρετε δ' ὑμεῖς πᾶσαι. ἐμεῖο δὲ καὶ μετόπισθε
μνήσασθ', ὁππότε κέν τις ἐπιχθονίων ἀνθρώπων
ἐνθάδ' ἀνείρηται ταλαπείριος ἄλλος ἐπελθών·
"'Ω κοῦραι, τίς δ' ὑμῖν ἀνὴρ ἥδιστος ἀοιδῶν
ἐνθάδε πωλεῖται καὶ τέῳ τέρπεσθε μάλιστα;"
ὑμεῖς δ' εὖ μάλα πᾶσαι ὑποκρίνασθαι εὐφήμως·[1]
"Τυφλὸς ἀνήρ, οἰκεῖ δὲ Χίῳ ἔνι παιπαλοέσσῃ."

6   Τοσαῦτα μὲν Ὅμηρος ἐτεκμηρίωσεν ὅτι ἦν καὶ
τὸ πάλαι μεγάλη ξύνοδος καὶ ἑορτὴ ἐν τῇ Δήλῳ·
ὕστερον δὲ τοὺς μὲν χοροὺς οἱ νησιῶται καὶ οἱ
Ἀθηναῖοι μεθ' ἱερῶν ἔπεμπον, τὰ δὲ περὶ τοὺς
ἀγῶνας καὶ τὰ πλεῖστα κατελύθη ὑπὸ ξυμφορῶν,
ὡς εἰκός, πρὶν δὴ οἱ Ἀθηναῖοι τότε τὸν ἀγῶνα
ἐποίησαν καὶ ἱπποδρομίας, ὃ πρότερον οὐκ ἦν.

CV. Τοῦ δ' αὐτοῦ χειμῶνος Ἀμπρακιῶται,
ὥσπερ ὑποσχόμενοι Εὐρυλόχῳ τὴν στρατιὰν
κατέσχον, ἐκστρατεύονται ἐπὶ Ἄργος τὸ Ἀμφι-
λοχικὸν τρισχιλίοις ὁπλίταις, καὶ ἐσβαλόντες ἐς
τὴν Ἀργείαν καταλαμβάνουσιν Ὄλπας, τεῖχος
ἐπὶ λόφου ἰσχυρὸν πρὸς τῇ θαλάσσῃ, ὅ ποτε
Ἀκαρνᾶνες τειχισάμενοι κοινῷ δικαστηρίῳ
ἐχρῶντο· ἀπέχει δὲ ἀπὸ τῆς Ἀργείων πόλεως

[1] εὐφήμως, Hude ἀφήμως.

---

[1] i.e. either a federal court of the Acarnanians, as Steup
maintains (see Schoemann, *Gr. Alterthümer*, ii³. p 76), or a
court of justice common to the Acarnanians and Amphilo-

184

women he ends his praise of them with the following verses, in which he also mentions himself:

"Come now, let Apollo be gracious and Artemis likewise, and farewell, all ye maidens. Yet remember me even in after times, whenever some other toil-enduring man, a dweller upon the earth, shall visit this isle and ask: 'O maidens, what man is the sweetest of minstrels to you of all who wander hither, and in whom do you take most delight?' Do you make answer, all with one accord, in gentle words, 'The blind man who dwells in rugged Chios.'"

Such is Homer's testimony, showing that in ancient times also there was a great concourse and festival in Delos. And in later times the people of the islands and the Athenians continued to send their choruses with sacrifices, but the contests, and indeed most of the ceremonies, fell into disuse in consequence, probably, of calamities, until the Athenians, at the time of which we now speak, restored the contests and added horse-races, of which there had been none before.

CV. During the same winter the Ambraciots, fulfilling the promise by which they had induced Eurylochus to keep his army there, made an expedition against Amphilochian Argos with three thousand hoplites, and invading its territory took Olpae, a stronghold on the hill near the sea, which the Acarnanians had fortified and had at one time used as a common tribunal [1] of justice; and it is

chians (see Kruse, *Hellas*, ii. p. 333), as Classen explains. The latter view has the support of Steph. Byz.: Ὄλπαι· φρούριον, κοινὸν Ἀκαρνάνων καὶ Ἀμφιλόχων δικαστήριον, Θουκυδίδης τρίτῃ.

ἐπιθαλασσίας οὔσης πέντε καὶ εἴκοσι σταδίους
2 μάλιστα. οἱ δὲ Ἀκαρνᾶνες οἱ μὲν ἐς Ἄργος
ξυνεβοήθουν, οἱ δὲ τῆς Ἀμφιλοχίας ἐν τούτῳ τῷ
χωρίῳ ὃ Κρῆναι καλεῖται, φυλάσσοντες τοὺς
μετὰ Εὐρυλόχου Πελοποννησίους μὴ λάθωσι πρὸς
τοὺς Ἀμπρακιώτας διελθόντες, ἐστρατοπεδεύ-
3 σαντο. πέμπουσι δὲ καὶ ἐπὶ Δημοσθένη τὸν ἐς
τὴν Αἰτωλίαν Ἀθηναίων στρατηγήσαντα, ὅπως
σφίσιν ἡγεμὼν γίγνηται, καὶ ἐπὶ τὰς εἴκοσι ναῦς
Ἀθηναίων αἳ ἔτυχον περὶ Πελοπόννησον οὖσαι,
ὧν ἦρχεν Ἀριστοτέλης τε ὁ Τιμοκράτους καὶ
4 Ἱεροφῶν ὁ Ἀντιμνήστου. ἀπέστειλαν δὲ καὶ
ἄγγελον οἱ περὶ τὰς Ὄλπας Ἀμπρακιῶται ἐς
τὴν πόλιν κελεύοντες σφίσι βοηθεῖν πανδημεί,
δεδιότες μὴ οἱ μετ' Εὐρυλόχου οὐ δύνωνται διελ-
θεῖν τοὺς Ἀκαρνᾶνας καὶ σφίσιν ἢ μονωθεῖσιν
ἡ μάχη γένηται ἢ ἀναχωρεῖν βουλομένοις οὐκ ᾖ
ἀσφαλές.

CVI. Οἱ μὲν οὖν μετ' Εὐρυλόχου Πελοποννήσιοι ὡς ᾔσθοντο τοὺς ἐν Ὄλπαις Ἀμπρακιώτας
ἥκοντας, ἄραντες ἐκ τοῦ Προσχίου ἐβοήθουν κατὰ
τάχος, καὶ διαβάντες τὸν Ἀχελῷον ἐχώρουν δι'
Ἀκαρνανίας οὔσης ἐρήμου διὰ τὴν ἐς Ἄργος
βοήθειαν, ἐν δεξιᾷ μὲν ἔχοντες τὴν Στρατίων
πόλιν καὶ τὴν φρουρὰν αὐτῶν, ἐν ἀριστερᾷ δὲ τὴν
2 ἄλλην Ἀκαρνανίαν. καὶ διελθόντες τὴν Στρα-

---

¹ After the return of the thirty ships (ch. xcviii. 5), these
twenty had been sent out again round the Peloponnesus.

about twenty-five stadia from the city of Argos, which is by the sea. Meanwhile some of the Acarnanian troops came to the relief of Argos, while the rest encamped at a place in Amphilochia which is called Crenae, keeping guard to prevent the Peloponnesians with Eurylochus from passing through unobserved to join the Ambraciots. They also sent for Demosthenes, who had led the army of the Athenians into Aetolia, to come and be their leader, as well as for the twenty Athenian ships[1] which happened to be off the coast of Peloponnesus under the command of Aristotle son of Timocrates and Hierophon son of Antimnestus. A messenger was also sent by the Ambraciots at Olpae to the city of Ambracia with a request that all the forces of the town should be dispatched to their aid, for they feared that Eurylochus and his troops might not be able to make their way through the Acarnanians, and, in that case, that they themselves would either have to fight single-handed, or, if they wished to retreat, would find that unsafe.

CVI. Now the Peloponnesian forces under Eurylochus, when they learned that the Ambraciots had arrived at Olpae, set out from Proschium with all speed to reinforce them, and crossing the Acheloüs advanced through Acarnania, which was without defenders because of the reinforcements which had been sent to Argos, and as they advanced they had the city of Stratus with its garrison on their right, and the rest of Acarnania on their left. Then traversing the territory of the Stratians they advanced through

Their real goal was Naupactus (ch. cxiv. 2), but answering the appeal of the Acarnanians they turned aside for the moment to the Ambracian Gulf (ch. cvii. 1).

τίων γῆν ἐχώρουν διὰ τῆς Φυτίας καὶ αὖθις Μεδεῶνος παρ' ἔσχατα, ἔπειτα διὰ Λιμναίας· καὶ ἐπέβησαν τῆς Ἀγραίων, οὐκέτι Ἀκαρνανίας,
3 φιλίας δὲ σφίσιν. λαβόμενοι δὲ τοῦ Θυάμου ὄρους, ὅ ἐστιν Ἀγραϊκόν,[1] ἐχώρουν δι' αὐτοῦ καὶ κατέβησαν ἐς τὴν Ἀργείαν νυκτὸς ἤδη, καὶ διεξελθόντες μεταξὺ τῆς τε Ἀργείων πόλεως καὶ τῆς ἐπὶ Κρήναις Ἀκαρνάνων φυλακῆς ἔλαθον καὶ προσέμειξαν τοῖς ἐν Ὄλπαις Ἀμπρακιώταις.
CVII. Γενόμενοι δὲ ἄθρόοι ἅμα τῇ ἡμέρᾳ καθίζουσιν ἐπὶ τὴν Μητρόπολιν καλουμένην καὶ στρατόπεδον ἐποιήσαντο. Ἀθηναῖοι δὲ ταῖς εἴκοσι ναυσὶν οὐ πολλῷ ὕστερον παραγίγνονται ἐς τὸν Ἀμπρακικὸν κόλπον βοηθοῦντες τοῖς Ἀργείοις, καὶ Δημοσθένης Μεσσηνίων μὲν ἔχων διακοσίους ὁπλίτας, ἑξήκοντα δὲ τοξότας Ἀθη-
2 ναίων. καὶ αἱ μὲν νῆες περὶ τὰς Ὄλπας τὸν λόφον[2] ἐκ θαλάσσης ἐφώρμουν· οἱ δὲ Ἀκαρνᾶνες καὶ Ἀμφιλόχων ὀλίγοι (οἱ γὰρ πλείους ὑπὸ Ἀμπρακιωτῶν βίᾳ κατείχοντο) ἐς τὸ Ἄργος ἤδη ξυνεληλυθότες παρεσκευάζοντο ὡς μαχούμενοι τοῖς ἐναντίοις, καὶ ἡγεμόνα τοῦ παντὸς ξυμμαχικοῦ αἱροῦνται Δημοσθένη μετὰ τῶν σφετέρων
3 στρατηγῶν. ὁ δὲ προσαγαγὼν ἐγγὺς τῆς Ὄλπης ἐστρατοπεδεύσατο· χαράδρα δ' αὐτοὺς μεγάλη διεῖργεν. καὶ ἡμέρας μὲν πέντε ἡσύχαζον, τῇ δ' ἕκτῃ ἐτάσσοντο ἀμφότεροι ὡς ἐς μάχην. καὶ (μεῖζον γὰρ ἐγένετο καὶ περιέσχε τὸ τῶν Πελοποννησίων στρατόπεδον) ὁ Δημοσθένης δείσας

---

[1] Ἀγραϊκόν, for ἄγροικον or ἀγροῖκον of the MSS., corrected by O. Mueller.
[2] τὸν λόφον, deleted by van Herwerden, followed by Hude.

Phytia, from there skirted the borders of Medeon, and then passed through Limnaea; and finally they reached the country of the Agraeans, being now outside of Acarnania and in a friendly country. Arriving next at Mt. Thyamus, which belongs to the Agraeans, they went through the pass over it and came down into Argive territory after nightfall, whence they succeeded in passing unobserved between the city of Argos and the Acarnanian guard at Crenae, finally joining the Ambraciots at Olpae.

CVII. After the two armies had effected a junction, at daybreak they took post at a place called Metropolis and made camp. Not long afterwards the Athenians with their twenty ships arrived in the Ambracian Gulf, reinforcing the Argives; and Demosthenes also came with two hundred Messenian hoplites and sixty Athenian bowmen. The ships lay at sea about the hill of Olpae, blockading it; but the Acarnanians and a few of the Amphilochians—for most of these were kept from moving by the Ambraciots—had already gathered at Argos and were preparing for battle with their opponents, having chosen Demosthenes to command the whole allied force in concert with their own generals. And he, leading them close to Olpae, encamped; and a great ravine separated the two armies. For five days they kept quiet, but on the sixth both sides drew up in order of battle. Now the army of the Peloponnesians was larger than that of Demosthenes and outflanked it; he, therefore, fearing that he

THUCYDIDES

μὴ κυκλωθῇ λοχίζει ἐς ὁδόν τινα κοίλην καὶ
λοχμώδη ὁπλίτας καὶ ψιλοὺς ξυναμφοτέρους ἐς
τετρακοσίους, ὅπως κατὰ τὸ ὑπερέχον τῶν ἐναντίων ἐν τῇ ξυνόδῳ αὐτῇ ἐξαναστάντες οὗτοι κατὰ
4 νώτου γίγνωνται. ἐπεὶ δὲ παρεσκεύαστο ἀμφοτέροις, ᾖσαν ἐς χεῖρας, Δημοσθένης μὲν τὸ δεξιὸν
κέρας ἔχων μετὰ Μεσσηνίων καὶ Ἀθηναίων
ὀλίγων· τὸ δὲ ἄλλο Ἀκαρνᾶνες ὡς ἕκαστοι τεταγμένοι ἐπεῖχον καὶ Ἀμφιλόχων οἱ παρόντες ἀκον-
τισταί· Πελοποννήσιοι δὲ καὶ Ἀμπρακιῶται
ἀναμὶξ τεταγμένοι πλὴν Μαντινέων· οὗτοι δὲ ἐν
τῷ εὐωνύμῳ μᾶλλον καὶ οὐ τὸ κέρας ἄκρον ἔχοντες ἁθρόοι ᾖσαν, ἀλλ' Εὐρύλοχος ἔσχατον εἶχε τὸ
εὐώνυμον καὶ οἱ μετ' αὐτοῦ, κατὰ Μεσσηνίους καὶ
Δημοσθένη.

CVIII. Ὡς δ' ἐν χερσὶν ἤδη ὄντες περιέσχον
τῷ κέρᾳ οἱ Πελοποννήσιοι καὶ ἐκυκλοῦντο τὸ
δεξιὸν τῶν ἐναντίων, οἱ ἐκ τῆς ἐνέδρας Ἀκαρνᾶνες
ἐπιγενόμενοι αὐτοῖς κατὰ νώτου προσπίπτουσί
τε καὶ τρέπουσιν, ὥστε μήτε ἐς ἀλκὴν ὑπομεῖναι
φοβηθέντας τε ἐς φυγὴν καὶ τὸ πλέον τοῦ στρατεύματος καταστῆσαι· ἐπειδὴ γὰρ εἶδον τὸ κατ'
Εὐρύλοχον καὶ ὃ κράτιστον ἦν διαφθειρόμενον,
πολλῷ μᾶλλον ἐφοβοῦντο. καὶ οἱ Μεσσήνιοι
ὄντες ταύτῃ μετὰ τοῦ Δημοσθένους τὸ πολὺ τοῦ
2 ἔργου ἐπεξῆλθον. οἱ δὲ Ἀμπρακιῶται καὶ οἱ
κατὰ τὸ δεξιὸν κέρας ἐνίκων τὸ καθ' ἑαυτοὺς καὶ
πρὸς τὸ Ἄργος ἐπεδίωξαν.[1] καὶ γὰρ μαχιμώτατοι

[1] ἐπεδίωξαν, for ἀπεδίωξαν of the MSS., Haase's conjecture.

might be surrounded, stationed in a sunken road overgrown with bushes an ambush of hoplites and light-troops, about four hundred all together, his purpose being that in the very moment of collision these troops should leap from their hiding-place and take the enemy in the rear at the point where his line overlapped. When both sides were ready they came to close quarters. Demosthenes with the Messenians and a few Athenian troops had the right wing; the rest of the line was held by the Acarnanians, arrayed by tribes, and such Amphilochian javelin-men as were present. But the Peloponnesians and Ambraciots were mingled together, except the Mantineans; these were massed more on the left wing, though not at its extremity, for that position, which was opposite Demosthenes and the Messenians, was held by Eurylochus and the troops under him.

CVIII. When finally the armies were at close quarters and the Peloponnesians outflanked with their left the right wing of their opponents and were about to encircle it, the Acarnanians, coming upon them from their ambush, fell upon their rear and routed them, so that they did not stand to make resistance and in their panic caused the greater part of their army to take to flight also; for when they saw the division under Eurylochus, their best troops, being cut to pieces, they were far more panic-stricken. And it was the Messenians, who were in this part of the field under the command of Demosthenes, that bore the brunt of the battle. On the other hand, the Ambraciots and those on the enemy's right wing defeated the troops opposed to themselves, and pursued them to Argos; and indeed

τῶν περὶ ἐκεῖνα τὰ χωρία τυγχάνουσιν ὄντες.
3 ἐπαναχωροῦντες δὲ ὡς ἑώρων τὸ πλέον νενικημένον
καὶ οἱ ἄλλοι Ἀκαρνᾶνες σφίσι προσέκειντο,
χαλεπῶς διεσῴζοντο ἐς τὰς Ὄλπας, καὶ πολλοὶ
ἀπέθανον αὐτῶν, ἀτάκτως καὶ οὐδενὶ κόσμῳ
προσπίπτοντες πλὴν Μαντινέων· οὗτοι δὲ μάλιστα ξυντεταγμένοι παντὸς τοῦ στρατοῦ ἀνεχώρησαν. καὶ ἡ μὲν μάχη ἐτελεύτα ἐς ὀψέ.

CIX. Μενεδάϊος δὲ τῇ ὑστεραίᾳ Εὐρυλόχου
τεθνεῶτος καὶ Μακαρίου αὐτὸς παρειληφὼς τὴν
ἀρχὴν καὶ ἀπορῶν μεγάλης τῆς [1] ἥσσης γεγενημένης ὅτῳ τρόπῳ ἢ μένων πολιορκήσεται, ἔκ τε
γῆς καὶ ἐκ θαλάσσης ταῖς Ἀττικαῖς ναυσὶν
ἀποκεκλημένος, ἢ καὶ ἀναχωρῶν διασωθήσεται,
προσφέρει λόγον περὶ σπονδῶν καὶ ἀναχωρήσεως
Δημοσθένει καὶ τοῖς Ἀκαρνάνων στρατηγοῖς καὶ
2 περὶ νεκρῶν ἅμα ἀναιρέσεως. οἱ δὲ νεκροὺς
μὲν ἀπέδοσαν καὶ τροπαῖον αὐτοὶ ἔστησαν καὶ
τοὺς ἑαυτῶν τριακοσίους μάλιστα ἀποθανόντας
ἀνείλοντο· ἀναχώρησιν δὲ ἐκ μὲν τοῦ προφανοῦς
οὐκ ἐσπείσαντο ἅπασι, κρύφα δὲ Δημοσθένης
μετὰ τῶν ξυστρατήγων τῶν [2] Ἀκαρνάνων σπέν-
δονται Μαντινεῦσι καὶ Μενεδαΐῳ καὶ τοῖς ἄλλοις
ἄρχουσι τῶν Πελοποννησίων καὶ ὅσοι αὐτῶν
ἦσαν ἀξιολογώτατοι ἀποχωρεῖν κατὰ τάχος,
βουλόμενος ψιλῶσαι τοὺς Ἀμπρακιώτας τε καὶ
τὸν μισθοφόρον ὄχλον,[3] μάλιστα δὲ Λακεδαι-

---

[1] τῆς added by Hude.
[2] τῶν, before Ἀκαρνάνων, added by Krüger, followed by Hude.
[3] τὸν ξενικόν, given in MSS. after ὄχλον, deleted by van Herwerden, followed by Hude.

these are the best fighters of all the peoples of that region. When, however, they returned and saw that their main army had been defeated, and the victorious division of the Acarnanians began to press hard upon them, they made their escape with difficulty to Olpae; and many of them were killed, for they rushed on with broken ranks and in disorder, all except the Mantineans, who kept their ranks together during the retreat better than any other part of the army. And it was late in the evening before the battle ended.

CIX. On the next day, since Eurylochus and Macarius had been slain, Menedaïus had on his own responsibility assumed the command, but the defeat had been so serious that he was at his wit's end how, if he remained, he could stand a siege, blockaded as he was by both land and sea by the Athenian fleet, or, if he retreated, could get away safely. He therefore made overtures to Demosthenes and the Athenian generals regarding a truce for his retreat and also about the recovery of his dead. And they gave back the dead, set up a trophy themselves, and took up their own dead, about three hundred in number. They would not, however, openly agree to a retreat for the whole army, but Demosthenes with his Acarnanian colleagues secretly agreed that the Mantineans and Menedaïus and the other Peloponnesian commanders and the most influential men among them might go back home, if they did so speedily. Their object was to isolate the Ambraciots and the miscellaneous crowd of mercenaries,[1] and above all to

---

[1] Opinions differ as to who are meant. They were probably mercenaries from the neighbouring Epirote tribes in the pay of the Ambraciots.

μονίους καὶ Πελοποννησίους διαβαλεῖν ἐς τοὺς
ἐκείνῃ χρήζων "Ελληνας ὡς καταπροδόντες τὸ
3 ἑαυτῶν προυργιαίτερον ἐποιήσαντο. καὶ οἱ μὲν
τούς τε νεκροὺς ἀνείλοντο καὶ διὰ τάχους ἔθαπτον,
ὥσπερ ὑπῆρχε, καὶ τὴν ἀποχώρησιν κρύφα οἷς
ἐδέδοτο ἐπεβούλευον.

CX. Τῷ δὲ Δημοσθένει καὶ τοῖς Ἀκαρνᾶσιν
ἀγγέλλεται τοὺς Ἀμπρακιώτας τοὺς ἐκ τῆς
πόλεως πανδημεὶ κατὰ τὴν πρώτην ἐκ τῶν
Ὀλπῶν ἀγγελίαν ἐπιβοηθεῖν διὰ τῶν Ἀμφιλόχων, βουλομένους τοῖς ἐν Ὀλπαις ξυμμεῖξαι
2 εἰδότας οὐδὲν τῶν γεγενημένων. καὶ πέμπει
εὐθὺς τοῦ στρατοῦ μέρος τι τὰς ὁδοὺς προλο-
χιοῦντας καὶ τὰ καρτερὰ προκαταληψομένους,
καὶ τῇ ἄλλῃ στρατιᾷ ἅμα παρεσκευάζετο βοηθεῖν ἐπ' αὐτούς.

CXI. Ἐν τούτῳ δ' οἱ Μαντινῆς καὶ οἷς ἔσπειστο
πρόφασιν ἐπὶ λαχανισμὸν καὶ φρυγάνων ξυλ-
λογὴν ἐξελθόντες ὑπαπῆσαν κατ' ὀλίγους, ἅμα
ξυλλέγοντες ἐφ' ἃ ἐξῆλθον δῆθεν· προκεχωρη-
κότες δὲ ἤδη ἄπωθεν τῆς Ὀλπης θᾶσσον ἀπε-
2 χώρουν. οἱ δ' Ἀμπρακιῶται καὶ οἱ ἄλλοι ὅσοι
μὲν¹ ἐτύγχανον οὕτως ἀθρόοι ξυνελθόντες, ὡς
ἔγνωσαν ἀπιόντας, ὥρμησαν καὶ αὐτοὶ καὶ ἔθεον
3 δρόμῳ, ἐπικαταλαβεῖν βουλόμενοι. οἱ δὲ Ἀκαρνᾶνες τὸ μὲν πρῶτον καὶ πάντας ἐνόμισαν ἀπιέναι

¹ Hude reads ὅσοι μὴ ἐτύγχανον τούτοις ἀθρόοι ξυνεξελθόντες.

---

¹ As distinguished from the Ambraciots who after the
battle were shut up in Olpae (ch. cxi. 2).
² The text is most probably corrupt. Classen offers
the best remedy: οἱ δὲ Ἀμπρακιῶται καὶ οἱ ἄλλοι ὅσοι
μονούμενοι ἐτύγχανον οὕτως, ἐθρόοι ξυνελθόντες ὡς ἔγνωσαν

discredit the Lacedaemonians and the Peloponnesians with the Hellenes of this region, on the ground that they had committed an act of treachery through preference for their own selfish interests. Accordingly the Peloponnesians took up their dead and hastily buried them as best they could, while those who had permission began secretly to plan their retreat.

CX. Word was now brought to Demosthenes and the Acarnanians that the inhabitants of the city of Ambracia,[1] in response to the first message that came from Olpae, were marching in full force through the Amphilochian territory, wishing to join the forces in Olpae, and that they were quite unaware of what had happened. So he immediately sent a part of his army to forestall these troops by setting ambuscades along the roads and occupying the strong positions, and at the same time began preparations to lead the rest of the army against them.

CXI. In the meantime the Mantineans and the others who were included in the agreement, leaving camp on the pretext of gathering pot-herbs and fire-wood, stole away in small groups, gathering at the same time what they pretended to have gone to seek; then when they had already got some distance from Olpae they quickened their pace. But the Ambraciots and all the others who happened to have come together in a body, when they realized that these were taking their departure, also set out themselves and ran at full speed, wishing to overtake them.[2] But the Acarnanians at first thought that all the fugitives were going away without covenant

ἀπιόντας, ὥρμησαν καὶ αὐτοὶ . . : "But the Ambraciots and all the others who chanced to be left came together in a body, and when they realised that they were taking their departure set off also themselves . . ."

ἀσπόνδους ὁμοίως καὶ τοὺς Πελοποννησίους ἐπε-
δίωκον, καί τινας αὐτῶν τῶν στρατηγῶν κωλύ-
οντας καὶ φάσκοντας ἐσπεῖσθαι αὐτοῖς ἠκόντισέ
τις, νομίσας καταπροδίδοσθαι σφᾶς· ἔπειτα
μέντοι τοὺς μὲν Μαντινέας καὶ τοὺς Πελοποννησίους ἀφίεσαν, τοὺς δ᾽ Ἀμπρακιώτας ἔκτεινον.
4 καὶ ἦν πολλὴ ἔρις καὶ ἄγνοια εἴτε Ἀμπρακιώτης
τίς ἐστιν εἴτε Πελοποννήσιος. καὶ ἐς διακοσίους
μέν τινας αὐτῶν ἀπέκτειναν· οἱ δ᾽ ἄλλοι διέ-
φυγον ἐς τὴν Ἀγραΐδα ὅμορον οὖσαν, καὶ Σαλύν-
θιος αὐτοὺς ὁ βασιλεὺς τῶν Ἀγραίων φίλος ὢν
ὑπεδέξατο.

CXII. Οἱ δ᾽ ἐκ τῆς πόλεως Ἀμπρακιῶται
ἀφικνοῦνται ἐπ᾽ Ἰδομενήν. ἐστὸν δὲ δύο λόφω ἡ
Ἰδομένη ὑψηλώ· τούτοιν τὸν μὲν μείζω νυκτὸς
ἐπιγενομένης οἱ προαποσταλέντες ὑπὸ τοῦ Δημοσθένους ἀπὸ τοῦ στρατοπέδου ἔλαθόν τε καὶ
ἔφθασαν προκαταλαβόντες, τὸν δ᾽ ἐλάσσω [1] ἔτυχον οἱ Ἀμπρακιῶται προαναβάντες καὶ ηὐλί-
2 σαντο. ὁ δὲ Δημοσθένης δειπνήσας ἐχώρει καὶ
τὸ ἄλλο στράτευμα ἀπὸ ἑσπέρας εὐθύς, αὐτὸς
μὲν τὸ ἥμισυ ἔχων ἐπὶ τῆς ἐσβολῆς, τὸ δ᾽ ἄλλο
3 διὰ τῶν Ἀμφιλοχικῶν ὁρῶν. καὶ ἅμα ὄρθρῳ
ἐπιπίπτει τοῖς Ἀμπρακιώταις ἔτι ἐν ταῖς εὐναῖς
καὶ οὐ προῃσθημένοις τὰ γεγενημένα, ἀλλὰ πολὺ
4 μᾶλλον νομίσασι τοὺς ἑαυτῶν εἶναι· καὶ γὰρ
τοὺς Μεσσηνίους πρώτους ἐπίτηδες ὁ Δημοσθένης
προύταξε καὶ προσαγορεύειν ἐκέλευε, Δωρίδα τε
γλῶσσαν ἱέντας καὶ τοῖς προφύλαξι πίστιν παρε-
χομένους, ἅμα δὲ καὶ οὐ καθορωμένους τῇ ὄψει

---

[1] ἐς is inserted before τὸν δ᾽ ἐλάσσω by Hude, following
Krüger.

196

or truce and therefore set off in pursuit of the Peloponnesians; and when some of the generals tried to prevent this, saying that a truce had been made with them, someone hurled javelins at them, believing that they had been betrayed. Afterwards, however, they let the Mantineans and Peloponnesians go, but began to kill the Ambraciots. And there was much dispute and uncertainty as to whether a man was an Ambraciot or a Peloponnesian. About two hundred of the Ambraciots were slain; the rest of the fugitives escaped into the neighbouring country of Agraea, and were received by Salynthius the king of the Agraeans, who was friendly to them.

CXII. Meanwhile the troops from the city of Ambracia arrived at Idomene. Now it consists of two lofty hills, and of these the higher had already been seized unobserved during the night by the troops which Demosthenes had sent forward from his main army; but the lower had previously, as it chanced, been ascended by the Ambraciots, who spent the night there. After dinner Demosthenes and the rest of the army set out immediately after nightfall, he himself with half of them making for the pass, while the rest took the road through the Amphilochian mountains. And at dawn he fell upon the Ambraciots, who were still in their beds and had no knowledge at all of what had previously happened. On the contrary, they supposed these troops to be their own men, for Demosthenes had purposely put the Messenians in front and directed them to accost the enemy in the Doric dialect, thus getting themselves trusted by the outposts; besides, they were indistinguishable to the sight, since it was still dark.

5 νυκτὸς ἔτι οὔσης. ὡς οὖν ἐπέπεσε τῷ στρατεύματι αὐτῶν, τρέπουσι, καὶ τοὺς μὲν πολλοὺς
αὐτοῦ διέφθειραν, οἱ δὲ λοιποὶ κατὰ τὰ ὄρη ἐς
6 φυγὴν ὥρμησαν. προκατειλημμένων δὲ τῶν ὁδῶν,
καὶ ἅμα τῶν μὲν Ἀμφιλόχων ἐμπείρων ὄντων
τῆς ἑαυτῶν γῆς καὶ ψιλῶν πρὸς ὁπλίτας, τῶν δὲ
ἀπείρων καὶ ἀνεπιστημόνων ὅπῃ τράπωνται,
ἐσπίπτοντες ἔς τε χαράδρας καὶ τὰς προλελο-
7 χισμένας ἐνέδρας διεφθείροντο. καὶ ἐς πᾶσαν
ἰδέαν χωρήσαντες τῆς φυγῆς ἐτράποντό τινες καὶ
ἐς τὴν θάλασσαν οὐ πολὺ ἀπέχουσαν, καὶ ὡς
εἶδον τὰς Ἀττικὰς ναῦς παραπλεούσας ἅμα τοῦ
ἔργου τῇ ξυντυχίᾳ, προσένευσαν, ἡγησάμενοι ἐν
τῷ αὐτίκα φόβῳ κρεῖσσον εἶναι σφίσιν ὑπὸ τῶν
ἐν ταῖς ναυσίν, εἰ δεῖ, διαφθαρῆναι ἢ ὑπὸ τῶν
8 βαρβάρων καὶ ἐχθίστων Ἀμφιλόχων. οἱ μὲν
οὖν Ἀμπρακιῶται τοιούτῳ τρόπῳ κακωθέντες
ὀλίγοι ἀπὸ πολλῶν ἐσώθησαν ἐς τὴν πόλιν·
Ἀκαρνᾶνες δὲ σκυλεύσαντες τοὺς νεκροὺς καὶ
τροπαῖα στήσαντες ἀπεχώρησαν ἐς Ἄργος.

CXIII. Καὶ αὐτοῖς τῇ ὑστεραίᾳ ἦλθε κῆρυξ
ἀπὸ τῶν ἐς Ἀγραίους καταφυγόντων ἐκ τῆς
Ὄλπης Ἀμπρακιωτῶν, ἀναίρεσιν αἰτήσων τῶν
νεκρῶν οὓς ἀπέκτειναν ὕστερον τῆς πρώτης μάχης, ὅτε μετὰ τῶν Μαντινέων καὶ τῶν ὑποσπόν-
2 δων ξυνεξῆσαν ἄσπονδοι. ἰδὼν δ' ὁ κῆρυξ τὰ
ὅπλα τῶν ἀπὸ τῆς πόλεως Ἀμπρακιωτῶν ἐθαύ-
μαζε τὸ πλῆθος· οὐ γὰρ ᾔδει τὸ πάθος, ἀλλ' ᾤετο

So they fell upon the army of the Ambraciots and put them to rout, slaying the majority of them on the spot; the rest took to flight over the mountains. But as the roads had already been occupied, and as, moreover, the Amphilochians were well acquainted with their own country and were light infantry opposing heavy-armed troops, whereas the Ambraciots were ignorant of the country and did not know which way to turn, under these circumstances the fleeing men fell into ravines and into ambushes which had previously been set for them and perished. And some of them, after resorting to every manner of flight, even turned to the sea, which was not far distant, and seeing the Athenian ships, which were sailing along the coast at the very time when the action was taking place, swam toward them, thinking in the panic of the moment that it was better for them to be slain, if slain they must be, by the crews of the ships than by the barbarian and detested Amphilochians. In this manner, then, the Ambraciots suffered disaster, and but few out of many returned in safety to their city; the Acarnanians, on the other hand, after stripping the dead and setting up trophies, returned to Argos.

CXIII. On the next day a herald came to the Athenians from the Ambraciots who had escaped from Olpae and taken refuge among the Agraeans, to ask for the bodies of those who had been slain after the first battle, at the time when unprotected by a truce these attempted to leave Olpae along with the Mantineans and the others who were included in the truce. Now when the herald saw the arms taken from the Ambraciots who came from the city, he was amazed at their number; for he did not know of the recent disaster, but thought that

3 τῶν μετὰ σφῶν εἶναι. καί τις αὐτὸν ἤρετο ὅ τι
θαυμάζοι καὶ ὁπόσοι αὐτῶν τεθνᾶσιν, οἰόμενος
αὖ ὁ ἐρωτῶν εἶναι τὸν κήρυκα ἀπὸ τῶν ἐν Ἰδο-
μεναῖς. ὁ δ᾽ ἔφη διακοσίους μάλιστα. ὑπολα-
4 βὼν δ᾽ ὁ ἐρωτῶν εἶπεν· "Οὔκουν τὰ ὅπλα ταυτὶ
διακοσίων¹ φαίνεται, ἀλλὰ πλέον ἢ χιλίων."
αὖθις δὲ εἶπεν ἐκεῖνος· "Οὐκ ἄρα τῶν μεθ᾽ ἡμῶν
μαχομένων ἐστίν." ὁ δ᾽ ἀπεκρίνατο· "Εἴπερ γε
ὑμεῖς ἐν Ἰδομενῇ χθὲς ἐμάχεσθε." "᾽Αλλ᾽ ἡμεῖς
γε οὐδενὶ ἐμαχόμεθα χθές, ἀλλὰ πρῴην ἐν τῇ
ἀποχωρήσει." "Καὶ μὲν δὴ τούτοις γε ἡμεῖς
χθὲς ἀπὸ τῆς πόλεως βοηθήσασι τῆς Ἀμπρακιω-
5 τῶν ἐμαχόμεθα." ὁ δὲ κῆρυξ ὡς ἤκουσε καὶ
ἔγνω ὅτι ἡ ἀπὸ τῆς πόλεως βοήθεια διέφθαρται,
ἀνοιμώξας καὶ ἐκπλαγεὶς τῷ μεγέθει τῶν παρόντων κακῶν ἀπῆλθεν εὐθὺς ἄπρακτος καὶ οὐκέτι
6 ἀπῄτει τοὺς νεκρούς. πάθος γὰρ τοῦτο μιᾷ πόλει Ἑλληνίδι ἐν ἴσαις ἡμέραις μέγιστον δὴ τῶν
κατὰ τὸν πόλεμον τόνδε ἐγένετο. καὶ ἀριθμὸν
οὐκ ἔγραψα τῶν ἀποθανόντων, διότι ἄπιστον τὸ
πλῆθος λέγεται ἀπολέσθαι ὡς πρὸς τὸ μέγεθος
τῆς πόλεως. Ἀμπρακίαν μέντοι οἶδα ὅτι, εἰ
ἐβουλήθησαν Ἀκαρνᾶνες καὶ Ἀμφίλοχοι Ἀθηναίοις καὶ Δημοσθένει πειθόμενοι ἐπελθεῖν, αὐτοβοεὶ ἂν εἶλον· νῦν δ᾽ ἔδεισαν μὴ οἱ Ἀθηναῖοι

¹ διακοσίων, added by Krüger.

the arms belonged to the men of his own division. And someone asked him why he was amazed, and how many of his comrades had been slain, the questioner on his part supposing that the herald had come from the forces which had fought at Idomene. The herald answered, "About two hundred." The questioner said in reply, "These arms, though, are clearly not those of two hundred men, but of more than a thousand." And again the herald said, "Then they are not the arms of our comrades in the battle." The other answered, "They are, if it was you who fought yesterday at Idomene." "But we did not fight with anyone yesterday; it was the day before yesterday, on the retreat." "And it is certain that we fought yesterday with these men, who were coming to your aid from the city of the Ambraciots." When the herald heard this and realized that the force which was coming to their relief from the city had perished, he lifted up his voice in lamentation and, stunned by the magnitude of the calamity before him, departed at once, forgetting his errand and making no request for the dead. Indeed this was the greatest calamity that befell any one Hellenic city in an equal number of days during the course of this whole war. The number of those who fell I have not recorded, seeing that the multitude reported to have perished is incredible when compared with the size of the city. I know, however, that if the Acarnanians and Amphilochians had been willing to hearken to the Athenians and Demosthenes and had made an attack upon Ambracia they would have taken it at the first onset; but as it was, they were afraid that the Athenians, if they

ἔχοντες αὐτὴν χαλεπώτεροι σφίσι πάροικοι ὦσιν.

CXIV. Μετὰ δὲ ταῦτα τρίτον μέρος νείμαντες τῶν σκύλων τοῖς Ἀθηναίοις τὰ ἄλλα κατὰ τὰς πόλεις διείλοντο. καὶ τὰ μὲν τῶν Ἀθηναίων πλέοντα ἑάλω, τὰ δὲ νῦν ἀνακείμενα ἐν τοῖς Ἀττικοῖς ἱεροῖς Δημοσθένει ἐξῃρέθησαν τριακόσιαι πανοπλίαι, καὶ ἄγων αὐτὰς κατέπλευσεν· καὶ ἐγένετο ἅμα αὐτῷ μετὰ τὴν ἐκ τῆς Αἰτωλίας ξυμφορὰν ἀπὸ ταύτης τῆς πράξεως ἀδεεστέρα ἡ 2 κάθοδος. ἀπῆλθον δὲ καὶ οἱ ἐν ταῖς εἴκοσι ναυσὶν Ἀθηναῖοι ἐς Ναύπακτον. Ἀκαρνᾶνες δὲ καὶ Ἀμφίλοχοι ἀπελθόντων Ἀθηναίων καὶ Δημοσθένους τοῖς ὡς Σαλύνθιον καὶ Ἀγραίους καταφυγοῦσιν Ἀμπρακιώταις καὶ Πελοποννησίοις ἀναχώρησιν ἐσπείσαντο ἐξ Οἰνιαδῶν οἵπερ καὶ μετ- 3 έστησαν παρὰ Σαλυνθίου. καὶ ἐς τὸν ἔπειτα χρόνον σπονδὰς καὶ ξυμμαχίαν ἐποιήσαντο ἑκατὸν ἔτη Ἀκαρνᾶνες καὶ Ἀμφίλοχοι πρὸς Ἀμπρακιώτας ἐπὶ τοῖσδε, ὥστε μήτε Ἀμπρακιώτας μετὰ Ἀκαρνάνων στρατεύειν ἐπὶ Πελοποννησίους μήτε Ἀκαρνᾶνας μετὰ Ἀμπρακιωτῶν ἐπ' Ἀθηναίους, βοηθεῖν δὲ τῇ ἀλλήλων, καὶ ἀποδοῦναι Ἀμπρακιώτας ὁπόσα ἢ χωρία ἢ ὁμήρους Ἀμφιλόχων ἔχουσι, καὶ ἐπὶ Ἀνακτόριον μὴ βοηθεῖν 4 πολέμιον ὃν Ἀκαρνᾶσιν. ταῦτα ξυνθέμενοι διέλυσαν τὸν πόλεμον. μετὰ δὲ ταῦτα Κορίνθιοι

had the town in their possession, would be more troublesome neighbours than the Ambraciots.

CXIV. After this the Acarnanians apportioned a third of the booty to the Athenians and distributed the rest among their cities. The portion which fell to the Athenians was captured from them on the voyage home; but the dedicatory offerings now to be seen in the Athenian temples, consisting of three hundred panoplies, were set apart as Demosthenes' share, and were brought home by him when he returned. Furthermore, his return could now, in consequence of this exploit, be made with less apprehension after his earlier misfortune in Aetolia. The Athenians in the twenty ships also departed, returning to Naupactus. As for the Acarnanians and Amphilochians, after the Athenians and Demosthenes had gone home, they concluded a truce with the Ambraciots and Peloponnesians who had taken refuge with Salynthius and the Agraeans, allowing them to withdraw from Oeniadae, whither they had gone after leaving Salynthius. The Acarnanians and Amphilochians also concluded for the future a treaty of alliance with the Ambraciots to last for one hundred years, on the following terms: The Ambraciots were not to join the Acarnanians in any expedition against the Peloponnesians; nor were the Acarnanians to join the Ambraciots against the Athenians, but they were to give aid in defence of one another's territory; the Ambraciots were to restore all places or hostages belonging to the Amphilochians which they now held; and they were not to give aid to Anactorium, which was hostile to the Acarnanians. On these terms of agreement they brought the war to an end. But

φυλακὴν ἑαυτῶν ἐς τὴν Ἀμπρακίαν ἀπέστειλαν
ἐς τριακοσίους ὁπλίτας καὶ Ξενοκλείδαν τὸν Εὐ-
θυκλέους ἄρχοντα· οἱ κομιζόμενοι χαλεπῶς διὰ
τῆς ἠπείρου ἀφίκοντο. τὰ μὲν κατ᾽ Ἀμπρακίαν
οὕτως ἐγένετο.

CXV. Οἱ δ᾽ ἐν τῇ Σικελίᾳ Ἀθηναῖοι τοῦ αὐτοῦ
χειμῶνος ἔς τε τὴν Ἱμεραίαν ἀπόβασιν ἐποιήσαντο ἐκ τῶν νεῶν μετὰ τῶν Σικελῶν τῶν ἄνωθεν
ἐσβεβληκότων ἐς τὰ ἔσχατα τῆς Ἱμεραίας καὶ
2 ἐπὶ τὰς Αἰόλου νήσους ἔπλευσαν. ἀναχωρήσαντες δὲ ἐς Ῥήγιον Πυθόδωρον τὸν Ἰσολόχου,
Ἀθηναίων στρατηγόν, καταλαμβάνουσιν ἐπὶ τὰς
3 ναῦς διάδοχον ὧν ὁ Λάχης ἦρχεν. οἱ γὰρ ἐν
Σικελίᾳ ξύμμαχοι πλεύσαντες ἔπεισαν τοὺς
Ἀθηναίους βοηθεῖν σφίσι πλείοσι ναυσίν· τῆς
μὲν γὰρ γῆς αὐτῶν οἱ Συρακόσιοι ἐκράτουν, τῆς
δὲ θαλάσσης ὀλίγαις ναυσὶν εἰργόμενοι παρεσκευάζοντο ναυτικὸν ξυναγείροντες ὡς οὐ περι-
4 οψόμενοι. καὶ ἐπλήρουν ναῦς τεσσαράκοντα οἱ
Ἀθηναῖοι ὡς ἀποστελοῦντες αὐτοῖς, ἅμα μὲν
ἡγούμενοι θᾶσσον τὸν ἐκεῖ πόλεμον καταλυθή-
σεσθαι, ἅμα δὲ βουλόμενοι μελέτην τοῦ ναυτικοῦ
5 ποιεῖσθαι. τὸν μὲν οὖν ἕνα τῶν στρατηγῶν ἀπέστειλαν Πυθόδωρον ὀλίγαις ναυσί, Σοφοκλέα δὲ
τὸν Σωστρατίδου καὶ Εὐρυμέδοντα τὸν Θουκλέους
6 ἐπὶ τῶν πλειόνων νεῶν ἀποπέμψειν ἔμελλον. ὁ
δὲ Πυθόδωρος ἤδη ἔχων τὴν τοῦ Λάχητος τῶν
νεῶν ἀρχὴν ἔπλευσε τελευτῶντος τοῦ χειμῶνος

after this the Corinthians sent to Ambracia a
garrison of their own troops, consisting of about
three hundred hoplites, under the command of
Xenocleidas son of Euthycles, who, making their
way with difficulty across the mainland, finally
reached their destination. Such was the course of
events at Ambracia.

CXV. During the same winter the Athenians in
Sicily made a descent from their ships upon the
territory of Himera, in concert with the Sicels
from the interior who had invaded the extreme
border[1] of Himeraea; and they also sailed against
the islands of Aeolus. Returning thence to Rhegium, they found that Pythodorus son of Isolochus,
an Athenian general, had come to succeed Laches
in command of the fleet. For their allies in Sicily
had sailed to Athens and persuaded them to aid
them with a larger fleet; for though their territory
was dominated by the Syracusans, yet since they
were kept from the sea by only a few ships they
were collecting a fleet and making preparations
with the determination not to submit. And the
Athenians manned forty ships to send to them, partly
because they believed that the war in Sicily could
sooner be brought to an end in this way, and partly
because they wished to give practice to their fleet.
Accordingly they despatched one of their generals,
Pythodorus, with a few ships, and were planning
later on to send Sophocles son of Sostratidas and
Eurymedon son of Thucles with the main body
of the fleet. Pythodorus, now that he had taken
over the command of Laches' ships, sailed toward
the end of the winter against the Locrian fort which

[1] i.e. toward the interior.

ἐπὶ τὸ Λοκρῶν φρούριον ὃ πρότερον Λάχης εἶλεν·
καὶ νικηθεὶς μάχῃ ὑπὸ τῶν Λοκρῶν ἀπεχώρησεν.

CXVI. Ἐρρύη δὲ περὶ αὐτὸ τὸ ἔαρ τοῦτο ὁ
ῥύαξ τοῦ πυρὸς ἐκ τῆς Αἴτνης, ὥσπερ καὶ πρότερον. καὶ γῆν τινα ἔφθειρε τῶν Καταναίων, οἳ
ὑπὸ τῇ Αἴτνῃ τῷ ὄρει οἰκοῦσιν, ὅπερ μέγιστόν
2 ἐστιν ὄρος ἐν τῇ Σικελίᾳ. λέγεται δὲ πεντη-
κοστῷ ἔτει ῥυῆναι τοῦτο μετὰ τὸ πρότερον ῥεῦμα,
τὸ δὲ ξύμπαν τρὶς γεγενῆσθαι τὸ ῥεῦμα ἀφ' οὗ
3 Σικελία ὑπὸ Ἑλλήνων οἰκεῖται. ταῦτα μὲν κατὰ
τὸν χειμῶνα τοῦτον ἐγένετο, καὶ ἕκτον ἔτος τῷ
πολέμῳ ἐτελεύτα τῷδε ὃν Θουκυδίδης ξυνέγραψεν.

---

[1] cf. ch. xcix.
[2] The eruption of Aetna mentioned in the Parian Marble,
lii. 67 f., as contemporaneous with the battle of Plataea
(479 B.C.); so that the expression "fiftieth year" is not quite
exact. From his form of expression in what follows, it

Laches had previously captured;[1] but he was defeated in battle by the Locrians and returned to Rhegium.

CXVI. At the beginning of the following spring the stream of fire burst from Aetna, as it had on former occasions. And it devastated a portion of the territory of the Catanaeans who dwell on the slope of Mount Aetna, the highest mountain in Sicily. This eruption took place, it is said, fifty years after the last preceding one;[2] and three eruptions all told are reported to have occurred since Sicily has been inhabited by the Hellenes.[3] Such was the course of events in this winter, and therewith ended the sixth year of this war of which Thucydides composed the history.

is clear that Thucydides, when he wrote this passage, could have had no knowledge of an eruption later than 425 B.C. He must therefore have died before that of 396 B.C. or, if he lived after that date, never revised this passage.

[3] *i.e.*, since the eighth century; see the account at the beginning of Book vi.

BOOK IV

Δ

I. Τοῦ δ' ἐπιγιγνομένου θέρους περὶ σίτου ἐκ-
βολὴν Συρακοσίων δέκα νῆες πλεύσασαι καὶ
Λοκρίδες ἴσαι Μεσσήνην τὴν ἐν Σικελίᾳ κατέλαβον, αὐτῶν ἐπαγαγομένων, καὶ ἀπέστη Μεσσήνη
2 Ἀθηναίων. ἔπραξαν δὲ τοῦτο μάλιστα οἱ μὲν
Συρακόσιοι ὁρῶντες προσβολὴν ἔχον τὸ χωρίον
τῆς Σικελίας καὶ φοβούμενοι τοὺς Ἀθηναίους μὴ
ἐξ αὐτοῦ ὁρμώμενοί ποτε σφίσι μείζονι παρι-
σκευῇ ἐπέλθωσιν, οἱ δὲ Λοκροὶ κατὰ ἔχθος τὸ
Ῥηγίνων, βουλόμενοι ἀμφοτέρωθεν αὐτοὺς κατα-
3 πολεμεῖν. καὶ ἐσεβεβλήκεσαν ἅμα ἐς τὴν Ῥηγίνων οἱ Λοκροὶ πανστρατιᾷ, ἵνα μὴ ἐπιβοηθῶσι
τοῖς Μεσσηνίοις, ἅμα δὲ καὶ ξυνεπαγόντων Ῥηγίνων φυγάδων, οἳ ἦσαν παρ' αὐτοῖς· τὸ γὰρ
Ῥήγιον ἐπὶ πολὺν χρόνον ἐστασίαζε καὶ ἀδύνατα
ἦν ἐν τῷ παρόντι τοὺς Λοκροὺς ἀμύνεσθαι, ᾗ καὶ
4 μᾶλλον ἐπετίθεντο. δῃώσαντες δὲ οἱ μὲν Λοκροὶ
τῷ πεζῷ ἀπεχώρησαν, αἱ δὲ νῆες Μεσσήνην
ἐφρούρουν· καὶ ἄλλαι[1] πληρούμεναι ἔμελλον αὐτόσε ἐγκαθορμισάμεναι τὸν πόλεμον ἐντεῦθεν
ποιήσεσθαι.

[1] αἱ, in the MSS. before πληρούμεναι, deleted by Classen,
followed by Hude.

BOOK IV

I. THE next summer, about the time of the earing of the grain, ten Syracusan and as many Locrian ships sailed to Messene in Sicily and occupied it, going thither on the invitation of the inhabitants; and Messene revolted from Athens. The chief reason for this act, on the part of the Syracusans, was that they saw that the place offered a point of attack upon Sicily and were afraid that the Athenians might some time make it a base from which to move against Syracuse with a larger force; the motive of the Locrians was their hostility to the Rhegians, whom they desired to subdue by both land and sea. And, indeed, the Locrians had at this same time invaded the territory of the Rhegians with all their forces in order to prevent them from giving any aid to the Messenians; and, besides, some Rhegians who were living in exile among the Locrians also urged them to make the invasion; for Rhegium had for a long time been in a state of revolution, and it was impossible at the moment to make any defence against the Locrians, who were consequently the more eager to attack. The Locrians first ravaged the country and then withdrew their land forces, but their ships continued guarding Messene; and still other ships were now being manned to be stationed at Messene and to carry on war from there.

II. Ὑπὸ δὲ τοὺς αὐτοὺς χρόνους τοῦ ἦρος, πρὶν τὸν σῖτον ἐν ἀκμῇ εἶναι, Πελοποννήσιοι καὶ οἱ ξύμμαχοι ἐσέβαλον ἐς τὴν Ἀττικήν (ἡγεῖτο δὲ Ἆγις ὁ Ἀρχιδάμου, Λακεδαιμονίων βασιλεύς), 2 καὶ ἐγκαθεζόμενοι ἐδῄουν τὴν γῆν. Ἀθηναῖοι δὲ τάς τε τεσσαράκοντα ναῦς ἐς Σικελίαν ἀπέστειλαν, ὥσπερ παρεσκευάζοντο, καὶ στρατηγοὺς τοὺς ὑπολοίπους Εὐρυμέδοντα καὶ Σοφοκλέα· Πυθόδωρος γὰρ ὁ τρίτος αὐτῶν ἤδη προαφῖκτο ἐς Σικε- 3 λίαν. εἶπον δὲ τούτοις καὶ Κερκυραίων ἅμα παραπλέοντας τῶν ἐν τῇ πόλει ἐπιμεληθῆναι, οἳ ἐλῃστεύοντο ὑπὸ τῶν ἐν τῷ ὄρει φυγάδων· καὶ Πελοποννησίων αὐτόσε νῆες ἑξήκοντα παρεπεπλεύκεσαν τοῖς ἐν τῷ ὄρει τιμωροὶ καὶ λιμοῦ ὄντος μεγάλου ἐν τῇ πόλει νομίζοντες κατασχή- 4 σειν ῥᾳδίως τὰ πράγματα. Δημοσθένει δὲ ὄντι ἰδιώτῃ μετὰ τὴν ἀναχώρησιν τὴν ἐξ Ἀκαρνανίας αὐτῷ δεηθέντι εἶπον χρῆσθαι ταῖς ναυσὶ ταύταις, ἢν βούληται, περὶ τὴν Πελοπόννησον.

III. Καὶ ὡς ἐγένοντο πλέοντες κατὰ τὴν Λακωνικὴν καὶ ἐπυνθάνοντο ὅτι αἱ νῆες ἐν Κερκύρᾳ ἤδη εἰσὶ τῶν Πελοποννησίων, ὁ μὲν Εὐρυμέδων καὶ Σοφοκλῆς ἠπείγοντο ἐς τὴν Κέρκυραν, ὁ δὲ Δημοσθένης ἐς τὴν Πύλον πρῶτον ἐκέλευε σχόντας αὐτοὺς καὶ πράξαντας ἃ δεῖ τὸν πλοῦν ποιεῖσθαι· ἀντιλεγόντων δὲ κατὰ τύχην χειμὼν ἐπιγενόμενος κατήνεγκε τὰς ναῦς ἐπὶ τὴν Πύλον. 2 καὶ ὁ Δημοσθένης εὐθὺς ἠξίου τειχίζεσθαι τὸ

II. About the same time that spring, before the grain was ripe, the Peloponnesians and their allies made an invasion of Attica, under the command of Agis son of Archidamus, king of the Lacedaemonians; and encamping there they ravaged the land. But the Athenians despatched the forty ships[1] to Sicily, as they had previously planned, together with the two remaining generals, Eurymedon and Sophocles, who were still at home; for Pythodorus, the third general, had already arrived in Sicily. These had instructions, as they sailed past Corcyra, to have a care for the inhabitants of the city, who were being plundered by the exiles on the mountain,[2] and the Peloponnesians with sixty ships had already sailed thither, with the purpose of aiding the party on the mountain and also in the belief that, since a great famine prevailed in the city, they would easily get control of affairs. Demosthenes also, who had retired into private life after his return from Acarnania,[3] now, at his own request, received permission from the Athenians to use the forty ships at his discretion in operations about the Peloponnesus.

III. Now when the Athenians arrived off the coast of Laconia and learned that the Peloponnesian fleet was already at Corcyra, Eurymedon and Sophocles were for pressing on to Corcyra, but Demosthenes urged them to put in at Pylos first, do there what was to be done, and then continue their voyage. They objected; but a storm came on, as it happened, and carried the fleet to Pylos. And Demosthenes at once urged them to fortify the place, as it was for

[1] cf. III. cxv. 4.   [2] cf. III. lxxxv. 4.
[3] cf. III. cxiv. 1.

χωρίον (ἐπὶ τοῦτο γὰρ ξυνεκπλεῦσαι), καὶ ἀπέ-
φαινε πολλὴν εὐπορίαν ξύλων τε καὶ λίθων καὶ
φύσει καρτερὸν ὂν καὶ ἐρῆμον αὐτό τε καὶ ἐπὶ
πολὺ τῆς χώρας· ἀπέχει γὰρ σταδίους μάλιστα ἡ
Πύλος τῆς Σπάρτης τετρακοσίους καὶ ἔστιν ἐν τῇ
Μεσσηνίᾳ ποτὲ οὔσῃ γῇ, καλοῦσι δὲ αὐτὴν οἱ
3 Λακεδαιμόνιοι Κορυφάσιον. οἱ δὲ πολλὰς ἔφασαν εἶναι ἄκρας ἐρήμους τῆς Πελοποννήσου, ἣν
βούληται καταλαμβάνων τὴν πόλιν δαπανᾶν.
τῷ δὲ διάφορόν τι ἐδόκει εἶναι τοῦτο τὸ χωρίον
ἑτέρου μᾶλλον, λιμένος τε προσόντος καὶ τοὺς
Μεσσηνίους οἰκείους ὄντας αὐτῷ τὸ ἀρχαῖον καὶ
ὁμοφώνους τοῖς Λακεδαιμονίοις πλεῖστ᾽ ἂν βλάπ-
τειν ἐξ αὐτοῦ ὁρμωμένους καὶ βεβαίους ἅμα τοῦ
χωρίου φύλακας ἔσεσθαι.

IV. Ὡς δὲ οὐκ ἔπειθεν οὔτε τοὺς στρατηγοὺς
οὔτε τοὺς στρατιώτας, ὕστερον καὶ τοῖς ταξιάρ-
χοις κοινώσας, ἡσύχαζον ὑπὸ ἀπλοίας, μέχρι
αὐτοῖς τοῖς στρατιώταις σχολάζουσιν ὁρμὴ ἐνέ-
2 πεσε περιστᾶσιν ἐκτειχίσαι τὸ χωρίον. καὶ
ἐγχειρήσαντες εἰργάζοντο, σιδήρια μὲν λιθουργὰ
οὐκ ἔχοντες, λογάδην δὲ φέροντες λίθους, καὶ
ξυνετίθεσαν ὡς ἕκαστόν τι ξυμβαίνοι· καὶ τὸν
πηλόν, εἴ που δέοι χρῆσθαι, ἀγγείων ἀπορίᾳ ἐπὶ
τοῦ νώτου ἔφερον ἐγκεκυφότες τε, ὡς μάλιστα
μέλλοι ἐπιμένειν, καὶ τὼ χεῖρε ἐς τοὐπίσω ξυμ-

this purpose that he had sailed with them; and he showed them that there was at hand an abundance of wood and stone, that the position was naturally a strong one, and that not only the place itself but also the neighbouring country for a considerable distance was unoccupied; for Pylos is about four hundred stadia distant from Sparta and lies in the land that was once Messenia; but the Lacedaemonians call the place Coryphasium. The other generals said there were many unoccupied headlands in the Peloponnesus, which he could seize if he wished to put the city to expense. Demosthenes, however, thought that this place had advantages over any other; not only was there a harbour close by, but also the Messenians, who originally owned this land and spoke the same dialect as the Lacedaemonians, would do them the greatest injury if they made this place their base of operations, and would at the same time be a trustworthy garrison of it.

IV. But Demosthenes could not win either the generals or the soldiers to his view, nor yet the commanders of divisions to whom he later communicated his plan; the army, therefore, since the weather was unfavourable for sailing, did nothing. But at length the soldiers themselves, having nothing to do, were seized with the impulse to station themselves around the place and fortify it. So they set their hands to this task and went to work; they had no iron tools for working stone, but picked up stones and put them together just as they happened to fit; and where mortar was needed, for want of hods, they carried it on their backs, bending over in such a way as would make it stay on best, and clasping both hands behind them to prevent it from falling

3 πλέκοντες, ὅπως μὴ ἀποπίπτοι. παντί τε τρόπῳ
ἠπείγοντο φθῆναι τοὺς Λακεδαιμονίους τὰ ἐπιμα-
χώτατα ἐξεργασάμενοι πρὶν ἐπιβοηθῆσαι. τὸ
γὰρ πλέον τοῦ χωρίου αὐτὸ καρτερὸν ὑπῆρχε καὶ
οὐδὲν ἔδει τείχους. V. οἱ δὲ ἑορτήν τινα ἔτυχον
ἄγοντες, καὶ ἅμα πυνθανόμενοι ἐν ὀλιγωρίᾳ
ἐποιοῦντο, ὡς, ὅταν ἐξέλθωσιν, ἢ οὐχ ὑπομενοῦν-
τας σφᾶς ἢ ῥᾳδίως ληψόμενοι βίᾳ· καί τι καὶ
αὐτοὺς ὁ στρατὸς ἔτι ἐν ταῖς Ἀθήναις ὢν ἐπέσχεν.
2 τειχίσαντες δὲ οἱ Ἀθηναῖοι τοῦ χωρίου τὰ πρὸς
ἤπειρον καὶ ἃ μάλιστα ἔδει ἐν ἡμέραις ἓξ τὸν μὲν
Δημοσθένη μετὰ νεῶν πέντε αὐτοῦ φύλακα κατα-
λείπουσι, ταῖς δὲ πλείοσι ναυσὶ τὸν ἐς τὴν Κέρκυραν πλοῦν καὶ Σικελίαν ἠπείγοντο.

VI. Οἱ δ' ἐν τῇ Ἀττικῇ ὄντες Πελοποννήσιοι
ὡς ἐπύθοντο τῆς Πύλου κατειλημμένης, ἀνεχώρουν κατὰ τάχος ἐπ' οἴκου, νομίζοντες μὲν οἱ
Λακεδαιμόνιοι καὶ Ἆγις ὁ βασιλεὺς οἰκεῖον σφίσι
τὸ περὶ τὴν Πύλον· ἅμα δὲ πρῲ ἐσβαλόντες καὶ
τοῦ σίτου ἔτι χλωροῦ ὄντος ἐσπάνιζον τροφῆς
τοῖς πολλοῖς, χειμών τε ἐπιγενόμενος μείζων παρὰ
τὴν καθεστηκυῖαν ὥραν ἐπίεσε τὸ στράτευμα.
2 ὥστε πολλαχόθεν ξυνέβη ἀναχωρῆσαί τε θᾶσσον
αὐτοὺς καὶ βραχυτάτην γενέσθαι τὴν ἐσβολὴν
ταύτην· ἡμέρας γὰρ πέντε καὶ δέκα ἔμειναν ἐν τῇ
Ἀττικῇ.

off. And in every way they made haste that they might complete the fortification of the most vulnerable points before the Lacedaemonians came out against them; for the greater part of the place was so strong by nature that it had no need of a wall. V. As for the Lacedaemonians, they happened to be celebrating a festival when they got word of the undertaking, and made light of it, thinking that the Athenians would not await their attack when they got ready to take the field, or, if they should, that they could easily take the place by force; and the fact also that their army was still in Attica had something to do with their delay. The Athenians in six days completed the wall on the side toward the land and at such other points as most needed it, and left Demosthenes there with five ships to defend it; they then took the main body of the fleet and hastened on their voyage to Corcyra and Sicily.

VI. But the Peloponnesians who were in Attica, when they heard that Pylos had been occupied, returned home in haste; for King Agis and the Lacedaemonians thought that the Athenian operations at Pylos were a matter of deep concern to them. And at the same time, since they had made their invasion early in the season when the grain was still green, most of them [1] were short of food, and bad weather, which came on with storms of greater violence than was to be expected so late in the spring, distressed the army. Consequently there were many reasons why they hastened their retirement from Attica and made this the shortest of their invasions; for they remained there only fifteen days.

[1] Each division had its own commissariat, and some were better provisioned than the main body. Classen explains, "were short of food for *so large* an army" (τοῖς πολλοῖς).

THUCYDIDES

VII. Κατὰ δὲ τὸν αὐτὸν χρόνον Σιμωνίδης
Ἀθηναίων στρατηγὸς Ἠιόνα τὴν ἐπὶ Θράκης
Μενδαίων ἀποικίαν, πολεμίαν δὲ οὖσαν, ξυλλέξας Ἀθηναίους τε ὀλίγους ἐκ τῶν φρουρίων καὶ
τῶν ἐκείνῃ ξυμμάχων πλῆθος προδιδομένην κατέ-
λαβεν. καὶ παραχρῆμα ἐπιβοηθησάντων Χαλκιδέων καὶ Βοττιαίων ἐξεκρούσθη τε καὶ ἀπέβαλε
πολλοὺς τῶν στρατιωτῶν.

VIII. Ἀναχωρησάντων δὲ τῶν ἐκ τῆς Ἀττικῆς
Πελοποννησίων οἱ Σπαρτιᾶται αὐτοὶ μὲν καὶ οἱ
ἐγγύτατα τῶν περιοίκων εὐθὺς ἐβοήθουν ἐπὶ τὴν
Πύλον, τῶν δὲ ἄλλων Λακεδαιμονίων βραδυτέρα
ἐγίγνετο ἡ ἔξοδος, ἄρτι ἀφιγμένων ἀφ᾽ ἑτέρας
2 στρατείας. περιήγγελλον δὲ καὶ κατὰ τὴν Πελοπόννησον βοηθεῖν ὅτι τάχιστα ἐπὶ Πύλον καὶ ἐπὶ
τὰς ἐν τῇ Κερκύρᾳ ναῦς σφῶν τὰς ἑξήκοντα
ἔπεμψαν, αἳ ὑπερενεχθεῖσαι τὸν Λευκαδίων
ἰσθμὸν καὶ λαθοῦσαι τὰς ἐν Ζακύνθῳ Ἀττικὰς
ναῦς ἀφικνοῦνται ἐπὶ Πύλον· παρῆν δὲ ἤδη καὶ ὁ
3 πεζὸς στρατός. Δημοσθένης δὲ προσπλεόντων
ἔτι τῶν Πελοποννησίων ὑπεκπέμπει φθάσας δύο
ναῦς ἀγγεῖλαι Εὐρυμέδοντι καὶ τοῖς ἐν ταῖς ναυσὶν
ἐν Ζακύνθῳ Ἀθηναίοις παρεῖναι ὡς τοῦ χωρίου
4 κινδυνεύοντος. καὶ αἱ μὲν νῆες κατὰ τάχος ἔπλεον
κατὰ τὰ ἐπεσταλμένα ὑπὸ Δημοσθένους· οἱ δὲ
Λακεδαιμόνιοι παρεσκευάζοντο ὡς τῷ τειχίσματι προσβαλοῦντες κατά τε γῆν καὶ κατὰ θάλασσαν, ἐλπίζοντες ῥᾳδίως αἱρήσειν οἰκοδόμημα
διὰ ταχέων εἰργασμένον καὶ ἀνθρώπων ὀλίγων

VII. About the same time Simonides, an Athenian general, getting together a few Athenians from the garrisons in Thrace and a large force from the allies in that neighbourhood, got, by the treachery of its inhabitants, possession of Eion in Thrace, a colony of the Mendaeans and hostile to Athens. But succour came promptly from the Chalcidians and the Bottiaeans and he was driven out with the loss of many of his soldiers.

VIII. On the return of the Peloponnesians from Attica, the Spartans themselves and the Perioeci who were in the neighbourhood of Pylos at once came to its relief; but the other Lacedaemonians were slower in coming, since they had just got back from another campaign. Word was also sent round to the states of the Peloponnesus, summoning them to come to the relief of Pylos as quickly as possible, and also to the sixty ships that were at Corcyra.[1] These were hauled across the Leucadian isthmus, and without being discovered by the Attic ships, which were now at Zacynthus, reached Pylos, where their land forces had already arrived. But before the Peloponnesian fleet had yet reached Pylos, Demosthenes managed to send out secretly ahead of them two ships which were to notify Eurymedon and the Athenian fleet at Zacynthus to come at once to his aid, as the place was in danger. And so the fleet proceeded in haste in compliance with Demosthenes' summons; meanwhile, however, the Lacedaemonians were busy with their preparations to attack the fortification both by land and by sea, and they thought that they would have no difficulty in capturing a structure which had been built hastily and was occupied by only a few

---

[1] cf. ch. ii. 3.

THUCYDIDES

5 ἐνόντων. προσδεχόμενοι δὲ τὴν ἀπὸ τῆς Ζακύνθου τῶν Ἀττικῶν νεῶν βοήθειαν ἐν νῷ εἶχον, ἢν
ἄρα μὴ πρότερον ἕλωσι, καὶ τοὺς ἔσπλους τοῦ
λιμένος ἐμφάρξαι, ὅπως μὴ ᾖ τοῖς Ἀθηναίοις
ἐφορμίσασθαι ἐς αὐτόν.

6 Ἡ γὰρ νῆσος ἡ Σφακτηρία καλουμένη τόν τε
λιμένα, παρατείνουσα καὶ ἐγγὺς ἐπικειμένη, ἐχυρὸν ποιεῖ καὶ τοὺς ἔσπλους στενούς, τῇ μὲν δυοῖν
νεοῖν διάπλουν κατὰ τὸ τείχισμα τῶν Ἀθηναίων
καὶ τὴν Πύλον, τῇ δὲ πρὸς τὴν ἄλλην ἤπειρον
ὀκτὼ ἢ ἐννέα· ὑλώδης τε καὶ ἀτριβὴς πᾶσα ὑπ'
ἐρημίας ἦν καὶ μέγεθος περὶ πέντε καὶ δέκα
7 σταδίους μάλιστα. τοὺς μὲν οὖν ἔσπλους ταῖς
ναυσὶν ἀντιπρώροις βύζην κλῄσειν ἔμελλον· τὴν
δὲ νῆσον ταύτην φοβούμενοι μὴ ἐξ αὐτῆς τὸν

---

[1] The harbour of Pylos is regarded by Classen and nearly
all recent commentators as identical with the modern Bay of
Navarino, the ἔσπλοι τοῦ λιμένος being the entrances north
and south of Sphacteria or Sphagia. But the entrance to
the harbour of Navarino south of Sphagia is now—and must
have been in Thucydides' time—a channel more than three-
quarters of a mile wide, and deep all the way across, so that
it does not answer to Thucydides' description of a passage
only wide enough to admit eight or nine triremes ; rather,
as Arnold says, "a hundred Greek ships might have found
room to sail abreast quite as easily as eight or nine."
Clearly, then, Thucydides could not have been personally
acquainted with the scene, and was misinformed as to the
breadth of the harbour's mouth, as Leake supposed. Or we
must assume that the dimensions of the entrances mentioned
by Thucydides were rather of those north and south of
Coryphasium, the modern Palaeo-Kastro, and the "harbour" was not the Bay of Navarino, as Thucydides sup-

men. But since they expected the Athenian fleet
to arrive soon from Zacynthus, it was their intention,
in case they should fail to take the place before
these came, to block up the entrances to the harbour
and thus make it impossible for the Athenians to
anchor inside and blockade them.

Now the island called Sphacteria stretches along
the mainland, lying quite close to it, and thus makes
the harbour safe and the entrances to it narrow;
on one side, opposite the Athenian fortifications
and Pylos, there is only room for two ships to pass
through, on the other side, next to the other part
of the mainland, there is room for eight or nine.[1]
The whole island was covered with timber and, since
it was uninhabited, had no roads, its length being
somewhere near fifteen stadia. Now it was the
intention of the Lacedaemonians to close up the
entrances tight by means of ships placed with their
prows outward; and as for the island, since they
were afraid that the Athenians would use it as

posed, but the Lagoon or Lake of Osmyn Aga, north of the
bay, and now cut off from it by a sandbar. This is the view
of Grundy—who in August, 1895, spent fourteen days there
making a survey—as to the lower entrance. The upper
entrance, he thinks, was closed already in Thucydides' time,
and the historian seems never to have apprehended that
fact. Grundy's view as to the lagoon being the harbour
meant by Thucydides is accepted by Steup, but he does not
approve of Grundy's assumption that Thucydides, without
personal knowledge of the region, following at different
points reports of different informants, confused statements
with reference to the harbour of Pylos and as to the bay as
referring to one and the same. See Arnold in App. to
Book IV. on Sphacteria; Grundy, "Investigation of the
Topography of the Region of Sphacteria and Pylos," in
Journal of Hellen. Studies, xvi. 1-54; Steup, App. on IV.
viii. 5.

πόλεμον σφίσι ποιῶνται, ὁπλίτας διεβίβασαν
ἐς αὐτὴν καὶ παρὰ τὴν ἤπειρον ἄλλους ἔταξαν·
8 οὕτω γὰρ τοῖς Ἀθηναίοις τήν τε νῆσον πολεμίαν
ἔσεσθαι τήν τε ἤπειρον ἀπόβασιν οὐκ ἔχουσαν
(τὰ γὰρ αὐτῆς τῆς Πύλου ἔξω τοῦ ἔσπλου πρὸς
τὸ πέλαγος ἀλίμενα ὄντα οὐχ ἕξειν ὅθεν ὁρμώμενοι ὠφελήσουσι τοὺς αὐτῶν), σφεῖς δὲ ἄνευ τε
ναυμαχίας καὶ κινδύνου ἐκπολιορκήσειν τὸ χωρίον
κατὰ τὸ εἰκός, σίτου τε οὐκ ἐνόντος καὶ δι᾽ ὀλίγης
9 παρασκευῆς κατειλημμένον. ὡς δ᾽ ἐδόκει αὐτοῖς
ταῦτα, καὶ διεβίβαζον ἐς τὴν νῆσον τοὺς ὁπλίτας
ἀποκληρώσαντες ἀπὸ πάντων τῶν λόχων. καὶ
διέβησαν μὲν καὶ ἄλλοι πρότερον κατὰ διαδοχήν,
οἱ δὲ τελευταῖοι καὶ ἐγκαταληφθέντες εἴκοσι καὶ
τετρακόσιοι ἦσαν καὶ Εἵλωτες οἱ περὶ αὐτούς·
ἦρχε δ᾽ αὐτῶν Ἐπιτάδας ὁ Μολόβρου.

IX. Δημοσθένης δὲ ὁρῶν τοὺς Λακεδαιμονίους
μέλλοντας προσβάλλειν ναυσί τε ἅμα καὶ πεζῷ,
παρεσκευάζετο καὶ αὐτός, καὶ τὰς τριήρεις αἳ
περιῆσαν αὐτῷ ἀπὸ τῶν καταλειφθεισῶν ἀνα-
σπάσας ὑπὸ τὸ τείχισμα προσεσταύρωσε, καὶ
τοὺς ναύτας ἐξ αὐτῶν ὥπλισεν ἀσπίσι[1] φαύλαις
καὶ οἰσυΐναις ταῖς πολλαῖς· οὐ γὰρ ἦν ὅπλα ἐν
χωρίῳ ἐρήμῳ πορίσασθαι, ἀλλὰ καὶ ταῦτα ἐκ

---

[1] τε, after ἀσπίσι in the MSS., deleted by Hude as not read by Suidas.

---

[1] i.e., north of the entrance, on the western side.
[2] Only three: five had been left him (ch. v. 2), but two of these he had sent to warn the squadron at Zacynthus.

a base for carrying on the war against them, they conveyed some hoplites across, at the same time posting others along the mainland. By these measures, they thought, the Athenians would find not only the island hostile to them, but also the mainland, since this afforded no landing-place; for there were no harbours along the shore of Pylos itself outside the entrance,[1] on the side toward the sea, and therefore the Athenians would have no base from which they could aid their countrymen. Consequently the Lacedaemonians believed that, without running the risk of a battle at sea, they could probably reduce the place by siege, since it had been occupied on short notice and was not supplied with provisions. As soon as they reached this conclusion they proceeded to convey the hoplites over to the island, drafting them by lot from all the companies. Several detachments had before this time crossed over, one group relieving another; the last to do so—and this is the force that was captured—numbering four hundred and twenty, besides the Helots who accompanied them, and they were under the command of Epitadas son of Molobrus.

IX. Meanwhile Demosthenes also, seeing that the Lacedaemonians intended to attack him by sea and by land at the same time, set about making his preparations. He drew ashore, close up under the fortification, the triremes [2] remaining to him out of those which had been left in his charge and enclosed them in a stockade; he then armed their crews with shields—poor ones, indeed, most of which were made of plaited willow; for it was not possible to procure arms in an uninhabited country, and such

ληστρικῆς Μεσσηνίων τριακοντέρου καὶ κέλητος
ἔλαβον, οἳ ἔτυχον παραγενόμενοι. ὁπλῖταί τε
τῶν Μεσσηνίων τούτων ὡς τεσσαράκοντα ἐγέ-
2 νοντο, οἷς ἐχρῆτο μετὰ τῶν ἄλλων. τοὺς μὲν
οὖν πολλοὺς τῶν τε ἀόπλων καὶ ὡπλισμένων ἐπὶ
τὰ τετειχισμένα μάλιστα καὶ ἐχυρὰ τοῦ χωρίου
πρὸς τὴν ἤπειρον ἔταξε, προειπὼν ἀμύνασθαι
τὸν πεζόν, ἢν προσβάλῃ· αὐτὸς δὲ ἀπολεξάμενος
ἐκ πάντων ἑξήκοντα ὁπλίτας καὶ τοξότας ὀλίγους
ἐχώρει ἔξω τοῦ τείχους ἐπὶ τὴν θάλασσαν, ᾗ
μάλιστα ἐκείνους προσεδέχετο πειράσειν ἀποβαίνειν, ἐς χωρία μὲν χαλεπὰ καὶ πετρώδη πρὸς
τὸ πέλαγος τετραμμένα, σφίσι δὲ τοῦ τείχους
ταύτῃ ἀσθενεστάτου ὄντος ἐσβιάσασθαι[1] αὐτοὺς
3 ἡγεῖτο προθυμήσεσθαι· οὔτε γὰρ αὐτοὶ ἐλπί-
ζοντές ποτε ναυσὶ κρατήσεσθαι οὐκ ἰσχυρὸν
ἐτείχιζον, ἐκείνοις τε βιαζομένοις τὴν ἀπόβασιν
4 ἁλώσιμον τὸ χωρίον γίγνεσθαι. κατὰ τοῦτο οὖν
πρὸς αὐτὴν τὴν θάλασσαν χωρήσας ἔταξε τοὺς
ὁπλίτας ὡς εἴρξων, ἢν δύνηται, καὶ παρεκελεύ-
σατο τοιάδε.

X. "Ἄνδρες οἱ ξυναράμενοι τοῦδε τοῦ κινδύνου, μηδεὶς ὑμῶν ἐν τῇ τοιᾷδε ἀνάγκῃ ξυνετὸς
βουλέσθω δοκεῖν εἶναι, ἐκλογιζόμενος ἅπαν τὸ
περιεστὸς ἡμᾶς δεινόν, μᾶλλον ἢ ἀπερισκέπτως
εὔελπις ὁμόσε χωρῆσαι τοῖς ἐναντίοις καὶ ἐκ
τούτων ἂν περιγενόμενος. ὅσα γὰρ ἐς ἀνάγκην

---

[1] ἐσβιάσασθαι: so Hude, after Leeuwen, for ἐπισπάσασθαι.

as they had they took from a thirty-oared privateer and a light boat belonging to some Messenians who chanced to come along, and included among them about forty hoplites, whom Demosthenes used along with the rest. He then posted the greater part of his troops, the unarmed as well as the armed, at the best fortified and strongest points of the place, on the side toward the mainland, giving them orders to ward off the enemy's infantry if it should attack. But he himself selected from the whole body of his troops sixty hoplites and a few archers, and with them sallied forth from the fort to the point on the seashore where he thought that the enemy would be most likely to attempt a landing. The ground, indeed, was difficult of access and rocky where it faced the sea, yet since the Athenian wall was weakest at this place the enemy would, he thought, be only too eager to make an assault there ; in fact the Athenians themselves had left their fortification weak at this spot merely because they never expected to be defeated at sea, and Demosthenes knew that if the enemy could force a landing there the place could be taken. Accordingly he posted his hoplites at this point, taking them to the very brink of the sea, determined to keep the enemy off if he could ; and then he exhorted them as follows :

X. "Soldiers, my comrades in this present hazard, let no one of you at such a time of necessity seek to prove his keenness of wit by calculating the full extent of the danger that encompasses us ; let him rather come to grips with the enemy in a spirit of unreflecting confidence that he will survive even these perils. For whenever it has come, as now

ἀφῖκται ὥσπερ τάδε, λογισμὸν ἥκιστα ἐνδεχό-
2 μενα, κινδύνου τοῦ ταχίστου προσδεῖται. ἐγὼ δὲ
καὶ τὰ πλείω ὁρῶ πρὸς ἡμῶν ὄντα, ἢν ἐθέλωμέν γε
μεῖναι καὶ μὴ τῷ πλήθει αὐτῶν καταπλαγέντες
τὰ ὑπάρχοντα ἡμῖν κρείσσω καταπροδοῦναι.
3 τοῦ τε γὰρ χωρίου τὸ δυσέμβατον ἡμέτερον
νομίζω, ὃ¹ μενόντων μὲν ἡμῶν ξύμμαχον γίγνεται, ὑποχωρήσασι² δὲ καίπερ χαλεπὸν ὂν εὔπορον ἔσται μηδενὸς κωλύοντος, καὶ τὸν πολέμιον
δεινότερον ἕξομεν μὴ ῥᾳδίας αὐτῷ πάλιν οὔσης
τῆς ἀναχωρήσεως, ἢν καὶ ὑφ' ἡμῶν βιάζηται· ἐπὶ
γὰρ ταῖς ναυσὶ ῥᾷστοί εἰσιν ἀμύνεσθαι, ἀπο-
4 βάντες δ' ἐν τῷ ἴσῳ ἤδη. τό τε πλῆθος αὐτῶν οὐκ
ἄγαν δεῖ φοβεῖσθαι· κατ' ὀλίγον γὰρ μαχεῖται
καίπερ πολὺ ὂν ἀπορίᾳ τῆς προσορμίσεως, καὶ
οὐκ ἐν γῇ στρατός ἐστιν ἐκ τοῦ ὁμοίου μείζων,
ἀλλ' ἀπὸ νεῶν, αἷς πολλὰ τὰ καίρια δεῖ ἐν τῇ
5 θαλάσσῃ ξυμβῆναι. ὥστε τὰς τούτων ἀπορίας
ἀντιπάλους ἡγοῦμαι τῷ ἡμετέρῳ πλήθει, καὶ ἅμα
ἀξιῶ ὑμᾶς, Ἀθηναίους ὄντας καὶ ἐπισταμένους
ἐμπειρίᾳ τὴν ναυτικὴν ἐπ' ἄλλους ἀπόβασιν ὅτι,
εἴ τις ὑπομένοι καὶ μὴ φόβῳ ῥοθίου καὶ νεῶν
δεινότητος κατάπλου ὑποχωροίη, οὐκ ἄν ποτε
βιάζοιτο, καὶ αὐτοὺς νῦν μεῖναί τε καὶ ἀμυνομέ-

¹ ὃ, Dion. Hal., MSS. omit.
² ὑποχωρήσασι, the genitive was to be expected after
μενόντων, and Poppo conjectures ὑποχωρησάντων. It is
dative of relation.

with us, to a case of necessity, where there is no room
for reflection, what is needed is to accept the hazard
with the least possible delay. However, as I see the
matter, the odds are on our side, if we are resolved
to stand our ground and are not so terrified by
their numbers as to sacrifice the advantages we
possess. As regards the position, the difficulty of
approach I regard as in our favour, since if we stand
firm that becomes a support, but once we give way,
even though the ground be rugged it will be easy of
access when there is none to resist; and we shall
then find the enemy more formidable, since it will
be no easy matter for them to turn and retreat, if
they should be hard-pressed by us; for though very
easily repelled while on board their ships, when once
they have landed they are on an equal footing with
us. And, as regards their numbers, we need have
no very great fear; for however numerous they are,
they will have to fight in small detachments on account of the difficulty of bringing their ships to
shore. And we have not to deal with an army,
which, though superior in numbers, is fighting on
land under like conditions with ourselves, but fighting on ships, and these require many favouring circumstances on the sea.[1] I therefore consider that
their disadvantages counterbalance our inferiority
in point of numbers. At the same time I call now
upon you, who are Athenians and know by experience that it is impossible to force a landing
from ships against an enemy on shore, if the
latter but stand their ground and do not give
way through fear of the splashing oars and of the
awe-inspiring sight of ships bearing down upon
them—I call upon you, in your turn to stand your

[1] c.g. a fair wind, space for manœuvring, etc.

νους παρ' αὐτὴν τὴν ῥαχίαν σῴζειν ὑμᾶς τε
αὐτοὺς καὶ τὸ χωρίον."

XI. Τοσαῦτα τοῦ Δημοσθένους παρακελευσαμένου οἱ Ἀθηναῖοι ἐθάρσησάν τε μᾶλλον καὶ
ἐπικαταβάντες ἐτάξαντο παρ' αὐτὴν τὴν θάλασ-
2 σαν. οἱ δὲ Λακεδαιμόνιοι ἄραντες τῷ τε κατὰ
γῆν στρατῷ προσέβαλλον τῷ τειχίσματι καὶ
ταῖς ναυσὶν ἅμα οὔσαις τεσσαράκοντα καὶ τρισί,
ναύαρχος δὲ αὐτῶν ἐπέπλει Θρασυμηλίδας ὁ
Κρατησικλέους, Σπαρτιάτης. προσέβαλλε δὲ
3 ᾗπερ ὁ Δημοσθένης προσεδέχετο. καὶ οἱ μὲν
Ἀθηναῖοι ἀμφοτέρωθεν, ἔκ τε γῆς καὶ ἐκ θαλάσσης, ἠμύνοντο· οἱ δὲ κατ' ὀλίγας ναῦς διελόμενοι,
διότι οὐκ ἦν πλείοσι προσσχεῖν, καὶ ἀναπαύοντες
ἐν τῷ μέρει τοὺς ἐπίπλους ἐποιοῦντο, προθυμίᾳ
τε πάσῃ χρώμενοι καὶ παρακελευσμῷ, εἴ πως
ὠσάμενοι ἕλοιεν τὸ τείχισμα. πάντων δὲ φανε-
4 ρώτατος Βρασίδας ἐγένετο. τριηραρχῶν γὰρ καὶ
ὁρῶν τοῦ χωρίου χαλεποῦ ὄντος τοὺς τριηράρχους
καὶ κυβερνήτας, εἴ που καὶ δοκοίη δυνατὸν εἶναι
σχεῖν, ἀποκνοῦντας καὶ φυλασσομένους τῶν νεῶν
μὴ ξυντρίψωσιν, ἐβόα λέγων ὡς οὐκ εἰκὸς εἴη
ξύλων φειδομένους τοὺς πολεμίους ἐν τῇ χώρᾳ
περιιδεῖν τεῖχος πεποιημένους, ἀλλὰ τάς τε σφετέρας ναῦς βιαζομένους τὴν ἀπόβασιν καταγνύ-
ναι ἐκέλευε καὶ τοὺς ξυμμάχους μὴ ἀποκνῆσαι
ἀντὶ μεγάλων εὐεργεσιῶν τὰς ναῦς τοῖς Λακεδαιμονίοις ἐν τῷ παρόντι ἐπιδοῦναι, ὀκείλαντας δὲ
καὶ παντὶ τρόπῳ ἀποβάντας τῶν τε ἀνδρῶν καὶ

ground, and, warding off the foe at the very water's edge, to save both yourselves and the stronghold."

XI. Thus encouraged by Demosthenes, the Athenians became yet more confident and going still nearer the water took up their position at the very brink of the sea. The Lacedaemonians, on the other hand, moved forward, and attacked the fortification at the same time with their land-army and with their ships, of which there were forty-three, the admiral in command of them being Thrasymelidas son of Cratesicles, a Spartan. And he attacked just where Demosthenes expected. The Athenians, on their part, proceeded to defend themselves in both directions, by land and by sea; but the enemy, dividing their ships into small detachments, because it was impossible for a larger number to approach the shore, and resting by turns, kept charging upon the Athenians, showing no lack of zeal and cheering each other on, in the hope that they might force the enemy back and take the fortification. Brasidas showed himself most conspicuous of all. Being captain of a galley, he noticed that the captains and pilots, because the shore was rocky, were inclined to hesitate and be careful of their ships, even when it seemed to be practicable to make a landing, for fear of dashing them to pieces. He would therefore shout that it ill became them through being thrifty of timber to allow their enemy to have built a fort in their country; nay, he urged, they must break their own ships so as to force a landing; and the allies he bade, in return for great benefits received from the Lacedaemonians, not to shrink from making them a free gift of their ships in the present emergency, but to run them aground, get ashore in any

τοῦ χωρίου κρατῆσαι. XII. καὶ ὁ μὲν τούς τε
ἄλλους τοιαῦτα ἐπέσπερχε καὶ τὸν ἑαυτοῦ κυβερ-
νήτην ἀναγκάσας ὀκεῖλαι τὴν ναῦν ἐχώρει ἐπὶ
τὴν ἀποβάθραν· καὶ πειρώμενος ἀποβαίνειν ἀνε-
κόπη ὑπὸ τῶν Ἀθηναίων, καὶ τραυματισθεὶς
πολλὰ ἐλιποψύχησέ τε καὶ πεσόντος αὐτοῦ ἐς
τὴν παρεξειρεσίαν ἡ ἀσπὶς περιερρύη ἐς τὴν
θάλασσαν, καὶ ἐξενεχθείσης αὐτῆς ἐς τὴν γῆν οἱ
Ἀθηναῖοι ἀνελόμενοι ὕστερον πρὸς τὸ τροπαῖον
ἐχρήσαντο ὃ ἔστησαν τῆς προσβολῆς ταύτης.

2   Οἱ δ' ἄλλοι προυθυμοῦντο μέν, ἀδύνατοι δ' ἦσαν
ἀποβῆναι τῶν τε χωρίων χαλεπότητι καὶ τῶν
3 Ἀθηναίων μενόντων καὶ οὐδὲν ὑποχωρούντων. ἐς
τοῦτό τε περιέστη ἡ τύχη ὥστε Ἀθηναίους μὲν ἐκ
γῆς τε καὶ ταύτης Λακωνικῆς ἀμύνεσθαι ἐκείνους
ἐπιπλέοντας, Λακεδαιμονίους δὲ ἐκ νεῶν τε καὶ ἐς
τὴν ἑαυτῶν πολεμίαν οὖσαν ἐπ' Ἀθηναίους ἀπο-
βαίνειν· ἐπὶ πολὺ γὰρ ἐποίει τῆς δόξης ἐν τῷ
τότε τοῖς μὲν ἠπειρώταις μάλιστα εἶναι καὶ τὰ
πεζὰ κρατίστοις, τοῖς δὲ θαλασσίοις τε καὶ ταῖς
ναυσὶ πλεῖστον προύχειν.

XIII. Ταύτην μὲν οὖν τὴν ἡμέραν καὶ τῆς
ὑστεραίας μέρος τι προσβολὰς ποιησάμενοι ἐπέ-
παυντο· καὶ τῇ τρίτῃ ἐπὶ ξύλα ἐς μηχανὰς παρέ-
πεμψαν τῶν νεῶν τινας ἐς Ἀσίνην, ἐλπίζοντες τὸ
κατὰ τὸν λιμένα τεῖχος ὕψος μὲν ἔχον, ἀπο-
2 βάσεως δὲ μάλιστα οὔσης ἑλεῖν ἂν [1] μηχαναῖς. ἐν
τούτῳ δὲ αἱ ἐκ τῆς Ζακύνθου νῆες τῶν Ἀθηναίων

---

[1] ἂν added by Madvig.

way they could, and master both the men and the place. XII. And he not only urged on the rest in this way, but, compelling his own pilot to beach his ship, he made for the gangway; and in trying to land he was knocked back by the Athenians, and after receiving many wounds fainted away. As he fell into the forward part of the ship his shield slipped off into the sea, and, being carried ashore, was picked up by the Athenians, who afterward used it for the trophy which they set up in commemoration of this attack.

The crews of the other Peloponnesian ships showed no lack of zeal, but were unable to land, both by reason of the difficulty of the ground and because the Athenians stood firm and would not give way at all. In such fashion had fortune swung round that the Athenians, fighting on land, and Laconian land at that, were trying to ward off a Lacedaemonian attack from the sea, while the Lacedaemonians, fighting in ships, were trying to effect a landing upon their own territory, now hostile, in the face of the Athenians. For at this time it was the special renown of the Lacedaemonians that they were a land power and invincible with their army, and of the Athenians that they were seamen and vastly superior with their fleet.

XIII. After making attacks that day and part of the next the Peloponnesians desisted. On the third day they sent some of the ships to Asine for wood with which to make engines, hoping that by means of engines they should be able to take the wall opposite the harbour in spite of its height, since here it was quite practicable to make a landing. Meanwhile, the Athenian fleet from Zacynthus arrived,

παραγίγνονται πεντήκοντα· προσεβοήθησαν γὰρ
τῶν τε φρουρίδων τινὲς αὐτοῖς τῶν ἐκ Ναυπάκτου
3 καὶ Χῖαι τέσσαρες. ὡς δὲ εἶδον τήν τε ἤπειρον
ὁπλιτῶν περίπλεων τήν τε νῆσον, ἔν τε τῷ λιμένι
οὔσας τὰς ναῦς καὶ οὐκ ἐκπλεούσας, ἀπορήσαντες
ὅπῃ καθορμίσωνται, τότε μὲν ἐς Πρωτὴν τὴν
νῆσον, ἣ οὐ πολὺ ἀπέχει ἐρῆμος οὖσα, ἔπλευσαν
καὶ ηὐλίσαντο, τῇ δ᾽ ὑστεραίᾳ παρασκευασάμενοι
ὡς ἐπὶ ναυμαχίαν ἀνήγοντο, ἢν μὲν ἀντεκπλεῖν
ἐθέλωσι σφίσιν ἐς τὴν εὐρυχωρίαν, εἰ δὲ μή, ὡς
αὐτοὶ ἐπεσπλευσούμενοι.

4 Καὶ οἱ μὲν οὔτε ἀντανήγοντο οὔτε ἃ διενοήθη-
σαν, φάρξαι τοὺς ἔσπλους, ἔτυχον ποιήσαντες,
ἡσυχάζοντες δ᾽ ἐν τῇ γῇ τάς τε ναῦς ἐπλήρουν
καὶ παρεσκευάζοντο, ἢν ἐσπλέῃ τις, ὡς ἐν τῷ
λιμένι ὄντι οὐ σμικρῷ ναυμαχήσοντες. XIV. οἱ δ᾽
Ἀθηναῖοι γνόντες καθ᾽ ἑκάτερον τὸν ἔσπλουν
ὥρμησαν ἐπ᾽ αὐτούς, καὶ τὰς μὲν πλείους καὶ
μετεώρους ἤδη τῶν νεῶν καὶ ἀντιπρώρους προσπεσόντες ἐς φυγὴν κατέστησαν, καὶ ἐπιδιώκοντες
ὡς διὰ βραχέος ἔτρωσαν μὲν πολλάς, πέντε δὲ
ἔλαβον καὶ μίαν τούτων αὐτοῖς ἀνδράσιν· ταῖς δὲ
λοιπαῖς ἐν τῇ γῇ καταπεφευγυίαις ἐνέβαλλον. αἱ
δὲ καὶ πληρούμεναι ἔτι πρὶν ἀνάγεσθαι ἐκόπτοντο·
καί τινας καὶ ἀναδούμενοι κενὰς εἷλκον τῶν ἀν-
2 δρῶν ἐς φυγὴν ὡρμημένων. ἃ ὁρῶντες οἱ Λακεδαι-

now numbering fifty ships, for it had been reinforced
by some of the ships on guard at Naupactus and by
four Chian vessels. But they saw that both the mainland and the island were full of hoplites, and that
the Lacedaemonian ships were in the harbour and
not intending to come out; they therefore, being at
a loss where to anchor, sailed for the present to
Prote, an uninhabited island not far from Pylos, and
bivouacked there. The next day they set sail, having
first made preparations to give battle in case the
enemy should be inclined to come out into the open
water to meet them ; if not, they intended to sail
into the harbour themselves.

Now the Lacedaemonians did not put out to meet
the Athenians, and somehow they had neglected to
block up the entrances as they had purposed; on
the contrary, they remained inactive on the shore,
engaged in manning their ships and making ready,
in case any one sailed into the harbour, to fight
there, since there was plenty of room. XIV. As for
the Athenians, when they saw the situation, they
rushed in upon them by both entrances and falling
upon their ships, most of which were by now afloat
and facing forward, put them to flight, and since
there was only a short distance for the pursuit,[1] not
only damaged many of them but also captured five,
one of them with all her crew ; the rest they kept on
ramming even after they had fled to the shore. Yet
other ships were being cut to pieces while still being
manned, before they could put to sea; and some they
took in tow empty, their crews having taken to flight,
and began to haul them away. At this sight the

---

[1] Or, "giving chase so far as the short distance allowed,
not only damaged . . ."

μόνιοι καὶ περιαλγοῦντες τῷ πάθει, ὅτιπερ αὐτῶν
οἱ ἄνδρες ἀπελαμβάνοντο ἐν τῇ νήσῳ, παρεβοή-
θουν, καὶ ἐπεσβαίνοντες ἐς τὴν θάλασσαν ξὺν
τοῖς ὅπλοις ἀνθεῖλκον ἐπιλαμβανόμενοι τῶν νεῶν·
καὶ ἐν τούτῳ κεκωλῦσθαι ἐδόκει ἕκαστος ᾧ μή
3 τινι καὶ αὐτὸς ἔργῳ παρῆν. ἐγένετό τε ὁ θόρυβος
μέγας, καὶ ἀντηλλαγμένου τοῦ ἑκατέρων τρόπου
περὶ τὰς ναῦς· οἵ τε γὰρ Λακεδαιμόνιοι ὑπὸ προ-
θυμίας καὶ ἐκπλήξεως ὡς εἰπεῖν ἄλλο οὐδὲν ἢ ἐκ
γῆς ἐναυμάχουν, οἵ τε Ἀθηναῖοι κρατοῦντες καὶ
βουλόμενοι τῇ παρούσῃ τύχῃ ὡς ἐπὶ πλεῖστον
4 ἐπεξελθεῖν ἀπὸ νεῶν ἐπεζομάχουν. πολύν τε πόνον
παρασχόντες ἀλλήλοις καὶ τραυματίσαντες διεκρίθησαν, καὶ οἱ Λακεδαιμόνιοι τὰς κενὰς ναῦς
5 πλὴν τῶν τὸ πρῶτον ληφθεισῶν διέσωσαν. καταστάντες δὲ ἑκάτεροι ἐς τὸ στρατόπεδον οἱ μὲν τροπαῖόν τε ἔστησαν καὶ νεκροὺς ἀπέδοσαν καὶ
ναυαγίων ἐκράτησαν, καὶ τὴν νῆσον εὐθὺς περιέπλεον καὶ ἐν φυλακῇ εἶχον, ὡς τῶν ἀνδρῶν
ἀπειλημμένων· οἱ δ᾽ ἐν τῇ ἠπείρῳ Πελοποννήσιοι
καὶ ἀπὸ πάντων ἤδη βεβοηθηκότες ἔμενον κατὰ
χώραν ἐπὶ τῇ Πύλῳ.

XV. Ἐς δὲ τὴν Σπάρτην ὡς ἠγγέλθη τὰ γεγενημένα περὶ Πύλου, ἔδοξεν αὐτοῖς ὡς ἐπὶ ξυμφορᾷ
μεγάλῃ τὰ τέλη καταβάντας ἐς τὸ στρατόπεδον
2 βουλεύειν παραχρῆμα ὁρῶντας ὅ τι ἂν δοκῇ. καὶ
ὡς εἶδον ἀδύνατον ὂν τιμωρεῖν τοῖς ἀνδράσι καὶ

Lacedaemonian soldiers on the shore, beside themselves with grief at the impending calamity, in that their comrades were being cut off on the island, rushed to the rescue, and going down into the sea in full armour took hold of the ships and tried to drag them back. Indeed, each man felt that no progress was being made where he himself was not at hand to help. The tumult that arose was great, especially since in this battle for the ships each side adopted the other's manner of fighting; for the Lacedaemonians in their eagerness and excitement were virtually waging a sea-fight from the land, while the Athenians, who were winning and wanted to follow up their success to the utmost while their good fortune lasted, were fighting a land-battle from their ships. Finally, after causing each other great distress and inflicting much damage, they separated, the Lacedaemonians saving all their empty ships except those which had been taken at first. Both sides then returned to their camps. The Athenians thereupon set up a trophy, gave back the dead, secured possession of the wrecks, and immediately began to sail round the island and keep it under guard, considering that the men on it were now cut off; on the other hand, the Peloponnesians on the mainland, and the reinforcements that had now arrived from all directions, remained in position at Pylos.

XV. At Sparta, when they received the news of what had happened at Pylos, regarding it as a great calamity they decided that the magistrates should go down to the camp, see the situation for themselves, and then determine on the spot what should be done. Now when these saw that no help could be given to the men on the island, and at the same

κινδυνεύειν οὐκ ἐβούλοντο ἢ ὑπὸ λιμοῦ τι παθεῖν
αὐτοὺς ἢ ὑπὸ πλήθους βιασθέντας κρατηθῆναι,¹
ἔδοξεν αὐτοῖς πρὸς τοὺς στρατηγοὺς τῶν Ἀθηναίων, ἢν ἐθέλωσι, σπονδὰς ποιησαμένους τὰ
περὶ Πύλον ἀποστεῖλαι ἐς τὰς Ἀθήνας πρέσβεις περὶ ξυμβάσεως καὶ τοὺς ἄνδρας ὡς τάχιστα
πειρᾶσθαι κομίσασθαι.

XVI. Δεξαμένων δὲ τῶν στρατηγῶν τὸν λόγον
ἐγίγνοντο σπονδαὶ τοιαίδε· Λακεδαιμονίους μὲν
τὰς ναῦς ἐν αἷς ἐναυμάχησαν καὶ τὰς ἐν τῇ
Λακωνικῇ πάσας, ὅσαι ἦσαν μακραί, παραδοῦναι
κομίσαντας ἐς Πύλον Ἀθηναίοις, καὶ ὅπλα μὴ
ἐπιφέρειν τῷ τειχίσματι μήτε κατὰ γῆν μήτε
κατὰ θάλασσαν, Ἀθηναίους δὲ τοῖς ἐν τῇ νήσῳ
ἀνδράσι σῖτον ἐᾶν τοὺς ἐν τῇ ἠπείρῳ Λακεδαιμονίους ἐσπέμπειν τακτὸν καὶ μεμαγμένον, δύο
χοίνικας ἑκάστῳ Ἀττικὰς ἀλφίτων καὶ δύο
κοτύλας οἴνου καὶ κρέας, θεράποντι δὲ τούτων
ἡμίσεα· ταῦτα δὲ ὁρώντων τῶν Ἀθηναίων ἐσπέμπειν καὶ πλοῖον μηδὲν ἐσπλεῖν λάθρα· φυλάσσειν
δὲ καὶ τὴν νῆσον Ἀθηναίους μηδὲν ἧσσον, ὅσα μὴ
ἀποβαίνοντας, καὶ ὅπλα μὴ ἐπιφέρειν τῷ Πελοποννησίων στρατῷ μήτε κατὰ γῆν μήτε κατὰ
2 θάλασσαν. ὅ τι δ' ἂν τούτων παραβαίνωσιν
ἑκάτεροι καὶ ὁτιοῦν, τότε λελύσθαι τὰς σπονδάς.
ἐσπεῖσθαι δὲ αὐτὰς μέχρι οὗ ἐπανέλθωσιν οἱ ἐκ
τῶν Ἀθηνῶν Λακεδαιμονίων πρέσβεις· ἀποστεῖλαι
δὲ αὐτοὺς τριήρει Ἀθηναίους καὶ πάλιν κομίσαι.
ἐλθόντων δὲ τάς τε σπονδὰς λελύσθαι ταύτας καὶ
τὰς ναῦς ἀποδοῦναι Ἀθηναίους ὁμοίας οἵασπερ ἂν

¹ κρατηθῆναι, CG, ἢ κρατηθῆναι, ABFM.

time were unwilling to run the risk of their being starved to death or forced to succumb to superior numbers, they decided, so far as Pylos was concerned, to conclude a truce with the Athenian generals, if they should consent, and to send envoys to Athens to propose an agreement, and thus try to recover their men as quickly as possible.

XVI. The generals accepted the proposal and a truce was concluded upon the following terms: The Lacedaemonians were to surrender to the Athenians the ships in which they had fought the battle, and were to bring to Pylos and deliver to them all the other ships of war which were in Laconia, and they were not to attack the fortification either by land or by sea. The Athenians were to permit the Lacedaemonians on the mainland to send flour to the men on the island, a fixed amount and already-kneaded, for each soldier two quarts [1] of barley-meal and a pint of wine and a ration of meat, and for each servant half as much; and they were to send these things to the island under the supervision of the Athenians, and no boat was to sail thither secretly. The Athenians were to go on guarding the island as before, but without landing on it, and were not to attack the army of the Peloponnesians either by land or sea. If either party should violate this agreement in any particular whatsoever, the truce should forthwith be at an end. The truce was to hold good until the Lacedaemonian envoys should get back from Athens; and the Athenians were to conduct them thither in a trireme and bring them back. On their return this truce was to be at an end, and the Athenians were then to restore the ships in as good condition as when

[1] The choinix was about two pints, dry measure; the cotyle, about half a pint.

3 παραλάβωσιν.   αἱ μὲν σπονδαὶ ἐπὶ τούτοις ἐγένοντο, καὶ αἱ νῆες παρεδόθησαν οὖσαι περὶ
ἑξήκοντα, καὶ οἱ πρέσβεις ἀπεστάλησαν. ἀφικόμενοι δὲ ἐς τὰς Ἀθήνας ἔλεξαν τοιάδε.

XVII. "Ἔπεμψαν ἡμᾶς Λακεδαιμόνιοι, ὦ
Ἀθηναῖοι, περὶ τῶν ἐν τῇ νήσῳ ἀνδρῶν πράξον-
τας ὅ τι ἂν ὑμῖν τε ὠφέλιμον ὂν τὸ αὐτὸ πείθωμεν
καὶ ἡμῖν ἐς τὴν ξυμφορὰν[1] ὡς ἐκ τῶν παρόντων
2 κόσμον μάλιστα μέλλῃ οἴσειν. τοὺς δὲ λόγους
μακροτέρους οὐ παρὰ τὸ εἰωθὸς μηκυνοῦμεν, ἀλλ᾽
ἐπιχώριον ὂν ἡμῖν οὗ μὲν βραχεῖς ἀρκῶσι μὴ
πολλοῖς χρῆσθαι, πλείοσι δὲ ἐν ᾧ ἂν καιρὸς ᾖ
διδάσκοντάς τι τῶν προύργου λόγοις τὸ δέον
3 πράσσειν. λάβετε δὲ αὐτοὺς μὴ πολεμίως μηδ᾽
ὡς ἀξύνετοι διδασκόμενοι, ὑπόμνησιν δὲ τοῦ καλῶς
4 βουλεύσασθαι πρὸς εἰδότας ἡγησάμενοι. ὑμῖν
γὰρ εὐτυχίαν τὴν παροῦσαν ἔξεστι καλῶς θέσθαι,
ἔχουσι μὲν ὧν κρατεῖτε, προσλαβοῦσι δὲ τιμὴν
καὶ δόξαν, καὶ μὴ παθεῖν ὅπερ οἱ ἀήθως τι ἀγαθὸν λαμβάνοντες τῶν ἀνθρώπων· αἰεὶ γὰρ τοῦ
πλέονος ἐλπίδι ὀρέγονται διὰ τὸ καὶ τὰ παρόντα
5 ἀδοκήτως εὐτυχῆσαι. οἷς δὲ πλεῖσται μεταβολαὶ
ἐπ᾽ ἀμφότερα ξυμβεβήκασι, δίκαιοί εἰσι καὶ
ἀπιστότατοι εἶναι ταῖς εὐπραγίαις· ὃ τῇ τε ὑμετέρᾳ πόλει δι᾽ ἐμπειρίαν καὶ ἡμῖν μάλιστ᾽ ἂν ἐκ
τοῦ εἰκότος προσείη.

---

[1] ἐς τὴν ξυμφοράν, bracketed by Hude.

they received them. The truce was concluded on these terms, the ships, sixty in number, were delivered up, and the envoys dispatched. When they arrived at Athens they spoke as follows:

XVII. "The Lacedaemonians, men of Athens, have sent us to arrange, in behalf of our men on the island, such terms as we may show to be at once advantageous to you and also most likely under present circumstances, in view of our misfortune, to bring credit to ourselves. If we speak at some length we shall not be departing from our custom; on the contrary, though it is the fashion of our country not to use many words where few suffice, yet, whenever occasion arises to expound an important matter and thereby to accomplish by speech the end we have in view, we use words more freely. And do not receive what we say in a hostile spirit, nor feel that you are being instructed as though you were without understanding, but regard our words as merely a reminder to men who know how to come to a good decision. For it is in your power to turn your present favourable fortune to good account, not only keeping what you have got, but acquiring honour and reputation besides. You may thus avoid the experience of those who achieve some unwonted success; for these are always led on by hope to grasp at more because of their unexpected good fortune in the present. And yet those who have most often undergone a change of fortune for better or for worse have best reason to be distrustful of prosperity; and this would naturally hold true of both your state and ours in an exceptional degree, in view of our past experience.

XVIII. "Γνῶτε δὲ καὶ ἐς τὰς ἡμετέρας νῦν ξυμφορὰς ἀπιδόντες, οἵτινες ἀξίωμα μέγιστον τῶν Ἑλλήνων ἔχοντες ἥκομεν παρ' ὑμᾶς, πρότερον αὐτοὶ κυριώτεροι νομίζοντες εἶναι δοῦναι ἐφ' ἃ νῦν 2 ἀφιγμένοι ὑμᾶς αἰτούμεθα. καίτοι οὔτε δυνάμεως ἐνδείᾳ ἐπάθομεν αὐτὸ οὔτε μείζονος προσγενομένης ὑβρίσαντες, ἀπὸ δὲ τῶν αἰεὶ ὑπαρχόντων γνώμῃ σφαλέντες, ἐν ᾧ πᾶσι τὸ αὐτὸ ὁμοίως ὑπάρχει. 3 ὥστε οὐκ εἰκὸς ὑμᾶς διὰ τὴν παροῦσαν νῦν ῥώμην πόλεώς τε καὶ τῶν προσγεγενημένων καὶ τὸ τῆς 4 τύχης οἴεσθαι αἰεὶ μεθ' ὑμῶν ἔσεσθαι. σωφρόνων δὲ ἀνδρῶν οἵτινες τἀγαθὰ ἐς ἀμφίβολον[1] ἀσφαλῶς ἔθεντο (καὶ ταῖς ξυμφοραῖς οἱ αὐτοὶ εὐξυνετώτερον ἂν προσφέροιντο), τόν τε πόλεμον νομίσωσι μὴ καθ' ὅσον ἄν τις αὐτοῦ μέρος βούληται μεταχειρίζειν, τούτῳ ξυνεῖναι, ἀλλ' ὡς ἂν αἱ τύχαι αὐτῶν ἡγήσωνται, καὶ ἐλάχιστ' ἂν οἱ τοιοῦτοι πταίοντες διὰ τὸ μὴ τῷ ὀρθουμένῳ αὐτοῦ πιστεύοντες ἐπαίρεσθαι ἐν τῷ εὐτυχεῖν ἂν μάλιστα 5 καταλύοιντο· ὃ νῦν ὑμῖν, ὦ Ἀθηναῖοι, καλῶς ἔχει πρὸς ἡμᾶς πρᾶξαι, καὶ μήποτε ὕστερον, ἢν ἄρα μὴ πειθόμενοι σφαλῆτε, ἃ πολλὰ ἐνδέχεται, νομισθῆναι τύχῃ καὶ τὰ νῦν προχωρήσαντα κρατῆσαι,

---

[1] ἀμφίβολον, MSS.; Hude reads ἀναμφίβολον.

---

[1] Or, "make sure of their advantages having regard to changes of luck."

XVIII. "To be convinced of this, you need only look at our present misfortunes. We who of all the Hellenes formerly were held in the highest consideration have come before you, although we have been wont to regard ourselves as better entitled to confer such favours as we have now come to beg of you. And yet it was neither through lack of power that we met with this misfortune, nor because our power became too great and we waxed insolent; nay, our resources were what they always were and we merely erred in judgment—a thing to which all are alike liable. Accordingly there is no reason why you, because of the strength both of your city and of its new acquisitions at the present moment, should expect that the favour of fortune will always be with you. Prudent men take the safe course of accounting prosperity mutable [1]—the same men, too, would deal more sagaciously with misfortunes—and consider that when anyone is at war he may not limit his participation to whatever portion of it he may choose to carry on,[2] but that he must follow where his fortune leads. Such men are least likely to come to grief, since they do not allow themselves to become elated by overconfidence in military success, and are therefore most likely to seize the moment of good fortune for concluding peace. And this, Athenians, is the policy which it is good for you to adopt towards us to-day, and not at some future time, should you perchance through rejecting our overtures incur disaster—and of this there are many possibilities—be credited with having won even your present successes through good fortune, when it is possible to

[2] *i.e.* in warfare one cannot accept only the successes and avoid the reverses by stopping before the latter set in; one is in the hands of fortune.

ἐξὸν ἀκίνδυνον δόκησιν ἰσχύος καὶ ξυνέσεως ἐς τὸ
ἔπειτα καταλιπεῖν.

XIX. "Λακεδαιμόνιοι δὲ ὑμᾶς προκαλοῦνται
ἐς σπονδὰς καὶ διάλυσιν πολέμου, διδόντες μὲν
εἰρήνην καὶ ξυμμαχίαν καὶ ἄλλην φιλίαν πολλὴν
καὶ οἰκειότητα ἐς ἀλλήλους ὑπάρχειν, ἀνται-
τοῦντες δὲ τοὺς ἐκ τῆς νήσου ἄνδρας, καὶ ἄμεινον
ἡγούμενοι ἀμφοτέροις μὴ διακινδυνεύεσθαι, εἴτε
βίᾳ ἂν¹ διαφύγοιεν παρατυχούσης τινὸς σωτηρίας
εἴτε καὶ ἐκπολιορκηθέντες μᾶλλον ἂν χειρωθεῖεν.
2 νομίζομέν τε τὰς μεγάλας ἔχθρας μάλιστ' ἂν
διαλύεσθαι βεβαίως, οὐκ ἢν ἀνταμυνόμενός τις
καὶ ἐπικρατήσας τὰ πλείω τοῦ πολέμου κατ'
ἀνάγκην ὅρκοις ἐγκαταλαμβάνων μὴ ἀπὸ τοῦ
ἴσου ξυμβῇ, ἀλλ' ἤν, παρὸν τὸ αὐτὸ δρᾶσαι πρὸς
τὸ ἐπιεικές, καὶ ἀρετῇ αὐτὸν νικήσας παρὰ ἃ
3 προσεδέχετο μετρίως ξυναλλαγῇ. ὀφείλων γὰρ
ἤδη ὁ ἐναντίος μὴ ἀνταμύνεσθαι ὡς βιασθείς,
ἀλλ' ἀνταποδοῦναι ἀρετήν, ἑτοιμότερός ἐστιν
4 αἰσχύνῃ ἐμμένειν οἷς ξυνέθετο. καὶ μᾶλλον πρὸς
τοὺς μείζονως ἐχθροὺς τοῦτο δρῶσιν οἱ ἄνθρωποι
ἢ πρὸς τοὺς μέτρια διενεχθέντας· πεφύκασί τε
τοῖς μὲν ἑκουσίως ἐνδοῦσιν ἀνθησσᾶσθαι μεθ'
ἡδονῆς, πρὸς δὲ τὰ ὑπεραυχοῦντα καὶ παρὰ
γνώμην διακινδυνεύειν.

¹ ἄν, Krüger's conjecture.

leave to posterity an unhazarded reputation at once for strength and sagacity.

XIX. "The Lacedaemonians therefore invite you to accept terms and bring the war to an end, offering you peace and alliance, and apart from this the maintenance of hearty friendship and intimacy one with the other; and asking on their side merely the return of the men on the island. They think it better for both parties not to take the risk either of the besieged making their escape in spite of you, should some chance of safety present itself, or of their being reduced by siege to a still harder lot. We believe, too, that a permanent reconciliation of bitter enmities is more likely to be secured, not when one party seeks revenge and, because he has gained a decided mastery in the war, tries to bind his opponent by compulsory oaths and thus makes peace with him on unequal terms, but when, having it in his power to secure the same result by clemency, he vanquishes his foe by generosity also, offering him terms of reconciliation which are moderate beyond all his expectations. For the adversary, finding himself now under obligation to repay the generosity in kind, instead of striving for vengeance for having had terms forced upon him, is moved by a sense of honour and is more ready to abide by his agreements. Furthermore, men are more inclined to act thus toward their more serious enemies than toward those with whom they have had but trifling differences. And, finally, it is natural for men cheerfully to accept defeat at the hands of those who first make willing concessions, but to fight to the bitter end, even contrary to their better judgment, against an overbearing foe.

XX. "'Ημῖν δὲ καλῶς εἴπερ ποτέ, ἔχει ἀμφοτέροις ἡ ξυναλλαγή, πρίν τι ἀνήκεστον διὰ μέσου
γενόμενον ἡμᾶς καταλαβεῖν, ἐν ᾧ ἀνάγκη ἀίδιον
ἡμῖν[1] ἔχθραν πρὸς τῇ κοινῇ καὶ ἰδίαν ἔχειν,
2 ὑμᾶς[2] δὲ στερηθῆναι ὧν νῦν προκαλούμεθα. ἔτι
δ' ὄντων ἀκρίτων καὶ ὑμῖν μὲν δόξης καὶ ἡμετέρας
φιλίας προσγιγνομένης, ἡμῖν δὲ πρὸ αἰσχροῦ
τινος τῆς ξυμφορᾶς μετρίως κατατιθεμένης διαλ-
λαγῶμεν, καὶ αὐτοί τε ἀντὶ πολέμου εἰρήνην
ἑλώμεθα καὶ τοῖς ἄλλοις Ἕλλησιν ἀνάπαυσιν
κακῶν ποιήσωμεν· οἳ καὶ ἐν τούτῳ ὑμᾶς αἰτιω-
τέρους ἡγήσονται. πολεμοῦνται μὲν γὰρ ἀσαφῶς
ὁποτέρων ἀρξάντων· καταλύσεως δὲ γενομένης,
ἧς νῦν ὑμεῖς τὸ πλέον κύριοί ἐστε, τὴν χάριν
3 ὑμῖν προσθήσουσιν. ἤν τε γνῶτε, Λακεδαιμονίοις ἔξεστιν ὑμῖν φίλους γενέσθαι βεβαίως,
αὐτῶν τε προκαλεσαμένων χαρισαμένοις τε μᾶλ-
4 λον ἢ βιασαμένοις.[3] καὶ ἐν τούτῳ τὰ ἐνόντα
ἀγαθὰ σκοπεῖτε ὅσα εἰκὸς εἶναι· ἡμῶν γὰρ καὶ
ὑμῶν ταὐτὰ λεγόντων τό γε ἄλλο Ἑλληνικὸν
ἴστε ὅτι ὑποδεέστερον ὂν τὰ μέγιστα τιμήσει."
XXI. Οἱ μὲν οὖν Λακεδαιμόνιοι τοσαῦτα
εἶπον, νομίζοντες τοὺς Ἀθηναίους ἐν τῷ πρὶν
χρόνῳ σπονδῶν μὲν ἐπιθυμεῖν, σφῶν δὲ ἐναν-
τιουμένων κωλύεσθαι, διδομένης δὲ εἰρήνης ἀσμέ-

---

[1] ἡμῖν, with F. Haase and Classen; Hude retains the MSS.
reading ὑμῖν, with Stahl, following the Scholiast.
[2] Hude reads ἡμᾶς, with C.
[3] Hude reads βιασαμένων, with C.

---

[1] Or, reading ἀίδιον ὑμῖν ... ἡμᾶς δέ, as Hude does, " you
Athenians would have our undying hatred . . . and we
Spartans would be deprived of the advantages we now offer."

XX. "Now, if ever, reconciliation is desirable for us both, before some irreparable disaster has come upon either of us and prevented it; should that befall, we shall inevitably cherish toward each other an undying personal hatred, over and above that which we now feel as public enemies, and you [1] will be deprived of the advantages [2] we now offer. While, therefore, the issue of the war is still in doubt, while your reputation is enhanced and you may have our friendship also, and while our disaster admits of a reasonable settlement and no disgrace as yet has befallen us, let us be reconciled; and let us for ourselves choose peace instead of war, and give a respite from evils to all the other Hellenes. And they will count you especially the authors of the peace; for although they were drawn into the war without knowing which of us began it, yet if a settlement is effected, the decision of which at this time rests chiefly with you, it is to you they will ascribe their gratitude. And so, if you decide for peace, it is in your power to win the steadfast friendship of the Lacedaemonians, which they freely offer and you may secure by acting, not with violence, but with generosity. Pray consider all the advantages which may well be involved in such a course; for if you and we agree be assured that the rest of the Hellenic world, since it will be inferior to us in power, will pay us the greatest deference."

XXI. Such were the words of the Lacedaemonians. They thought that, since the Athenians had at an earlier period [3] been eager to end the war and had been prevented by the opposition of Sparta, they

[2] *i.e.* peace, alliance, intimate friendship (ch. xix. 1).
[3] *i.e.* after the plague and the second invasion of Attica, in 430 B.C. *cf.* II. lix.

νους δέξεσθαί τε καὶ τοὺς ἄνδρας ἀποδώσειν.
2 οἱ δὲ τὰς μὲν σπονδάς, ἔχοντες τοὺς ἄνδρας ἐν τῇ
νήσῳ, ἤδη σφίσιν ἐνόμιζον ἑτοίμους εἶναι, ὁπόταν
βούλωνται ποιεῖσθαι πρὸς αὐτούς, τοῦ δὲ πλέονος
3 ὠρέγοντο. μάλιστα δὲ αὐτοὺς ἐνῆγε Κλέων ὁ
Κλεαινέτου, ἀνὴρ δημαγωγὸς κατ' ἐκεῖνον τὸν
χρόνον ὢν[1] τῷ πλήθει πιθανώτατος· καὶ ἔπεισεν
ἀποκρίνασθαι ὡς χρὴ τὰ μὲν ὅπλα καὶ σφᾶς
αὐτοὺς τοὺς ἐν τῇ νήσῳ παραδόντας πρῶτον
κομισθῆναι Ἀθήναζε, ἐλθόντων δὲ ἀποδόντας
Λακεδαιμονίους Νίσαιαν καὶ Πηγὰς καὶ Τροζῆνα
καὶ Ἀχαιΐαν, ἃ οὐ πολέμῳ ἔλαβον, ἀλλ' ἀπὸ
τῆς προτέρας ξυμβάσεως Ἀθηναίων ξυγχωρη-
σάντων κατὰ ξυμφορὰς καὶ ἐν τῷ τότε δεομένων
τι μᾶλλον σπονδῶν, κομίσασθαι τοὺς ἄνδρας καὶ
σπονδὰς ποιήσασθαι ὁπόσον ἂν δοκῇ χρόνον
ἀμφοτέροις.

XXII. Οἱ δὲ πρὸς μὲν τὴν ἀπόκρισιν οὐδὲν
ἀντεῖπον, ξυνέδρους δὲ σφίσιν ἐκέλευον ἑλέσθαι
οἵτινες λέγοντες καὶ ἀκούοντες περὶ ἑκάστου
ξυμβήσονται κατὰ ἡσυχίαν ὅ τι ἂν πείθωσιν
2 ἀλλήλους· Κλέων δὲ ἐνταῦθα δὴ πολὺς ἐνέκειτο,
λέγων γιγνώσκειν μὲν καὶ πρότερον οὐδὲν ἐν νῷ
ἔχοντας δίκαιον αὐτούς, σαφὲς δ' εἶναι καὶ νῦν,
οἵτινες τῷ μὲν πλήθει οὐδὲν ἐθέλουσιν εἰπεῖν,
ὀλίγοις δὲ ἀνδράσι ξύνεδροι βούλονται γίγνεσθαι·
ἀλλὰ εἴ τι ὑγιὲς διανοοῦνται, λέγειν ἐκέλευσεν[2]
3 ἅπασιν. ὁρῶντες δὲ οἱ Λακεδαιμόνιοι οὔτε σφίσιν
οἷόν τε ὂν ἐν πλήθει εἰπεῖν, εἴ τι καὶ ὑπὸ τῆς

---

[1] καί, before τῷ πλήθει, deleted by Krüger.
[2] Hude inserts ἐν before ἅπασιν, with Cobet.

would, if peace were offered to them, gladly accept
it and give up the men. But the Athenians believed
that, since they held the men on the island, peace
could be theirs the moment they cared to make it,
and meanwhile they were greedy for more. They
were urged to this course chiefly by Cleon son of
Cleaenetus, a popular leader at that time who had
very great influence with the multitude. He persuaded them to reply that the men on the island
must first give up themselves and their arms and be
brought to Athens; on their arrival, the Lacedaemonians must give back Nisaea, Pegae, Troezen, and
Achaea, which had not been taken in war but had
been ceded by the Athenians [1] in an agreement
made some time before as a result of misfortunes,
when they were somewhat more eager for peace
than now. They could then recover the men and
make a treaty which should be binding for as long a
time as both parties should agree.

XXII. To this reply the envoys said nothing,
but they requested the appointment of commissioners who should confer with them, and after
a full discussion of all the details should at their
leisure agree upon such terms as they could mutually
approve. Thereupon Cleon attacked them violently,
saying that he had known before this that they had
no honourable intention, and now it was clear,
since they were unwilling to speak out before the
people, but wished to meet a few men in conference;
he bade them, on the contrary, if their purpose was
honest, to declare it there before them all. But the
Lacedaemonians, seeing that it was impossible to
announce in full assembly such concessions as they

[1] cf. I. cxv. 1.

THUCYDIDES

ξυμφορᾶς ἐδόκει αὐτοῖς ξυγχωρεῖν, μὴ ἐς τοὺς ξυμμάχους διαβληθῶσιν εἰπόντες καὶ οὐ τυχόντες, οὔτε τοὺς Ἀθηναίους ἐπὶ μετρίοις ποιήσοντας ἃ προυκαλοῦντο, ἀνεχώρησαν ἐκ τῶν Ἀθηνῶν ἄπρακτοι.

XXIII. Ἀφικομένων δὲ αὐτῶν διελέλυντο[1] εὐθὺς αἱ σπονδαὶ αἱ περὶ Πύλον, καὶ τὰς ναῦς οἱ Λακεδαιμόνιοι ἀπῄτουν, καθάπερ ξυνέκειτο· οἱ δ᾽ Ἀθηναῖοι ἐγκλήματα ἔχοντες ἐπιδρομήν τε τῷ τειχίσματι παράσπονδον καὶ ἄλλα οὐκ ἀξιόλογα δοκοῦντα εἶναι οὐκ ἀπεδίδοσαν, ἰσχυριζόμενοι ὅτι δὴ εἴρητο, ἐὰν καὶ ὁτιοῦν παραβαθῇ, λελύσθαι τὰς σπονδάς. οἱ δὲ Λακεδαιμόνιοι ἀντέλεγόν τε καὶ ἀδίκημα ἐπικαλέσαντες τὸ τῶν νεῶν ἀπελ-
2 θόντες ἐς πόλεμον καθίσταντο. καὶ τὰ περὶ Πύλον ὑπ᾽ ἀμφοτέρων κατὰ κράτος ἐπολεμεῖτο, Ἀθηναῖοι μὲν δυοῖν νεοῖν ἐναντίαιν αἰεὶ τὴν νῆσον περιπλέοντες τῆς ἡμέρας (τῆς δὲ νυκτὸς καὶ ἅπασαι περιώρμουν, πλὴν τὰ πρὸς τὸ πέλαγος, ὁπότε ἄνεμος εἴη· καὶ ἐκ τῶν Ἀθηνῶν αὐτοῖς εἴκοσι νῆες ἀφίκοντο ἐς τὴν φυλακήν, ὥστε αἱ πᾶσαι ἑβδομήκοντα ἐγένοντο), Πελοποννήσιοι δὲ ἔν τε τῇ ἠπείρῳ στρατοπεδευόμενοι καὶ προσβολὰς ποιούμενοι τῷ τείχει, σκοποῦντες καιρὸν εἴ τις παραπέσοι ὥστε τοὺς ἄνδρας σῶσαι.

XXIV. Ἐν τούτῳ δὲ[2] ἐν τῇ Σικελίᾳ Συρακόσιοι καὶ οἱ ξύμμαχοι πρὸς ταῖς ἐν Μεσσήνῃ φρουρούσαις ναυσὶ τὸ ἄλλο ναυτικὸν ὃ παρεσκευάζοντο προσκομίσαντες τὸν πόλεμον ἐποιοῦντο ἐκ

---

[1] With Cobet, for διελύοντο of the MSS.
[2] οἱ of the MSS., before ἐν τῇ Σικελίᾳ, deleted by Hude.

might think it best to make in view of their misfortune, lest they might be discredited with their allies if they proposed them and were rebuffed, and seeing also that the Athenians would not grant their proposals on tolerable conditions, withdrew from Athens, their mission a failure.

XXIII. When they returned, the truce at Pylos was terminated at once, and the Lacedaemonians demanded the return of their ships according to the agreement; but the Athenians accused them of having made a raid against the fort in violation of the truce, and of other acts that do not seem worth mentioning, and refused to give up the ships, stoutly maintaining that it had been stipulated that, if there should be any violation of the truce whatsoever, it should be at an end forthwith. The Lacedaemonians contradicted this, and after protesting that the detention of the ships was an act of injustice went away and renewed the war. And so the warfare at Pylos was carried on vigorously by both sides. The Athenians kept sailing round the island by day with two ships going in opposite directions, and at night their whole fleet lay at anchor on all sides of it, except to seaward when there was a wind; while to assist them in the blockade twenty additional ships came from Athens, so that they now had seventy in all. As for the Peloponnesians, they were encamped on the mainland, and kept making assaults upon the fort, watching for any opportunity which might offer of rescuing their men.

XXIV. Meanwhile in Sicily the Syracusans and their allies, having reinforced the ships which were keeping guard at Messene by bringing up the other naval force which they had been equipping,[1] were

[1] cf. ch. i. 4.

THUCYDIDES

2 τῆς Μεσσήνης (καὶ μάλιστα ἐνῆγον οἱ Λοκροὶ τῶν
  Ῥηγίνων κατὰ ἔχθραν, καὶ αὐτοὶ δὲ ἐσεβεβλή-
3 κεσαν πανδημεὶ ἐς τὴν γῆν αὐτῶν), καὶ ναυμαχίας ἀποπειρᾶσθαι ἐβούλοντο, ὁρῶντες τοῖς
  Ἀθηναίοις τὰς μὲν παρούσας ναῦς ὀλίγας, ταῖς
  δὲ πλείοσι καὶ μελλούσαις ἥξειν πυνθανόμενοι
4 τὴν νῆσον πολιορκεῖσθαι. εἰ γὰρ κρατήσειαν
  τῷ ναυτικῷ, τὸ Ῥήγιον ἤλπιζον πεζῇ τε καὶ
  ναυσὶν ἐφορμοῦντες ῥᾳδίως χειρώσεσθαι, καὶ ἤδη
  σφῶν ἰσχυρὰ τὰ πράγματα γίγνεσθαι. ξύνεγγυς
  γὰρ κειμένου τοῦ τε Ῥηγίου ἀκρωτηρίου τῆς
  Ἰταλίας τῆς τε Μεσσήνης τῆς Σικελίας, τοῖς
  Ἀθηναίοις[1] οὐκ ἂν εἶναι ἐφορμεῖν καὶ τοῦ
  πορθμοῦ κρατεῖν. ἔστι δὲ ὁ πορθμὸς ἡ μεταξὺ
  Ῥηγίου θάλασσα καὶ Μεσσήνης, ᾗπερ βραχύ-
  τατον Σικελία τῆς ἠπείρου ἀπέχει· καὶ ἔστιν ἡ
  Χάρυβδις κληθεῖσα τοῦτο, ᾗ Ὀδυσσεὺς λέγεται
  διαπλεῦσαι. διὰ στενότητα δὲ καὶ ἐκ μεγάλων
  πελαγῶν, τοῦ τε Τυρσηνικοῦ καὶ τοῦ Σικελικοῦ,
  ἐσπίπτουσα ἡ θάλασσα ἐς αὐτὸ[2] καὶ ῥοώδης
  οὖσα εἰκότως χαλεπὴ ἐνομίσθη.

XXV. Ἐν τούτῳ οὖν τῷ μεταξὺ οἱ Συρακόσιοι
  καὶ οἱ ξύμμαχοι ναυσὶν ὀλίγῳ πλείοσιν ἢ τριάκοντα ἠναγκάσθησαν ὀψὲ τῆς ἡμέρας ναυμαχῆσαι
  περὶ πλοίου διαπλέοντος, ἀντεπαναγόμενοι πρός
  τε Ἀθηναίων ναῦς ἑκκαίδεκα καὶ Ῥηγίνας ὀκτώ.
2 καὶ νικηθέντες ὑπὸ τῶν Ἀθηναίων διὰ τάχους
  ἀπέπλευσαν ὡς ἕκαστοι ἔτυχον ἐς τὰ οἰκεῖα στρα-

---

[1] τε, after Ἀθηναίοις in all MSS. except Cod. Danicus, is
bracketed by all later editors.
[2] αὐτὸ the MSS.; Hude emends to ταὐτό.

carrying on the war from Messene. To this they were instigated chiefly by the Locrians on account of their hatred of the Rhegians, whose territory they had themselves invaded in full force. The Syracusans wanted also to try their fortune in a sea-fight, seeing that the Athenians had only a few ships at hand, and hearing that the most of their fleet, the ships that were on the way to Sicily, were employed in blockading the island of Sphacteria. For, in case they won a victory with the fleet, they could then invest Rhegium both by land and by sea and, as they believed, capture it without difficulty; and from that moment their situation would be a strong one, since Rhegium, the extreme point of Italy, and Messene in Sicily are only a short distance apart, and so the Athenians would not be able to keep a fleet there [1] and command the strait. Now the strait is that arm of the sea between Rhegium and Messene, at the point where Sicily is nearest the mainland; and it is the Charybdis, so called, through which Odysseus is said to have sailed. On account of its narrowness and because the water falls into it from two great seas, the Etruscan and the Sicilian, and is full of currents, it has naturally been considered dangerous.

XXV. Now it was in this strait that the Syracusans and their allies were compelled one day toward evening to fight for a vessel which was making the passage; and with thirty odd ships they put out against sixteen Athenian and eight Rhegian ships. They were defeated by the Athenians, and hastily sailed back, each contingent as best it could, to their own

---

[1] i.e. in case Rhegium were taken by the Syracusans.

τόπεδα¹ μίαν ναῦν ἀπολέσαντες· καὶ νὺξ ἐπεγέ-
3 νετο τῷ ἔργῳ. μετὰ δὲ τοῦτο οἱ μὲν Λοκροὶ
ἀπῆλθον ἐκ τῆς 'Ρηγίνων, ἐπὶ δὲ τὴν Πελωρίδα
τῆς Μεσσήνης ξυλλεγεῖσαι αἱ τῶν Συρακοσίων
καὶ ξυμμάχων νῆες ὥρμουν καὶ ὁ πεζὸς αὐτοῖς
4 παρῆν. προσπλεύσαντες δὲ οἱ 'Αθηναῖοι καὶ
'Ρηγῖνοι ὁρῶντες τὰς ναῦς κενὰς ἐνέβαλον, καὶ
χειρὶ σιδηρᾷ ἐπιβληθείσῃ μίαν ναῦν αὐτοὶ ἀπώ-
5 λεσαν τῶν ἀνδρῶν ἀποκολυμβησάντων. καὶ μετὰ
τοῦτο τῶν Συρακοσίων ἐσβάντων ἐς τὰς ναῦς καὶ
παραπλεόντων ἀπὸ κάλω ἐς τὴν Μεσσήνην, αὖθις
προσβαλόντες οἱ 'Αθηναῖοι, ἀποσιμωσάντων
ἐκείνων καὶ προεμβαλόντων, ἑτέραν ναῦν ἀπολ-
6 λύουσιν. καὶ ἐν τῷ παράπλῳ καὶ τῇ ναυμαχίᾳ
τοιουτοτρόπῳ γενομένῃ οὐκ ἔλασσον ἔχοντες οἱ
Συρακόσιοι παρεκομίσθησαν ἐς τὸν ἐν τῇ Μεσσήνῃ λιμένα.
7 Καὶ οἱ μὲν 'Αθηναῖοι, Καμαρίνης ἀγγελθείσης
προδίδοσθαι Συρακοσίοις ὑπ' 'Αρχίου καὶ τῶν
μετ' αὐτοῦ, ἔπλευσαν ἐκεῖσε· Μεσσήνιοι δ' ἐν
τούτῳ πανδημεὶ κατὰ γῆν καὶ ταῖς ναυσὶν ἅμα
ἐστράτευσαν ἐπὶ Νάξον τὴν Χαλκιδικὴν ὅμορον
8 οὖσαν. καὶ τῇ πρώτῃ ἡμέρᾳ τειχήρεις ποιήσαντες τοὺς Ναξίους ἐδῄουν τὴν γῆν, τῇ δ' ὑστεραίᾳ ταῖς μὲν ναυσὶ περιπλεύσαντες κατὰ τὸν
'Ακεσίνην ποταμὸν τὴν γῆν ἐδῄουν, τῷ δὲ πεζῷ
9 πρὸς τὴν πόλιν προσέβαλλον.² ἐν τούτῳ δὲ οἱ
Σικελοὶ³ ὑπὲρ τῶν ἄκρων πολλοὶ κατέβαινον

¹ τό τε ἐν τῇ Μεσσήνῃ καὶ ἐν τῷ 'Ρηγίῳ, in the MSS.
after στρατόπεδα, rejected by Hude, after Stahl and van
Herwerden.
² For ἐσέβαλλον of the MSS., Poppo's correction, accepted
by most editors.

camps, having lost one ship; and night came on while they were in action. After this the Locrians left the territory of the Rhegians; and the ships of the Syracusans and their allies assembled at Peloris in Messene, where they anchored and were joined by their land-forces. The Athenians and the Rhegians sailed up, and seeing that the Syracusan ships were unmanned attacked them; but they themselves lost one ship, which was caught by a grappling-iron cast upon it, the crew having leaped overboard. After this the Syracusans embarked and their ships were being towed along the shore by ropes toward Messene when the Athenians attacked again, but lost another ship, since the Syracusans made a sudden turn outwards and charged them first. In the passage along the shore, then, and in the sea-fight that followed in this unusual fashion, the Syracusans had the best of it, and at length gained the harbour at Messene.

But the Athenians, on the report that Camarina was to be betrayed to the Syracusans by Archias and his faction, sailed thither. The Messenians meanwhile took all their land-forces and also the allied fleet and made an expedition against Naxos, the Chalcidian settlement on their borders. On the first day they confined the Naxians within their walls and ravaged their lands; on the next day, while their fleet sailed round to the river Acesines and ravaged the land there, their army assaulted the city of Naxos. Meanwhile the Sicels came down over the heights in

---

³ οἱ, before ὑπὲρ, Krüger's suggestion following a scholium (ἀντὶ τοῦ οἱ ἐπὶ τῶν ἀκρῶν ὄντες κ.τ.λ.), is adopted by Hude.

253

βοηθοῦντες ἐπὶ τοὺς Μεσσηνίους. καὶ οἱ Νάξιοι
ὡς εἶδον, θαρσήσαντες καὶ παρακελευόμενοι ἐν
ἑαυτοῖς ὡς οἱ Λεοντῖνοι σφίσι καὶ οἱ ἄλλοι
Ἕλληνες ξύμμαχοι ἐς τιμωρίαν ἐπέρχονται, ἐκ-
δραμόντες ἄφνω ἐκ τῆς πόλεως προσπίπτουσι
τοῖς Μεσσηνίοις, καὶ τρέψαντες ἀπέκτεινάν τε
ὑπὲρ χιλίους καὶ οἱ λοιποὶ χαλεπῶς ἀπεχώρησαν
ἐπ' οἴκου· καὶ γὰρ οἱ βάρβαροι ἐν ταῖς ὁδοῖς
10 ἐπιπεσόντες τοὺς πλείστους διέφθειραν. καὶ αἱ
νῆες σχοῦσαι ἐς τὴν Μεσσήνην ὕστερον ἐπ' οἴκου
ἕκασται διεκρίθησαν. Λεοντῖνοι δὲ εὐθὺς καὶ οἱ
ξύμμαχοι μετὰ Ἀθηναίων ἐς τὴν Μεσσήνην ὡς
κεκακωμένην ἐστράτευον, καὶ προσβάλλοντες οἱ
μὲν Ἀθηναῖοι κατὰ τὸν λιμένα ταῖς ναυσὶν ἐπεί-
11 ρων, ὁ δὲ πεζὸς πρὸς τὴν πόλιν. ἐπεκδρομὴν δὲ
ποιησάμενοι οἱ Μεσσήνιοι καὶ Λοκρῶν τινες μετὰ
τοῦ Δημοτέλους, οἳ μετὰ τὸ πάθος ἐγκατελείφθη-
σαν φρουροί, ἐξαπιναίως προσπεσόντες τρέπουσι
τοῦ στρατεύματος τῶν Λεοντίνων τὸ πολὺ καὶ
ἀπέκτειναν πολλούς. ἰδόντες δὲ οἱ Ἀθηναῖοι καὶ
ἀποβάντες ἀπὸ τῶν νεῶν ἐβοήθουν, καὶ κατεδίωξαν τοὺς Μεσσηνίους πάλιν ἐς τὴν πόλιν, τε-
ταραγμένοις ἐπιγενόμενοι· καὶ τροπαῖον στήσαν-
12 τες ἀνεχώρησαν ἐς τὸ Ῥήγιον. μετὰ δὲ τοῦτο οἱ
μὲν ἐν τῇ Σικελίᾳ Ἕλληνες ἄνευ τῶν Ἀθηναίων
κατὰ γῆν ἐστράτευον ἐπ' ἀλλήλους.

XXVI. Ἐν δὲ τῇ Πύλῳ ἔτι ἐπολιόρκουν τοὺς
ἐν τῇ νήσῳ Λακεδαιμονίους οἱ Ἀθηναῖοι, καὶ τὸ
ἐν τῇ ἠπείρῳ στρατόπεδον τῶν Πελοποννησίων
2 κατὰ χώραν ἔμενεν. ἐπίπονος δ' ἦν τοῖς Ἀθηναίοις ἡ φυλακὴ σίτου τε ἀπορίᾳ καὶ ὕδατος· οὐ

large numbers to help in resisting the Messenians.
When the Naxians saw them coming, they took heart,
and calling to each other that the Leontines and their
other Hellenic allies were approaching to defend
them rushed suddenly out of the city and fell upon
the Messenians, putting them to flight and killing
over a thousand of them. The rest got back home with
difficulty; for the barbarians attacked them in the
roads and killed most of them. And the allied fleet,
after putting in at Messene, dispersed to their
several homes. Thereupon the Leontines and their
allies, in company with the Athenians, immediately
made an expedition against Messene, believing it to
be weakened, and attempted an assault upon it, the
Athenians attacking with their ships on the side of
the harbour, while the land forces moved against the
town. But the Messenians and some of the Locrians,
who, under the command of Demoteles, had been
left there as a garrison after the disaster at Naxos,
made a sortie, and falling suddenly upon them routed
the larger part of the army of the Leontines and
killed many of them. Seeing this the Athenians
disembarked and came to their aid, and attacking the
Messenians while they were in disorder pursued them
back into the city; they then set up a trophy and withdrew to Rhegium. After this the Hellenes in Sicily,
without the cooperation of the Athenians, continued
to make expeditions against one another by land.

XXVI. At Pylos, meanwhile, the Athenians were
still besieging the Lacedaemonians on the island, and
the army of the Peloponnesians on the mainland
remained in its former position. The blockade, however, was harassing to the Athenians on account of
the lack of both food and water; for there was only

γὰρ ἦν κρήνη ὅτι μὴ μία ἐν αὐτῇ τῇ ἀκροπόλει
τῆς Πύλου καὶ αὕτη οὐ μεγάλη, ἀλλὰ διαμώμενοι
τὸν κάχληκα οἱ πλεῖστοι ἐπὶ τῇ θαλάσσῃ ἔπινον
3 οἷον εἰκὸς ὕδωρ.   στενοχωρία τε ἐν ὀλίγῳ στρατο-
πεδευομένοις ἐγίγνετο, καὶ τῶν νεῶν οὐκ ἐχουσῶν
ὅρμον αἱ μὲν σῖτον ἐν τῇ γῇ ᾑροῦντο κατὰ μέρος,
4 αἱ δὲ μετέωροι ὥρμουν.   ἀθυμίαν τε πλείστην ὁ
χρόνος παρεῖχε παρὰ λόγον ἐπιγιγνόμενος, οὓς
ᾤοντο ἡμερῶν ὀλίγων ἐκπολιορκήσειν, ἐν νήσῳ τε
5 ἐρήμῃ καὶ ὕδατι ἁλμυρῷ χρωμένους.   αἴτιον δὲ
ἦν οἱ Λακεδαιμόνιοι προειπόντες ἐς τὴν νῆσον
ἐσάγειν σῖτόν τε τὸν βουλόμενον ἀληλεμένον καὶ
οἶνον καὶ τυρὸν καὶ εἴ τι ἄλλο βρῶμα, οἷ᾽ ἂν ἐς
πολιορκίαν ξυμφέρῃ, τάξαντες ἀργυρίου πολλοῦ
καὶ τῶν Εἱλώτων τῷ ἐσαγαγόντι ἐλευθερίαν ὑπι-
6 σχνούμενοι.   καὶ ἐσῆγον ἄλλοι τε παρακινδυνεύ-
οντες καὶ μάλιστα οἱ Εἵλωτες, ἀπαίροντες ἀπὸ
τῆς Πελοποννήσου ὁπόθεν τύχοιεν καὶ καταπλέ-
οντες ἔτι νυκτὸς ἐς τὰ πρὸς τὸ πέλαγος τῆς νήσου.
7 μάλιστα δὲ ἐτήρουν ἀνέμῳ καταφέρεσθαι· ῥᾷον
γὰρ τὴν φυλακὴν τῶν τριήρων ἐλάνθανον, ὁπότε
πνεῦμα ἐκ πόντου εἴη· ἄπορον γὰρ ἐγίγνετο περι-
ορμεῖν, τοῖς δὲ ἀφειδὴς ὁ κατάπλους καθειστήκει·
ἐπώκελλον γὰρ τὰ πλοῖα τετιμημένα χρημάτων,
καὶ οἱ ὁπλῖται περὶ τὰς κατάρσεις τῆς νήσου

---

[1] The reference is to the ships which kept up a patrol
round the island.   There was no anchorage near the shore

one spring, high up on the acropolis of Pylos, and a
small one at that, and the soldiers for the most part
scraped away the shingle upon the beach and drank
water such as one might expect to find there. And
there was scant room for them, encamping as they
did in a small space, and since there was no anchorage for the ships,[1] the crews would take their food on
land by turns, while the rest of the fleet lay at anchor
out at sea. Very great discouragement, too, was
caused by the surprisingly long duration of the siege,
whereas they had expected to reduce the enemy in
a few days, since they were on a desert island and
had only brackish water to drink. But the cause of
their holding out was that the Lacedaemonians had
called for volunteers to convey to the island ground
corn and wine and cheese and other food such as might
be serviceable in a siege, fixing a high price and
also promising freedom to any Helot who should
get food in. Many took the risk, especially the
Helots, and actually brought it in, putting out from
any and every point in the Peloponnesus and coming
to shore during the night on the side of the island
facing the sea. If possible they waited for a wind
to bear them to the shore; for they found it easier
to elude the guard of triremes when the breeze was
from the sea, since then it was impossible for the
ships to lie at their moorings off the island, whereas
they themselves ran ashore regardless of conse-
quences, as a value had been set upon the boats
which they drove upon the beach, and the hoplites would be on watch for them at the landing-

on the seaward side (ch. viii. 8), so at meal-times the crews
of one part of the fleet would make a landing somewhere and
eat, while the other part would be out at sea on guard.

ἐφύλασσον. ὅσοι δὲ γαλήνῃ κινδυνεύσειαν, ἠλί-
8 σκοντο. ἐσένεον δὲ καὶ κατὰ τὸν λιμένα κολυμ-
βηταὶ ὕφυδροι, καλῳδίῳ ἐν ἀσκοῖς ἐφέλκοντες
μήκωνα μεμελιτωμένην καὶ λίνου σπέρμα κεκομ-
μένον· ὧν τὸ πρῶτον λανθανόντων φυλακαὶ
9 ὕστερον ἐγένοντο. παντί τε τρόπῳ ἑκάτεροι
ἐτεχνῶντο, οἱ μὲν ἐσπέμπειν τὰ σιτία, οἱ δὲ μὴ
λανθάνειν σφᾶς.

XXVII. Ἐν δὲ ταῖς Ἀθήναις πυνθανόμενοι
περὶ τῆς στρατιᾶς ὅτι ταλαιπωρεῖται καὶ σῖτος
τοῖς ἐν τῇ νήσῳ ὅτι ἐσπλεῖ, ἠπόρουν καὶ ἐδεδοί-
κεσαν μὴ σφῶν χειμὼν τὴν φυλακὴν ἐπιλάβοι,
ὁρῶντες τῶν τε ἐπιτηδείων τὴν περὶ τὴν Πελοπόννησον κομιδὴν ἀδύνατον ἐσομένην, ἅμα ἐν
χωρίῳ ἐρήμῳ καὶ οὐδ᾽ ἐν θέρει οἷοί τε ὄντες ἱκανὰ
περιπέμπειν, τόν τε ἔφορμον χωρίων ἀλιμένων
ὄντων οὐκ ἐσόμενον, ἀλλ᾽ ἢ σφῶν ἀνέντων τὴν
φυλακὴν περιγενήσεσθαι τοὺς ἄνδρας ἢ τοῖς πλοίοις ἃ τὸν σῖτον αὐτοῖς ἦγε χειμῶνα τηρήσαντας
2 ἐκπλεύσεσθαι. πάντων τε ἐφοβοῦντο μάλιστα
τοὺς Λακεδαιμονίους, ὅτι ἔχοντάς τι ἰσχυρὸν αὐτοὺς ἐνόμιζον οὐκέτι σφίσιν ἐπικηρυκεύεσθαι· καὶ
3 μετεμέλοντο τὰς σπονδὰς οὐ δεξάμενοι. Κλέων
δὲ γνοὺς αὐτῶν τὴν ἐς αὐτὸν ὑποψίαν περὶ τῆς
κωλύμης τῆς ξυμβάσεως οὐ τἀληθῆ ἔφη λέγειν
τοὺς ἐξαγγέλλοντας.[1] παραινούντων δὲ τῶν ἀφιγ-

---

[1] So the MSS.: Hude adopts Krüger's conjecture, ἐσαγ-
γέλλοντας.

places on the island. All, on the other hand, who made the venture in calm weather were captured. At the harbour, too, there were divers who swam to the island under water, towing after them by a cord skins filled with poppy-seed mixed with honey and bruised linseed; at first they were not discovered, but afterwards watches were set for them. And so both sides kept resorting to every device, the one to get food in, the other to catch them doing it.

XXVII. At Athens, meanwhile, when they heard that their army was in distress and that food was being brought in to the men on the island, they were perplexed and became apprehensive that the winter would overtake them while still engaged in the blockade. They saw that conveyance of supplies round the Peloponnesus would be impossible—Pylos being a desolate place at best, to which they were unable even in summer to send round adequate supplies—and that, since there were no harbours in the neighbourhood, the blockade would be a failure. Either their own troops would relax their watch and the men on the island would escape, or else, waiting for bad weather, they would sail away in the boats which brought them food. Above all they were alarmed about the attitude of the Lacedaemonians, thinking that it was because they had some ground for confidence that they were no longer making overtures to them; and they repented having rejected their proposals for peace. But Cleon, knowing that their suspicions were directed against him because he had prevented the agreement, said that the messengers who had come from Pylos were not telling the truth. Whereupon these messengers advised, if their own

μένων, εἰ μὴ σφίσι πιστεύουσι, κατασκόπους
τινὰς πέμψαι, ἡρέθη κατάσκοπος αὐτὸς μετὰ
4 Θεογένους ὑπὸ Ἀθηναίων. καὶ γνοὺς ὅτι ἀναγ-
κασθήσεται ἢ ταὐτὰ λέγειν οἷς διέβαλλεν ἢ τά-
ναντία εἰπὼν ψευδὴς φανήσεσθαι,[1] παρῄνει τοῖς
Ἀθηναίοις, ὁρῶν αὐτοὺς καὶ ὡρμημένους τι τὸ
πλέον τῇ γνώμῃ στρατεύειν, ὡς χρὴ κατασκόπους
μὲν μὴ πέμπειν μηδὲ διαμέλλειν καιρὸν παριέντας,
εἰ δὲ δοκεῖ αὐτοῖς ἀληθῆ εἶναι τὰ ἀγγελλόμενα,
5 πλεῖν ἐπὶ τοὺς ἄνδρας. καὶ ἐς Νικίαν τὸν Νικηράτου στρατηγὸν ὄντα ἀπεσήμαινεν, ἐχθρὸς ὢν
καὶ ἐπιτιμῶν, ῥᾴδιον εἶναι παρασκευῇ, εἰ ἄνδρες
εἶεν οἱ στρατηγοί, πλεύσαντας λαβεῖν τοὺς ἐν
τῇ νήσῳ, καὶ αὐτός γ' ἄν, εἰ ἦρχε, ποιῆσαι
τοῦτο.

XXVIII. Ὁ δὲ Νικίας τῶν τε Ἀθηναίων τι
ὑποθορυβησάντων ἐς τὸν Κλέωνα, ὅ τι οὐ καὶ νῦν
πλεῖ, εἰ ῥᾴδιόν γε αὐτῷ φαίνεται, καὶ ἅμα ὁρῶν
αὐτὸν ἐπιτιμῶντα, ἐκέλευεν ἥντινα βούλεται δύ-
2 ναμιν λαβόντα τὸ ἐπὶ σφᾶς εἶναι ἐπιχειρεῖν. ὁ δὲ
τὸ μὲν πρῶτον οἰόμενος αὐτὸν λόγῳ μόνον ἀφιέναι,
ἕτοιμος ἦν, γνοὺς δὲ τῷ ὄντι παραδωσείοντα ἀνε-
χώρει καὶ οὐκ ἔφη αὐτὸς ἀλλ' ἐκεῖνον στρατη-
γεῖν, δεδιὼς ἤδη καὶ οὐκ ἂν οἰόμενός οἱ αὐτὸν
3 τολμῆσαι ὑποχωρῆσαι. αὖθις δὲ ὁ Νικίας ἐκέλευε καὶ ἐξίστατο τῆς ἐπὶ Πύλῳ ἀρχῆς καὶ μάρ-

---

[1] So all MSS. except B (γενήσεσθαι): Hude adopts, with
Krüger, Rauchenstein's conjecture φανήσεται.

reports were not believed, that commissioners be sent
to see for themselves, and Cleon himself was chosen by
the Athenians, with Theagenes as his colleague.
Realizing now that he would either be obliged to bring
the same report as the messengers whose word he
was impugning, or, if he contradicted them, be convicted of falsehood, and also seeing that the Athenians
were now somewhat more inclined to send an expedition, he told them that they ought not to send
commissioners, or by dallying to let slip a favourable
opportunity, but urged them, if they themselves
thought the reports to be true, to send a fleet and
fetch the men. And pointing at Nicias son of
Niceratus, who was one of the generals and an
enemy of his, and taunting him, he said that it was
an easy matter, if the generals were men, to sail
there with a proper force and take the men on the
island, declaring that this was what he himself would
have done had he been in command.

XXVIII. The Athenians thereupon began to
clamour against Cleon, asking him why he did not sail
even now, if it seemed to him so easy a thing; and
Nicias, noticing this and Cleon's taunt, told him that
as far as the generals were concerned he might take
whatever force he wished and make the attempt.
As for Cleon, he was at first ready to go, thinking it
was only in pretence that Nicias offered to relinquish
the command; but when he realized that Nicias
really desired to yield the command to him, he
tried to back out, saying that not he but Nicias was
general; for by now he was alarmed, and never
thought that Nicias would go so far as to retire in
his favour. But again Nicias urged him to go and
offered to resign his command of the expedition

τυρας τοὺς Ἀθηναίους ἐποιεῖτο. οἱ δέ, οἷον ὄχλος
φιλεῖ ποιεῖν, ὅσῳ μᾶλλον ὁ Κλέων ὑπέφευγε τὸν
πλοῦν καὶ ἐξανεχώρει τὰ εἰρημένα, τόσῳ ἐπεκε-
λεύοντο τῷ Νικίᾳ παραδιδόναι τὴν ἀρχὴν καὶ
4 ἐκείνῳ ἐπεβόων πλεῖν· ὥστε οὐκ ἔχων ὅπως τῶν
εἰρημένων ἔτι ἐξαπαλλαγῇ, ὑφίσταται τὸν πλοῦν,
καὶ παρελθὼν οὔτε φοβεῖσθαι ἔφη Λακεδαιμονίους
πλεύσεσθαί τε λαβὼν ἐκ μὲν τῆς πόλεως οὐδένα,
Λημνίους δὲ καὶ Ἰμβρίους τοὺς παρόντας καὶ
πελταστὰς οἳ ἦσαν ἔκ τε Αἴνου βεβοηθηκότες καὶ
ἄλλοθεν τοξότας τετρακοσίους· ταῦτα δὲ ἔχων
ἔφη[1] πρὸς τοῖς ἐν Πύλῳ στρατιώταις ἐντὸς ἡμερῶν εἴκοσι ἢ ἄξειν Λακεδαιμονίους ζῶντας ἢ
5 αὐτοῦ ἀποκτενεῖν· τοῖς δὲ Ἀθηναίοις ἐνέπεσε
μέν τι καὶ γέλωτος τῇ κουφολογίᾳ αὐτοῦ, ἀσμένοις δ' ὅμως ἐγίγνετο τοῖς σώφροσι τῶν ἀνθρώπων,
λογιζομένοις δυοῖν ἀγαθοῖν τοῦ ἑτέρου τεύξεσθαι,
ἢ Κλέωνος ἀπαλλαγήσεσθαι, ὃ μᾶλλον ἤλπιζον,
ἢ σφαλεῖσι γνώμης Λακεδαιμονίους σφίσι χειρώσεσθαι.[2]

XXIX. Καὶ πάντα διαπραξάμενος ἐν τῇ
ἐκκλησίᾳ καὶ ψηφισαμένων Ἀθηναίων αὐτῷ τὸν
πλοῦν, τῶν τε ἐν Πύλῳ στρατηγῶν ἕνα προσελό-
μενος, Δημοσθένη, τὴν ἀναγωγὴν διὰ τάχους
2 ἐποιεῖτο. τὸν δὲ Δημοσθένη προσέλαβε πυνθανόμενος τὴν ἀπόβασιν αὐτὸν ἐς τὴν νῆσον διανοεῖ-
σθαι. οἱ γὰρ στρατιῶται κακοπαθοῦντες τοῦ
χωρίου τῇ ἀπορίᾳ καὶ μᾶλλον πολιορκούμενοι ἢ
πολιορκοῦντες ὥρμηντο διακινδυνεῦσαι. καὶ αὐτῷ

---

[1] Omitted by Hude, following M.
[2] χειρώσασθαι ABFM.

against Pylos, calling the Athenians to witness that he did so. And the more Cleon tried to evade the expedition and to back out of his own proposal, the more insistently the Athenians, as is the way with a crowd, urged Nicias to give up the command and shouted to Cleon to sail. And so, not knowing how he could any longer escape from his own proposal, he undertook the expedition, and, coming forward, said that he was not afraid of the Lacedaemonians, and that he would sail without taking a single Athenian soldier, but only the Lemnian and Imbrian troops which were in Athens and a body of targeteers which had come from Aenos, and four hundred archers from other places. With these, in addition to the troops now at Pylos, he said that within twenty days he would either bring back the Lacedaemonians alive or slay them on the spot. At this vain talk of his there was a burst of laughter on the part of the Athenians, but nevertheless the sensible men among them were glad, for they reflected that they were bound to obtain one of two good things— either they would get rid of Cleon, which they preferred, or if they were disappointed in this, he would subdue the Lacedaemonians for them.

XXIX. When he had arranged everything in the assembly and the Athenians had voted in favour of his expedition, he chose as his colleague Demosthenes, one of the generals at Pylos, and made haste to set sail. He selected Demosthenes because he had heard that he was planning to make his landing on the island. For his soldiers, who were suffering because of the discomforts of their position, where they were rather besieged than besiegers, were eager to run all risks. And Demosthenes himself had also

THUCYDIDES

ἔτι ῥώμην καὶ ἡ νῆσος ἐμπρησθεῖσα παρέσχεν.
3 πρότερον μὲν γὰρ οὔσης αὐτῆς ὑλώδους ἐπὶ τὸ
πολὺ καὶ ἀτριβοῦς διὰ τὴν αἰεὶ ἐρημίαν ἐφοβεῖτο
καὶ πρὸς τῶν πολεμίων τοῦτο ἐνόμιζε μᾶλλον
εἶναι· πολλῷ γὰρ ἂν στρατοπέδῳ ἀποβάντι ἐξ
ἀφανοῦς χωρίου προσβάλλοντας αὐτοὺς βλάπ-
τειν. σφίσι μὲν γὰρ τὰς ἐκείνων ἁμαρτίας καὶ
παρασκευὴν ὑπὸ τῆς ὕλης οὐκ ἂν ὁμοίως δῆλα
εἶναι, τοῦ δὲ αὐτῶν στρατοπέδου καταφανῆ ἂν
εἶναι πάντα τὰ ἁμαρτήματα, ὥστε προσπίπτειν
ἂν αὐτοὺς ἀπροσδοκήτως ᾗ βούλοιντο· ἐπ'
4 ἐκείνοις γὰρ εἶναι ἂν τὴν ἐπιχείρησιν. εἰ δ'
αὖ ἐς δασὺ χωρίον βιάζοιτο ὁμόσε ἰέναι, τοὺς
ἐλάσσους, ἐμπείρους δὲ τῆς χώρας, κρείσσους
ἐνόμιζε τῶν πλεόνων ἀπείρων· λανθάνειν τε ἂν
τὸ ἑαυτῶν στρατόπεδον πολὺ ὂν διαφθειρόμενον,
οὐκ οὔσης τῆς προσόψεως ᾗ χρῆν ἀλλήλοις
ἐπιβοηθεῖν.

XXX. Ἀπὸ δὲ τοῦ Αἰτωλικοῦ πάθους, ὃ διὰ
τὴν ὕλην μέρος τι ἐγένετο, οὐχ ἥκιστα αὐτὸν
2 ταῦτα ἐσῄει. τῶν δὲ στρατιωτῶν ἀναγκασθέντων
διὰ τὴν στενοχωρίαν τῆς νήσου τοῖς ἐσχάτοις
προσίσχοντας ἀριστοποιεῖσθαι διὰ προφυλακῆς
καὶ ἐμπρήσαντός τινος κατὰ μικρὸν τῆς ὕλης
ἄκοντος καὶ ἀπὸ τούτου πνεύματος ἐπιγενομένου
3 τὸ πολὺ αὐτῆς ἔλαθε κατακαυθέν. οὕτω δὴ

been emboldened by a conflagration which had swept the island. For hitherto, since the island was for the most part covered with woods and had no roads, having never been inhabited, he had been afraid to land, thinking that the terrain was rather in the enemy's favour; for they could attack from an unseen position and inflict damage upon a large army after it had landed. To his own troops, indeed, the mistakes and the preparations of the enemy would not be equally clear by reason of the woods, whereas all their own mistakes would be manifest to their opponents, and so they could fall upon them unexpectedly wherever they wished, since the power of attack would rest with them. If, on the other hand, he should force his way into the thicket and there close with the enemy, the smaller force which was acquainted with the ground would, he thought, be stronger than the larger number who were unacquainted with it; and his own army, though large, would be destroyed piece-meal before he knew it, because there was no possible way of seeing the points at which the detachments should assist one another.

XXX. It was especially owing to his experience in Aetolia,[1] when his reverse was in some measure due to the forest, that these thoughts occurred to Demosthenes. But the soldiers were so cramped in their quarters that they were obliged to land on the edge of the island and take their meals under cover of a picket, and one of their number accidentally set fire to a small portion of the forest, and from this, when a breeze had sprung up, most of the forest was burned before they knew it. Thus it happened that

[1] cf. III. xcvii., xcviii.

τούς τε Λακεδαιμονίους μᾶλλον κατιδὼν πλείους
ὄντας, ὑπονοῶν πρότερον ἐλάσσοσι τὸν σῖτον
αὐτοὺς[1] ἐσπέμπειν, τήν τε νῆσον εὐαποβατω-
τέραν οὖσαν, τότε ὡς ἐπ᾿ ἀξιόχρεων τοὺς Ἀθηναίους μᾶλλον σπουδὴν ποιεῖσθαι τὴν ἐπιχείρησιν παρεσκευάζετο, στρατιάν τε μεταπέμπων
ἐκ τῶν ἐγγὺς ξυμμάχων καὶ τὰ ἄλλα ἑτοιμάζων.

4 Κλέων δὲ ἐκείνῳ τε προπέμψας ἄγγελον ὡς
ἥξων καὶ ἔχων στρατιὰν ἣν ᾐτήσατο, ἀφικνεῖται
ἐς Πύλον. καὶ ἅμα γενόμενοι πέμπουσι πρῶτον
ἐς τὸ ἐν τῇ ἠπείρῳ στρατόπεδον κήρυκα, προκα-
λούμενοι, εἰ βούλοιντο, ἄνευ κινδύνου τοὺς ἐν τῇ
νήσῳ ἄνδρας σφίσι τά τε ὅπλα καὶ σφᾶς αὐτοὺς
κελεύειν παραδοῦναι, ἐφ᾿ ᾧ φυλακῇ τῇ μετρίᾳ
τηρήσονται, ἕως ἄν τι περὶ τοῦ πλέονος ξυμβαθῇ.
XXXI. οὐ προσδεξαμένων δὲ αὖ μίαν μὲν
ἡμέραν ἐπέσχον, τῇ δ᾿ ὑστεραίᾳ ἀνηγάγοντο μὲν
νυκτὸς ἐπ᾿ ὀλίγας ναῦς τοὺς ὁπλίτας πάντας
ἐπιβιβάσαντες, πρὸ δὲ τῆς ἕω ὀλίγον ἀπέβαινον
τῆς νήσου ἑκατέρωθεν, ἔκ τε τοῦ πελάγους καὶ
πρὸς τοῦ λιμένος, ὀκτακόσιοι μάλιστα ὄντες
ὁπλῖται, καὶ ἐχώρουν δρόμῳ ἐπὶ τὸ πρῶτον
2 φυλακτήριον τῆς νήσου. ὧδε γὰρ διετετάχατο·
ἐν ταύτῃ μὲν τῇ πρώτῃ[2] φυλακῇ ὡς τριάκοντα
ἦσαν ὁπλῖται, μέσον δὲ καὶ ὁμαλώτατόν τε καὶ

---

[1] Bekker's conjecture for αὐτοῦ of the MSS. Hude reads
αὐτόσε, with Krüger.
[2] Hude deletes, with Krüger.

Demosthenes, who could now get a better view of the Lacedaemonians, found that they were more numerous than he had thought; for he had previously suspected that the number for which they were sending provisions was smaller than they stated.[1] He also found that the island was less difficult to make a landing upon than he had supposed. He now, therefore, believing that the object in view was well worth a more serious effort on the part of the Athenians, began preparations for the attempt, summoning troops from the allies in the neighbourhood and getting everything else ready.

Cleon, meanwhile, having first sent word to Demosthenes that he would soon be there, arrived at Pylos, bringing the army for which he had asked. As soon as they had joined forces, they sent a herald to the enemy's camp on the mainland, giving them the option, if they wished to avoid a conflict, of ordering the men on the island to surrender themselves and their arms, on condition that they should be held in mild custody until some agreement should be reached about the main question.[2] XXXI. This offer being rejected, the Athenians waited for one day, but on the next day while it was still dark they embarked all their hoplites on a few vessels and put off, landing a little before dawn on both sides of the island, on the side toward the open sea and on that facing the harbour, their number being about eight hundred, all hoplites. They then advanced at a run against the first guard-post on the island. For the forces of the enemy were disposed as follows: in this, the first post, there were about thirty hoplites; the central and most level part of the island, near their

---

[1] cf. ch. xvi. 1. [2] i.e. a general peace.

περὶ τὸ ὕδωρ οἱ πλεῖστοι αὐτῶν καὶ Ἐπιτάδας ὁ
ἄρχων εἶχε, μέρος δέ τι οὐ πολὺ αὐτὸ[1] τὸ
ἔσχατον ἐφύλασσε τῆς νήσου τὸ πρὸς τὴν Πύλον,
ὃ ἦν ἔκ τε θαλάσσης ἀπόκρημνον καὶ ἐκ τῆς γῆς
ἥκιστα ἐπίμαχον· καὶ γάρ τι καὶ ἔρυμα αὐτόθι
ἦν παλαιὸν λίθων λογάδην πεποιημένον, ὃ ἐνόμιζον σφίσιν ὠφέλιμον ἂν εἶναι, εἰ καταλαμβάνοι
ἀναχώρησις βιαιοτέρα. οὕτω μὲν τεταγμένοι
ἦσαν.

XXXII. Οἱ δὲ Ἀθηναῖοι τοὺς μὲν πρώτους
φύλακας, οἷς ἐπέδραμον, εὐθὺς διαφθείρουσιν, ἔν
τε ταῖς εὐναῖς ἔτι κἀναλαμβάνοντας τὰ ὅπλα καὶ
λαθόντες τὴν ἀπόβασιν, οἰομένων αὐτῶν τὰς
ναῦς κατὰ τὸ ἔθος ἐς ἔφορμον τῆς νυκτὸς πλεῖν.
2 ἅμα δὲ ἕῳ γιγνομένῃ καὶ ὁ ἄλλος στρατὸς ἀπέβαινον, ἐκ μὲν νεῶν ἑβδομήκοντα καὶ ὀλίγῳ
πλειόνων πάντες πλὴν θαλαμιῶν, ὡς ἕκαστοι
ἐσκευασμένοι, τοξόται δὲ ὀκτακόσιοι καὶ πελτασταὶ οὐκ ἐλάσσους τούτων, Μεσσηνίων τε οἱ
βεβοηθηκότες καὶ οἱ ἄλλοι ὅσοι περὶ Πύλον κατεῖχον πάντες πλὴν τῶν ἐπὶ τοῦ τείχους φυλάκων.
3 Δημοσθένους δὲ τάξαντος διέστησαν κατὰ διακοσίους καὶ πλείους, ἔστι δ᾽ ᾗ ἐλάσσους, τῶν
χωρίων τὰ μετεωρότατα λαβόντες, ὅπως ὅτι
πλείστη ἀπορία ᾖ τοῖς πολεμίοις πανταχόθεν
κεκυκλωμένοις καὶ μὴ ἔχωσι πρὸς ὅ τι ἀντιτά-

[1] αὐτὸ, Bauer's correction ; MSS. αὐτοῦ.

---

[1] cf. ch. xxvi 4.
[2] Not hewn, but brought just as they picked them out.
[3] cf. ch. xxiii. 2.
[4] The θαλαμῖται, or oarsmen of the lowest tier. At this

water supply,[1] was held by the main body of troops, under the command of Epitadas; and a small detachment guarded the very extremity of the island where it looks toward Pylos. This point was precipitous on the side toward the sea and least assailable toward the land; there was also here an old fortification, built of stones picked up,[2] which the Lacedaemonians thought would be useful to them in case they should have to retreat under strong pressure. Such, then, was the disposition of the enemy's forces.

XXXII. As for the Athenians, they immediately destroyed the men of the first post, upon whom they charged at full speed, finding them still in their beds or endeavouring to snatch up their arms; for they had not noticed the Athenians' landing, supposing that the ships were merely sailing as usual to their watch-station for the night.[3] Then as soon as day dawned the rest of the army began to disembark. These were the crews of somewhat more than seventy ships (with the single exception of the rowers of the lowest benches[4]), equipped each in his own way, besides eight hundred archers and as many targeteers, and also the Messenians who had come to reinforce them, and all the others who were on duty about Pylos except the men left to guard the fort. Under Demosthenes' direction they were divided into companies of two hundred more or less, which occupied the highest points of the island, in order that the enemy, being surrounded on all sides, might be in the greatest possible perplexity and not know which

time a trireme was manned by fifty-four θαλαμῖται, fifty-four ζυγῖται (occupants of the middle bank), sixty-two θρανῖται (upper bank), and thirty περίνεῳ (reserve oarsmen), including ὑπηρέται and ἐπιβάται.

ξωνται, ἀλλ' ἀμφίβολοι γίγνωνται τῷ πλήθει,
εἰ μὲν τοῖς πρόσθεν ἐπίοιεν, ὑπὸ τῶν κατόπιν
βαλλόμενοι, εἰ δὲ τοῖς πλαγίοις, ὑπὸ τῶν ἑκατέ-
4 ρωθεν παρατεταγμένων. κατὰ νώτου τε αἰεὶ
ἔμελλον αὐτοῖς, ᾗ χωρήσειαν, οἱ πολέμιοι ἔσεσθαι
ψιλοί, καὶ οἱ ἀπορώτατοι, τοξεύμασι καὶ ἀκοντίοις καὶ λίθοις καὶ σφενδόναις ἐκ πολλοῦ
ἔχοντες ἀλκήν· οἷς μηδὲ ἐπελθεῖν οἷόν τε ἦν·
φεύγοντές τε γὰρ ἐκράτουν καὶ ἀναχωροῦσιν
ἐπέκειντο. τοιαύτῃ μὲν γνώμῃ ὁ Δημοσθένης τό
τε πρῶτον τὴν ἀπόβασιν ἐπενόει καὶ ἐν τῷ ἔργῳ
ἔταξεν.

XXXIII. Οἱ δὲ περὶ τὸν Ἐπιτάδαν καὶ ὅπερ
ἦν πλεῖστον τῶν ἐν τῇ νήσῳ, ὡς εἶδον τό τε
πρῶτον φυλακτήριον διεφθαρμένον καὶ στρατὸν
σφίσιν ἐπιόντα, ξυνετάξαντο καὶ τοῖς ὁπλίταις
τῶν Ἀθηναίων ἐπῇσαν, βουλόμενοι ἐς χεῖρας
ἐλθεῖν· ἐξ ἐναντίας γὰρ οὗτοι καθειστήκεσαν, ἐκ
2 πλαγίου δὲ οἱ ψιλοὶ καὶ κατὰ νώτου. τοῖς μὲν
οὖν ὁπλίταις οὐκ ἐδυνήθησαν προσμεῖξαι οὐδὲ τῇ
σφετέρᾳ ἐμπειρίᾳ χρήσασθαι· οἱ γὰρ ψιλοὶ
ἑκατέρωθεν βάλλοντες εἶργον, καὶ ἅμα ἐκεῖνοι
οὐκ ἀντεπῇσαν, ἀλλ' ἡσύχαζον. τοὺς δὲ ψιλούς,
ᾗ μάλιστα αὐτοῖς προσθέοντες προσκέοιντο, ἔτρε-
πον, καὶ οἳ ὑποστρέφοντες ἠμύνοντο, ἄνθρωποι
κούφως τε ἐσκευασμένοι καὶ προλαμβάνοντες

attack to face, but be exposed to missiles on every side from the host of their opponents—if they attacked those in front, from those behind; if those on either flank, from those arrayed on the other. And they would always find in their rear, whichever way they moved, the light-armed troops of the enemy, which were the most difficult to deal with, since they fought at long range with arrows, javelins, stones, and slings. Nay, they could not even get at them, for they were victorious even as they fled, and as soon as their pursuers turned they were hard upon them again. Such was the idea which Demosthenes had in mind when he devised the plan of landing, and such were his tactics when he put this into effect.

XXXIII. Now when the troops under Epitadas, constituting the main body of the Lacedaemonians on the island, saw that the first outpost was destroyed and that an army was advancing against them, they drew up in line and set out to attack the Athenian hoplites, wishing to come to close quarters with them; for these were stationed directly in front of them, while the light-armed troops were on their flank and rear. They were not able, however, to engage with the hoplites or to avail themselves of their own peculiar skill in fighting; for the light-armed troops kept attacking them with missiles from either side and thus held them in check, and at the same time the hoplites did not advance against them, but remained quiet. They did, however, put the light-armed troops to flight wherever they pressed most closely upon them in their charges; and then these latter would wheel about and keep fighting, being lightly equipped and therefore finding it easy

ῥᾳδίως τῆς φυγῆς χωρίων τε χαλεπότητι καὶ
ὑπὸ τῆς πρὶν ἐρημίας τραχέων ὄντων, ἐν οἷς
οἱ Λακεδαιμόνιοι οὐκ ἐδύναντο διώκειν ὅπλα
ἔχοντες.

XXXIV. Χρόνον μὲν οὖν τινα ὀλίγον οὕτω
πρὸς ἀλλήλους ἠκροβολίσαντο· τῶν δὲ Λακεδαιμονίων οὐκέτι ὀξέως ἐπεκθεῖν ᾗ προσπίπτοιεν δυνα-
μένων, γνόντες αὐτοὺς οἱ ψιλοὶ βραδυτέρους ἤδη
ὄντας τῷ ἀμύνασθαι, καὶ αὐτοὶ τῇ τε ὄψει τοῦ
θαρσεῖν τὸ πλεῖστον εἰληφότες πολλαπλάσιοι
φαινόμενοι καὶ ξυνειθισμένοι μᾶλλον μηκέτι
δεινοὺς αὐτοὺς ὁμοίως σφίσι φαίνεσθαι, ὅτι οὐκ
εὐθὺς ἄξια τῆς προσδοκίας ἐπεπόνθεσαν, ὥσπερ
ὅτε πρῶτον ἀπέβαινον τῇ γνώμῃ δεδουλωμένοι ὡς
ἐπὶ Λακεδαιμονίους, καταφρονήσαντες καὶ ἐμβοή-
σαντες ἀθρόοι ὥρμησαν ἐπ᾽ αὐτοὺς καὶ ἔβαλλον
λίθοις τε καὶ τοξεύμασι καὶ ἀκοντίοις, ὡς ἕκαστός
2 τι πρόχειρον εἶχεν. γενομένης δὲ τῆς βοῆς ἅμα
τῇ ἐπιδρομῇ ἔκπληξίς τε ἐνέπεσεν ἀνθρώποις
ἀήθεσι τοιαύτης μάχης καὶ ὁ κονιορτὸς τῆς ὕλης
νεωστὶ κεκαυμένης ἐχώρει πολὺς ἄνω, ἄπορόν τε
ἦν ἰδεῖν τὸ πρὸ αὑτοῦ ὑπὸ τῶν τοξευμάτων καὶ
λίθων ἀπὸ πολλῶν ἀνθρώπων μετὰ τοῦ κονιορτοῦ
3 ἅμα φερομένων. τό τε ἔργον ἐνταῦθα χαλεπὸν
τοῖς Λακεδαιμονίοις καθίστατο. οὔτε γὰρ οἱ
πῖλοι ἔστεγον τὰ τοξεύματα, δοράτιά τε ἐναπε-

to take to flight in good time, since the ground was difficult and, because it had never been inhabited, was naturally rough. Over such a terrain the Lacedaemonians, who were in heavy armour, were unable to pursue them.

XXXIV. For some little time they skirmished thus with one another; but when the Lacedaemonians were no longer able to dash out promptly at the point where they were attacked, the light-armed troops noticed that they were slackening in their defence, and also conceived the greatest confidence in themselves, now that they could see that they were undoubtedly many times more numerous than the enemy, and, since their losses had from the outset been less heavy than they had expected, they had gradually become accustomed to regarding their opponents as less formidable than they had seemed at their first landing when their own spirits were oppressed by the thought that they were going to fight against Lacedaemonians. Conceiving, therefore, a contempt for them, with a shout they charged upon them in a body, hurling at them stones, arrows or javelins, whichever each man had at hand. The shouting with which the Athenians accompanied their charge caused consternation among the Lacedaemonians, who were unaccustomed to this manner of fighting; and the dust from the newly-burned forest rose in clouds to the sky, so that a man could not see what was in front of him by reason of the arrows and stones, hurled, in the midst of the dust, by many hands. And so the battle began to go hard with the Lacedaemonians; for their felt cuirasses afforded them no protection against the arrows, and the points of the javelins broke off and clung there when the

κέκλαστο βαλλομένων, εἶχόν τε οὐδὲν σφίσιν
αὐτοῖς χρήσασθαι ἀποκεκλημένοι μὲν τῇ ὄψει
τοῦ προορᾶν, ὑπὸ δὲ τῆς μείζονος βοῆς τῶν
πολεμίων τὰ ἐν αὐτοῖς παραγγελλόμενα οὐκ
ἐσακούοντες, κινδύνου τε πανταχόθεν περιεστῶτος
καὶ οὐκ ἔχοντες ἐλπίδα καθ᾽ ὅ τι χρὴ ἀμυνομένους σωθῆναι.

XXXV. Τέλος δὲ τραυματιζομένων ἤδη πολλῶν
διὰ τὸ ἀεὶ ἐν τῷ αὐτῷ ἀναστρέφεσθαι, ξυγκλή-
σαντες ἐχώρησαν ἐς τὸ ἔσχατον ἔρυμα τῆς νήσου,
2 ὃ οὐ πολὺ ἀπεῖχε, καὶ τοὺς ἑαυτῶν φύλακας. ὡς
δὲ ἐνέδοσαν, ἐνταῦθα ἤδη πολλῷ ἔτι πλέονι βοῇ
τεθαρσηκότες οἱ ψιλοὶ ἐπέκειντο, καὶ τῶν Λακεδαιμονίων ὅσοι μὲν ὑποχωροῦντες ἐγκατελαμβά-
νοντο, ἀπέθνησκον, οἱ δὲ πολλοὶ διαφυγόντες ἐς
τὸ ἔρυμα μετὰ τῶν ταύτῃ φυλάκων ἐτάξαντο
3 παρὰ πᾶν ὡς ἀμυνούμενοι ᾗπερ ἦν ἐπίμαχον. καὶ
οἱ Ἀθηναῖοι ἐπισπόμενοι περίοδον μὲν αὐτῶν καὶ
κύκλωσιν χωρίου ἰσχύι οὐκ εἶχον, προσιόντες δὲ
ἐξ ἐναντίας ὤσασθαι ἐπειρῶντο, καὶ χρόνον μὲν
πολὺν καὶ τῆς ἡμέρας τὸ πλεῖστον ταλαιπωρού-
μενοι ἀμφότεροι ὑπό τε τῆς μάχης καὶ δίψης καὶ
ἡλίου ἀντεῖχον, πειρώμενοι οἱ μὲν ἐξελάσασθαι
ἐκ τοῦ μετεώρου, οἱ δὲ μὴ ἐνδοῦναι· ῥᾶον δ᾽ οἱ
Λακεδαιμόνιοι ἡμύνοντο ἢ ἐν τῷ πρίν, οὐκ οὔσης
σφῶν τῆς κυκλώσεως ἐς τὰ πλάγια.

XXXVI. Ἐπειδὴ δὲ ἀπέραντον ἦν, προσελθὼν
ὁ τῶν Μεσσηνίων στρατηγὸς Κλέωνι καὶ Δημο-

men were struck. They were, therefore, quite at their wits' end, since the dust shut off their view ahead and they could not hear the word of command on their own side because the enemy's shouts were louder. Danger encompassed them on every side and they despaired of any means of defence availing to save them.

XXXV. At last when they saw that their men were being wounded in large numbers because they had to move backwards and forwards always on the same ground, they closed ranks and fell back to the farthermost fortification on the island, which was not far distant, and to their own garrison stationed there. But the moment they began to give way, the light-armed troops, now emboldened, fell upon them with a louder outcry than ever. Those of the Lacedae-monians who were intercepted in their retreat were slain, but the majority of them escaped to the fortifi-cation, where they ranged themselves with the garrison there, resolved to defend it at every point where it was assailable. The Athenians followed, but the position was so strong that they could not outflank and surround the defenders. They, there-fore, tried to dislodge them by a frontal attack. Now for a long time, and indeed during the greater part of the day, in spite of the distress from the battle, from thirst, and from the heat of the sun, both sides held out, the one trying to drive the enemy from the heights, the other merely to hold their ground; the Lacedaemonians, however, now found it easier than before to defend themselves, since they could not be taken in flank.

XXXVI. But when the business seemed intermin-able, the general [1] of the Messenians came to Cleon

_____
[1] Named Comon, according to Paus. IV. xxvi. 2.

σθένει ἄλλως ἔφη πονεῖν σφᾶς· εἰ δὲ βούλονται
ἑαυτῷ δοῦναι τῶν τοξοτῶν μέρος τι καὶ τῶν
ψιλῶν περιιέναι κατὰ νώτου αὐτοῖς ὁδῷ ᾗ ἂν
αὐτὸς εὕρῃ, δοκεῖν βιάσασθαι [1] τὴν ἔφοδον.
2 λαβὼν δὲ ἃ ᾐτήσατο, ἐκ τοῦ ἀφανοῦς ὁρμήσας
ὥστε μὴ ἰδεῖν ἐκείνους, κατὰ τὸ αἰεὶ παρεῖκον
τοῦ κρημνώδους τῆς νήσου προβαίνων καὶ ᾗ οἱ
Λακεδαιμόνιοι χωρίου ἰσχύι πιστεύσαντες οὐκ
ἐφύλασσον, χαλεπῶς τε καὶ μόλις περιελθὼν
ἔλαθε, καὶ ἐπὶ τοῦ μετεώρου ἐξαπίνης ἀναφανεὶς
κατὰ νώτου αὐτῶν τοὺς μὲν τῷ ἀδοκήτῳ ἐξέ-
πληξε, τοὺς δὲ ἃ προσεδέχοντο ἰδόντας πολλῷ
3 μᾶλλον ἐπέρρωσεν. καὶ οἱ Λακεδαιμόνιοι βαλλό-
μενοί τε ἀμφοτέρωθεν ἤδη καὶ γιγνόμενοι ἐν τῷ
αὐτῷ ξυμπτώματι, ὡς μικρὸν μεγάλῳ εἰκάσαι,
τῷ ἐν Θερμοπύλαις (ἐκεῖνοί τε γὰρ τῇ ἀτραπῷ
περιελθόντων τῶν Περσῶν διεφθάρησαν οὗτοί
τε), ἀμφίβολοι ἤδη ὄντες οὐκέτι ἀντεῖχον, ἀλλὰ
πολλοῖς τε ὀλίγοι μαχόμενοι καὶ ἀσθενείᾳ σωμάτων διὰ τὴν σιτοδείαν ὑπεχώρουν· καὶ οἱ
Ἀθηναῖοι ἐκράτουν ἤδη τῶν ἐφόδων.

XXXVII. Γνοὺς δὲ ὁ Κλέων καὶ ὁ Δημοσθένης,
εἰ καὶ ὁποσονοῦν μᾶλλον ἐνδώσουσι, διαφθαρη-
σομένους αὐτοὺς ὑπὸ τῆς σφετέρας στρατιᾶς,
ἔπαυσαν τὴν μάχην καὶ τοὺς ἑαυτῶν ἀπεῖρξαν,
βουλόμενοι ἀγαγεῖν αὐτοὺς Ἀθηναίοις ζῶντας, εἴ

---

[1] As the MSS.; Hude βιάσεσθαι, after Madvig.

and Demosthenes and said that their side was wasting its pains; but if they were willing to give him a portion of their bowmen and light-armed troops, so that he could get round in the enemy's rear by some path or other which he might himself discover, he thought that he could force the approach. Obtaining what he asked for, he started from a point out of the enemy's sight, so as not to be observed by them, and advanced along the precipitous shore of the island, wherever it offered a foothold, to a point where the Lacedaemonians, trusting to the strength of the position, maintained no guard. Thus with great difficulty he barely succeeded in getting round unobserved and suddenly appeared on the high ground in the enemy's rear, striking them with consternation by this unexpected move, but far more encouraging his friends, who now saw what they were expecting. The Lacedaemonians were now assailed on both sides, and—to compare a small affair with a great one—were in the same evil case as they had been at Thermopylae; for there they had perished when the Persians got in their rear by the path,[1] and here they were caught in the same way. Since, then, they were now assailed on both sides they no longer held out, but, fighting few against many and withal weak in body from lack of food, they began to give way. And the Athenians by this time were in possession of the approaches.

XXXVII. But Cleon and Demosthenes, realizing that if the enemy should give back ever so little more they would be destroyed by the Athenian army, put a stop to the battle and held back their own men, wishing to deliver them alive to the Athenians

---

[1] cf. Hdt. vii. 213.

πως τοῦ κηρύγματος ἀκούσαντες ἐπικλασθεῖεν
τῇ γνώμῃ[1] καὶ ἡσσηθεῖεν τοῦ παρόντος δεινοῦ,
2 ἐκήρυξάν τε, εἰ βούλονται, τὰ ὅπλα παραδοῦναι
καὶ σφᾶς αὐτοὺς Ἀθηναίοις ὥστε βουλεῦσαι ὅ τι
ἂν ἐκείνοις δοκῇ.

XXXVIII. Οἱ δὲ ἀκούσαντες παρεῖσαν τὰς
ἀσπίδας οἱ πλεῖστοι καὶ τὰς χεῖρας ἀνέσεισαν
δηλοῦντες προσίεσθαι τὰ κεκηρυγμένα. μετὰ δὲ
ταῦτα γενομένης τῆς ἀνοκωχῆς ξυνῆλθον ἐς λόγους
ὅ τε Κλέων καὶ ὁ Δημοσθένης καὶ ἐκείνων Στύφων
ὁ Φάρακος, τῶν πρότερον ἀρχόντων τοῦ μὲν
πρώτου τεθνηκότος, Ἐπιτάδου, τοῦ δὲ μετ' αὐτὸν
Ἱππαγρέτου ἐφῃρημένου ἐν τοῖς νεκροῖς ἔτι ζῶντος
κειμένου ὡς τεθνεῶτος. αὐτὸς τρίτος ἐφῃρημένος
2 ἄρχειν κατὰ νόμον, εἴ τι ἐκεῖνοι πάσχοιεν. ἔλεξε
δὲ ὁ Στύφων καὶ οἱ μετ' αὐτοῦ ὅτι βούλονται
διακηρυκεύσασθαι πρὸς τοὺς ἐν τῇ ἠπείρῳ Λακε-
3 δαιμονίους ὅ τι χρὴ σφᾶς ποιεῖν. καὶ ἐκείνων
μὲν οὐδένα ἀφιέντων, αὐτῶν δὲ τῶν Ἀθηναίων
καλούντων ἐκ τῆς ἠπείρου κήρυκας καὶ γενομένων
ἐπερωτήσεων δὶς ἢ τρίς, ὁ τελευταῖος διαπλεύσας
αὐτοῖς ἀπὸ τῶν ἐκ τῆς ἠπείρου Λακεδαιμονίων
ἀνὴρ ἀπήγγειλεν ὅτι " Λακεδαιμόνιοι κελεύουσιν
ὑμᾶς αὐτοὺς περὶ ὑμῶν αὐτῶν βουλεύεσθαι μηδὲν
αἰσχρὸν ποιοῦντας." οἱ δὲ καθ' ἑαυτοὺς βου-
λευσάμενοι τὰ ὅπλα παρέδοσαν καὶ σφᾶς αὐτούς.

---

[1] After τῇ γνώμῃ the MSS. have τὰ ὅπλα παραδοῦναι, which
most recent editors delete, after Krüger.

and in hopes that possibly, when they heard the herald's proclamation, they would be broken in spirit and submit to the present danger. Accordingly, they caused the herald to proclaim that they might, if they wished, surrender themselves and their arms to the Athenians, these to decide their fate as should seem good to them.

XXXVIII. When the Lacedaemonians heard this, most of them lowered their shields and waved their hands, indicating that they accepted the terms proposed. An armistice was then arranged and a conference was held, Cleon and Demosthenes representing the Athenians and Styphon son of Pharax the Lacedaemonians. Of the earlier Lacedaemonian commanders the first, Epitadas, had been slain and Hippagretas, who had been chosen as next in succession, now lay among the fallen and was accounted dead, though he was still alive; and Styphon was third in succession, having been originally chosen, as the law prescribed, to be in command in case anything should happen to the other two. He then, and those with him, said that they wished to send a herald over to the Lacedaemonians on the mainland to ask what they must do. The Athenians, however, would not let any of them go, but themselves summoned heralds from the mainland; then, after interrogatories had been exchanged two or three times, the last man who came over to them from the Lacedaemonians on the mainland brought this message: "The Lacedaemonians bid you decide your case for yourselves, but do nothing dishonourable." So they took counsel with one another and then surrendered themselves and their arms. During

4 καὶ ταύτην μὲν τὴν ἡμέραν καὶ τὴν ἐπιοῦσαν
νύκτα ἐν φυλακῇ εἶχον αὐτοὺς οἱ Ἀθηναῖοι· τῇ δ'
ὑστεραίᾳ οἱ μὲν Ἀθηναῖοι τροπαῖον στήσαντες ἐν
τῇ νήσῳ τἆλλα διεσκευάζοντο ὡς ἐς πλοῦν καὶ
τοὺς ἄνδρας τοῖς τριηράρχοις διέδοσαν ἐς φυλακήν, οἱ δὲ Λακεδαιμόνιοι κήρυκα πέμψαντες τοὺς
5 νεκροὺς διεκομίσαντο. ἀπέθανον δ' ἐν τῇ νήσῳ
καὶ ζῶντες ἐλήφθησαν τοσοίδε· εἴκοσι μὲν ὁπλῖται
διέβησαν καὶ τετρακόσιοι οἱ πάντες· τούτων
ζῶντες ἐκομίσθησαν ὀκτὼ ἀποδέοντες τριακόσιοι,
οἱ δὲ ἄλλοι ἀπέθανον. καὶ Σπαρτιᾶται τούτων
ἦσαν τῶν ζώντων περὶ εἴκοσι καὶ ἑκατόν. Ἀθηναίων δὲ οὐ πολλοὶ διεφθάρησαν· ἡ γὰρ μάχη οὐ
σταδία ἦν.

XXXIX. Χρόνος δὲ ὁ ξύμπας ἐγένετο ὅσον οἱ
ἄνδρες ἐν τῇ νήσῳ ἐπολιορκήθησαν, ἀπὸ τῆς
ναυμαχίας μέχρι τῆς ἐν τῇ νήσῳ μάχης, ἑβδομή-
2 κοντα ἡμέραι καὶ δύο. τούτων περὶ εἴκοσι
ἡμέρας, ἐν αἷς οἱ πρέσβεις περὶ τῶν σπονδῶν ἀπῆσαν, ἐσιτοδοτοῦντο, τὰς δὲ ἄλλας τοῖς ἐσπλέουσι
λάθρα διετρέφοντο· καὶ ἦν σῖτός τις ἐν τῇ νήσῳ
καὶ ἄλλα βρώματα ἐγκατελήφθη· ὁ γὰρ ἄρχων
Ἐπιτάδας ἐνδεεστέρως ἑκάστῳ παρεῖχεν ἢ πρὸς
τὴν ἐξουσίαν.

3 Οἱ μὲν δὴ Ἀθηναῖοι καὶ οἱ Πελοποννήσιοι
ἀνεχώρησαν τῷ στρατῷ ἐκ τῆς Πύλου ἑκάτεροι
ἐπ' οἴκου, καὶ τοῦ Κλέωνος καίπερ μανιώδης
οὖσα ἡ ὑπόσχεσις ἀπέβη· ἐντὸς γὰρ εἴκοσι
ἡμερῶν ἤγαγε τοὺς ἄνδρας, ὥσπερ ὑπέστη.
XL. παρὰ γνώμην τε δὴ μάλιστα τῶν κατὰ τὸν
πόλεμον τοῦτο τοῖς Ἕλλησιν ἐγένετο· τοὺς γὰρ

that day and the following night the Athenians kept them under guard; but on the next day, after setting up a trophy on the island, they made all their preparations to sail, distributing the prisoners among the trierarchs for safe-keeping; and the Lacedaemonians sent a herald and brought their dead to the mainland. The number of those who had been killed or taken alive on the island was as follows: four hundred and twenty hoplites had crossed over in all; of these two hundred and ninety two were brought to Athens alive; all the rest had been slain. Of those who survived one hundred and twenty were Spartans.[1] Of the Athenians, however, not many perished; for it was not a pitched battle.

XXXIX. The time during which the men on the island were under blockade, from the sea fight up to the battle on the island, amounted all told to seventy-two days. For about twenty of these days, the period during which the envoys were absent negotiating the truce, they were regularly provisioned, but the rest of the time they lived on what was smuggled in. And indeed some grain was found on the island at the time of the capture, as well as other articles of food; for the commander Epitadas was accustomed to give each man a scantier ration than his supplies would have allowed.

The Athenians and Peloponnesians now withdrew from Pylos and returned home with their respective forces, and Cleon's promise, mad as it was, had been fulfilled; for within twenty days he brought the men as he had undertaken to do. XL. Of all the events of this war this came as the greatest surprise to the Hellenic world; for men could not conceive that the

---

[1] i.e. citizens of Sparta, the rest being from the neighbouring towns of the Perioeci; cf. ch. viii. 1.

Λακεδαιμονίους οὔτε λιμῷ οὔτ᾽ ἀνάγκῃ οὐδεμιᾷ
ἠξίουν τὰ ὅπλα παραδοῦναι, ἀλλὰ ἔχοντας καὶ
2 μαχομένους ἕως ἐδύναντο ἀποθνήσκειν, ἀπιστοῦντες[1] μὴ εἶναι τοὺς παραδόντας τοῖς τεθνεῶ-
σιν ὁμοίους. καί τινος ἐρομένου ποτὲ ὕστερον
τῶν Ἀθηναίων ξυμμάχων δι᾽ ἀχθηδόνα[2] ἕνα τῶν
ἐκ τῆς νήσου αἰχμαλώτων εἰ οἱ τεθνεῶτες αὐτῶν
καλοὶ κἀγαθοί, ἀπεκρίνατο αὐτῷ πολλοῦ ἂν ἄξιον
εἶναι τὸν ἄτρακτον, λέγων τὸν οἰστόν, εἰ τοὺς
ἀγαθοὺς διεγίγνωσκε, δήλωσιν ποιούμενος ὅτι ὁ
ἐντυγχάνων τοῖς τε λίθοις καὶ τοξεύμασι διεφ-
θείρετο.

XLI. Κομισθέντων δὲ τῶν ἀνδρῶν οἱ Ἀθηναῖοι
ἐβούλευσαν δεσμοῖς μὲν αὐτοὺς φυλάσσειν μέχρι
οὗ τι ξυμβῶσιν, ἢν δ᾽ οἱ Πελοποννήσιοι πρὸ
τούτου ἐς τὴν γῆν ἐσβάλλωσιν, ἐξαγαγόντες
2 ἀποκτεῖναι. τῆς δὲ Πύλου φυλακὴν κατεστήσαντο, καὶ οἱ ἐκ τῆς Ναυπάκτου Μεσσήνιοι ὡς
ἐς πατρίδα ταύτην (ἔστι γὰρ ἡ Πύλος τῆς Μεσση-
νίδος ποτὲ οὔσης γῆς) πέμψαντες σφῶν αὐτῶν
τοὺς ἐπιτηδειοτάτους ἐλῄζοντό τε τὴν Λακωνικὴν
3 καὶ πλεῖστα ἔβλαπτον ὁμόφωνοι ὄντες. οἱ δὲ
Λακεδαιμόνιοι ἀμαθεῖς ὄντες ἐν τῷ πρὶν χρόνῳ
λῃστείας καὶ τοῦ τοιούτου πολέμου, τῶν τε
Εἱλώτων αὐτομολούντων καὶ φοβούμενοι μὴ καὶ
ἐπὶ μακρότερον σφίσι τι νεωτερισθῇ τῶν κατὰ
τὴν χώραν, οὐ ῥᾳδίως ἔφερον, ἀλλά, καίπερ οὐ
βουλόμενοι ἔνδηλοι εἶναι τοῖς Ἀθηναίοις, ἐπρεσ-

---

[1] So Hude, with M; most other MSS. ἀπιστοῦντές τε.
[2] δι᾽ ἀχθηδόνα, deleted by Hude, after Rutherford.

Lacedaemonians would ever be induced by hunger or any other compulsion to give up their arms, but thought that they would keep them till they died, fighting as long as they were able; and they could not believe that those who had surrendered were as brave as those who had fallen. And when one of the Athenian allies sometime afterwards sneeringly asked one of the captives taken on the island, whether the Lacedaemonians who had been slain were brave men and true,[1] the answer was, that the shaft, meaning the arrow, would be worth a great deal if it could distinguish the brave, intimating that it was a mere matter of chance who was hit and killed by stones and bow-shots.

XLI. When the captives were brought to Athens, the Athenians determined to keep them in prison until some agreement should be reached, but if before that the Peloponnesians should invade their territory, to bring them out and put them to death. They also placed a garrison in Pylos, and the Messenians at Naupactus, regarding this territory as their fatherland—for Pylos belongs to the country that was once Messenia—sent thither such of their own number as were best fitted for the task and proceeded to ravage the Laconian territory, and they did a great deal of damage, since they were men of the same speech as the inhabitants. As for the Lacedaemonians, they had never before experienced predatory warfare of this kind, and therefore, when the Helots began to desert and there was reason to fear that the revolutionary movement might gain still further headway in their territory, they were uneasy, and, in spite of their desire not to betray their alarm

---

[1] Implying that the survivors were not.

βεύοντο παρ' αὐτοὺς καὶ ἐπειρῶντο τήν τε Πύλον
4 καὶ τοὺς ἄνδρας κομίζεσθαι. οἱ δὲ μειζόνων τε
ὠρέγοντο καὶ πολλάκις φοιτώντων αὐτοὺς ἀπράκ-
τους ἀπέπεμπον. ταῦτα μὲν τὰ περὶ Πύλον
γενόμενα.

XLII. Τοῦ δ' αὐτοῦ θέρους μετὰ ταῦτα εὐθὺς
Ἀθηναῖοι ἐς τὴν Κορινθίαν ἐστράτευσαν ναυσὶν
ὀγδοήκοντα καὶ δισχιλίοις ὁπλίταις ἑαυτῶν καὶ
ἐν ἱππαγωγοῖς ναυσὶ διακοσίοις ἱππεῦσιν· ἠκολούθουν δὲ καὶ τῶν ξυμμάχων Μιλήσιοι καὶ
Ἄνδριοι καὶ Καρύστιοι, ἐστρατήγει δὲ Νικίας
2 ὁ Νικηράτου τρίτος αὐτός. πλέοντες δὲ ἅμα ἔῳ
ἔσχον μεταξὺ Χερσονήσου τε καὶ Ῥείτου ἐς τὸν
αἰγιαλὸν τοῦ χωρίου ὑπὲρ οὗ ὁ Σολύγειος λόφος
ἐστίν, ἐφ' ὃν Δωριῆς τὸ πάλαι ἱδρυθέντες τοῖς ἐν
τῇ πόλει Κορινθίοις ἐπολέμουν οὖσιν Αἰολεῦσιν·
καὶ κώμη νῦν ἐπ' αὐτοῦ Σολύγεια καλουμένη
ἐστίν. ἀπὸ δὲ τοῦ αἰγιαλοῦ τούτου ἔνθα αἱ νῆες
κατέσχον ἡ μὲν κώμη αὕτη δώδεκα σταδίους
ἀπέχει, ἡ δὲ Κορινθίων πόλις ἑξήκοντα, ὁ δὲ
3 ἰσθμὸς εἴκοσι. Κορίνθιοι δὲ προπυθόμενοι ἐξ
Ἄργους ὅτι ἡ στρατιὰ ἥξει τῶν Ἀθηναίων ἐκ
πλείονος ἐβοήθησαν ἐς ἰσθμὸν πάντες πλὴν τῶν
ἔξω ἰσθμοῦ· καὶ ἐν Ἀμπρακίᾳ καὶ ἐν Λευκάδι
ἀπῆσαν αὐτῶν πεντακόσιοι φρουροί· οἱ δ' ἄλλοι
πανδημεὶ ἐπετήρουν τοὺς Ἀθηναίους οἱ κατα-

---

[1] At the time when the Dorians, under the leadership of
the Heracleidae, got possession of the Peloponnesus (cf. I.
xii. 3). See Busolt, Gr. Gesch. i². 208.

to the Athenians, kept sending envoys to them in the endeavour to recover Pylos and the prisoners. But the Athenians constantly made greater demands and the envoys, although they came again and again, were always sent home unsuccessful. Such were the events at Pylos.

XLII. During the same summer and directly after these events the Athenians made an expedition into Corinthian territory with eighty ships and two thousand Athenian hoplites, together with two hundred cavalry on board horse-transports; allied forces also went with them, namely Milesian, Andrian, and Carystian troops, the whole being under the command of Nicias son of Niceratus and two others. These sailed and at day-break landed midway between the peninsula Chersonesus and the stream Rheitus, at a point on the beach over which rises the Solygeian hill—the hill where the Dorians in olden times[1] established themselves when they made war upon the Corinthians in the city, who were Aeolians; and there is still on the hill a village called Solygeia. From this point on the beach where the ships put in to shore this village is twelve stadia distant, the city of Corinth sixty, and the Isthmus twenty. But the Corinthians, having previous information from Argos that the Athenian army would come, had long before occupied the Isthmus with all their forces, except those who dwelt north of the Isthmus and five hundred Corinthians who were away doing garrison duty in Ambracia[2] and Leucas; all the rest to a man were now there, watching to see where the Athenians

[2] Three hundred of these had been sent the previous winter to Ambracia, which was a Corinthian colony; cf. III. cxiv. 4.

4 σχήσουσιν. ὡς δὲ αὐτοὺς ἔλαθον νυκτὸς κατα-
πλεύσαντες καὶ τὰ σημεῖα αὐτοῖς ἤρθη, καταλιπόντες τοὺς ἡμίσεις αὐτῶν ἐν Κεγχρειᾷ, ἢν ἄρα
οἱ Ἀθηναῖοι ἐπὶ τὸν Κρομμυῶνα ἴωσιν, ἐβοήθουν
κατὰ τάχος.

XLIII. Καὶ Βάττος μὲν ὁ ἕτερος τῶν στρατηγῶν (δύο γὰρ ἦσαν ἐν τῇ μάχῃ οἱ παρόντες)
λαβὼν λόχον ἦλθεν ἐπὶ τὴν Σολύγειαν κώμην
φυλάξων ἀτείχιστον οὖσαν, Λυκόφρων δὲ τοῖς
2 ἄλλοις ξυνέβαλεν. καὶ πρῶτα μὲν τῷ δεξιῷ
κέρᾳ τῶν Ἀθηναίων εὐθὺς ἀποβεβηκότι πρὸ τῆς
Χερσονήσου οἱ Κορίνθιοι ἐπέκειντο, ἔπειτα δὲ καὶ
τῷ ἄλλῳ στρατεύματι. καὶ ἦν ἡ μάχη καρτερὰ
3 καὶ ἐν χερσὶ πᾶσα. καὶ τὸ μὲν δεξιὸν κέρας τῶν
Ἀθηναίων καὶ Καρυστίων (οὗτοι γὰρ παρα-
τεταγμένοι ἦσαν ἔσχατοι) ἐδέξαντό τε τοὺς
Κορινθίους καὶ ἐώσαντο μόλις· οἱ δὲ ὑποχωρή-
σαντες πρὸς αἱμασιάν (ἦν γὰρ τὸ χωρίον πρόσ-
αντες πᾶν) βάλλοντες τοῖς λίθοις καθύπερθεν
ὄντες καὶ παιανίσαντες ἐπῇσαν αὖθις, δεξαμένων
δὲ τῶν Ἀθηναίων ἐν χερσὶν ἦν πάλιν ἡ μάχη.
4 λόχος δέ τις τῶν Κορινθίων ἐπιβοηθήσας τῷ
εὐωνύμῳ κέρᾳ ἑαυτῶν ἔτρεψε τῶν Ἀθηναίων τὸ
δεξιὸν κέρας καὶ ἐπεδίωξεν ἐς τὴν θάλασσαν
πάλιν δὲ ἀπὸ τῶν νεῶν ἀνέστρεψαν οἵ τε Ἀθηναῖοι καὶ οἱ Καρύστιοι. τὸ δὲ ἄλλο στρατόπεδον
ἀμφοτέρωθεν ἐμάχετο ξυνεχῶς, μάλιστα δὲ τὸ
δεξιὸν κέρας τῶν Κορινθίων, ἐφ᾽ ᾧ ὁ Λυκόφρων

---

[1] The Corinthian eastern haven, seventy stadia from the city.
[2] The chief place on this coast-line between the Isthmus

would land. But when the Athenians eluded them by making their landing by night and the Corinthians were notified by the raising of fire-signals, these left half of their troops at Cenchraeae,[1] in case the Athenians should after all go against Crommyon,[2] and in haste rushed to the defence.

XLIII. Thereupon Battus, one of the two Corinthian generals present at the battle, took a company and went to the village of Solygeia, which was unwalled, to guard it, while Lycophron attacked with the remainder of their troops. Now at first the Corinthians assailed the right wing of the Athenians, which had just disembarked in front of Chersonesus, and afterwards engaged the rest of the army also. The battle was stubbornly contested throughout and fought at close quarters. The Athenian right wing, at whose extremity were stationed the Carystians, received the charge of the Corinthians and drove them back, though with difficulty; but the latter retreated to a stone fence and, since the ground was everywhere a steep slope, pelted the Athenians with stones, being on higher ground, and then, raising the paean, charged a second time. The Athenians received the charge and the battle was again waged at close quarters. Then a company of the Corinthians, reinforcing their own left wing, routed the right wing of the Athenians and pursued it to the sea; but again upon reaching the ships the Athenians and Carystians rallied. The other divisions of the two armies were continuously engaged, especially the right wing of the Corinthians, where Lycophron was in command against the

and Megara, some 120 stadia from Corinth, known as the haunt of the wild boar killed by Theseus (Paus. I. xxvii. 9; II. i. 3).

THUCYDIDES

ὧν κατὰ τὸ εὐώνυμον τῶν Ἀθηναίων ἠμύνετο·
ἤλπιζον γὰρ αὐτοὺς ἐπὶ τὴν Σολύγειαν κώμην
πειράσειν.

XLIV. Χρόνον μὲν οὖν πολὺν ἀντεῖχον οὐκ ἐνδι-
δόντες ἀλλήλοις· ἔπειτα (ἦσαν γὰρ τοῖς Ἀθηναίοις
οἱ ἱππῆς ὠφέλιμοι ξυμμαχόμενοι, τῶν ἑτέρων οὐκ
ἐχόντων ἵππους) ἐτράποντο οἱ Κορίνθιοι καὶ
ὑπεχώρησαν πρὸς τὸν λόφον καὶ ἔθεντο τὰ ὅπλα
2 καὶ οὐκέτι κατέβαινον, ἀλλ᾽ ἡσύχαζον. ἐν δὲ τῇ
τροπῇ ταύτῃ κατὰ τὸ δεξιὸν κέρας οἱ πλεῖστοί τε
αὐτῶν ἀπέθανον καὶ Λυκόφρων ὁ στρατηγός. ἡ
δὲ ἄλλη στρατιὰ τούτῳ τῷ τρόπῳ οὐ κατὰ δίωξιν
πολλὴν οὐδὲ ταχείας φυγῆς γενομένης, ἐπεὶ
ἐβιάσθη, ἐπαναχωρήσασα πρὸς τὰ μετέωρα
ἱδρύθη. οἱ δὲ Ἀθηναῖοι, ὡς οὐκέτι αὐτοῖς ἐπῇσαν
3 ἐς μάχην, τούς τε νεκροὺς ἐσκύλευον καὶ τοὺς
ἑαυτῶν ἀνῃροῦντο, τροπαῖόν τε εὐθέως ἔστησαν.
4 τοῖς δ᾽ ἡμίσεσι τῶν Κορινθίων, οἳ ἐν τῇ Κεγχρειᾷ
ἐκάθηντο φύλακες, μὴ ἐπὶ τὸν Κρομμυῶνα πλεύ-
σωσι, τούτοις οὐ κατάδηλος ἡ μάχη ἦν ὑπὸ τοῦ
ὄρους τοῦ Ὀνείου· κονιορτὸν δὲ ὡς εἶδον καὶ ὡς
ἔγνωσαν, ἐβοήθουν εὐθύς. ἐβοήθησαν δὲ καὶ οἱ ἐκ
τῆς πόλεως πρεσβύτεροι τῶν Κορινθίων αἰσθό-
5 μενοι τὸ γεγενημένον. ἰδόντες δὲ οἱ Ἀθηναῖοι
ξύμπαντας αὐτοὺς ἐπιόντας καὶ νομίσαντες τῶν
ἐγγὺς ἀστυγειτόνων Πελοποννησίων βοήθειαν
ἐπιέναι, ἀνεχώρουν κατὰ τάχος ἐπὶ τὰς ναῦς,
ἔχοντες τὰ σκυλεύματα καὶ τοὺς ἑαυτῶν νεκροὺς
πλὴν δυοῖν, οὓς ἐγκατέλιπον οὐ δυνάμενοι εὑρεῖν.

Athenian left and kept it in check; for they expected the Athenians to make an attempt against the village of Solygeia.

XLIV. For a long time they held out, neither side yielding to the other. Then as the Athenians had an advantage in the support of their cavalry, whereas the other side had no horses, the Corinthians turned and retired to the hill, where they halted, and did not come down again but remained quiet. In this repulse it was on their right wing that most of the Corinthians that were lost were killed, among them Lycophron the general. But the rest of the Corinthian army retired in this manner—there was no long pursuit nor hasty flight, but when it was forced back, it withdrew to the higher ground and there established itself. As for the Athenians, when the enemy no longer came against them and offered battle, they stripped the corpses, took up their own dead, and straightway set up a trophy. Meanwhile the other half of the Corinthian forces, which was stationed at Cenchraeae as a garrison to prevent the Athenians from making a descent upon Crommyon, were unable to see the battle because Mt. Oneium intervened; but when they saw the cloud of dust and realized what was going on, they rushed thither at once, as did also the older men in the city of Corinth when they perceived what had happened. But the Athenians, seeing the whole throng advancing and thinking it to be a detachment of the neighbouring Peloponnesians coming to assist the Corinthians, withdrew in haste to their ships, having their spoils and the bodies of their own dead, except two, which they left behind because they were not able to find them.

6 καὶ ἀναβάντες ἐπὶ τὰς ναῦς ἐπεραιώθησαν ἐς τὰς
ἐπικειμένας νήσους, ἐκ δ' αὐτῶν ἐπικηρυκευσά-
μενοι τοὺς νεκροὺς οὓς ἐγκατέλιπον ὑποσπόνδους
ἀνείλοντο. ἀπέθανον δὲ Κορινθίων μὲν ἐν τῇ
μάχῃ δώδεκα καὶ διακόσιοι, Ἀθηναίων δὲ ὀλίγῳ
ἐλάσσους πεντήκοντα.

XLV. Ἄραντες δὲ ἐκ τῶν νήσων οἱ Ἀθηναῖοι
ἔπλευσαν αὐθημερὸν ἐς Κρομμυῶνα τῆς Κοριν-
θίας· ἀπέχει δὲ τῆς πόλεως εἴκοσι καὶ ἑκατὸν
σταδίους. καὶ καθορμισάμενοι τήν τε γῆν ἐδῄωσαν
2 καὶ τὴν νύκτα ηὐλίσαντο. τῇ δ' ὑστεραίᾳ παρα-
πλεύσαντες ἐς τὴν Ἐπιδαυρίαν πρῶτον καὶ ἀπό-
βασίν τινα ποιησάμενοι ἀφίκοντο ἐς Μέθανα[1] τὴν
μεταξὺ Ἐπιδαύρου καὶ Τροιζῆνος, καὶ ἀπολαβόν-
τες τὸν τῆς χερσονήσου ἰσθμὸν ἐτείχισαν ἐν ᾗ ἡ
Μέθανα ἐστί. καὶ φρούριον καταστησάμενοι
ἐλῄστευον τὸν ἔπειτα χρόνον τήν τε Τροιζηνίαν
γῆν καὶ Ἁλιάδα καὶ Ἐπιδαυρίαν. ταῖς δὲ ναυσίν,
ἐπειδὴ ἐξετείχισαν τὸ χωρίον, ἀπέπλευσαν ἐπ'
οἴκου.

XLVI. Κατὰ δὲ τὸν αὐτὸν χρόνον, καθ' ὃν[2]
ταῦτα ἐγίγνετο, καὶ Εὐρυμέδων καὶ Σοφοκλῆς,
ἐπειδὴ ἐκ τῆς Πύλου ἀπῆραν ἐς τὴν Σικελίαν
ναυσὶν Ἀθηναίων, ἀφικόμενοι ἐς Κέρκυραν ἐστράτευσαν μετὰ τῶν ἐκ τῆς πόλεως ἐπὶ τοὺς ἐν τῷ
ὄρει τῆς Ἰστώνης Κερκυραίων καθιδρυμένους, οἳ
τότε μετὰ τὴν στάσιν διαβάντες ἐκράτουν τε τῆς
2 γῆς καὶ πολλὰ ἔβλαπτον. προσβαλόντες δὲ τὸ

---

[1] MSS. give Μεθώνη, but Strabo states that the true name is
Μέθανα. Lower down the MSS. read ἐν ᾧ ἡ Μεθώνη ἐστί, which
many editors bracket. If it is retained, ἐν ᾗ must be read for
ἐν ᾧ, as Μέθανα lay, not on the Isthmus, but on the west coast
of the peninsula.   [2] καθ' ὃν, with CGM, omitted by ABEF.

So they embarked and crossed over to the adjacent islands, and sending thence a herald recovered under truce the bodies which they had left behind. There were slain in this battle two hundred and twelve of the Corinthians, and of the Athenians somewhat fewer than fifty.

XLV. Setting out from the islands, the Athenians sailed the same day to Crommyon in Corinthian territory, which is distant a hundred and twenty stadia from the city, and coming to anchor ravaged the land and bivouacked during the night. The next day sailing along the coast they came first to the territory of Epidaurus, where they made a landing, and then to Methana, between Epidaurus and Troezen, where they walled off the neck of the peninsula on which Methana lies. Here they left a garrison, which afterward occupied itself with marauding excursions into the territory of Troezen, Halieis, and Epidaurus. But the fleet sailed back to Athens as soon as the fortifications at Methana had been completed.

XLVI. It was at this time, while these events were occurring, that Eurymedon and Sophocles,[1] setting sail from Pylos for Sicily with an Athenian fleet, arrived at Corcyra. There they took part with the men from the city[2] in an expedition against the Corcyraeans who had established themselves on Mt. Istone, and who at this time, after crossing over thither subsequently to the revolution, were dominating the country and doing a great deal of damage. The stronghold was taken by assault, but the men in

---

[1] cf. ch. viii. 3 ; xxix. 1.
[2] The democrats who had held the city since 427 B.C. (cf. III. lxxxv.).

μὲν τείχισμα εἷλον, οἱ δὲ ἄνδρες καταπεφευγότες
ἀθρόοι πρὸς μετέωρόν τι ξυνέβησαν ὥστε τοὺς
μὲν ἐπικούρους παραδοῦναι, περὶ δὲ σφῶν τὰ
ὅπλα παραδόντων τὸν Ἀθηναίων δῆμον διαγνῶναι.
3 καὶ αὐτοὺς ἐς τὴν νῆσον οἱ στρατηγοὶ τὴν Πτυ-
χίαν ἐς φυλακὴν διεκόμισαν ὑποσπόνδους, μέχρι
οὗ Ἀθήναζε πεμφθῶσιν, ὥστ' ἐάν τις ἁλῷ ἀποδι-
4 δράσκων, ἅπασι λελύσθαι τὰς σπονδάς. οἱ δὲ τοῦ
δήμου προστάται τῶν Κερκυραίων, δεδιότες μὴ οἱ
Ἀθηναῖοι τοὺς ἐλθόντας οὐκ ἀποκτείνωσι, μη-
5 χανῶνται τοιόνδε τι· τῶν ἐν τῇ νήσῳ πείθουσί
τινας ὀλίγους, ὑποπέμψαντες φίλους καὶ διδά-
ξαντες ὡς κατ' εὔνοιαν δὴ λέγειν ὅτι κράτιστον
αὐτοῖς εἴη ὡς τάχιστα ἀποδρᾶναι, πλοῖον δέ τι
αὐτοὶ ἑτοιμάσειν· μέλλειν γὰρ δὴ τοὺς στρατηγοὺς τῶν Ἀθηναίων παραδώσειν αὐτοὺς τῷ δήμῳ
τῶν Κερκυραίων. XLVII. ὡς δὲ ἐπείσθησαν καὶ
μηχανησαμένων τὸ πλοῖον ἐκπλέοντες ἐλήφθησαν,
ἐλέλυντό τε αἱ σπονδαὶ καὶ τοῖς Κερκυραίοις
2 παρεδίδοντο οἱ πάντες. ξυνελάβοντο δὲ τοῦ τοιούτου οὐχ ἥκιστα, ὥστε ἀκριβῆ τὴν πρόφασιν
γενέσθαι καὶ τοὺς τεχνησαμένους ἀδεέστερον
ἐγχειρῆσαι, οἱ στρατηγοὶ τῶν Ἀθηναίων κατά-
δηλοι ὄντες τοὺς ἄνδρας μὴ ἂν βούλεσθαι ὑπ'
ἄλλων κομισθέντας, διότι αὐτοὶ ἐς Σικελίαν
ἔπλεον, τὴν τιμὴν τοῖς ἄγουσι προσποιῆσαι.
3 παραλαβόντες δὲ αὐτοὺς οἱ Κερκυραῖοι ἐς οἴκημα

it fled in a body to some high ground and there
capitulated, on condition that they should surrender
their mercenary troops and give up their arms,
leaving it to the Athenian people to decide upon
their own fate. The generals accordingly conveyed
the men under truce to the island of Ptychia[1] to be
kept under custody there until they should be sent
to Athens, and the understanding was that if anyone
should be caught trying to run away the truce should
be regarded as broken for them all. But the leaders
of the popular party at Corcyra were afraid that the
Athenians would not put them to death on their
arrival at Athens, and therefore resorted to the
following stratagem. They first tried to persuade a
few of the men on the island to run away, by secretly
sending thither friends who were instructed to say,
with a show of good will, that the best course for
them was to do this with no loss of time, and
promising to have a boat ready; for the Athenian
generals, they explained, were intending to deliver
them up to the Corcyraean populace. XLVII. And
when the men had been persuaded, and were caught
sailing away in the boat which the others had provided, the truce was broken and the whole party
was delivered up to the Corcyraeans. But what
chiefly contributed to such a result, so that the
pretext seemed quite plausible and that those who
devised the scheme felt little fear about putting it
into effect, was the fact that the Athenian generals
showed that they would not be willing, as they
were bound for Sicily themselves, to have the men
conveyed to Athens by others, who would thus
get the credit for conducting them. Now the
Corcyraeans took over the prisoners and shut them

_____
[1] cf. III. lxxv. 5 ; now called Vido.

μέγα κατεῖρξαν, καὶ ὕστερον ἐξάγοντες κατὰ
εἴκοσι ἄνδρας διῆγον διὰ δυοῖν στοίχοιν ὁπλιτῶν
ἑκατέρωθεν παρατεταγμένων, δεδεμένους τε πρὸς
ἀλλήλους καὶ παιομένους καὶ κεντουμένους ὑπὸ
τῶν παρατεταγμένων, εἴ πού τίς τινα ἴδοι ἐχθρὸν
ἑαυτοῦ· μαστιγοφόροι τε παριόντες ἐπετάχυνον
τῆς ὁδοῦ τοὺς σχολαίτερον προϊόντας.

XLVIII. Καὶ ἐς μὲν ἄνδρας ἑξήκοντα ἔλαθον
τοὺς ἐν τῷ οἰκήματι τούτῳ τῷ τρόπῳ ἐξαγαγόντες
καὶ διαφθείραντες (ᾤοντο γὰρ αὐτοὺς μεταστή-
σοντάς ποι ἄλλοσ' ἐξάγειν)· ὡς δὲ ᾔσθοντο καί
τις αὐτοῖς ἐδήλωσε, τούς τε Ἀθηναίους ἐπεκα-
λοῦντο καὶ ἐκέλευον σφᾶς, εἰ βούλονται, αὐτοὺς
διαφθείρειν, ἔκ τε τοῦ οἰκήματος οὐκέτι ἤθελον
ἐξιέναι, οὐδ' ἐσιέναι ἔφασαν κατὰ δύναμιν περιό-
2 ψεσθαι οὐδένα. οἱ δὲ Κερκυραῖοι κατὰ μὲν τὰς
θύρας οὐδ' αὐτοὶ διενοοῦντο βιάζεσθαι, ἀναβάντες
δὲ ἐπὶ τὸ τέγος τοῦ οἰκήματος καὶ διελόντες τὴν
ὀροφὴν ἔβαλλον τῷ κεράμῳ καὶ ἐτόξευον κάτω.
3 οἱ δὲ ἐφυλάσσοντό τε ὡς ἐδύναντο καὶ ἅμα οἱ
πολλοὶ σφᾶς αὐτοὺς διέφθειρον, οἰστούς τε οὓς
ἀφίεσαν ἐκεῖνοι ἐς τὰς σφαγὰς καθιέντες καὶ ἐκ
κλινῶν τινων, αἳ ἔτυχον αὐτοῖς ἐνοῦσαι, τοῖς
σπάρτοις καὶ ἐκ τῶν ἱματίων παραιρήματα ποιοῦντες ἀπαγχόμενοι. παντί τε ¹ τρόπῳ τὸ πολὺ τῆς
νυκτός (ἐπεγένετο γὰρ νὺξ τῷ παθήματι) ἀνα-
λοῦντες σφᾶς αὐτοὺς καὶ βαλλόμενοι ὑπὸ τῶν

¹ τε added by Poppo.

up in a large building; afterwards they led them out in groups of twenty and marched them down between two lines of hoplites stationed on either side, the prisoners being bound to one another and receiving blows and stabs from the men who stood in the lines, if any of these perchance saw among them a personal enemy; and men with scourges walked by their sides to quicken the steps of such as proceeded too slowly on the way.

XLVIII. In this manner about sixty men were led out and killed without the knowledge of the men who remained in the house, who supposed that their companions were being led out in order to be transferred to some other place. But when they perceived what was going on, or were told by somebody, they appealed to the Athenians and urged them, if they wished to kill them, to do so with their own hands; and they refused thenceforth to leave the house, and declared that they would not allow anyone to enter if they could prevent it. Nor had the Corcyraeans themselves any intention of trying to force their way in by the doors, but climbing on to the top of the building and breaking through the roof they hurled tiles and shot arrows upon them from above. The men inside tried to defend themselves as best as they could, and at the same time most of them set to work to destroy themselves by thrusting into their throats the arrows which the enemy had shot or by strangling themselves with the cords from some beds that happened to be in the place or with strips made from their own garments. Thus for the greater part of the night—for night fell upon their misery—dispatching themselves in every fashion and struck by the missiles of the men on

4 ἄνω διεφθάρησαν. καὶ αὐτοὺς οἱ Κερκυραῖοι,
ἐπειδὴ ἡμέρα ἐγένετο, φορμηδὸν ἐπὶ ἁμάξας
ἐπιβαλόντες ἀπήγαγον ἔξω τῆς πόλεως. τὰς
δὲ γυναῖκας, ὅσαι ἐν τῷ τειχίσματι ἑάλωσαν,
5 ἠνδραποδίσαντο. τοιούτῳ μὲν τρόπῳ οἱ ἐκ τοῦ
ὄρους Κερκυραῖοι ὑπὸ τοῦ δήμου διεφθάρησαν, καὶ
ἡ στάσις πολλὴ γενομένη ἐτελεύτησεν ἐς τοῦτο,
ὅσα γε κατὰ τὸν πόλεμον τόνδε· οὐ γὰρ ἔτι ἦν
6 ὑπόλοιπον τῶν ἑτέρων ὅ τι καὶ ἀξιόλογον. οἱ δὲ
Ἀθηναῖοι ἐς τὴν Σικελίαν, ἵναπερ τὸ πρῶτον ὥρμηντο, ἀποπλεύσαντες μετὰ τῶν ἐκεῖ ξυμμάχων
ἐπολέμουν.

XLIX. Καὶ οἱ ἐν τῇ Ναυπάκτῳ Ἀθηναῖοι καὶ
Ἀκαρνᾶνες ἅμα τελευτῶντος τοῦ θέρους στρατευ-
σάμενοι Ἀνακτόριον Κορινθίων πόλιν, ἣ κεῖται
ἐπὶ τῷ στόματι τοῦ Ἀμπρακικοῦ κόλπου, ἔλαβον
προδοσίᾳ· καὶ ἐκπέμψαντες Κορινθίους [1] αὐτοὶ
Ἀκαρνᾶνες οἰκήτορας [2] ἀπὸ πάντων ἔσχον τὸ
χωρίον. καὶ τὸ θέρος ἐτελεύτα.

L. Τοῦ δ᾽ ἐπιγιγνομένου χειμῶνος Ἀριστείδης ὁ
Ἀρχίππου, εἷς τῶν ἀργυρολόγων νεῶν Ἀθηναίων
στρατηγός, αἳ ἐξεπέμφθησαν πρὸς τοὺς ξυμμάχους, Ἀρταφέρνη, ἄνδρα Πέρσην, παρὰ βασιλέως πορευόμενον ἐς Λακεδαίμονα ξυλλαμβάνει
2 ἐν Ἠιόνι τῇ ἐπὶ Στρυμόνι. καὶ αὐτοῦ κομισθέντος
οἱ Ἀθηναῖοι τὰς μὲν ἐπιστολὰς μεταγραψάμενοι
ἐκ τῶν Ἀσσυρίων γραμμάτων ἀνέγνωσαν, ἐν αἷς
πολλῶν ἄλλων γεγραμμένων κεφάλαιον ἦν πρὸς
Λακεδαιμονίους οὐ γιγνώσκειν ὅ τι βούλονται·
πολλῶν γὰρ ἐλθόντων πρέσβεων οὐδένα ταὐτὰ

---

[1] Hude deletes Κορινθίους, after Dobree.
[2] Hude reads οἰκήτορες, with CE.

the roof, they perished. When day came the Corcyraeans loaded the bodies on wagons, laying them lengthwise and crosswise, and hauled them out of the city; but the women who had been captured in the fort were sold into captivity. In such fashion the Corcyraeans from the mountain were destroyed by the popular party, and the revolution, which had lasted long, ended thus, so far at least as this war was concerned; for there were no longer enough of the oligarchs left to be of any account. But the Athenians sailed for Sicily, whither they had set out in the first place, and proceeded to carry on the war in conjunction with their allies in the island.

XLIX. At the end of the same summer the Athenians at Naupactus and the Acarnanians made a campaign, and took by the treachery of its inhabitants Anactorium, a city belonging to the Corinthians which is situated at the mouth of the Ambracian Gulf; and the Acarnanians, expelling the Corinthians, occupied the place with colonists drawn from all their tribes. And the summer ended.

L. During the following winter Aristides [1] son of Archippus, one of the commanders of the Athenian ships which had been sent to the allies to collect the revenues, arrested at Eion on the Strymon Artaphernes, a Persian, who was on his way from the King to Lacedaemon. He was conveyed to Athens, and the Athenians caused his letters to be transcribed from the Assyrian characters and read them. Many other matters were touched upon therein, but the most important, with reference to the Lacedaemonians, was that the King did not know what they wanted; for though many envoys had come to him, no two

---

[1] Mentioned again ch. lxxv. 1 as general in these waters.

λέγειν· εἰ οὖν τι βούλονται σαφὲς λέγειν, πέμψαι
3 μετὰ τοῦ Πέρσου ἄνδρας ὡς αὐτόν. τὸν δὲ Ἀρταφέρνη ὕστερον οἱ Ἀθηναῖοι ἀποστέλλουσι τριήρει
ἐς Ἔφεσον καὶ πρέσβεις ἅμα· οἱ πυθόμενοι αὐτόθι
βασιλέα Ἀρταξέρξην τὸν Ξέρξου νεωστὶ τεθνη-
κότα (κατὰ γὰρ τοῦτον τὸν χρόνον ἐτελεύτησεν)
ἐπ' οἴκου ἀνεχώρησαν.

LI. Τοῦ δ' αὐτοῦ χειμῶνος καὶ Χῖοι τὸ τεῖχος
περιεῖλον τὸ καινὸν κελευσάντων Ἀθηναίων καὶ
ὑποπτευσάντων ἐς αὐτούς τι νεωτεριεῖν, ποιησάμενοι μέντοι πρὸς Ἀθηναίους πίστεις καὶ
βεβαιότητα ἐκ τῶν δυνατῶν μηδὲν περὶ σφᾶς
νεώτερον βουλεύσειν. καὶ ὁ χειμὼν ἐτελεύτα, καὶ
ἕβδομον ἔτος τῷ πολέμῳ ἐτελεύτα τῷδε ὃν
Θουκυδίδης ξυνέγραψεν.

LII. Τοῦ δ' ἐπιγιγνομένου θέρους εὐθὺς τοῦ τε
ἡλίου ἐκλιπές τι ἐγένετο περὶ νουμηνίαν καὶ τοῦ
2 αὐτοῦ μηνὸς ἱσταμένου ἔσεισεν. καὶ οἱ Μυτιληναίων φυγάδες καὶ τῶν ἄλλων Λεσβίων, ὁρμώμενοι οἱ πολλοὶ ἐκ τῆς ἠπείρου καὶ μισθωσάμενοι
ἔκ τε Πελοποννήσου ἐπικουρικὸν καὶ αὐτόθεν
ξυναγείραντες, αἱροῦσι Ῥοίτειον, καὶ λαβόντες
δισχιλίους στατῆρας Φωκαΐτας ἀπέδοσαν πάλιν,
3 οὐδὲν ἀδικήσαντες· καὶ μετὰ τοῦτο ἐπὶ Ἄντανδρον
στρατεύσαντες προδοσίας γενομένης λαμβάνουσι
τὴν πόλιν. καὶ ἦν αὐτῶν ἡ διάνοια τάς τε ἄλλας

---

[1] After a reign of forty years (465–425 B.C.).

told the same tale; if therefore they had any definite proposal to make, they should send men to him in company with the Persian. As for Artaphernes, the Athenians afterwards sent him to Ephesus in a trireme, together with some envoys; these, however, hearing there of the recent death of King Artaxerxes son of Xerxes—for he died about that time [1]—returned to Athens.

LI. The same winter the Chians demolished their new wall at the bidding of the Athenians, who suspected them of planning an insurrection against themselves; they, however, obtained from the Athenians pledges and such security as they could that they would adopt no harsh measures against them. And the winter ended, and with it the seventh year of this war of which Thucydides composed the history.

LII. At the very beginning of the next summer a 424 B.C. partial eclipse of the sun took place at new moon, and in the early part of the same month an earthquake. Also the citizens of Mytilene and of the other cities of Lesbos who were in exile, the majority of them setting out from the mainland, hired some mercenaries from the Peloponnesus, gathered still others on the spot, and took Rhoeteum; but they restored it again without having done any damage, on receiving two thousand Phocaean staters.[2] After this they made an expedition against Antandros and took the city through treachery on the part of the inhabitants. It was, in fact, their plan to free the

---

[2] The Phocaean stater was notorious for the badness of the gold (or rather electron); cf. Dem. xi. 36. It was worth about twenty-three silver drachmas. See Hultsch, *Gr. und röm. Metrologie*[2], 184.

πόλεις τὰς Ἀκταίας καλουμένας, ἃς πρότερον
Μυτιληναίων νεμομένων Ἀθηναῖοι εἶχον, ἐλευθεροῦν, καὶ πάντων μάλιστα τὴν Ἄντανδρον· καὶ
κρατυνάμενοι αὐτήν (ναῦς τε γὰρ εὐπορία ἦν
ποιεῖσθαι, αὐτόθεν ξύλων ὑπαρχόντων καὶ τῆς
Ἴδης ἐπικειμένης, καὶ τὰ ἄλλα σκεύη) ῥᾳδίως ἀπ᾽
αὐτῆς ὁρμώμενοι τήν τε Λέσβον ἐγγὺς οὖσαν
κακώσειν καὶ τὰ ἐν τῇ ἠπείρῳ Αἰολικὰ πολίσματα
4 χειρώσεσθαι. καὶ οἱ μὲν ταῦτα παρασκευάζεσθαι
ἔμελλον.

LIII. Ἀθηναῖοι δὲ ἐν τῷ αὐτῷ θέρει ἑξήκοντα
ναυσὶ καὶ δισχιλίοις ὁπλίταις ἱππεῦσί τε ὀλίγοις
καὶ τῶν ξυμμάχων Μιλησίους καὶ ἄλλους τινὰς
ἄγοντες ἐστράτευσαν ἐπὶ Κύθηρα· ἐστρατήγει δὲ
αὐτῶν Νικίας ὁ Νικηράτου καὶ Νικόστρατος ὁ
2 Διειτρέφους καὶ Αὐτοκλῆς ὁ Τολμαίου. τὰ δὲ
Κύθηρα νῆσός ἐστιν, ἐπίκειται δὲ τῇ Λακωνικῇ
κατὰ Μαλέαν· Λακεδαιμόνιοι δ᾽ εἰσὶ τῶν περιοίκων, καὶ κυθηροδίκης ἀρχὴ ἐκ τῆς Σπάρτης διέ-
βαινεν αὐτόσε κατὰ ἔτος, ὁπλιτῶν τε φρουρὰν
διέπεμπον αἰεὶ καὶ πολλὴν ἐπιμέλειαν ἐποιοῦντο.
3 ἦν γὰρ αὐτοῖς τῶν τε ἀπ᾽ Αἰγύπτου καὶ Λιβύης
ὁλκάδων προσβολή, καὶ λῃσταὶ ἅμα τὴν Λακωνικὴν ἧσσον ἐλύπουν ἐκ θαλάσσης, ᾗπερ μόνον
οἷόν τε ἦν κακουργεῖσθαι· πᾶσα γὰρ ἀνέχει
πρὸς τὸ Σικελικὸν καὶ Κρητικὸν πέλαγος. LIV.
κατασχόντες οὖν οἱ Ἀθηναῖοι τῷ στρατῷ δέκα

---

[1] i.e. of the ἀκτή or promontory of the mainland north of
Lesbos. These had been taken from Mytilene by Paches
(cf. III. l. 3). They are mentioned also C.I.A. i. 37.
[2] i.e. if Cythera were well guarded.

rest of the cities known as the Actaean cities,[1] which had hitherto been in the possession of the Athenians, though inhabited by Mytilenaeans, and above all Antandros. Having strengthened this place, where there was every facility for building ships—timber being available on the spot and Ida being near at hand —as well as for providing other equipments of war, they could easily, making it the base of their operations, not only ravage Lesbos, which was near, but also master the Aeolic towns on the mainland. Such were the plans upon which they were preparing to embark.

LIII. During the same summer the Athenians with sixty ships, two thousand hoplites, and a small detachment of cavalry, taking with them also some Milesians and others of their allies, made an expedition against Cythera. In command of the expedition were Nicias son of Niceratus, Nicostratus son of Dieitrephes, and Autocles son of Tolmaeus. Now Cythera is an island adjacent to Laconia, lying off Malea; its inhabitants are Lacedaemonians of the class of the Perioeci, and an official called the Bailiff of Cythera used to cross over thither once a year from Sparta; they also used regularly to send over a garrison of hoplites and paid much attention to the place. For it served them as a port of call for merchant ships from Egypt and Libya, and, moreover, pirates would be less likely to annoy Laconia from the sea,[2] on which side alone it could be harmed; for the whole coast runs out towards the Sicilian and the Cretan seas.[3] LIV. So then the Athenians, putting in at Cythera with their armament, consisting of ten

---

[3] Others take πᾶσα of the island, which forms as it were a bastion "running out into the Sicilian and Cretan seas."

μὲν ναυσὶ καὶ δισχιλίοις Μιλησίων ὁπλίταις τὴν ἐπὶ θαλάσσῃ πόλιν Σκάνδειαν καλου- μένην αἱροῦσι, τῷ δὲ ἄλλῳ στρατεύματι ἀπο- βάντες τῆς νήσου ἐς τὰ πρὸς Μαλέαν τετραμ- μένα ἐχώρουν ἐπὶ τὴν ἀπὸ θαλάσσης[1] πόλιν τῶν Κυθηρίων, καὶ ηὗρον εὐθὺς αὐτοὺς ἐστρα- 2 τοπεδευμένους ἅπαντας. καὶ μάχης γενομένης ὀλίγον μέν τινα χρόνον ὑπέστησαν οἱ Κυθήριοι, ἔπειτα τραπόμενοι κατέφυγον ἐς τὴν ἄνω πόλιν, καὶ ὕστερον ξυνέβησαν πρὸς Νικίαν καὶ τοὺς ξυνάρχοντας Ἀθηναίοις ἐπιτρέψαι περὶ σφῶν 3 αὐτῶν πλὴν θανάτου. ἦσαν δέ τινες καὶ γενόμενοι τῷ Νικίᾳ λόγοι πρότερον πρός τινας τῶν Κυθη- ρίων, δι' ὃ καὶ θᾶσσον καὶ ἐπιτηδειότερον τό τε παραυτίκα καὶ τὸ ἔπειτα τὰ[2] τῆς ὁμολογίας ἐπράχθη αὐτοῖς· ἀνέστησαν γὰρ ἂν[3] οἱ Ἀθηναῖοι Κυθηρίους, Λακεδαιμονίους τε ὄντας καὶ ἐπὶ τῇ 4 Λακωνικῇ τῆς νήσου οὕτως ἐπικειμένης. μετὰ δὲ τὴν ξύμβασιν οἱ Ἀθηναῖοι τήν τε Σκάνδειαν τὸ ἐπὶ τῷ λιμένι πόλισμα παραλαβόντες καὶ τῶν Κυθήρων φυλακὴν ποιησάμενοι ἔπλευσαν ἔς τε Ἀσίνην καὶ Ἕλος καὶ τὰ πλεῖστα τῶν περὶ θάλασσαν, καὶ ἀποβάσεις ποιούμενοι καὶ ἐναυλι-

---

[1] Stahl's conjecture for ἐπὶ θαλάσσῃ of the MSS., which is deleted by Hude, following Krüger.
[2] τά, omitted by the best MSS. [3] ἄν, added by Heilmann.

---

[1] An incredibly large number. In VIII. xxv. 2, where they are in their own land, the Milesians can oppose to the enemy only 800 hoplites. Nor would ten ships suffice for so many epibatae. Perhaps there is a confusion in the numeri- cal sign, due to a copyist.
[2] The haven of Cythera, some ten stadia distant from that city.

ships and two thousand Milesian hoplites,[1] took the
city by the sea called Scandeia[2]; then, with the rest
of their forces landing on the part of the island
which looks toward Malea, they advanced against
the city of Cythera which is away from the sea,[3]
where they found that all the inhabitants had immediately established themselves in camp. A fight
ensued, in which the Cytherians stood their ground
for some little time, then turned and fled to the
upper town, but afterwards capitulated to Nicias
and his colleagues, agreeing to leave the question of
their own fate, except as to a penalty of death, to
the arbitration of the Athenians. Some negotiations
between Nicias and certain of the Cytherians had
already taken place, and for this reason the settlement
of the terms, both for the present and the future,
was arranged more speedily and with better advantage to them; for otherwise the Athenians would
have expelled the inhabitants, since they were Lacedaemonians and the island lay in that position on
the coast of Laconia. After the capitulation the
Athenians took possession of Scandeia, the town at
the harbour, and having taken precautions for
guarding Cythera, then sailed to Asine, Helus, and
most of the other towns on the seacoast; here they
made raids or bivouacked at whatever place they

---

[3] It seems necessary to adopt Stahl's conjecture ἀπὸ θαλάσσης, or delete ἐπὶ θαλάσσῃ. "One division of the Athenian
force landed at Scandeia, another, disembarking on the
N.E coast, marched on the capital. The second force found
the Cytherians prepared to meet them; in the battle which
ensued the Cytherians were routed, and fled to the upper
city, i.e. the capital. This explanation is borne out by
existing remains. See Frazer's Pausanias, iii. 385, 386; also
Weil in *Mittheil. d. Arch. Inst. in Athen.* v. 224-243." (Spratt.)

ζόμενοι τῶν χωρίων οὗ καιρὸς εἴη ἐδῄουν τὴν γῆν ἡμέρας μάλιστα ἑπτά.

LV. Οἱ δὲ Λακεδαιμόνιοι, ἰδόντες μὲν τοὺς Ἀθηναίους τὰ Κύθηρα ἔχοντας, προσδεχόμενοι δὲ καὶ ἐς τὴν γῆν σφῶν ἀποβάσεις τοιαύτας ποιήσεσθαι, ἀθρόᾳ μὲν οὐδαμοῦ τῇ δυνάμει ἀντετάξαντο, κατὰ δὲ τὴν χώραν φρουρὰς διέπεμψαν, ὁπλιτῶν πλῆθος, ὡς ἑκασταχόσε ἔδει, καὶ τὰ ἄλλα ἐν φυλακῇ πολλῇ ἦσαν, φοβούμενοι μὴ σφίσι νεώτερόν τι γένηται τῶν περὶ τὴν κατάστασιν, γεγενημένου μὲν τοῦ ἐν τῇ νήσῳ πάθους ἀνελπίστου καὶ μεγάλου, Πύλου δὲ ἐχομένης καὶ Κυθήρων καὶ πανταχόθεν σφᾶς περιεστῶτος πολέμου
2 ταχέος καὶ ἀπροφυλάκτου, ὥστε παρὰ τὸ εἰωθὸς ἱππέας τετρακοσίους κατεστήσαντο καὶ τοξότας, ἔς τε τὰ πολεμικά, εἴπερ ποτέ, μάλιστα δὴ ὀκνηρότεροι ἐγένοντο ξυνεστῶτες παρὰ τὴν ὑπάρχουσαν σφῶν ἰδέαν τῆς παρασκευῆς ναυτικῷ ἀγῶνι, καὶ τούτῳ πρὸς Ἀθηναίους, οἷς τὸ μὴ ἐπιχειρούμενον αἰεὶ ἐλλιπὲς ἦν τῆς δοκήσεώς τι πράξειν·
3 καὶ ἅμα τὰ τῆς τύχης πολλὰ καὶ ἐν ὀλίγῳ ξυμβάντα παρὰ λόγον αὐτοῖς ἔκπληξιν μεγίστην παρεῖχε, καὶ ἐδέδισαν μή ποτε αὖθις ξυμφορά τις
4 αὐτοῖς περιτύχῃ οἵα καὶ ἐν τῇ νήσῳ, ἀτολμότεροι δὲ δι᾽ αὐτὸ ἐς τὰς μάχας ἦσαν καὶ πᾶν ὅ τι κινήσειαν ᾤοντο ἁμαρτήσεσθαι διὰ τὸ τὴν γνώμην ἀνεχέγγυον γεγενῆσθαι ἐκ τῆς πρὶν ἀηθείας τοῦ κακοπραγεῖν.

found convenient, and ravaged the land for about seven days.

LV. The Lacedaemonians, though they saw the Athenians in possession of Cythera and expected them to make such descents upon their own territory, nowhere massed their forces to oppose them, but sent garrisons here and there throughout the country, determining the number of hoplites by the strength needed at each point, and otherwise were very watchful, fearing lest some revolution should take place which would affect their constitution; for the calamity which had befallen them at the island of Sphacteria had been great and unexpected, Pylos and Cythera were occupied, and on all sides they were encompassed by a war which moved with a swiftness which defied precaution. Consequently they organized, contrary to their custom, a force of four hundred cavalry and bowmen, and in military matters they now became more timid than at any time before they were involved in a naval struggle which was outside their own existing scheme of military organisation, and that too against Athenians, with whom an attempt foregone was always so much lost of what they had reckoned on accomplishing.[1] Besides, the reverses of fortune, which had befallen them unexpectedly in such numbers and in so short a time, caused very great consternation, and they were afraid that some time a calamity might again come upon them like that which had happened on the island; and on this account they showed less spirit in their fighting, and whatever move they might make they thought would be a failure, because they had lost all self-confidence in consequence of having been hitherto unused to adversity.

[1] *cf.* I. lxx. 7.

THUCYDIDES

LVI. Τοῖς δὲ Ἀθηναίοις τότε τὴν παραθαλάσσιον δῃοῦσι τὰ μὲν πολλὰ ἡσύχασαν, ὡς καθ' ἑκάστην φρουρὰν γίγνοιτό τις ἀπόβασις, πλήθει τε ἐλάσσους ἕκαστοι ἡγούμενοι εἶναι καὶ ἐν τῷ τοιούτῳ· μία δὲ φρουρά, ἥπερ καὶ ἡμύνατο περὶ Κοτύρταν καὶ Ἀφροδιτίαν, τὸν μὲν ὄχλον τῶν ψιλῶν ἐσκεδασμένον ἐφόβησεν ἐπιδρομῇ, τῶν δὲ ὁπλιτῶν δεξαμένων ὑπεχώρησε πάλιν, καὶ ἄνδρες τέ τινες ἀπέθανον αὐτῶν ὀλίγοι καὶ ὅπλα ἐλήφθη, τροπαῖόν τε στήσαντες οἱ Ἀθηναῖοι ἀπέπλευσαν
2 ἐς Κύθηρα. ἐκ δὲ αὐτῶν περιέπλευσαν ἐς Ἐπίδαυρον τὴν Λιμηράν, καὶ δῃώσαντες μέρος τι τῆς γῆς ἀφικνοῦνται ἐπὶ Θυρέαν, ἥ ἐστι μὲν τῆς Κυνουρίας γῆς καλουμένης, μεθορία δὲ τῆς Ἀργείας καὶ Λακωνικῆς. νεμόμενοι δὲ αὐτὴν ἔδοσαν Λακεδαιμόνιοι Αἰγινήταις ἐκπεσοῦσιν ἐνοικεῖν διά τε τὰς ὑπὸ τὸν σεισμὸν σφίσι γενομένας καὶ τῶν Εἱλώτων τὴν ἐπανάστασιν εὐεργεσίας καὶ ὅτι Ἀθηναίων ὑπακούοντες ὅμως πρὸς τὴν ἐκείνων γνώμην αἰεὶ ἑστᾶσιν.

LVII. Προσπλεόντων οὖν ἔτι τῶν Ἀθηναίων οἱ Αἰγινῆται τὸ μὲν ἐπὶ τῇ θαλάσσῃ ὃ ἔτυχον οἰκοδομοῦντες τεῖχος ἐκλείπουσιν, ἐς δὲ τὴν ἄνω πόλιν, ἐν ᾗ ᾤκουν, ἀπεχώρησαν ἀπέχουσαν σταδίους μάλιστα δέκα τῆς θαλάσσης.
2 καὶ αὐτοῖς τῶν Λακεδαιμονίων φρουρὰ μία τῶν περὶ τὴν χώραν, ἥπερ καὶ ξυνετείχιζε, ξυνεσελθεῖν μὲν ἐς τὸ τεῖχος οὐκ ἠθέλησαν δεομένων τῶν Αἰγινητῶν, ἀλλ' αὐτοῖς κίνδυνος ἐφαίνετο ἐς τὸ τεῖχος κατακλῄεσθαι· ἀναχωρήσαντες δὲ ἐπὶ τὰ μετέωρα ὡς οὐκ ἐνόμιζον ἀξιόμα-
3 χοι εἶναι, ἡσύχαζον. ἐν τούτῳ δὲ οἱ Ἀθηναῖοι

LVI. Accordingly, while the Athenians were at that time ravaging their seaboard, they generally kept quiet when any descent was made upon any particular garrison, each thinking itself inferior in number and there being such depression. One garrison, however, which offered resistance in the region of Cotyrta and Aphrodisia, frightened the scattered crowd of light-armed troops by a charge, but when it encountered hoplites retreated again, a few of their men being killed and some of their arms taken; and the Athenians, after setting up a trophy, sailed back to Cythera. From there they sailed to Epidaurus Limera, and after ravaging some part of the land came to Thyrea, which belongs to the district called Cynuria, on the border between the Argive and Laconian territories. This district the Lacedaemonians who occupied it had given to the expelled Aeginetans to dwell in, on account of the kind services shown themselves at the time of the earthquake and the uprising of the Helots, and because they had always sided with their policy, in spite of being subject to the Athenians.

LVII. While, then, the Athenians were still sailing up, the Aeginetans left the fort by the sea which they happened to be building and withdrew to the upper town, where they dwelt, at a distance of about ten stadia from the sea. Now a detachment of the Lacedaemonian troops which were distributed in garrisons about the country was assisting the Aeginetans to build this fort. But they refused to enter the fort with them, as they requested, since it seemed to them dangerous to be cooped up in it; but retreating to high ground they kept quiet, thinking themselves no match for the enemy. Meanwhile the

κατασχόντες καὶ χωρήσαντες εὐθὺς πάσῃ τῇ
στρατιᾷ αἱροῦσι τὴν Θυρέαν. καὶ τήν τε πόλιν
κατέκαυσαν καὶ τὰ ἐνόντα ἐξεπόρθησαν, τούς τε
Αἰγινήτας, ὅσοι μὴ ἐν χερσὶ διεφθάρησαν, ἄγοντες
ἀφίκοντο ἐς τὰς Ἀθήνας καὶ τὸν ἄρχοντα ὃς παρ'
αὐτοῖς ἦν τῶν Λακεδαιμονίων, Τάνταλον τὸν
4 Πατροκλέους· ἐζωγρήθη γὰρ τετρωμένος. ἦγον
δέ τινας καὶ ἐκ τῶν Κυθήρων ἄνδρας ὀλίγους, οὓς
ἐδόκει ἀσφαλείας ἕνεκα μεταστῆσαι. καὶ τούτους
μὲν οἱ Ἀθηναῖοι ἐβουλεύσαντο καταθέσθαι ἐς τὰς
νήσους, καὶ τοὺς ἄλλους Κυθηρίους οἰκοῦντας τὴν
ἑαυτῶν φόρον τέσσαρα τάλαντα φέρειν, Αἰγινήτας
δὲ ἀποκτεῖναι πάντας ὅσοι ἑάλωσαν διὰ τὴν
5 προτέραν αἰεί ποτε ἔχθραν, Τάνταλον δὲ παρὰ
τοὺς ἄλλους τοὺς ἐν τῇ νήσῳ[1] Λακεδαιμονίους
καταδῆσαι.

LVIII. Τοῦ δ' αὐτοῦ θέρους ἐν Σικελίᾳ Καμα-
ριναίους καὶ Γελῴοις ἐκεχειρία γίγνεται πρῶτον
πρὸς ἀλλήλους· εἶτα καὶ οἱ ἄλλοι Σικελιῶται
ξυνελθόντες ἐς Γέλαν, ἀπὸ πασῶν τῶν πόλεων
πρέσβεις, ἐς λόγους κατέστησαν ἀλλήλοις, εἰ
πως ξυναλλαγεῖεν. καὶ ἄλλαι τε πολλαὶ γνῶμαι
ἐλέγοντο ἐπ' ἀμφότερα, διαφερομένων καὶ ἀξιούν-
των, ὡς ἕκαστοί τι ἐλασσοῦσθαι ἐνόμιζον, καὶ
Ἑρμοκράτης ὁ Ἕρμωνος Συρακόσιος, ὅσπερ καὶ
ἔπεισε μάλιστα αὐτούς, ἐς τὸ κοινὸν τοιούτους
δὴ λόγους εἶπεν.

LIX. "Οὔτε πόλεως ὢν ἐλαχίστης, ὦ Σικελιῶται, τοὺς λόγους ποιήσομαι οὔτε πονουμένης
μάλιστα τῷ πολέμῳ, ἐς κοινὸν δὲ τὴν δοκοῦσαν

─────────
[1] τοὺς ἐν τῇ νήσῳ, Hude deletes, after van Herwerden.

Athenians landed, and advancing straightway with
their whole force took Thyrea. They burned the
city and pillaged what was in it; but they carried to
Athens all the Aeginetans who did not perish in
the action, together with their Lacedaemonian
commander who was present, Tantalus son of Patro-
cles, who was wounded and taken prisoner. They
brought also a few men from Cythera, whom they
thought best to remove for the sake of safety.
These the Athenians determined to place for safe-
keeping on the islands, and to permit the rest of the
Cytherians to occupy their own territory on payment
of a tribute of four talents,[1] but to put to death all
the Aeginetans who had been captured, because
of their former inveterate enmity, and to imprison
Tantalus along with the other Lacedaemonians captured on the island of Sphacteria.

LVIII. During the same summer, in Sicily, an
armistice was first concluded between the Camarinaeans and Geloans; then representatives from all
the other Sicilian cities came together in Gela and
held a conference, to see whether they might not
become reconciled. Many opinions were expressed
for and against, the several envoys disputing and
making demands according as they believed that
their own rights were being prejudiced; and among
the rest Hermocrates son of Hermon, the Syracusan,
whose word proved to have the greatest weight with
the others, spoke in the general interest[2] words to
this effect:

LIX. "The city which I represent, Siceliots, is
not the weakest, nor is it suffering most in the war; but
I propose to speak in the general interest, declaring

[1] £800, $3,840.   [2] Or, "before the meeting."

μοι βελτίστην γνώμην εἶναι ἀποφαινόμενος τῇ
2 Σικελίᾳ πάσῃ. καὶ περὶ μὲν τοῦ πολεμεῖν ὡς
χαλεπὸν τί ἄν τις πᾶν τὸ ἐνὸν ἐκλέγων ἐν εἰδόσι
μακρηγοροίη; οὐδεὶς γὰρ οὔτε ἀμαθίᾳ ἀναγκά-
ζεται αὐτὸ δρᾶν, οὔτε φόβῳ, ἢν οἴηταί τι πλέον
σχήσειν, ἀποτρέπεται. ξυμβαίνει δὲ τοῖς μὲν
τὰ κέρδη μείζω φαίνεσθαι τῶν δεινῶν, οἱ δὲ τοὺς
κινδύνους ἐθέλουσιν ὑφίστασθαι πρὸ τοῦ αὐτίκα
3 τι ἐλασσοῦσθαι· αὐτὰ δὲ ταῦτα εἰ μὴ ἐν καιρῷ
τύχοιεν ἑκάτεροι πράσσοντες, αἱ παραινέσεις
4 τῶν ξυναλλαγῶν ὠφέλιμοι. ὃ καὶ ἡμῖν ἐν τῷ
παρόντι πειθομένοις πλείστου ἂν ἄξιον γένοιτο·
τὰ γὰρ ἴδια ἕκαστοι εὖ βουλόμενοι δὴ θέσθαι τό
τε πρῶτον ἐπολεμήσαμεν καὶ νῦν πρὸς ἀλλήλους
δι' ἀντιλογιῶν πειρώμεθα καταλλαγῆναι καί, ἢν
ἄρα μὴ προχωρήσῃ ἴσον ἑκάστῳ ἔχοντι ἀπελθεῖν,
πάλιν πολεμήσομεν.

LX. "Καίτοι γνῶναι χρὴ ὅτι οὐ περὶ τῶν
ἰδίων μόνον, εἰ σωφρονοῦμεν, ἡ ξύνοδος ἔσται,
ἀλλ' εἰ ἐπιβουλευομένην τὴν πᾶσαν Σικελίαν,
ὡς ἐγὼ κρίνω, ὑπ' Ἀθηναίων δυνησόμεθα ἔτι
διασῶσαι, καὶ διαλλακτὰς πολὺ τῶν ἐμῶν λόγων
ἀναγκαιοτέρους περὶ τῶνδε Ἀθηναίους νομίσαι,
οἳ δύναμιν ἔχοντες μεγίστην τῶν Ἑλλήνων τάς

the opinion which seems to me the best for Sicily as a whole. As for the miseries which war entails, why should one by expressly stating all that can be said make a long harangue in the presence of those who know? For no one is either forced to make war through ignorance of what it is, or deterred from making it by fear, if he thinks he will get some advantage from it. What really happens is this, that to one side the gains appear greater than the terrors, while the other deliberately prefers to undergo the dangers rather than submit to a temporary disadvantage; but if it should turn out that these two lines of action are both inopportune, each for the side which adopts it, then some profit may come from exhortations which advise a compromise. And so with us at the present time, if we could be persuaded of the wisdom of this course it would be to our great advantage; for each of us began the war in the first place because we desired to promote our private interests. So now let us endeavour by setting forth our conflicting claims to become reconciled with each other; and then, if we do not after all succeed in securing, each of us, what is fair and just before we part, we shall go to war again.

LX. "And yet we should recognise the fact that the subject of our conference will not, if we are wise, be our private interests merely, but rather the question whether we shall still be able to save Sicily as a whole, for it is against it, in my judgment, that the Athenians are plotting; and we must consider that we have an argument far more cogent to bring us together on these matters than my words, namely, the Athenians, who possess a military power greater than that of any other Hellenic state and are now at

THUCYDIDES

τε ἁμαρτίας ἡμῶν τηροῦσιν ὀλίγαις ναυσὶ παρόντες, καὶ ὀνόματι ἐννόμῳ ξυμμαχίας τὸ φύσει
πολέμιον εὐπρεπῶς ἐς τὸ ξυμφέρον καθίστανται.
2 πόλεμον γὰρ αἰρομένων ἡμῶν καὶ ἐπαγομένων
αὐτούς, ἄνδρας οἳ καὶ τοῖς μὴ ἐπικαλουμένοις
αὐτοὶ ἐπιστρατεύουσι, κακῶς τε ἡμᾶς αὐτοὺς
ποιούντων τέλεσι τοῖς οἰκείοις, καὶ τῆς ἀρχῆς
ἅμα προκοπτόντων ἐκείνοις, εἰκός, ὅταν γνῶσιν
ἡμᾶς τετρυχωμένους, καὶ πλέονί ποτε στόλῳ
ἐλθόντας αὐτοὺς τάδε πάντα πειράσασθαι ὑπὸ
σφᾶς ποιεῖσθαι.
LXI. "Καίτοι τῇ ἑαυτῶν ἑκάστους, εἰ σωφρονοῦμεν, χρὴ τὰ μὴ προσήκοντα ἐπικτωμένους
μᾶλλον ἢ τὰ ἑτοῖμα βλάπτοντας ξυμμάχους τε
ἐπαγέσθαι καὶ τοὺς κινδύνους προσλαμβάνειν,
νομίσαι τε στάσιν μάλιστα φθείρειν τὰς πόλεις
καὶ τὴν Σικελίαν, ἧς γε οἱ ἔνοικοι ξύμπαντες μὲν
2 ἐπιβουλευόμεθα, κατὰ πόλεις δὲ διέσταμεν. ἃ
χρὴ γνόντας καὶ ἰδιώτην ἰδιώτῃ καταλλαγῆναι
καὶ πόλιν πόλει, καὶ πειρᾶσθαι κοινῇ σῴζειν τὴν
πᾶσαν Σικελίαν, παρεστάναι δὲ μηδενὶ ὡς οἱ
μὲν Δωριῆς ἡμῶν πολέμιοι τοῖς Ἀθηναίοις, τὸ
3 δὲ Χαλκιδικὸν τῇ Ἰάδι ξυγγενείᾳ ἀσφαλές. οὐ
γὰρ τοῖς ἔθνεσιν, ὅτι δίχα πέφυκε, τοῦ ἑτέρου
ἔχθει ἐπίασιν, ἀλλὰ τῶν ἐν Σικελίᾳ ἀγαθῶν
4 ἐφιέμενοι, ἃ κοινῇ κεκτήμεθα. ἐδήλωσαν δὲ νῦν
ἐν τῇ τοῦ Χαλκιδικοῦ γένους παρακλήσει· τοῖς
γὰρ οὐδεπώποτε σφίσι κατὰ τὸ ξυμμαχικὸν

hand with a few ships watching for our mistakes, and under the lawful name of alliance are speciously trying to turn to their own advantage our natural hostility to them. For if we begin war and call them in—men who of their own accord are ready enough to intrude their forces even on those who do not ask for their intervention—and if we spend our own revenues in doing hurt to ourselves, and at the same time pave the way for their supremacy, we may well expect them, when they see that we are worn out, to come sometime with a larger armament and try to bring everything here under their sway.

LXI. "And yet, if we are prudent, we ought, each of us in behalf of his own state, to call in allies and incur dangers only when we are seeking to win what does not belong to us and not when we imperil what is already ours; and we should remember that faction is the chief cause of ruin to states and indeed to Sicily, seeing that we her inhabitants, although we are all being plotted against, are disunited, each city by itself. Recognizing these facts, we must be reconciled with each other, citizen with citizen and state with state, and join in a common effort to save all Sicily. And let no one imagine that only the Dorians among us are enemies of the Athenians, while the Chalcidians, because of their kinship with the Ionians, are safe. For it is not through hatred of one of the two races into which we are divided that they will attack us, but because they covet the good things of Sicily which we possess in common. They have just made this clear by their response to the appeal which the people of Chalcidic stock made to them; [1] for to those who have never given them aid

---

[1] cf. III. lxxxvi. 3.

προσβοηθήσασιν αὐτοὶ τὸ δίκαιον μᾶλλον τῆς
5 ξυνθήκης προθύμως παρέσχοντο. καὶ τοὺς μὲν
Ἀθηναίους ταῦτα πλεονεκτεῖν τε καὶ προνοεῖσθαι
πολλὴ ξυγγνώμη, καὶ οὐ τοῖς ἄρχειν βουλομένοις
μέμφομαι, ἀλλὰ τοῖς ὑπακούειν ἑτοιμοτέροις
οὖσιν· πέφυκε γὰρ τὸ ἀνθρώπειον διὰ παντὸς
ἄρχειν μὲν τοῦ εἴκοντος, φυλάσσεσθαι δὲ τὸ
6 ἐπιόν. ὅσοι δὲ γιγνώσκοντες αὐτὰ μὴ ὀρθῶς
προσκοποῦμεν, μηδὲ τοῦτό τις πρεσβύτατον ἥκει
κρίνας, τὸ κοινῶς φοβερὸν ἅπαντας εὖ θέσθαι,
7 ἁμαρτάνομεν. τάχιστα δ' ἂν ἀπαλλαγὴ αὐτοῦ
γένοιτο, εἰ πρὸς ἀλλήλους ξυμβαῖμεν· οὐ γὰρ
ἀπὸ τῆς αὑτῶν ὁρμῶνται Ἀθηναῖοι, ἀλλ' ἐκ τῆς
8 τῶν ἐπικαλεσαμένων. καὶ οὕτως οὐ πόλεμος
πολέμῳ, εἰρήνη δὲ διαφοραὶ ἀπραγμόνως παύ-
ονται, οἵ τ' ἐπίκλητοι εὐπρεπῶς ἄδικοι ἐλθόντες
εὐλόγως ἄπρακτοι ἀπίασιν.

LXII. "Καὶ τὰ μὲν πρὸς τοὺς Ἀθηναίους
τοσοῦτον ἀγαθὸν εὖ βουλευομένοις εὑρίσκεται·
2 τὴν δὲ ὑπὸ πάντων ὁμολογουμένην ἄριστον εἶναι
εἰρήνην πῶς οὐ χρὴ καὶ ἐν ἡμῖν αὐτοῖς ποιήσασθαι; ἢ δοκεῖ γε, εἴ τῴ τι ἔστιν ἀγαθὸν ἢ εἴ
τῳ τὰ ἐναντία, οὐχ ἡσυχία μᾶλλον ἢ πόλεμος τὸ
μὲν παῦσαι ἂν ἑκατέρῳ, τὸ δὲ ξυνδιασῶσαι, καὶ
τὰς τιμὰς καὶ λαμπρότητας ἀκινδυνοτέρας ἔχειν
τὴν εἰρήνην, ἄλλα τε ὅσα ἐν μήκει λόγων ἄν τις

according to the terms of their alliance they of their own accord have fulfilled an ally's obligations with a zeal exceeding their compact. That the Athenians entertain these designs of aggrandisement is quite pardonable; and I have no word of blame for those who wish to rule, but only for those who are too ready to submit; for it is an instinct of man's nature always to rule those who yield, but to guard against those who are ready to attack. If any of us, knowing how matters really stand, fails to take proper precautions, or if anyone has come here not accounting it of paramount importance that we must all together deal wisely with the common peril, we are making a mistake. The speediest relief from this peril would be gained by our entering into an understanding with one another; for the base from which the Athenians propose to move is not their own territory, but that of the people who asked them to intervene. And if we follow this course, war will not end in another war, but without trouble quarrels will end quietly in peace, and those who have been invited to intervene, having come with a fair pretext for injustice, will depart home with a fair plea for failure.

LXII. "So far, then, as the Athenians are concerned, this is the great advantage we win if we are well advised; but as to the question of peace, which all men agree is a most desirable thing, why should we not make it here among ourselves? Or, think you, if one person now enjoys a blessing and another labours under adversity, it is not tranquillity far more than war that will put an end to the latter and perpetuate the former? And has not peace its honours and less hazardous splendours, and all the

διέλθοι ὥσπερ περὶ τοῦ πολεμεῖν;[1] ἃ χρὴ σκεψα-
μένους μὴ τοὺς ἐμοὺς λόγους ὑπεριδεῖν, τὴν δὲ
αὐτοῦ τινα σωτηρίαν μᾶλλον ἀπ᾽ αὐτῶν προϊδεῖν.
3 καὶ εἴ τις βεβαίως τι ἢ τῷ δικαίῳ ἢ βίᾳ πράξειν
οἴεται, τῷ παρ᾽ ἐλπίδα μὴ χαλεπῶς σφαλλέσθω,
γνοὺς ὅτι πλείους ἤδη, καὶ τιμωρίαις μετιόντες
τοὺς ἀδικοῦντας καὶ ἐλπίσαντες ἕτεροι δυνάμει τι
πλεονεκτήσειν, οἱ μὲν οὐχ ὅσον οὐκ ἠμύναντο
ἀλλ᾽ οὐδ᾽ ἐσώθησαν, τοὺς δ᾽ ἀντὶ τοῦ πλέον ἔχειν
4 προσκαταλιπεῖν τὰ αὑτῶν ξυνέβη. τιμωρία γὰρ
οὐκ εὐτυχεῖ δικαίως, ὅτι καὶ ἀδικεῖται· οὐδὲ ἰσχὺς
βέβαιον, διότι καὶ εὔελπι. τὸ δὲ ἀστάθμητον τοῦ
μέλλοντος ὡς ἐπὶ πλεῖστον κρατεῖ, πάντων τε
σφαλερώτατον ὂν ὅμως καὶ χρησιμώτατον φαίνε-
ται· ἐξ ἴσου γὰρ δεδιότες προμηθίᾳ μᾶλλον ἐπ᾽
ἀλλήλους ἐρχόμεθα.

LXIII. "Καὶ νῦν τοῦ ἀφανοῦς τε τούτου διὰ τὸ
ἀτέκμαρτον δέος καὶ διὰ τὸ ἤδη, φοβεροὺς παρόντας Ἀθηναίους, κατ᾽ ἀμφότερα ἐκπλαγέντες, καὶ
τὸ ἐλλιπὲς τῆς γνώμης ὧν ἕκαστός τι ᾠήθημεν
πράξειν ταῖς κωλύμαις ταύταις ἱκανῶς νομίσαντες
εἰρχθῆναι, τοὺς ἐφεστῶτας πολεμίους ἐκ τῆς
χώρας ἀποπέμπωμεν, καὶ αὐτοὶ μάλιστα μὲν ἐς
ἀίδιον ξυμβῶμεν, εἰ δὲ μή, χρόνον ὡς πλεῖστον
σπεισάμενοι τὰς ἰδίας διαφορὰς ἐς αὖθις ἀνα-

---

[1] ὥσπερ περὶ τοῦ πολεμεῖν, deleted by Hude, after Krüger.

[1] i.e. "most of our plans are baffled by the uncertainty of the future."

other advantages on which one might dilate as easily as on the horrors of war? Considering these things, you should not overlook my advice, but should rather look forward each to his own salvation thereby. And if any of you cherishes the confident belief that he can gain anything either by insisting on his rights or by an appeal to force, let him not, through the baffling of his hopes, suffer a grievous disappointment; for he knows that many men ere now, whether pursuing with vengeance those who have wronged them, or in other cases, hoping to gain some advantage by the exercise of power, have, on the one hand, not only not avenged themselves but have not even come out whole, and, on the other hand, instead of gaining more, have sacrificed what was their own. For revenge has no right to expect success just because a wrong has been done; nor is strength sure just because it is confident. But as regards the future, it is uncertainty that for the most part prevails,[1] and this uncertainty, utterly treacherous as it is, proves nevertheless to be also most salutary; for since both sides alike fear it, we proceed with a greater caution in attacking one another.

LXIII. "So let us now, taking alarm on account of both these things—the vague fear of this hidden future and the immediate fear of the dread Athenian presence—and charging to these obstacles, as effectually blocking our way, any failure in the plans which any one of us had hoped to realize, let us dismiss from the country the enemy who is at our gates, and if possible let us make peace among ourselves for evermore; but if that may not be, let us conclude a truce for the longest practicable period, and put off our

2 βαλώμεθα. τὸ ξύμπαν τε δὴ γνῶμεν πιθόμενοι μὲν ἐμοὶ πόλιν ἕξοντες ἕκαστος ἐλευθέραν, ἀφ' ἧς αὐτοκράτορες ὄντες τὸν εὖ καὶ κακῶς δρῶντα ἐξ ἴσου ἀρετῇ ἀμυνούμεθα, ἢν δ' ἀπιστήσαντες ἄλλοις ὑπακούσωμεν, οὐ περὶ τοῦ τιμωρήσασθαί τινα, ἀλλὰ καὶ ἄγαν εἰ τύχοιμεν, φίλοι μὲν ἂν τοῖς ἐχθίστοις, διάφοροι δὲ οἷς οὐ χρὴ κατ' ἀνάγκην γιγνοίμεθα.

LXIV. "Καὶ ἐγὼ μέν, ἅπερ καὶ ἀρχόμενος εἶπον, πόλιν τε μεγίστην παρεχόμενος καὶ ἐπιὼν τῳ μᾶλλον ἢ ἀμυνόμενος¹ ἀξιῶ προϊδόμενος² αὐτῶν ξυγχωρεῖν, καὶ μὴ τοὺς ἐναντίους οὕτω κακῶς δρᾶν ὥστε αὐτὸς τὰ πλείω βλάπτεσθαι, μηδὲ μωρίᾳ φιλονικῶν ἡγεῖσθαι τῆς τε οἰκείας γνώμης ὁμοίως αὐτοκράτωρ εἶναι καὶ ἧς οὐκ
2 ἄρχω τύχης, ἀλλ' ὅσον εἰκὸς ἡσσᾶσθαι. καὶ τοὺς ἄλλους δικαιῶ ταὐτό μοι ποιῆσαι, ὑφ' ὑμῶν αὐτῶν καὶ μὴ ὑπὸ τῶν πολεμίων τοῦτο παθεῖν·
3 οὐδὲν γὰρ αἰσχρὸν οἰκείους οἰκείων ἡσσᾶσθαι, ἢ Δωριᾶ τινα Δωριῶς ἢ Χαλκιδέα τῶν ξυγγενῶν, τό τε ξύμπαν γείτονας ὄντας καὶ ξυνοίκους μιᾶς χώρας καὶ περιρρύτου καὶ ὄνομα ἓν κεκλημένους Σικελιώτας· οἳ πολεμήσομέν τε, οἶμαι, ὅταν ξυμβῇ, καὶ ξυγχωρησόμεθά γε πάλιν καθ' ἡμᾶς
4 αὐτοὺς λόγοις κοινοῖς χρώμενοι· τοὺς δὲ ἀλλοφύλους ἐπελθόντας ἀθρόοι αἰεί, ἢν σωφρονῶμεν, ἀμυνούμεθα, εἴπερ καὶ καθ' ἑκάστους βλαπτόμενοι ξύμπαντες κινδυνεύομεν, ξυμμάχους δὲ

---

¹ ἀμυνόμενος, Hude followed by Steup, for ἀμυνούμενος of the MSS.
² προϊδόμενος . . . ὥστε αὐτός, Reiske and Dobree, for προειδομένους . . . ὥστε αὐτούς of the MSS.

private differences to some other day. In fine, let us feel assured that if my advice is followed we shall each keep our city free, and from it, since we shall be arbiters of our own destiny, we shall with equal valour ward off both him who comes to benefit and him who comes to harm. But if, on the other hand, my advice is rejected and we give heed to others, it will not be a question of our taking vengeance on anybody, but, even if we should be never so successful, we should perforce become friends to our bitterest foes and at variance with those with whom we should not be.

LXIV. "As for me, as I said in the beginning, although I represent a most powerful city and am more ready for attacking another than for self-defence, I deem it my duty, with these dangers in view, to make concessions, and not to harm my enemies in such a way as to receive more injury myself, or in foolish obstinacy to think that I am as absolutely master of Fortune, which I do not control, as of my own judgment; nay, so far as is reasonable I will give way. And I require of the rest of you to follow my example and submit to this, not at the hands of the enemy, but of yourselves. For there is no disgrace in kinsmen giving way to kinsmen, a Dorian to a Dorian or a Chalcidian to men of the same race, since we are, in a word, neighbours and together are dwellers in a single land encircled by the sea and are called by a single name, Siceliots. We shall go to war, no doubt, whenever occasion arises—yes, and we shall make peace again by taking common counsel among ourselves; but when alien peoples invade us, we shall always act in concert, if we are prudent, and repel them, seeing that any injury suffered by one of us brings danger to us all; but never

οὐδέποτε τὸ λοιπὸν ἐπαξόμεθα οὐδὲ διαλλακτάς.
5 τάδε γὰρ ποιοῦντες ἔν τε τῷ παρόντι δυοῖν ἀγαθοῖν οὐ στερήσομεν τὴν Σικελίαν, 'Αθηναίων τε
ἀπαλλαγῆναι καὶ οἰκείου πολέμου, καὶ ἐς τὸ
ἔπειτα καθ' ἡμᾶς αὐτοὺς ἐλευθέραν νεμούμεθα
καὶ ὑπὸ ἄλλων ἧσσον ἐπιβουλευομένην."

LXV. Τοιαῦτα τοῦ Ἑρμοκράτους εἰπόντος πειθόμενοι οἱ Σικελιῶται αὐτοὶ μὲν κατὰ σφᾶς αὐτοὺς
ξυνηνέχθησαν γνώμῃ ὥστε ἀπαλλάσσεσθαι τοῦ
πολέμου ἔχοντες ἃ ἕκαστοι ἔχουσι, τοῖς δὲ
Καμαριναίοις Μοργαντίνην εἶναι ἀργύριον τακτὸν
2 τοῖς Συρακοσίοις ἀποδοῦσιν· οἱ δὲ τῶν 'Αθηναίων
ξύμμαχοι παρακαλέσαντες αὐτῶν τοὺς ἐν τέλει
ὄντας εἶπον ὅτι ξυμβήσονται καὶ αἱ σπονδαὶ
ἔσονται κἀκείνοις κοιναί. ἐπαινεσάντων δὲ αὐτῶν
ἐποιοῦντο τὴν ὁμολογίαν, καὶ αἱ νῆες τῶν 'Αθηναίων ἀπέπλευσαν μετὰ ταῦτα ἐκ Σικελίας.
3 ἐλθόντας δὲ τοὺς στρατηγοὺς οἱ ἐν τῇ πόλει
'Αθηναῖοι τοὺς μὲν φυγῇ ἐζημίωσαν, Πυθόδωρον
καὶ Σοφοκλέα, τὸν δὲ τρίτον Εὐρυμέδοντα χρήματα ἐπράξαντο, ὡς ἐξὸν αὐτοῖς τὰ ἐν Σικελίᾳ
καταστρέψασθαι δώροις πεισθέντες ἀποχωρή-
4 σειαν. οὕτω τῇ γε παρούσῃ εὐτυχίᾳ χρώμενοι
ἠξίουν σφίσι μηδὲν ἐναντιοῦσθαι, ἀλλὰ καὶ
τὰ δυνατὰ ἐν ἴσῳ καὶ τὰ ἀπορώτερα μεγάλῃ
τε ὁμοίως καὶ ἐνδεεστέρᾳ παρασκευῇ κατεργάζεσθαι. αἰτία δ' ἦν ἡ παρὰ λόγον τῶν
πλειόνων εὐπραγία αὐτοῖς ὑποτιθεῖσα ἰσχὺν
τῆς ἐλπίδος.

LXVI. Τοῦ δ' αὐτοῦ θέρους Μεγαρῆς οἱ ἐν τῇ
πόλει πιεζόμενοι ὑπό τε 'Αθηναίων τῷ πολέμῳ,

henceforth shall we ask outsiders to intervene, either as allies or as mediators. If we follow this policy, we shall at the present time not rob Sicily of two desirable things—getting rid of the Athenians and escaping from civil war—and for the future we shall dwell here by ourselves in a land that is free and less exposed to the plotting of others."

LXV. After Hermocrates had spoken to this effect the Siceliots, accepting his advice, came to an understanding among themselves. They agreed to end the war, each city keeping what it had, except that the Camarinaeans were to have Morgantina on payment of a stated sum of money to the Syracusans. The Sicilian allies of the Athenians then summoned the Athenian generals and said that they proposed to make peace and that the treaty would also include them. And when the generals assented, they proceeded to make the agreement, whereupon the Athenian fleet sailed away from Sicily. But when it arrived at Athens, the Athenians sentenced to exile two of the generals, Pythodorus and Sophocles, and fined Eurymedon, the third, on the charge that when it had been in their power to subdue Sicily they had been bribed to withdraw from it. To such an extent, because of their present good fortune, did they expect to be thwarted in nothing, and believed that, no matter whether their forces were powerful or deficient, they could equally achieve what was easy and what was difficult. The cause of this was the amazing success which attended most of their undertakings and inspired them with strong confidence.

LXVI. The same summer the people of the city of Megara, being harassed in the war by the Athenians,

αἰεὶ κατὰ ἔτος ἕκαστον δὶς ἐσβαλλόντων πανστρατιᾷ ἐς τὴν χώραν, καὶ ὑπὸ τῶν σφετέρων
φυγάδων τῶν ἐκ Πηγῶν, οἳ στασιασάντων ἐκ-
πεσόντες ὑπὸ τοῦ πλήθους χαλεποὶ ἦσαν λῃ-
στεύοντες, ἐποιοῦντο λόγους ἐν ἀλλήλοις ὡς χρὴ
δεξαμένους τοὺς φεύγοντας μὴ ἀμφοτέρωθεν τὴν
2 πόλιν φθείρειν. οἱ δὲ φίλοι τῶν ἔξω τὸν θροῦν
αἰσθόμενοι φανερῶς μᾶλλον ἢ πρότερον καὶ αὐτοὶ
3 ἠξίουν τούτου τοῦ λόγου ἔχεσθαι. γνόντες δὲ
οἱ τοῦ δήμου προστάται οὐ δυνατὸν τὸν δῆμον
ἐσόμενον ὑπὸ τῶν κακῶν μετὰ σφῶν καρτερεῖν,
ποιοῦνται λόγους δείσαντες πρὸς τοὺς τῶν Ἀθηναίων στρατηγούς, Ἱπποκράτη τε τὸν Ἀρίφρονος
καὶ Δημοσθένη τὸν Ἀλκισθένους, βουλόμενοι
ἐνδοῦναι τὴν πόλιν καὶ νομίζοντες ἐλάσσω σφίσι
τὸν κίνδυνον ἢ τοὺς ἐκπεσόντας ὑπὸ σφῶν κατελ-
4 θεῖν. ξυνέβησάν τε πρῶτα μὲν τὰ μακρὰ τείχη ἑλεῖν
Ἀθηναίους (ἦν δὲ σταδίων μάλιστα ὀκτὼ ἀπὸ τῆς
πόλεως ἐπὶ τὴν Νίσαιαν τὸν λιμένα αὐτῶν), ὅπως
μὴ ἐπιβοηθήσωσιν ἐκ τῆς Νισαίας οἱ Πελοποννήσιοι, ἐν ᾗ αὐτοὶ μόνοι ἐφρούρουν βεβαιότητος
ἕνεκα τῶν Μεγάρων, ἔπειτα δὲ καὶ τὴν ἄνω πόλιν
πειράσεσθαι ἐνδοῦναι· ῥᾷον δ' ἤδη ἔμελλον προσ-
χωρήσειν τούτου γεγενημένου.

LXVII. Οἱ οὖν Ἀθηναῖοι, ἐπειδὴ ἀπό τε τῶν
ἔργων καὶ τῶν λόγων παρεσκεύαστο ἀμφοτέροις,
ὑπὸ νύκτα πλεύσαντες ἐς Μινῴαν τὴν Μεγαρέων
νῆσον ὁπλίταις ἑξακοσίοις, ὧν Ἱπποκράτης ἦρ-

who regularly invaded their country in full force
twice every year, and also by their own exiles in Pegae,
who had been expelled in a revolution by the popular
party and kept annoying them by raiding the country,
began to say to one another that they ought to
receive the fugitives back, so that the city should not
be exposed to ruin from both directions at once.
And the friends of the exiles, noticing the murmuring
of the people, all began more openly than before to
urge that this proposal be adopted.   But the leaders
of the popular party, realizing that the populace
under the pressure of their distress would not be
able to hold out with them, became frightened and
made overtures to the Athenian generals, Hippocrates
son of Ariphron and Demosthenes son of Alcisthenes,
proposing to surrender the city to them; for they
thought that this course would be less dangerous to
themselves than the restoration of the citizens whom
they had banished.   They agreed, in the first place,
that the Athenians should take possession of the
long walls (the distance between the city and the
harbour at Nisaea was about eight stadia), in order to
prevent the Peloponnesians from sending reinforcements from Nisaea, where they formed the sole
garrison to keep their hold on Megara, and, in the
second place, that they would do their best to hand
over to them the upper-town as well, believing that,
as soon as this was done, their fellow-citizens would
more readily go over to the Athenian side.

LXVII. So, then, as soon as due preparations, both
in word and act, had been made by both parties, the
Athenians sailed under cover of night to Minoa, the
island which lies off Megara, taking six hundred
hoplites under the command of Hippocrates, and took

THUCYDIDES

χεν, ἐν ὀρύγματι ἐκαθέζοντο, ὅθεν ἐπλίνθευον τὰ
2 τείχη καὶ ἀπεῖχεν οὐ πολύ· οἱ δὲ μετὰ τοῦ
Δημοσθένους τοῦ ἑτέρου στρατηγοῦ Πλαταιῆς
τε ψιλοὶ καὶ ἕτεροι περίπολοι ἐνήδρευσαν ἐς τὸ
Ἐννάλιον, ὅ ἐστιν ἔλασσον ἄπωθεν. καὶ ἤσθετο
οὐδεὶς εἰ μὴ οἱ ἄνδρες οἷς ἐπιμελὲς ἦν εἰδέναι τὴν
3 νύκτα ταύτην. καὶ ἐπειδὴ ἕως ἔμελλε γίγνεσθαι,
οἱ προδιδόντες τῶν Μεγαρέων¹ οὗτοι τοιόνδε
ἐποίησαν. ἀκάτιον ἀμφηρικὸν ὡς λῃσταί, ἐκ
πολλοῦ τεθεραπευκότες τὴν ἄνοιξιν τῶν πυλῶν,
εἰώθεσαν ἐπὶ ἁμάξῃ, πείθοντες τὸν ἄρχοντα, διὰ
τῆς τάφρου κατακομίζειν τῆς νυκτὸς ἐπὶ τὴν
θάλασσαν καὶ ἐκπλεῖν· καὶ πρὶν ἡμέραν εἶναι
πάλιν αὐτὸ τῇ ἁμάξῃ κομίσαντες ἐς τὸ τεῖχος
κατὰ τὰς πύλας ἐσῆγον, ὅπως τοῖς ἐκ τῆς Μινῴας
Ἀθηναίοις ἀφανὴς δὴ εἴη ἡ φυλακή, μὴ ὄντος
4 ἐν τῷ λιμένι πλοίου φανεροῦ μηδενός. καὶ τότε
πρὸς ταῖς πύλαις ἤδη ἦν ἡ ἅμαξα, καὶ ἀνοιχθεισῶν κατὰ τὸ εἰωθὸς ὡς τῷ ἀκατίῳ οἱ Ἀθηναῖοι
(ἐγίγνετο γὰρ ἀπὸ ξυνθήματος τὸ τοιοῦτον)
ἰδόντες ἔθεον δρόμῳ ἐκ τῆς ἐνέδρας, βουλόμενοι
φθάσαι πρὶν ξυγκλῃσθῆναι πάλιν τὰς πύλας
καὶ ἕως ἔτι ἡ ἅμαξα ἐν αὐταῖς ἦν, κώλυμα οὖσα
προσθεῖναι· καὶ αὐτοῖς ἅμα καὶ οἱ ξυμπράσσοντες
Μεγαρῆς τοὺς κατὰ πύλας φύλακας κτείνουσιν.
5 καὶ πρῶτον μὲν οἱ περὶ τὸν Δημοσθένη Πλαταιῆς
τε καὶ περίπολοι ἐσέδραμον οὗ νῦν τὸ τροπαῖον
ἐστι, καὶ εὐθὺς ἐντὸς τῶν πυλῶν (ᾔσθοντο γὰρ

¹ οἱ προδιδόντες τῶν Μεγαρέων, deleted by Hude.

cover in a ditch, not far from the town, where bricks had been made for the walls. A second company consisting of light-armed Plataeans and frontier-patrols under the command of the other general, Demosthenes, set an ambuscade at Enyalius, which is somewhat nearer. And all that night no one perceived what was going on except the men whose business it was to know. Then, at the approach of dawn, these would-be Megarian traitors began their work as follows. For a long time before this they had been carefully preparing for the opening of the gates by regularly assuming the guise of pirates and taking a sculling boat, drawn on a cart, through the ditch and down to the sea, where they would put out. This they did every night, first securing the consent of the commander.[1] Then before daybreak they would cart the boat back into the fortifications, taking it in by way of the gates, their object being, as they pretended, to keep the Athenian garrison, which was stationed at Minoa, in the dark, as no boat would be visible in the harbour. On the night in question the cart was already at the gates, and when these were opened as usual as if to let the boat pass through, the Athenians, who were acting throughout in accordance with an agreement, seeing it, ran at top speed from their ambush, wishing to get there before the gates were closed again and while the cart was still in the passage, thus forming an obstacle to the shutting of the gates; and at the same time their Megarian accomplices killed the guards at the gates. And first the Plataeans and the patrols under Demosthenes' command rushed into the place where the trophy now stands, and as soon as they were inside the gates the Plataeans engaged with the

[1] i.e., of the Peloponnesian garrison.

οἱ ἐγγύτατα Πελοποννήσιοι) μαχόμενοι τοὺς
προσβοηθοῦντας οἱ Πλαταιῆς ἐκράτησαν καὶ τοῖς
τῶν Ἀθηναίων ὁπλίταις ἐπιφερομένοις βεβαίους
τὰς πύλας παρέσχον.   LXVIII. ἔπειτα δὲ καὶ
τῶν Ἀθηναίων ἤδη ὁ αἰεὶ ἐντὸς γιγνόμενος χωρεῖ
2 ἐπὶ τὸ τεῖχος. καὶ οἱ Πελοποννήσιοι φρουροὶ τὸ
μὲν πρῶτον ἀντισχόντες ἠμύνοντο ὀλίγοι, καὶ
ἀπέθανόν τινες αὐτῶν, οἱ δὲ πλείους ἐς φυγὴν
κατέστησαν, φοβηθέντες ἐν νυκτί τε πολεμίων
προσπεπτωκότων καὶ τῶν προδιδόντων Μεγαρέων
ἀντιμαχομένων νομίσαντες τοὺς ἅπαντας σφᾶς
3 Μεγαρέας προδεδωκέναι. ξυνέπεσε γὰρ καὶ τὸν
τῶν Ἀθηναίων κήρυκα ἀφ' ἑαυτοῦ γνώμης κη-
ρύξαι τὸν βουλόμενον ἰέναι Μεγαρέων μετὰ
Ἀθηναίων θησόμενον τὰ ὅπλα. οἱ δ' ὡς ἤκουσαν,
οὐκέτι ἀνέμενον, ἀλλὰ τῷ ὄντι νομίσαντες κοινῇ
4 πολεμεῖσθαι κατέφυγον ἐς τὴν Νίσαιαν. ἅμα δὲ
ἕῳ ἑαλωκότων ἤδη τῶν τειχῶν καὶ τῶν ἐν τῇ
πόλει Μεγαρέων θορυβουμένων οἱ πρὸς τοὺς
Ἀθηναίους πράξαντες καὶ ἄλλο μετ' αὐτῶν
πλῆθος, ὃ ξυνῄδει, ἔφασαν χρῆναι ἀνοίγειν τὰς
5 πύλας καὶ ἐπεξιέναι ἐς μάχην. ξυνέκειτο δὲ
αὐτοῖς τῶν πυλῶν ἀνοιχθεισῶν ἐσπίπτειν τοὺς
Ἀθηναίους, αὐτοὶ δὲ διάδηλοι ἔμελλον ἔσεσθαι
(λίπα γὰρ ἀλείψεσθαι), ὅπως μὴ ἀδικῶνται.
ἀσφάλεια δὲ αὐτοῖς μᾶλλον ἐγίγνετο τῆς ἀνοίξεως·
καὶ γὰρ οἱ ἀπὸ τῆς Ἐλευσῖνος κατὰ τὸ ξυγκεί-
μενον τετρακισχίλιοι ὁπλῖται τῶν Ἀθηναίων καὶ

reinforcements which came up — for the nearest
Peloponnesians had become aware of what was going
on—and defeated them, thus securing the gates for
the onrushing Athenian hoplites.   LXVIII. After
that every Athenian who got inside immediately made
for the wall.   A few of the Peloponnesian garrison at
first stood their ground and defended themselves,
some of them being killed, but most of them took to
flight, being seized with panic, both because the
enemy had attacked them at night, and also
because they thought the Megarian traitors were
fighting against them; and they supposed that all the
Megarians had betrayed them.   For it so happened
also that the Athenian herald, acting on his own
responsibility, made a proclamation that any Megarian
who so desired might espouse the cause of the
Athenians.   When the garrison heard this proclamation it no longer held out, but, verily believing that
a concerted attack was being made upon them, fled to
Nisaea.   And at daybreak, when the walls had already
been taken and the Megarians in the city were in a
tumult, those who had negotiated with the Athenians,
and a large number besides who were privy to the
plot, expressed the opinion that they ought to open
the gates and go out to battle.   It had, in fact, been
agreed between them and the Athenians, that as soon
as the gates were opened the Athenians should rush
in, and, in order that they might themselves escape
injury, they were to be distinguished from the rest by
being anointed with oil.   They were also to have
additional security in thus opening the gates, since
the men who according to the compact were to
march by night from Eleusis, four thousand Athenian

ἱππῆς ἑξακόσιοι οἱ τὴν νύκτα πορευσόμενοι[1]
6 παρῆσαν. ἀληλιμμένων δὲ αὐτῶν καὶ ὄντων ἤδη
περὶ τὰς πύλας καταγορεύει τις ξυνειδὼς τοῖς
ἑτέροις τὸ ἐπιβούλευμα. καὶ οἱ ξυστραφέντες
ἀθρόοι ἦλθον καὶ οὐκ ἔφασαν χρῆναι οὔτε
ἐπεξιέναι (οὐδὲ γὰρ πρότερόν πω τοῦτο ἰσχύοντες
μᾶλλον τολμῆσαι) οὔτε ἐς κίνδυνον φανερὸν τὴν
πόλιν καταγαγεῖν. εἴ τε μὴ πείσεταί τις, αὐτοῦ
τὴν μάχην ἔσεσθαι. ἐδήλουν δὲ οὐδὲν ὅτι ἴσασι
τὰ πρασσόμενα, ἀλλὰ ὡς τὰ βέλτιστα βουλεύ-
οντες ἰσχυρίζοντο, καὶ ἅμα περὶ τὰς πύλας
παρέμενον φυλάσσοντες, ὥστε οὐκ ἐγένετο τοῖς
ἐπιβουλεύουσι πρᾶξαι ὃ ἔμελλον.

LXIX. Γνόντες δὲ οἱ τῶν Ἀθηναίων στρατηγοὶ
ὅτι ἐναντίωμά τι ἐγένετο καὶ τὴν πόλιν βίᾳ οὐχ
οἷοί τε ἔσονται λαβεῖν, τὴν Νίσαιαν εὐθὺς περιε-
τείχιζον, νομίζοντες, εἰ πρὶν ἐπιβοηθῆσαί τινας
ἐξέλοιεν, θᾶσσον ἂν καὶ τὰ Μέγαρα προσχωρῆ-
2 σαι (παρεγένετο δὲ σίδηρός τε ἐκ τῶν Ἀθηνῶν
ταχὺ καὶ λιθουργοὶ καὶ τἆλλα ἐπιτήδεια)· ἀρξάμενοι δ' ἀπὸ τοῦ τείχους ὃ εἶχον καὶ διοικοδομή-
σαντες τὸ πρὸς Μεγαρέας, ἀπ' ἐκείνου ἑκατέρωθεν
ἐς θάλασσαν τῆς Νισαίας[2] τάφρον τε καὶ τείχη
διελομένη ἦγεν[3] ἡ στρατιά, ἔκ τε τοῦ προαστείου
λίθοις καὶ πλίνθοις χρώμενοι, καὶ κόπτοντες τὰ
δένδρα καὶ ὕλην ἀπεσταύρουν εἴ πη δέοιτό τι

---

[1] πορευσόμενοι, Rutherford's conjecture for πορευόμενοι of
the MSS.   [2] Hude deletes τῆς Νισαίας, after Stahl.
[3] ἦγεν added by Stahl and Rauchenstein.

hoplites and six hundred cavalry, were now at hand.[1]
But after they had anointed themselves and were
already near the gates, an accomplice divulged the
plot to the other party. And they, gathering in a
body, came and declared that they ought neither to
march out to fight—for they had never ventured to do
such a thing before, even when they were stronger
—nor to bring the city into manifest danger; and,
they added, should anyone refuse to obey, the fight
would take place on the spot. But they gave no signs
whatever that they were aware of the plot which was
going on, but stoutly maintained that their advice
was for the best, and at the same time stayed about
the gates keeping watch, so that the plotters had
no opportunity to carry out their intentions.

LXIX. The Athenian generals, however, saw that
some obstacle had arisen and that they would not be
able to take the city by force, and therefore at once
began to invest Nisaea with a wall, thinking that, if
they could take this town before any succour came,
Megara also would soon capitulate. A supply of iron
quickly arrived from Athens, as well as stonemasons
and whatever else was needed. Beginning then at
the part of the fortification which they already held
and building a cross-wall on the side of it facing
Megara, from that point they built out on either side
of Nisaea as far as the sea, the army apportioning
among them the ditch and the walls and using stones
and bricks from the suburbs. Moreover, they cut
down fruit-trees and forest-wood and built stockades

---

[1] Or, retaining πορευόμενοι with the MSS. and rejecting οἱ
before τὴν νύκτα, "since the men from Eleusis, four thousand
Athenian hoplites and six hundred cavalry, according to the
compact had marched all night and were now at hand."

καὶ αἱ οἰκίαι τοῦ προαστείου ἐπάλξεις λαμβά-
νουσαι αὐταὶ ὑπῆρχον ἔρυμα. καὶ ταύτην μὲν
3 τὴν ἡμέραν ὅλην εἰργάζοντο· τῇ δὲ ὑστεραίᾳ περὶ
δείλην τὸ τεῖχος ὅσον οὐκ ἀπετετέλεστο, καὶ οἱ ἐν
τῇ Νισαίᾳ δείσαντες, σίτου τε ἀπορίᾳ (ἐφ᾽ ἡμέραν
γὰρ ἐκ τῆς ἄνω πόλεως ἐχρῶντο) καὶ τοὺς Πελοποννησίους οὐ νομίζοντες ταχὺ ἐπιβοηθήσειν, τούς
τε Μεγαρέας πολεμίους ἡγούμενοι, ξυνέβησαν
τοῖς Ἀθηναίοις ῥητοῦ μὲν ἕκαστον ἀργυρίου ἀπο-
λυθῆναι ὅπλα παραδόντας, τοῖς δὲ Λακεδαιμονίοις, τῷ τε ἄρχοντι καὶ εἴ τις ἄλλος ἐνῆν,
χρῆσθαι Ἀθηναίους ὅ τι ἂν βούλωνται. ἐπὶ τού-
4 τοις ὁμολογήσαντες ἐξῆλθον. καὶ οἱ Ἀθηναῖοι
τὰ μακρὰ τείχη ἀπορρήξαντες ἀπὸ τῆς τῶν
Μεγαρέων πόλεως καὶ τὴν Νίσαιαν παραλαβόντες
τἆλλα παρεσκευάζοντο.

LXX. Βρασίδας δὲ ὁ Τέλλιδος Λακεδαιμόνιος
κατὰ τοῦτον τὸν χρόνον ἐτύγχανε περὶ Σικυῶνα
καὶ Κόρινθον ὤν, ἐπὶ Θρᾴκης στρατείαν παρα-
σκευαζόμενος. καὶ ὡς ᾔσθετο τῶν τειχῶν τὴν
ἅλωσιν, δείσας περί τε τοῖς ἐν τῇ Νισαίᾳ Πελοποννησίοις καὶ μὴ τὰ Μέγαρα ληφθῇ, πέμπει ἔς
τε τοὺς Βοιωτοὺς κελεύων κατὰ τάχος στρατιᾷ
ἀπαντῆσαι ἐπὶ Τριποδίσκον (ἔστι δὲ κώμη τῆς
Μεγαρίδος ὄνομα τοῦτο ἔχουσα ὑπὸ τῷ ὄρει τῇ
Γερανείᾳ), καὶ αὐτὸς ἔχων ἦλθεν ἑπτακοσίους μὲν
καὶ δισχιλίους Κορινθίων ὁπλίτας, Φλειασίων δὲ
τετρακοσίους, Σικυωνίων δὲ ἑξακοσίους καὶ τοὺς

wherever they were needed; and the houses of the suburbs with the addition of battlements of themselves furnished a rampart. They worked the whole of this first day, but on the next day toward evening when the wall was all but finished the garrison of Nisaea, becoming alarmed by the shortage of food, seeing that they received provisions from the upper-city for only a day at a time, and not anticipating any speedy relief from the Peloponnesians, and believing the Megarians to be hostile, capitulated to the Athenians on condition that they should give up their arms and pay a ransom of a stipulated amount for each man; as for the Lacedaemonians in the garrison, the commander or anyone else, they were to be disposed of as the Athenians might wish. On these terms they came to an agreement and marched out. The Athenians then made a breach in the long walls in order to separate them from the wall of the city of Megara, took possession of Nisaea, and proceeded with their other preparations.

LXX. At this time Brasidas son of Tellis, a Lacedaemonian, happened to be in the neighbourhood of Sicyon and Corinth, preparing a force for use in the region of Thrace. And when he heard of the capture of the walls, fearing for the safety of the Peloponnesians in Nisaea and apprehensive lest Megara should be taken, he sent to the Boeotians requesting them to come in haste with an army and to meet him at Tripodiscus, which is the name of a village in the district of Megara at the foot of Mount Geraneia. He himself set out with two thousand seven hundred Corinthian hoplites, four hundred from Phlius, seven hundred from Sicyon, and such troops

μεθ' αὑτοῦ ὅσοι ἤδη ξυνειλεγμένοι ἦσαν, οἰόμενος
2 τὴν Νίσαιαν ἔτι καταλήψεσθαι ἀνάλωτον. ὡς δὲ
ἐπύθετο, (ἔτυχε γὰρ νυκτὸς ἐπὶ τὸν Τριποδίσκον
ἐξελθών) ἀπολέξας τριακοσίους τοῦ στρατοῦ, πρὶν
ἔκπυστος γενέσθαι, προσῆλθε τῇ τῶν Μεγαρέων
πόλει λαθὼν τοὺς Ἀθηναίους ὄντας περὶ τὴν
θάλασσαν, βουλόμενος μὲν τῷ λόγῳ καὶ ἅμα εἰ
δύναιτο ἔργῳ τῆς Νισαίας πειρᾶσαι, τὸ δὲ μέγιστον, τὴν τῶν Μεγαρέων πόλιν ἐσελθὼν βεβαιώ-
σασθαι. καὶ ἠξίου δέξασθαι σφᾶς λέγων ἐν
ἐλπίδι εἶναι ἀναλαβεῖν Νίσαιαν. LXXI. αἱ δὲ
τῶν Μεγαρέων στάσεις φοβούμεναι, οἱ μὲν μὴ
τοὺς φεύγοντας σφίσιν ἐσαγαγὼν αὐτοὺς ἐκβάλῃ,
οἱ δὲ μὴ αὐτὸ τοῦτο ὁ δῆμος δείσας ἐπίθηται
σφίσι καὶ ἡ πόλις ἐν μάχῃ καθ' αὑτὴν οὖσα ἐγγὺς
ἐφεδρευόντων Ἀθηναίων ἀπόληται, οὐκ ἐδέξαντο,
ἀλλ' ἀμφοτέροις ἐδόκει ἡσυχάσασι τὸ μέλλον
2 περιιδεῖν. ἤλπιζον γὰρ καὶ μάχην ἑκάτεροι
ἔσεσθαι τῶν τε Ἀθηναίων καὶ τῶν προσβοηθη-
σάντων, καὶ οὕτω σφίσιν ἀσφαλεστέρως ἔχειν,
οἷς τις εἴη εὔνους, κρατήσασι προσχωρῆσαι· ὁ δὲ
Βρασίδας ὡς οὐκ ἔπειθεν, ἀνεχώρησε πάλιν ἐς τὸ
ἄλλο στράτευμα.

LXXII. Ἅμα δὲ τῇ ἕῳ οἱ Βοιωτοὶ παρῆσαν,
διανενοημένοι μὲν καὶ πρὶν Βρασίδαν πέμψαι
βοηθεῖν ἐπὶ τὰ Μέγαρα, ὡς οὐκ ἀλλοτρίου ὄντος
τοῦ κινδύνου, καὶ ἤδη ὄντες πανστρατιᾷ Πλα-
ταιᾶσιν· ἐπειδὴ δὲ καὶ ἦλθεν ὁ ἄγγελος, πολλῷ
μᾶλλον ἐρρώσθησαν, καὶ ἀποστείλαντες διακο-

of his own as had already been levied, thinking that he would arrive before Nisaea had been taken. But when he learned the truth—for he happened to have gone out by night to Tripodiscus—he selected three hundred of his own army, and before his approach was known reached the city of Megara unobserved by the Athenians, who were down by the sea. His plan was, ostensibly—and really, too, if it should prove possible—to make an attempt upon Nisaea, but most of all to get into the city of Megara and secure it. And he demanded that they should receive him, saying that he was in hopes of recovering Nisaea. LXXI. But the rival factions of Megara were afraid, the one that he might bring in the exiles and drive them out, the other that the populace, fearing this very thing, might attack them, and that the city, being at war with itself, while the Athenians were lying in wait near at hand, might be ruined. They, therefore, did not admit Brasidas, both parties thinking it best to wait and see what would happen. For each party expected that there would be a battle between the Athenians and the relieving army, and so it was safer for them not to join the side which anyone favoured until it was victorious. So then Brasidas, when he could not persuade them, withdrew once more to his own army.

LXXII. At daybreak the Boeotians arrived. They had intended, even before Brasidas summoned them, to go to the aid of Megara, feeling that the danger was not alien to them, and were already at Plataea with all their forces; but when the summons actually came, they were greatly strengthened in their purpose, and sent on two thousand two hundred hoplites

333

σίους καὶ δισχιλίους ὁπλίτας καὶ ἱππέας ἑξακο-
2 σίους τοῖς πλείοσιν ἀπῆλθον πάλιν. παρόντος
δὲ ἤδη ξύμπαντος τοῦ στρατεύματος, ὁπλιτῶν
οὐκ ἔλασσον ἑξακισχιλίων, καὶ τῶν Ἀθηναίων
τῶν μὲν ὁπλιτῶν περί τε τὴν Νίσαιαν ὄντων καὶ
τὴν θάλασσαν ἐν τάξει, τῶν δὲ ψιλῶν ἀνὰ τὸ
πεδίον ἐσκεδασμένων, οἱ ἱππῆς οἱ τῶν Βοιωτῶν
ἀπροσδοκήτοις ἐπιπεσόντες τοῖς ψιλοῖς ἔτρεψαν
ἐπὶ τὴν θάλασσαν (ἐν γὰρ τῷ πρὸ τοῦ οὐδεμία
βοήθειά πω τοῖς Μεγαρεῦσιν οὐδαμόθεν ἐπῆλθεν)·
3 ἀντεπεξελάσαντες δὲ καὶ οἱ τῶν Ἀθηναίων ἐς
χεῖρας ἦσαν, καὶ ἐγένετο ἱππομαχία ἐπὶ πολύ, ἐν
4 ᾗ ἀξιοῦσιν ἑκάτεροι οὐχ ἥσσους γενέσθαι. τὸν
μὲν γὰρ ἵππαρχον τῶν Βοιωτῶν καὶ ἄλλους τινὰς
οὐ πολλοὺς πρὸς αὐτὴν τὴν Νίσαιαν προσελά-
σαντας [1] οἱ Ἀθηναῖοι καὶ ἀποκτείναντες ἐσκύλευ-
σαν, καὶ τῶν τε νεκρῶν τούτων κρατήσαντες
ὑποσπόνδους ἀπέδοσαν καὶ τροπαῖον ἔστησαν·
οὐ [2] μέντοι ἔν γε τῷ παντὶ ἔργῳ βεβαίως οὐδέτεροι τελευτήσαντες ἀπεκρίθησαν ἀλλ᾽ [3] οἱ μὲν
Βοιωτοὶ πρὸς τοὺς ἑαυτῶν, οἱ δὲ ἐπὶ τὴν Νίσαιαν.
LXXIII. Μετὰ δὲ τοῦτο Βρασίδας καὶ τὸ
στράτευμα ἐχώρουν ἐγγυτέρω τῆς θαλάσσης καὶ
τῆς τῶν Μεγαρέων πόλεως, καὶ καταλαβόντες
χωρίον ἐπιτήδειον παραταξάμενοι ἡσύχαζον,
οἰόμενοι σφίσιν ἐπιέναι τοὺς Ἀθηναίους καὶ τοὺς
Μεγαρέας ἐπιστάμενοι περιορωμένους ὁποτέρων ἢ
2 νίκη ἔσται. καλῶς δὲ ἐνόμιζον σφίσιν ἀμφότερα
ἔχειν, ἅμα μὲν τὸ μὴ ἐπιχειρεῖν προτέρους μηδὲ

---

[1] Portus' correction for προσελάσαντες of the MSS.
[2] Hude adopts Rutherford's conjecture οὐδέν.
[3] ἀλλ᾽, Hude deletes, as not translated by Valla.

and six hundred cavalry, returning home with the larger part of their army. Then, finally, when their whole army was at hand, consisting of not less than six thousand hoplites, and the Athenian hoplites were in line about Nisaea and the sea, while the light-armed troops were scattered up and down the plain, the Boeotian cavalry fell upon the latter and drove them to the sea. The attack was unexpected, for hitherto no reinforcements had ever come to the Megarians from any quarter. But the Athenian horsemen charged upon them in turn and a prolonged cavalry action ensued, in which both sides claimed to have held their own. The Athenians did succeed in killing the commander of the Boeotian cavalry and a few others who had charged to the very walls of Nisaea and despoiled them, and having got possession of their bodies they gave them back under a truce and set up a trophy; in the action as a whole, however, neither side finally gained a decisive advantage, and so they separated, the Boeotians going to their own army, the Athenians to Nisaea.

LXXIII. After this Brasidas and his army advanced nearer to the sea and the city of Megara, and there, taking up an advantageous position, they drew up their lines and kept quiet, thinking that the Athenians would come against them, and feeling assured that the Megarians would wait to see which side would be victorious. And they thought that matters stood well with them in both of two respects: in the first place, they were not forcing an

μάχης καὶ κινδύνου ἑκόντας ἄρξαι, ἐπειδή γε ἐν
φανερῷ ἔδειξαν ἑτοῖμοι ὄντες ἀμύνεσθαι, καὶ
αὐτοῖς ὥσπερ ἀκονιτὶ τὴν νίκην δικαίως ἀνατίθε-
σθαι· ἐν τῷ αὐτῷ δὲ καὶ πρὸς τοὺς Μεγαρέας
3 ὀρθῶς ξυμβαίνειν· εἰ μὲν γὰρ μὴ ὤφθησαν
ἐλθόντες, οὐκ ἂν ἐν τύχῃ γίγνεσθαι σφίσιν, ἀλλὰ
σαφῶς ἂν ὥσπερ ἡσσηθέντων στερηθῆναι εὐθὺς
τῆς πόλεως· νῦν δὲ κἂν τυχεῖν αὐτοὺς Ἀθηναίους
μὴ βουληθέντας ἀγωνίζεσθαι, ὥστε ἀμαχητὶ ἂν
περιγενέσθαι αὐτοῖς ὧν ἕνεκα ἦλθον. ὅπερ καὶ
4 ἐγένετο. οἱ γὰρ Μεγαρῆς, ὡς οἱ Ἀθηναῖοι
ἐτάξαντο μὲν παρὰ τὰ μακρὰ τείχη ἐξελθόντες,
ἡσύχαζον δὲ καὶ αὐτοὶ μὴ ἐπιόντων, λογιζόμενοι
καὶ οἱ ἐκείνων στρατηγοὶ μὴ ἀντίπαλον εἶναι
σφίσι τὸν κίνδυνον, ἐπειδὴ καὶ τὰ πλείω αὐτοῖς
προυκεχωρήκει, ἄρξασι μάχης πρὸς πλείονας
αὐτῶν ἢ λαβεῖν νικήσαντας Μέγαρα ἢ σφαλέντας
τῷ βελτίστῳ τοῦ ὁπλιτικοῦ βλαφθῆναι, τοῖς δὲ
ξυμπάσης τῆς δυνάμεως καὶ τῶν παρόντων μέρος
ἕκαστον κινδυνεύειν εἰκότως ἐθέλειν τολμᾶν,
χρόνον δὲ ἐπισχόντες καὶ ὡς οὐδὲν ἀφ' ἑκατέρων
ἐπεχειρεῖτο, ἀπῆλθον πρότεροι οἱ Ἀθηναῖοι ἐς
τὴν Νίσαιαν καὶ αὖθις οἱ Πελοποννήσιοι ὅθενπερ
ὡρμήθησαν· οὕτω δὴ τῷ μὲν Βρασίδᾳ αὐτῷ καὶ

---

[1] Apparently there is an anacoluthon, the sentence beginning as if τῷ Βρασίδᾳ ἀνοίγουσι τὰς πύλας were to be the
predicate, but after the long parenthesis the subject is
resumed in partitive form, αἱ τῶν φευγόντων φίλοι Μεγαρῆς.

engagement and had not deliberately courted the
risk of a battle, although they had at least plainly
shown that they were ready to defend themselves,
so that the victory would justly be accredited to
them almost without a blow; and at the same time
they thought that things were turning out right as
regards the Megarians also. For if they had failed
to put in an appearance there would have been no
chance for them, but they would clearly have lost
the city at once just as though they had been defeated; but by this move there was the possible
chance that the Athenians themselves would not care
to fight, with the result that they would have gained
what they came for without a battle. And this is
just what happened. For the Megarians did what
was expected of them.[1] When the Athenians came
out and drew up their lines before the long walls,
they too kept quiet, since the Peloponnesians did
not attack, and their generals also reckoned that
they were running an unequal risk, now that almost
all their plans had turned out well, to begin a battle
against larger numbers, and either be victorious and
take Megara, or, if defeated, have the flower of their
hoplite force damaged; whereas the Peloponnesians
would naturally be willing to risk an engagement
which would involve, for each contingent, only a
portion of the entire army or of the troops there at
hand.[2] Both armies therefore waited for some time,
and when no attack was made from either side, the
Athenians were the first to withdraw, retiring to
Nisaea, and next the Peloponnesians, returning to
the place from which they had set out. So then,
finally, the Megarians who were friends of the exiles

[2] The text is clearly corrupt, but the general sense seems
to be that given above.

τοῖς ἀπὸ τῶν πόλεων ἄρχουσιν οἱ τῶν φευγόντων
φίλοι Μεγαρῆς, ὡς ἐπικρατήσαντι καὶ τῶν
Ἀθηναίων οὐκέτι ἐθελησάντων μάχεσθαι, θαρ-
σοῦντες μᾶλλον ἀνοίγουσί τε τὰς πύλας καὶ
δεξάμενοι καταπεπληγμένων ἤδη τῶν πρὸς τοὺς
Ἀθηναίους πραξάντων ἐς λόγους ἔρχονται.

LXXIV. Καὶ ὕστερον ὁ μὲν διαλυθέντων τῶν
ξυμμάχων κατὰ πόλεις ἐπανελθὼν καὶ αὐτὸς ἐς
τὴν Κόρινθον, τὴν ἐπὶ Θράκης στρατείαν παρε-
2 σκεύαζεν, ἵναπερ καὶ τὸ πρῶτον ὥρμητο· οἱ δὲ
ἐν τῇ πόλει Μεγαρῆς, ἀποχωρησάντων καὶ τῶν
Ἀθηναίων ἐπ᾽ οἴκου, ὅσοι μὲν τῶν πραγμάτων πρὸς
τοὺς Ἀθηναίους μάλιστα μετέσχον, εἰδότες ὅτι
ὤφθησαν εὐθὺς ὑπεξῆλθον, οἱ δὲ ἄλλοι κοινολο-
γησάμενοι τοῖς τῶν φευγόντων φίλοις κατάγουσι
τοὺς ἐκ Πηγῶν, ὁρκώσαντες πίστεσι μεγάλαις
μηδὲν μνησικακήσειν, βουλεύσειν δὲ τῇ πόλει τὰ
3 ἄριστα. οἱ δὲ ἐπειδὴ ἐν ταῖς ἀρχαῖς ἐγένοντο καὶ
ἐξέτασιν ὅπλων ἐποιήσαντο, διαστήσαντες τοὺς
λόχους ἐξελέξαντο τῶν τε ἐχθρῶν καὶ οἳ ἐδόκουν
μάλιστα ξυμπρᾶξαι τὰ πρὸς τοὺς Ἀθηναίους,
ἄνδρας ὡς ἑκατόν, καὶ τούτων πέρι ἀναγκάσαντες
τὸν δῆμον ψῆφον φανερὰν διενεγκεῖν, ὡς κατε-
γνώσθησαν, ἔκτειναν, καὶ ἐς ὀλιγαρχίαν τὰ
4 μάλιστα κατέστησαν τὴν πόλιν. καὶ πλεῖστον
δὴ χρόνον αὕτη ὑπ᾽ ἐλαχίστων γενομένη ἐκ στάσεως μετάστασις ξυνέμεινεν.

plucked up courage, and opened the gates to Brasidas and the commanders from the various cities, in the feeling that he had won the victory and that the Athenians had finally declined battle.[1] And receiving them into the town they entered into a conference with them, the party which had been intriguing with the Athenians being now quite cowed.

LXXIV. Afterwards, when the Peloponnesian allies had been dismissed to their several cities, Brasidas went back to Corinth and began preparations for the expedition to Thrace, whither he had originally been bound. But when the Athenians also returned home, all the Megarians who had been most implicated in the negotiations with the Athenians, knowing that they had been detected, immediately withdrew secretly from the city, while the rest, communicating with the friends of the exiles, brought them back from Pegae, after first binding them on their oath by strong pledges not to harbour ill-will, but to consult for the best interests of the city. But as soon as these men attained office and had made an inspection of arms, separating the companies they selected about one hundred of their personal enemies and of those who seemed to have had the largest part in the negotiations with the Athenians, and compelling the popular assembly to take an open vote concerning these, when they had been condemned, slew them, and established an extreme oligarchy in the city. And there was never a change of government, effected by so small a number of men through the triumph of a faction, that lasted so long.

[1] Or, adopting Rutherford's conjecture, ἐθελησόντων, "and that the Athenians would not care to fight again."

THUCYDIDES

LXXV. Τοῦ δ' αὐτοῦ θέρους τῆς Ἀντάνδρου
ὑπὸ τῶν Μυτιληναίων, ὥσπερ διενοοῦντο, μελλούσης κατασκευάζεσθαι, οἱ τῶν ἀργυρολόγων
Ἀθηναίων νεῶν στρατηγοί, Δημόδοκος καὶ Ἀριστείδης, ὄντες περὶ Ἑλλήσποντον (ὁ γὰρ τρίτος
αὐτῶν Λάμαχος δέκα ναυσὶν ἐς τὸν Πόντον
ἐσεπεπλεύκει) ὡς ᾐσθάνοντο τὴν παρασκευὴν τοῦ
χωρίου καὶ ἐδόκει αὐτοῖς δεινὸν εἶναι μὴ ὥσπερ
τὰ Ἄναια ἐπὶ τῇ Σάμῳ γένηται, ἔνθα οἱ φεύγοντες τῶν Σαμίων καταστάντες τούς τε Πελοποννησίους ὠφέλουν ἐς τὰ ναυτικὰ κυβερνήτας πέμ-
ποντες καὶ τοὺς ἐν τῇ πόλει Σαμίους ἐς ταραχὴν
καθίστασαν καὶ τοὺς ἐξιόντας ἐδέχοντο· οὕτω δὴ
ξυναγείραντες ἀπὸ τῶν ξυμμάχων στρατιὰν καὶ
πλεύσαντες, μάχῃ τε νικήσαντες τοὺς ἐκ τῆς
Ἀντάνδρου ἐπεξελθόντας, ἀναλαμβάνουσι τὸ
2 χωρίον πάλιν. καὶ οὐ πολὺ ὕστερον ἐς τὸν
Πόντον ἐσπλεύσας Λάμαχος, ἐν τῇ Ἡρακλεώτιδι
ὁρμίσας ἐς τὸν Κάλητα ποταμὸν ἀπόλλυσι τὰς
ναῦς ὕδατος ἄνωθεν γενομένου καὶ κατελθόντος
αἰφνιδίου τοῦ ῥεύματος· αὐτὸς δὲ καὶ ἡ στρατιὰ
πεζῇ διὰ Βιθυνῶν Θρᾳκῶν, οἵ εἰσι πέραν ἐν τῇ
Ἀσίᾳ, ἀφικνεῖται ἐς Καλχηδόνα, τὴν ἐπὶ τῷ
στόματι τοῦ Πόντου Μεγαρέων ἀποικίαν.

LXXVI. Ἐν δὲ τῷ αὐτῷ θέρει καὶ Δημοσθένης
Ἀθηναίων στρατηγὸς τεσσαράκοντα ναυσὶν ἀφικνεῖται ἐς Ναύπακτον, εὐθὺς μετὰ τὴν ἐκ τῆς
2 Μεγαρίδος ἀναχώρησιν. τῷ γὰρ Ἱπποκράτει καὶ
ἐκείνῳ τὰ Βοιώτια πράγματα ἀπό τινων ἀνδρῶν

LXXV. During the same summer, when Antandros was about to be strengthened[1] by the Mytilenaeans as they had planned, the generals in command of the Athenian ships which were collecting the tribute, namely, Demodocus and Aristides, who were in the neighbourhood of the Hellespont—for Lamachus, their colleague, had sailed into the Pontus with ten ships—heard of the fortification of the place and thought that there was danger of its becoming a menace to Lesbos, just as Anaea was to Samos[2]; for the Samian exiles, establishing themselves at Anaea, kept aiding the Peloponnesians by sending them pilots for their fleet, and also brought the Samians who lived in the city into a state of turmoil and continually offered a refuge to those who were sent into exile. The Athenian generals, therefore, collected an army from among the allies, sailed thither, defeated in battle those who came out against them from Antandros, and recovered the city. And not long afterwards Lamachus, who had sailed into the Pontus and anchored in the river Cales in Heraclean territory, lost his ships in consequence of a rain which fell in the uplands and brought down a sudden flood. He and his army, however, going by land through the Bithynian Thracians, who were on the other side, in Asia, arrived at Chalcedon, the Megarian colony at the mouth of the Pontus.

LXXVI. During the same summer, immediately after the Athenians retired from Megara, Demosthenes, the Athenian general, arrived with forty ships at Naupactus. For he and Hippocrates were engaged in negotiations about affairs in Boeotia, at the

---

[1] cf. ch. lii. 3.   [2] cf. III. xix. 2, xxxii. 2.

ἐν ταῖς πόλεσιν ἐπράσσετο, βουλομένων μεταστῆσαι τὸν κόσμον καὶ ἐς δημοκρατίαν ὥσπερ
οἱ Ἀθηναῖοι[1] τρέψαι· καὶ Πτοιοδώρου μάλιστ'
ἀνδρὸς φυγάδος ἐκ Θηβῶν ἐσηγουμένου τάδε
3 αὐτοῖς παρεσκευάσθη. Σίφας μὲν ἔμελλόν τινες
προδώσειν (αἱ δὲ Σῖφαι εἰσὶ τῆς Θεσπικῆς γῆς ἐν
τῷ Κρισαίῳ κόλπῳ ἐπιθαλασσίδιοι)· Χαιρώνειαν
δέ, ἢ ἐς Ὀρχομενὸν τὸν Μινύειον πρότερον καλού-
μενον, νῦν δὲ Βοιώτιον, ξυντελεῖ, ἄλλοι ἐξ Ὀρχο-
μενοῦ ἐνεδίδοσαν, καὶ οἱ Ὀρχομενίων φυγάδες
ξυνέπρασσον τὰ μάλιστα καὶ ἄνδρας ἐμισθοῦντο
ἐκ Πελοποννήσου (ἔστι δὲ ἡ Χαιρώνεια ἔσχατον
τῆς Βοιωτίας πρὸς τῇ Φανοτίδι τῆς Φωκίδος), καὶ
4 Φωκέων μετεῖχόν τινες. τοὺς δὲ Ἀθηναίους ἔδει
Δήλιον καταλαβεῖν, τὸ ἐν τῇ Ταναγραίᾳ πρὸς
Εὔβοιαν τετραμμένον Ἀπόλλωνος ἱερόν, ἅμα δὲ
ταῦτα ἐν ἡμέρᾳ ῥητῇ γίγνεσθαι, ὅπως μὴ ξυμβοη-
θήσωσιν ἐπὶ τὸ Δήλιον οἱ Βοιωτοὶ ἀθρόοι, ἀλλ'
5 ἐπὶ τὰ σφέτερα αὐτῶν ἕκαστοι κινούμενα. καὶ εἰ
κατορθοῖτο ἡ πεῖρα καὶ τὸ Δήλιον τειχισθείη,
ῥᾳδίως ἤλπιζον, εἰ καὶ μὴ παραυτίκα νεωτερίζοιτο
τι τῶν κατὰ τὰς πολιτείας τοῖς Βοιωτοῖς, ἐχο-
μένων τούτων τῶν χωρίων καὶ λῃστευομένης τῆς
γῆς καὶ οὔσης ἑκάστοις διὰ βραχέος ἀποστροφῆς,
οὐ μενεῖν κατὰ χώραν τὰ πράγματα, ἀλλὰ χρόνῳ
τῶν Ἀθηναίων μὲν προσιόντων τοῖς ἀφεστηκόσι,

[1] ὥσπερ οἱ Ἀθηναῖοι, bracketed by Hude, after Rutherford.

instance of certain men in several cities who wished
to bring about a change in their form of government and to transform it into a democracy, such as
the Athenians had. The leading spirit in these
transactions was Ptoeodorus, an exile from Thebes,
through whom Demosthenes and Hippocrates had
brought about the following state of affairs. Siphae,
a town on the shore of the Crisaean Gulf in the territory of Thespiae, was to be betrayed by certain men ;
and Chaeronea, a city which is tributary to Orchomenus—the city which was formerly called Minyan,
but is now called Boeotian—was to be put into the
hands of the Athenians by others, the fugitives from
Orchomenus, who also took into their pay some Peloponnesians, being especially active in the conspiracy.
Some Phocians also had a share in the plot, Chaeronea
being on the borders of Boeotia, and adjacent to
Phanotis, which is in Phocis. The Athenians were
to occupy Delium, the sanctuary of Apollo which is
in the territory of Tanagra and opposite Euboea ;
and all these events were to take place simultaneously
on an appointed day, in order that the Boeotians
might not concentrate their forces at Delium, but
that the several states might be occupied with their
own disaffected districts. And if the attempt should
succeed and Delium should be fortified, they con-
fidently expected, even if no immediate change
occurred in the constitutions of the Boeotian states,
nevertheless, so long as these places were in their
possession, from which Boeotian territory could be
ravaged and where everyone might find a convenient
place of refuge, the situation would not remain as it
was, but in time, when the Athenians should come
to the support of the rebels and the forces of the

τοῖς δὲ οὐκ οὔσης ἀθρόας τῆς δυνάμεως, καταστήσειν αὐτὰ ἐς τὸ ἐπιτήδειον.

LXXVII. Ἡ μὲν οὖν ἐπιβουλὴ τοιαύτη παρε-
σκευάζετο· ὁ δὲ Ἱπποκράτης αὐτὸς μὲν ἐκ τῆς
πόλεως δύναμιν ἔχων, ὁπότε καιρὸς εἴη, ἔμελλε
στρατεύειν ἐς τοὺς Βοιωτούς, τὸν δὲ Δημοσθένη
προαπέστειλε ταῖς τεσσαράκοντα ναυσὶν ἐς τὴν
Ναύπακτον, ὅπως ἐξ ἐκείνων τῶν χωρίων στρατὸν
ξυλλέξας Ἀκαρνάνων τε καὶ τῶν ἄλλων ξυμμάχων πλέοι ἐπὶ τὰς Σίφας ὡς προδοθησομένας·
ἡμέρα δ' αὐτοῖς εἴρητο ᾗ ἔδει ταῦτα πράσσειν.
2 καὶ ὁ μὲν Δημοσθένης ἀφικόμενος, Οἰνιάδας δὲ
ὑπό τε Ἀκαρνάνων πάντων κατηναγκασμένους
καταλαβὼν ἐς τὴν Ἀθηναίων ξυμμαχίαν καὶ
αὐτὸς ἀναστήσας τὸ ξυμμαχικὸν τὸ ἐκείνῃ πᾶν,
ἐπὶ Σαλύνθιον καὶ Ἀγραίους στρατεύσας πρῶτον
καὶ προσποιησάμενος τἆλλα ἡτοιμάζετο ὡς ἐπὶ
τὰς Σίφας, ὅταν δέῃ, ἀπαντησόμενος.

LXXVIII. Βρασίδας δὲ κατὰ τὸν αὐτὸν χρόνον
τοῦ θέρους πορευόμενος ἑπτακοσίοις καὶ χιλίοις
ὁπλίταις ἐς τὰ ἐπὶ Θρᾴκης ἐπειδὴ ἐγένετο ἐν
Ἡρακλείᾳ τῇ ἐν Τραχῖνι καί, προπέμψαντος
αὐτοῦ ἄγγελον ἐς Φάρσαλον παρὰ τοὺς ἐπιτηδείους ἀξιοῦντος διάγειν ἑαυτὸν καὶ τὴν στρατιάν,
ἦλθον ἐς Μελίτειαν τῆς Ἀχαΐας Πάναιρός τε καὶ
Δῶρος καὶ Ἱππολοχίδας καὶ Τορύλαος καὶ Στρό-
φακος πρόξενος ὢν Χαλκιδέων, τότε δὴ ἐπορεύετο.
2 ἦγον δὲ καὶ ἄλλοι Θεσσαλῶν αὐτὸν καὶ ἐκ Λαρί-

oligarchs were scattered, they could settle matters to their own advantage.

LXXVII. Such was the plot which was then under way. It was the purpose of Hippocrates, when the proper moment should arrive, to take troops from Athens and in person make an expedition into Boeotia; meanwhile he was sending Demosthenes in advance with a fleet of forty ships to Naupactus, in order that he should first collect in this region an army of Acarnanians and of other allies of Athens and then sail to Siphae, in expectation of its being betrayed; and a day was agreed upon between the two generals for doing these two things simultaneously. Upon his arrival at Naupactus, Demosthenes found that Oeniadae had already been forced by all the rest of the Acarnanians to join the Athenian alliance; he himself then raised all the allied forces in that district, and after first making an expedition against Salynthius and the Agraeans [1] and securing these, proceeded with his other preparations so as to be present at Siphae when needed.

LXXVIII. About the same time in the course of this summer, Brasidas, who was on his way to Thrace with one thousand seven hundred hoplites, reached Heracleia in Trachis and sent forward a messenger to his friends at Pharsalus requesting them to conduct him and his army through. Accordingly he was met at Meliteia in Achaia by Panaerus, Dorus, Hippolochidas, Torylaüs, and Strophacus, who was proxenus of the Chalcidians, and then proceeded on his march. He was conducted by several Thessalians also, among whom were Niconidas of Larisa, a

[1] *cf.* III. cxi. 4; cxiv. 2.

σης Νικονίδας Περδίκκᾳ ἐπιτήδειος ὤν. τὴν γὰρ
Θεσσαλίαν ἄλλως τε οὐκ εὔπορον ἦν διιέναι ἄνευ
ἀγωγοῦ καὶ μετὰ ὅπλων γε δή, καὶ τοῖς πᾶσί γε
ὁμοίως Ἕλλησιν ὕποπτον καθεστήκει τὴν τῶν
πέλας μὴ πείσαντας διιέναι· τοῖς τε Ἀθηναίοις
αἰεί ποτε τὸ πλῆθος τῶν Θεσσαλῶν εὔνουν ὑπῆρ-
3 χεν. ὥστε εἰ μὴ δυναστείᾳ μᾶλλον ἢ ἰσονομίᾳ
ἐχρῶντο τὸ ἐγχώριον¹ οἱ Θεσσαλοί, οὐκ ἄν ποτε
προῆλθεν, ἐπεὶ καὶ τότε πορευομένῳ αὐτῷ ἀπαν-
τήσαντες ἄλλοι τῶν τἀναντία τούτοις βουλομένων
ἐπὶ τῷ Ἐνιπεῖ ποταμῷ ἐκώλυον καὶ ἀδικεῖν ἔφα-
4 σαν ἄνευ τοῦ πάντων κοινοῦ πορευόμενον. οἱ δὲ
ἄγοντες οὔτε ἀκόντων ἔφασαν διάξειν, αἰφνίδιόν
τε παραγενόμενον ξένοι ὄντες κομίζειν. ἔλεγε δὲ
καὶ αὐτὸς ὁ Βρασίδας τῇ Θεσσαλῶν γῇ καὶ αὐτοῖς
φίλος ὢν ἰέναι καὶ Ἀθηναίοις πολεμίοις οὖσι καὶ
οὐκ ἐκείνοις ὅπλα ἐπιφέρειν, Θεσσαλοῖς τε οὐκ
εἰδέναι καὶ Λακεδαιμονίοις ἔχθραν οὖσαν ὥστε τῇ
ἀλλήλων γῇ μὴ χρῆσθαι, νῦν τε ἀκόντων ἐκείνων
οὐκ ἂν προελθεῖν (οὐδὲ γὰρ ἂν δύνασθαι), οὐ
5 μέντοι ἀξιοῦν γε εἴργεσθαι. καὶ οἱ μὲν ἀκούσαντες
ταῦτα ἀπῆλθον· ὁ δὲ κελευόντων τῶν ἀγωγῶν,
πρίν τι πλέον ξυστῆναι τὸ κωλῦσον, ἐχώρει οὐδὲν
ἐπισχὼν δρόμῳ. καὶ ταύτῃ μὲν τῇ ἡμέρᾳ, ᾗ ἐκ

___

¹ τὸ ἐγχώριον, Hude changes to ἐγχωρίῳ, after τῷ ἐγχωρίῳ
of Dion. Hal.

friend of Perdiccas. Indeed, Thessaly was not in any case an easy country to traverse without an escort, and especially with an armed force; and among all the Hellenes alike to traverse the territory of neighbours without their consent was looked on with suspicion. Besides, the common people of Thessaly had always been well disposed to the Athenians. If, therefore, the Thessalians had not been under the sway of a few powerful men, as is usual in that country, rather than under a free democracy, Brasidas would not have made headway; even as it was, he was confronted on his march, when he reached the river Enipeus, by other Thessalians belonging to the opposite party. These tried to stop him, warning him that he was doing wrong in proceeding without the consent of the whole people. But his conductors reassured them, saying that, if they were unwilling, they would not conduct him further, and that they were merely playing the part of hosts in escorting an unexpected visitor. Brasidas himself explained that he came as a friend to Thessaly and its inhabitants and was bearing arms against the Athenians, who were enemies, and not against them; moreover, he was not aware of any such hostility between the Thessalians and the Lacedaemonians as to debar them from access to each other's territory, but if in this instance they were unwilling, he would go no further, nor indeed could he do so; he hoped, however, that they would not bar his progress. On hearing this the Thessalians departed; but Brasidas, taking the advice of his escort, before a larger force could be collected to hinder him, set out at full speed and without making any halt. In fact, he finished the journey to Pharsalus

τῆς Μελιτείας ἀφώρμησεν, ἐς Φάρσαλόν τε ἐτέλεσε
καὶ ἐστρατοπεδεύσατο ἐπὶ τῷ Ἀπιδανῷ ποταμῷ,
ἐκεῖθεν δὲ ἐς Φάκιον, καὶ ἐξ αὐτοῦ ἐς Περραιβίαν·
6 ἀπὸ δὲ τούτου ἤδη οἱ μὲν Θεσσαλῶν ἀγωγοὶ πάλιν
ἀπῆλθον, οἱ δὲ Περραιβοὶ αὐτόν, ὑπήκοοι ὄντες
Θεσσαλῶν, κατέστησαν ἐς Δῖον τῆς Περδίκκου
ἀρχῆς, ὃ ὑπὸ τῷ Ὀλύμπῳ Μακεδονίας πρὸς
Θεσσαλοὺς πόλισμα κεῖται.

LXXIX. Τούτῳ τῷ τρόπῳ Βρασίδας Θεσσαλίαν φθάσας διέδραμε πρίν τινα κωλύειν παρα-
σκευάσασθαι, καὶ ἀφίκετο ὡς Περδίκκαν καὶ ἐς
2 τὴν Χαλκιδικήν. ἐκ γὰρ τῆς Πελοποννήσου, ὡς
τὰ τῶν Ἀθηναίων ηὐτύχει, δείσαντες οἵ τε ἐπὶ
Θράκης ἀφεστῶτες Ἀθηναίων καὶ Περδίκκας
ἐξήγαγον τὸν στρατόν, οἱ μὲν Χαλκιδῆς νομίζοντες ἐπὶ σφᾶς πρῶτον ὁρμήσειν τοὺς Ἀθηναίους
(καὶ ἅμα αἱ πλησιόχωροι πόλεις αὐτῶν αἱ οὐκ
ἀφεστηκυῖαι ξυνεπῆγον κρύφα), Περδίκκας δὲ
πολέμιος μὲν οὐκ ὢν ἐκ τοῦ φανεροῦ, φοβούμενος
δὲ καὶ αὐτὸς τὰ παλαιὰ διάφορα τῶν Ἀθηναίων
καὶ μάλιστα βουλόμενος Ἀρράβαιον τὸν Λυγκη-
3 στῶν βασιλέα παραστήσασθαι. ξυνέβη δὲ αὐτοῖς
ὥστε ῥᾷον ἐκ τῆς Πελοποννήσου στρατὸν ἐξαγα-
γεῖν, ἡ τῶν Λακεδαιμονίων ἐν τῷ παρόντι κακο-
πραγία.

LXXX. Τῶν γὰρ Ἀθηναίων ἐγκειμένων τῇ
Πελοποννήσῳ καὶ οὐχ ἥκιστα τῇ ἐκείνων γῇ,
ἤλπιζον ἀποτρέψειν αὐτοὺς μάλιστα, εἰ ἀντι-
παραλυποῖεν πέμψαντες ἐπὶ τοὺς ξυμμάχους

on the same day on which he had set out from
Meliteia, and encamped on the river Apidanus;
thence he proceeded to Phacium, and from there to
Perrhaebia. Here his Thessalian escort at length
turned back, and the Perrhaebians, who are subjects
of the Thessalians, brought him safely to Dium in the
dominions of Perdiccas, a small town in Macedonia at
the foot of Mt. Olympus, facing Thessaly.

LXXIX. It was in this manner that Brasidas
succeeded in rushing through Thessaly before anyone
could get ready to hinder him and reached Perdiccas
and the Chalcidic peninsula. The reason why the
peoples in Thrace who had revolted from Athens
had, in conjunction with Perdiccas, brought this army
all the way from the Peloponnesus was that they
were filled with alarm at the success of the Athenians.
The Chalcidians thought that the Athenians would
take the field against them first, and the cities in this
neighbourhood which had not yet revolted nevertheless took part secretly in inviting the Peloponnesians
to intervene. As for Perdiccas, although he was
not yet openly hostile to Athens, he also was afraid
of the long-standing differences between himself and
the Athenians, and above all he was anxious to
reduce Arrhabaeus, the king of the Lyncestians. A
further circumstance which rendered it easier for
them to procure an army from the Peloponnesus
was the evil fortune which at the present time
attended the Lacedaemonians.

LXXX. For since the Athenians kept harassing the
Peloponnesians, and especially the territory of the
Lacedaemonians, the latter thought that the best
way of diverting them would be to retaliate by
sending an army against their allies, especially since

αὐτῶν στρατιάν, ἄλλως τε καὶ ἑτοίμων ὄντων
τρέφειν τε καὶ ἐπὶ ἀποστάσει σφᾶς ἐπικαλου-
2 μένων. καὶ ἅμα τῶν Εἱλώτων βουλομένοις ἦν
ἐπὶ προφάσει ἐκπέμψαι, μή τι πρὸς τὰ παρόντα
3 τῆς Πύλου ἐχομένης νεωτερίσωσιν. ἐπεὶ καὶ τόδε
ἔπραξαν φοβούμενοι αὐτῶν τὴν νεότητα καὶ τὸ
πλῆθος (αἰεὶ γὰρ τὰ πολλὰ Λακεδαιμονίοις πρὸς
τοὺς Εἵλωτας τῆς φυλακῆς πέρι μάλιστα καθέ-
στηκεν)· προεῖπον αὐτῶν ὅσοι ἀξιοῦσιν ἐν τοῖς
πολεμίοις γεγενῆσθαι σφίσιν ἄριστοι, κρίνεσθαι,
ὡς ἐλευθερώσοντες, πεῖραν ποιούμενοι καὶ ἡγούμενοι τούτους σφίσιν ὑπὸ φρονήματος, οἵπερ καὶ
ἠξίωσαν πρῶτος ἕκαστος ἐλευθεροῦσθαι, μάλιστα
4 ἂν καὶ ἐπιθέσθαι. καὶ προκρινάντων ἐς δισχιλίους
οἱ μὲν ἐστεφανώσαντό τε καὶ τὰ ἱερὰ περιῆλθον
ὡς ἠλευθερωμένοι, οἱ δὲ οὐ πολλῷ ὕστερον ἠφάνι-
σάν τε αὐτοὺς καὶ οὐδεὶς ᾔσθετο ὅτῳ τρόπῳ
5 ἕκαστος διεφθάρη. καὶ τότε προθύμως τῷ Βρασίδᾳ
αὐτῶν ξυνέπεμψαν ἑπτακοσίους ὁπλίτας, τοὺς δ'
ἄλλους ἐκ τῆς Πελοποννήσου μισθῷ πείσας ἐξή-
γαγεν.

LXXXI. Αὐτόν τε Βρασίδαν βουλόμενον[1]
μάλιστα Λακεδαιμόνιοι ἀπέστειλαν (προυθυμή-
θησαν δὲ καὶ οἱ Χαλκιδῆς), ἄνδρα ἔν τε τῇ Σπάρτῃ

---

[1] βουλόμενον, with the MSS. Hude reads βουλόμενοι.

these allies were ready to maintain an army and were calling upon the Lacedaemonians for help in order that they might revolt. Furthermore, the Lacedaemonians were glad to have an excuse for sending out some of the Helots, in order to forestall their attempting a revolt at the present juncture when Pylos was in the possession of the enemy. Indeed, through fear of their youth [1] and numbers —for in fact most of their measures have always been adopted by the Lacedaemonians with a view to guarding against the Helots—they had once even resorted to the following device. They made proclamation that all Helots who claimed to have rendered the Lacedaemonians the best service in war should be set apart, ostensibly to be set free. They were, in fact, merely testing them, thinking that those who claimed, each for himself, the first right to be set free would be precisely the men of high spirit who would be the most likely to attack their masters. About two thousand of them were selected and these put crowns on their heads and made the rounds of the temples, as though they were already free, but the Spartans not long afterwards made away with them, and nobody ever knew in what way each one perished. So, on the present occasion, the Spartans gladly sent with Brasidas seven hundred Helots as hoplites, the rest of his forces being drawn from the Peloponnesus by the inducement of pay.

LXXXI. As for Brasidas himself, the Lacedaemonians sent him chiefly at his own desire, though the Chalcidians also were eager to have him. He was a man esteemed at Sparta as being energetic in

---

[1] Most MSS. read νεότητα, B σκαιότητα, but some word meaning "boldness" or "recklessness" seems to be required. Hude adopts Widmann's conjecture καινότητα.

δοκοῦντα δραστήριον εἶναι ἐς τὰ πάντα καὶ ἐπειδὴ
ἐξῆλθε πλείστου ἄξιον Λακεδαιμονίοις γενόμενον.
2 τό τε γὰρ παραυτίκα ἑαυτὸν παρασχὼν δίκαιον
καὶ μέτριον ἐς τὰς πόλεις ἀπέστησε τὰ πολλά, τὰ
δὲ προδοσίᾳ εἷλε τῶν χωρίων, ὥστε τοῖς Λακεδαιμονίοις γίγνεσθαι ξυμβαίνειν τε βουλομένοις,
ὅπερ ἐποίησαν, ἀνταπόδοσιν καὶ ἀποδοχὴν χωρίων
καὶ τοῦ πολέμου ἀπὸ τῆς Πελοποννήσου λώφησιν·
ἔς τε τὸν χρόνῳ ὕστερον μετὰ τὰ ἐκ Σικελίας
πόλεμον ἡ τότε Βρασίδου ἀρετὴ καὶ ξύνεσις, τῶν
μὲν πείρᾳ αἰσθομένων, τῶν δὲ ἀκοῇ νομισάντων,
μάλιστα ἐπιθυμίαν ἐνεποίει τοῖς Ἀθηναίων ξυμ-
3 μάχοις ἐς τοὺς Λακεδαιμονίους. πρῶτος γὰρ ἐξελ-
θὼν καὶ δόξας εἶναι κατὰ πάντα ἀγαθὸς ἐλπίδα
ἐγκατέλιπε βέβαιον ὡς καὶ οἱ ἄλλοι τοιοῦτοί
εἰσιν.

LXXXII. Τότε δ᾽ οὖν ἀφικομένου αὐτοῦ ἐς τὰ
ἐπὶ Θρᾴκης οἱ Ἀθηναῖοι πυθόμενοι τόν τε Περδίκκαν πολέμιον ποιοῦνται, νομίσαντες αἴτιον
εἶναι τῆς παρόδου, καὶ τῶν ταύτῃ ξυμμάχων
φυλακὴν πλέονα κατεστήσαντο. LXXXIII. Περδίκκας δὲ Βρασίδαν καὶ τὴν στρατιὰν εὐθὺς λαβὼν
μετὰ τῆς ἑαυτοῦ δυνάμεως στρατεύει ἐπὶ Ἀρράβαιον τὸν Βρομεροῦ, Λυγκηστῶν Μακεδόνων
βασιλέα, ὅμορον ὄντα, διαφορᾶς τε αὐτῷ οὔσης
2 καὶ βουλόμενος καταστρέψασθαι. ἐπεὶ δὲ ἐγένετο
τῷ στρατῷ μετὰ τοῦ Βρασίδου ἐπὶ τῇ ἐσβολῇ τῆς

everything he did, and indeed, after he had gone abroad, he proved invaluable to the Lacedaemonians. For, at the present crisis, by showing himself just and moderate in his dealings with the cities he caused most of the places to revolt, and secured possession of others by the treachery of their inhabitants, so that when the Lacedaemonians wished to make terms with Athens, as they did ultimately,[1] they had places to offer in exchange for places they wished to recover and were able to secure for the Peloponnesus a respite from the war; and in the later part of the war, after the events in Sicily, it was the virtue and tact which Brasidas had displayed at this time—qualities of which some had had experience, while others knew of them by report—that did most to inspire in the allies of the Athenians a sentiment favourable to the Lacedaemonians. For since he was the first Lacedaemonian abroad who gained a reputation for being in all respects a good man, he left behind him a confident belief that the other Lacedaemonians also were of the same stamp.

LXXXII. On the arrival of Brasidas in Thrace at the time referred to,[2] the Athenians, on hearing of it, declared Perdiccas an enemy, regarding him as responsible for his coming, and they established a stricter watch over their allies in that region. LXXXIII. But Perdiccas immediately took Brasidas and his army, together with his own forces, and made an expedition against his neighbour Arrhabaeus, son of Bromerus, king of the Lyncestian Macedonians; for he had a quarrel with him and wished to subdue him. . But when he and Brasidas arrived with their combined armies at the pass leading

[1] 421 B.C.; cf. V. xvii. [2] cf. ch. lxxix. 1.

Λύγκου, Βρασίδας ἐς λόγους[1] ἔφη βούλεσθαι
πρῶτον ἐλθὼν πρὸ πολέμου Ἀρράβαιον ξύμμαχον
3 Λακεδαιμονίων, ἢν δύνηται, ποιῆσαι. καὶ γάρ τι
καὶ Ἀρράβαιος ἐπεκηρυκεύετο, ἑτοῖμος ὢν Βρασίδᾳ
μέσῳ δικαστῇ ἐπιτρέπειν· καὶ οἱ Χαλκιδέων
πρέσβεις ξυμπαρόντες ἐδίδασκον αὐτὸν μὴ ὑπεξ-
ελεῖν τῷ Περδίκκᾳ τὰ δεινά, ἵνα προθυμοτέρῳ
4 ἔχοιεν καὶ ἐς τὰ ἑαυτῶν χρῆσθαι. ἅμα δέ τι καὶ
εἰρήκεσαν τοιοῦτον οἱ παρὰ τοῦ Περδίκκου ἐν τῇ
Λακεδαίμονι, ὡς πολλὰ αὐτοῖς τῶν περὶ αὐτὸν
χωρίων ξύμμαχα ποιήσοι, ὥστε ἐκ τοῦ τοιούτου
κοινῇ μᾶλλον ὁ Βρασίδας τὰ τοῦ Ἀρραβαίου
5 ἠξίου πράσσειν. Περδίκκας δὲ οὔτε δικαστὴν ἔφη
Βρασίδαν τῶν σφετέρων διαφορῶν ἀγαγεῖν, μᾶλλον δὲ καθαιρέτην ὧν ἂν αὐτὸς ἀποφαίνῃ πολεμίων, ἀδικήσειν τε εἰ αὐτοῦ τρέφοντος τὸ ἥμισυ
6 τοῦ στρατοῦ ξυνέσται Ἀρραβαίῳ. ὁ δὲ ἄκοντος
καὶ ἐκ διαφορᾶς ξυγγίγνεται, καὶ πεισθεὶς τοῖς
λόγοις ἀπήγαγε τὴν στρατιὰν πρὶν ἐσβαλεῖν ἐς
τὴν χώραν. Περδίκκας δὲ μετὰ τοῦτο τρίτον
μέρος ἀνθ' ἡμίσεος τῆς τροφῆς ἐδίδου, νομίζων
ἀδικεῖσθαι.

LXXXIV. Ἐν δὲ τῷ αὐτῷ θέρει εὐθὺς ὁ
Βρασίδας ἔχων καὶ Χαλκιδέας ἐπὶ Ἄκανθον τὴν
Ἀνδρίων ἀποικίαν ὀλίγον πρὸ τρυγήτου ἐστρά-
2 τευσεν. οἱ δὲ περὶ τοῦ δέχεσθαι αὐτὸν κατ'

---

[1] ἐς λόγους, van Herwerden's correction for λόγοις of the MSS.

to Lyncus, Brasidas said that he wished, before appealing to arms, to have a conference with Arrhabaeus and make him an ally of the Lacedaemonians, if he could. For it seemed that Arrhabaeus had made some overtures and was ready to submit the question at issue to Brasidas' arbitration; the Chalcidian envoys who were present also kept urging him not to remove the difficulties from the path of Perdiccas, since they wished to have in him a more zealous helper in their own affairs. Furthermore, the envoys of Perdiccas, when they were at Lacedaemon, had given a hint to the effect that he would bring many of the places in his neighbourhood into alliance with the Lacedaemonians; consequently Brasidas was inclined to insist upon having a freer hand in dealing with Arrhabaeus. But Perdiccas said that he had not brought Brasidas to be a judge of their quarrels, but rather to be a destroyer of any enemies whom he himself might designate, and that Brasidas would do wrong if, when he himself maintained half the army, he should parley with Arrhabaeus. But Brasidas, in spite of Perdiccas and after a quarrel with him, held the conference, and finding the king's arguments convincing, withdrew his army without invading his country. After this Perdiccas contributed only a third instead of one-half of the maintenance, considering himself to be aggrieved.

LXXXIV. Immediately afterwards during the same summer and a short time before the vintage season, Brasidas took some Chalcidians in addition to his own force and made an expedition against Acanthus, the colony of the Andrians. But on the question of admitting him the Acanthians were

ἀλλήλους ἐστασίαζον, οἵ τε μετὰ τῶν Χαλκιδέων
ξυνεπάγοντες καὶ ὁ δῆμος. ὅμως δὲ διὰ τοῦ
καρποῦ τὸ δέος ἔτι ἔξω ὄντος πεισθὲν τὸ πλῆθος
ὑπὸ τοῦ Βρασίδου δέξασθαί τε αὐτὸν μόνον καὶ
ἀκούσαντες βουλεύσασθαι, δέχεται· καὶ καταστὰς
ἐπὶ τὸ πλῆθος (ἦν δὲ οὐδὲ ἀδύνατος, ὡς Λακεδαιμόνιος, εἰπεῖν) ἔλεγε τοιάδε.

LXXXV. "'Η μὲν ἔκπεμψίς μου καὶ τῆς
στρατιᾶς ὑπὸ Λακεδαιμονίων, ὦ Ἀκάνθιοι,
γεγένηται τὴν αἰτίαν ἐπαληθεύουσα ἣν ἀρχόμενοι
τοῦ πολέμου προείπομεν, Ἀθηναίοις ἐλευθεροῦντες
2 τὴν Ἑλλάδα πολεμήσειν· εἰ δὲ χρόνῳ ἐπήλθομεν,
σφαλέντες τῆς ἀπὸ τοῦ ἐκεῖ πολέμου δόξης, ᾗ
διὰ τάχους αὐτοὶ ἄνευ τοῦ ὑμετέρου κινδύνου
ἠλπίσαμεν Ἀθηναίους καθαιρήσειν, μηδεὶς
μεμφθῇ· νῦν γάρ, ὅτε παρέσχεν, ἀφιγμένοι καὶ
μετὰ ὑμῶν πειρασόμεθα κατεργάζεσθαι αὐτούς.
3 θαυμάζω δὲ τῇ τε ἀποκλῄσει μου τῶν πυλῶν καὶ
4 εἰ μὴ ἀσμένοις ὑμῖν ἀφῖγμαι. ἡμεῖς μὲν γὰρ οἱ
Λακεδαιμόνιοι οἰόμενοί τε παρὰ ξυμμάχους, καὶ
πρὶν ἔργῳ ἀφικέσθαι, τῇ γοῦν γνώμῃ ἥξειν καὶ
βουλομένοις ἔσεσθαι, κίνδυνόν τε τοσόνδε ἀνερρί-
ψαμεν διὰ τῆς ἀλλοτρίας πολλῶν ἡμερῶν ὁδὸν
ἰόντες καὶ πᾶν τὸ πρόθυμον παρεσχόμεθα.[1]
5 ὑμεῖς δὲ εἴ τι ἄλλο ἐν νῷ ἔχετε ἢ εἰ ἐναντιώσεσθε
τῇ τε ὑμετέρᾳ αὐτῶν ἐλευθερίᾳ καὶ τῶν ἄλλων

[1] Rutherford's correction for παρεχόμενοι of the MSS.

divided among themselves, on the one side being those who, in concert with the Chalcidians, asked him to intervene, and on the other side the popular party. However, when Brasidas urged them to admit him unattended and then, after hearing what he had to say, to deliberate on the matter, the populace consented, for they had fears concerning the grapes, which had not yet been gathered. So he came before the people—and indeed, for a Lacedaemonian, he was not wanting in ability as a speaker—and addressed them as follows:

LXXXV. "Citizens of Acanthus, the Lacedaemonians have sent me and my army to prove the truth of what we proclaimed at the beginning to be the cause of the war, when we said that we were going to war with the Athenians for the liberation of Hellas. But if we have arrived late, disappointed as we have been with regard to the war at home, where we had hoped to destroy the Athenians quite speedily, by our own efforts and without involving you in the danger, do not blame us; for we are here now, having come as soon as opportunity offered, and together with you we shall try to subdue them. But I am amazed at the closing of your gates against me, and that my coming has been unwelcome to you. For we Lacedaemonians, thinking, even before we actually came, that we should find ourselves among men who were allies in spirit at least and that we should be welcomed, have hazarded the great danger of travelling a journey of many days through an alien territory and have shown all possible zeal. But if you have aught else in mind, or intend to stand in the way of your own freedom and that of the rest of the Hellenes, that would be

6 Ἑλλήνων, δεινὸν ἂν εἴη. καὶ γὰρ οὐχ ὅτι αὐτοὶ
ἀνθίστασθε, ἀλλὰ καὶ οἷς ἂν ἐπίω, ἧσσόν τις
ἐμοὶ πρόσεισι, δυσχερὲς ποιούμενοι εἰ ἐπὶ οὓς
πρῶτον ἦλθον ὑμᾶς, καὶ πόλιν ἀξιόχρεων παρεχο-
μένους καὶ ξύνεσιν δοκοῦντας ἔχειν, μὴ ἐδέξασθε,
καὶ τὴν αἰτίαν οὐ δόξω[1] πιστὴν ἀποδεικνύναι,
ἀλλ' ἢ ἄδικον τὴν ἐλευθερίαν ἐπιφέρειν ἢ ἀσθενὴς
καὶ ἀδύνατος τιμωρῆσαι τὰ πρὸς Ἀθηναίους, ἢν
7 ἐπίωσιν, ἀφῖχθαι. καίτοι στρατιᾷ γε τῇδ' ἣν νῦν
ἔχω ἐπὶ Νίσαιαν ἐμοῦ βοηθήσαντος οὐκ ἠθέλησαν Ἀθηναῖοι πλέονες ὄντες προσμεῖξαι, ὥστε
οὐκ εἰκὸς νηίτῃ[2] γε αὐτοὺς τῷ ἐν Νισαίᾳ[3]
στρατῷ ἴσον πλῆθος ἐφ' ὑμᾶς ἀποστεῖλαι.

LXXXVI. "Αὐτός τε οὐκ ἐπὶ κακῷ, ἐπ' ἐλευθερώσει δὲ τῶν Ἑλλήνων παρελήλυθα, ὅρκοις τε
Λακεδαιμονίων καταλαβὼν τὰ τέλη τοῖς μεγίστοις
ἦ μὴν οὓς ἂν ἔγωγε προσαγάγωμαι ξυμμάχους
ἔσεσθαι αὐτονόμους, καὶ ἅμα οὐχ ἵνα ξυμμάχους
ὑμᾶς ἔχωμεν ἢ βίᾳ ἢ ἀπάτῃ προσλαβόντες, ἀλλὰ
τοὐναντίον ὑμῖν δεδουλωμένοις ὑπὸ Ἀθηναίων
2 ξυμμαχήσοντες. οὔκουν ἀξιῶ οὔτ' αὐτὸς ὑποπ-
τεύεσθαι, πίστεις γε διδοὺς τὰς μεγίστας, οὔτε
τιμωρὸς ἀδύνατος νομισθῆναι, προσχωρεῖν δὲ
ὑμᾶς θαρσήσαντας.

3 "Καὶ εἴ τις ἰδίᾳ τινὰ δεδιὼς ἄρα, μὴ ἐγώ τισι
προσθῶ τὴν πόλιν, ἀπρόθυμός ἐστι, πάντων

[1] Sauppe's correction for οὐχ ἕξω of the MSS.
[2] So the MSS.; Hude emends to νηίτην.
[3] For ἐν Νισαίᾳ Hude adopts ἐκεῖ, with E, against the
other MSS.

monstrous. For it is not merely that you yourselves oppose me, but that all to whom I may apply will be less inclined to join me, raising the objection that you to whom I first came, representing as you do an important city and reputed to be men of sense, did not receive me. And it will seem[1] that the reason which I give for your refusal is not to be believed, but that either the freedom I offered you is not honourable, or that when I came to you I was powerless and unable to defend you against the Athenians if they should attack you. And yet when I brought aid to Nisaea with the very army which I now have, the Athenians were unwilling, though superior in numbers, to engage us, so that they are not likely to send against you by sea a number equal to the armament they had at Nisaea.

LXXXVI. "As for myself, I have come here not to harm but to liberate the Hellenes, having bound the government of the Lacedaemonians by the most solemn oaths that in very truth those whom I should win as allies should enjoy their own laws; and further, we are come, not that we may have you as allies, winning you over either by force or fraud, but to offer our alliance to you who have been enslaved by the Athenians. I claim, therefore, that I ought not either myself to be suspected, offering as I do the most solemn pledges, or to be accounted an impotent champion, but that you should boldly come over to me.

"And if anyone, possibly, being privately afraid of somebody is half-hearted through fear that I may put the city into the hands of some party or

[1] Or, reading οὐχ ἕξω, "And I shall have to submit to the charge of not being able to give a reason for your refusal that can be believed, but of offering, etc."

4 μάλιστα πιστευσάτω. οὐ γὰρ ξυστασιάσων
ἥκω, οὐδὲ ἂν σαφῆ[1] τὴν ἐλευθερίαν νομίζω ἐπιφέρειν, εἰ τὸ πάτριον παρεὶς τὸ πλέον τοῖς
ὀλίγοις ἢ τὸ ἔλασσον τοῖς πᾶσι δουλώσαιμι.
5 χαλεπωτέρα γὰρ ἂν τῆς ἀλλοφύλου ἀρχῆς εἴη,
καὶ ἡμῖν τοῖς Λακεδαιμονίοις οὐκ ἂν ἀντὶ πόνων
χάρις καθίσταιτο, ἀντὶ δὲ τιμῆς καὶ δόξης αἰτία
μᾶλλον· οἷς τε τοὺς Ἀθηναίους ἐγκλήμασι
καταπολεμοῦμεν, αὐτοὶ ἂν φαινοίμεθα ἐχθίονα
6 ἢ ὁ μὴ ὑποδείξας ἀρετὴν κατακτώμενοι. ἀπάτῃ
γὰρ εὐπρεπεῖ αἴσχιον[2] τοῖς γε ἐν ἀξιώματι
πλεονεκτῆσαι ἢ βίᾳ ἐμφανεῖ· τὸ μὲν γὰρ ἰσχύος
δικαιώσει, ἣν ἡ τύχη ἔδωκεν, ἐπέρχεται, τὸ δὲ
γνώμης ἀδίκου ἐπιβουλῇ. LXXXVII. οὕτω
πολλὴν περιωπὴν τῶν ἡμῖν[3] ἐς τὰ μέγιστα
διαφόρων ποιούμεθα, καὶ οὐκ ἂν μείζω πρὸς
τοῖς ὅρκοις βεβαίωσιν λάβοιτε, ἢ[4] οἷς τὰ ἔργα
ἐκ τῶν λόγων ἀναθρούμενα δόκησιν ἀναγκαίαν
παρέχεται ὡς καὶ ξυμφέρει ὁμοίως ὡς εἶπον.

2   "Εἰ δ' ἐμοῦ ταῦτα προϊσχομένου ἀδύνατοι μὲν
φήσετε εἶναι, εὖνοι δ' ὄντες ἀξιώσετε μὴ κακού-
μενοι διωθεῖσθαι, καὶ τὴν ἐλευθερίαν μὴ ἀκίνδυνον
ὑμῖν φαίνεσθαι, δίκαιόν τε εἶναι, οἷς καὶ δυνατὸν
δέχεσθαι αὐτήν, τούτοις καὶ ἐπιφέρειν, ἄκοντα δὲ

[1] ἂν σαφῆ, Bauer's correction for ἀσαφῆ of the MSS.
[2] Hude writes αἴσχιόν τι, after Stobaeus.
[3] Hude writes ὑμῖν, with Stahl.   [4] Deleted by Hude.

other,[1] let him most of all have confidence. For I am not come to join a faction, nor do I think that the freedom I am offering would be a real one if, regardless of your ancestral institutions, I should enslave the majority to the few or the minority to the multitude. That would be more galling than foreign rule, and for us Lacedaemonians the result would be, not thanks for our pains, but, instead of honour and glory, only reproach; and the very charges on which we are waging war to the death against the Athenians we should be found to be bringing home to ourselves in a more odious form than the power which has made no display of virtue. For it is more shameful, at least to men of reputation, to gain advantage by specious deceit than by open force; for the one makes assault by the assertion of power, which is the gift of fortune, the other by the intrigues of deliberate injustice. LXXXVII. Consequently we Lacedaemonians use great circumspection as regards matters that concern us in the highest degree[2]; and you could not get better security, in addition to our oaths, than where you have men whose actions scrutinized in the light of their professions furnish the irresistible conviction that their interests are indeed exactly as they have said.

"But if you meet these offers of mine with the plea that you cannot join us, but, because you are well-disposed to us, claim that you should not suffer by your refusal, and maintain that the liberty I offer seems to you to be not without its dangers, and that it is right to offer it to those who can receive it but not to force

---

[1] *i.e.* the dreaded ὀλίγοι.
[2] Referring to Sparta's reputation for justice.

μηδένα προσαναγκάζειν, μάρτυρας μὲν θεοὺς καὶ
ἥρως τοὺς ἐγχωρίους ποιήσομαι ὡς ἐπ' ἀγαθῷ
ἥκων οὐ πείθω, γῆν δὲ τὴν ὑμετέραν δῃῶν πειρά-
3 σομαι βιάζεσθαι, καὶ οὐκ ἀδικεῖν ἔτι νομιῶ,
προσεῖναι δέ τί μοι καὶ κατὰ δύο ἀνάγκας τὸ
εὔλογον, τῶν μὲν Λακεδαιμονίων, ὅπως μὴ τῷ
ὑμετέρῳ εὔνῳ, εἰ μὴ προσαχθήσεσθε, τοῖς ἀπὸ
ὑμῶν χρήμασι φερομένοις παρ' Ἀθηναίους βλάπ-
τωνται, οἱ δὲ Ἕλληνες ἵνα μὴ κωλύωνται ὑφ'
4 ὑμῶν δουλείας ἀπαλλαγῆναι. οὐ γὰρ δὴ εἰκότως
γ' ἂν τάδε πράσσοιμεν, οὐδὲ ὀφείλομεν οἱ Λακεδαιμόνιοι μὴ κοινοῦ τινος ἀγαθοῦ αἰτίᾳ τοὺς μὴ
5 βουλομένους ἐλευθεροῦν· οὐδ' αὖ ἀρχῆς ἐφιέμεθα,
παῦσαι δὲ μᾶλλον ἑτέρους σπεύδοντες τοὺς
πλείους ἂν ἀδικοῖμεν, εἰ ξύμπασιν αὐτονομίαν
ἐπιφέροντες ὑμᾶς τοὺς ἐναντιουμένους περιίδοιμεν.
6 πρὸς ταῦτα βουλεύεσθε εὖ, καὶ ἀγωνίσασθε τοῖς
τε Ἕλλησιν ἄρξαι πρῶτοι ἐλευθερίας καὶ ἀίδιον
δόξαν καταθέσθαι, καὶ αὐτοὶ τά τε ἴδια μὴ
βλαφθῆναι καὶ ξυμπάσῃ τῇ πόλει τὸ κάλλιστον
ὄνομα περιθεῖναι."

LXXXVIII. Ὁ μὲν Βρασίδας τοσαῦτα εἶπεν.
οἱ δὲ Ἀκάνθιοι, πολλῶν λεχθέντων πρότερον ἐπ'
ἀμφότερα, κρύφα διαψηφισάμενοι, διά τε τὸ
ἐπαγωγὰ εἰπεῖν τὸν Βρασίδαν καὶ περὶ τοῦ
καρποῦ φόβῳ ἔγνωσαν οἱ πλείους ἀφίστασθαι
Ἀθηναίων, καὶ πιστώσαντες αὐτὸν τοῖς ὅρκοις
οὓς τὰ τέλη τῶν Λακεδαιμονίων ὀμόσαντα αὐτὸν
ἐξέπεμψαν, ἦ μὴν ἔσεσθαι ξυμμάχους αὐτονόμους

it on anyone against his will, I shall make the gods
and heroes of your country my witnesses that, though
I come for your good, I cannot persuade you, and I
shall try, by ravaging your territory, to compel you;
and in that case I shall not consider that I am doing
wrong, but that I have some justification, for two
compelling reasons: first, in the interest of the
Lacedaemonians, that with all your professed goodwill toward them they may not, in case you shall
not be brought over, be injured by the money you
pay as tribute to the Athenians; secondly, that the
Hellenes may not be prevented by you from escaping
bondage. For otherwise we should not be justified
in acting thus, nor are we Lacedaemonians bound,
except on the plea of some common good, to confer
liberty on those who do not wish it. Nor, again, are
we seeking after empire, but rather we are eager
to stop others from acquiring it; and we should
do wrong to the majority, if, when we are bringing
independence to all, we permitted you to stand in
the way. In view of these things, deliberate wisely,
and strive to be the first to inaugurate freedom
for the Hellenes and to lay up for yourselves undying fame; thus you will save your own property
from injury and confer upon your whole state the
fairest name."

LXXXVIII. Such was the speech of Brasidas. But
the Acanthians, after much had been said on both
sides of the question, took a secret vote, and, on
account of Brasidas' impassioned words and their fears
about the harvest, the majority decided to revolt from
the Athenians; then having bound him with the
oaths which the authorities of the Lacedaemonians
swore when they sent him out, namely, that those

THUCYDIDES

οὓς ἂν προσαγάγηται, οὕτω δέχονται τὸν στρατόν.
2 καὶ οὐ πολὺ ὕστερον καὶ Στάγιρος Ἀνδρίων
ἀποικία ξυναπέστη. ταῦτα μὲν οὖν ἐν τῷ θέρει
τούτῳ ἐγένετο.

LXXXIX. Τοῦ δ' ἐπιγιγνομένου χειμῶνος εὐθὺς
ἀρχομένου, ὡς τῷ Ἱπποκράτει καὶ Δημοσθένει
στρατηγοῖς οὖσιν Ἀθηναίων τὰ ἐν τοῖς Βοιωτοῖς
ἐνεδίδοτο καὶ ἔδει τὸν μὲν Δημοσθένη ταῖς ναυσὶν
ἐς τὰς Σίφας ἀπαντῆσαι, τὸν δ' ἐπὶ τὸ Δήλιον,
γενομένης διαμαρτίας τῶν ἡμερῶν ἐς ἃς ἔδει
ἀμφοτέρους στρατεύειν, ὁ μὲν Δημοσθένης πρότερον πλεύσας πρὸς τὰς Σίφας καὶ ἔχων ἐν ταῖς
ναυσὶν Ἀκαρνᾶνας καὶ τῶν ἐκεῖ πολλοὺς ξυμμάχων, ἄπρακτος γίγνεται μηνυθέντος τοῦ
ἐπιβουλεύματος ὑπὸ Νικομάχου, ἀνδρὸς Φωκέως
ἐκ Φανοτέως, ὃς Λακεδαιμονίοις εἶπεν, ἐκεῖνοι δὲ
2 Βοιωτοῖς· καὶ βοηθείας γενομένης πάντων
Βοιωτῶν (οὐ γάρ πω Ἱπποκράτης παρελύπει ἐν
τῇ γῇ ὤν) προκαταλαμβάνονται αἵ τε Σίφαι καὶ
ἡ Χαιρώνεια. ὡς δὲ ᾔσθοντο οἱ πράσσοντες
τὸ ἁμάρτημα, οὐδὲν ἐκίνησαν τῶν ἐν ταῖς
πόλεσιν.

XC. Ὁ δὲ Ἱπποκράτης ἀναστήσας Ἀθηναίους
πανδημεί, αὐτοὺς καὶ τοὺς μετοίκους καὶ ξένων
ὅσοι παρῆσαν, ὕστερος ἀφικνεῖται ἐπὶ τὸ Δήλιον,
ἤδη τῶν Βοιωτῶν ἀνακεχωρηκότων ἀπὸ τῶν
Σιφῶν· καὶ καθίσας τὸν στρατὸν Δήλιον ἐτείχιζε
2 τοιῷδε τρόπῳ.[1] τάφρον μὲν κύκλῳ περὶ τὸ ἱερὸν
καὶ τὸν νεὼν ἔσκαπτον, ἐκ δὲ τοῦ ὀρύγματος
ἀνέβαλλον ἀντὶ τείχους τὸν χοῦν, καὶ σταυροὺς

[1] τὸ ἱερὸν τοῦ Ἀπόλλωνος, after τρόπῳ in the MSS., deleted by Dobree.

whom he might win over should be autonomous allies, they finally received the army. And not long afterwards Stagirus,[1] a colony of the Andrians, joined in the revolt. Such then, were the events of that summer.

LXXXIX. At the very beginning of the following winter,[2] when the places in Boeotia were to be delivered to Hippocrates and Demosthenes, the Athenian generals, Demosthenes was to have been present with his ships at Siphae, the other general at Delium. But a mistake was made as to the days when both were to start, and Demosthenes sailed too soon to Siphae, having Acarnanians and many allies from that region on board, and so proved unsuccessful; for the plot had been betrayed by Nicomachus, a Phocian from Phanotis, who told the Lacedaemonians, and they the Boeotians. Accordingly succour came from all the Boeotians—for Hippocrates was not yet in their country to annoy them—and both Siphae and Chaeroneia were occupied in advance; and the conspirators, learning of the mistake, attempted no disturbance in the towns.

XC. Meanwhile Hippocrates levied all the forces of Athens, both citizens and resident aliens, and such foreigners as were in the city. But he arrived at Delium too late, after the Boeotians had already withdrawn from Siphae. Then, after settling his army in camp, he proceeded to fortify Delium in the following manner. They dug a ditch round the temple and the sacred precinct and threw up the earth from the ditch to serve for a wall, fixing stakes along

---

[1] About twelve miles north of Acanthus, known also as Stageira, the birthplace of Aristotle.

[2] Resumption of the narrative of ch. lxxix.

παρακαταπηγνύντες ἄμπελον κόπτοντες τὴν περὶ
τὸ ἱερὸν ἐσέβαλλον καὶ λίθους ἅμα καὶ πλίνθον
ἐκ τῶν οἰκοπέδων τῶν ἐγγὺς καθαιροῦντες, καὶ
παντὶ τρόπῳ ἐμετεώριζον τὸ ἔρυμα. πύργους τε
ξυλίνους κατέστησαν ᾗ καιρὸς ἦν καὶ τοῦ ἱεροῦ
οἰκοδόμημα οὐδὲν ὑπῆρχεν· ἥπερ γὰρ ἦν στοὰ
3 κατεπεπτώκει. ἡμέρᾳ δὲ ἀρξάμενοι τρίτῃ ὡς
οἴκοθεν ὥρμησαν ταύτῃ τε εἰργάζοντο καὶ τὴν
4 τετάρτην καὶ τῆς πέμπτης μέχρι ἀρίστου. ἔπειτα,
ὡς τὰ πλεῖστα ἀπετετέλεστο, τὸ μὲν στρατόπεδον
προαπεχώρησεν ἀπὸ τοῦ Δηλίου οἷον δέκα
σταδίους ὡς ἐπ᾽ οἴκου πορευόμενον, καὶ οἱ μὲν
ψιλοὶ οἱ πλεῖστοι εὐθὺς ἐχώρουν, οἱ δ᾽ ὁπλῖται
θέμενοι τὰ ὅπλα ἡσύχαζον· Ἱπποκράτης δὲ
ὑπομένων ἔτι καθίστατο φυλακάς τε καὶ τὰ περὶ
τὸ προτείχισμα, ὅσα ἦν ὑπόλοιπα, ὡς χρὴν
ἐπιτελέσαι.

XCI. Οἱ δὲ Βοιωτοὶ ἐν ταῖς ἡμέραις ταύταις
ξυνελέγοντο ἐς τὴν Τάναγραν· καὶ ἐπειδὴ
ἀπὸ πασῶν τῶν πόλεων παρῆσαν καὶ ᾐσθάνοντο τοὺς Ἀθηναίους προχωροῦντας ἐπ᾽ οἴκου,
τῶν ἄλλων βοιωταρχῶν, οἵ εἰσιν ἕνδεκα, οὐ
ξυνεπαινούντων μάχεσθαι, ἐπειδὴ οὐκ ἐν τῇ
Βοιωτίᾳ ἔτι εἰσί (μάλιστα γὰρ ἐν μεθορίοις τῆς
Ὠρωπίας οἱ Ἀθηναῖοι ἦσαν, ὅτε ἔθεντο τὰ ὅπλα),
Παγώνδας ὁ Αἰολάδου βοιωταρχῶν ἐκ Θηβῶν
μετ᾽ Ἀριανθίδου τοῦ Λυσιμαχίδου καὶ ἡγεμονίας
οὔσης αὐτοῦ βουλόμενος τὴν μάχην ποιῆσαι καὶ
νομίζων ἄμεινον εἶναι κινδυνεῦσαι, προσκαλῶν
ἑκάστους κατὰ λόχους, ὅπως μὴ ἀθρόοι ἐκλίποιεν
τὰ ὅπλα, ἔπειθε τοὺς Βοιωτοὺς ἰέναι ἐπὶ τοὺς
Ἀθηναίους καὶ τὸν ἀγῶνα ποιεῖσθαι, λέγων τοιάδε.

it; and cutting down the grape-vines round the sanctuary, they threw them in, as well as stones and bricks from the neighbouring homesteads which they pulled down, and in every way strove to increase the height of the fortification. Wooden towers, too, were erected wherever there was occasion for them and no temple-structure was ready to hand; for the cloister that once existed had fallen down. Beginning on the third day after they started from home, they worked that day and the fourth and until dinner-time on the fifth. Then, when most of it had been finished, the main body withdrew from Delium about ten stadia on their way home; and most of the light-armed troops went straight on, while the hoplites grounded arms and halted there. Hippocrates, however, remained behind and was busy posting pickets and arranging to complete whatever was unfinished about the outwork.

XCI. But during these days the Boeotians were gathering at Tanagra; and when they had come in from all the cities and perceived that the Athenians were going home, the rest of the eleven Boeotarchs disapproved of fighting, as the enemy were no longer in Boeotia—for the Athenians were just about on the borders of Oropia when they halted. But Pagondas son of Aeolidas, who, with Arianthidas son of Lysimachidas, was Boeotarch from Thebes and then in chief command, wishing to bring on the battle and thinking it was better to take the risk, called the men by companies one after another, that they might not leave their arms all at once, and tried to persuade the Boeotians to go against the Athenians and bring on the contest, speaking as follows:

XCII. "Χρῆν μέν, ὦ ἄνδρες Βοιωτοί, μηδ᾽ ἐς
ἐπίνοιάν τινα ἡμῶν ἐλθεῖν τῶν ἀρχόντων ὡς οὐκ
εἰκὸς Ἀθηναίοις, ἢν ἄρα μὴ ἐν τῇ Βοιωτίᾳ ἔτι
καταλάβωμεν αὐτούς, διὰ μάχης ἐλθεῖν. τὴν
γὰρ Βοιωτίαν ἐκ τῆς ὁμόρου ἐλθόντες τεῖχος
ἐνοικοδομησάμενοι μέλλουσι φθείρειν, καὶ εἰσὶ
δήπου πολέμιοι ἐν ᾧ τε ἂν χωρίῳ καταληφθῶσι
2 καὶ ὅθεν ἐπελθόντες πολέμια ἔδρασαν. νυνὶ δ᾽
εἴ τῳ καὶ ἀσφαλέστερον ἔδοξεν εἶναι, μετα-
γνώτω. οὐ γὰρ τὸ προμηθές, οἷς ἂν ἄλλος ἐπίῃ,
περὶ τῆς σφετέρας ὁμοίως ἐνδέχεται λογισμὸν καὶ
ὅστις τὰ μὲν ἑαυτοῦ ἔχει, τοῦ πλείονος δὲ ὀρεγό-
3 μενος ἑκών τινι ἐπέρχεται. πάτριόν τε ὑμῖν
στρατὸν ἀλλόφυλον ἐπελθόντα καὶ ἐν τῇ οἰκείᾳ
καὶ ἐν τῇ τῶν πέλας ὁμοίως ἀμύνεσθαι· Ἀθηναίους δὲ καὶ προσέτι ὁμόρους ὄντας πολλῷ
4 μάλιστα δεῖ. πρός τε γὰρ τοὺς ἀστυγείτονας
πᾶσι τὸ ἀντίπαλον καὶ ἐλεύθερον καθίσταται, καὶ
πρὸς τούτους[1] γε δή, οἳ καὶ μὴ τοὺς ἐγγύς, ἀλλὰ
καὶ τοὺς ἄπωθεν πειρῶνται δουλοῦσθαι, πῶς οὐ
χρὴ καὶ ἐπὶ τὸ ἔσχατον ἀγῶνος ἐλθεῖν (παράδειγμα δὲ ἔχομεν τούς τε ἀντιπέρας Εὐβοέας καὶ
τῆς ἄλλης Ἑλλάδος τὸ πολὺ ὡς αὐτοῖς διάκειται),
καὶ γνῶναι ὅτι τοῖς μὲν ἄλλοις οἱ πλησιόχωροι
περὶ γῆς ὅρων τὰς μάχας ποιοῦνται, ἡμῖν δὲ ἐς
πᾶσαν, ἢν νικηθῶμεν, εἰς ὅρος οὐκ ἀντίλεκτος
παγήσεται· ἐσελθόντες γὰρ βίᾳ τὰ ἡμέτερα
5 ἕξουσιν. τοσούτῳ ἐπικινδυνοτέραν ἑτέρων τὴν

---

[1] Duker's correction for τούτοις of the MSS.

XCII. "It should never, men of Boeotia, have even entered the mind of any of us who are in command that we ought not to come to battle with the Athenians unless we should overtake them while still on Boeotian soil. For it was to ravage Boeotia that they came from across the frontier and built a fort in our territory, and they are assuredly equally our enemies wherever they may be caught, and especially on that soil from which they advanced to do the work of enemies. But as matters stand, if anyone did indeed think that course safer, let him change his mind. For where men are attacked prudence does not admit of such nice calculation regarding their own land as is permitted to those who, secure in their own possessions, in their greed for more wantonly attack others. Furthermore, it is hereditary with you when an alien army comes against you to ward it off, alike in your own land and in that of your neighbours; and most of all when the invaders are Athenians and moreover upon your borders. For in dealing with neighbours, it is always equality of force that guarantees liberty; and when the contest is against men like these, who are trying to enslave not only those near by but those far away, is it not necessary to fight to the very last? We have as a warning example their policy toward the Euboeans across the strait as well as toward the greater part of Hellas, and must realize that, whereas others make war with their neighbours about territorial boundaries, for us, if we are conquered, one boundary beyond dispute will be fixed for our whole land; for they will come and take by force all that we have. So much more dangerous is the neighbourhood of the Athenians

παροίκησιν τῶνδε ἔχομεν. εἰώθασί τε οἱ ἰσχύος
που θράσει τοῖς πέλας, ὥσπερ Ἀθηναῖοι νῦν,
ἐπιόντες τὸν μὲν ἡσυχάζοντα καὶ ἐν τῇ ἑαυτοῦ
μόνον ἀμυνόμενον ἀδεέστερον ἐπιστρατεύειν, τὸν
δὲ ἔξω ὅρων προαπαντῶντα καί, ἢν καιρὸς ᾖ,
6 πολέμου ἄρχοντα ἧσσον ἑτοίμως κατέχειν. πεῖραν δὲ ἔχομεν ἡμεῖς αὐτοῦ ἐς τούσδε· νικήσαντες
γὰρ ἐν Κορωνείᾳ αὐτούς, ὅτε τὴν γῆν ἡμῶν
στασιαζόντων κατέσχον, πολλὴν ἄδειαν τῇ
7 Βοιωτίᾳ μέχρι τοῦδε κατεστήσαμεν. ὧν χρὴ
μνησθέντας ἡμᾶς τούς τε πρεσβυτέρους ὁμοιω-
θῆναι τοῖς πρὶν ἔργοις, τούς τε νεωτέρους πατέρων
τῶν τότε ἀγαθῶν γενομένων παῖδας πειρᾶσθαι μὴ
αἰσχῦναι τὰς προσηκούσας ἀρετάς, πιστεύσαντας
δὲ τῷ θεῷ πρὸς ἡμῶν ἔσεσθαι, οὗ τὸ ἱερὸν ἀνόμως
τειχίσαντες νέμονται, καὶ τοῖς ἱεροῖς ἃ ἡμῖν
θυσαμένοις καλὰ φαίνεται, ὁμόσε χωρῆσαι τοῖσδε
καὶ δεῖξαι ὅτι ὧν μὲν ἐφίενται πρὸς τοὺς μὴ
ἀμυνομένους ἐπιόντες κτάσθων, οἷς δὲ γενναῖον
τήν τε αὐτῶν αἰεὶ ἐλευθεροῦν μάχῃ καὶ τὴν
ἄλλων μὴ δουλοῦσθαι ἀδίκως, ἀνανταγώνιστοι
ἀπ᾽ αὐτῶν οὐκ ἀπίασιν."

XCIII. Τοιαῦτα ὁ Παγώνδας τοῖς Βοιωτοῖς
παραινέσας ἔπεισεν ἰέναι ἐπὶ τοὺς Ἀθηναίους.
καὶ κατὰ τάχος ἀναστήσας ἦγε τὸν στρατόν (ἤδη
γὰρ καὶ τῆς ἡμέρας ὀψὲ ἦν), καὶ ἐπειδὴ προσέ-
μειξεν ἐγγὺς τοῦ στρατεύματος αὐτῶν, ἐς χωρίον
καθίσας ὅθεν λόφου ὄντος μεταξὺ οὐκ ἐθεώρουν
ἀλλήλους, ἔτασσέ τε καὶ παρεσκευάζετο ὡς ἐς

than that of others. Besides, people who in the confidence of strength attack their neighbours, as the Athenians now do, are wont to march more fearlessly against one who keeps quiet and defends himself only in his own land, but are less ready to grapple with him who meets them outside of his own boundaries and, if opportunity offers, makes the first attack. We have a proof of this in these Athenians; for at Coronea,[1] when owing to our internal dissensions they had occupied our land, we defeated them and won for Boeotia great security which has lasted to this day. Remembering these things, let the older men among us emulate their former deeds, and the younger, sons of fathers who then were brave, try not to disgrace the virtues which are their heritage. Trusting that the god whose sanctuary they have impiously fortified and now occupy will be on our side, and relying on the sacrifices, which appear to be propitious to us, who have offered them, let us advance to meet them and show that if they would get what they covet they must attack those who will not defend themselves, but that men whose noble spirit impels them always to fight for the liberty of their own land and not to enslave that of others unjustly will never let them depart without a battle."

XCIII. With such exhortations Pagondas persuaded the Boeotians to attack the Athenians, then quickly broke camp and led on his army, for it was already late in the day. When he drew near their army he halted at a place from which, because of an intervening hill, the two armies could not see each other, and there drew up and prepared for battle.

---

[1] 447 B.C.; cf. I. cxiii. 2; III. lxii. 5.

2 μάχην. τῷ δὲ Ἱπποκράτει[1] ὄντι περὶ τὸ Δήλιον
ὡς αὐτῷ ἠγγέλθη ὅτι Βοιωτοὶ ἐπέρχονται, πέμπει
ἐς τὸ στράτευμα κελεύων ἐς τάξιν καθίστασθαι,
καὶ αὐτὸς οὐ πολλῷ ὕστερον ἐπῆλθε, καταλιπὼν
ὡς τριακοσίους ἱππέας περὶ τὸ Δήλιον, ὅπως
φύλακές τε ἅμα εἶεν, εἴ τις ἐπίοι αὐτῷ, καὶ τοῖς
Βοιωτοῖς καιρὸν φυλάξαντες ἐπιγένοιντο ἐν τῇ
3 μάχῃ. Βοιωτοὶ δὲ πρὸς τούτους ἀντικατέστησαν
τοὺς ἀμυνουμένους, καὶ ἐπειδὴ καλῶς αὐτοῖς
εἶχεν, ὑπερεφάνησαν τοῦ λόφου καὶ ἔθεντο τὰ
ὅπλα τεταγμένοι ὥσπερ ἔμελλον, ὁπλῖται
ἑπτακισχίλιοι μάλιστα καὶ ψιλοὶ ὑπὲρ μυρίους,
ἱππῆς δὲ χίλιοι καὶ πελτασταὶ πεντακόσιοι.
4 εἶχον δὲ δεξιὸν μὲν κέρας Θηβαῖοι καὶ οἱ ξύμ-
μοροι αὐτοῖς· μέσοι δὲ Ἁλιάρτιοι καὶ Κορωναῖοι
καὶ Κωπαιῆς καὶ οἱ ἄλλοι οἱ περὶ τὴν λίμνην·
τὸ δὲ εὐώνυμον εἶχον Θεσπιῆς καὶ Ταναγραῖοι
καὶ Ὀρχομένιοι. ἐπὶ δὲ τῷ κέρα ἑκατέρῳ οἱ
ἱππῆς καὶ ψιλοὶ ἦσαν. ἐπ᾽ ἀσπίδας δὲ πέντε
μὲν καὶ εἴκοσι Θηβαῖοι ἐτάξαντο, οἱ δὲ ἄλλοι ὡς
5 ἕκαστοι ἔτυχον. αὕτη μὲν Βοιωτῶν παρασκευὴ
καὶ διάκοσμος ἦν.

XCIV. Ἀθηναῖοι δὲ οἱ μὲν ὁπλῖται ἐπὶ ὀκτὼ
πᾶν τὸ στρατόπεδον ἐτάξαντο ὄντες πλήθει
ἰσοπαλεῖς τοῖς ἐναντίοις, ἱππῆς δὲ ἐφ᾽ ἑκατέρῳ
τῷ κέρα. ψιλοὶ δὲ ἐκ παρασκευῆς μὲν ὡπλι-
σμένοι οὔτε τότε παρῆσαν οὔτε ἐγένοντο τῇ
πόλει· οἵπερ δὲ ξυνεσέβαλον, ὄντες πολλαπλάσιοι τῶν ἐναντίων, ἄοπλοί τε πολλοὶ ἠκολού-
θησαν, ἅτε πανστρατιᾶς ξένων τῶν παρόντων[2]

---

[1] Hude inserts ἔτι before ὄντι, with Rutherford, and deletes
αὐτῷ before ἠγγέλθη, with Krüger.   [2] Deleted by Hude.

Meanwhile Hippocrates, who was at Delium, on being informed that the Boeotians were coming on, sent orders to the army to fall in line, and himself not long afterwards joined them, leaving about three hundred cavalry at Delium, to guard it in case of attack and also to watch for an opportunity to fall upon the Boeotians in the course of the battle. But the Boeotians set a detachment to ward these off. Then when everything was ready they appeared over the hill and halted, drawn up in the order in which they were to fight, about seven thousand hoplites, over ten thousand light-armed troops, one thousand cavalry, and five hundred peltasts. On the right were the Thebans and their allies; in the centre the Haliartians, Coronaeans, Copaeans, and the other people around the lake;[1] on the left the Thespians, Tanagraeans and Orchomenians. On either wing were the cavalry and the light-armed troops. The Thebans were marshalled in ranks twenty-five shields deep, the rest as chance directed in each case. Such were the preparations of the Boeotians and their order of battle.

XCIV. On the Athenian side the whole body of hoplites, who were equal in number to those of the enemy, were marshalled eight deep, and the cavalry on either wing. But light-armed troops, regularly armed, were neither then present, nor did the city possess any; but such lighter forces as had joined in the invasion, while they were many times more numerous than the enemy, followed in large part without arms, as there had been a levy in mass of strangers that were in Athens as well as of citizens;

[1] Lake Copais.

καὶ ἀστῶν γενομένης, καὶ ὡς τὸ πρῶτον ὥρμησαν
2 ἐπ᾿ οἴκου, οὐ παρεγένοντο ὅτι μὴ ὀλίγοι. καθε-
στώτων δὲ ἐς τὴν τάξιν καὶ ἤδη μελλόντων
ξυνιέναι, Ἱπποκράτης ὁ στρατηγὸς ἐπιπαριὼν τὸ
στρατόπεδον τῶν Ἀθηναίων παρεκελεύετό τε καὶ
ἔλεγε τοιάδε.

XCV. "῏Ω Ἀθηναῖοι, δι᾿ ὀλίγου μὲν ἡ παραί-
νεσις γίγνεται, τὸ ἴσον δὲ πρός γε τοὺς ἀγαθοὺς
ἄνδρας δύναται καὶ ὑπόμνησιν μᾶλλον ἔχει ἢ
2 ἐπικέλευσιν. παραστῇ δὲ μηδενὶ ὑμῶν ὡς ἐν τῇ
ἀλλοτρίᾳ οὐ προσῆκον τοσόνδε κίνδυνον ἀναρρι-
πτοῦμεν. ἐν γὰρ τῇ τούτων ὑπὲρ τῆς ἡμετέρας ὁ
ἀγὼν ἔσται· καὶ ἢν νικήσωμεν, οὐ μή ποτε ὑμῖν
Πελοποννήσιοι ἐς τὴν χώραν ἄνευ τῆς τῶνδε
ἵππου ἐσβάλωσιν, ἐν δὲ μιᾷ μάχῃ τήνδε τε
προσκτᾶσθε καὶ ἐκείνην μᾶλλον ἐλευθεροῦτε·
3 χωρήσατε οὖν ἀξίως ἐς αὐτοὺς τῆς τε πόλεως,
ἣν ἕκαστος πατρίδα ἔχων πρώτην ἐν τοῖς Ἕλλησιν ἀγάλλεται, καὶ τῶν πατέρων, οἳ τούσδε μάχῃ
κρατοῦντες μετὰ Μυρωνίδου ἐν Οἰνοφύτοις τὴν
Βοιωτίαν ποτὲ ἔσχον."

XCVI. Τοιαῦτα τοῦ Ἱπποκράτους παρακε-
λευομένου καὶ μέχρι μὲν μέσου τοῦ στρατοπέδου
ἐπελθόντος, τὸ δὲ πλέον οὐκέτι φθάσαντος, οἱ
Βοιωτοί, παρακελευσαμένου καὶ σφίσιν ὡς διὰ
ταχέων καὶ ἐνταῦθα Παγώνδου, παιανίσαντες
ἐπῇσαν ἀπὸ τοῦ λόφου. ἀντεπῇσαν δὲ καὶ οἱ
2 Ἀθηναῖοι καὶ προσέμειξαν δρόμῳ. καὶ ἑκατέρων
τῶν στρατοπέδων τὰ ἔσχατα οὐκ ἦλθεν ἐς χεῖρας,
ἀλλὰ τὸ αὐτὸ ἔπαθεν· ῥύακες γὰρ ἐκώλυσαν.
τὸ δὲ ἄλλο καρτερᾷ μάχῃ καὶ ὠθισμῷ ἀσπίδων
3 ξυνειστήκει. καὶ τὸ μὲν εὐώνυμον τῶν Βοιωτῶν

and, having once started homewards, they were not present at the action, except a few. When they were arranged in line and were about to engage, Hippocrates the general, passing along the Athenian line, exhorted them and spoke as follows:

XCV. " Men of Athens, my exhortation will not be long, but to brave men it will mean as much, and will be a reminder rather than an appeal. Let none of you think that because we are on foreign soil it is without cause that we are hazarding this great danger. For though the contest is on Boeotian soil, it will be in defence of our own ; and, if we win, the Peloponnesians, deprived of the Boeotian cavalry, will never again invade your territory, and in one battle you not only win this land but make more sure the freedom of your own. Advance to meet them, therefore, in a spirit worthy both of that state, the foremost in Hellas, which every one of you is proud to claim as his fatherland, and of the fathers who under Myronides vanquished these men at Oenophyta,[1] and became at one time masters of Boeotia."

XCVI. Hippocrates was thus exhorting his men and had got as far as the centre of the army, but no further, when the Boeotians, after they too had again been briefly harangued by Pagondas, raised the paean and came on from the hill. And the Athenians also advanced against them and met them on a run. The extremities of the line on either side never came to close quarters, for both had the same difficulty—they were hindered by swollen torrents. The rest were engaged in stubborn conflict, with shield pressed against shield. And the Boeotian left, as

---

[1] 456 b.c.

THUCYDIDES

καὶ μέχρι μέσου ἡσσᾶτο ὑπὸ τῶν Ἀθηναίων, καὶ
ἐπίεσαν τούς τε ἄλλους ταύτῃ καὶ οὐχ ἥκιστα
τοὺς Θεσπιᾶς. ὑποχωρησάντων γὰρ αὐτοῖς τῶν
παρατεταγμένων καὶ κυκλωθέντες [1] ἐν ὀλίγῳ,
οἵπερ διεφθάρησαν Θεσπιῶν, ἐν χερσὶν ἀμυνόμενοι κατεκόπησαν· καί τινες καὶ τῶν Ἀθηναίων
διὰ τὴν κύκλωσιν ταραχθέντες ἠγνόησάν τε καὶ
4 ἀπέκτειναν ἀλλήλους.   τὸ μὲν οὖν ταύτῃ ἡσσᾶτο
τῶν Βοιωτῶν καὶ πρὸς τὸ μαχόμενον κατέφυγε,
τὸ δὲ δεξιόν, ᾗ οἱ Θηβαῖοι ἦσαν, ἐκράτει τῶν
Ἀθηναίων καὶ ὠσάμενοι κατὰ βραχὺ τὸ πρῶτον
5 ἐπηκολούθουν.   καὶ ξυνέβη, Παγώνδου περιπέμ-
ψαντος δύο τέλη τῶν ἱππέων ἐκ τοῦ ἀφανοῦς
περὶ τὸν λόφον, ὡς ἐπόνει τὸ εὐώνυμον αὐτῶν,
καὶ ὑπερφανέντων αἰφνιδίως, τὸ νικῶν τῶν
Ἀθηναίων κέρας, νομίσαν ἄλλο στράτευμα
6 ἐπιέναι, ἐς φόβον καταστῆναι· καὶ ἀμφοτέρωθεν
ἤδη, ὑπό τε τοῦ τοιούτου καὶ ὑπὸ τῶν Θηβαίων
ἐφεπομένων καὶ παραρρηγνύντων, φυγὴ καθει-
στήκει παντὸς τοῦ στρατοῦ τῶν Ἀθηναίων.
7 καὶ οἱ μὲν πρὸς τὸ Δήλιόν τε καὶ τὴν θάλασσαν
ὥρμησαν, οἱ δὲ ἐπὶ τοῦ Ὠρωποῦ, ἄλλοι δὲ πρὸς
Πάρνηθα τὸ ὄρος, οἱ δὲ ὡς ἕκαστοί τινα εἶχον
8 ἐλπίδα σωτηρίας. Βοιωτοὶ δὲ ἐφεπόμενοι ἔκτεινον,
καὶ μάλιστα οἱ ἱππῆς οἵ τε αὐτῶν καὶ οἱ Λοκροὶ
βεβοηθηκότες ἄρτι τῆς τροπῆς γιγνομένης·
νυκτὸς δὲ ἐπιλαβούσης τὸ ἔργον ῥᾷον τὸ πλῆθος
τῶν φευγόντων διεσώθη. καὶ τῇ ὑστεραίᾳ οἵ τε
ἐκ τοῦ Ὠρωποῦ καὶ οἱ ἐκ τοῦ Δηλίου φυλακὴν
ἐγκαταλιπόντες (εἶχον γὰρ αὐτὸ ὅμως ἔτι)
ἀπεκομίσθησαν κατὰ θάλασσαν ἐπ' οἴκου.

[1] Krüger's correction for κυκλωθέντων of the MSS.

376

far as the centre, was worsted by the Athenians, who pressed hard upon all the rest in that quarter, and especially upon the Thespians. For when they saw that the ranks on either side had given way and that they were surrounded, those of the Thespians who perished were cut down fighting hand to hand. And some also of the Athenians, getting into confusion owing to their surrounding the enemy, mistook and killed one another. Here, then, the Boeotians were defeated and fled to the part of their army which was still fighting; but the right wing, where the Thebans were, had the better of the Athenians, and pushing them back step by step at first followed after them. It happened also that Pagondas, when their left was in distress, sent two squadrons of cavalry round the hill from a point out of sight, and when these suddenly appeared, the victorious wing of the Athenians, thinking that another army was coming on, was thrown into a panic. At this time, consequently, owing both to this manœuvre [1] and to the Thebans following them up and breaking their line, a rout of the whole Athenian army ensued. Some hastened to Delium and the sea, others toward Oropus, others to Mt. Parnes, others wherever each had any hope of safety. And the Boeotians, especially their cavalry and that of the Locrians who had come up just as the rout began, followed after and slew them; but when night closed down upon the action the mass of the fugitives escaped more easily. On the next day the troops from Oropus and those from Delium, leaving a garrison at the latter place, which they still held, were conveyed home by sea.[2]

[1] *i.e.* the attack of the two squadrons of cavalry.
[2] It is interesting to know that Socrates fought in the battle of Delium and saved Alcibiades' life (Plato, *Symp.* 221 e).

XCVII. Καὶ οἱ Βοιωτοὶ τροπαῖον στήσαντες καὶ τοὺς ἑαυτῶν ἀνελόμενοι νεκροὺς τούς τε τῶν πολεμίων σκυλεύσαντες καὶ φυλακὴν καταλιπόντες ἀνεχώρησαν ἐς τὴν Τάναγραν, καὶ τῷ 2 Δηλίῳ ἐπεβούλευον ὡς προσβαλοῦντες. ἐκ δὲ τῶν Ἀθηναίων κῆρυξ πορευόμενος ἐπὶ τοὺς νεκροὺς ἀπαντᾷ κήρυκι Βοιωτῷ, ὃς αὐτὸν ἀποστρέψας καὶ εἰπὼν ὅτι οὐδὲν πράξει πρὶν ἂν αὐτὸς ἀναχωρήσῃ πάλιν, καταστὰς ἐπὶ τοὺς Ἀθηναίους ἔλεγε τὰ παρὰ τῶν Βοιωτῶν, ὅτι οὐ δικαίως δράσειαν παραβαίνοντες τὰ νόμιμα τῶν 3 Ἑλλήνων· πᾶσι γὰρ εἶναι καθεστηκὸς ἰόντας ἐπὶ τὴν ἀλλήλων ἱερῶν τῶν ἐνόντων ἀπέχεσθαι, Ἀθηναίους δὲ Δήλιον τειχίσαντας ἐνοικεῖν, καὶ ὅσα ἄνθρωποι ἐν βεβήλῳ δρῶσι πάντα γίγνεσθαι αὐτόθι, ὕδωρ τε ὃ ἦν ἄψαυστον σφίσι πλὴν πρὸς τὰ ἱερὰ χέρνιβι χρῆσθαι, ἀνασπάσαντας ὑδρεύ- 4 εσθαι· ὥστε ὑπέρ τε τοῦ θεοῦ καὶ ἑαυτῶν Βοιωτούς, ἐπικαλουμένους τοὺς ὁμωχέτας δαίμονας καὶ τὸν Ἀπόλλω, προαγορεύειν αὐτοὺς ἐκ τοῦ ἱεροῦ ἀπιόντας ἀποφέρεσθαι τὰ σφέτερα αὐτῶν.

XCVIII. Τοσαῦτα τοῦ κήρυκος εἰπόντος οἱ Ἀθηναῖοι πέμψαντες παρὰ τοὺς Βοιωτοὺς ἑαυτῶν κήρυκα τοῦ μὲν ἱεροῦ οὔτε ἀδικῆσαι ἔφασαν οὐδὲν οὔτε τοῦ λοιποῦ ἑκόντες βλάψειν· οὐδὲ γὰρ τὴν ἀρχὴν ἐσελθεῖν ἐπὶ τούτῳ, ἀλλ᾽ ἵνα ἐξ αὐτοῦ τοὺς 2 ἀδικοῦντας μᾶλλον σφᾶς ἀμύνωνται. τὸν δὲ

XCVII. The Boeotians set up a trophy and took up their own dead ; then, having stripped the dead of the enemy and left a guard over them, they retired to Tanagra, and there planned an assault upon Delium. Meanwhile a herald from Athens, coming to ask for their dead, met a Boeotian herald, who turned him back, telling him he would accomplish nothing until he himself returned.[1] The latter then came before the Athenians and gave them the message from the Boeotians : that they had not done right in transgressing the usages of the Hellenes ; for it was an established custom of them all, when invading one another's country to abstain from the sanctuaries therein, whereas the Athenians had fortified Delium and now dwelt in it, doing there whatsoever men do in a profane place, even drawing for common use the water which was untouched by themselves except for use in lustrations connected with the sacrifices. Wherefore the Boeotians, in behalf of the god and of themselves, invoking the deities worshipped at the common altars and also Apollo, gave them notice to come out themselves from the temple and carry off what belonged to them.[2]

XCVIII. When the herald had spoken, the Athenians sent a herald of their own to the Boeotians, saying that they had done no injury to the temple, and would not damage it wilfully in the future ; for they had not entered it at the outset with any such intent, but rather that from it they might defend themselves against those who were wronging them. And the law of the

---

[1] i.e. to the Boeotian camp from the Athenian, to which he was carrying a message.　[2] i.e. their dead.

νόμον τοῖς Ἕλλησιν εἶναι, ὧν ἂν ᾖ τὸ κράτος τῆς
γῆς ἑκάστης, ἤν τε πλέονος ἤν τε βραχυτέρας,
τούτων καὶ τὰ ἱερὰ αἰεὶ γίγνεσθαι, τρόποις
θεραπευόμενα οἷς ἂν πρὸ τοῦ[1] εἰωθόσι καὶ
3 δύνωνται. καὶ γὰρ Βοιωτοὺς καὶ τοὺς πολλοὺς
τῶν ἄλλων, ὅσοι ἐξαναστήσαντές τινα βίᾳ
νέμονται γῆν, ἀλλοτρίοις ἱεροῖς τὸ πρῶτον
4 ἐπελθόντας οἰκεῖα νῦν κεκτῆσθαι. καὶ αὐτοί, εἰ
μὲν ἐπὶ πλέον δυνηθῆναι τῆς ἐκείνων κρατῆσαι,
τοῦτ᾽ ἂν ἔχειν· νῦν δὲ ἐν ᾧ μέρει εἰσίν, ἑκόντες
5 εἶναι ὡς ἐκ σφετέρου οὐκ ἀπιέναι. ὕδωρ τε
ἐν τῇ ἀνάγκῃ κινῆσαι, ἣν οὐκ αὐτοὶ ὕβρει
προσθέσθαι, ἀλλ᾽ ἐκείνους προτέρους ἐπὶ τὴν
σφετέραν ἐλθόντας ἀμυνόμενοι βιάζεσθαι χρῆ-
6 σθαι. πᾶν δ᾽ εἰκὸς εἶναι τὸ πολέμῳ καὶ δεινῷ τινι
κατειργόμενον ξύγγνωμόν τι γίγνεσθαι καὶ πρὸς
τοῦ θεοῦ. καὶ γὰρ τῶν ἀκουσίων ἁμαρτημάτων
καταφυγὴν εἶναι τοὺς βωμούς, παρανομίαν τε
ἐπὶ τοῖς μὴ ἀνάγκῃ κακοῖς ὀνομασθῆναι καὶ οὐκ
7 ἐπὶ τοῖς ἀπὸ τῶν ξυμφορῶν τι τολμήσασιν. τούς
τε νεκροὺς πολὺ μειζόνως ἐκείνους ἀντὶ ἱερῶν
ἀξιοῦντας ἀποδιδόναι ἀσεβεῖν ἢ τοὺς μὴ ἐθέλον-
8 τας ἱεροῖς τὰ πρέποντα κομίζεσθαι. σαφῶς τε
ἐκέλευον σφίσιν εἰπεῖν μὴ ἀπιοῦσιν ἐκ τῆς

---

[1] Stahl's conjecture for πρὸς τοῖς of the MSS.

Hellenes was, they said, that whosoever had dominion over any country, be it larger or smaller, to them the sanctuaries also always belonged, to be tended, so far as might be possible, with whatsoever rites had hitherto been customary.[1] Indeed the Boeotians, and most others who had driven out any people and taken forcible possession of their country, had at first attacked the temples as alien but now possessed them as their own. And they themselves, if they had been able to conquer more of the Boeotian territory, would have held it; but as it was, they would not depart from that portion in which they were, at least of their free will, considering it their own. The water, moreover, they had disturbed in their sore need, which they had not wantonly brought upon themselves; they had been forced to use the water while defending themselves against the Boeotians who had first invaded their land. And anything done under the constraint of war and danger might reasonably meet with some indulgence, even from the god. For altars were a refuge in cases of involuntary misdeeds, and transgression was a term applied to those who do evil without compulsion and not to those who are driven by misfortunes to some act of daring. Moreover, the Boeotians in presuming to give up the bodies of the dead in return for temples were impious in a much higher degree than they who refused by the exchange of temples to procure that which they had a right to recover. And they bade the Boeotians plainly tell them they might take up their dead, not

[1] Or, reading πρὸς τοῖς εἰωθόσι with the MSS., "to be tended, besides the usual rites, with such others as they might be able to use."

Βοιωτῶν γῆς (οὐ γὰρ ἐν τῇ ἐκείνων ἔτι εἶναι, ἐν ᾗ δὲ δορὶ ἐκτήσαντο), ἀλλὰ κατὰ τὰ πάτρια τοὺς νεκροὺς σπένδουσιν ἀναιρεῖσθαι.

XCIX. Οἱ δὲ Βοιωτοὶ ἀπεκρίναντο, εἰ μὲν ἐν τῇ Βοιωτίᾳ εἰσίν, ἀπιόντας ἐκ τῆς ἑαυτῶν ἀποφέρεσθαι τὰ σφέτερα, εἰ δὲ ἐν τῇ ἐκείνων, αὐτοὺς γιγνώσκειν τὸ ποιητέον, νομίζοντες τὴν μὲν Ὠρωπίαν, ἐν ᾗ τοὺς νεκροὺς ἐν μεθορίοις τῆς μάχης γενομένης κεῖσθαι ξυνέβη, Ἀθηναίων κατὰ τὸ ὑπήκοον εἶναι, καὶ οὐκ ἂν αὐτοὺς βίᾳ σφῶν κρατῆσαι αὐτῶν (οὐδ' αὖ ἐσπένδοντο δῆθεν ὑπὲρ τῆς ἐκείνων [1])· τὸ δὲ "ἐκ τῆς ἑαυτῶν" εὐπρεπὲς εἶναι ἀποκρίνασθαι "ἀπιόντας καὶ ἀπολαβεῖν ἃ ἀπαιτοῦσιν." ὁ δὲ κῆρυξ τῶν Ἀθηναίων ἀκούσας ἀπῆλθεν ἄπρακτος.

C. Καὶ οἱ Βοιωτοὶ εὐθὺς μεταπεμψάμενοι ἔκ τε τοῦ Μηλιῶς κόλπου ἀκοντιστὰς καὶ σφενδονήτας, καὶ βεβοηθηκότων αὐτοῖς μετὰ τὴν μάχην Κορινθίων τε δισχιλίων ὁπλιτῶν καὶ τῶν ἐκ Νισαίας ἐξεληλυθότων Πελοποννησίων φρουρῶν καὶ Μεγαρέων ἅμα, ἐστράτευσαν ἐπὶ τὸ Δήλιον καὶ προσέβαλον τῷ τειχίσματι, ἄλλῳ τε τρόπῳ πειράσαντες καὶ μηχανὴν προσήγαγον, ἥπερ εἷλεν αὐτό, τοιάνδε.

2 κεραίαν μεγάλην δίχα πρίσαντες ἐκοίλαναν ἅπασαν καὶ ξυνήρμοσαν πάλιν ἀκριβῶς ὥσπερ αὐλόν, [2] καὶ ἐπ' ἄκραν λέβητά τε ἤρτησαν ἁλύσεσι καὶ ἀκροφύσιον ἀπὸ τῆς κεραίας σιδηροῦν ἐς αὐτὸν νεῦον καθεῖτο, καὶ ἐσεσιδήρωτο ἐπὶ μέγα

---

[1] Parenthetical according to Poppo.
[2] ὥσπερ αὐλόν, deleted by Hude.

"on condition of quitting Boeotia "—for they were no longer in Boeotian territory, but in land which they had won by the spear,—but "on making a truce according to ancestral custom."

XCIX. The Boeotians made answer, if they were in Boeotia, they might carry off their dead on quitting their land; but if they were in their own territory, they could determine themselves what to do. For they thought that though Oropia, in which the bodies happened to be lying—for the battle occurred on the boundaries — belonged to the Athenians by right of its subjection, yet that they could not get possession of the bodies without their leave (nor indeed were they going to make a truce, forsooth, about territory belonging to the Athenians); but they thought it was fair to answer, "when they had quitted Boeotian territory they could get back what they asked for." And the herald of the Athenians, on hearing this, went away without accomplishing his object.

C. The Boeotians sent off at once for darters and slingers from the Maliac Gulf, and with two thousand Corinthian hoplites, who reinforced them after the battle, as well as the Peloponnesian garrison which had evacuated Nisaea, and some Megarians also, made an expedition against Delium and attacked the fortification. After trying other forms of assault they took it by bringing up an engine made in the following manner. Having sawed in two a great beam they hollowed it throughout, and fitted it together again nicely like a pipe; then they hung a cauldron at one end of it with chains, and into the cauldron an iron bellows-pipe was let down in a curve[1] from the beam, which was itself in great part plated

[1] *i.e.* it was bent into the cauldron.

3 καὶ τοῦ ἄλλου ξύλου. προσῆγον δὲ ἐκ πολλοῦ
ἁμάξαις τῷ τείχει, ᾗ μάλιστα τῇ ἀμπέλῳ καὶ
τοῖς ξύλοις ᾠκοδόμητο· καὶ ὁπότε εἴη ἐγγύς,
φύσας μεγάλας ἐσθέντες ἐς τὸ πρὸς ἑαυτῶν ἄκρον
4 τῆς κεραίας ἐφύσων. ἡ δὲ πνοὴ ἰοῦσα στεγανῶς
ἐς τὸν λέβητα, ἔχοντα ἄνθρακάς τε ἡμμένους
καὶ θεῖον καὶ πίσσαν, φλόγα ἐποίει μεγάλην καὶ
ἧψε τοῦ τείχους, ὥστε μηδένα ἔτι ἐπ' αὐτοῦ
μεῖναι, ἀλλὰ ἀπολιπόντας ἐς φυγὴν καταστῆναι
5 καὶ τὸ τείχισμα τούτῳ τῷ τρόπῳ ἁλῶναι. τῶν
δὲ φρουρῶν οἱ μὲν ἀπέθανον, διακόσιοι δὲ
ἐλήφθησαν· τῶν δὲ ἄλλων τὸ πλῆθος ἐς τὰς
ναῦς ἐσβὰν ἀπεκομίσθη ἐπ' οἴκου.

CI. Τοῦ δὲ Δηλίου ἑβδόμῃ καὶ δεκάτῃ [1] ἡμέρᾳ
ληφθέντος μετὰ τὴν μάχην καὶ τοῦ ἀπὸ τῶν
Ἀθηναίων κήρυκος οὐδὲν ἐπισταμένου τῶν
γεγενημένων ἐλθόντος οὐ πολὺ ὕστερον αὖθις
περὶ τῶν νεκρῶν, ἀπέδοσαν οἱ Βοιωτοὶ καὶ
2 οὐκέτι ταὐτὰ ἀπεκρίναντο. ἀπέθανον δὲ Βοιωτῶν
μὲν ἐν τῇ μάχῃ ὀλίγῳ ἐλάσσους πεντακοσίων,
Ἀθηναίων δὲ ὀλίγῳ ἐλάσσους χιλίων καὶ
Ἱπποκράτης ὁ στρατηγός, ψιλῶν δὲ καὶ σκευο-
φόρων πολὺς ἀριθμός.

3 Μετὰ δὲ τὴν μάχην ταύτην καὶ ὁ Δημοσθένης
ὀλίγῳ ὕστερον, ὡς αὐτῷ τότε πλεύσαντι τὰ περὶ
τὰς Σίφας τῆς προδοσίας πέρι οὐ προυχώρησεν,
ἔχων τὸν στρατὸν ἐπὶ τῶν νεῶν τῶν τε Ἀκαρνάνων καὶ Ἀγραίων, καὶ Ἀθηναίων τετρακοσίους
ὁπλίτας, ἀπόβασιν ἐποιήσατο ἐς τὴν Σικυωνίαν.
4 καὶ πρὶν πάσας τὰς ναῦς καταπλεῦσαι βοηθή-
σαντες οἱ Σικυώνιοι τοὺς ἀποβεβηκότας ἔτρεψαν
καὶ κατεδίωξαν ἐς τὰς ναῦς, καὶ τοὺς μὲν ἀπέ-

---

[1] Krüger's correction for ἑπτακαιδεκάτῃ of the MSS.

with iron. This engine they brought up from a distance on carts to the part of the wall where it was built chiefly of vines and wood; and when it was near, they inserted a large bellows into the end of the beam next to them and blew through it. And the blast passing through the air-tight tube into the cauldron, which contained lighted coals, sulphur, and pitch, made a great blaze and set fire to the wall, so that no one could stay on it longer, but all left it and took to flight; and in this way the fortification was taken. Of the garrison some were slain, and two hundred were captured; but most of the rest got on board their ships and were conveyed home.

CI. So Delium was taken seventeen days after the battle, and when the Athenian herald, who knew nothing of what had happened, came back not long after to ask for the dead, the Boeotians did not again make the same answer but gave them up. And there were slain in the battle, of the Boeotians a little more than five hundred, of the Athenians a little less than one thousand, including Hippocrates their general, besides a great number of light-armed troops and baggage-carriers.

Not long after this battle Demosthenes, since he had failed in his negotiations about the betrayal of Siphae, when he sailed thither at the time mentioned above,[1] took on his ships his force of Acarnanians and Agraeans and four hundred Athenian hoplites and made a descent upon the territory of Sicyon. But before all his ships had come to shore the Sicyonians came to the rescue, and routing those who had disembarked pursued them to their ships,

---

[1] cf. ch. lxxxix. 1.

κτειναν, τοὺς δὲ ζῶντας ἔλαβον. τροπαῖον δὲ
στήσαντες τοὺς νεκροὺς ὑποσπόνδους ἀπέδοσαν.

5 Ἀπέθανε δὲ καὶ Σιτάλκης Ὀδρυσῶν βασιλεύς
ὑπὸ τὰς αὐτὰς ἡμέρας τοῖς ἐπὶ Δηλίῳ, στρατεύσας
ἐπὶ Τριβαλλοὺς καὶ νικηθεὶς μάχῃ. Σεύθης δὲ ὁ
Σπαραδόκου ἀδελφιδοῦς ὢν αὐτοῦ ἐβασίλευσεν
Ὀδρυσῶν τε καὶ τῆς ἄλλης Θρᾴκης ἧσπερ καὶ
ἐκεῖνος.

CII. Τοῦ δ' αὐτοῦ χειμῶνος Βρασίδας ἔχων
τοὺς ἐπὶ Θρᾴκης ξυμμάχους ἐστράτευσεν ἐς
Ἀμφίπολιν τὴν ἐπὶ Στρυμόνι ποταμῷ Ἀθη-
2 ναίων ἀποικίαν. τὸ δὲ χωρίον τοῦτο ἐφ' οὗ νῦν
ἡ πόλις ἐστὶν ἐπείρασε μὲν πρότερον καὶ Ἀρι-
σταγόρας ὁ Μιλήσιος φεύγων βασιλέα Δαρεῖον
κατοικίσαι, ἀλλὰ ὑπὸ Ἠδώνων ἐξεκρούσθη,
ἔπειτα δὲ καὶ οἱ Ἀθηναῖοι ἔτεσι δύο καὶ τριάκοντα ὕστερον, ἐποίκους μυρίους σφῶν τε αὐτῶν
καὶ τῶν ἄλλων τὸν βουλόμενον πέμψαντες, οἳ
3 διεφθάρησαν ἐν Δραβησκῷ ὑπὸ Θρακῶν. καὶ
αὖθις ἑνὸς δέοντι τριακοστῷ ἔτει ἐλθόντες οἱ
Ἀθηναῖοι, Ἅγνωνος τοῦ Νικίου οἰκιστοῦ ἐκπεμ-
φθέντος, Ἠδώνας ἐξελάσαντες ἔκτισαν τὸ χωρίον
τοῦτο, ὅπερ πρότερον Ἐννέα ὁδοὶ ἐκαλοῦντο.
4 ὡρμῶντο δὲ ἐκ τῆς Ἠιόνος, ἣν αὐτοὶ εἶχον ἐμ-
πόριον ἐπὶ τῷ στόματι τοῦ ποταμοῦ ἐπιθαλάσ-
σιον, πέντε καὶ εἴκοσι σταδίους ἀπέχον ἀπὸ τῆς
νῦν πόλεως, ἣν Ἀμφίπολιν Ἅγνων ὠνόμασεν,
ὅτι ἐπ' ἀμφότερα περιρρέοντος τοῦ Στρυμόνος [1]
τείχει μακρῷ ἀπολαβὼν ἐκ ποταμοῦ ἐς ποταμὸν

---

[1] διὰ τὸ περιέχειν αὐτήν ("with a view to enclosing it") in
the MSS. after Στρυμόνος, deleted by Dobree.

killing some and taking others alive. Then setting up a trophy they gave up the dead under truce.

Sitalces,[1] too, king of the Odrysians, was killed about the same time as the events at Delium, having made an expedition against the Triballi,[2] who defeated him in battle. Seuthes[3] son of Sparadocus, his nephew, now became king of the Odrysians and of the rest of Thrace over which Sitalces had reigned.

CII. During the same winter, Brasidas, with his allies in Thrace, made an expedition against Amphipolis, the Athenian colony on the river Strymon. This place, where the city now stands, Aristagoras[4] the Milesian had tried to colonize before,[5] when fleeing from the Persian king, but he had been beaten back by the Edonians. Thirty-two years afterwards the Athenians also made another attempt, sending out ten thousand settlers of their own citizens and any others who wished to go; but these were destroyed by the Thracians at Drabescus. Again, twenty-nine years later, the Athenians, sending out Hagnon son of Nicias as leader of the colony, drove out the Edonians and settled the place, which was previously called Ennea-Hodoi or Nine-Ways. Their base of operations was Eion, a commercial seaport which they already held, at the mouth of the river, twenty-five stadia distant from the present city of Amphipolis,[6] to which Hagnon gave that name, because, as the Strymon flows round it on both sides, he cut off the site by a long wall running from one point of the river to another, and

---

[1] cf. ɪɪ. lxvii., xcv., ci.   [2] cf. ɪɪ. xcvi.
[3] cf. ɪɪ. ci. 5.   [4] cf. Hdt. v. 126.   [5] 497 B.C.
[6] The name means "a city looking both ways."

περιφανῆ ἐς θάλασσάν τε καὶ τὴν ἤπειρον
ᾤκισεν.

CIII. Ἐπὶ ταύτην οὖν ὁ Βρασίδας ἄρας ἐξ
Ἀρνῶν τῆς Χαλκιδικῆς ἐπορεύετο τῷ στρατῷ.
καὶ ἀφικόμενος περὶ δείλην ἐπὶ τὸν Αὐλῶνα καὶ
Βρομίσκον, ᾗ ἡ Βόλβη λίμνη ἐξίησιν ἐς θάλασσαν, καὶ δειπνοποιησάμενος ἐχώρει τὴν νύκτα.
2 χειμὼν δὲ ἦν καὶ ὑπένειφεν· ᾗ καὶ μᾶλλον
ὥρμησε, βουλόμενος λαθεῖν τοὺς ἐν τῇ Ἀμφι-
3 πόλει πλὴν τῶν προδιδόντων. ἦσαν γὰρ Ἀρ-
γιλίων τε ἐν αὐτῇ οἰκήτορες (εἰσὶ δὲ οἱ Ἀργίλιοι
Ἀνδρίων ἄποικοι) καὶ ἄλλοι οἳ ξυνέπρασσον
ταῦτα, οἱ μὲν Περδίκκᾳ πειθόμενοι, οἱ δὲ Χαλκι-
4 δεῦσιν. μάλιστα δὲ οἱ Ἀργίλιοι, ἐγγύς τε προσοι-
κοῦντες καὶ αἰεί ποτε τοῖς Ἀθηναίοις ὄντες
ὕποπτοι καὶ ἐπιβουλεύοντες τῷ χωρίῳ, ἐπειδὴ
παρέτυχεν ὁ καιρὸς καὶ Βρασίδας ἦλθεν, ἔπραξάν
τε ἐκ πλείονος πρὸς τοὺς ἐμπολιτεύοντας σφῶν
ἐκεῖ ὅπως ἐνδοθήσεται ἡ πόλις, καὶ τότε δεξάμενοι
αὐτὸν τῇ πόλει καὶ ἀποστάντες τῶν Ἀθηναίων
ἐκείνῃ τῇ νυκτὶ κατέστησαν τὸν στρατὸν πρὸ ἕω
ἐπὶ τὴν γέφυραν τοῦ ποταμοῦ (ἀπέχει δὲ τὸ πό-
5 λισμα πλέον τῆς διαβάσεως)· καὶ οὐ καθεῖτο
τείχη ὥσπερ νῦν, φυλακὴ δέ τις βραχεῖα καθει-
στήκει, ἣν βιασάμενος ῥᾳδίως ὁ Βρασίδας, ἅμα
μὲν τῆς προδοσίας οὔσης, ἅμα δὲ καὶ χειμῶνος
ὄντος καὶ ἀπροσδόκητος προσπεσών, διέβη τὴν
γέφυραν, καὶ τὰ ἔξω τῶν Ἀμφιπολιτῶν οἰκούντων
κατὰ πᾶν τὸ χωρίον εὐθὺς εἶχεν.

so established a city which was conspicuous both seaward and landward.

CIII. Against this place Brasidas marched with his army, setting out from Arnae in Chalcidice. Arriving about dusk at Aulon and Bromiscus,[1] where the lake Bolbe has its outlet into the sea, he took supper and then proceeded by night. The weather was bad and somewhat snowy, and for this reason he made the more haste, wishing to escape the notice of the people in Amphipolis, except those who were to betray it. For there were in the place some settlers from Argilus, an Andrian colony; these and some others were his accomplices in this intrigue, some instigated by Perdiccas, others by the Chalcidians. But the chief plotters were the Argilians, who dwelt near by, were always suspected by the Athenians, and were secret enemies of the place; now that opportunity offered and Brasidas had come, they had some time before negotiated with their countrymen who resided in Amphipolis with a view to the surrender of the place. So at this time they received Brasidas into their town, revolted from the Athenians that same night, and before dawn brought his army down to the bridge over the river, which is some distance from the town and not connected with it by walls as now. Brasidas easily forced the small guard stationed at the bridge, partly because there was treachery, partly because he had fallen upon them in stormy weather and unexpectedly; and as soon as he had crossed the bridge he was at once master of the property of the Amphipolitans outside the walls; for they had houses all over the neighbourhood.

[1] According to tradition, the scene of the death of Euripides.

CIV. Τῆς δὲ διαβάσεως αὐτοῦ ἄφνω τοῖς ἐν τῇ πόλει γεγενημένης, καὶ τῶν ἔξω πολλῶν μὲν ἁλισκομένων, τῶν δὲ καὶ καταφευγόντων ἐς τὸ τεῖχος, οἱ Ἀμφιπολῖται ἐς θόρυβον μέγαν κατέστησαν, ἄλλως τε καὶ ἀλλήλοις ὕποπτοι
2 ὄντες. καὶ λέγεται Βρασίδαν, εἰ ἠθέλησε μὴ ἐφ᾽ ἁρπαγὴν τῷ στρατῷ τραπέσθαι, ἀλλ᾽ εὐθὺς
3 χωρῆσαι πρὸς τὴν πόλιν, δοκεῖν ἂν ἑλεῖν. νῦν δὲ ὁ μὲν ἱδρύσας τὸν στρατόν, ἐπεὶ[1] τὰ ἔξω ἐπέδραμε καὶ οὐδὲν αὐτῷ ἀπὸ τῶν ἔνδον ὡς
4 προσεδέχετο ἀπέβαινεν, ἡσύχαζεν· οἱ δὲ ἐναντίοι τοῖς προδιδοῦσι, κρατοῦντες τῷ πλήθει ὥστε μὴ αὐτίκα τὰς πύλας ἀνοίγεσθαι, πέμπουσι μετὰ Εὐκλέους τοῦ στρατηγοῦ, ὃς ἐκ τῶν Ἀθηνῶν παρῆν αὐτοῖς φύλαξ τοῦ χωρίου, ἐπὶ τὸν ἕτερον στρατηγὸν τῶν ἐπὶ Θράκης, Θουκυδίδην τὸν Ὀλόρου, ὃς τάδε ξυνέγραψεν, ὄντα περὶ Θάσον (ἔστι δὲ ἡ νῆσος Παρίων ἀποικία, ἀπέχουσα τῆς Ἀμφιπόλεως ἡμίσεος ἡμέρας μάλιστα πλοῦν),
5 κελεύοντες σφίσι βοηθεῖν. καὶ ὁ μὲν ἀκούσας κατὰ τάχος ἑπτὰ ναυσὶν αἳ ἔτυχον παροῦσαι ἔπλει, καὶ ἐβούλετο φθάσαι μάλιστα μὲν οὖν τὴν Ἀμφίπολιν, πρίν τι ἐνδοῦναι, εἰ δὲ μή, τὴν Ἠιόνα προκαταλαβών.

CV. Ἐν τούτῳ δὲ ὁ Βρασίδας δεδιὼς καὶ τὴν ἀπὸ τῆς Θάσου τῶν νεῶν βοήθειαν καὶ πυνθανόμενος τὸν Θουκυδίδην κτῆσίν τε ἔχειν τῶν χρυσείων μετάλλων ἐργασίας ἐν τῇ περὶ ταῦτα Θράκῃ καὶ ἀπ᾽ αὐτοῦ δύνασθαι ἐν τοῖς πρώτοις τῶν ἠπειρωτῶν, ἠπείγετο προκατασχεῖν, εἰ δύναιτο, τὴν πόλιν, μὴ ἀφικνουμένου αὐτοῦ τὸ πλῆθος τῶν Ἀμφιπολιτῶν, ἐλπίσαν ἐκ θαλάσσης

---

[1] ἐπεί, with F and (ex corr.) C ; other MSS. ἐπί.

CIV. His crossing had surprised the people inside the city, and of those outside many were captured, while others took refuge within the walls; hence the Amphipolitans were thrown into great confusion, especially as they were suspicious of each other. Indeed the general impression was, it is said, that if Brasidas, instead of turning to pillage with his army, had decided to march straight against the city, he could have taken it. But as it was, when he had overrun the country outside and found that none of his plans were being carried out by his friends within the city, he merely settled his army in camp and kept quiet. Meanwhile the opponents of the traitors, being numerous enough to prevent the gates being opened to him at once, acting in concert with Eucles the general, who had come from Athens as warden of the place, sent to the other commander of the Thracian district, Thucydides son of Olorus, the author of this history, who was at Thasos, a Parian colony, about a half-day's sail from Amphipolis, and urged him to come to their aid. And he, on hearing this, sailed in haste with seven ships which happened to be at hand, wishing above all to secure Amphipolis before it yielded, or, failing in that, to seize Eion.

CV. Meanwhile, Brasidas, fearing the arrival of the ships from Thasos, and hearing that Thucydides possessed the right of working the gold-mines in that part of Thrace and in consequence had influence among the first men of the mainland, made haste to seize the city if possible before he should come; for he was afraid that, if Thucydides should arrive, the popular party in Amphipolis, in the expectation that

ξυμμαχικὸν καὶ ἀπὸ τῆς Θράκης ἀγείραντα αὐτὸν
2 περιποιήσειν σφᾶς, οὐκέτι προσχωροίη. καὶ τὴν
ξύμβασιν μετρίαν ἐποιεῖτο, κήρυγμα τόδε ἀνει-
πών, Ἀμφιπολιτῶν καὶ Ἀθηναίων τῶν ἐνόντων
τὸν μὲν βουλόμενον ἐπὶ τοῖς ἑαυτοῦ τῆς ἴσης καὶ
ὁμοίας μετέχοντα μένειν, τὸν δὲ μὴ ἐθέλοντα
ἀπιέναι τὰ ἑαυτοῦ ἐκφερόμενον πέντε ἡμερῶν.

CVI. Οἱ δὲ πολλοὶ ἀκούσαντες ἀλλοιότεροι
ἐγένοντο τὰς γνώμας, ἄλλως τε καὶ βραχὺ μὲν
Ἀθηναίων ἐμπολιτεῦον, τὸ δὲ πλέον ξύμμεικτον,
καὶ τῶν ἔξω ληφθέντων συχνοῖς οἰκεῖοι ἔνδον
ἦσαν· καὶ τὸ κήρυγμα πρὸς τὸν φόβον δίκαιον
εἶναι ἐλάμβανον, οἱ μὲν Ἀθηναῖοι διὰ τὸ ἄσμενοι
ἂν ἐξελθεῖν, ἡγούμενοι οὐκ ἐν ὁμοίῳ σφίσι τὰ
δεινὰ εἶναι καὶ ἅμα οὐ προσδεχόμενοι βοήθειαν
ἐν τάχει, ὁ δὲ ἄλλος ὅμιλος πόλεώς τε ἐν τῷ
ἴσῳ οὐ στερισκόμενοι καὶ κινδύνου παρὰ δόξαν
2 ἀφιέμενοι. ὥστε τῶν πρασσόντων τῷ Βρασίδᾳ
ἤδη καὶ ἐκ τοῦ φανεροῦ διαδικαιούντων αὐτά,
ἐπειδὴ καὶ τὸ πλῆθος ἑώρων τετραμμένον καὶ τοῦ
παρόντος Ἀθηναίων στρατηγοῦ οὐκέτι ἀκροώ-
μενον, ἐγένετο ἡ ὁμολογία καὶ προσεδέξαντο ἐφ'
3 οἷς ἐκήρυξεν. καὶ οἱ μὲν τὴν πόλιν τοιούτῳ
τρόπῳ παρέδοσαν, ὁ δὲ Θουκυδίδης καὶ αἱ νῆες
ταύτῃ τῇ ἡμέρᾳ ὀψὲ κατέπλεον ἐς τὴν Ἠιόνα.
4 καὶ τὴν μὲν Ἀμφίπολιν Βρασίδας ἄρτι εἶχε, τὴν
δὲ Ἠιόνα παρὰ νύκτα ἐγένετο λαβεῖν· εἰ γὰρ
μὴ ἐβοήθησαν αἱ νῆες διὰ τάχους, ἅμα ἔῳ ἂν
εἴχετο.

he would collect an allied force from the islands and from Thrace and relieve them, would refuse to yield. Accordingly, he offered moderate terms, making proclamation to this effect, that any citizen of Amphipolis or any resident Athenian, if he chose, might remain there, retaining possession of his own property and enjoying full equality; but that anyone who was not inclined to stay might go away within five days and take his property with him.

CVI. On hearing this the majority became irresolute, especially as few of the citizens were Athenians, the greater number being a mixed multitude, and a considerable number of those who had been captured outside had relatives inside the city. As compared with their fears they conceived the proclamation to be fair—the Athenians, because they were only too glad to be able to leave, since they realized that their share of the dangers was greater, and besides, did not expect any speedy relief; the general multitude, because they were not to lose their civil rights but to retain them as before and also, contrary to their expectation, were to be released from peril. And so, as the partisans of Brasidas were already quite openly justifying his proposals, since these saw that the populace had changed its attitude and no longer hearkened to the Athenian general who was in the city, the capitulation was made, and Brasidas was received on the terms of his proclamation. In this way they gave up the city, and on the evening of the same day Thucydides and his ships sailed into Eion. Brasidas had just got possession of Amphipolis, and he missed taking Eion only by a night; for if the ships had not come to the rescue with all speed, it would have been taken at dawn.

THUCYDIDES

CVII. Μετὰ δὲ τοῦτο ὁ μὲν τὰ ἐν τῇ Ἰόνι καθίστατο, ὅπως καὶ τὸ αὐτίκα, ἢν ἐπίῃ ὁ Βρασίδας, καὶ τὸ ἔπειτα ἀσφαλῶς ἕξει, δεξάμενος τοὺς ἐθελήσαντας ἐπιχωρῆσαι ἄνωθεν κατὰ τὰς 2 σπονδάς· ὁ δὲ πρὸς μὲν τὴν Ἰόνα κατά τε τὸν ποταμὸν πολλοῖς πλοίοις ἄφνω καταπλεύσας, εἴ πως τὴν προύχουσαν ἄκραν ἀπὸ τοῦ τείχους λαβὼν κρατοίη τοῦ ἔσπλου, καὶ κατὰ γῆν ἀποπειράσας ἅμα, ἀμφοτέρωθεν ἀπεκρούσθη, τὰ δὲ 3 περὶ τὴν Ἀμφίπολιν ἐξηρτύετο. καὶ Μύρκινός τε αὐτῷ προσεχώρησεν, Ἠδωνικὴ πόλις, Πιττακοῦ τοῦ Ἠδώνων βασιλέως ἀποθανόντος ὑπὸ τῶν Γοάξιος παίδων καὶ Βραυροῦς τῆς γυναικὸς αὐτοῦ, καὶ Γαληψὸς οὐ πολλῷ ὕστερον καὶ Οἰσύμη· εἰσὶ δὲ αὗται Θασίων ἀποικίαι. παρὼν δὲ καὶ Περδίκκας εὐθὺς μετὰ τὴν ἅλωσιν ξυγκαθίστη ταῦτα.

CVIII. Ἐχομένης δὲ τῆς Ἀμφιπόλεως οἱ Ἀθηναῖοι ἐς μέγα δέος κατέστησαν, ἄλλως τε καὶ ὅτι ἡ πόλις ἦν αὐτοῖς ὠφέλιμος ξύλων τε ναυπηγησίμων πομπῇ καὶ χρημάτων προσόδῳ, καὶ ὅτι μέχρι μὲν τοῦ Στρυμόνος ἦν πάροδος Θεσσαλῶν διαγόντων ἐπὶ τοὺς ξυμμάχους σφῶν τοῖς Λακεδαιμονίοις, τῆς δὲ γεφύρας μὴ κρατούντων, ἄνωθεν μὲν μεγάλης οὔσης ἐπὶ πολὺ λίμνης τοῦ ποταμοῦ, τὰ δὲ πρὸς Ἰόνα τριήρεσι τηρουμένων,[1] οὐκ ἂν δύνασθαι προελθεῖν· τότε δὲ

[1] Hude emends to τηρουμένου.

CVII. After this Thucydides proceeded to arrange matters at Eïon, in order to insure its safety for the present, if Brasidas should attack, and also for the future, receiving those who chose to come thither from the upper town according to the terms of the truce.[1] And Brasidas suddenly sailed down the river to Eïon with many boats, in the hope that by taking the point which juts out from the wall he might gain command of the entrance, and at the same time he made an attempt by land; but he was beaten back at both points, and then proceeded to put matters in order at Amphipolis. Myrcinus also, an Edonian town, came over to him, Pittacus, the king of the Edonians, having been killed by the sons of Goaxis and his own wife Brauro; and not long afterwards Galepsus and Oesyme, colonies of the Thasians, also came over. Perdiccas,[2] too, came to Amphipolis directly after its capture and joined in arranging these matters.

CVIII. The Athenians were greatly alarmed by the capture of Amphipolis. The chief reason was that the city was useful to them for the importation of timber for ship-building and for the revenue it produced, and also that, whereas hitherto the Lacedaemonians had possessed, under the guidance of the Thessalians, access to the Athenian allies as far as the Strymon, yet as long as they did not control the bridge—the river for a long way above the town being a great lake and triremes being on guard in the direction of Eïon—they could not have advanced further; but now at last the matter

---

[1] cf. ch. cv. 2.
[2] Now evidently reconciled with Brasidas, with whom he had quarrelled (ch. lxxxvi. 3); cf. ch. ciii. 3.

ῥάδια [1] ἤδη γεγενῆσθαι.[2] καὶ τοὺς ξυμμάχους
2 ἐφοβοῦντο μὴ ἀποστῶσιν. ὁ γὰρ Βρασίδας ἔν
τε τοῖς ἄλλοις μέτριον ἑαυτὸν παρεῖχε καὶ ἐν
τοῖς λόγοις πανταχοῦ ἐδήλου ὡς ἐλευθερώσων
3 τὴν Ἑλλάδα ἐκπεμφθείη. καὶ αἱ πόλεις πυν-
θανόμεναι αἱ τῶν Ἀθηναίων ὑπήκοοι [3] τῆς τε
Ἀμφιπόλεως τὴν ἅλωσιν καὶ ἃ παρέχεται, τήν
τε ἐκείνου πραότητα, μάλιστα δὴ ἐπήρθησαν ἐς
τὸ νεωτερίζειν, καὶ ἐπεκηρυκεύοντο πρὸς αὐτὸν
κρύφα, ἐπιπαριέναι τε κελεύοντες καὶ βουλόμενοι
4 αὐτοὶ ἕκαστοι πρῶτοι ἀποστῆναι. καὶ γὰρ καὶ
ἄδεια ἐφαίνετο αὐτοῖς, ἐψευσμένοις [4] μὲν τῆς
Ἀθηναίων δυνάμεως ἐπὶ τοσοῦτον ὅση ὕστερον
διεφάνη, τὸ δὲ πλέον βουλήσει κρίνοντες ἀσαφεῖ
ἢ προνοίᾳ ἀσφαλεῖ, εἰωθότες οἱ ἄνθρωποι οὗ μὲν
ἐπιθυμοῦσιν ἐλπίδι ἀπερισκέπτῳ διδόναι, ὃ δὲ
μὴ προσίενται λογισμῷ αὐτοκράτορι διωθεῖσθαι.
5 ἅμα δὲ τῶν Ἀθηναίων ἐν τοῖς Βοιωτοῖς νεωστὶ
πεπληγμένων καὶ τοῦ Βρασίδου ἐφολκὰ καὶ οὐ τὰ
ὄντα λέγοντος, ὡς αὐτῷ ἐπὶ Νίσαιαν τῇ ἑαυτοῦ
μόνῃ στρατιᾷ [5] οὐκ ἠθέλησαν οἱ Ἀθηναῖοι ξυμ-
βαλεῖν, ἐθάρσουν καὶ ἐπίστευον μηδένα ἂν ἐπὶ
6 σφᾶς βοηθῆσαι. τὸ δὲ μέγιστον, διὰ τὸ ἡδονὴν
ἔχον ἐν τῷ αὐτίκα καὶ ὅτι τὸ πρῶτον Λακεδαιμονίων ὀργώντων ἔμελλον πειράσεσθαι, κινδυνεύειν παντὶ τρόπῳ ἕτοιμοι ἦσαν. ὧν αἰσθανό-

---

[1] Kistemacher's correction for ῥᾳδία or ῥᾳδίαι of the MSS.
[2] Supply in thought here ἐνόμιζον before γεγενῆσθαι. Most
MSS. have ἐνόμιζεν (Vulg. ἐνομίζετο) ; Kistemacher deletes.
[3] αἱ τῶν Ἀθηναίων ὑπήκοοι, Hude deletes.
[4] Hude reads ἐψευσμένοι, with E.
[5] Linwood, followed by Stahl and Hude, inserts βοηθή-
σαντι, as indeed seems to have been in the mind of the
author.

had become easy.[1] And they feared, too, the revolt of their allies. For Brasidas in other things
showed himself moderate, and in his declarations
everywhere made plain that he had been sent out
for the liberation of Hellas. And the cities that
were subject to Athens, hearing of the capture of
Amphipolis and the assurances that were offered,
and of the gentleness of Brasidas, were more than
ever incited to revolution, and sent secret messengers to him, urging him to come on to them, and
wishing each for itself to be the first to revolt.
For it seemed to them that there was little ground
for fear, since they estimated the Athenian power
to be far less great than it afterwards proved to be,
and in their judgment were moved more by illusive
wishing than by cautious foresight; for men are wont,
when they desire a thing, to trust to unreflecting hope,
but to reject by arbitrary judgment whatever they
do not care for. Furthermore, because of the recent
defeat of the Athenians in Boeotia and the enticing
but untrue statements of Brasidas,[2] that the
Athenians had been unwilling to engage him when
he came to the relief of Nisaea with only his own
army, they grew bold, and believed that nobody
would come against them. Above all, they were
so moved by the pleasurable anticipations of the
moment, and by the fact that they were now for the
first time going to have a proof of what the Lacedaemonians would do when on their mettle, that
they were ready to take any risk. Being aware of

---

[1] Or, retaining ῥᾴδια of the MSS. and the Vulgate reading
ἐνομίζετο, "but now the access was thought to have become
easy."

[2] cf. ch. lxxiii.; lxxxv. 7.

μένοι οἱ μὲν Ἀθηναῖοι φυλακάς, ὡς ἐξ ὀλίγου καὶ
ἐν χειμῶνι, διέπεμπον ἐς τὰς πόλεις, ὁ δὲ ἐς τὴν
Λακεδαίμονα ἐφιέμενος στρατιάν τε προσαπο-
στέλλειν ἐκέλευε καὶ αὐτὸς ἐν τῷ Στρυμόνι
7 ναυπηγίαν τριήρων παρεσκευάζετο. οἱ δὲ Λακεδαιμόνιοι τὰ μὲν καὶ φθόνῳ ἀπὸ τῶν πρώτων
ἀνδρῶν οὐχ ὑπηρέτησαν αὐτῷ, τὰ δὲ καὶ βουλόμενοι μᾶλλον τούς τε ἄνδρας τοὺς ἐκ τῆς νήσου
κομίσασθαι καὶ τὸν πόλεμον καταλῦσαι.

CIX. Τοῦ δ᾽ αὐτοῦ χειμῶνος Μεγαρῆς τε τὰ
μακρὰ τείχη, ἃ σφῶν οἱ Ἀθηναῖοι εἶχον, κατέ-
σκαψαν ἑλόντες ἐς ἔδαφος, καὶ Βρασίδας μετὰ τὴν
Ἀμφιπόλεως ἅλωσιν ἔχων τοὺς ξυμμάχους
2 στρατεύει ἐπὶ τὴν Ἀκτὴν καλουμένην. ἔστι δὲ
ἀπὸ τοῦ βασιλέως διορύγματος ἔσω προύχουσα,
καὶ ὁ Ἄθως αὐτῆς ὄρος ὑψηλὸν τελευτᾷ ἐς τὸ
3 Αἰγαῖον πέλαγος. πόλεις δὲ ἔχει Σάνην μὲν
Ἀνδρίων ἀποικίαν παρ᾽ αὐτὴν τὴν διώρυχα, ἐς
τὸ πρὸς Εὔβοιαν πέλαγος τετραμμένην, τὰς δὲ
ἄλλας Θυσσὸν καὶ Κλεωνὰς καὶ Ἀκροθῴους καὶ
4 Ὀλόφυξον καὶ Δῖον· αἳ οἰκοῦνται ξυμμείκτοις
ἔθνεσι βαρβάρων διγλώσσων, καί τι καὶ Χαλκιδικὸν ἔνι βραχύ, τὸ δὲ πλεῖστον Πελασγικόν,
τῶν καὶ Λῆμνόν ποτε καὶ Ἀθήνας Τυρσηνῶν
οἰκησάντων, καὶ Βισαλτικὸν καὶ Κρηστωνικὸν
καὶ Ἠδῶνες· κατὰ δὲ μικρὰ πολίσματα οἰκοῦσιν.
5 καὶ οἱ μὲν πλείους προσεχώρησαν τῷ Βρασίδᾳ,
Σάνη δὲ καὶ Δῖον ἀντέστη, καὶ αὐτῶν τὴν χώραν
ἐμμείνας τῷ στρατῷ ἐδῄου.

these things, the Athenians, so far as was possible at short notice and in the winter season, sent out garrisons among the cities; while Brasidas sent to Lacedaemon and urgently begged them to send him reinforcements, and was himself making preparations for building ships in the Strymon. The Lacedaemonians, however, did not comply with his request, partly on account of the jealousy of the foremost men, partly also because they wished rather to recover the men taken on the island and to bring the war to an end.

CIX. The same winter the Megarians took and razed to the ground their long walls[1] which the Athenians had held; and Brasidas, after the capture of Amphipolis, made an expedition with his allies against the district called Acte. It is a promontory projecting from the King's canal[2] on the inner side of the isthmus, and its terminus at the Aegean Sea is the lofty Mt. Athos. Of the cities it contains, one is Sane, an Andrian colony close to the canal, facing the sea which is toward Euboea; the others are Thyssus, Cleonae, Acrothoï, Olophyxus and Dium, which are inhabited by mixed barbarian tribes speaking two languages. There is in it also a small Chalcidic element; but the greatest part is Pelasgic—belonging to those Etruscans that once inhabited Lemnos and Athens[3]—Bisaltic, Crestonic, and Edonian; and they live in small towns. Most of these yielded to Brasidas, but Sane and Dium held out against him; so he waited there with his army and laid waste their territory.

---

[1] cf. ch. lxix. 4.   [2] Xerxes' canal; cf. Hdt. vii. 22 ff.
[3] According to Herodotus (vi. 137 ff.), they were expelled from Attica, and afterwards, by Miltiades, from Lemnos.

CX. Ὡς δ' οὐκ ἐσήκουον, εὐθὺς στρατεύει ἐπὶ
Τορώνην τὴν Χαλκιδικήν, κατεχομένην ὑπὸ
Ἀθηναίων· καὶ αὐτὸν ἄνδρες ὀλίγοι ἐπήγοντο,
ἕτοιμοι ὄντες τὴν πόλιν παραδοῦναι. καὶ ἀφικόμενος νυκτὸς ἔτι καὶ περὶ ὄρθρον τῷ στρατῷ
ἐκαθέζετο πρὸς τὸ Διοσκόρειον, ὃ ἀπέχει τῆς
2 πόλεως τρεῖς μάλιστα σταδίους. τὴν μὲν οὖν
ἄλλην πόλιν τῶν Τορωναίων καὶ τοὺς Ἀθηναίους
τοὺς ἐμφρουροῦντας ἔλαθεν· οἱ δὲ πράσσοντες
αὐτῷ εἰδότες ὅτι ἥξοι, καὶ προελθόντες τινὲς
αὐτῶν λάθρᾳ ὀλίγοι ἐτήρουν τὴν πρόσοδον, καὶ
ὡς ᾔσθοντο παρόντα, ἐσκομίζουσι παρ' αὐτοὺς
ἐγχειρίδια ἔχοντας ἄνδρας ψιλοὺς ἑπτά (τοσοῦτοι
γὰρ μόνοι ἀνδρῶν εἴκοσι τὸ πρῶτον ταχθέντων οὐ
κατέδεισαν ἐσελθεῖν· ἦρχε δὲ αὐτῶν Λυσίστρατος
Ὀλύνθιος), οἳ διαδύντες διὰ τοῦ πρὸς τὸ πέλαγος
τείχους καὶ λαθόντες τούς τε ἐπὶ τοῦ ἀνωτάτω
φυλακτηρίου φρουρούς, οὔσης τῆς πόλεως πρὸς
λόφον, ἀναβάντες διέφθειραν καὶ τὴν κατὰ Κανα-
στραῖον πυλίδα διῄρουν.

CXI. Ὁ δὲ Βρασίδας τῷ μὲν ἄλλῳ στρατῷ
ἡσύχαζεν ὀλίγον προελθών, ἑκατὸν δὲ πελταστὰς
προπέμπει, ὅπως, ὁπότε πύλαι τινὲς ἀνοιχθεῖεν
καὶ τὸ σημεῖον ἀρθείη ὃ ξυνέκειτο, πρῶτοι
2 ἐσδράμοιεν. καὶ οἱ μὲν χρόνου ἐγγιγνομένου καὶ
θαυμάζοντες κατὰ μικρὸν ἔτυχον ἐγγὺς τῆς
πόλεως προσελθόντες· οἱ δὲ τῶν Τορωναίων
ἔνδοθεν παρασκευάζοντες μετὰ τῶν ἐσεληλυ-

CX. Since, however, they would not yield he marched at once against Torone,[1] in Chalcidice, which was held by the Athenians; for a few men, who were ready to betray the town, had invited him over. Arriving with his army toward dawn, but while it was still dark, he encamped near the temple of the Dioscuri, which is about three stadia distant from the city. The rest of the town of Torone and the Athenians of the garrison were unaware of his approach, but his partisans, knowing that he would come, and some few of them having secretly gone forward to meet him, were watching for his approach; and when they perceived that he was there, they introduced into the town seven light-armed men with daggers, under the command of Lysistratus an Olynthian, these men alone of the twenty first assigned to the task not being afraid to enter. These slipped through the seaward wall and escaping the notice of the guard at the uppermost watch-post of the town, which is on the slope of a hill, went up and slew these sentinels, and broke open the postern on the side towards the promontory of Canastraeum.

CXI. Meanwhile Brasidas, having gone forward a little, kept quiet with the rest of his army, but sent forward one hundred targeteers, in order that as soon as any gates were opened and the signal agreed upon was raised they might rush in first. These now, as time elapsed, were wondering at the delay and had come up little by little close to the town. Meanwhile the Toronaeans inside who were co-operating with the party which had entered, when the postern

---

[1] The chief town on the Sithonian peninsula.

θότων, ὡς αὐτοῖς ἥ τε πυλὶς διήρητο καὶ αἱ κατὰ
τὴν ἀγορὰν πύλαι τοῦ μοχλοῦ διακοπέντος ἀνεῴ-
γοντο, πρῶτον μὲν κατὰ τὴν πυλίδα τινὰς
περιαγαγόντες ἐσεκόμισαν, ὅπως κατὰ νώτου καὶ
ἀμφοτέρωθεν τοὺς ἐν τῇ πόλει οὐδὲν εἰδότας
ἐξαπίνης φοβήσειαν, ἔπειτα τὸ σημεῖόν τε τοῦ
πυρός, ὡς εἴρητο, ἀνέσχον καὶ διὰ τῶν κατὰ τὴν
ἀγορὰν πυλῶν τοὺς λοιποὺς ἤδη τῶν πελταστῶν
ἐσεδέχοντο.   CXII. καὶ ὁ Βρασίδας ἰδὼν τὸ
ξύνθημα ἔθει δρόμῳ, ἀναστήσας τὸν στρατὸν
ἐμβοήσαντάς τε ἁθρόον καὶ ἔκπληξιν πολλὴν
2 τοῖς ἐν τῇ πόλει παρασχόντας. καὶ οἱ μὲν κατὰ
τὰς πύλας εὐθὺς ἐσέπιπτον, οἱ δὲ κατὰ δοκοὺς
τετραγώνους, αἳ ἔτυχον τῷ τείχει πεπτωκότι
κἀνοικοδομουμένῳ πρὸς λίθων ἀνολκὴν προσκεί-
3 μεναι. Βρασίδας μὲν οὖν καὶ τὸ πλῆθος εὐθὺς
ἄνω καὶ ἐπὶ τὰ μετέωρα τῆς πόλεως ἐτράπετο,
βουλόμενος κατ' ἄκρας καὶ βεβαίως ἑλεῖν αὐτήν·
ὁ δὲ ἄλλος ὅμιλος κατὰ πάντα ὁμοίως ἐσκεδάν-
νυντο.

CXIII. Τῶν δὲ Τορωναίων γιγνομένης τῆς
ἁλώσεως τὸ μὲν πολὺ οὐδὲν εἰδὸς ἐθορυβεῖτο, οἱ
δὲ πράσσοντες καὶ οἷς ταῦτα ἤρεσκε μετὰ τῶν
2 ἐσελθόντων εὐθὺς ἦσαν. οἱ δὲ Ἀθηναῖοι (ἔτυχον
γὰρ ἐν τῇ ἀγορᾷ ὁπλῖται καθεύδοντες ὡς
πεντήκοντα) ἐπειδὴ ᾔσθοντο, οἱ μέν τινες ὀλίγοι
διαφθείρονται ἐν χερσὶν αὐτῶν, τῶν δὲ λοιπῶν οἱ
μὲν πεζῇ, οἱ δὲ ἐς τὰς ναῦς, αἳ ἐφρούρουν δύο,
καταφυγόντες διασῴζονται ἐς τὴν Λήκυθον τὸ
φρούριον, ὃ εἶχον αὐτοὶ καταλαβόντες, ἄκρον τῆς
πόλεως ἐς τὴν θάλασσαν ἀπειλημμένον ἐν στενῷ

had been broken down and the gates near the market-place had been opened by cutting the bar, first brought some men around to the postern and let them in, in order that they might take the townsmen unawares by a sudden attack in their rear and on both sides and throw them into a panic; after that they raised the fire-signal agreed upon and received the rest of the targeteers through the gates near the market-place. CXII. Brasidas, on seeing the signal, set off at a run, calling up his force, and they with one voice raised a shout and caused great dismay to the townsmen. Some burst in immediately by the gates, others over some square beams which chanced to have been placed, for the purpose of drawing up stones, against the wall that had fallen in and was now being rebuilt. Brasidas, then, and the main body made at once for the high points of the town, wishing to make its capture complete and decisive; but the rest of the multitude[1] scattered in all directions.

CXIII. While the capture was being effected, most of the Toronaeans, who knew nothing of the plot, were in a tumult, but the conspirators and such as were in sympathy with the movement at once joined those who had entered. When the Athenians became aware of it—for about fifty of their hoplites happened to be sleeping in the market-place—though some few of them were slain in hand-to-hand conflict, the rest fled, some by land, others to the two ships which were on guard, and got safely into the fort of Lecythus, which had been occupied and was held by their own men. It is the citadel of the city, projecting into the sea—a separate section[2] on a

---

[1] Macedonian and Thracian irregulars.

[2] There was probably a wall across the isthmus.

3 ἰσθμῷ. κατέφυγον δὲ καὶ τῶν Τορωναίων ἐς
αὐτοὺς ὅσοι ἦσαν σφίσιν ἐπιτήδειοι.

CXIV. Γεγενημένης δὲ ἡμέρας ἤδη καὶ βεβαίως
τῆς πόλεως ἐχομένης ὁ Βρασίδας τοῖς μὲν μετὰ
τῶν Ἀθηναίων Τορωναίοις καταπεφευγόσι κήρυγμα ἐποιήσατο τὸν βουλόμενον ἐπὶ τὰ ἑαυτοῦ
ἐσελθόντα ἀδεῶς πολιτεύειν, τοῖς δὲ Ἀθηναίοις
κήρυκα προσπέμψας ἐξιέναι ἐκέλευεν ἐκ τῆς
Ληκύθου ὑποσπόνδους καὶ τὰ ἑαυτῶν ἔχοντας ὡς
2 οὔσης Χαλκιδέων. οἱ δὲ ἐκλείψειν μὲν οὐκ
ἔφασαν, σπείσασθαι δὲ σφίσιν ἐκέλευον ἡμέραν
τοὺς νεκροὺς ἀνελέσθαι. ὁ δὲ ἐσπείσατο δύο.
ἐν ταύταις δὲ αὐτός τε τὰς ἐγγὺς οἰκίας ἐκρατύ-
3 νατο καὶ Ἀθηναῖοι τὰ σφέτερα. καὶ ξύλλογον
τῶν Τορωναίων ποιήσας ἔλεξε τοῖς ἐν τῇ Ἀκάνθῳ
παραπλήσια, ὅτι οὐ δίκαιον εἴη οὔτε τοὺς πράξαντας πρὸς αὐτὸν τὴν λῆψιν τῆς πόλεως χείρους
οὐδὲ προδότας ἡγεῖσθαι (οὐ γὰρ ἐπὶ δουλείᾳ οὐδὲ
χρήμασι πεισθέντας δρᾶσαι τοῦτο, ἀλλ' ἐπὶ
ἀγαθῷ καὶ ἐλευθερίᾳ τῆς πόλεως), οὔτε τοὺς μὴ
μετασχόντας οἴεσθαι μὴ τῶν αὐτῶν τεύξεσθαι·
ἀφῖχθαι γὰρ οὐ διαφθερῶν οὔτε πόλιν οὔτε ἰδιώ-
4 την οὐδένα. τὸ δὲ κήρυγμα ποιήσασθαι τούτου
ἕνεκα τοῖς παρ' Ἀθηναίους καταπεφευγόσιν, ὡς
ἡγούμενος οὐδὲν χείρους τῇ ἐκείνων φιλίᾳ· οὐδ'
ἂν σφῶν πειρασαμένους αὐτοὺς τῶν Λακεδαιμονίων[1] δοκεῖν ἧσσον, ἀλλὰ πολλῷ μᾶλλον, ὅσῳ

[1] τῶν Λακεδαιμονίων, deleted by Cobet, followed by Hude.

narrow isthmus. And such of the Toronaeans as were
friendly to the Athenians took refuge there also.

CXIV. When day had come and the town was
securely in his possession, Brasidas made proclamation
to the Toronaeans who had taken refuge with the
Athenians, that whoever wished might return to his
property and exercise citizenship without fear ; but
to the Athenians he sent a herald, ordering them to
come out of Lecythus under truce, bringing all their
property, as the place belonged to the Chalcidians.
They, however, refused to leave, but requested him
to make a truce with them for a day, that they
might take up their dead. He granted a truce for
two days, during which he himself fortified the
houses near by and the Athenians strengthened
their defences. Then calling a meeting of the
Toronaeans, Brasidas spoke to them much as he had
done to the people at Acanthus.[1] He said that it
was not just either to regard as villains or as
traitors those who had negotiated with him for
the capture of the town—for they had done this,
not to enslave it, nor because they were bribed,
but for the welfare and freedom of the city—or to
think that those who had not taken part would not
get the same treatment as the others ; for he had
not come to destroy either the city or any private
citizen. He explained that he made his proclamation to those who had taken refuge with the Athenians for the reason that he thought none the worse
of them for their friendship with these ; and when
they had proved his countrymen, the Lacedaemonians,
they would not, he thought, be less but rather far
more kindly disposed toward them than toward the

[1] cf. chs. lxxxv.–lxxxvii.

δικαιότερα πράσσουσιν, εὔνους ἂν σφίσι γενέσθαι,
5 ἀπειρίᾳ δὲ νῦν πεφοβῆσθαι. τούς τε πάντας
παρασκευάζεσθαι ἐκέλευεν ὡς βεβαίους τε ἐσομένους ξυμμάχους καὶ τὸ ἀπὸ τοῦδε ἤδη ὅ τι ἂν
ἁμαρτάνωσιν αἰτίαν ἔξοντας· τὰ δὲ πρότερα οὐ
σφεῖς ἀδικεῖσθαι, ἀλλ᾽ ἐκείνους μᾶλλον ὑπ᾽ ἄλλων
κρεισσόνων, καὶ ξυγγνώμην εἶναι εἴ τι ἠναντιοῦντο.

CXV. Καὶ ὁ μὲν τοιαῦτα εἰπὼν καὶ παραθαρ-
σύνας διελθουσῶν τῶν σπονδῶν τὰς προσβολὰς
ἐποιεῖτο τῇ Ληκύθῳ· οἱ δὲ Ἀθηναῖοι ἠμύνοντό τε
ἐκ φαύλου τειχίσματος καὶ ἀπ᾽ οἰκιῶν ἐπάλξεις
ἐχουσῶν, καὶ μίαν μὲν ἡμέραν ἀπεκρούσαντο·
2 τῇ δ᾽ ὑστεραίᾳ μηχανῆς μελλούσης προσάξεσθαι
αὐτοῖς ἀπὸ τῶν ἐναντίων, ἀφ᾽ ἧς πῦρ ἐνήσειν
διενοοῦντο ἐς τὰ ξύλινα παραφράγματα, καὶ
προσιόντος ἤδη τοῦ στρατεύματος, ᾗ ᾤοντο
μάλιστα αὐτοὺς προσκομιεῖν τὴν μηχανὴν καὶ ἦν
ἐπιμαχώτατον, πύργον ξύλινον ἐπ᾽ οἴκημα ἀντέστησαν, καὶ ὕδατος ἀμφορέας πολλοὺς καὶ πίθους
ἀνεφόρησαν καὶ λίθους μεγάλους, ἄνθρωποί τε
3 πολλοὶ ἀνέβησαν. τὸ δὲ οἴκημα λαβὸν μεῖζον
ἄχθος ἐξαπίνης κατερράγη καὶ ψόφου πολλοῦ
γενομένου τοὺς μὲν ἐγγὺς καὶ ὁρῶντας τῶν
Ἀθηναίων ἐλύπησε μᾶλλον ἢ ἐφόβησεν, οἱ δὲ
ἄπωθεν, καὶ μάλιστα οἱ διὰ πλείστου, νομίσαντες
ταύτῃ ἑαλωκέναι ἤδη τὸ χωρίον, φυγῇ ἐς τὴν
θάλασσαν καὶ τὰς ναῦς ὥρμησαν.

CXVI. Καὶ ὁ Βρασίδας ὡς ᾔσθετο αὐτοὺς
ἀπολείποντάς τε τὰς ἐπάλξεις καὶ τὸ γιγνόμενον

Athenians, inasmuch as their conduct was more just; whereas now they had been afraid of them through inexperience. Moreover, he told them all to prepare to show themselves staunch allies and to be held responsible for whatever mistakes they might make from this time on; as to their former actions, it was not the Lacedaemonians who had been wronged by them, but the Toronaeans rather by others [1] who were stronger, and it was pardonable if the Toronaeans had made any opposition to him.

CXV. Having said such things and encouraged them, when the truce expired he proceeded to make assaults upon Lecythus; but the Athenians defended themselves from a paltry fort and from such houses as had battlements, and beat them back for one day. On the next day, however, when the enemy were about to bring against them an engine from which it was intended to throw fire upon the wooden defences, and the army was already coming up, they set up a wooden tower on a house at the point where they thought the enemy most likely to bring up his engine and where the wall was most assailable, and carried up many jars and casks of water and big stones, and many men also ascended. But the house, being over-weighted, collapsed suddenly and with a great noise, annoying rather than frightening the Athenians who were near and saw it; but those who were at a distance, and especially those furthest off, thinking that in that quarter the place had already been taken, set off in flight for the sea and their ships.

CXVI. When Brasidas perceived that they were leaving the battlements and saw what was going on,

[1] The Athenians.

ὁρῶν, ἐπιφερόμενος τῷ στρατῷ εὐθὺς τὸ τείχισμα
λαμβάνει, καὶ ὅσους ἐγκατέλαβε διέφθειρεν.
2 καὶ οἱ μὲν Ἀθηναῖοι τοῖς τε πλοίοις καὶ ταῖς
ναυσὶ τούτῳ τῷ τρόπῳ ἐκλιπόντες τὸ χωρίον ἐς
Παλλήνην διεκομίσθησαν· ὁ δὲ Βρασίδας (ἔστι
γὰρ ἐν τῇ Ληκύθῳ Ἀθηναίας ἱερόν, καὶ ἔτυχε
κηρύξας, ὅτε ἔμελλε προσβάλλειν, τῷ ἐπιβάντι
πρώτῳ τοῦ τείχους τριάκοντα μνᾶς ἀργυρίου
δώσειν) νομίσας ἄλλῳ τινὶ τρόπῳ ἢ ἀνθρωπείῳ
τὴν ἅλωσιν γενέσθαι, τάς τε τριάκοντα μνᾶς τῇ
θεῷ ἀπέδωκεν ἐς τὸ ἱερὸν καὶ τὴν Λήκυθον
καθελὼν καὶ ἀνασκευάσας τέμενος ἀνῆκεν ἅπαν.
3 καὶ ὁ μὲν τὸ λοιπὸν τοῦ χειμῶνος ἅ τε εἶχε τῶν
χωρίων καθίστατο καὶ τοῖς ἄλλοις ἐπεβούλευεν·
καὶ τοῦ χειμῶνος διελθόντος ὄγδοον ἔτος ἐτελεύτα
τῷ πολέμῳ.

CXVII. Λακεδαιμόνιοι δὲ καὶ Ἀθηναῖοι ἅμα
ἦρι τοῦ ἐπιγιγνομένου θέρους εὐθὺς ἐκεχειρίαν
ἐποιήσαντο ἐνιαύσιον, νομίσαντες Ἀθηναῖοι μὲν
οὐκ ἂν ἔτι τὸν Βρασίδαν σφῶν προσαποστῆσαι
οὐδὲν πρὶν παρασκευάσαιντο καθ' ἡσυχίαν, καὶ
ἅμα, εἰ καλῶς σφίσιν ἔχοι, κἂν ξυμβῆναι τὰ
πλείω, Λακεδαιμόνιοι δὲ ταῦτα τοὺς Ἀθηναίους
ἡγούμενοι ἅπερ ἐδέδισαν φοβεῖσθαι, καὶ γενομένης
ἀνοκωχῆς κακῶν καὶ ταλαιπωρίας μᾶλλον ἐπιθυ-
μήσειν αὐτοὺς πειρασαμένους ξυναλλαγῆναί τε
καὶ τοὺς ἄνδρας σφίσιν ἀποδόντας σπονδὰς

he bore down at once with the army and took the
fort, destroying all that he found in it. And so the
Athenians left the place in their small boats and ships
and were thus conveyed to Pallene. Now there is a
temple of Athena in Lecythus, and it chanced that
Brasidas, when he was on the point of making the
assault, had proclaimed that he would give thirty
minas [1] in silver to him who first mounted the wall;
but thinking now that the capture had been effected
by some other means than human, he paid the thirty
minas to the goddess for the temple, and after razing
Lecythus and clearing the ground consecrated the
whole place as a sacred precinct. Then for the rest
of the winter he proceeded to set in order the
affairs of the places that he held and to plot against
the other towns; and with the conclusion of this
winter ended the eighth year of the war.

CXVII. But at the opening of spring in the following summer season, the Lacedaemonians and
Athenians at once concluded an armistice for a year.
The Athenians believed that Brasidas would thus not
be able to cause any more of their allies to revolt
and they meanwhile could make preparations at
their leisure, and at the same time that, should it
be to their advantage, they might make further
agreements; the Lacedaemonians, on their part,
thought that the Athenians were moved by precisely
the fears which actuated them,[2] and that, when once
they had enjoyed a respite from troubles and hard-
ships, they would, after such an experience, be more
anxious to be reconciled, restore their men and make

423 B C.

---

[1] £122, $580.
[2] i.e., if an armistice did not intervene, Brasidas might
detach still other allies from them.

2 ποιήσασθαι καὶ ἐς τὸν πλείω χρόνον. τοὺς γὰρ
δὴ ἄνδρας περὶ πλείονος ἐποιοῦντο κομίσασθαι,
ἕως ¹ ἔτι Βρασίδας ηὐτύχει. καὶ ἔμελλον ἐπὶ
μεῖζον χωρήσαντος αὐτοῦ καὶ ἀντίπαλα κατα-
στήσαντος τῶν μὲν στέρεσθαι, τοῖς δ' ἐκ τοῦ ἴσου
ἀμυνόμενοι κινδυνεύειν, εἰ ² καὶ κρατήσειαν.
3 γίγνεται οὖν ἐκεχειρία αὐτοῖς τε καὶ τοῖς ξυμμάχοις ἥδε·

CXVIII. "Περὶ μὲν τοῦ ἱεροῦ καὶ τοῦ μαντείου
τοῦ Ἀπόλλωνος τοῦ Πυθίου δοκεῖ ἡμῖν χρῆσθαι
τὸν βουλόμενον ἀδόλως καὶ ἀδεῶς κατὰ τοὺς
2 πατρίους νόμους. τοῖς μὲν Λακεδαιμονίοις ταῦτα
δοκεῖ καὶ τοῖς ξυμμάχοις τοῖς παροῦσιν· Βοιωτοὺς
δὲ καὶ Φωκέας πείσειν φασὶν ἐς δύναμιν προσκη-
ρυκευόμενοι.

3 "Περὶ δὲ τῶν χρημάτων τῶν τοῦ θεοῦ ἐπιμέ-
λεσθαι ὅπως τοὺς ἀδικοῦντας ἐξευρήσομεν, ὀρθῶς
καὶ δικαίως τοῖς πατρίοις νόμοις χρώμενοι καὶ
ὑμεῖς καὶ ἡμεῖς καὶ τῶν ἄλλων οἱ βουλόμενοι,
4 τοῖς πατρίοις νόμοις χρώμενοι πάντες. περὶ μὲν
οὖν τούτων ἔδοξε Λακεδαιμονίοις καὶ τοῖς ἄλλοις
ξυμμάχοις κατὰ ταῦτα.

"Τάδε δὲ ἔδοξε Λακεδαιμονίοις καὶ τοῖς ἄλλοις
ξυμμάχοις, ἐὰν σπονδὰς ποιῶνται οἱ Ἀθηναῖοι,
ἐπὶ τῆς αὐτῶν μένειν ἑκατέρους ἔχοντας ἅπερ νῦν
ἔχομεν, τοὺς μὲν ἐν τῷ Κορυφασίῳ ἐντὸς τῆς
Βουφράδος καὶ τοῦ Τομέως μένοντας, τοὺς δὲ ἐν

---

¹ ἕως, so Hude and van Herwerden from schol. on Ar.
Pax 479 ; MSS. ὡς.
² εἰ καὶ κρατήσειαν, Madvig's conjecture, for καὶ κρατήσειν
of the MSS.

a truce for a longer time. For it was their men they made a special point of recovering, while Brasidas was still in good luck. If he were still further successful and established the contending forces on an even footing, the likelihood was that they would still be deprived of these men, and it would be doubtful whether, fighting on equal terms, they could prevail with the remainder. Accordingly an armistice was concluded for them and their allies on the following terms :

CXVIII. "Concerning the temple and oracle of the Pythian Apollo, we agree that whosoever will shall consult it without fraud and without fear, according to the usages of our forefathers. These things seem good to the Lacedaemonians and the allies that are present; and they promise to send heralds to the Boeotians and Phocians and persuade them so far as they can.

"Concerning the treasure of the god we agree to take care to find out all wrong-doers, rightly and justly following the usages of our forefathers, you and we and all others that wish to do so, all following the usages of our forefathers. Concerning these things, then, it is so agreed by the Lacedaemonians and the rest of the confederates on such terms.

"The following agreements also are made by the Lacedaemonians and the rest of the confederates, that in case the Athenians make a treaty, we shall each of us remain on our own territory, keeping what we now have : the Athenian garrison in Coryphasium[1] shall keep within Buphras and Tomeus;

---

[1] The Lacedaemonian name of Pylos (ch. iii. 2). Buphras and Tomeus were two high points on the coast.

THUCYDIDES

Κυθήροις μὴ ἐπιμισγομένους ἐς τὴν ξυμμαχίαν,
μήτε ἡμᾶς πρὸς αὐτοὺς μήτε αὐτοὺς πρὸς ἡμᾶς,
τοὺς δ' ἐν Νισαίᾳ καὶ Μινῴᾳ μὴ ὑπερβαίνοντας
τὴν ὁδὸν τὴν ἀπὸ τῶν πυλῶν τῶν παρὰ¹ τοῦ
Νίσου ἐπὶ τὸ Ποσειδώνιον, ἀπὸ δὲ τοῦ Ποσει-
δωνίου εὐθὺς ἐπὶ τὴν γέφυραν τὴν ἐς Μινῴαν
(μηδὲ Μεγαρέας καὶ τοὺς ξυμμάχους ὑπερβαίνειν
τὴν ὁδὸν ταύτην), καὶ τὴν νῆσον, ἥνπερ ἔλαβον
οἱ Ἀθηναῖοι, ἔχοντας, μηδὲ ἐπιμισγομένους μηδετέρους μηδετέρωσε, καὶ τὰ ἐν Τροιζῆνι, ὅσαπερ
νῦν ἔχουσι καθ' ἃ² ξυνέθεντο πρὸς Ἀθηναίους.

5 "Καὶ τῇ θαλάσσῃ χρωμένους, ὅσα ἂν κατὰ
τὴν ἑαυτῶν καὶ κατὰ τὴν ξυμμαχίαν, Λακεδαιμονίους καὶ τοὺς ξυμμάχους πλεῖν μὴ μακρᾷ νηί,
ἄλλῳ δὲ κωπήρει πλοίῳ ἐς πεντακόσια τάλαντα
ἄγοντι μέτρα.

6 "Κήρυκι δὲ καὶ πρεσβείᾳ καὶ ἀκολούθοις,
ὁπόσοις ἂν δοκῇ, περὶ καταλύσεως τοῦ πολέμου
καὶ δικῶν ἐς Πελοπόννησον καὶ Ἀθήναζε σπονδὰς
εἶναι ἰοῦσι καὶ ἀπιοῦσι, καὶ κατὰ γῆν καὶ κατὰ
θάλασσαν.

7 "Τοὺς δὲ αὐτομόλους μὴ δέχεσθαι ἐν τούτῳ τῷ
χρόνῳ, μήτε ἐλεύθερον μήτε δοῦλον, μήτε ὑμᾶς
μήτε ἡμᾶς.

8 "Δίκας τε διδόναι ὑμᾶς τε ἡμῖν καὶ ἡμᾶς ὑμῖν
κατὰ τὰ πάτρια, τὰ ἀμφίλογα δίκῃ διαλύοντας
ἄνευ πολέμου.

¹ M reads ἀπὸ τοῦ Νισαίου.
² Kirchhoff's correction for καὶ οἷα of the MSS.

---

¹ cf. chs. liii., liv.   ² cf. ch. lxix.
³ cf. III. li.; IV. lxvii.
⁴ Lit. "the gates leading from the shrine [or statue, as παρά might indicate] of Nisus."

412

that in Cythera[1] shall have no communication with
the territory of the Lacedaemonian allies, neither we
with them nor they with us; that in Nisaea[2] and
Minoa[3] shall not cross the road leading from the
gates of the shrine of Nisus[4] to the Poseidonium,
and from the Poseidonium straight to the bridge[5]
at Minoa (nor shall the Megarians or their allies
cross this road); as to the island[6] which the Athenians took, they shall retain it, and neither party shall
communicate with the other; and finally, in the
territory of Troezen,[7] the Athenians shall retain
whatever they now have in accordance with the
agreements which the Troezenians have made with
the Athenians.

"As to the use of the sea, in so far as they use it
along their own coast and along that of their confederacy, the Lacedaemonians and their allies may
sail, not with a ship of war, but with any rowing-
vessel up to five hundred talents burden.[8]

"There shall be safe conduct for herald and envoys
and their attendants, as many as shall seem proper,
on their way to the Peloponnesus and to Athens for
the purpose of bringing the war to an end and for the
arbitration of disputes, both going and coming, by
land and by sea.

"Deserters shall not be received during this time,
whether freemen or slaves, either by you or by us.

"You shall give satisfaction to us and we to you
according to our ancestral customs, settling disputed
points by arbitration without war.

[5] Connecting Minoa with the mainland; *cf.* III. li. 3.
[6] Probably Atalante is meant; *cf.* III. lxxxix. 3; v. xviii. 7.
[7] The Athenian fortification on the isthmus of Methana;
cf. ch. xlv. 2.
[8] About 12½ tons.

" Τοῖς μὲν Λακεδαιμονίοις καὶ τοῖς ξυμμάχοις
9 ταῦτα δοκεῖ· εἰ δέ τι ὑμῖν εἴτε κάλλιον εἴτε
δικαιότερον τούτων δοκεῖ εἶναι, ἰόντες ἐς Λακεδαίμονα διδάσκετε· οὐδενὸς γὰρ ἀποστήσονται,
ὅσα ἂν δίκαια λέγητε, οὔτε οἱ Λακεδαιμόνιοι
10 οὔτε οἱ ξύμμαχοι. οἱ δὲ ἰόντες τέλος ἔχοντες
ἰόντων, ᾗπερ καὶ ὑμεῖς ἡμᾶς ἐκελεύετε. αἱ δὲ
σπονδαὶ ἐνιαυτὸν ἔσονται."

11 Ἔδοξεν τῷ δήμῳ. Ἀκαμαντὶς ἐπρυτάνευε,
Φαίνιππος ἐγραμμάτευε, Νικιάδης ἐπεστάτει.
Λάχης εἶπε, τύχῃ ἀγαθῇ τῇ Ἀθηναίων, ποιεῖσθαι
τὴν ἐκεχειρίαν, καθ᾽ ἃ ξυγχωροῦσι Λακεδαιμόνιοι
καὶ οἱ ξύμμαχοι αὐτῶν· καὶ ὡμολόγησαν ἐν τῷ
12 δήμῳ τὴν[1] ἐκεχειρίαν εἶναι ἐνιαυτόν, ἄρχειν δὲ
τήνδε τὴν ἡμέραν, τετράδα ἐπὶ δέκα τοῦ Ἐλαφη-
13 βολιῶνος μηνός. ἐν τούτῳ τῷ χρόνῳ ἰόντας ὡς
ἀλλήλους πρέσβεις καὶ κήρυκας ποιεῖσθαι τοὺς
λόγους, καθ᾽ ὅ τι ἔσται ἡ κατάλυσις τοῦ πολέμου.
14 ἐκκλησίαν δὲ ποιήσαντας τοὺς στρατηγοὺς καὶ
τοὺς πρυτάνεις[2] πρῶτον περὶ τῆς εἰρήνης βουλεύσασθαι Ἀθηναίους καθ᾽ ὅ τι ἂν ἐσίῃ[3] ἡ πρεσβεία
περὶ τῆς καταλύσεως τοῦ πολέμου. σπείσασθαι
δὲ αὐτίκα μάλα τὰς πρεσβείας ἐν τῷ δήμῳ τὰς
παρούσας ἦ μὴν ἐμμενεῖν ἐν ταῖς σπονδαῖς τὸν
ἐνιαυτόν.

CXIX. Ταῦτα ξυνέθεντο Λακεδαιμόνιοι καὶ
ὤμοσαν[4] καὶ οἱ ξύμμαχοι Ἀθηναίοις καὶ τοῖς

---

[1] Hude inserts δ᾽, after Kirchhoff.
[2] The change of subject implies a relative clause ; something like ἐν ᾗ may have dropped out.
[3] Hude reads ἂν εἶσιν, after Kirchhoff.
[4] καὶ ὤμοσαν (Vulg. καὶ ὡμολόγησαν) deleted by Hude, after
Kirchhoff.

"To the Lacedaemonians and their allies these things seem good; but if anything seems to you fairer or juster than these things, come to Lacedaemon and set forth your view; for neither the Lacedaemonians nor their allies will reject any just proposal you may make. And let those who come come with full powers, as you also desired of us. And the truce shall be for a year."

[1] *Decreed by the people. The tribe Acamantis held the prytany, Phaenippus was clerk, Niciades was president. Laches, invoking good fortune for the people of Athens, moved to conclude the armistice according to the terms to which the Lacedaemonians and their allies had consented;* and it was agreed in the popular assembly that the armistice should be for a year, and should begin on that day, the fourteenth of the month Elaphebolion. During this time envoys and heralds were to go from one state to the other and discuss proposals looking to the termination of the war. And the generals and prytanes were to call an assembly in which the Athenians should deliberate first of all about peace, on what terms the Lacedaemonian embassy for ending the war should be admitted. And the embassies now present should pledge themselves at once, in the presence of the people, to abide by the truce for the year.

CXIX. These agreements the Lacedaemonians and their allies made with the Athenians and their allies

---

[1] The prescript of the Athenian decree which ratified the truce is quoted verbatim (italics above).

ξυμμάχοις μηνὸς ἐν Λακεδαίμονι Γεραστίου
2 δωδεκάτῃ. ξυνετίθεντο δὲ καὶ ἐσπένδοντο Λακεδαιμονίων μὲν οἵδε· Ταῦρος Ἐχετιμίδα, Ἀθήναιος Περικλείδα, Φιλοχαρίδας Ἐρυξιλᾴδα·
Κορινθίων δὲ Αἰνέας Ὠκύτου, Εὐφαμίδας
Ἀριστωνύμου· Σικυωνίων δὲ Δαμότιμος Ναυ-
κράτους, Ὀνάσιμος Μεγακλέους· Μεγαρέων δὲ
Νίκασος Κεκάλου, Μενεκράτης Ἀμφιδώρου·
Ἐπιδαυρίων δὲ Ἀμφίας Εὐπαλίδα·¹ Ἀθηναίων δὲ
οἱ στρατηγοὶ Νικόστρατος Διειτρέφους, Νικίας
Νικηράτου, Αὐτοκλῆς Τολμαίου.
3   Ἡ μὲν δὴ ἐκεχειρία αὕτη ἐγένετο, καὶ ξυνῆσαν
ἐν αὐτῇ περὶ τῶν μειζόνων σπονδῶν διὰ παντὸς
ἐς λόγους.

CXX. Περὶ δὲ τὰς ἡμέρας ταύτας αἷς ἐπήρ-
χοντο Σκιώνη ἐν τῇ Παλλήνῃ πόλις ἀπέστη ἀπ᾽
Ἀθηναίων πρὸς Βρασίδαν. φασὶ δὲ οἱ Σκιωναῖοι
Πελληνῆς μὲν εἶναι ἐκ Πελοποννήσου, πλέοντας
δ᾽ ἀπὸ Τροίας σφῶν τοὺς πρώτους κατενεχθῆναι
ἐς τὸ χωρίον τοῦτο τῷ χειμῶνι ᾧ ἐχρήσαντο
2 Ἀχαιοί, καὶ αὐτοῦ οἰκῆσαι. ἀποστᾶσι δ᾽ αὐτοῖς
ὁ Βρασίδας διέπλευσε νυκτὸς ἐς τὴν Σκιώνην,
τριήρει μὲν φιλίᾳ προπλεούσῃ, αὐτὸς δὲ ἐν κελη-
τίῳ ἄπωθεν ἐφεπόμενος, ὅπως, εἰ μέν τινι τοῦ

¹ Hude's conjecture; Bekker Εὐπαῖδα, for Εὐπαῖδα of
most MSS.

---

¹ Grote is probably right in assuming that the twelfth of
Gerastius corresponded to the fourteenth of Elaphebolion.
² These consisted of formal libations.

and ratified them by oath at Lacedaemon on the twelfth day of the Spartan month Gerastius.[1] And those who concluded and ratified the truce on behalf of the Lacedaemonians were the following: Taurus son of Echetimidas, Athenaeus son of Pericleidas, Philocharidas son of Eryxilaidas; on behalf of the Corinthians, Aeneas son of Ocytus, Euphamidas son of Aristonymus; on behalf of the Sicyonians, Damotimus son of Naucrates, Onasimus son of Megacles; on behalf of the Megarians, Nicasus son of Cecalus, Menecrates son of Amphidorus; on behalf of the Epidaurians, Amphias son of Eupalidas; on behalf of the Athenians, the generals Nicostratus son of Dieitrephes, Nicias son of Niceratus, Autocles son of Tolmaeus.

Such, then, were the terms on which the armistice was concluded, and during its continuance they were constantly conferring about a truce of longer duration.

CXX. About the very time when they were performing the rites of confirmation,[2] Scione, a city in Pallene, revolted from the Athenians and went over to Brasidas. The Scionaeans assert that they came originally from Pellene[3] in the Peloponnesus, and that the first settlers in Scione were driven to this place on their way back from Troy by the storm[4] which the Achaeans encountered, and settled here. On their revolt, Brasidas crossed over[5] by night to Scione, a friendly trireme sailing ahead and he himself following in a skiff at some distance behind. His idea was that, if he should meet with any boat

---

[3] Pellene was in Achaea, near Sicyon; the people are mentioned as allies of Sparta in II. ix. 2.

[4] Referred to again in VI. ii. 3.   [5] *i.e.* from Torone.

κέλητος μείζονι πλοίῳ περιτυγχάνοι, ἡ τριήρης
ἀμύνοι αὐτῷ,¹ ἀντιπάλου δὲ ἄλλης τριήρους
ἐπιγενομένης οὐ πρὸς τὸ ἔλασσον νομίζων
τρέψεσθαι, ἀλλ' ἐπὶ τὴν ναῦν, καὶ ἐν τούτῳ
3 αὐτὸν διασώσειν. περαιωθεὶς δὲ καὶ ξύλλογον
ποιήσας τῶν Σκιωναίων ἔλεγεν ἅ τε ἐν τῇ
'Ακάνθῳ καὶ Τορώνῃ, καὶ προσέτι πάντων² ἀξιω-
τάτους αὐτοὺς εἶναι ἐπαίνου, οἵτινες τῆς Παλ-
λήνης ἐν τῷ ἰσθμῷ ἀπειλημμένης ὑπὸ 'Αθηναίων
Ποτείδαιαν ἐχόντων καὶ ὄντες οὐδὲν ἄλλο ἢ
νησιῶται αὐτεπάγγελτοι ἐχώρησαν πρὸς τὴν
ἐλευθερίαν καὶ οὐκ ἀνέμειναν ἀτολμίᾳ ἀνάγκην
σφίσι προσγενέσθαι περὶ τοῦ φανερῶς οἰκείου
ἀγαθοῦ· σημεῖόν τ' εἶναι τοῦ καὶ ἄλλο τι ἂν
αὐτοὺς τῶν μεγίστων ἀνδρείως ὑπομεῖναι· εἴ τε³
τεθήσεται κατὰ νοῦν τὰ πράγματα, πιστοτάτους
τε τῇ ἀληθείᾳ ἡγήσεσθαι αὐτοὺς Λακεδαιμονίων
φίλους καὶ τἆλλα τιμήσειν.

CXXI. Καὶ οἱ μὲν Σκιωναῖοι ἐπήρθησάν τε
τοῖς λόγοις καὶ θαρσήσαντες πάντες ὁμοίως, καὶ
οἷς πρότερον μὴ ἤρεσκε τὰ πρασσόμενα, τόν τε
πόλεμον διενοοῦντο προθύμως οἴσειν καὶ τὸν
Βρασίδαν τά τ' ἄλλα καλῶς ἐδέξαντο καὶ δημοσίᾳ μὲν χρυσῷ στεφάνῳ ἀνέδησαν ὡς ἐλευθε-
ροῦντα τὴν Ἑλλάδα, ἰδίᾳ δὲ ἐταινίουν τε καὶ
2 προσήρχοντο ὥσπερ ἀθλητῇ. ὁ δὲ τό τε παραυτίκα φυλακήν τινα αὐτοῖς ἐγκαταλιπὼν διέβη
πάλιν καὶ ὕστερον οὐ πολλῷ στρατιὰν πλείω

---

¹ The corrected reading of two minor MSS.; all the better
MSS. αὐτῇ. Hude deletes, after Poppo.
² πάντων, Hude adopts Krüger's conjecture, φάσκων.
³ τε added by Krüger.

larger than a skiff, the trireme would protect him, but if another trireme of equal strength should come along it would turn, not against the smaller boat, but against the ship, and in the meantime he could get safely across. He succeeded in crossing, and having called a meeting of the Scionaeans repeated what he had said at Acanthus and Torone, adding that their own conduct had been most praiseworthy of all because, when Pallene was cut off at the isthmus by the Athenians who held Potidaea and when they were nothing but islanders, they had not supinely awaited the compulsion of necessity in a matter that was manifestly for their own good, but had of their own free will taken the side of freedom ; and that, he said, was a proof that they would endure like men any other peril however great ; and if things should be settled according to his wish, he would consider them in very truth most loyal friends of the Lacedaemonians and would honour them in other respects.

CXXI. The Scionaeans were elated at his words, and all alike, even those who before were not satisfied with what was being done, took courage and determined to carry on the war with spirit. Brasidas they not only welcomed with other honours but publicly crowned him with a golden crown as liberator of Hellas, and privately decked him with garlands and made offerings as for a victor in the games. And he, leaving them a guard for the present, crossed back, but not long afterwards he led over a

ἐπεραίωσε, βουλόμενος μετ' αὐτῶν τῆς τε Μένδης
καὶ τῆς Ποτειδαίας ἀποπειρᾶσαι, ἡγούμενος καὶ
τοὺς Ἀθηναίους βοηθῆσαι ἂν ὡς ἐς νῆσον καὶ
βουλόμενος φθάσαι· καί τι αὐτῷ καὶ ἐπράσσετο
ἐς τὰς πόλεις ταύτας προδοσίας πέρι.

CXXII. Καὶ ὁ μὲν ἔμελλεν ἐγχειρήσειν ταῖς
πόλεσι ταύταις· ἐν τούτῳ δὲ τριήρει οἱ τὴν
ἐκεχειρίαν περιαγγέλλοντες ἀφικνοῦνται παρ'
αὐτόν, Ἀθηναίων μὲν Ἀριστώνυμος, Λακεδαι-
2 μονίων δὲ Ἀθήναιος. καὶ ἡ μὲν στρατιὰ πάλιν
διέβη ἐς Τορώνην, οἱ δὲ τῷ¹ Βρασίδᾳ ἀνήγγελλον
τὴν ξυνθήκην, καὶ ἐδέξαντο πάντες οἱ ἐπὶ Θράκης
3 ξύμμαχοι Λακεδαιμονίων τὰ πεπραγμένα. Ἀριστώνυμος δὲ τοῖς μὲν ἄλλοις κατῄνει, Σκιω-
ναίους δὲ αἰσθόμενος ἐκ λογισμοῦ τῶν ἡμερῶν
ὅτι ὕστερον ἀφεστήκοιεν, οὐκ ἔφη ἐνσπόνδους
ἔσεσθαι. Βρασίδας δὲ ἀντέλεγε πολλά, ὡς
4 πρότερον, καὶ οὐκ ἀφίει τὴν πόλιν. ὡς δ' ἀπήγ-
γελλεν ἐς τὰς Ἀθήνας ὁ Ἀριστώνυμος περὶ
αὐτῶν, οἱ Ἀθηναῖοι εὐθὺς ἕτοιμοι ἦσαν στρατεύειν ἐπὶ τὴν Σκιώνην. οἱ δὲ Λακεδαιμόνιοι
πρέσβεις πέμψαντες παραβήσεσθαι ἔφασαν αὐτοὺς τὰς σπονδάς, καὶ τῆς πόλεως ἀντεποιοῦντο
Βρασίδᾳ πιστεύοντες, δίκῃ τε ἕτοιμοι ἦσαν περὶ
5 αὐτῆς κρίνεσθαι. οἱ δὲ δίκῃ μὲν οὐκ ἤθελον
κινδυνεύειν, στρατεύειν δὲ ὡς τάχιστα, ὀργὴν
ποιούμενοι εἰ καὶ οἱ ἐν ταῖς νήσοις ἤδη ὄντες
ἀξιοῦσι σφῶν ἀφίστασθαι, τῇ κατὰ γῆν Λακε-
6 δαιμονίων ἰσχύι ἀνωφελεῖ πιστεύοντες· εἶχε δὲ
καὶ ἡ ἀλήθεια περὶ τῆς ἀποστάσεως μᾶλλον ᾗ

_____

¹ τῷ deleted by Hude, after Stahl.

larger army, wishing in concert with them to make an attempt upon Mende and Potidaea; for he thought the Athenians would bring succour to Pallene as though it were an island, and he wished to anticipate them; besides, he was negotiating with these towns with a view to their betrayal.

CXXII. So he was about to attack these towns; but in the meantime those who were carrying round the news of the armistice arrived at his head-quarters in a trireme, Aristonymus from Athens and Athenaeus from Lacedaemon. Whereupon his army crossed back to Torone; and the messengers formally announced the agreement to Brasidas, and all the Thracian allies of the Lacedaemonians acquiesced in what had been done. Aristonymus assented for the other places, but, finding on a calculation of the days that the Scionaeans had revolted after the agreement, he said that they would not be included in the truce. Brasidas, however, earnestly maintained that they had revolted before, and would not give up the city. Whereupon Aristonymus sent word to Athens about these matters, and the Athenians were ready at once to make an expedition against Scione. But the Lacedaemonians sent envoys, saying that the Athenians would be violating the truce, and trusting the word of Brasidas they laid claim to the town and were ready to arbitrate about it. The Athenians, however, were inclined, not to risk arbitration, but to make an expedition as quickly as possible, being enraged to think that even the inhabitants of the islands now presumed to revolt, relying on the strength which the Lacedaemonians had on land, useless though it was to them.[1] Moreover, the truth about the

---

[1] Because the Athenians commanded the sea.

οἱ Ἀθηναῖοι ἐδικαίουν· δύο γὰρ ἡμέραις ὕστερον
ἀπέστησαν οἱ Σκιωναῖοι. ψήφισμά τ' εὐθὺς
ἐποιήσαντο, Κλέωνος γνώμῃ πεισθέντες, Σκιω-
ναίους ἐξελεῖν τε καὶ ἀποκτεῖναι. καὶ τἆλλα
ἡσυχάζοντες ἐς τοῦτο παρεσκευάζοντο.

CXXIII. Ἐν τούτῳ δὲ Μένδη ἀφίσταται
αὐτῶν, πόλις ἐν τῇ Παλλήνῃ, Ἐρετριῶν ἀποικία.
καὶ αὐτοὺς ἐδέξατο ὁ Βρασίδας, οὐ νομίζων
ἀδικεῖν, ὅτι ἐν τῇ ἐκεχειρίᾳ φανερῶς προσε-
χώρησαν· ἔστι γὰρ ἃ καὶ αὐτὸς ἐνεκάλει τοῖς
2 Ἀθηναίοις παραβαίνειν τὰς σπονδάς. δι' ὃ καὶ
οἱ Μενδαῖοι μᾶλλον ἐτόλμησαν, τήν τε τοῦ
Βρασίδου γνώμην ὁρῶντες ἑτοίμην, τεκμαιρόμενοι
καὶ ἀπὸ τῆς Σκιώνης ὅτι οὐ προυδίδου, καὶ ἅμα
τῶν πρασσόντων σφίσιν[1] ὀλίγων τε ὄντων καὶ
ὡς τότε ἐμέλλησαν, οὐκέτι ἀνέντων, ἀλλὰ περὶ
σφίσιν αὐτοῖς φοβουμένων τὸ κατάδηλον καὶ
καταβιασαμένων παρὰ γνώμην τοὺς πολλούς.
3 οἱ δὲ Ἀθηναῖοι εὐθὺς πυθόμενοι, πολλῷ ἔτι
μᾶλλον ὀργισθέντες παρεσκευάζοντο ἐπ' ἀμφοτέ-
4 ρας τὰς πόλεις. καὶ Βρασίδας προσδεχόμενος
τὸν ἐπίπλουν αὐτῶν ὑπεκκομίζει ἐς Ὄλυνθον τὴν
Χαλκιδικὴν παῖδας καὶ γυναῖκας τῶν Σκιωναίων
καὶ Μενδαίων, καὶ τῶν Πελοποννησίων αὐτοῖς
πεντακοσίους ὁπλίτας διέπεμψε καὶ πελταστὰς
τριακοσίους Χαλκιδέων, ἄρχοντά τε τῶν ἁπάντων
Πολυδαμίδαν. καὶ οἱ μὲν τὰ περὶ σφᾶς αὐτούς,
ὡς ἐν τάχει παρεσομένων τῶν Ἀθηναίων, κοινῇ
ηὐτρεπίζοντο.

CXXIV. Βρασίδας δὲ καὶ Περδίκκας ἐν τούτῳ
στρατεύουσιν ἅμα ἐπὶ Ἀρράβαιον τὸ δεύτερον

---

[1] σφίσιν, Krüger deletes, followed by Hude.

revolt was rather as the Athenians claimed; for the Scionaeans revolted two days after the agreement. The Athenians, then, immediately passed a vote, on the motion of Cleon, to destroy Scione and put the citizens to death. And so, keeping quiet in other matters, they made preparations for this.

CXXIII. Meanwhile Mende revolted from them, a city in Pallene, and an Eretrian colony. And Brasidas received them, thinking they were not doing wrong in coming over to him, though clearly it was in the time of the armistice; for there were some points in which he himself charged the Athenians with breaking the truce. Wherefore the Mendaeans also became more bold, for they saw the resolute attitude of Brasidas, and also inferred it from the fact that he did not give up Scione. Moreover, the conspirators among them were few in number, and, once they had formed the design, from that moment showed no slackness, but were in fear of their lives in case of detection and coerced the multitude even against their will. But the Athenians, when they heard the news, were far more enraged, and straightway made preparations against both cities. And Brasidas, expecting their coming, conveyed away to Olynthus in Chalcidice the women and children of the Scionaeans and Mendaeans, and sent over to protect them five hundred Peloponnesian hoplites and three hundred Chalcidian targeteers, with Polydamidas as commander of the whole. And the two cities together made preparations for their defence, in the belief that the Athenians would soon be at hand.

CXXIV. Brasidas and Perdiccas meanwhile marched together a second time[1] to Lyncus against

[1] *cf.* ch. lxxxiii.

ἐς Λύγκον. καὶ ἦγον ὁ μὲν ὧν ἐκράτει Μακεδόνων τὴν δύναμιν καὶ τῶν ἐνοικούντων Ἑλλήνων
ὁπλίτας, ὁ δὲ πρὸς τοῖς αὑτοῦ περιλοίποις τῶν
Πελοποννησίων Χαλκιδέας καὶ Ἀκανθίους καὶ
τῶν ἄλλων κατὰ δύναμιν ἑκάστων. ξύμπαν δὲ
τὸ ὁπλιτικὸν τῶν Ἑλλήνων τρισχίλιοι μάλιστα,
ἱππῆς δ' οἱ πάντες ἠκολούθουν Μακεδόνων ξὺν
Χαλκιδεῦσιν ὀλίγου ἐς χιλίους, καὶ ἄλλος ὅμιλος
2 τῶν βαρβάρων πολύς. ἐσβαλόντες δὲ ἐς τὴν
Ἀρραβαίου καὶ εὑρόντες ἀντεστρατοπεδευμένους
αὑτοῖς τοὺς Λυγκηστάς, ἀντεκαθέζοντο καὶ
3 αὑτοί. καὶ ἐχόντων τῶν μὲν πεζῶν λόφον ἑκατέρωθεν, πεδίου δὲ τοῦ μέσου ὄντος, οἱ ἱππῆς ἐς
αὐτὸ καταδραμόντες ἱππομάχησαν πρῶτα ἀμφοτέρων, ἔπειτα δὲ καὶ ὁ Βρασίδας καὶ ὁ Περδίκκας,
προελθόντων προτέρων ἀπὸ τοῦ λόφου μετὰ τῶν
ἱππέων τῶν Λυγκηστῶν ὁπλιτῶν καὶ ἑτοίμων
ὄντων μάχεσθαι, ἀντεπαγαγόντες καὶ αὐτοὶ ξυνέβαλον καὶ ἔτρεψαν τοὺς Λυγκηστάς, καὶ πολλοὺς μὲν διέφθειραν, οἱ δὲ λοιποὶ διαφυγόντες
4 πρὸς τὰ μετέωρα ἡσύχαζον. μετὰ δὲ τοῦτο
τροπαῖον στήσαντες δύο μὲν ἢ τρεῖς ἡμέρας
ἐπέσχον, τοὺς Ἰλλυριοὺς μένοντες, οἳ ἔτυχον
τῷ Περδίκκᾳ μισθοῦ μέλλοντες ἥξειν. ἔπειτα
ὁ Περδίκκας ἐβούλετο προϊέναι ἐπὶ τὰς τοῦ
Ἀρραβαίου κώμας καὶ μὴ καθῆσθαι, Βρασίδας δὲ
τῆς τε Μένδης περιορώμενος, μὴ τῶν Ἀθηναίων
πρότερον ἐπιπλευσάντων τι πάθῃ, καὶ ἅμα τῶν
Ἰλλυριῶν οὐ παρόντων, οὐ πρόθυμος ἦν, ἀλλὰ
ἀναχωρεῖν μᾶλλον.

CXXV. Καὶ ἐν τούτῳ διαφερομένων αὐτῶν
ἠγγέλθη ὅτι καὶ οἱ Ἰλλυριοὶ μετ' Ἀρραβαίου,

Arrhabaeus. The latter led the force of the Macedonians, over whom he held sway, and a body of Hellenic hoplites resident among them; the former led not only the Peloponnesian troops which were left in the country, but also such forces from Chalcidice, Acanthus and the other towns as they could each furnish. The total Hellenic force was about three thousand; the cavalry that went with them, Macedonians and Chalcidians, were all told a little less than one thousand, and there was besides a great multitude of barbarians. Invading the country of Arrhabaeus and finding the Lyncestians encamped against them, they also took up a position facing them. The infantry occupied a hill on either side, with a plain between, while the cavalry of both armies at first galloped down into the plain and engaged in battle; then Brasidas and Perdiccas, after the Lyncestian hoplites had come forward from the hill in conjunction with their own cavalry and were ready to fight, advanced also in their turn and joined battle, routing the Lyncestians and destroying many, while the rest escaped to the high places and kept quiet. After this they set up a trophy and halted for two or three days, awaiting the Illyrians, who had been hired by Perdiccas and were momentarily expected. Then Perdiccas wished, on their arrival, to go forward against the villages of Arrhabaeus instead of sitting idle; but Brasidas was solicitous about Mende, fearing that it might suffer some harm if the Athenians should sail there before his return; and, besides, the Illyrians had not appeared, so that he was not eager to go on, but rather to retreat.

CXXV. Meanwhile, as they were disputing, it was announced that the Illyrians had betrayed Perdiccas

προδόντες Περδίκκαν, γεγένηνται· ὥστε ἤδη ἀμφοτέροις μὲν δοκοῦν ἀναχωρεῖν διὰ τὸ δέος αὐτῶν,
ὄντων ἀνθρώπων μαχίμων, κυρωθὲν δὲ οὐδὲν ἐκ
τῆς διαφορᾶς ὁπηνίκα χρὴ ὁρμᾶσθαι, νυκτός τε
ἐπιγενομένης, οἱ μὲν Μακεδόνες καὶ τὸ πλῆθος
τῶν βαρβάρων εὐθὺς φοβηθέντες, ὅπερ φιλεῖ
μεγάλα στρατόπεδα ἀσαφῶς ἐκπλήγνυσθαι, καὶ
νομίσαντες πολλαπλασίους μὲν ἢ ἦλθον ἐπιέναι,
ὅσον δὲ οὔπω παρεῖναι, καταστάντες ἐς αἰφνίδιον
φυγὴν ἐχώρουν ἐπ' οἴκου, καὶ τὸν Περδίκκαν τὸ
πρῶτον οὐκ αἰσθανόμενον, ὡς ἔγνω, ἠνάγκασαν
πρὶν τὸν Βρασίδαν ἰδεῖν (ἄπωθεν γὰρ πολὺ
2 ἀλλήλων ἐστρατοπεδεύοντο) προαπελθεῖν. Βρασίδας δὲ ἅμα τῇ ἕῳ ὡς εἶδε τοὺς Μακεδόνας
προκεχωρηκότας,[1] τούς τε Ἰλλυριοὺς καὶ τὸν
Ἀρράβαιον μέλλοντας ἐπιέναι, ξυναγαγὼν καὶ
αὐτὸς ἐς τετράγωνον τάξιν τοὺς ὁπλίτας καὶ τὸν
ψιλὸν ὅμιλον ἐς μέσον λαβών, διενοεῖτο ἀνα-
3 χωρεῖν. ἐκδρόμους δέ, εἴ πῃ προσβάλλοιεν
αὐτοῖς, ἔταξε τοὺς νεωτάτους, καὶ αὐτὸς λογάδας
ἔχων τριακοσίους τελευταῖος γνώμην εἶχεν ὑπο-
χωρῶν τοῖς τῶν ἐναντίων πρώτοις προσκεισο-
4 μένοις ἀνθιστάμενος ἀμύνεσθαι. καὶ πρὶν τοὺς
πολεμίους ἐγγὺς εἶναι, ὡς διὰ ταχέων παρεκελεύ-
σατο τοῖς στρατιώταις τοιάδε.

CXXVI. "Εἰ μὲν μὴ ὑπώπτευον, ἄνδρες
Πελοποννήσιοι, ὑμᾶς τῷ τε μεμονῶσθαι καὶ ὅτι
βάρβαροι οἱ ἐπιόντες καὶ πολλοὶ ἔκπληξιν ἔχειν,
οὐκ ἂν ὁμοίως διδαχὴν ἅμα τῇ παρακελεύσει

---

[1] Hude adopts van Herwerden's conjecture, προανακε-
χωρηκότας.

and taken sides with Arrhabaeus; consequently, because of their fear of these people, who were warlike, both generals now agreed that it was best to retreat. But in consequence of their dispute nothing had been determined as to when they should set out; and when night came on the Macedonians and the mass of the barbarians immediately took fright, as large armies are wont to be smitten with unaccountable panic, and thinking that the advancing enemy were many times more numerous than they really were and were all but on them, betook themselves to sudden flight and hastened homewards. Perdiccas, who at first was not aware of their movement, was compelled, when he did learn of it, to go away without seeing Brasidas; for they were encamped far away from each other. But at daybreak, when Brasidas saw that the Macedonians had already decamped and that the Illyrians and Arrhabaeus were about to come against him, he formed his hoplites into a square, put the crowd of light-armed troops in the centre, and was himself intending to retreat. He so stationed the youngest of his troops that they might dash out against the enemy, in case they attacked at any point, and proposed to take himself three hundred picked men and, bringing up the rear, to make a stand and beat off the foremost of the enemy whenever they pressed him hard. And before the enemy were near he exhorted his soldiers, so far as haste allowed, in the following words:

CXXVI. "Did I not suspect, men of Peloponnesus, that you are in a state of panic because you have been left alone, and because your assailants are barbarous and numerous, I should not offer you

ἐποιούμην· νῦν δὲ πρὸς μὲν τὴν ἀπόλειψιν τῶν
ἡμετέρων καὶ τὸ πλῆθος τῶν ἐναντίων βραχεῖ
ὑπομνήματι καὶ παραινέσει τὰ μέγιστα πειρά-
2 σομαι πείθειν. ἀγαθοῖς γὰρ εἶναι ὑμῖν προσήκει
τὰ πολέμια οὐ διὰ ξυμμάχων παρουσίαν ἑκά-
στοτε, ἀλλὰ δι' οἰκείαν ἀρετήν, καὶ μηδὲν πλῆθος
πεφοβῆσθαι ἑτέρων, οἵγε μηδὲ ἀπὸ πολιτειῶν
τοιούτων ἥκετε, ἐν αἷς οὐ¹ πολλοὶ ὀλίγων ἄρχουσιν, ἀλλὰ πλειόνων μᾶλλον ἐλάσσους, οὐκ
ἄλλῳ τινὶ κτησάμενοι τὴν δυναστείαν ἢ τῷ μαχό-
3 μενοι κρατεῖν. βαρβάρους δὲ οὓς νῦν ἀπειρίᾳ
δέδιτε, μαθεῖν χρή, ἐξ ὧν τε προηγώνισθε τοῖς
Μακεδόσιν αὐτῶν καὶ ἀφ' ὧν ἐγὼ εἰκάζων τε καὶ
4 ἄλλων ἀκοῇ ἐπίσταμαι, οὐ δεινοὺς ἐσομένους. καὶ
γὰρ ὅσα μὲν τῷ ὄντι ἀσθενῆ ὄντα τῶν πολεμίων
δόκησιν ἔχει ἰσχύος, διδαχὴ ἀληθὴς προσγενομένη²
περὶ αὐτῶν ἐθάρσυνε μᾶλλον τοὺς ἀμυνομένους·
οἷς δὲ βεβαίως τι πρόσεστιν ἀγαθόν, μὴ προειδώς
5 τις ἂν αὐτοῖς τολμηρότερον προσφέροιτο. οὗτοι
δὲ τὴν μέλλησιν μὲν ἔχουσι τοῖς ἀπείροις φο-
βεράν· καὶ γὰρ πλήθει ὄψεως δεινοὶ καὶ βοῆς
μεγέθει ἀφόρητοι, ἥ τε διὰ κενῆς ἐπανάσεισις
τῶν ὅπλων ἔχει τινὰ δήλωσιν ἀπειλῆς. προσμεῖξαι δὲ τοῖς ὑπομένουσιν αὐτὰ οὐχ ὁμοῖοι· οὔτε

---

¹ οὐ, Hude deletes, after Stephanus.
² Hude adopts προγενομένη, after Bekker.

instruction combined with encouragement. But as it is, in view of our abandonment by our allies and of the multitude of our opponents, I shall try by a brief reminder and by advice to impress upon you the most important considerations. For it is proper that you should be brave in war, not because of the presence of allies each and every time, but because of innate valour; nor should you be afraid of any number of aliens, you who do not come from states like theirs, but states in which, not the many rule the few, but rather the minority rule the majority, having acquired their power by no other means but superiority in fighting. And as for the barbarians, whom now in your inexperience you fear, you ought to know, both from the contest you have already had with the Macedonians among them,[1] and may gather from the knowledge I gain by inference and from reports of others, that they will not be formidable. For whenever the enemy's power conveys an impression of strength, but is in reality weak, correct information about them, when once it has been gained, tends rather to embolden their opponents; whereas, when the enemy possesses some solid advantage, if one has no previous knowledge of it, one would be only too bold in attacking them. Now as for these Illyrians, for those who have had no experience of them, the menace of their attack has terror; for their number is indeed dreadful to behold and the loudness of their battle-cry is intolerable, and the idle brandishing of their arms has a threatening effect. But for hand to hand fighting,

---

[1] *i.e.* the Lyncestians, who, according to ch. lxxxiii. 1 and II. xcix. 2, belonged to the Macedonians, and had been beaten, as stated in ch. cxxiv. 3.

γὰρ ταξιν ἔχοντες αἰσχυνθεῖεν ἂν λιπεῖν τινα
χώραν βιαζόμενοι, ἥ τε φυγὴ καὶ ἡ ἔφοδος αὐτῶν
ἴσην ἔχουσα δόξαν τοῦ καλοῦ ἀνεξέλεγκτον καὶ
τὸ ἀνδρεῖον ἔχει (αὐτοκράτωρ δὲ μάχη μάλιστ᾽
ἂν καὶ πρόφασιν τοῦ σῴζεσθαί τινι πρεπόντως
πορίσειε), τοῦ τε ἐς χεῖρας ἐλθεῖν πιστότερον τὸ
ἐκφοβήσειν[1] ὑμᾶς ἀκινδύνως ἡγοῦνται· ἐκείνῳ γὰρ
6 ἂν πρὸ τούτου ἐχρῶντο. σαφῶς τε πᾶν τὸ
προϋπάρχον δεινὸν ἀπ᾽ αὐτῶν ὁρᾶτε ἔργῳ μὲν
βραχὺ ὄν, ὄψει δὲ καὶ ἀκοῇ κατασπέρχον. ὃ
ὑπομείναντες ἐπιφερόμενον καί, ὅταν καιρὸς ᾖ,
κόσμῳ καὶ τάξει αὖθις ὑπαγαγόντες, ἔς τε τὸ
ἀσφαλὲς θᾶσσον ἀφίξεσθε καὶ γνώσεσθε τὸ
λοιπὸν ὅτι οἱ τοιοῦτοι ὄχλοι τοῖς μὲν τὴν πρώτην
ἔφοδον δεξαμένοις ἄπωθεν ἀπειλαῖς τὸ ἀνδρεῖον
μελλήσει ἐπικομποῦσιν, οἳ δ᾽ ἂν εἴξωσιν αὐτοῖς,
κατὰ πόδας τὸ εὔψυχον ἐν τῷ ἀσφαλεῖ ὀξεῖς
ἐνδείκνυνται."

CXXVII. Τοιαῦτα ὁ Βρασίδας παραινέσας
ὑπῆγε τὸ στράτευμα. οἱ δὲ βάρβαροι ἰδόντες
πολλῇ βοῇ καὶ θορύβῳ προσέκειντο, νομίσαντες
φεύγειν τε αὐτὸν καὶ καταλαβόντες διαφθερεῖν.
2 καὶ ὡς αὐτοῖς αἵ τε ἐκδρομαὶ ὅπῃ προσπίπτοιεν
ἀπήντων, καὶ αὐτὸς ἔχων τοὺς λογάδας ἐπικει-
μένοις ὑφίστατο, τῇ τε πρώτῃ ὁρμῇ παρὰ γνώμην

---

[1] Hude emends to ἐκφοβῆσαι, after Torstrick.

if their opponents but endure such threats, they are
not the men they seem; for having no regular order,
they would not be ashamed to abandon any position
when hard pressed; and since flight and attack are
considered equally honourable with them, their
courage cannot be put to the test. Besides, a mode
of fighting in which everyone is his own master will
provide a man the best excuse for saving himself
becomingly. They think, too, that it is a less risky
game to try to frighten you from a safe distance
than to meet you hand to hand; otherwise they
would not have taken this course in preference to
that. And so you clearly see that all that was at
first formidable about them is but little in reality,
startling merely to eye and ear. If you withstand
all this in the first onrush, and then, whenever
opportunity offers, withdraw again in orderly array,
you will the sooner reach safety, and will hereafter
know that mobs like these, if an adversary but
sustain their first onset, merely make a flourish of
valour with threats from afar in menace [1] of attack,
but if one yields to them, they are right upon his
heels, quick enough to display their courage when
all is safe."

CXXVII. After such words of admonition, Brasidas
began to withdraw his army. On seeing this the
barbarians came on with a mighty shouting and uproar, thinking that he was fleeing and that they
could overtake and destroy his army. But the
troops who had been selected to dash out met them
wherever they charged, and Brasidas himself with
his picked men sustained their attack; and so the
Peloponnesians to their surprise withstood their first

[1] Possibly μελλήσει = "without coming to action."

ἀντέστησαν καὶ τὸ λοιπὸν ἐπιφερομένους μὲν
δεχόμενοι ἡμύνοντο, ἡσυχαζόντων δὲ αὐτοὶ ὑπεχώρουν, τότε δὴ τῶν μετὰ τοῦ Βρασίδου Ἑλλήνων
ἐν τῇ εὐρυχωρίᾳ οἱ πολλοὶ τῶν βαρβάρων ἀπέ-
σχοντο, μέρος δέ τι καταλιπόντες αὐτοῖς ἐπακο-
λουθοῦν προσβάλλειν, οἱ λοιποὶ χωρήσαντες
δρόμῳ ἐπί τε τοὺς φεύγοντας τῶν Μακεδόνων
οἷς ἐντύχοιεν ἔκτεινον καὶ τὴν ἐσβολήν, ἥ ἐστι
μεταξὺ δυοῖν λόφοιν στενὴ ἐς τὴν Ἀρραβαίου,
φθάσαντες προκατέλαβον, εἰδότες οὐκ οὖσαν
ἄλλην τῷ Βρασίδᾳ ἀναχώρησιν. καὶ προσιόντος
αὐτοῦ ἐς αὐτὸ ἤδη τὸ ἄπορον τῆς ὁδοῦ κυκλοῦνται
ὡς ἀποληψόμενοι.

CXXVIII. Ὁ δὲ γνοὺς προεῖπε τοῖς μεθ' αὑτοῦ
τριακοσίοις, ὃν ᾤετο μᾶλλον ἂν ἑλεῖν τῶν λόφων,
χωρήσαντας πρὸς αὐτὸν δρόμῳ ὡς τάχιστα
ἕκαστος δύναται ἄνευ τάξεως, πειρᾶσαι ἀπ'
αὐτοῦ ἐκκροῦσαι τοὺς ἤδη ἐπόντας[1] βαρβάρους,
πρὶν καὶ τὴν πλείονα κύκλωσιν σφῶν αὐτόσε
2 προσμεῖξαι. καὶ οἱ μὲν προσπεσόντες ἐκράτησάν
τε τῶν ἐπὶ τοῦ λόφου, καὶ ἡ πλείων ἤδη στρατιὰ
τῶν Ἑλλήνων ῥᾷον πρὸς αὐτὸν ἐπορεύοντο· οἱ
γὰρ βάρβαροι καὶ ἐφοβήθησαν, τῆς τροπῆς
αὐτοῖς ἐνταῦθα γενομένης σφῶν ἀπὸ τοῦ μετεώρου,
καὶ ἐς τὸ πλέον οὐκέτ' ἐπηκολούθουν, νομίζοντες
καὶ ἐν μεθορίοις εἶναι αὐτοὺς ἤδη καὶ διαπεφευ-
3 γέναι. Βρασίδας δὲ ὡς ἀντελάβετο τῶν μετεώ-
ρων, κατὰ ἀσφάλειαν μᾶλλον ἰὼν αὐθημερὸν
ἀφικνεῖται ἐς Ἄρνισαν πρῶτον τῆς Περδίκκου
4 ἀρχῆς. καὶ αὐτοὶ ὀργιζόμενοι οἱ στρατιῶται τῇ
προαναχωρήσει τῶν Μακεδόνων, ὅσοις ἐνέτυχον

[1] Poppo's correction for ἐπιόντας of the MSS.

onset and continued to receive their attacks and repulse them, but when they ceased, themselves retired. Thereupon most of the barbarians refrained from attacking the Hellenes under Brasidas in the open country, and leaving a portion of their force to follow and harass them, the rest, advancing on the run after the fleeing Macedonians, slew them as they came upon them, and getting ahead of them occupied the narrow pass between two hills which led into the country of Arrhabaeus, knowing that there was no other way of retreat for Brasidas. And just as he was coming to the most difficult part of the road, they began to encircle him with a view to cutting him off.

CXXVIII. But he perceived their intention and told his three hundred to break ranks and go at a run, each as fast as he could, to that one of the hills which he thought could be taken more easily and try to dislodge the barbarians already there before the larger outflanking body could come up. They accordingly attacked and overcame the men on the hill, and so the main body of the Hellenes now more easily made their way to it; for the barbarians, finding that their own men had been dislodged from the high ground, became alarmed and followed no further, thinking that the enemy were already on the frontier and had made good their escape. Brasidas, however, when he had gained the heights, proceeded in more security and arrived the same day at Arnisa, the first town in the dominions of Perdiccas. As for his soldiers, they were enraged at the Macedonians for having gone ahead in retreat, and whenever they came upon any ox-teams of

κατὰ τὴν ὁδὸν ζεύγεσιν αὐτῶν βοεικοῖς ἢ εἴ τινι
σκεύει ἐκπεπτωκότι, οἷα ἐν νυκτερινῇ καὶ φοβερᾷ
ἀναχωρήσει εἰκὸς ἦν ξυμβῆναι, τὰ μὲν ὑπολύ-
οντες κατέκοπτον, τῶν δὲ οἰκείωσιν ἐποιοῦντο.
5 ἀπὸ τούτου τε πρῶτον Περδίκκας Βρασίδαν τε
πολέμιον ἐνόμισε καὶ ἐς τὸ λοιπὸν Πελοποννησίων τῇ μὲν γνώμῃ δι' Ἀθηναίους οὐ ξύνηθες
μῖσος εἶχε, τῶν δὲ ἀναγκαίων ξυμφόρων δια-
ναστὰς[1] ἔπρασσεν ὅτῳ τρόπῳ τάχιστα τοῖς μὲν
ξυμβήσεται, τῶν δὲ ἀπαλλάξεται.

CXXIX. Βρασίδας δὲ ἀναχωρήσας ἐκ Μακεδονίας ἐς Τορώνην καταλαμβάνει Ἀθηναίους
Μένδην ἤδη ἔχοντας, καὶ αὐτοῦ ἡσυχάζων ἐς μὲν
τὴν Παλλήνην ἀδύνατος ἤδη ἐνόμιζεν εἶναι διαβὰς τιμωρεῖν, τὴν δὲ Τορώνην ἐν φυλακῇ εἶχεν.
2 ὑπὸ γὰρ τὸν αὐτὸν χρόνον τοῖς ἐν τῇ Λύγκῳ
ἐξέπλευσαν ἐπί τε τὴν Μένδην καὶ τὴν Σκιώνην οἱ
Ἀθηναῖοι, ὥσπερ παρεσκευάζοντο, ναυσὶ μὲν
πεντήκοντα, ὧν ἦσαν δέκα Χῖαι, ὁπλίταις δὲ
χιλίοις ἑαυτῶν καὶ τοξόταις ἑξακοσίοις καὶ Θρᾳξὶ
μισθωτοῖς χιλίοις καὶ ἄλλοις τῶν αὐτόθεν ξυμμάχων πελτασταῖς· ἐστρατήγει δὲ Νικίας ὁ
Νικηράτου καὶ Νικόστρατος ὁ Διειτρέφους.
3 ἄραντες δὲ ἐκ Ποτειδαίας ταῖς ναυσὶ καὶ σχόντες
κατὰ τὸ Ποσειδώνιον ἐχώρουν ἐς τοὺς Μενδαίους.
οἱ δὲ αὐτοί τε καὶ Σκιωναίων τριακόσιοι βεβοηθηκότες Πελοποννησίων τε οἱ ἐπίκουροι, ξύμπαντες[2] ἑπτακόσιοι ὁπλῖται, καὶ Πολυδαμίδας ὁ
ἄρχων αὐτῶν, ἔτυχον ἐξεστρατοπεδευμένοι ἔξω τῆς

---

[1] Hude adopts Madvig's correction, τῷ δὲ ἀναγκαίῳ ξυμφόρῳ
διαστάς, "However, such was the urgency of his situation
that he stood aside and began to devise how . . ."

[2] δέ, in the MSS. after ξύμπαντες, deleted by Krüger.

theirs in the road or upon any baggage that had
been dropped, as was likely to happen in a retreat
made by night and in a panic, of their own accord
they loosed the oxen and slaughtered them, but
appropriated the baggage. And from this time
Perdiccas began to regard Brasidas as an enemy, and
thenceforth he cherished a hatred of the Peloponnesians, which was indeed not consistent with his
feeling against the Athenians. However, disregard-
ing his own urgent interests, he was devising how
he might in the quickest way come to terms with
the latter and get rid of the former.

CXXIX. Returning from Macedonia to Torone,
Brasidas found the Athenians already in possession
of Mende; and thinking it now impossible to cross
over to Pallene and give aid, he remained quiet
where he was, but kept watch over Torone. For
about the same time as the events in Lyncus the
Athenians had sailed against Mende and Scione, as
they had been preparing to do,[1] with fifty ships, of
which ten were Chian, and with one thousand hoplites of their own, six hundred bowmen, a thousand
Thracian mercenaries, and in addition targeteers
from their allies in that neighbourhood. They were
under the command of Nicias son of Niceratus and
Nicostratus son of Diitrephes. Setting out with the
fleet from Potidaea and putting in at the temple of
Poseidon, they advanced into the country of the
Mendaeans. Now these and three hundred Scionaeans who had come to their support, and the
Peloponnesian auxiliaries, seven hundred hoplites in
all, with Polydamidas as their commander, had just

---

[1] cf. ch. cxxii. 6; cxxiii. 3.

4 πόλεως ἐπὶ λόφου καρτεροῦ. καὶ αὐτοῖς Νικίας
μέν, Μεθωναίους τε ἔχων εἴκοσι καὶ ἑκατὸν ψιλοὺς
καὶ λογάδας τῶν Ἀθηναίων ὁπλιτῶν ἑξήκοντα καὶ
τοὺς τοξότας ἅπαντας, κατὰ ἀτραπόν τινα τοῦ
λόφου πειρώμενος προσβῆναι καὶ τραυματιζόμενος
ὑπ' αὐτῶν οὐκ ἐδυνήθη βιάσασθαι· Νικόστρατος
δὲ ἄλλῃ ἐφόδῳ ἐκ πλείονος παντὶ τῷ ἄλλῳ στρατοπέδῳ ἐπιὼν τῷ λόφῳ ὄντι δυσπροσβάτῳ καὶ
πάνυ ἐθορυβήθη, καὶ ἐς ὀλίγον ἀφίκετο πᾶν τὸ
5 στράτευμα τῶν Ἀθηναίων νικηθῆναι. καὶ ταύτῃ
μὲν τῇ ἡμέρᾳ, ὡς οὐκ ἐνέδοσαν οἱ Μενδαῖοι καὶ οἱ
ξύμμαχοι, οἱ Ἀθηναῖοι ἀναχωρήσαντες ἐστρατο-
πεδεύσαντο, καὶ οἱ Μενδαῖοι νυκτὸς ἐπελθούσης
ἐς τὴν πόλιν ἀπῆλθον.

CXXX. Τῇ δ' ὑστεραίᾳ οἱ μὲν Ἀθηναῖοι περιπλεύσαντες ἐς τὸ πρὸς Σκιώνης τό τε προάστειον
εἷλον καὶ τὴν ἡμέραν ἅπασαν ἐδῄουν τὴν γῆν
οὐδενὸς ἐπεξιόντος (ἦν γάρ τι καὶ στασιασμοῦ ἐν
τῇ πόλει), οἱ δὲ τριακόσιοι τῶν Σκιωναίων τῆς
2 ἐπιούσης νυκτὸς ἀπεχώρησαν ἐπ' οἴκου. καὶ τῇ
ἐπιγιγνομένῃ ἡμέρᾳ Νικίας μὲν τῷ ἡμίσει τοῦ
στρατοῦ προϊὼν ἅμα ἐς τὰ μεθόρια τῶν Σκιωναίων
τὴν γῆν ἐδῄου, Νικόστρατος δὲ τοῖς λοιποῖς κατὰ
τὰς ἄνω πύλας, ᾗ ἐπὶ Ποτειδαίας ἔρχονται, προσ-
3 εκάθητο τῇ πόλει. ὁ δὲ Πολυδαμίδας (ἔτυχε γὰρ
ταύτῃ τοῖς Μενδαίοις καὶ ἐπικούροις ἐντὸς τοῦ
τείχους τὰ ὅπλα κείμενα) διατάσσει τε ὡς ἐς
4 μάχην καὶ παρῄνει τοῖς Μενδαίοις ἐπεξιέναι. καὶ
τινος αὐτῷ τῶν ἀπὸ τοῦ δήμου ἀντειπόντος κατὰ
τὸ στασιωτικὸν ὅτι οὐκ ἐπέξεισιν οὐδὲ δέοιτο
πολεμεῖν, καὶ ὡς ἀντεῖπεν ἐπισπασθέντος τε τῇ

encamped outside the city in a strong position on a hill. Nicias tried to reach them by a path up the hill, having with him one hundred and twenty light-armed Methonaeans, sixty picked men of the Athenian hoplites, and all the bowmen, but his troops suffered in the attempt and he was unable to carry this position. Nicostratus, however, with all the rest of the army, advancing against the hill, which was difficult of access, by another and longer route, was thrown into utter confusion, and the whole Athenian army narrowly escaped defeat. So on this day, as the Mendaeans and their allies did not yield, the Athenians withdrew and encamped, and the Mendaeans, when night came on, returned to the city.

CXXX. On the next day the Athenians sailed round to the side of the town facing Scione and took the suburb, and all that day they ravaged the land. No one came out against them, as there was some sort of uprising in the town; and during the following night the three hundred Scionaeans returned home. On the next day Nicias with half of the army advanced as far as the boundary of the Scionaeans and ravaged the land, while Nicostratus with the rest sat down before the city at the upper gates, on the road leading to Potidaea. But it chanced that in that quarter of the town, inside the walls, the arms of the Mendaeans and their auxiliaries were deposited, and Polydamidas was there drawing his troops up for battle and exhorting the Mendaeans to make a sortie. Some one of the popular party mutinously answered him that he would not go out and had no use for war, but no sooner had he answered than Polydamidas seized

χειρὶ ὑπ' αὐτοῦ καὶ θορυβηθέντος,[1] ὁ δῆμος εὐθὺς
ἀναλαβὼν τὰ ὅπλα περιοργὴς ἐχώρει ἐπί τε
Πελοποννησίους καὶ τοὺς τὰ ἐναντία σφίσι μετ'
5 αὐτῶν πράξαντας. καὶ προσπεσόντες τρέπουσιν
ἅμα μὲν μάχῃ αἰφνιδίῳ, ἅμα δὲ τοῖς Ἀθηναίοις
τῶν πυλῶν ἀνοιγομένων φοβηθέντων· ᾠήθησαν
γὰρ ἀπὸ προειρημένου τινὸς αὐτοῖς τὴν ἐπιχείρη-
6 σιν γενέσθαι. καὶ οἱ μὲν ἐς τὴν ἀκρόπολιν, ὅσοι
μὴ αὐτίκα διεφθάρησαν, κατέφυγον, ἥνπερ καὶ τὸ
πρότερον αὐτοὶ εἶχον· οἱ δὲ Ἀθηναῖοι (ἤδη γὰρ καὶ
ὁ Νικίας ἐπαναστρέψας πρὸς τῇ πόλει ἦν) ἐσπε-
σόντες ἐς τὴν πόλιν,[2] ἅτε οὐκ ἀπὸ ξυμβάσεως
ἀνοιχθεῖσαν, ἁπάσῃ τῇ στρατιᾷ ὡς κατὰ κράτος
ἑλόντες διήρπασαν, καὶ μόλις οἱ στρατηγοὶ κατέσχον ὥστε μὴ καὶ τοὺς ἀνθρώπους διαφθείρεσθαι.
7 καὶ τοὺς μὲν Μενδαίους μετὰ ταῦτα πολιτεύειν
ἐκέλευον ὥσπερ εἰώθεσαν, αὐτοὺς κρίναντας ἐν
σφίσιν αὐτοῖς εἴ τινας ἡγοῦνται αἰτίους εἶναι τῆς
ἀποστάσεως· τοὺς δ' ἐν τῇ ἀκροπόλει ἀπετεί-
χισαν ἑκατέρωθεν τείχει ἐς θάλασσαν καὶ φυλακὴν
ἐπικαθίσταντο.[3] ἐπειδὴ δὲ τὰ περὶ τὴν Μένδην
κατέσχον, ἐπὶ τὴν Σκιώνην ἐχώρουν.

CXXXI. Οἱ δὲ ἀντεπεξελθόντες αὐτοὶ καὶ
Πελοποννήσιοι ἱδρύθησαν ἐπὶ λόφου καρτεροῦ
πρὸ τῆς πόλεως, ὃν εἰ μὴ ἕλοιεν οἱ ἐναντίοι, οὐκ
2 ἐγίγνετο σφῶν περιτείχισις. προσβαλόντες δ'
αὐτῷ κατὰ κράτος οἱ Ἀθηναῖοι καὶ μάχῃ ἐκκρού-
σαντες τοὺς ἐπόντας[4] ἐστρατοπεδεύσαντό τε καὶ
ἐς τὸν περιτειχισμὸν τροπαῖον στήσαντες παρε-

---

[1] θορυβηθέντος, Hude καταθορυβηθέντος.
[2] τὴν Μένδην πόλιν, MSS.; Dobree deletes Μένδην.
[3] Poppo's correction for ἐπεκαθίσαντο of the MSS.
[4] Dobree's correction for ἐπιόντας of the MSS.

him with violence and roughly handled him;
whereupon the populace in great anger at once
caught up their arms and advanced upon the Peloponnesians and the opposite party who were in
league with them. Falling upon them they put
them to rout, partly by the suddenness of their
onslaught, partly because the others were terrified
when the gates were opened to the Athenians; for
they thought that the attack had been made upon
them by a preconcerted agreement. Those of the
Peloponnesians who were not killed on the spot
took refuge on the acropolis, which they already
had possession of; but the Athenians—for Nicias
had already turned back and was near the city—
burst into the city with their whole force, and, as
the gates had been opened without an agreement,
plundered the city as though they had taken it by
storm; and the generals with difficulty kept them
from destroying the inhabitants also. They then
directed the Mendaeans henceforth to retain their
former constitution, and bring to trial among themselves any whom they thought guilty of the revolt;
but the men on the acropolis they fenced off with
a wall extending on either side down to the sea, and
set a guard over them. And when they had thus
secured Mende, they proceeded against Scione.

CXXXI. The Scionaeans and the Peloponnesians
had come out against them and taken position on a
strong hill before the city, which had to be taken by
the enemy before the city could be invested with a
wall. So the Athenians made a furious assault upon
the hill and dislodged those that were upon it; they
then encamped and, after raising a trophy, prepared

3 σκευάζοντο. καὶ αὐτῶν οὐ πολὺ ὕστερον ἤδη ἐν
ἔργῳ ὄντων οἱ ἐκ τῆς ἀκροπόλεως ἐν τῇ Μένδῃ
πολιορκούμενοι ἐπίκουροι βιασάμενοι παρὰ θάλασσαν τὴν φυλακὴν νυκτὸς ἀφικνοῦνται, καὶ
διαφυγόντες οἱ πλεῖστοι τὸ ἐπὶ τῇ Σκιώνῃ στρατόπεδον ἐσῆλθον ἐς αὐτήν.

CXXXII. Περιτειχιζομένης δὲ τῆς Σκιώνης
Περδίκκας τοῖς τῶν Ἀθηναίων στρατηγοῖς ἐπι-
κηρυκευσάμενος ὁμολογίαν ποιεῖται πρὸς τοὺς
Ἀθηναίους διὰ τὴν τοῦ Βρασίδου ἔχθραν περὶ
τῆς ἐκ τῆς Λύγκου ἀναχωρήσεως, εὐθὺς τότε
2 ἀρξάμενος πράσσειν. καὶ ἐτύγχανε γὰρ τότε
Ἰσχαγόρας ὁ Λακεδαιμόνιος στρατιὰν μέλλων
πεζῇ πορεύσειν ὡς Βρασίδαν, ὁ δὲ ¹ Περδίκκας,
ἅμα μὲν κελεύοντος τοῦ Νικίου, ἐπειδὴ ξυνεβε-
βήκει, ἔνδηλόν τι ποιεῖν τοῖς Ἀθηναίοις βεβαιότητος πέρι, ἅμα δ' αὐτὸς οὐκέτι βουλόμενος
Πελοποννησίους ἐς τὴν αὐτοῦ ἀφικνεῖσθαι,
παρασκευάσας τοὺς ἐν Θεσσαλίᾳ ξένους, χρώ-
μενος αἰεὶ τοῖς πρώτοις, διεκώλυσε τὸ στράτευμα
καὶ τὴν παρασκευήν, ὥστε μηδὲ πειρᾶσθαι Θεσ-
3 σαλῶν. Ἰσχαγόρας μέντοι καὶ Ἀμεινίας καὶ
Ἀριστεὺς αὐτοί τε ὡς Βρασίδαν ἀφίκοντο, ἐπιδεῖν
πεμψάντων Λακεδαιμονίων τὰ πράγματα, καὶ
τῶν ἡβώντων αὐτῶν ² παρανόμως ἄνδρας ἐξῆγον
ἐκ Σπάρτης, ὥστε τῶν πόλεων ἄρχοντας καθι-
στάναι καὶ μὴ τοῖς ἐντυχοῦσιν ἐπιτρέπειν. καὶ
Κλεαρίδαν μὲν τὸν Κλεωνύμου καθίστησιν ἐν
Ἀμφιπόλει, Πασιτελίδαν ³ δὲ τὸν Ἡγησάνδρου
ἐν Τορώνῃ.

¹ δέ, deleted by Hude, following Dobree.
² αὐτῶν, Hude reads αὐτῷ, after Stahl.
³ Dobree's correction for Ἐπιτελίδαν of the MSS. ; cf. v. 3.

for the circumvallation. But not long afterwards, when they were already at work, the auxiliaries who were besieged on the acropolis of Mende forced their way by night along the shore through the guard and reached Scione; and most of them escaped through the besieging army and got into the city.

CXXXII. While the circumvallation of Scione was in progress, Perdiccas sent a herald to the Athenian generals and made an agreement with them; he was moved to this by the hatred he bore Brasidas for his retreat from Lyncus, at which time indeed he had begun his negotiations.[1] Now it happened at that time that Ischagoras, the Lacedaemonian, was on the point of taking an army by land to join Brasidas, but Perdiccas, partly because Nicias urged him, since he had made terms with the Athenians, to give them some token of his sincerity, partly also because he himself no longer wished the Peloponnesians to enter his territory, now worked upon his friends in Thessaly, with the foremost of whom he was always on good terms, and effectually stopped the army and the expedition, to such a degree that they did not even try to obtain permission from the Thessalians. Ischagoras, however, with Ameinias and Aristeus, came by themselves to Brasidas, having been commissioned by the Lacedaemonians to look into the situation. And they brought from Sparta, contrary to custom, some of their young men, intending to place them as governors over the cities instead of entrusting these to anybody that might chance to offer. Accordingly, they placed at Amphipolis Clearidas son of Cleonymus and at Torone Pasitelidas son of Hegesander.

---

[1] cf. ch. cxxviii. 5.

CXXXIII. Ἐν δὲ τῷ αὐτῷ θέρει Θηβαῖοι Θεσπιῶν τεῖχος περιεῖλον ἐπικαλέσαντες ἀττικισμόν, βουλόμενοι μὲν καὶ αἰεί, παρεστηκὸς δὲ ῥᾷον ἐπειδὴ καὶ ἐν τῇ πρὸς Ἀθηναίους μάχῃ ὅ τι 2 ἦν αὐτῶν ἄνθος ἀπολώλει. καὶ ὁ νεὼς τῆς Ἥρας τοῦ αὐτοῦ θέρους ἐν Ἄργει κατεκαύθη, Χρυσίδος τῆς ἱερείας λύχνον τινὰ θείσης ἡμμένον πρὸς τὰ στέμματα καὶ ἐπικαταδαρθούσης, ὥστε ἔλαθεν 3 ἀφθέντα πάντα καὶ καταφλεχθέντα. καὶ ἡ Χρυσὶς μὲν εὐθὺς τῆς νυκτὸς δείσασα τοὺς Ἀργείους ἐς Φλειοῦντα φεύγει· οἱ δὲ ἄλλην ἱέρειαν ἐκ τοῦ νόμου τοῦ προκειμένου κατεστήσαντο Φαεινίδα ὄνομα. ἔτη δὲ ἡ Χρυσὶς τοῦ πολέμου τοῦδε ἐπέλαβεν ὀκτὼ καὶ ἔνατον ἐκ μέσου, ὅτε ἐπε- 4 φεύγει. καὶ ἡ Σκιώνη τοῦ θέρους ἤδη τελευτῶντος περιετετείχιστό τε παντελῶς, καὶ οἱ Ἀθηναῖοι ἐπ᾽ αὐτῇ φυλακὴν καταλιπόντες ἀνεχώρησαν τῷ ἄλλῳ στρατῷ.

CXXXIV. Ἐν δὲ τῷ ἐπιόντι χειμῶνι τὰ μὲν Ἀθηναίων καὶ Λακεδαιμονίων ἡσύχαζε διὰ τὴν ἐκεχειρίαν, Μαντινῆς δὲ καὶ Τεγεᾶται καὶ οἱ ξύμμαχοι ἑκατέρων ξυνέβαλον ἐν Λαοδοκείῳ [1] τῆς Ὀρεσθίδος, καὶ νίκη ἀμφιδήριτος ἐγένετο· κέρας γὰρ ἑκάτεροι τρέψαντες τὸ καθ᾽ αὑτοὺς τροπαῖά τε ἀμφότεροι ἔστησαν καὶ σκῦλα ἐς Δελφοὺς 2 ἀπέπεμψαν. διαφθαρέντων μέντοι πολλῶν ἑκατέροις καὶ ἀγχωμάλου τῆς μάχης γενομένης καὶ

[1] Bursian's correction for Λαοδικίῳ of the MSS.

CXXXIII. In the same summer the Thebans dismantled the wall of the Thespians, accusing them of favouring the Athenians. Indeed they had always wished to do this, but now found it easier, since the flower of the Thespians had perished in the battle with the Athenians.[1] In this same summer, too, the temple of Hera at Argos was burned down, Chrysis[2] the priestess having placed a lighted torch near the garlands and then gone to sleep, so that the whole place took fire and was ablaze before she was aware. And Chrysis that very night, in fear of the Argives, fled to Phlius; but they appointed another priestess according to the custom prescribed, Phäeinis by name. Chrysis had been priestess during eight years of this war and half of the ninth when she fled. Toward the close of the summer Scione was at length completely invested, and the Athenians, leaving a guard there, withdrew with the rest of their army.

CXXXIV. In the following winter, on account of the armistice, matters were quiet with the Athenians and the Lacedaemonians; but the Mantineans and the Tegeans with their respective allies fought a battle at Laodoceum in the district of Oresthis. The victory was disputed; for each side routed the wing opposed to themselves, and both set up trophies[3] and sent spoils to Delphi. Certain it is at any rate that after many had fallen on both sides and night had cut short the action, the issue of battle being

[1] At Delium ; cf. ch. xciii. 4; xcvi. 3.
[2] The same who in 431 B.C. had held her office forty-eight years; cf. II. ii. 1.
[3] It seems that the Mantineans and Tegeans each defeated the other's allies, which were on the left wings of the opposing armies.

ἀφελομένης νυκτὸς τὸ ἔργον οἱ Τεγεᾶται μὲν ἐπηυλίσαντό τε καὶ εὐθὺς ἔστησαν τροπαῖον, Μαντινῆς δὲ ἀπεχώρησάν τε ἐς Βουκολιῶνα καὶ ὕστερον ἀντέστησαν.

CXXXV. Ἀπεπείρασε δὲ τοῦ αὐτοῦ χειμῶνος καὶ ὁ Βρασίδας τελευτῶντος καὶ πρὸς ἔαρ ἤδη Ποτειδαίας. προσελθὼν γὰρ νυκτὸς καὶ κλίμακα προσθεὶς μέχρι μὲν τούτου ἔλαθεν· τοῦ γὰρ κώδωνος παρενεχθέντος οὕτως ἐς τὸ διάκενον, πρὶν ἐπανελθεῖν τὸν παραδιδόντα αὐτόν, ἡ πρόσθεσις ἐγένετο· ἔπειτα μέντοι εὐθὺς αἰσθομένων, πρὶν προσβῆναι, ἀπήγαγε πάλιν κατὰ τάχος τὴν 2 στρατιὰν καὶ οὐκ ἀνέμεινεν ἡμέραν γενέσθαι. καὶ ὁ χειμὼν ἐτελεύτα, καὶ ἔνατον ἔτος τῷ πολέμῳ ἐτελεύτα τῷδε ὃν Θουκυδίδης ξυνέγραψεν.

still undecided, the Tegeans bivouacked on the field and set up a trophy at once, while the Mantineans retreated to Bucolion, and afterwards set up a rival trophy.

CXXXV. Toward the close of the same winter, when spring was near at hand, Brasidas made an attempt on Potidaea. He came up by night and placed a ladder against the wall, up to this point escaping detection; for the ladder was planted precisely at the interval of time after the bell had been carried by and before the patrol who passed it on had come back.[1] The guards, however, discovered it immediately, before an ascent could be made, and Brasidas made haste to lead his army back again, not waiting for day to come. So ended the winter and with it the ninth year of this war of which Thucydides wrote the history.

[1] It appears that the bell was passed from one sentinel to the next. Another, and probably more common, way of testing the watchfulness of the sentinels was to have a patrol with a bell make the round, each sentinel having to answer the signal.

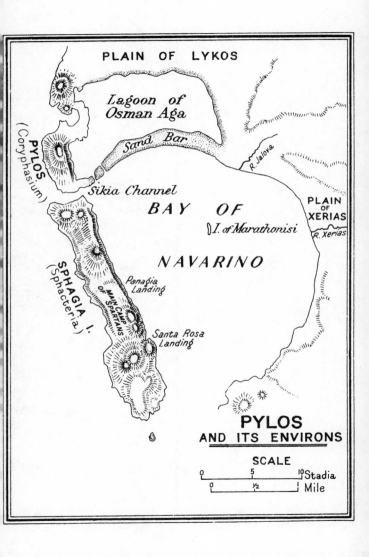

PLAIN OF LYKOS

Lagoon of Osman Aga

PYLOS
(Coryphasium)

Sand Bar

R. Jalova

Sikia Channel

PLAIN
OF
XERIAS

BAY OF

I. of Marathonisi

R. Xerias

NAVARINO

Panagia Landing

SPHAGIA I.
(Sphacteria)

MAIN CAMP OF SPARTANS

Santa Rosa Landing

PYLOS
AND ITS ENVIRONS

SCALE

| 0 | 5 | 10 Stadia |

| 0 | ½ | 1 Mile |

CENTRAL GREECE
AND
PELOPONNESUS

English Miles

0   50   100

Stadia

0   100   200   300   400   500   600

Pieria

Peneus

Magnesia

Larisa

Crannon

Pherae

Sin
Pagasaeus

Pharsalus

THESSALIA

MALIS

Heraclea

Thermopylae

Doris

Elatea

Amphissa

Delphi

Daulis

LOCRIS

Oreus

Scyros

EUBOEA

Opus

Cenaeum Pr.

Orchomenus

Chalcis

Copais L.

Chaeronea

Lebadea

Coronea

Aulis

Corinthiacus

BOEOTIA

Thespiae

Leuctra

Thebae

Plataea

Oenophyta

Tanagra

Eretria

M. Cyllene

Pellene

Sicyon

ACHAIA

Phlius

Corinthus

M. Parnes

Decelea

Acharnae

Marathon

Eleusis

Megara

Salamis

ATTICA

ATHENAE

Piraeus

Carystus

Geraestus Pr.

Andros

Mycenae

Cenchreae

Orchomenus

Argos

ARGOLIS

Nauplia

Tiryns

Tegea

ARCADIA

Aegina

Saronicus S.

Epidaurus

Calauria

Thoricus

Sunium Pr.

Ceos

Tenos

Myconos

Delos

Megalopolis

Thyrea

Inachus

Hermione

Scyllaeum Pr.

PELOPONNESUS

Naxos

Paros

LACONICA

Prasiae

SPARTA

Amyclae

Eurotas

Melos

Epidaurus

Limera

Sinus

Laconicus

Taenarum Pr.

Malea Pr.

Cythera

Thera